Lecture Notes in Computer Science 1479

Edited by G. Goos, J. Hartmanis and J. van Leeuwen

Springer

Berlin
Heidelberg
New York
Barcelona
Budapest
Hong Kong
London
Milan
Paris
Singapore
Tokyo

Jim Grundy   Malcolm Newey (Eds.)

Theorem Proving
in Higher Order Logics

11th International Conference, TPHOLs '98
Canberra, Australia
September 27 – October 1, 1998
Proceedings

 Springer

Series Editors

Gerhard Goos, Karlsruhe University, Germany
Juris Hartmanis, Cornell University, NY, USA
Jan van Leeuwen, Utrecht University, The Netherlands

Volume Editors

Jim Grundy
Malcolm Newey
The Australian National University, Department of Computer Science
Canberra ACT 0200, Australia
E-mail: {Jim.Grundy,Malcolm.Newey}@anu.edu.au

Cataloging-in-Publication data applied for

Die Deutsche Bibliothek - CIP-Einheitsaufnahme

Theorem proving in higher order logics : 11th international
conference ; proceedings / TPHOLs '98, Canberra, Australia,
September 27 - October 2, 1998 / Jim Grundy ; Malcolm Newey
(ed.). - Berlin ; Heidelberg ; New York ; Barcelona ; Budapest ; Hong
Kong ; London ; Milan ; Paris ; Singapore ; Tokyo : Springer, 1998
   (Lecture notes in computer science ; Vol. 1479)
   ISBN 3-540-64987-5

CR Subject Classification (1991): B.6.3, D.2.4, F.3.1, F.4.1, I.2.3

ISSN 0302-9743
ISBN 3-540-64987-5 Springer-Verlag Berlin Heidelberg New York

© Springer-Verlag Berlin Heidelberg 1998
Printed in Germany

Typesetting: Camera-ready by author
SPIN 10638740   06/3142 – 5 4 3 2 1 0   Printed on acid-free paper

Preface

This volume contains the proceedings of *The 11th International Conference on Theorem Proving in Higher Order Logics* (TPHOLs'98), which was held in Canberra at The Australian National University, between September 27 and October 2, 1998. Each of the fifty-two papers submitted as completed research contributions was refereed by at least three reviewers appointed by the program committee. Because of the limited space in the program and proceedings, only twenty-six could be accepted for publication in this volume. The competition was tough, and many good papers were unsuccessful.

TPHOLs'98 continues the tradition of its predecessors in providing a venue for the presentation of work in progress, where researchers invite discussion of preliminary results by means of a short talk, a display at a poster session, and inclusion of a paper in a supplementary proceedings. For TPHOLs'98, the supplementary proceedings takes the form of a book entitled *Theorem Proving in Higher Order Logics: Emerging Trends, 1998* and published by the Computer Science Department of The Australian National University,

The invited speakers for TPHOLs'98 were Tobias Nipkow and Joakim von Wright; the organizers were delighted that both accepted the invitation and provided original papers for inclusion in the proceedings. Professor Nipkow plays a leading role in the Isabelle community, while Dr. von Wright is noted for his contributions both to theorem proving in higher order logics and to the area of program refinement. This is particularly pertinent since TPHOLs'98 was run in federation with *The 1998 International Refinement Workshop and Formal Methods Pacific* (IRW/FMP'98).

Although the TPHOLs conferences have their genesis in HOL Users Meetings, recent years have seen a high rate of contribution from the other major groups, particularly the user communities of Coq, Isabelle, LAMBDA, LEGO, NuPrl, and PVS. Since 1993 the proceedings have been published by Springer as Volumes 780, 859, 971, 1125, 1275, and 1479 of *Lecture Notes in Computer Science*. More history of TPHOLs can be found with further information about the 1998 event at http://cs.anu.edu.au/TPHOLs98/.

The conference was sponsored by the Computer Science Department of The Australian National University (ANU), Intel, the Defence Science and Technology Organisation (DSTO), The Australian Research Council, and ACSys (the Cooperative Research Centre for Advanced Computational Systems). The financial support of these groups is gratefully acknowledged.

Canberra, September 1998   Jim Grundy and Malcolm Newey

Conference Organisation

Jim Grundy (ANU)
Malcolm Newey (ANU)

Program Committee

Mark Aagaard (Intel)
Sten Agerholm (IFAD)
David Basin (Freiburg)
Richard Boulton (Edinburgh)
Albert Camilleri (HP)
Tony Cant (DSTO)
Robert Constable (Cornell)
Gilles Dowek (INRIA)
Amy Felty (Bell Labs)
Mike Gordon (Cambridge)
Jim Grundy (ANU)
Elsa Gunter (Bell Labs)
Joshua Guttman (Mitre)
John Harrison (Intel)

Paul Jackson (Edinburgh)
Sara Kalvala (Warwick)
Thomas Kropf (Karlsruhe)
Tim Leonard (Compaq)
Paul Loewenstein (Sun)
Tom Melham (Glasgow)
Paul Miner (NASA)
Malcolm Newey (ANU)
Sam Owre (SRI)
Christine Paulin-Mohring (LRI)
Lawrence Paulson (Cambridge)
Laurent Théry (INRIA)
Phil Windley (Brigham Young)
Wai Wong (Hong Kong Baptist)

Invited Speakers

Tobias Nipkow (TU München)
Jockum von Wright (Åbo Akademi)

Additional Reviewers

Abdelwaheb Ayari
Robert Beers
Yves Bertot
Michael Butler
Ricky Butler
Victor Carreño
David Cyrluk
Joelle Despeyroux
Ben DiVito
Katherine Eastaughffe
Andy Gordon

Rajev Goré
Trent Larson
Patrick Lincoln
Chuchang Liu
Brendan Mahony
Andrew Martin
Monica Nesi
Michael Norrish
Maris Ozols
Randy Pollack

Peter Robinson
Shankar
Rob Shaw
John Slaney
Srivas
Mark Staples
Myra VanInwegen
Luca Vigano
Jockum von Wright
Jon Whittle
Burkhart Wolff

Contents

Invited Papers

Verified Lexical Analysis 1
Tobias Nipkow

Extending Window Inference 17
Joakim von Wright

Refereed Papers

Program Abstraction in a Higher-Order Logic Framework 33
Marco Benini, Sara Kalvala, and Dirk Nowotka

The Village Telephone System:
A Case Study in Formal Software Engineering 49
Karthikeyan Bhargavan, Carl A. Gunter, Elsa L. Gunter,
Michael Jackson, Davor Obradovic, and Pamela Zave

Generating Embeddings from Denotational Descriptions 67
Richard J. Boulton

An Interface between CLᴬM and HOL............................... 87
Richard Boulton, Konrad Slind, Alan Bundy, and Mike Gordon

Classical Propositional Decidability via Nuprl Proof Extraction 105
James L. Caldwell

A Comparison of PVS and Isabelle/HOL............................. 123
David Griffioen and Marieke Huisman

Adding External Decision Procedures to HOL90 Securely 143
Elsa L. Gunter

Formalizing Basic First Order Model Theory 153
John Harrison

Formalizing Dijkstra 171
John Harrison

Mechanical Verification of Total Correctness through
Diversion Verification Conditions 189
Peter V. Homeier and David F. Martin

A Type Annotation Scheme for Nuprl 207
Douglas J. Howe

Verifying a Garbage Collection Algorithm 225
Paul B. Jackson

HOT: A Concurrent Automated Theorem Prover
Based on Higher-Order Tableaux.. 245
Karsten Konrad

Free Variables and Subexpressions in Higher-Order Meta Logic 263
Chuck Liang

An LPO-based Termination Ordering for Higher-Order Terms
without λ-abstraction 277
Maxim Lifantsev and Leo Bachmair

Proving Isomorphism of First-Order Logic Proof Systems in HOL 295
Anna Mikhajlova and Joakim von Wright

Exploiting Parallelism in Interactive Theorem Provers 315
Roderick Moten

I/O Automata and Beyond:
Temporal Logic and Abstraction in Isabelle 331
Olaf Müller

Object-Oriented Verification Based on Record Subtyping in
Higher-Order Logic.. 349
Wolfgang Naraschewski and Markus Wenzel

On the Effectiveness of Theorem Proving Guided Discovery of Formal
Assertions for a Register Allocator in a High-Level Synthesis System 367
Naren Narasimhan and Ranga Vemuri

Co-inductive Axiomatization of a Synchronous Language................. 387
David Nowak, Jean-René Beauvais, and Jean-Pierre Talpin

Formal Specification and Theorem Proving Breakthroughs in
Geometric Modeling... 401
François Puitg and Jean-François Dufourd

A Tool for Data Refinement 423
Rimvydas Rukšėnas and Joakim von Wright

Mechanizing Relevant Logics with HOL 443
Hajime Sawamura and Daisaku Asanuma

Case Studies in Meta-Level Theorem Proving......................... 461
Friedrich W. von Henke, Stephan Pfab, Holger Pfeifer, and Harald Rueß

Formalization of Graph Search Algorithms and Its Applications.......... 479
*Mitsuharu Yamamoto, Koichi Takahashi, Masami Hagiya,
Shin-ya Nishizaki, and Tetsuo Tamai*

Author Index.. 497

Verified Lexical Analysis

Tobias Nipkow

Technische Universität München
Institut für Informatik, 80290 München, Germany
http://www.in.tum.de/~nipkow/

Abstract. This paper presents the development and verification of a (very simple) lexical analyzer generator that takes a regular expression and yields a functional lexical analyzer. The emphasis is on simplicity and executability. The work was carried out with the help of the theorem prover Isabelle/HOL.

1 Introduction

Admittedly, lexical analysis is not exactly safety critical. But if the dream of a verified compiler is to be taken seriously, it must include the front end as well. Practical applications aside, lexical analysis is an excellent example of computational discrete mathematics, and as such an ideal test case for any aspiring theorem prover.

We formalize and verify the process of taking a regular expression and turning it into a lexical analyzer (also called *scanner*). The design goals are simplicity and executability. The result is an almost executable functional program, except for one place, where simplicity has prevailed over executability. The overall structure of both the verified theories and the main sections of the paper is shown in Fig. 1.

The vertical arrows describe the well-known translation of a regular expression into a deterministic automaton. This is the subject of Sects. 3–4. We follow the standard textbook treatment but rely on functions to represent automata.

The horizontal arrows describe the actual scanner. Roughly speaking, a scanner converts a string into a list of 'tokens'. We have simplified the model by replacing the tokens by the substrings themselves. In addition, the scanner returns the unrecognized suffix of the input. Thus function scan takes a string w and returns a pair of

- a list $[u_1, \ldots, u_n]$ that is obtained by repeatedly chopping off the remaining input the maximal nonempty prefix u_i that is recognized by A,
- and the remaining unrecognized suffix v.

In particular this means the concatenation $u_1 \ldots u_n v$ yields the input w. Although this scanning process is not given much attention in the literature, a precise specification and a verified implementation of scan turns out to be very interesting and is the subject of Sect. 5. All theories are available online at http://www.in.tum.de/~isabelle/library/HOL/Lex/.

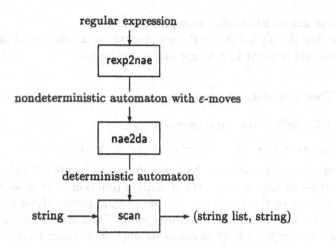

Fig. 1. The structure

We assume that the reader is familiar with the standard theory of finite automata and regular expressions as described, for example, in the textbook by Hopcroft and Ullman [6].

1.1 Notation

Although we have talked about 'strings' above, there is no need for a new datatype: strings are simply lists, and we don't even need to fix the alphabet. In the sequel, type variable α always represents this alphabet and we use 'string' as a synonym for 'list over type α'.

A few words about notation in Isabelle/HOL (abbreviated to HOL below). List notation is similar to ML (e.g. @ is 'append' and concat distributes @ over a list of lists) except that the 'cons' operation is denoted by # instead of ::. There is also the function set that returns the set of elements of a list. Set comprehension syntax is $\{e \ . \ P\}$. Function types are denoted by $\Rightarrow$.

Thanks to Markus Wenzel, Isabelle has recently acquired *long identifiers* of the form $T.n$ where T is the name of a theory and n a name defined in T.

To distinguish variables from constants, the latter are shown in sans-serif.

2 Automata

All our automata will be triples of a start state, a next state function and a test for final states. We define three corresponding projections start, next and fin:

$$\mathsf{start}(q,d,f) \equiv q \qquad \mathsf{next}(q,d,f) \equiv d \qquad \mathsf{fin}(q,d,f) \equiv f$$

Our formalization differs from standard automata theory in the following aspects:

- there are no finiteness assumptions;
- neither the alphabet nor the set of states is a component of the automaton; both are implicit in the *type* of the components.

2.1 Deterministic Automata

Theory DA defines the parameterized type

$$(\alpha,\sigma)\text{da} = \sigma \times (\alpha \Rightarrow \sigma \Rightarrow \sigma) \times (\sigma \Rightarrow \text{bool})$$

of deterministic automata, where σ is the type of states. The only painful choice is the order of arguments of the transition function: $\sigma \Rightarrow \alpha \Rightarrow \sigma$ or $\alpha \Rightarrow \sigma \Rightarrow \sigma$? Both appear in the literature and have their minor advantages and disadvantages. I prefer the state transformer view. Final states are encoded via a test function rather than a set of states to allow direct execution.

The extension of next to strings is called delta:[1]

```
delta :: (α,σ)da ⇒ α list ⇒ σ ⇒ σ
delta A []    s = s
delta A (a#w) s = delta A w (next A a s)
```

A word is accepted by a da if delta maps the start state to a final state:

```
accepts ::  (α,σ)da ⇒ α list ⇒ bool
accepts A w ≡ fin A (delta A w (start A))
```

2.2 Nondeterministic Automata

Nondeterministic automata come in two flavours, with and without ε-moves. The latter are defined by the type

$$(\alpha,\sigma)\text{na} = \sigma \times (\alpha \Rightarrow \sigma \Rightarrow \sigma \text{ set}) \times (\sigma \Rightarrow \text{bool})$$

and merely serve as the stepping stone towards the former. Adjoining a new element ε to the alphabet is naturally modeled by the standard datatype

$$(\alpha)\text{option} = \text{None} \mid \text{Some } \alpha$$

where None represents ε. By this device a nondeterministic automaton with ε-moves over alphabet α is simply a nondeterministic automaton without ε-moves over alphabet (α)option:

$$(\alpha,\sigma)\text{nae} = (\alpha \text{ option},\sigma)\text{na}$$

That was easy. The only choice we had was whether to model the transition function as a set-valued function (as we did) or as a relation. The argument in favour of a set-valued function is purely computational: provided the set of next states of every state is finite, it can be represented by a list, and hence the transition function is computable. Using a relation, it is unclear in what sense the set of next states is computable.

---

[1] With a different order of arguments we could have defined delta A ≡ foldl (next A).

Although relations are not so nice for computing, they are handy for reasoning. Hence we define step, the relational version of next:

```
step :: (α,σ)nae ⇒ α option ⇒ (σ × σ)set
step A a ≡ {(p,q) . q ∈ next A a p}
```

The term eps A is short for step A None and denotes all ε-moves.

Before we can continue, we need two operations from the standard theory of relations: $r\hat{}*$ is the reflexive transitive closure of r and s ⊙ r is the composition of r and s (mind the order!):

```
s ⊙ r ≡ {(x,z). ∃ y. (x,y) ∈ r ∧ (y,z) ∈ s}
```

The extension of step to lists is straightforward:[2]

```
steps :: (α,σ)nae ⇒ α list ⇒ (σ × σ)set
steps A []    = (eps A)^*
steps A (a#w) = steps A w ⊙ step A (Some a) ⊙ (eps A)^*
```

The term (eps A)$\hat{}*$ is the so-called *epsilon closure* of an nae A that relates state s to state t iff t is reachable from s by a finite sequence of ε-moves.

The words accepted by an nae are defined as usual:

```
accepts :: (α,σ)nae ⇒ α list ⇒ bool
accepts A w ≡ ∃ q. (start A,q) ∈ steps A w ∧ fin A q
```

Note that step, steps and accepts are used only in proofs. Hence their non-executability is of no concern.

All the definitions in this subsection reside in theory NAe. Thus we can distinguish, for example, DA.accepts and NAe.accepts.

2.3 Discussion of Nondeterministic Automata

Apart from the fact that transition functions are arbitrary functions and hence automata need not be finite, the above treatment of nondeterministic automata is standard. However, it was not until after a number of painful iterations that I arrived at this formulation. There are three different options when dealing with the extension of the next state function to words, which behave quite differently in proofs:

1. The standard one is of type (α,σ)nae ⇒ (α)list ⇒ σ ⇒ (σ)set. This is how we started, but it leads to proofs with a lot of duplication because of the asymmetry between input (single states) and output (sets of states).
2. A much slicker version is defined directly on sets of states, i.e. it is of type (α,σ)nae ⇒ (α)list ⇒ (σ)set ⇒ (σ)set. This eliminates the asymmetry of the first version and results in some compact algebraic laws like

```
delta A (u@v) = delta A v o delta A u
```

Unfortunately it also leads to very complicated arguments in those cases where only single states are involved, e.g. the start state.

---

[2] I have used delta for functions and steps for relations.

3. steps is an excellent compromise because it it only talks about individual states in the input and output, and it is close to our intuition. On the other hand, there are also some drawbacks that we discuss in Sect. 4.

The touchstone for these different formulations was the correctness proof of the translation of a regular expression into an **nae** (see Sect. 4). Our conclusion is corroborated by the corresponding textbook proof [6]: the latter does not use a set-valued transition function at all (although it has been defined) but argues informally in terms of 'paths', which corresponds to the relation **steps**.

2.4   Equivalences

Every **nae** can be translated into an equivalent **na** which can then be translated into an equivalent **da**. Since we are not interested in **nas**, we have defined a direct translation from **naes** into **das** which combines the power set and ε-closure construction:

```
nae2da :: (α,σ)nae ⇒ (α,σ set)da
nae2da A ≡ ({start A},
            λ a Q. ⋃(next A (Some a) '' ((eps A)^* ^^ Q)),
            λ Q. ∃ p ∈ (eps A)^* ^^ Q. fin A p)
```

We use two further standard constructs, the image of a set under a function and a relation:

```
f '' S ≡ {f x . x ∈ S}
r ^^ S ≡ {y. ∃ x ∈ S. (x,y) ∈ r}
```

The actual equivalence proof, i.e. the proof of

$$\text{DA.accepts (nae2da A) w = NAe.accepts A w} \qquad (1)$$

is by rewriting with the lemma

```
(eps A)^* ^^ (DA.delta (nae2da A) w S) = steps A w ^^ S
```

which is proved by induction on w.

3   Regular Expressions

Regular expressions represent *regular sets*. The latter are sets of strings finitely generated from finite sets by union, concatenation and iteration (the star operation). Concatenation is defined explicitly

```
conc :: α list set ⇒ α list set ⇒ α list set
conc A B ≡ {xs@ys . xs ∈ A ∧ ys ∈ B}
```

whereas the star operation is defined inductively:

```
star :: α list set ⇒ α list set
[] ∈ star A
a ∈ A ∧ as ∈ star A ⟹ a@as ∈ star A
```

Two easy inductions yield an alternative characterization of star:

w ∈ star A = (∃ as. (∀ a ∈ set as. a ∈ A) ∧ (w = concat as))

Regular expressions are defined as usual

```
datatype α rexp = Empty
                | Atom α
                | Union (α rexp) (α rexp)
                | Conc (α rexp) (α rexp)
                | Star (α rexp)
```

as is the language denoted by a regular expression:

```
lang :: α rexp ⇒ α list set
lang Empty       = {}
lang (Atom a)    = {[a]}
lang (Union r s) = (lang r) ∪ (lang s)
lang (Conc r s)  = conc (lang r) (lang s)
lang (Star r)    = star (lang r)
```

Note that there is no separate constructor for a regular expression denoting the set {[]} because Star Empty does just that.

4   Regular Expressions into Nondeterministic Automata

This section is the core of the paper. It discusses the transformation of regular expressions into nondeterministic automata with ε-transitions. We follow the spirit of the standard inductive construction [6], but simplify things a little: we do not insist that each automaton has only one final state and no transitions out of this state. The simplified construction of the union and iteration of automata is shown in Fig. 2. The capital F represents a set of final states.

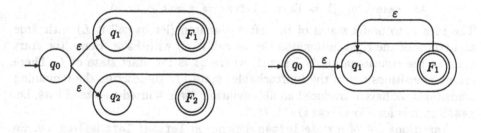

Fig. 2. Union and iteration of automata

The function we want to define has to be of type (α)rexp ⇒ (α,σ)nae. It remains to be determined what σ should be. The main criterion is the ease of renaming the states of an automaton to ensure they are disjoint from some other automaton. Graphically, this is easy: simply draw the two automata in nonoverlapping areas (e.g. as in Fig. 2 on the left). Adding offsets to natural numbers comes to mind, but this can be messy in proofs. Instead we use lists of Booleans and stick True or False in front to guarantee distinctness. Thus the above σ is simply (bool)list and we define the type

```
(α)bitsNAe = (α,(bool)list)nae
```

and the function

```
rexp2nae :: α rexp ⇒ α bitsNAe
rexp2nae Empty      = ([], λ a s. {}, λ s. False)
rexp2nae(Atom a)    = atom a
rexp2nae(Union r s) = union (rexp2nae r) (rexp2nae s)
rexp2nae(Conc r s)  = conc (rexp2nae r) (rexp2nae s)
rexp2nae(Star r)    = star (rexp2nae r)
```

Let us first examine the translation of Empty. The initial state is the empty list. The transition function always returns the empty set. Hence there is no transition out of any state, in particular not out of []. Thus the only reachable state is []. There is no final state because the last component (fin) always returns False. Hence the automaton accepts no word, as required by Empty.

The definition of atom is analogous.

We could now go through the remaining constructions one by one, but it will suffice to examine conc in detail:

```
conc :: α bitsNAe ⇒ α bitsNAe ⇒ α bitsNAe
conc ≡ λ(ql,dl,fl)(qr,dr,fr).
    (True#ql,
      λa s. case s of
               [] ⇒ {}
             | left#s ⇒ if left then (True ## dl a s) ∪
                                        (if fl s ∧ a=None then {False#qr}
                                                          else {})
                                 else False ## dr a s,
      λs. case s of [] ⇒ False | left#s ⇒ ¬left ∧ fr s)
```

The idea is to prefix states of the left automaton (let us call it L) with True and states of the right automaton (let us call it R) with False. Hence the start state of the concatenation is True#ql, where ql is the start state of L. There are no transitions out of the (unreachable) state []. To describe the remaining transitions we have introduced an abbreviation: ## is # lifted to sets of lists, i.e. x##XS stands for (λxs. x#xs) `` XS.

Transitions out of a state left#s depend on left. If left is True, i.e. we are in L, we take the transitions of L out of s together with an ε-transition to False#qr, where qr is the start state of R, in case s is a final state of R. If left is False, we simply take the transitions of R. The operation ## lifts states of L and R to states of their concatenation. The final states are those of R.

The definitions of union and star are analogous.

If the reader finds the above treatment in terms of bit lists revoltingly concrete, I cannot disagree. A more abstract approach is clearly desirable.

4.1 The Proof

The proof plan in the large is easy: show

$$\text{accepts (rexp2nae } r) \; w = (w \in \text{lang } r) \tag{2}$$

by induction on r using the obvious lemmas

```
accepts (atom a) w    = (w = [a])
accepts (union L R) w  = (accepts L w ∨ accepts R w)
accepts (conc L R) w   = (∃ u v. w = u@v ∧ accepts L u ∧ accepts R v)
accepts (star A) w     = (∃ us. (∀ u ∈ set us. accepts A u)
                              ∧ (w = concat us))
```

The realization of this plan is, unfortunately, a textbook example of the gap
between graphical intuition and formal proof. All of the lemmas appear obvious
given a picture of the composition of automata such as Fig. 2. Yet their proofs
require a painful amount of detail. For your amusement, the lemmas for the
conc-case are shown in Fig. 3.

```
fin (conc L R) (True#p) = False
fin (conc L R) (False#p) = fin R p
(True#p,q) ∈ step (conc L R) a =
   ((∃ r. q=True#r ∧ (p,r) ∈ step L a) ∨ (fin L p ∧ a=None ∧ q=False#start R))
(False#p,q) ∈ step (conc L R) a = (∃ r. q = False#r ∧ (p,r) ∈ step R a)
(False#p,fq) ∈ (eps(conc L R))^* ⟹ ∃ q. (p,q) ∈ (eps R)^* ∧ fq = False#q
(p,q) ∈ (eps R)^* ⟹ (False#p, False#q) ∈ (eps(conc L R))^*
(False#p,fq) ∈ (eps(conc L R))^* = (∃ q. fq = False#q ∧ (p,q) ∈ (eps R)^*)
(False#p,fq) ∈ steps (conc L R) w = (∃ q. fq = False#q ∧ (p,q)∈ steps R w)
(p,q) ∈ (eps L)^* ⟹ (True#p, True#q) ∈ (eps(conc L R))^*
(p,q) ∈ steps L w ⟹ (True#p, True#q) ∈ steps (conc L R) w
(True#p,tq) ∈ (eps(conc L R))^* ⟹
    (∃ q. tq = True#q ∧ (p,q) ∈ (eps L)^*) ∨
    (∃ q r. tq = False#q ∧ (p,r)∈(eps L)^* ∧ fin L r ∧ (start R,q) ∈ (eps R)^*)
(p,q) ∈ (eps L)^* ⟹ (True#p, True#q) ∈ (eps(conc L R))^*
(p,q) ∈ step R None ⟹ (False#p,False#q) ∈ step (conc L R) None
(p,q) ∈ (eps R)^* ⟹ (False#p,False#q) ∈ (eps(conc L R))^*
fin L p ⟹ (True#p,False#start R) ∈ eps(conc L R)
((True#p,q) ∈ (eps(conc L R))^*) =
    ((∃ r. (p,r) ∈ (eps L)^* ∧ q = True#r) ∨
     (∃ r. (p,r) ∈ (eps L)^* ∧ fin L r ∧
         (∃ s. (start R, s) ∈ (eps R)^* ∧ q = False#s)))
(True#p,q) ∈ steps (conc L R) w ⟹
    ((∃ r. (p,r) ∈ steps L w ∧ q = True#r) ∨
     (∃ u v. w = u@v ∧ (∃ r. (p,r) ∈ steps L u ∧ fin L r ∧
         (∃ s. (start R,s) ∈ steps R v ∧ q = False#s))))
```

Fig. 3. Lemmas for correctness of conc

If you examine the lemmas in Fig. 3 carefully, you will find that each one
is very reasonable, i.e. none of them is contrived to fit the needs of the theorem prover. Apart from the last two, which require 10 and 24 steps respectively,
all of them are proved in 3 or 4 steps: induction plus (automatic) predicate
calculus reasoning and a bit of simplification. However, because of the form of
the lemmas, predicate calculus reasoning dominates. Fortunately, Isabelle now

provides the right kind of automation [10], whereas the previous generation of Isabelle's predicate calculus reasoning tools [9] floundered on some of the lemmas. Unfortunately, predicate calculus reasoning is inherently less pleasant than simplification because a failed attempt of an automatic procedure yields no information on what is missing. Hence you have to start your own manual single step proof to discover where things go wrong, which is how we found the lemmas in Fig. 3. This is in contrast to simplification, where a failed proof attempt results in a new goal that, in many cases, is a strong clue as to what the missing lemma is. Hence the design decision for a relational treatment as discussed in Sect. 2.3 also has its drawbacks. For example, in a functional style, the lemma

```
(False#p,fq) ∈ steps (conc L R) w =
  (∃ q. fq = False#q ∧ (p,q) ∈ steps R w)
```

becomes

```
delta (conc L R) a (False ## Q) = False ## delta R a Q
```

Despite these difficulties, the relational approach appears simpler. Proponents of relation algebra might point out that the reduction to predicate calculus is responsible for all complications, and a purely relation-algebraic treatment would have been much slicker. They may well be right.

The derivation of the lemmas for union and star is entirely similar. If we now put (1) and (2) together, we obtain the main correctness theorem:

```
DA.accepts (nae2da(rexp2nae r)) w = (w ∈ lang r)
```

5   The Scanner

We will now turn deterministic automata into scanners as described in the introduction. It is easy to see that the concept of repeatedly chopping a maximal prefix off a string is independent of automata theory and can be parameterized by an arbitrary predicate on strings. Thus we will first do a bit of list processing, followed by two applications: the scanner, and, as an afterthought, paragraph filling. The nice thing is that the hard part of the development, including most of the proofs, is confined to the generic list processing functions.

5.1   Chopping Up Lists

We start by specifying the requirements. What does it mean to chop a list up into maximal prefixes? The prefix ordering on lists is defined as usual:

```
xs ≤ zs  ≡  ∃ ys. zs = xs@ys
```

Note the overloading of ≤. Then what is a maximal prefix of a list w.r.t. a predicate? The answer is almost obvious

```
is_maxpref P xs ys ≡
xs ≤ ys ∧ (xs=[] ∨ P xs) ∧ (∀ zs. zs ≤ ys ∧ P zs ⟶ zs ≤ xs)
```

except that we also allow [] to be a maximal prefix in case ys has no prefix that satisfies P. This definition makes sense in our context where the maximal prefix should never be empty (because chopping it off should reduce the list). Thus we can use [] as an indication that there is no nonempty prefix that satisfies P.

We now come to the main specification. The class of functions we want to specify are of type

$$\alpha \text{ chopper } = \alpha \text{ list} \Rightarrow \alpha \text{ list list} \times \alpha \text{ list}$$

The specification is a predicate

$$\text{is\_maxchopper} :: (\alpha \text{ list} \Rightarrow \text{bool}) \Rightarrow \alpha \text{ chopper} \Rightarrow \text{bool}$$

that expresses when its second argument correctly chops up lists according to its first argument:

```
is_maxchopper P chopper ≡
∀ xs zs yss.
    (chopper(xs) = (yss,zs)) =
    (xs = concat yss @ zs ∧ (∀ ys ∈ set yss. ys ≠ []) ∧
    (case yss of
        [] ⇒ is_maxpref P [] xs
      | us#uss ⇒ is_maxpref P us xs ∧
                    chopper(concat(uss)@zs) = (uss,zs)))
```

Let's recast this into words: chopper(xs) returns (yss,zs) iff

1. the concatenation of the outputs yields the input,
2. all elements of yss are nonempty, and
3. if yss is empty, then there is no nonempty prefix of xs that satisfies P, and if yss = us#uss, then us is the maximal prefix of xs w.r.t. P and chopping up the remaining list yields (uss,zs).

Note that instead of an unjustified axiom specifying a constant chopper, the predicate is_maxchopper is merely an abbreviation.

Note also that although the specification only says that the first element us of yss must be a maximal prefix, the remaining elements are covered by the "recursive" call of chopper in the final line. A direct specification of the maximal prefix property for all elements of yss is more involved because the list of which they are a prefix is not directly at hand.

Now that we have the main specification, let us look at an implementation:

1. function maxsplit splits a list into a maximal prefix and the remaining list;
2. function chop iterates the process of splitting off a prefix.

To make things more modular, we introduce the type

$$\alpha \text{ splitter } = \alpha \text{ list} \Rightarrow \alpha \text{ list} \times \alpha \text{ list}$$

and a separate specification

```
is_maxsplitter :: (α list ⇒ bool) ⇒ α splitter ⇒ bool
is_maxsplitter P splitf ≡
(∀ xs ps qs. (splitf xs = (ps,qs)) = (xs=ps@qs ∧ is_maxpref P ps xs))
```

that maxsplit should satisfy. The definition of

```
maxsplit :: (α list ⇒ bool) ⇒ α list × α list ⇒ α list
             ⇒ α splitter
maxsplit P r ps []    = (if P ps then (ps,[]) else r)
maxsplit P r ps (q#qs) = maxsplit P (if P ps then (ps,q#qs) else r)
                                 (ps@[q]) qs
```

is fairly easy: r is the maximal result found so far, ps the prefix accumulated since the initial call, and qs is the suffix that remains to be examined; r is updated every time a longer prefix that satisfies P is found.

Once you come up with and prove (by induction on qs) the lemma

```
(maxsplit P r ps qs = (xs,ys)) =
(if ∃ us. us ≤ qs ∧ P(ps@us)
  then xs@ys=ps@qs ∧ is_maxpref P xs (ps@qs) else (xs,ys)=r)
```

it follows easily that maxsplit, suitably initialized, meets its specification:

```
is_maxsplitter P (λ xs. maxsplit P ([],xs) [] xs)
```

Note that maxsplit traverses the whole list. Iterating maxsplit may therefore lead to quadratic run times. This problem could be overcome if there were an additional test whether ps can at all be extended to a list satisfying P. In terms of automata theory, this corresponds to a test whether the current state is an 'error' state which does not lead to any final state.

We now come to our main function chop that turns splitters into choppers by iterating them:

```
chop :: α splitter ⇒ α chopper
reducing splitf ⟹
  chop splitf xs = (let (pre,post) = splitf xs
                    in if pre=[] then ([],xs)
                       else let (xss,zs) = chop splitf post
                            in (pre#xss,zs))
```

Note that this a direct consequence of the actual definition by wellfounded recursion, which is not shown. The precondition involving

```
reducing :: α splitter ⇒ bool
reducing splitf ≡
∀ xs ys zs. splitf xs = (ys,zs) ∧ ys ≠ [] ⟶ length zs < length xs
```

is necessary to guarantee termination of chop. With the help of a few lemmas (proved by induction on the length of a list) one can establish

```
is_maxsplitter P splitf ⟹ is_maxchopper P (chop splitf)
```

5.2 Scanning

Now we specialize the above generic functions to perform scanning, i.e. chopping up strings based on the acceptance by a deterministic automaton. A naïve solution is to call maxsplit with the predicate (accepts A). But since accepts is applied to longer and longer prefixes, this leads to quadratic run times.

Thus we need to re-implement maxsplit, replacing the predicate by an accepting da together with its current state:

```
auto_split :: (α,σ)da ⇒ σ  ⇒ α list × α list ⇒ α list
                          ⇒ α splitter
auto_split A q r ps []    = (if fin A q then (ps,[]) else r)
auto_split A q r ps (x#xs) =
  auto_split A (next A x q) (if fin A q then (ps,x#xs) else r) (ps@[x]) xs
```

Although it may seem that maxsplit is completely superseded by auto_split and need never have been defined, the opposite is true: it is now trivial (an induction on xs) to show

```
auto_split A (delta A ps q) r ps xs =
maxsplit (λ ys. fin A (delta A ys q)) r ps xs
```

which, putting the results of Sect. 5.1 together, yields the corollary

```
is_maxchopper (accepts A) (scan A)
```

where

```
scan :: (α,σ)da ⇒ α chopper
scan A ≡ chop (λ xs. auto_split A (start A) ([],xs) [] xs)
```

is our main function. As predicted above, specializing the generic development to automata is easy.

If the whole development appears overly modular, I recommend the following more direct definition of the scanner

```
acc A s r ps []    ys = (if ys=[] then r else (ys#fst(r),snd(r)))
acc A s r ps (x#xs) ys = (let t = next A x s in
    if fin A t
    then acc A t (acc A (start A) ([],xs) [] xs [])
               (ps@[x]) xs (ps@[x])
    else acc A t r (ps@[x]) xs ys)
```

due to Roland Handl [5]. It mixes the generic and the specific and, on top of that, is primitive recursive.[3] Although acc confuses me to this day, Richard Mayr managed to verify it. However, the proof is sufficiently unpleasant that there had to be a better way to do it. What I presented above is the result of my quest for a more appealing solution.

5.3   Filling Paragraphs

After the completion of the above development I suddenly remembered that Bird and Wadler [1] also define a function scan. On looking it up, I found that

---

[3] Nested primitive recursion can be reduced to ordinary primitive recursion [3]. Handl was forced to use primitive recursion because at the time HOL did not provide easy access to wellfounded recursion.

it is used in a similar application, namely filling paragraphs (pages 91–92). This made me realize that one can define their function

fill :: **nat** $\Rightarrow$ (α list list) $\Rightarrow$ (α list list list)

that takes a list of words and returns a list of lines that are no longer than the given line width (the first parameter), as an instance of our scan:

fill n $\equiv$ fst(scan (0, λ **xs** i. i+length(**xs**)+1, λ i. i $\leq$ n+1))

The second component of the result of scan is dropped (fst selects the first component) to make the function conform to the type in [1]. If none of the input words is longer than the line width, the second component is always [].

6 Does it Run?

To be more precise: can the definitions of the main functions rexp2nae, nae2da and scan (and of their supporting functions) be interpreted directly in a functional programming language? For scan, the answer is yes: only primitive or wellfounded recursion on lists is used. Deterministic automata are also easy, but nondeterministic automata cause a little problem: we need to implement sets. In full generality, this is impossible, but finite sets can be represented as lists, which is one of the standard examples of implementation concepts for abstract data types. Fortunately, the sets arising in rexp2nae are all finite, thanks to the finite nature of regular expressions. Hence rexp2nae is also executable (although a replacement of finite sets by lists would be tricky to perform automatically in HOL).

The real problem arises with the definition of nae2da, which contains the inductively defined transitive closure operator ^* and is therefore definitely not directly executable. Even if all sets in sight are finite, we would still need a recursive function for computing the transitive closure. Hence the answer to the section title is 'almost'.

There are a number of solutions to this problem:

- Show that rexp2nae only produces finite automata and define a recursive version of ^* that operates on finite relations. This is possible but most likely messier than the next alternative.
- Generate a nondeterministic automaton *without* ε-steps directly from a regular expression. Although this complicates the construction a little, I expect the proofs actually become simpler because ε-steps are eliminated.
- Give a concrete finite representation of the transition function of automata in terms of, for example, association lists. This does entail rephrasing rexp2nae in terms of this representation, but I believe that one can reuse most of the proofs by showing that the concrete representation is a correct implementation of the abstract automaton model of this paper.

We intend to investigate the last two options in the near future. Note that there is a fundamental difference between them. Performing the conversion of nondeterministic automata on our functional representation postpones most of the work until run time, where states of the da are represented as sets of states of the na, all of which have to be processed. Given a concrete data structure for the transition function of the na, it is possible to eliminate this overhead by representing each of the (finitely many!) sets of states by a single new state. Nevertheless, the speedup is only a constant factor that depends on the size of the state space. Both representations allow DA.accepts to operate in time linear in the size of the input string. Scanning, however, is quadratic, because the recognition of each maximal prefix requires traversing the whole (remaining) string.

7   Related Work

I am aware of three other papers on formalized automata theory [7, 4, 2], all of which use constructive type theory (i.e. they extract their algorithms from the proofs rather than providing them as part of the definitions) and follow [6] closely. The main result of Kreitz [7] is the pumping lemma and the main result of Constable et al. [2] the Myhill/Nerode theorem. Both of them use the Nuprl system.

Closest to our work is that by Filliâtre [4] who gives a constructive proof for the translation of regular expressions into nondeterministic finite automata with ε-moves in the Coq system.[4] Although the transition relation of the resulting automaton has a nice concrete representation as a finite set of triples, he does not consider the further conversion into a deterministic automaton (nor the scanning aspect). It is the latter conversion where executability breaks down for us because we use the transitive closure operator ^*.

Thompson [11] presents an implementation (no proofs) of regular expressions and finite automata in Miranda.

8   Conclusion

We have seen a formalization of a (very simple) lexical analyzer generator taking us from a regular expression right to the actual scanner. Almost all of the functions involved are directly executable. Ignoring the small executability gap in our development (see Sect. 6), this work shows that HOL is eminently suitable to verify (total) functional programs, although HOL is neither constructive (where you often worry if the extracted program will be what you think it should be) nor a quantifier-free logic of recursively defined functions.

The size of the combined theories and proofs is quite acceptable: roughly 1000 lines dedicated to automata and regular expressions, and fewer than 400 lines involving the scanner. My first attempts in this direction go back a number of

---

[4] Contrary to the title of that paper, the opposite direction is not mentioned. I have formalized and verified the translation of automata into regular sets as a recursive algorithm similar to Warshall's. The details are beyond the current paper.

years and include dead alleys explored by students. The bulk of the development presented in this paper took me about 3 intensive weeks.

Although the work was not intended as a formalization of a specific textbook (in contrast to [2] or [8]), I feel that Hopcroft and Ullman's treatment has influenced me more than necessary, and that a development bypassing ε-moves might have been better. This will be explored in the future.

Acknowledgements

Stefan Weber helped with an initial version of the proofs in Sect. 4. David Basin, David von Oheimb, Larry Paulson and Markus Wenzel read a draft and commented on it at short notice, for which I am very grateful.

References

1. R. Bird and P. Wadler. *Introduction to Functional Programming.* Prentice-Hall, 1988.
2. R. Constable, P. Jackson, P. Naumov, and J. Uribe. Constructively formalizing automata. In G. Plotkin and M. Tofte, editors, *Proof, Language and Interaction: Essays in Honour of Robin Milner.* MIT Press, 1998. To appear.
3. W. Felscher. *Berechenbarkeit.* Springer-Verlag, 1993.
4. J.-C. Filliâtre. Finite automata theory in Coq. A constructive proof of Kleene's theorem. Technical Report 97-04, Laboratoire de l'Informatique du Parallélisme, Ecole Normale Supérieure de Lyon, 1997.
5. R. Handl. Verifikation eines Scanners (mit Isabelle). Master's thesis, Institut für Informatik, TU München, 1993.
6. J. E. Hopcroft and J. D. Ullman. *Introduction to Automata Theory, Languages, and Computation.* Addison-Wesley, 1979.
7. C. Kreitz. Constructive automata theory implemented with the Nuprl proof development system. Technical Report TR 86-779, Dept. of Computer Science, Cornell University, 1986.
8. T. Nipkow. Winskel is (almost) right: Towards a mechanized semantics textbook. In V. Chandru and V. Vinay, editors, *Foundations of Software Technology and Theoretical Computer Science,* volume 1180 of *Lect. Notes in Comp. Sci.,* pages 180–192. Springer-Verlag, 1996.
9. L. C. Paulson. Generic automatic proof tools. In R. Veroff, editor, *Automated Reasoning and its Applications.* MIT Press, 1997. Also Report 396, Computer Laboratory, University of Cambridge.
10. L. C. Paulson. A generic tableau prover and its integration with Isabelle. Technical Report 441, University of Cambridge, Computer Laboratory, 1998.
11. S. Thompson. Regular expressions and automata using Miranda. Available at http://www.cs.ukc.ac.uk/pubs/1995/212, 1995.

Extending Window Inference

Joakim von Wright

Åbo Akademi University and Turku Centre for Computer Science (TUCS)
Lemminkäisenkatu 14A, 20520 Turku, Finland
jwright@abo.fi

Abstract. Window inference is a proof paradigm where a theorem is proved by stepwise transformation, including transformations that change subterms while taking the context of these subterms into account. Originally developed for mathematical equivalence reasoning, window inference has proved powerful in other fields as well, and in particular for reasoning about refinement of programs. Although window inference is powerful and flexible, it has many limitations. The paper shows how some restrictions can be relaxed without compromising the elegance and simplicity of the window inference paradigm. We suggest a number of extensions, discuss their possible implementations and give examples of their use.

1 Introduction

Window inference is a proof paradigm where a theorem of the form $\vdash E\ R\ E'$ (where E and E' are expressions and R is a relation) is proved by stepwise transformation, including transformations that change subterms while taking the context of these subterms into account. Window inference was originally developed for mathematical reasoning with equivalence relations, but it has proved a powerful method for general logical reasoning, and in particular for reasoning about refinement of programs.

Grundy formalised window inference in higher-order logic and implemented a tool for the HOL theorem proving system [8]. His system did not require the addition of axioms or inference rules; instead, it translates proof steps of window inference to corresponding proof steps in higher-order logic. This gives a guarantee that every proof is sound. The use of higher-order logic also makes it possible to formulate very general rules that can use powerful matching techniques.

Although window inference is very powerful and flexible, it has certain built-in limitations. When building a tool for program refinement based on window inference [5] we have repeatedly encountered situations where slight generalisations of the window inference paradigm would make it possible to provide support for refinement features that are now outside the scope of window inference. The aim of this paper is to show how some restrictions can be relaxed without compromising the elegance and simplicity of the window inference paradigm. We suggest a number of extensions, discuss their possible implementations and give examples of their use.

Window inference (with certain extensions) has been considered and implemented in other contexts than the HOL system as well. The Ergo system [4] is a generic proof tool with window inference as its main theorem proving paradigm. Staples [14] has implemented window inference in the Isabelle system, in a "lightweight" way that reuses much of the built-in theorem proving infrastructure of Isabelle.

The paper uses standard logical notation, with T and F for the truth values, with $\equiv$ for logical equivalence, with the range of quantifiers delimited by parentheses, and with $f\ x$ standing for the application of (function) f to argument x.

2   Window Inference

In this section we briefly describe window inference, including its implementation and applications and its relation to other proof methods. For more details, we refer the reader to the references given in the text.

2.1   Window Inference

Window inference is a method for doing transformational proofs, originally described by Robinson and Staples [13] and later extended by Grundy [7]. An *initial focus* E_0 is transformed step by step while preserving a preorder (i.e., a reflexive and transitive relation) R. The result of the sequence of transformations (called a *derivation*)

$$E_0\ R\ E_1\ R\ \cdots\ R\ E_n$$

is (by transitivity of R) that $E_0\ R\ E_n$ holds.

A major feature of window inference is that we can at any time focus our attention on a subterm of the current focus (this is called *opening a window* on the subterm). The subterm is transformed as described above (in a *subderivation*) and when we *close the subwindow*, the result of the subderivation is substituted for the term that we focused our attention on.

The opening and closing of subwindows is governed by *window rules* of the form

$$\frac{\Gamma' \vdash\ e\ r\ e'}{\Gamma \vdash\ E[e]\ R\ E[e']} \tag{1}$$

where r and R are preorders (reflexive and transitive relations), $E[e]$ is a term with e occurring as a subterm and $E[e']$ is the same term but with e' substituted for e, and Γ and Γ' are sets of formulas. Logically, this is an inference rule in a sequent formulation of a logic (in our case higher-order logic). As a window rule, it should be read starting in the lower left corner. The rule can be applied in a situation when we are preserving the relation R and focusing on the subterm e of the current focus $E[e]$ and when the assumptions that we are working under are Γ. The rule then states that we may assume Γ' and transform e while preserving r in the subderivation.

An example of a window rule is the following:

$$\frac{\Gamma, t_2 \ \vdash \ t_1 \Rightarrow t_1'}{\Gamma \ \vdash \ (t_1 \wedge t_2) \ \Rightarrow \ (t_1' \wedge t_2)}$$

which states that we can transform a conjunct (under implication) and that we may then assume the other conjunct. Slightly less obvious examples are the following:

$$\frac{\Gamma, \neg t_1 \ \vdash \ t_2 \Rightarrow t_2'}{\Gamma \ \vdash \ (t_1 \vee t_2) \ \Rightarrow \ (t_1 \vee t_2')} \qquad \frac{\Gamma, \neg t_2 \ \vdash \ t_1 \Leftarrow t_1'}{\Gamma \ \vdash \ (t_1 \Rightarrow t_2) \ \Rightarrow \ (t_1' \Rightarrow t_2)}$$

Window rules can be chained together. For example, if the focus is $t_1 \vee (t \wedge t_2)$ and we are preserving implication, then we may focus on t and preserve backward implication, assuming $\neg t_1$ and t_2.

2.2   Tool Support

Grundy's tool for window inference [8] handles a derivation using a *stack* of *windows* in the metalanguage of the HOL system [6]. When a stack is *created*, a focus E, a relation R and a set Γ of assumptions are given and entered into the first window in the stack. The window can be characterised by the *window theorem* $\Gamma \vdash E \ R \ E$ (recall that R must be reflexive). The system has a database of relations that are known to be reflexive and transitive. Initially equality and (forward and backward) implication are available, but the user can add new relations to the database (after the reflexivity and transitivity properties have been proved).

A transformation is applied by specifying a theorem in the HOL logic of the form $\Phi \vdash t \ R \ t'$ where E matches t and a subset of Γ matches Φ. The system then deduces $\Gamma \vdash E \ R \ E'$ and this becomes the new window theorem. After the next transformation (of the form $\Gamma \vdash E' \ R \ E''$) the window theorem is $\Gamma \vdash E \ R \ E''$ (by transitivity) and so on.

The tool stores window rules in a database. When the user selects a subterm e of the current focus, a suitable sequence of window rules is chained together and from these the assumptions Γ' and the relation r of the *subwindow* (or *child window*) which is pushed onto the stack. After this, the focus of the child window can be transformed and new subwindows can be opened. When a subwindow is closed at a point when the window theorem is $\Gamma' \vdash e \ r \ e'$, the window is popped from the stack and the window rule is applied to make $\Gamma \vdash E[e] \ R \ E[e']$ the window theorem of the parent window.

The assumptions (Γ) of a window can be flagged as being *conjectures*, i.e., assumptions that have been added in a transformation step and need to be discharged (by a proof). This flagging has no logical meaning, it simply distinguish the original assumptions from those that have been added because the correctness of some transformations depends on them. The assumptions can also include *lemmas*, i.e., formulas that have been derived from the other assumptions.

2.3 Structured Derivations

There is a close correspondence between window inference and the format of *structured derivations* (or *structured calculational proofs*) described by Back, Grundy and von Wright [2]. The following example should make this proof format clear. It is a simple proof of the tautology $p \wedge (p \Rightarrow q) \equiv p \wedge q$:

$$p \wedge {}_{\llcorner}(p \Rightarrow q)_{\lrcorner}$$
$$\equiv \{\text{replace subterm } p \Rightarrow q \text{ in context}\}$$
$$1 \triangleright \qquad \langle p \rangle$$
$$p \Rightarrow q$$
$$\equiv \{\text{use assumption (which is equivalent to } p \equiv \mathsf{T})\}$$
$$\mathsf{T} \Rightarrow q$$
$$\equiv \{\mathsf{T} \text{ is top element}\}$$
$$q$$
$$\triangleleft \quad p \wedge {}^{\ulcorner}q^{\urcorner}$$

In this format, an indented subproof (a *subderivation*) corresponds to proving a hypothesis of an inference rule; in this case the rule is

$$\frac{t \vdash t_1 \equiv t_2}{\vdash t \wedge t_1 \equiv t \wedge t_2}$$

where the added assumption of the subderivation (p) is indicated in angle brackets. Note also the last justification in the subderivation: implication is a partial ordering on the booleans.

Structured derivations fit nicely with the refinement-oriented formulation of higher-order logic given by Back and von Wright [3]. In this formulation, an inference rule has the general format

$$\frac{\Phi_1 \vdash t_1 \sqsubseteq_1 t'_1 \quad \cdots \quad \Phi_n \vdash t_n \sqsubseteq_n t'_n}{\Phi \vdash t \sqsubseteq t'}$$

and an inference using this rule is written with n indented subderivations. The subderivations that occur in window inference are then a special case, where an inference rules has the special form (1).

2.4   Applications and Limitations of Window Inference

Window inference was originally developed for working with equality and equivalence in mathematical and logical reasoning. Grundy extended window inference to work with preorders, with the explicit idea of applying it to program refinement. In this, he was inspired by Back's refinement diagrams [1] which give a graphical description of program refinement by stepwise transformation of program subcomponents. Grundy used his system for program refinement in a relational framework [8] but it was later used for program development in a predicate transformer framework [5].

Although window inference is a general and powerful proof method, it has certain built-in limitations. The window relation is required to be reflexive and transitive. Furthermore, window inference is inherently linear; there is always a single current focus that we are working with (in the implementation, this allows the simple stack structure to be used). Finally, window inference only works with subderivations that replace a subterm of the focus. The main aim of this paper is to show how restrictions such as these can be relaxed without compromising the elegance and simplicity of the window inference paradigm.

3   Nonreflexive Relations

The requirement that the window relation must be reflexive is not essential. Reflexivity is used in the initial theorem of a subderivation; when we open a subwindow according to a rule of the form

$$\frac{\Gamma' \vdash e \; r \; e'}{\Gamma \vdash E[e] \; R \; E[e']}$$

the initial window theorem is $e \; r \; e$. However, as pointed out by Staples [14] we can just as well use $e = e'$ as the initial theorem. As long as we do equality steps, the window theorem is of the form $\Gamma \vdash e = e'$ (even though the window relation is not equality). When we do the first step according to the nonreflexive relation r the theorem changes form to $\Gamma \vdash e \; r \; e'$ and from that point on it has that form.

A simple-minded solution would be to work with a nonreflexive (but transitive) relation in the same way as with a reflexive one. However, if we require that every step in a derivation that is supposed to preserve, say, $<$ on the integers, then a three-step derivation of the form $t_0 < t_1 < t_2 < t_3$ in fact requires that $t_0 < t_3 - 2$. Thus we must make a distinction between two different relations: the *intended* window relation and the *actual* relation that has been preserved so far (and which must be stronger than the intended relation; usually equality). The example below illustrates this idea.

The following example illustrates two derivations with a nonreflexive relation (in this case the strict ordering $<$ on the real numbers).

$$
\begin{array}{l}
\quad\quad \dfrac{5\epsilon}{4} - \dfrac{\epsilon}{2} \\[4pt]
< \; \{\text{subderivation in antimonotonic context}\} \\[4pt]
1 \rhd \quad\quad \dfrac{\epsilon}{2} \\[4pt]
\quad\quad\quad > \; \{\text{arithmetic}\} \\[4pt]
\quad\quad\quad \dfrac{\epsilon}{4} \\[4pt]
\lhd \quad \dfrac{5\epsilon}{4} - \dfrac{\epsilon}{4} \\[4pt]
= \; \{\text{arithmetic}\} \\[4pt]
\quad\quad \dfrac{4\epsilon}{4} \\[4pt]
= \; \{\text{arithmetic}\} \\[4pt]
\quad\quad \epsilon
\end{array}
$$

and

$$\frac{5\epsilon}{4} - \frac{\epsilon}{2}$$
$$= \{\text{subderivation}\}$$
$$1 \triangleright \qquad \frac{\epsilon}{2}$$
$$= \{\text{arithmetic}\}$$
$$\frac{2\epsilon}{4}$$
$$\triangleleft \qquad \frac{5\epsilon}{4} - \frac{2\epsilon}{4}$$
$$= \{\text{arithmetic}\}$$
$$\frac{3\epsilon}{4}$$
$$< \{\text{arithmetic}\}$$
$$\epsilon$$

In the first derivation, the window relation changes from equality to the non-reflexive relation already in the subderivation (where antimonotonicity justifies using > as window relation). In the second derivation, the relation of the window theorem is equality up until the last step. Of course, it may happen that we do only equality steps, even though the window relation is nonreflexive. The only result of this is that our final theorem is an equality rather that the kind of theorem that we were looking for.

From the example we see why dropping the reflexivity requirement also affects the closing of subwindows, in the sense that we must distinguish two separate cases. If the actual and the intended relation are the same, then closing works as for reflexive relations. However, if the window theorem in the child window is an equality, then closing gives an equality in the parent window, and the nonreflexive relation is still waiting to be "realised".

This idea for handling nonreflexive relations is extended to allow not only equalities but also the use of relations that are between the reflexive relation and equality in strength. For example, if we preserve <, then we may do steps according to both = and ≤ on the way.

4 Nontransitive Window Relations

Dropping transitivity is not as simple as dropping reflexivity. In principle, it is possible to work in the style of window inference arbitrary relations and simply compute the composition of relations as we go along:

$$t_1$$
$$R_1 \{\text{first transformation step}\}$$
$$t_2$$
$$R_2 \{\text{second transformation step}\}$$
$$t_3$$

In this case the window theorem after the two steps is t_1 $(R_1; R_2)$ t_3. However, that means we are not preserving a specific relation in our derivation. This may not seem like a problem, but it makes it difficult to build a useful collection of window rules. To see this, consider the format for window rules

$$\frac{\Gamma' \vdash e \ r \ e'}{\Gamma \vdash E[e] \ R \ E[e']}$$

Even if we do not know R when focusing on e in $E[e]$, we can do transformation steps on e and if the window theorem at the time of closing matches $\Gamma' \vdash e \ r \ e'$ then the window theorem in the parent window will become $\Gamma \vdash E[e] \ R \ E[e']$. However, closing is not possible unless there is an exact match, and this makes it hard to work with anything other than equality in subderivations. Furthermore, if the relation R is not known at the time when the subwindow is opened, then it may not be possible to decide what window rule to use at closing, and this means that it may not be possible to compute the additional context information (i.e., the formulas in Γ' that are not in Γ).

4.1 Indexed Relations

A simple solution to the problem is to use *indexed relations*. An indexed relation is simply a relation of higher order than two, but where some arguments are handled in a special way. An indexed relation on a type Σ is a constant $R: \alpha \rightarrow \Sigma \rightarrow \Sigma \rightarrow$ Bool, where α is a type equipped with an associative operation $\circ$ so that the following holds for arbitrary x and y of type α:

$$R \ x; R \ y = R \ (x \circ y) \tag{2}$$

Writing $R \ x$ as R_x (and using infix notation) this can be stated as follows

$$t_1 \ R_x \ t_2 \ \wedge \ t_2 \ R_y \ t_3 \Rightarrow t_1 \ R_{x \circ y} \ t_3$$

which shows that (2) is a generalised transitivity property. Higher-order relations for data refinement by window inference were proposed by Nickson [11], but he did not employ the idea of composing indices.

The idea is that we preserve a general indexed relation R, but the index is computed (composed) as we move along. Window rules can be stated in terms of the general indexed relation, so that the right rule can be identified and the context information computed at the time a subwindow is opened. A window rule will have the following form:

$$\frac{\Gamma' \vdash e \ r_x \ e'}{\Gamma \vdash E[e] \ R_X \ E[e']}$$

When the subwindow is opened, Γ, $E[e]$ and R are known. These should be sufficient to compute Γ' and r. After a sequence of transformation steps we then know e' and x and from these it should be possible to compute X and close the subwindow.

If the indexing type is a monoid with respect to the operation $\circ$ and R_1 is always reflexive (where 1 is the unit element of $\circ$), then the initial theorem can be of the form $\vdash t\ R_1\ t$ and we can start composing relations immediately. However, this requirement is not necessary, since we can let the initial window theorem be the equality $\vdash t = t$, as explained in Sect.3.

4.2 Examples

An example where indexed relations can be used is when following computation paths according to axioms and rules for a transition relation. Rules are often given on the form of a structured operational semantics, e.g.

$$\frac{}{\alpha; P \xrightarrow{\alpha} P} \qquad \frac{P \xrightarrow{\alpha} P'}{P|Q \xrightarrow{\alpha} P'|Q}$$

where P and Q stand for some kind of processes, α stands for an action, and ; and $|$ are operators used to build processes. A sequence of steps according to such rules can be collected, by defining composition of indices to be simple concatenation:

$$\xrightarrow{\alpha}; \xrightarrow{\beta} = \xrightarrow{\alpha\beta}$$

Window inference can then be used to prove that a given process P can perform a certain sequence of actions $\alpha_1\alpha_2\cdots\alpha_n$ and become some other process P'.

As another example consider computing partial derivatives of a term with respect to certain variables. If $t \xrightarrow{x} t'$ means that t is the derivative of t with respect to x, then a sequence

$$t \xrightarrow{x} t' \xrightarrow{y} t''$$

allows us to deduce $t\xrightarrow{xy}t'$ (in this case, the composition operation on indices is commutative, since the variable order does not matter in partial derivatives).

4.3 Data Refinement

A further example where indexed relations are needed is in data refinement of programs. In data refinement, the refinement relation $\sqsubseteq$ is indexed by an *abstraction relation* R that relates the new (*concrete*) state space to the original (*abstract*) state space. The following general theorem of data refinement shows that we in fact have an indexed relation:

$$S \sqsubseteq_R S' \land S' \sqsubseteq_Q S'' \Rightarrow S \sqsubseteq_{Q;R} S'' \tag{3}$$

so the operation on indices is (reverse) relation composition.

A window rule for data refinement is the following rule, which shows how local variables can be replaced in a data refinement.

$$\frac{\Gamma \vdash S \sqsubseteq_R S'}{\Gamma \vdash \text{begin var } x \bullet S \text{ end} \sqsubseteq \text{begin var } x' \bullet [\exists x \bullet R]; S' \text{ end}}$$

with the side condition that R only refers to the local variables (x and x'). Here the relation R need not be given when the subwindow is opened. Instead, we can do stepwise data refinements as shown in (3), with the abstraction relations being composed, until we are satisfied.

If there are nested blocks, so that the statement S contains an inner block, then part of the data refinement on the outer level can be a data refinement of this inner block, using the following rule:

$$\frac{\Gamma \vdash S \sqsubseteq_{R \wedge Q} S'}{\Gamma \vdash \textsf{begin var } y \bullet S \textsf{ end} \sqsubseteq_R \textsf{begin var } y' \bullet [\exists y \bullet Q]; S' \textsf{ end}}$$

Here, the indexed relation is of the more complex form ($\lambda X \bullet \sqsubseteq_{R \wedge X}$).

5 Nonfocusing Subderivations

An important difference between window inference and the structured derivations format is that the latter allows more freedom when it comes to starting subderivations. A subderivation in window inference is always started on a subcomponent of the current focus (or on a term in the context of the current focus). This gives a uniform structure to subderivations (and it allows the rules to be chained together automatically when opening a window on a subterm deep inside the focus) but it is at the same time a restriction.

Grundy has shown [9] that window inference is complete for first-order logic, in the sense that to any natural deduction proof there is a corresponding window inference proof. However, from this it does not follow that any proof in higher-order logic can be done using window inference. Also, we believe there are situations where nonfocusing subderivations are in many situations easier to work with than the possible restructuring that is needed in order to make proof fit the window inference format.

Although traditional window inference does not support nonfocusing subderivations, Grundy has implemented an extension to his window inference tool, which allows the user to define nonfocusing subderivations. These are stored in the same database as the window rules, but they are invoked explicitly by the user, who also supplies the extra information that is needed to set up the subderivation and to close it.

5.1 General Subderivations

In the style of structured derivations, inference rules have the general format

$$\frac{\Gamma_1 \vdash t_1 \sqsubseteq_1 t_1' \quad \cdots \quad \Gamma_n \vdash t_n \sqsubseteq_n t_n'}{\Gamma \vdash t \sqsubseteq t'}$$

where it may not be possible to compute the initial terms of the subderivations (i.e., $t_1, \ldots, t_n$) from the focus t.

Let us first consider the case when there is only one subderivation. If we allow the opening of a subwindow to have arguments connected to it, then it is sufficient that the rule and the initial focus of the child window can be computed from the current focus and the arguments given. In the most general case, we can think of both the rule name and the initial focus of the child window being given as arguments.

As an example, consider the principle of *complete induction*. We can state it as an inference rule (preserving backward implication), as follows:

$$\frac{\Gamma, (\forall k \mid k < n \bullet t[n := k]) \vdash t \Leftarrow \mathsf{T}}{\Gamma \vdash (\forall n \bullet t) \Leftarrow \mathsf{T}}$$

Although the initial focus of the subderivation is a subterm of the parent focus, this is not a focusing subderivation (since the rule is not a monotonicity rule). Note also that we require the endpoint of the subderivation to reach a very specific focus (T) before the subwindow can be closed. This is a typical feature for many nonfocusing subderivations.

In certain cases, nonfocusing subderivations can be replaced by normal transformations. In this case, we can get away with the simple rule

$$\frac{}{\vdash (\forall n \bullet t) \ \Leftarrow \ ((\forall k \mid k < n \bullet t[n := k]) \Rightarrow t)}$$

(and some may say this is just as natural). Applying this transformation rule to a focus of the form $(\forall n \bullet t)$ and then focusing on the consequent gives essentially the same effect as starting a subderivation according to the previous rule.

5.2   Multiple Subderivations

As noted earlier, linear derivations with multiple subderivations give us a system that matches natural deduction (with proofs written in the format of structured derivations). Window inference can be extended to allow for multiple subderivations, by adding a number of subwindows onto the stack and then closing them one by one, keeping track of all the window theorems proved. For example, the meet introduction rule for lattices:

$$\frac{\Gamma \vdash t \sqsubseteq t_1 \qquad \Gamma \vdash t \sqsubseteq t_2}{\Gamma \vdash t \ \sqsubseteq \ t_1 \sqcap t_2}$$

can be applied by pushing two subwindows onto the stack, both with initial theorem $\Gamma \vdash t \sqsubseteq t$ (or $\Gamma \vdash t = t$ if we allow nonreflexive relations). When the first subwindow is closed at $\Gamma \vdash t \sqsubseteq t_1$, this theorem could be stored temporarily and the second subderivation started. When this second derivation is closed, the theorems of the two subderivations together allow us to deduce $\Gamma \vdash t \sqsubseteq t_1 \sqcap t_2$ in the parent window.

Although this is theoretically simple, it requires an elaboration of the basic stack structure used in window inference tools. In addition, it may be desirable to move between different subderivations so that errors in one subderivation can be corrected without undoing the independent work done in other subderivations. For this to be possible, the windows must be organised in a tree-like structure (see Sect.6).

Again, there are cases where multiple subderivations can be avoided by using alternative strategies. For example, meet introduction can be simulated by first transforming t into $t \sqcap t$ (using the idempotence rule for meet) and then separately transforming the first t to t_1 and the second t to t_2. An example where this is not as easily done is when proving equivalence by mutual implication:

$$\frac{\Gamma \vdash t \Rightarrow t' \quad \Gamma \vdash t \Leftarrow t'}{\Gamma \vdash t \equiv t'}$$

5.3 Recursion Introduction

As an example where it is not as simple to reduce a nonfocusing subderivation to a combination of transforming and focusing, consider the following well-known refinement rule for *recursion introduction* in program refinement:

$$\frac{\Gamma \vdash \{t = w\}; S \sqsubseteq f(\{t < w\}; S)}{\Gamma \vdash S \sqsubseteq \mu f}$$

where t is a variant expression that ranges over some well-founded set and w is a fresh variable. If this rule is applied at a certain point in a program derivation when the focus is S, then a subwindow is opened (i.e., a subderivation is started) with $\{t = w\}; S$ as focus. The variant t must be given as an argument, since it cannot be computed from the information available. The fact that the recursion introduction rule should be used, rather than some other rule, must also be indicated. Note also that for a rule such as this one, it is not possible to close the subwindow at an arbitrary point, since the focus has to match $f(\{t < w\}; S)$ when the subwindow is closed. Note that f is a higher-order variable; the use of this rule requires second-order matching.

6 Nonsequential Derivations

Window inference is sequential in nature. The top window of the stack is the only one that can be accessed and the proof always moves in a forward direction. From a practical point of view, more flexibility could be helpful. For example, one may want to open two subwindows on different subterms of the focus of a window and then work on them in parallel.

6.1 Parallel Derivations

In parallel window inference the windows would have to be organised as a tree rather than a stack. This would allow us to open subwindows on different subterms of the current focus, and switch between working with them.

It is easily seen that parallel derivations cannot be permitted without introducing some restrictions. For example, if we focus in parallel on both conjuncts of $t \wedge t$ and transform under equivalence, then the rules of context allow us to transform each t to T (using the other conjunct as context information):

$$t \wedge t$$
$$\equiv \{\text{parallel subderivations, one on each conjunct}\}$$

1▷	$\langle t \rangle$	$\langle t \rangle$
	t	t
	$\equiv \{\text{use assumption}\}$	$\equiv \{\text{use assumption}\}$
	T	T

$$\triangleleft \ \mathsf{T} \wedge \mathsf{T}$$
$$\equiv \{\text{propositional calculus}\}$$
$$\mathsf{T}$$

The final theorem would be $t \wedge t \equiv \mathsf{T}$ which is obviously not true in general.

If we are to work on two subwindows in parallel, we must require that at most one of them contains context information derived from the initial focus of the other. We also need to keep added information local to the subderivation where it was generated, since such information may not be available after the subwindow is closed. One solution is to give the subwindow that is opened first the maximal context information, another is to start off with maximal context information in both subwindows, but as soon as a piece of information is used, it is deleted from the other subwindow. This calls for a much more elaborate implementation than Grundy's current stack implementation.

6.2 Derivations with Gaps

The value of parallel derivations can be questioned. A more obviously useful way of making window inference nonsequential is to allow gaps in derivations. When working with focus t under relation $\sqsubseteq$, we can simply assert that an unknown number of transformations should give us the result t'. This corresponds to leaving a gap in the derivation, with the intention of filling it in later:

$$\vdots$$
$$\sqsubseteq \{\text{justification}\}$$
$$t$$
$$- - - \ \langle \text{gap} \rangle \ - - -$$
$$t'$$
$$\sqsubseteq \{\text{justification}\}$$
$$\vdots$$

If the window theorem before the gap is $\Gamma \vdash t_0 \sqsubseteq t$, then immediately after the gap it is $\Gamma, t \sqsubseteq t' \vdash t_0 \sqsubseteq t'$, where the added assumption is flagged as a conjecture. Since window inference allows us to work with relation $\sqsupseteq$ as well as $\sqsubseteq$, we can choose to fill in the gap from either end (which amounts to focusing on either t or t' in the added assumption). This strategy is particularly useful when we already from the start know that we want to prove $t \sqsubseteq t'$ and both t and t' are complicated terms that can be transformed to some simpler term t_1 such that $t \sqsubseteq t_1 \sqsubseteq t'$. This is common practice in pen-and-paper proofs of formulas of the form $t_1 \Rightarrow t_2$; it is often a good strategy to try to transform (simplify) both t_1 an t_2, independently of each other but using the other to help find the right direction.

Derivations with gaps are still compatible with the stack structure of traditional window inference. The gaps are visible as undischarged conjectures, and the user can at any time open a subwindow on such a conjecture and try to fill in (part of) the gap. Thus, one could say that this kind of gap is already handled by the way assumptions are handled in window inference. However, it would be useful to have visual support for the idea that these special conjectures actually correspond to gaps in a subderivation.

Heuberger [10] has suggested using ("silently failing") decision procedures that try to fill in the gap in the background and only attract the attention of the user if they manage to fill in the gap. As soon as the gap has been made smaller (by an explicit transformation by the user) the decision procedure would stop working on the old gap and starts on the new one instead.

7   Uninstantiated Terms

In practical problem solving, we often know approximately what the result should look like or what auxiliary information to use. As we move toward a solution, we get more information about the problem and may be able to make the information more precise. We shall now consider a way of representing such approximate or incomplete information.

7.1   Metavariables

In higher-order logic, variables can have arbitrary type and theorems can contain free (implicitly universally quantified) variables. By a *metavariable* we mean a free variable that can be instantiated, at which point every occurrence in the stack is instantiated. Thus, instantiating a metavariable leads to a change in all window theorems of the stack in question. This is justified by the following inference rule of higher-order logic:

$$\frac{\Gamma \vdash t}{\Gamma[t'/x] \vdash t[t'/x]}$$

An implementation of metavariables requires facilities to make nonlocal changes in the window stack; we must make a pass through the whole stack, updating every window and proving the correctness of the instantiation in question.

Metavariables should not be confused with a *schematic variable*, which (in the metalogic) stands for a term or a set of terms. Schematic variables are often used when giving theorem schemes or inference rules (we have generally used t, Γ and Φ in this way).

Mark Staples's implementation of window inference in Isabelle [14] reuses the built-in schematic variables of Isabelle as metavariables in approximately the way we have described here. This is possible because the Isabelle system has a formalised metalogic. The Ergo system [15] also provides metalogical metavariables.

7.2   Example: The Incomplete Invariant

Invariant reasoning in correctness proofs for loops provide a good example of how metavariables can be used. We consider the proof obligation for the proof of correctness of the loop

$$\text{do } i < n \rightarrow i, s := i + 1, s + a[i] \text{ od}$$

with respect to precondition $i = 0 \land s = 0$ and postcondition $s = \text{sum}(a[0..n-1])$. As invariant we use the following:

$$s = \text{sum}(a[0..i-1]) \land X(i, s)$$

where $X(i, s)$ stands for a conjunct that we suspect we have omitted. Here the metavariable X is a function of the program variables i and s (since we are working in higher-order logic, such function variables are allowed). X does not need to refer to a and n; since they are not changed by the program they can be thought of as constants.

The proof obligation is then the following:

$$(\forall i\, s \bullet i = 0 \land s = 0 \Rightarrow s = \text{sum}(a[0..i-1]) \land X(i, s))$$
$$\land (\forall i\, s \bullet i < n \land s = \text{sum}(a[0..i-1]) \land X(i, s)$$
$$\Rightarrow s + a[i] = \text{sum}(a[0..i]) \land X(i + 1, s + a[i]))$$
$$\land (\forall i\, s \bullet i \geq n \land s = \text{sum}(a[0..i-1]) \land X(i, s) \Rightarrow s = \text{sum}(a[0..n-1]))$$

We can work on it (under backward implication) and open a subwindow on any conjunct. We decide to rewrite the first conjunct to

$$(\forall i\, s \bullet i = 0 \land s = 0 \Rightarrow X(i, s))$$

After this we open a subwindow on the third conjunct and reduce it to

$$(\forall i\, s \bullet i \geq n \land X(i, s) \Rightarrow \text{sum}(a[0..i-1]) = \text{sum}(a[0..n-1]))$$

Here the right hand side gives a hint; we would want $i = n$ to hold. To achieve this, we instantiate X to $(\lambda i, s \bullet i \leq n \land Y(i, s))$, so that we replace $X(i, s)$ by $i \leq n \land Y(i, s)$. This discharges the third conjunct and we are left with the instantiated parent focus

$$(\forall i\, s \bullet i = 0 \land s = 0 \Rightarrow i \leq n \land Y(i, s))$$
$$\land (\forall i\, s \bullet i < n \land s = \text{sum}(a[0..i-1]) \land i \leq n \land Y(i, s)$$
$$\Rightarrow s + a[i] = \text{sum}(a[0..i]) \land i + 1 \leq n \land Y(i + 1, s + a[i]))$$

Simplifying both conjuncts we get

$$(\forall i\, s \bullet i = 0 \land s = 0 \Rightarrow Y(i, s))$$
$$\land (\forall i\, s \bullet i < n \land s = \text{sum}(a[0..i-1]) \land Y(i, s) \Rightarrow Y(i + 1, s + a[i]))$$

Here we can instantiate Y to true, i.e., to $(\lambda i, s \cdot \mathsf{T})$. Then both conjuncts are reduced to T and the proof is finished. As a by-product, we have the complete invariant:

$$s = \mathsf{sum}(a[0..i-1]) \wedge i \leq n$$

Note that we are not in any way required to instantiate metavariables. Even if we leave Y uninstantiated, the result of our derivation is a valid theorem. Of course, the occurrences of the free variable Y in this theorem may make it useless and hard to interpret, but there is nothing logically wrong with it. In an implementation, a metavariable would simply be an ordinary free variable that is flagged in some way (e.g., using specific naming conventions).

8   Conclusion

We have described a number of possible extensions to the window inference proof paradigm, and in particular to window inference as it is implemented in Grundy's tool for the HOL system. Extensions such as these are always dangerous, since one may easily cross the line where an extension destroys some essential part of the original idea. We have tried to show how window inference can be significantly extended while still retaining the simplicity and flexibility of the original paradigm.

Our original motivation has been the application of window inference to program refinement (in particular in the refinement calculus framework where programs are predicate transformers, which are higher-order entities). The crucial problem in program refinement has been how to accommodate data refinement and simulation between distributed systems. However, our examples show that the extensions can be useful in a variety of applications.

Most of the extensions that are discussed in this paper have not been implemented in a tool, but we are currently starting up a project which has the development of a generalised tool for window inference as one of its goals.

Other researchers have also described extensions to the basic window inference paradigm. Nickson [11] suggests the use of higher-order relations to allow data refinement by window inference (though his model is less elaborate than our indexed relations). Nickson and Hayes [12] have developed a tool for refinement (using a modal logic) where the notion of context is extended to allow state-dependent context information to be used in program reasoning. Undoubtedly there are also many other directions in which window inference can be extended.

Acknowledgements

I want to thank Jim Grundy for his many detailed and helpful comments on a draft of this paper.

References

1. R. J. Back. Refinement diagrams. In J.M. Morris and R.C.F. Shaw, editors, *Proc. 4th Refinement Workshop*, Workshops in Computer Science, pages 125–137, Cambridge, England, 9–11 January 1991. Springer-Verlag.

2. R. J. Back, J. Grundy, and J. von Wright. Structured calculational proof. Tech. Rpt. 65, Turku Centre for Computer Science, November 1996. to appear in *Formal Aspects of Computing*.

3. R. J. Back and J. von Wright. *Refinement Calculus: A Systematic Introduction*. Springer-Verlag, 1998.

4. H. Becht, A. Bloesch, R. Nickson and I. Hayes. Ergo 4.1 Reference Manual. Tech.Rpt. 96-31, Dept. Computer Science, Queensland University, November 1996.

5. M. J. Butler, J. Grundy, T. Långbacka, R. Rukšėnas, and J. von Wright. The refinement calculator: Proof support for program refinement. In *Proc. FMP'97 – Formal Methods Pacific*, Discrete Mathematics and Theoretical Computer Science, Wellington, New Zealand, July 1997. Springer-Verlag.

6. M. J. C. Gordon and T. F. Melham. *Introduction to HOL*. Cambridge University Press, New York, 1993.

7. J. Grundy. A window inference tool for refinement. In Jones et al, editor, *Proc. 5th Refinement Workshop*, London, Jan. 1992. Springer-Verlag.

8. J. Grundy. *A Method of Program Refinement*. PhD thesis, University of Cambridge Computer Laboratory, Cambridge, England, 1993. Tech. Rpt. 318.

9. J. Grundy. Transformational Hierarchical Reasoning. *The Computer Journal*, 39(4):291–302, 1996.

10. P. Heuberger. The minimal user-interface of a simple refinement tool. In *Proc. 3rd Workshop on User Interfaces for Theorem Provers*, INRIA Sophia-Antipolis, September 1997.

11. R. Nickson. Window inference for data refinement. In *Proc. 5th Australasian Refinement Workshop*, University of Queensland, 1996.

12. R. Nickson and I. Hayes. Supporting contexts in program refinement. Tech.Rpt. 96-29, Dept. Computer Science, Queensland University, 1996.

13. P. J. Robinson and J. Staples. Formalising a hierarchical structure of practical mathematical reasoning. *Journal of Logic and Computation*, 3(1):47–61, 1993.

14. M. Staples. Window inference in Isabelle. In *Proc. Isabelle Users Workshop*, University of Cambridge Computer Laboratory, September 1995.

15. M. Utting. The Ergo 5 Generic Proof Engine. Tech.Rpt. 97-44, Dept. Computer Science, Queensland University, 1997.

Program Abstraction in a Higher-Order Logic Framework

Marco Benini, Sara Kalvala, and Dirk Nowotka

Department of Computer Science
University of Warwick, Coventry CV4 7AL, United Kingdom

Abstract. We present a hybrid approach to program verification: a higher-order logic, used as a specification language, and a human-driven proof environment, with a process-algebraic engine to allow the use of process simulation as an abstraction technique. The domain of application is the validation of object code, and our intent is to adapt and mix existing formalisms to make the verification of representative programs possible. In this paper, we describe the logic in question and an underlying semantics given in terms of a process algebra.

1 Introduction

Software validation through formal verification has been a topic of much research over the years, but widespread adoption of developed techniques is still elusive. One may attribute this to many factors – two of them being the difficulty in performing the verification and the relevance of the formal proof to actual trustworthiness of the software product.

Most of the techniques being developed have approached the problem by incorporating the semantics of the high-level language of the original program, proving a correspondence with the specification. However, this approach assumes the correct implementation of an abstract program (the high-level programming language) on some hardware. One can either rely on that implementation or show that the translation of high-level code to machine code by the involved compiler is sound. But, doing that is not trivial. Real compilers do not work by incorporating so called correctness-preserving transformations, but by invoking many optimising heuristics and practical but informal knowledge. One may therefore question the relevance of the verification exercise to the correctness of the actual code that is to be run. This does not invalidate the verification of high-level programs, as many design errors can still be found and corrected.

We believe that there is scope for verifying the compiled code itself, which relies only on the correctness of used hardware directly and no program code transformations. This gives a better assurance about the overall system, which is after all the object one would like to have confidence in. That approach is called *object code verification*.

A specification language has to be fixed. We decided to use logical specifications, and as such *higher-order logic*. This decision distinguishes our approach from others like Pavey and Winsborrow [9], who used a rather informal mapping of program code into MALPAS Intermediate Language, in mathematical rigour and Yu [11], who used the quantifier free, first-order logic of Nqthm, in expressiveness. Our decision was also influenced by the availability of automated theorem provers for higher-order logic like HOL [2] and Isabelle/HOL [6, 8].

However, there are difficulties in the verification of programs written in a low-level language. Such a language is, in a sense, further away from the specification language because it has to deal with a more concrete machine, considering registers, limited memory, and so on. There is a vast shift in granularity between code and specification. This gap strongly suggests the application of abstraction techniques on the data as well as control structure of a program.

The concept of simulation [3] and observational equivalence [5] in the framework of process algebra gives us a well-developed tool for abstraction. We use a variation of a traditional process algebra (Milner's CCS [5]), which is called ωCCS. In this setting – HOL and ωCCS – the verification effort would consist of abstraction steps interspersed with interesting *inference* steps where correctness properties are derived. So, one approach that can be used for structuring a verification task is to separate the inference steps from the abstraction steps, and support each of them in an optimal manner.

In this paper, we describe a system which allows the use of both inference in higher-order logic and abstraction in process algebra while still maintaining consistency. The use of this formalism allows us to structure the verification task as illustrated in Fig. 1. The left-hand side of the picture (grey arrows) is the way we assume the software to be developed, i.e., starting from a specification a program (in some high-level language) has been written, and the object code was generated from that. Formalising the specification, we obtain an higher-order formula. From the object code, by means of our tool, another higher-order formula is constructed; we call this formula the *representation* of our program. The usual process of formal verification (solid arrows in Fig. 1) is to try to *infer* the validity of the formalised specification assuming the representation.

Our tool provides the instruments to perform such deductions. But it also provides an abstraction mechanism based on ωCCS (right-hand side of Fig. 1): translating a program representation into an ωCCS expression, we can refine it, and we get as a result an abstracted ωCCS expression, we can then translate back to higher-order logic, and this is another representation of the original program, not equivalent to the original one, but preserving enough information so to ensure that, if we are able to deduce the specification from it, then there is (a more complex) derivation of the same specification from the original representation.

We will illustrate our approach by first introducing ωCCS, our process algebra, and showing how we model abstraction in this system. We then describe the logic used, which provides the syntax and a proof interface.

Our emphasis is on showing the correctness of the process algebraic formalism with respect to the logical representation, so we illustrate the correspondence between these two formalisms.

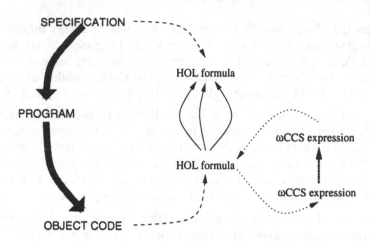

Fig. 1. Verification integrating inference and abstraction

Finally, we sketch a practical embodiment of this system as an extension to the Isabelle/HOL theorem prover.

A particular assembly language has been fixed to allow the comparison of our work with others in the field (e.g., [11]). We use the Motorola M68000 architecture here.

2 An Algebra for Processes

In this section we give a detailed overview of ωCCS, a variant of the Calculus of Communicating Systems (CCS). The motivation for this variant is given by explaining the main difficulty we have in using the standard CCS for our verification endeavours, namely in the characterisation of divergence.

2.1 Basic Notions

The CCS process algebra is an intuitive framework for describing processes. Our extension is based on *message passing CCS* [5, pp. 53–56], which models actions as objects capable of reading a value and co-actions as objects which are able to send a value.

As in CCS, we assume as given two distinct sets, Actions and Values, which are used to build processes, following the syntax in Fig. 2.

We refer to literature [3–5] for a detailed explanation of the intuitive and formal meaning of process constructors. The only syntactical differences we introduced with respect to CCS are:

- renaming involves values as well as actions;
- as in ACP [1], we have a sequential composition operator: P ;; Q should be read as "P then Q", and it is the process which behaves like P until P terminates, if ever, then it behaves like Q.

$$\langle Process \rangle ::= \langle Action \rangle . \langle Value \longrightarrow Process \rangle$$
$$| \quad \overline{\langle Action \rangle}(\langle Value \rangle) . \langle Process \rangle$$
$$| \quad \tau . \langle Process \rangle$$
$$| \quad \sum \langle Process\ set \rangle$$
$$| \quad \langle Process \rangle | \langle Process \rangle$$
$$| \quad \mu \langle Process \longrightarrow Process \rangle$$
$$| \quad \langle Process \rangle \setminus \langle Action\ set \rangle$$
$$| \quad \langle Process \rangle [\langle (Action \longrightarrow Action) \times (Value \longrightarrow Value) \rangle]$$
$$| \quad \langle Process \rangle ;; \langle Process \rangle$$

Fig. 2. Syntax of ωCCS processes

In the usual way, a transition relation is defined for ωCCS. The basic rules are shown in Fig. 3.

Since we are interested in observing only visible actions, because they corresponds in our frame to the execution of instructions, we use the so called *observational transition relation*:

$$P \xRightarrow{\alpha} Q \text{ iff } \alpha \neq \tau \wedge \exists P', Q'.P \xrightarrow{\tau^*} P' \wedge P' \xrightarrow{\alpha} Q' \wedge Q' \xrightarrow{\tau^*} Q .$$

The properties about these relations, not involving simulations, are the same as for CCS.

In our implementation, we designed an Isabelle/HOL theory that, representing processes as a datatype and defining by co-induction [7] the transition relations, give the possibility to prove all the lemmas and theorems concerning these basic definitions. We proved most of them.

2.2   Simulation and Divergence

As we said in the introduction, our goal is to use ωCCS to abstract over program representations. Let us suppose that a program is represented by the process P, we say that another process Q is an *abstraction* over P, if it is able to behave like P.

The process algebraic counterpart of this notion is *simulation*. Since we focus our attention to visible actions, a good candidate for modeling our notion of abstraction seems to be *weak simulation* [5]:

$$P \preccurlyeq Q \quad \text{iff} \quad \forall \beta, P'.P \xrightarrow{\beta} P' \rightarrow \exists Q'.Q \xRightarrow{\beta} Q' \wedge P' \preccurlyeq Q' .$$

It is easy to show that $\preccurlyeq$ is a precongruence [5, 10] with respect to all operators of ωCCS, with the exception of sequence. We will return to this point later.

Unfortunately, our intuitive notion of behaviour for a program does not correspond to the idea of behaviour embodied into the weak simulation. A behaviour, for weak simulation, is a sequence of visible actions a process may perform, and

$$\alpha \, . \, (\lambda w.P(w)) \xrightarrow{\alpha(v)} P(v) \qquad \overline{\alpha}(v) \, . \, P \xrightarrow{\overline{\alpha}(v)} P \qquad \tau \, . \, P \xrightarrow{\tau} P$$

$$\frac{P \xrightarrow{\beta} Q}{\sum (\{P\} \cup \Xi) \xrightarrow{\beta} Q}$$

$$\frac{P \xrightarrow{\beta} Q}{P \mid R \xrightarrow{\beta} Q \mid R} \qquad \frac{P \xrightarrow{\beta} Q}{R \mid P \xrightarrow{\beta} R \mid Q}$$

$$\frac{P \xrightarrow{\alpha(v)} P' \quad Q \xrightarrow{\overline{\alpha}(v)} Q'}{P \mid Q \xrightarrow{\tau} P' \mid Q'}$$

$$\frac{P(\mu \, (\lambda w.P(w))) \xrightarrow{\beta} Q}{\mu \, (\lambda w.P(w)) \xrightarrow{\beta} Q}$$

$$\frac{P \xrightarrow{\alpha(v)} Q \quad \alpha \notin \Delta}{P \setminus \Delta \xrightarrow{\alpha(v)} Q \setminus \Delta} \qquad \frac{P \xrightarrow{\overline{\alpha}(v)} Q \quad \alpha \notin \Delta}{P \setminus \Delta \xrightarrow{\overline{\alpha}(v)} Q \setminus \Delta} \qquad \frac{P \xrightarrow{\tau} Q}{P \setminus \Delta \xrightarrow{\tau} Q \setminus \Delta}$$

$$\frac{P \xrightarrow{\alpha(v)} Q}{P[\Phi] \xrightarrow{(\Phi(\alpha))(\Phi(v))} Q[\Phi]} \qquad \frac{P \xrightarrow{\overline{\alpha}(v)} Q}{P[\Phi] \xrightarrow{\overline{(\Phi(\alpha))(\Phi(v))}} Q[\Phi]} \qquad \frac{P \xrightarrow{\tau} Q}{P[\Phi] \xrightarrow{\tau} Q[\Phi]}$$

$$\frac{P \xrightarrow{\beta} Q}{P \, ;; R \xrightarrow{\beta} Q \, ;; R}$$

Where: v, w are variables ranging over values,
X is a variable ranging over processes,
P, Q, R are processes,
α is any action except τ,
β is of the form $\alpha(v)$, $\overline{\alpha}(v)$ or τ,
Δ is any set of actions,
Ξ is any set of processes.

Moreover, we know that $\sum \emptyset$ is the termination process, that $\sum \{P\} \equiv P$, that $\overline{\overline{\alpha}}(v) \equiv \alpha(v)$, and that $\sum \emptyset \, ;; P \equiv P$. Since in renaming, Φ denotes a pair of functions $\langle \phi, \theta \rangle$,

$$(\Phi(\alpha))(\Phi(v)) \equiv (\phi(\alpha))(\theta(v)) \ .$$

Fig. 3. The basic transition relation for ωCCS

a way to read $P \preccurlyeq Q$ is that "for every sequence of visible actions P can perform, the same sequence is a possible behaviour for Q".

Suppose now that P represent a program which is in an unrecoverable deadlock situation: it continues to request a service which is permanently unavailable. From the observer point of view, there is no visible action, but he is able to recognise that the program is "doing nothing", but it has not terminated its execution. Suppose $Q \equiv \sum \emptyset$, that means Q is the program which reached happily its last instruction, so it has finished its job with no troubles. Again, from the observer point of view, Q is unable to perform any visible action, but, this time, the observer knows that Q has terminated its execution.

But according to the definition of weak simulation, $P \preccurlyeq Q$, so we have lost an essential piece of information regarding the behaviour of P: in general, it is easy to figure out examples which show that situations like *starvation* and *deadlocks* are not preserved by weak simulation. Obviously, there is no hope to use weak simulation as an abstraction tool in a formal verification task, since, most of the time, the verifier must check exactly for the kind of faults which are not preserved by the $\preccurlyeq$ relation.

From a formal point of view, we want to preserve *divergence*:

$$\text{diverge}(P) \quad \text{iff} \quad \exists f. f(0) = P \wedge \forall n. f(n) \xrightarrow{\tau} f(n+1) .$$

A process is said to be divergent if it is able to produce an infinite trace which is composed only by τ actions.

Our main abstraction tool, we call it *div-simulation* is defined as:

$$P \overset{div}{\preccurlyeq} Q \quad \text{iff} \quad P \preccurlyeq Q \wedge (\text{diverge}(P) \to \text{diverge}(Q)) .$$

The main properties regarding this notion are shown in Fig. 4.

Compared to other results in literature (e.g., [1, 10]), our notion is more primitive and not so attractive from the mathematical point of view, since div-simulation is not a precongruence: the rule

$$\frac{P \overset{div}{\preccurlyeq} Q}{P ;; R \overset{div}{\preccurlyeq} Q ;; R} \tag{1}$$

does not hold; if $P \equiv \sum \emptyset$, $Q \equiv \overline{a}(v) . \sum \emptyset$, $R \equiv \overline{\gamma}(v) . \sum \emptyset$, where α and γ are different actions, it follows that $P \preccurlyeq Q$ and $\neg\text{diverge}(P)$, so $P \overset{div}{\preccurlyeq} Q$, but $P ;; R \xrightarrow{\gamma(v)} \sum \emptyset$ while $Q ;; R \overset{\gamma(v)}{\not\rightarrow} X$, for any process X, so $P ;; R \not\preccurlyeq Q ;; R$.

In this respect, it becomes evident that even weak simulation is not a precongruence when a sequencing operator is added to the process algebra. This result is not new, since it is already discussed in [5, Sect. 9.2], but the solution proposed there, i.e., using a special action which denotes termination, is impractical in most verification tasks, since it forces the verifier to use different representations for subsections of code. As an example, if we want to prove correctness of a loop, the algebraic representation must produce a "termination" action as

$$\frac{P \stackrel{div}{\preceq} Q}{\tau \, . \, P \stackrel{div}{\preceq} \tau \, . \, Q} \qquad \frac{P \stackrel{div}{\preceq} Q}{\overline{\alpha}(v) \, . \, P \stackrel{div}{\preceq} \overline{\alpha}(v) \, . \, Q} \qquad \frac{\forall w . P(w) \stackrel{div}{\preceq} Q(w)}{\alpha \, . \, P \stackrel{div}{\preceq} \alpha \, . \, Q}$$

$$\frac{P \stackrel{div}{\preceq} Q}{\sum \Xi \cup \{P\} \stackrel{div}{\preceq} \sum \Xi \cup \{Q\}} \qquad \frac{P \stackrel{div}{\preceq} P' \quad Q \stackrel{div}{\preceq} Q'}{P \,|\, Q \stackrel{div}{\preceq} P' \,|\, Q'}$$

$$\frac{P \stackrel{div}{\preceq} Q}{P \setminus \Delta \stackrel{div}{\preceq} Q \setminus \Delta} \qquad \frac{P \stackrel{div}{\preceq} Q}{P[\Phi] \stackrel{div}{\preceq} Q[\Phi]}$$

$$\frac{P(\mu \, P) \stackrel{div}{\preceq} Q(\mu \, Q)}{\mu \, P \stackrel{div}{\preceq} \mu \, Q} \qquad \frac{P \stackrel{div}{\preceq} Q}{R \,;; P \stackrel{div}{\preceq} R \,;; Q}$$

Fig. 4. Basic properties of div-simulation

the last step of the loop computation; if this loop is part of a bigger code, we cannot simply immerse it by using the sequence operator, so we are forced to use something like the *Before* operator [5, p. 173]. This is not satisfactory since we must know in advance where we plan to divide the code for verificational purposes, and this is not true in real practice.

Anyway, our notion is powerful enough to give us the right instrument to perform abstraction. In fact a restricted version of (1) holds:

$$\frac{P \stackrel{div}{\preceq} Q \quad Q \stackrel{div}{\preceq} P}{P \,;; R \stackrel{div}{\preceq} Q \,;; R}$$

Most of the time, this rule is just what we need for our purposes. We also note that if P is *finitary*, i.e., if P always reduces to $\sum \emptyset$, then $P \,;; Q$ can be converted to an equivalent process R, where sequencing is substituted with prefixing and summations.

Our implementation of ωCCS in Isabelle/HOL provides the notion of divergence, of weak simulation and of div-simulation, along with all lemmas presented in this section, plus many others. The coding of these notions is completely standard, using the coinduction package [7], and all proofs are carried on following the guidelines traced in [5].

2.3   An Illustrating Example

The main motivation for introducing a process algebra into our verification methodology is to cope with the interrupt system of a machine, or more generally, to cope with processes running in parallel. This is necessary when we want to verify programs for a "real-world" environment.

Let us have a look at interrupts triggered by the program itself, like for instance operating system calls (see Fig. 5).

Program	Operating System
A	case *interrupt* of
syscall 7	1: I_1
B	...
	7: I_7
	...
	esac
	return

Fig. 5. Software interrupts

This kind of interaction of a program with its environment does not necessarily need a concurrent model. It could simply be the sequential composition of the program parts, A and B, with the interrupt routine, I_7, which would be the way one would treat such a system following [11].

$$Program \stackrel{\text{def}}{=} A\,;;I_7\,;;B$$

Nevertheless, we prefer the following variant:

$$Prog \stackrel{\text{def}}{=} ((A\,;;\overline{syscall}(7)\,.\,rti\,.\,(\lambda State.B)) \mid OS) \setminus \{syscall, rti\}$$

$$OS \stackrel{\text{def}}{=} syscall\,.\,\lambda i.I_i\,;;\overline{rti}(State)\,.\,OS$$

Though it looks more complicated, this new approach allows us to handle external interrupts, that is, events that can interrupt the program at any possible time and change the state of the machine. Such a system could hardly be modeled with the first approach above.

The whole system, i.e. the program and its run-time environment, would then look like this:

$$System \stackrel{\text{def}}{=} (Prog \mid (Proc(InitState) \mid Env)) \setminus \{rd, wr, int, ret, rd_{int}, wr_{int}\}$$

where *InitState* is the initial state. The process components are defined below.

$$Prog \overset{\text{def}}{=} rd . (\lambda State.(\overline{wr}(State') . Prog))$$

$$Proc(State) \overset{\text{def}}{=} \overline{rd}(State) . Proc(State) + wr . (\lambda State'.Proc(State'))$$
$$+ int . Proc'(State)$$

$$Proc'(State) \overset{\text{def}}{=} \overline{rd_{int}}(State) . Proc'(State) + wr_{int} . (\lambda State'.Proc'(State'))$$
$$+ \overline{ret} . Proc(State)$$

$$Env \overset{\text{def}}{=} \overline{int} . Env + rd_{int} . (\lambda State.(\overline{wr_{int}}(State') . Env))$$
$$+ ret . Env$$

Every component of the system can now be subject to abstraction as long as its interaction with the system is not modified. The environment, for instance, could be altered in a way that the machine state is not changed by an interrupt routine.

$$System' \overset{\text{def}}{=} (Prog \mid (Proc''(InitState) \mid Env')) \setminus \{rd, wr, int, ret\}$$

Where we have:

$$Proc''(State) \overset{\text{def}}{=} \overline{rd}(State) . Proc''(State) + wr . (\lambda State'.Proc''(State'))$$
$$+ int . \overline{ret} . Proc''(State)$$

$$Env' \overset{\text{def}}{=} \overline{int} . Env' + ret . Env'$$

Since

$$(Proc(InitState) \mid Env) \overset{div}{\preccurlyeq} (Proc''(InitState) \mid Env')$$

and obviously $Prog \overset{div}{\preccurlyeq} Prog$, we have $System \overset{div}{\preccurlyeq} System'$. It is easy to see that our (simple) model can engage into starvation of the program, which is the case when interrupts occur continuously. That is why the following would be a wrong abstraction.

$$System'' \overset{\text{def}}{=} (Prog \mid (Proc'''(InitState) \mid Env'')) \setminus \{rd, wr\}$$

$$Proc'''(State) \overset{\text{def}}{=} \overline{rd}(State) . Proc'''(State) + wr . (\lambda State'.Proc'''(State'))$$

$$Env'' \overset{\text{def}}{=} \sum \emptyset$$

Because that abstraction does *not* preserve divergence.

$$(Proc(InitState) \mid Env) \overset{div}{\npreccurlyeq} (Proc'''(InitState) \mid Env'')$$

A termination result for *Prog* in *System''* does not ensure us that *Prog* actually terminates in *System*, too.

3   Program Representation in Higher Order Logic and ωCCS

The standard syntax used for higher-order logic is used here. However, when working with Isabelle/HOL the syntax is, of course, more "ASCII like", but the translation is straightforward and should pose no problems in understanding (see also [8]).

Terms are defined in a way that allows arithmetic on integer numbers. We also define functions to model registers ($D_0, \dots , D_7, A_0, \dots A_7$), the program counter (PC), and memory (Mem). These functions take a term, representing time, to a term, representing a value. (Mem also takes a term, representing an address, as argument.) Flags, i.e., elements of the condition code register, are represented by predicates (C, N, V, X, Z) taking a term, that represents time, as argument. See Fig. 6 and Fig. 7.

$$
\begin{aligned}
\langle Term \rangle ::= \; & 1 \mid 2 \mid 3 \mid \dots \\
\mid \; & \langle Variable \rangle \\
\mid \; & \langle Term \rangle + \langle Term \rangle \\
\mid \; & \langle Term \rangle - \langle Term \rangle \\
\mid \; & \langle Term \rangle \times \langle Term \rangle \\
\mid \; & \langle Term \rangle \div \langle Term \rangle \\
\mid \; & \langle Term \rangle^{\langle Term \rangle} \\
\mid \; & \langle Term \rangle \bmod \langle Term \rangle \\
\mid \; & \text{PC}(\langle Term \rangle) \\
\mid \; & \text{D}_0(\langle Term \rangle) \mid \text{D}_1(\langle Term \rangle) \mid \dots \mid \text{D}_7(\langle Term \rangle) \\
\mid \; & \text{A}_0(\langle Term \rangle) \mid \text{A}_1(\langle Term \rangle) \mid \dots \mid \text{A}_7(\langle Term \rangle) \\
\mid \; & \text{Mem}_{\langle Term \rangle}(\langle Term \rangle)
\end{aligned}
$$

Fig. 6. Term syntax

$$
\begin{aligned}
\langle Formula \rangle ::= \; & \text{true} \mid \text{false} \\
\mid \; & \text{C}(\langle Term \rangle) \mid \text{N}(\langle Term \rangle) \mid \text{V}(\langle Term \rangle) \mid \text{X}(\langle Term \rangle) \mid \text{Z}(\langle Term \rangle) \\
\mid \; & \langle Term \rangle = \langle Term \rangle \mid \langle Term \rangle < \langle Term \rangle \mid \langle Term \rangle \leq \langle Term \rangle \\
\mid \; & \neg \langle Formula \rangle \mid \langle Formula \rangle \wedge \langle Formula \rangle \mid \langle Formula \rangle \vee \langle Formula \rangle \\
\mid \; & \langle Formula \rangle \rightarrow \langle Formula \rangle \mid \langle Formula \rangle \leftrightarrow \langle Formula \rangle \\
\mid \; & \exists \langle Variable \rangle.\langle Formula \rangle \mid \forall \langle Variable \rangle.\langle Formula \rangle
\end{aligned}
$$

Fig. 7. Formula syntax

The meaning of the introduced functions is as one would expect and is best illustrated with an example program.

The instructions of a small program in assembly language, shown in Fig. 8, illustrate the program representation in higher-order logic. Every line in the table is numbered and shows one assembly instruction followed by its representation as a logical formula. This representation has already been manipulated: if one knows the specification, it is straightforward to cut irrelevant references to memory/registers from the representation. Since this procedure has been automated in our system and does not affect the verification validity (but improves performance and readability), we assume this simplification is being done implicitly.

1: `MOVE #0, D1` $PC(t) = 1 \land PC(t+1) = 2 \land D_0(t+1) = D_0(t) \land D_1(t+1) = 0$

2: `MOVE D1, D2` $PC(t) = 2 \land PC(t+1) = 3 \land D_0(t+1) = D_0(t)$
$\land D_1(t+1) = D_1(t) \land D_2(t+1) = D_1(t)$

3: `MULT D2, D2` $PC(t) = 3 \land PC(t+1) = 4 \land D_0(t+1) = D_0(t)$
$\land D_1(t+1) = D_1(t) \land D_2(t+1) = D_2(t)^2$

4: `CMP D2, D0` $PC(t) = 4 \land PC(t+1) = 5 \land (N(t+1) \leftrightarrow D_2(t) \leq D_0(t))$
$\land D_0(t+1) = D_0(t) \land D_1(t+1) = D_1(t)$

5: `BGT 8` $PC(t) = 5 \land (\neg N(t) \to PC(t+1) = 6) \land (N(t) \to PC(t+1) = 8)$
$\land D_0(t+1) = D_0(t) \land D_1(t+1) = D_1(t)$

6: `ADD #1, D1` $PC(t) = 6 \land PC(t+1) = 7 \land D_0(t+1) = D_0(t)$
$\land D_1(t+1) = 1 + D_1(t)$

7: `BRA 2` $PC(t) = 7 \land PC(t+1) = 2 \land D_0(t+1) = D_0(t)$
$\land D_1(t+1) = D_1(t)$

8: `SUB #1, D1` $PC(t) = 8 \land PC(t+1) = 9 \land D_0(t+1) = D_0(t)$
$\land D_1(t+1) = D_1(t) - 1$

Fig. 8. A small assembly program and its logical representation

Every instruction depends on a parameter t which represents the time flow. The actual program representation in higher-order logic is

$$\forall t. i_1(t) \lor i_2(t) \lor i_3(t) \lor i_4(t) \lor i_5(t) \lor i_6(t) \lor i_7(t) \lor i_8(t)$$

where $i_j(t)$ stands for the formula representing instruction j instantiated with t.

This program should calculate the integer square root of a natural number. It terminates with 9 as last program counter value, the argument of the computation is given in register D_0 and the result stands in register D_1. So the program ought to satisfy the following specification:

$$\exists t. PC(t) = 9 \land (D_1(t))^2 \leq D_0(t) \land D_0(t) \leq (D_1(t) + 1)^2. \tag{2}$$

The same program is represented in ωCCS. Due to space limitations that representation is sketched. Nonetheless, some definitions are necessary. Let

$$S = \{PC, D_0, \dots, D_7, A_0, \dots, A_7, Mem_i, C, N, V, X, Z\} \qquad 0 \leq i < 2^{32}$$

be a set of constants that represent the obvious machine parts. Let a state be of type $S \to \mathbf{N}$. Let a tuple of type $S \times \mathbf{N}$ denote the update of some memory cell/register. Let *overwrite* be a function that takes a state and a set of tuples to a new state. For instance, let $State(PC) = 1$ and $State(D_0) = 8$, then $State' = overwrite(State, \{(PC, 2)\})$ with now $State'(PC) = 2$ and $State'(D_0) = 8$.

See Fig. 9 for a representation of the first three assembly lines.

1: MOVE #0, D1 $Instr_1 \overset{\text{def}}{=} rd . \lambda State.\overline{wr}(overwrite$
$(State, \{(D_1, 0), (C, 0), (N, 0), (V, 0), (Z, 1)\})) . Instr_2$

2: MOVE D1, D2 $Instr_2 \overset{\text{def}}{=} rd . \lambda State.\overline{wr}(overwrite$
$(State, \{(D_2, State(D_1)), (C, 0), \dots\})) . Instr_3$

3: MULT D2, D2 $Instr_3 \overset{\text{def}}{=} rd . \lambda State.\overline{wr}(overwrite$
$(State, \{(D_2, State(D_2)^2), (C, 0), \dots\})) . Instr_4$

Fig. 9. A small assembly program and its ωCCS representation

The next section illustrates why we took the effort to represent the same program in two theories.

4   Abstraction

As mentioned in Sect. 1, verification of object code programs is characterised by starting with a program full of many details and eliminating the details which do not affect the properties of interest. By abstraction we mean forgetting about details and focusing on the essentials.

More precisely, if P is a process that represents a program, we can say that the process Q is an abstraction of P if:

− except for "irrelevant" details, Q is able to behave like P.
− the intrinsic properties of P are preserved.

The "irrelevant" details mentioned above have to do with the precise operation of the machine, while an example of an intrinsic property we may want to preserve is the divergence character.

4.1   Abstraction in ωCCS

Recalling from Sect. 2.2, if $P \overset{div}{\preccurlyeq} Q$ holds, we know that every behaviour satisfying P must satisfy Q and Q cannot be non-divergent if P is divergent.

Let us suppose that P is a process which encodes a program, and let us try to understand what Q is.

Every behaviour of the process P represents, in a formal sense, a computation of the program represented by P. Since Q simulates P, Q is able to perform every computation P may perform. But div-simulation preserves divergence so Q can be divergent even if P is not, and Q must be divergent whenever P is. With this interpretation, the strict nature of programs we chose to model is preserved and Q is a fair model for the program encoded in P, but Q is, in principle, more general since it can exhibit more behaviours than P. So Q, by our intuitive definition of abstraction, is an abstract version of P.

This kind of view can be considered a structural abstraction, something that, enlarging the set of possible behaviours, simplifies the structure of the program.

It is possible to gain data abstraction: if P is a process representing a program, and $P \overset{div}{\preccurlyeq} P[\Phi]$ for a proper Φ, we can use the renaming function to hide, in a fair way, useless variables and parts of the state. Again, having a simulation between P and $P[\Phi]$, we have an abstraction by our intuitive definition.

There are other ways to generate abstractions: essentially, given P, if we have an operation Γ depending on a set Δ of parameters, then $\Gamma_\Delta(P)$ is an abstraction over P if $P \overset{div}{\preccurlyeq} \Gamma_\Delta(P)$. Of course, the interesting part is to discover appropriate Γs in such a way as to generate useful abstractions for P. We have no definite answers in this direction, but it is promising to know that not only is Q an abstraction for P if $P \overset{div}{\preccurlyeq} Q$, but there are no abstractions for P which do not div-simulate P itself. In other words, our framework is rich enough to model every abstraction (in the sense introduced above), but it is not trivial to discriminate useful from useless ones.

From the practical point of view, it is difficult to use div-simulation to perform abstractions. The simplest example we have proved correct with our tool is illustrated in Sect. 2.3.

As explained in that example, the main reason why we are interested in div-simulation, is to abstract over the whole system, especially for dealing with situations where external interrupts, non predictable faults or asynchronous I/O are involved.

The way to perform abstraction is clear from the example: from the concrete representation P we produce, by means of some reasoning, usually in an heuristic way, an abstract representation Q. Our implementation of ωCCS aids the proof that Q is an abstraction with respect to P, that means, $P \overset{div}{\preccurlyeq} Q$. When the proof is "simple" the ωCCS theory is able to prove that goal by using Isabelle's simplifier, while, in more complex cases, the user has to drive to prover in order to establish the truth of the statement.

4.2 Abstraction in Higher Order Logic

Our abstraction paradigm could be modeled completely using div-simulation, but this is impractical for two reasons:

- some kinds of abstractions are simple, and used very often;
- the most natural way to conceive some abstractions is quite different from a process algebraic simulation.

For these reasons we enrich our framework in higher-order logic with tools in order to perform common abstractions directly in the logical level (opposing to use the ωCCS representation).

The first tool we provide takes the higher-order logic representation of an object code program along with the specification we want to prove and simplifies the representation itself by removing references to memory and registers which do not appear in the specification. The algorithm to do this simplification uses information about the flow of control of the program to choose what to remove and what to preserve.

In Fig. 8 is shown the result of this simplification with respect to the specification (2). Just as an example, the complete representation of instruction 7 will look like:

$$PC(t) = 7 \wedge PC(t+1) = 2 \wedge D_0(t+1) = D_0(t) \wedge D_1(t+1) = D_1(t)$$
$$\wedge D_2(t+1) = D_2(t) \wedge D_3(t+1) = D_3(t) \wedge D_4(t+1) = D_4(t)$$
$$\wedge D_5(t+1) = D_5(t) \wedge D_6(t+1) = D_6(t) \wedge D_7(t+1) = D_7(t)$$
$$\wedge A_0(t+1) = A_0(t) \wedge A_1(t+1) = A_1(t) \wedge A_2(t+1) = A_2(t)$$
$$\wedge A_3(t+1) = A_3(t) \wedge A_4(t+1) = A_4(t) \wedge A_5(t+1) = A_5(t)$$
$$\wedge A_6(t+1) = A_6(t) \wedge A_7(t+1) = A_7(t) \wedge (\forall x.\text{Mem}_x(t+1) = \text{Mem}_x(t))$$
$$\wedge (N(t+1) = N(t)) \wedge (Z(t+1) = Z(t)) \wedge (V(t+1) = V(t))$$
$$\wedge (C(t+1) = C(t)) \wedge (X(t+1) = X(t)) ,$$

while the simplified version is

$$PC(t) = 7 \wedge PC(t+1) = 2 \wedge D_0(t+1) = D_0(t) \wedge D_1(t+1) = D_1(t) .$$

Even if this kind of abstraction is sound with respect to div-simulation, we think it is more natural and efficient to provide it as an independent tool; of course, the same simplification is operated over the ωCCS representation.

Another important kind of abstraction which is described more naturally in higher-order logic than in ωCCS is the mapping between abstract data types and their concrete representations.

In this case we use a datatype declaration of Isabelle [7] with an explicit instance for the representation function.

datatype $string$ = null | char of $(byte, string)$

$$\text{rep(null)}(t) \qquad = 0$$
$$\text{rep(char}(x, s))(t) = n \rightarrow \text{Mem}_n(t) = x \wedge n \neq 0$$
$$\wedge (s = \text{null} \vee (s \neq \text{null} \wedge \text{rep}(s)(t) = n + 1))$$

Fig. 10. Abstraction over data type: C strings

Informally, it means that we define explicitly what is the map from the abstract data type to its concrete representation which is the one manipulated by the object code. As an example, Fig. 10 shows how a string (in the standard C representation) is coded following these guidelines. In this way we can describe by means of the data type operations what is performed by the program.

Of course, our main abstraction mechanism is div-simulation and, since the ωCCS theory is coded into higher-order logic, it is immediately available when it is necessary to perform abstraction steps which are beyond the capabilities of our other tools.

There is a simple map from ωCCS processes to logical formulas which enable us to translate the abstracted process into an abstract logical representation for the program. This map is essentially a formulation of semantics for ωCCS into higher-order logic and its definition is standard [5].

5   Summary and Further Work

A verification formalism based on two different frameworks – a higher-order logic and a process algebra – has been discussed in this paper. We have shown that a very general form of abstraction (simulation) can be coded into a logic using a process algebra. Since abstraction is a crucial issue in applying formal methods in practice, this method is a significant step towards a feasible object code verification of representative programs.

When emphasising the practical motivation of this paper, we have also introduced ωCCS as process algebra which is a slightly modified version of CCS. Our modifications allow a better application of this concept without sacrificing too many characteristics of CCS.

The results in this paper are direct spin-offs of an ongoing project concerned with the development and use of a system that applies formal methods to "real world" program verification. We use higher-order logic as specification language and proof environment, interfacing to the user, and ωCCS as machinery behind, to handle and modify the object of interest (in our case, programs in assembly language). So, two powerful techniques are applied to particular parts of the verification process. The fusion of these two frameworks is the key part of a successful application and has now been presented by this paper.

Moreover, the results of this work have actually been implemented and used. The ωCCS formalism has been coded within the Isabelle/HOL prover. Isabelle allows us to specify new object logics within the prover and immediately use these logics to drive new proofs. We have therefore been able to prove the correspondence between HOL and the lemmas regarding ωCCS, in particular div-simulation, within the prover. This gives us a useful framework to apply abstraction for practical purposes.

We are now in the process of using this proof infra-structure to aid in the verification of object code programs of significant size. The example suite we use is the GNU C Library compiled for the Motorola 68000 architecture.

This paper presents a general idea of "implementing" abstraction into a higher-order logic. We feel that we have developed an interesting verification methodology, which is practical and which builds on results of more than one theoretical framework. Our result encourages the application of this approach to other logics, as well.

Acknowledgements

Carl Pulley has been responsible for many of the ideas embodied in this work, and a substantial part of the implementation. Mathai Joseph proposed the project and provided much of the guidance. This work is sponsored by EPSRC under grant GR/K52447.

References

1. J. C. M. Baeten and W. P. Weijland. *Process Algebra*, volume 18 of *Cambridge Tracts in Theoretical Computer Science*. Cambridge University Press, 1990.
2. Michael J. C. Gordon and Tom F. Melham. *Introduction to HOL: A Theorem Proving Environment for Higher Order Logic*. Cambridge University Press, 1993.
3. Robin Milner. An algebraic definition of simulation between programs. In *Second Joint Conference on Artificial Intelligence*, pages 481–489, 1971.
4. Robin Milner. *A Calculus of Communicating Systems*, volume 92 of *Lecture Notes in Computer Science*. Springer-Verlag, 1980.
5. Robin Milner. *Communication and Concurrency*. International Series in Computer Science. Prentice Hall, London, 1989.
6. Lawrence C. Paulson. *Isabelle: A Generic Theorem Prover*. Number 828 in LNCS. Springer-Verlag, 1994.
7. Lawrence C. Paulson. A fixedpoint approach to (co)inductive and (co)datatype definitions. Technical Report 304, Computer Laboratory, University of Cambridge, May 1997.
8. Lawrence C. Paulson. Isabelle's object-logics. Technical Report 286, Computer Laboratory, University of Cambridge, May 1997.
9. D. Pavey and L. Winsborrow. Demonstrating equivalence of source code and PROM contents. *The Computer Journal*, 36(7):654–667, 1993.
10. David Walker. Bisimulation and divergence. *Information and Computation*, 85:202–241, 1990.
11. Yuan Yu. Automated proofs of object code for a widely used microprocessor. Research Report 114, Digital Equipment Corporation Systems Research Center, Palo Alto, CA, October 1993.

The Village Telephone System:
A Case Study in Formal Software Engineering

Karthikeyan Bhargavan[1], Carl A. Gunter[1], Elsa L. Gunter[2], Michael Jackson[3],
Davor Obradovic[1], and Pamela Zave[3]

[1] University of Pennsylvania, Pittsburgh, PA 19104, USA
{bkarthik,gunter,davor}@cis.upenn.edu
[2] Bell Labs, Lucent Technologies, Murray Hill, NJ 07974, USA
elsa@research.bell-labs.com
[3] AT&T Laboratories, Murray Hill, NJ 07974, USA
pamela@research.att.com   jacksonma@acm.org

Abstract. In this paper we illustrate the use of formal methods in the development of a benchmark application we call the *Village Telephone System* which is characteristic of a class of network and telecommunication protocols. The aim is to show an effective integration of methodology and tools in a software engineering task that proceeds from user-level requirements to an implementation. In particular, we employ a general methodology which we advocate for requirements capture and refinement based on a treatment of designated terminology, domain knowledge, requirements, specifications, and implementation. We show how a general-purpose theorem prover (HOL) can provide formal support for all of these components and how a model checker (Mocha) can provide formal support for the specifications and implementation. We develop a new HOL theory of inductive sequences that is suited to modelling reactive systems and provides a common basis for interoperability between HOL and Mocha.

1 Introduction

One of the key problems in the practical adoption of formal methods is that many are usable only at certain stages of the software engineering process and must work with a specific form of data. At AT&T and Bell Labs we have seen a number of instances where formal tools *might have been* useful in a project *if* the kinds of specifications on which such tools work were available. Unfortunately projects do not typically use formal methods in the development of specifications, so the information on which a formal method might be employed is unavailable, or would be very expensive to obtain. Indeed, once a project has chosen not to use formal language early in the development of requirements and specifications for software, it is difficult (or often impossible for all practical purposes) to introduce such formality at a later stage. This suggests that it is essential to find ways in which formal language can be introduced at *early* stages of requirements capture, and there must be effective refinement principles for moving from user-level requirements to an implementation.

Several approaches must be brought together to address this problem effectively. In this paper we explore the problems of modelling and tool integration on an illustrative problem we call the Village Telephone System (VTS). The VTS provides an accessible but non-trivial application similar to many others in the telecommunications and networking domains. We analyze it using a methodology we have developed in [5–7, 4] with formal support provided by the HOL90 general-purpose theorem prover and the Mocha model checker. First we provide a brief overview of the methodology, referring the reader to the cited work for more details. The main body of the paper is devoted to the treatment of the VTS using this methodology.

Principles of good requirements engineering [7] demand that we identify the primitive vocabulary that is available to describe the application domain, and that we provide a precise (albeit informal) explanation of the real-world meaning of each primitive term. The principles also demand that we separate logical assertions into two distinct moods. Assertions made in the indicative mood describe the environment as it would be regardless of the system – they represent domain knowledge. Assertions made in the optative mood describe the environment as we would like it to be because of the system – they represent requirements. A requirement is not necessarily directly implementable by a computer system [6]; it may involve concepts that are not directly visible to the implementor. If it is not, then it must be refined into an implementable specification, using domain knowledge as a resource. Formal requirements engineering culminates in an argument that the specifications and the domain knowledge are consistent, and in a proof that the domain knowledge and the specifications together entail the satisfaction of all the requirements. Similarly, on the development side, the aim is to ensure that the programming of the machine satisfies the specifications.

Our treatment of the Village Telephone System is accordingly organized into a collection of parts, each having a different significance:

Mathematical Foundations provide concepts not already available in existing libraries that are needed for the VTS.

Designated Terminology provides terms to describe the application domain (environment, world), and an informal explanation of their meaning in the real world.

Requirements indicate what the villagers need from their telephone system, described in terms of the designations.

Domain Knowledge provides presumed facts about the environment.

Specifications provide enough information for a programmer to build a system to satisfy the requirements.

Program implements the specification on the programming platform.

Programming Platform provides the basis for programming a machine to satisfy the requirements and specifications.

If we got the specifications right, then it will be possible to combine our (presumably correct) domain knowledge about the environment with the specifications of our system and show that the villagers will have the kind of telephone service they require.

The last five parts in the list above can be grouped into categories of environment and system to emphasize their roles, with the specifications acting as an intermediary between the system and its environment. The "Five Theory Model" can be illustrated as follows:

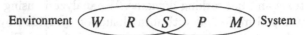

Environment W R S P M System

Generally speaking, the proof obligations are to show that the theories in question are consistent and that, under appropriate assumptions:

- the domain knowledge W, supplemented by the specifications S, satisfies the requirements R, and
- the programming platform M, with its programming P, implements the specifications.

The precise statement of these obligations in Higher-Order Logic is given in the section on designations below (Table 1) because it depends crucially on distinguishing variables (representing events and state) that are controlled by the environment (like a person taking a telephone off-hook) from those that are controlled by the system (like causing a telephone to ring). Details about our refinement principles can be found in [4].

Turning now to our benchmark problem, we shall illustrate our approach for a simple telephone service suited to the needs of a very friendly village. The telephones are fairly conventional: they have a microphone (or mouthpiece) and a speaker (or earpiece) and they ring to alert an incoming call. Taking the phone off-hook when it is ringing answers the incoming call. Putting it back on-hook terminates calls. Taking it off-hook when it is not ringing indicates a desire to make a call. They are less conventional in two respects. First, they have no dialing device, nor is there an operator in the telephone exchange: the exchange is entirely automatic. The maker of a call cannot therefore choose which number to call. The system makes the choice. This is acceptable because the villagers know each other and each other's business so well that a villager wanting to make a call is equally happy to talk to any fellow villager. The second difference is that a villager whose partner in a call has just hung up need only wait, keeping his own phone off-hook, and the system will immediately try to find him another conversation partner. A variant of this system we have investigated, but will not consider in this paper, has such phones enter a "drooping" state where they cannot be connected until they go back on-hook. There can, of course, be no guarantee that the system will always find a partner for every villager who wants to talk, because a ringing phone may be left unanswered indefinitely, and there may be no-one left available to be rung. However, we are guaranteed that the system will ring someone if this is possible.

Although VTS is not in itself a product of any telephone company, it is a fairly typical protocol resembling communication services such as anycast or chat lines. There is a variety of possible implementations representing trade-offs such as the likelihood of finding a partner and other factors. At one extreme (broadcast) an off-hook event could cause all on-hook telephones to alert and, at another extreme (hotlines), each telephone t could have its own pre-determined unique partner which alerts in response to an off-hook event of t. An intermediate solution (anycast) could cause an undetermined on-hook telephone to alert in response to an off-hook event. Each of these approaches has various refinements, such as allowing any off-hook event to make a connection to an existing off-hook telephone that has not yet received a connection. The VTS is therefore more interesting than its cousin, Plain Old Telephone Service (POTS), in which a uniquely designated telephone is alerted as a result of dialing an off-hook telephone. Between the two lie a range of interesting services in which an off-hook telephone seeks a connection with any of a specified collection of on-hook telephones. VTS represents the extreme in which every such telephone is a candidate for connection, while POTS represents the extreme in which only one other telephone is a candidate. In this middle ground fall services such as 800 numbers in the North American system where an incoming call is assigned to one of a group of operators, possibly with queueing if all operators are engaged.

We have used several systems in the development of the VTS: the HOL90 theorem prover, the Mocha model checker, and the SML programming language. This diversity was intended to help us explore the parts of the task best treated by each tool. We have allowed some overlap in order to carry out comparisons, but have also used the tools in exploring distinct solutions and in different parts of the development. In particular, HOL has been used for all phases of the development except the programming, whereas SML is used only for the programming. Mocha is used to provide a specification and also programming. Our SML implementation uses an anycast solution together with what we call the "greedy" connection rule while we considered a broadcast solution in the Mocha specification and implementation.

The paper is divided into sections representing each of the parts we discussed earlier for our methodology (the program and programming platform are combined in a single implementation section). Each section emphasizes what we view as the most interesting themes. For instance, the mathematical foundations section describes an HOL model that we have tuned for use on reactive systems like the VTS, and the implementation section considers the challenge of bridging between formal specification language and executable programs. Another issue is the set of tradeoffs involved in using a general-purpose system (HOL90) versus a special-purpose one (Mocha). The final section provides some conclusions.

2   Mathematical Foundations

As is usual with projects in HOL, we found it desirable to build up a body of fairly general purpose mathematics as a foundation of the requirements and specification of the village telephone system in HOL. This background should be useful for the description of reactive systems in general. There is a basic temporal theory given by inductive sequences, and a theory of finite state machines with a specialization to toggles.

2.1 Inductive Sequences

The formalization of reactive systems has typically been founded on some notion of sequences of events. The paper [3] discusses differences in four theorem prover formalizations of possibly infinite sequences. We have chosen to treat sequences in a way that differs from these in two fundamental ways. The approaches taken so far have been *explicit* in that they build a specific model for sequences and then derive properties. Here, we shall be taking an *implicit*, or axiomatic approach. The definition of a sequence is given by:

$\forall order\ domain.$ inductive_sequence $(order, domain)\ =$
  transitive $(order, domain)\ \wedge$ irreflexive $(order, domain)\ \wedge$
  nondense $(order, domain)\ \wedge\ (\exists\ f.$ least $(order, domain)\ f)\ \wedge$
  $(\forall Invar.\ ((\forall f.$ least $(order, domain)\ f\ \Rightarrow\ Invar(f))\ \wedge$
    $(\forall i\ j.$ successor$(order, domain)\ (i, j)\ \wedge\ Invar(i)\ \Rightarrow\ Invar(j)))\ \Rightarrow$
    $\forall i.\ domain(i)\ \Rightarrow\ Invar(i))$

An ordering is non-dense if every element that is not the least has an immediate predecessor, and if it has anything greater than it, then it has an immediate successor. The last clause is the principle of induction. Any set and ordering that is an inductive sequence is isomorphic to an initial segment of the natural numbers. Still, by not restricting ourselves to that particular model, we get certain properties practically for free. For example, we automatically get that any non-empty subset of an inductive sequence is again an inductive sequence.

Using inductive sequences, we can now develop a rich temporal theory appropriate for reasoning about reactive systems. For example, given a predicate P on events of an inductive sequence, we can define predicates like previously(P), which says that P holds of the previous event, and throughout(P) which says that P holds continuously throughout some interval. We have one-step induction (which is more conveniently used in conjunction with previously) and general induction. Thus, the same machinery that is available to the explicit versions of sequences is available for the implicit one.

The previous approaches also are based, directly or indirectly, on mappings from some ordered set to actions, telling what action occurred at a given time. We have taken the dual approach. Actions are represented as predicates stating at which events they occur. Thus on(t) is a predicate on events that indicates all those times when the telephone t went on-hook. If we fix the set of action predicates, then we can recreate the inverse mapping from events to actions. However, by doing the mapping this way around, we can more easily extend our system to include more actions and readily compose two systems in parallel. Also, to express a system with true concurrency requires no extra effort, while if the mapping is done the reverse of our way, then true concurrency requires switching from sequences of actions to sequences of sets of actions. On the whole, we believe this formalization of sequences of actions will prove to carry less overhead for many applications than previous methods.

2.2 Finite State Machines

Finite state machines (FSM's) are one of the most commonly used specification formalisms. A variety of descriptive techniques are based on FSM's, different techniques incorporating them in different ways. For example, we could be interested only in the sequence of *states* traversed, or only in the sequence of *transitions* taken. Our objective is to develop a reasonably general HOL model for FSM's that could handle different variations as special cases.

Finite state machines recognize inductive sequences. Formally, fsm is a predicate defined over the 5-tuples $(v, q, q0, f, r)$, where v is a predicate that provides a vocabulary of actions:

$v : (event \rightarrow bool) \rightarrow bool$	the set of transition *labels*
$q : state \rightarrow bool$	the set of *states*
$q0 : state \rightarrow bool$	the set of *initial states*
$f : state \rightarrow bool$	the set of *final states*
$r : state \times (event \rightarrow bool) \times state \rightarrow bool$	the set of *transitions*.

Notice that transitions are labeled with predicates whose role is to determine the availability of the transition at any given moment.

fsm $(v, q, q0, f, r)$ = (finite q) $\wedge$ ($q0 \subseteq q$) $\wedge$ ($f \subseteq q$) $\wedge$
  ($\forall l\ s1\ s2.\ ((s1, l, s2) \in r) \Rightarrow (s1 \in q \wedge s2 \in q \wedge l \in v)) \wedge$
  (pairwise_disjoint $\{l \mid \exists\ s1\ s2.\ (s1, l, s2) \in r\}$)

This models nondeterministic FSM's. We need to define the way in which an FSM interprets an inductive sequence. For that purpose, we define the relation pstates $e\ s$ that says when a state s can be entered after an event e. The relation is defined by rule induction:

$$\frac{least\ e \qquad s \in q0}{pstates\ e\ s}\ (Init)$$

$$\frac{pstates\ e1\ s \qquad successor\ (e1, e2) \qquad (s, l, t) \in r \qquad e2 \in l}{pstates\ e2\ t}\ (Step)$$

$$\frac{pstates\ e1\ s \qquad successor\ (e1, e2) \qquad \forall l \in v.\ e2 \notin l}{pstates\ e2\ s}\ (Stay).$$

The *Stay* rule says that all the events which the machine does not mention at all are ignored (filtered out).

An inductive sequence is accepted by an FSM if, at every point, it is guaranteed the ability to reach a final state. Formally,

accept $(v, q, q0, f, r)\ (order, domain)$ =
  $\forall\ e1.\ (e1 \in domain \Rightarrow$
    $\exists\ e2\ s.\ (s \in f) \wedge ((e1 = e2) \vee order(e1, e2)) \wedge pstates\ e2\ s).$

This definition takes care of both finite and infinite inductive sequences. In the finite case it coincides with the classical definition of acceptance by ending up in a final state. In the infinite case it coincides with acceptance by Buchi automata.

We also defined deterministic FSM's as a special case and proved some basic results about them. An interesting class of deterministic FSM's are *toggle FSM's*. A toggle FSM is an FSM with exactly two states and two disjointly labeled transitions between them. Given two sets of events *go_on* and *go_off* they determine a toggle FSM iff:

$$\text{toggle } (go\_on, go\_off) = \text{fsm } (\text{toggle\_fsm}(go\_on, go\_off) \land$$
$$\text{accept } (\text{toggle\_fsm}(go\_on, go\_off)) \ (order, domain)$$

where

$$\text{toggle\_fsm}(go\_on, go\_off) =$$
$$(\{go\_on; go\_off\}, \{0; 1\}, \{0\}, \{0; 1\}, \{(0, go\_on, 1), (1, go\_off, 0)\}$$

3 Designated Terminology

This part of the VTS description presents the primitive vocabulary that is available for use to describe the application domain (environment, world). It also explains the real-world meaning of each primitive term. Obviously these explanations are informal; if they were formal, then the terms would not be primitive. In general, designated terminology must be classified into one of four categories according to control and visibility: environment-controlled, system-hidden; environment-controlled, system-visible; system-controlled, environment-visible; and system-controlled, environment-hidden. When we need to represent these variables in mathematical formulae, we shall write them as eh, ev, sv, and sh, where each of these is to be viewed as a list of variables. The system-controlled and environment-hidden variables sh, only arise within the implementation and will not be covered here. The purpose of the designations is to clarify the role these terms may play in the formation of the domain knowledge, specification and requirements. It also is critical in formulating the basic theorems that need to relate these components. Using the variable classification, we can represent the domain knowledge by $W(eh, ev, sv)$, represent the requirements by $R(eh, ev, sv)$, represent the specification by $S(ev, sv)$, represent (as an input-output relation) a program implementing the specification by $P(ev, sv, sh)$ and represent knowledge of the programming platform (machine) on which the program will be run by $M(ev, sv, sh)$. Notice that the domain knowledge and the requirements cannot reference those variables controlled by the system and hidden from the environment, and that the specification can only reference those variables visible to both the system and the environment. Suppressing the arguments, the ultimate theorems we wish to hold are given in Table 1. Formulas (1) and (2) are consistency properties and (3) is the correctness of the implementation relative to the domain knowledge and requirements. From (2) and (3), we can prove the consistency of the requirements relative to the domain knowledge. To prove (2) and (3), we will factor through the specification. If we prove (4), (5) and (6) then we can derive both (2) and (3) from them. A major part of the point of

Table 1. Proof Obligations for Refinements

$$\exists \; eh \; ev \; sv.\mathsf{W} \tag{1}$$

$$\forall eh \; ev.(\exists \; sv.\mathsf{W}) \Rightarrow (\exists \; sv.\mathsf{W} \wedge \mathsf{M} \wedge \mathsf{P}) \tag{2}$$

$$\forall eh \; ev \; sv.\mathsf{W} \wedge \mathsf{M} \wedge \mathsf{P} \Rightarrow \mathsf{R} \tag{3}$$

$$\forall eh \; ev \; sv.\mathsf{W} \wedge \mathsf{S} \Rightarrow \mathsf{R} \tag{4}$$

$$\forall eh \; ev.(\exists \; sv.\mathsf{W}) \Rightarrow (\exists \; sv.\mathsf{S}) \wedge (\forall sv.\mathsf{S} \Rightarrow \mathsf{W}) \tag{5}$$

$$\forall ev.(\exists \; sv.\mathsf{S}) \Rightarrow (\exists \; sv \; sh.\mathsf{M} \wedge \mathsf{P}) \wedge (\forall sv \; sh.(\mathsf{M} \wedge \mathsf{P}) \Rightarrow \mathsf{S}) \tag{6}$$

this factorization is that on the one hand, the person writing the specification need only worry about satisfying (1), (4) and (5) without any concern for the particulars of any program that might implement it, while the person writing the program need only worry about satisfying (5) without any knowledge of the domain knowledge or the original requirements. Formula (5) for the specification is a bit stronger than the corresponding formula (2) for the program and programming platform. Formula (5) asserts that for all values from the environment that do not contradict the domain knowledge, the specification relates some value from the system, and all such values from the system must satisfy the domain knowledge. It turns out that the correspondingly stronger version of formula (2) also follows from (4), (5), and (6).

The designated terminology describing time, people, telephones, sounds, their actions and interactions is as follows:

- **Environment-controlled, system-visible:**
    - event(E): E is an atomic event.
    - earlier($E1, E2$): event $E1$ is earlier than event $E2$, and
    - tel(t) : t is a telephone in the village;
    - on(t)(E) : E is an event where telephone t goes onhook.
    - off(t)(E) : E is an event in which telephone t goes offhook.
- **Environment-controlled, system-hidden:**
    - person(p) : p is person in the village;
    - sound(s) : s is a unit instance (or packet) of sound.
    - go_near_phone(p, t)(E) : a person p goes near (enough to be heard over) a telephone t at an event E.
    - go_away_from_phone(p, t)(E) : a person p goes away (enough not to be heard over) a telephone t at an event E.
    - make_sound(p, s)(E) : a person p makes a sound s at an event E.
    - hear_sound(p, s)(E) : a person p hears the sound s at an event E.
    - transmit(t_1, t_2, s)(E) : the sound s is transmitted from telephone t_1 to telephone t_2 at an event E.
- **System-controlled, environment-visible:**
    - then_alerting(t)(E) : Immediately after event E, telephone t is in an alerting state (that is, the telephone is 'ringing').

- then_connected$(t1, t2)(E)$: Immediately after event E, telephones $t1$ and $t2$ have a talking connection.

The predicates tel, person, and sound are 'timeless' facts treated as constants. The other predicates above are partially curried on events to facilitate their use with the general temporal theory. Most of the predicates are just what would be expected. The treatment of sound is a little unusual. Since we are assuming that time is discrete, we assume that sound comes in discrete units as well. We also associate with a sound its origin so that sounds made by different people are different sounds.

The temporal theory assumes that events are instantaneous: the actions of the system (telephone system) are sufficiently fast that users perceive them as happening in no time, for all practical purposes. The state of the telephone system changes only at events, so state predicates are often defined using event boundaries. For instance, a telephone t that satisfies then_alerting$(t)(E)$ is one that began to alert at event E or was alerting prior to E and continued to alert after E. State is often viewed in terms of *immediately before* E (alerting_then) and *immediately after* E (then_alerting). The alerting state immediately before E is a defined predicate:

$$\forall E\ t.\ \text{alerting\_then}\ t\ E\ =\ \text{previously(then\_alerting}\ t)\ E.$$

We will use names prefixed or suffixed by then for state predicates; actions are not so modified.

Using the designated terminology, we have built up a considerable vocabulary of defined terminology. One such example is alerting_then. We omit the definitions here, but assume that the names are adequately suggestive to allow the reader to determine what the definitions are.

4 Requirements

Because this is a very friendly village we require the system to make it as easy as possible for villagers to talk to each other. Intuitively, the requirement is that if a villager wants to talk to somebody the system will make an effort to find a suitable partner – that is, another villager who is offhook and not engaged in another conversation, and therefore free to talk. This effort may include alerting one or more villagers whose phones are onhook in the hope that a phone will then go offhook and can be connected. There are many possible versions of these informal requirements. In all versions we assume that time is discrete (this is stipulated by the temporal theory) and that the system is fast enough to complete its response to each event before the next environment event occurs (this is sometimes called the "reactive system hypothesis"). In our case this means that then_connected and then_alerting can be viewed as instantaneous state changes.

The first thing that anybody would want out of a telephone system is that communication can happen:

PR0(near_phone_then, is_offhook_then, connected_then, make_sound,
  hear_sound) =
$\forall E$ $p1$ $p2$ $t1$ $t2$ s. (near_phone_then$(p1, t1)$ E $\wedge$ is_offhook_then $t1$ E $\wedge$
  near_phone_then$(p2, t2)$ E $\wedge$ is_offhook_then $t2$ E $\wedge$
  connected_then$(t1, t2)$ E $\wedge$ make_sound$(p1, s)$ $E)$ $\Rightarrow$ hear_sound$(p2, s)$ E

In what remains, we will leave the arguments to PRn implicit. Another thing people expect from their phone is a degree of privacy:

PR1 = $\forall E$ p s $t1$ $t2$.is_onhook_then $t1$ E $\Rightarrow$
      $(\neg$transmit_sound$(t1, t2)$ E $\wedge$ $\neg$transmit_sound$(t2, t1)$ $E)$

A bit of politeness is that an offhook telephone should not be alerting:

PR2 = $\forall E$ t. then_offhook t E $\Rightarrow$ $\neg$then_alerting t E

Connections are reliable in the sense that a connection is not broken (or even replaced by another connection) until one of its participants goes onhook:

PR3 = $\forall E$ $t1$ $t2$.
      (connected_then $(t1, t2)$ E $\wedge$ $\neg$then_connected $(t1, t2)$ $E)$
      $\Rightarrow$ (on $t1$ E $\vee$ on $t2$ $E)$

Alerting is also reliable in the sense that an answered phone (one that goes offhook while it is alerting) immediately enters the talking state (that is, it is connected to some other phone). That other phone may of course go onhook in the very next event, but between the two events the answered phone is in the talking state:

PR4 = $\forall E$ t. answer t E $\Rightarrow$ then_talking t E

When somebody is requesting a connection (by having taken their phone offhook when it was not alerting and not having been connected or having hung up yet) and there is an onhook phone, then some phone is alerting.

PR5 = $\forall E$ $t1$. then_requesting $t1$ E $\wedge$ $(\exists$ $t2$. then_onhook $t2$ $E)$ $\Rightarrow$
      $(\exists$ $t3$. then_alerting $t3$ $E)$

The partial requirements PR0 through PR5 are basic to any version of this telephone service, and we have included them in each of the speculative set of requirements we investigated. Let us therefore refer to the following formula as partial requirement B:

B = PR0 $\wedge$ PR1 $\wedge$ PR2 $\wedge$ PR3 $\wedge$ PR4 $\wedge$ PR5

In addition to the basic requirements, there are two alternative ways of handling phones that lose a connection. A telephone is said to *droop* if it was connected to another phone which hangs up, and remains drooping until it either hangs up or is connected to another phone. There are two evident options for how to handle a drooping phone. One option is to treat a drooping phone the same as a requesting phone. In which case we have a requirement for drooping phones that is the same as PR5 for requesting phones.

PR6 = $\forall E$ $t1$. then_drooping $t1$ E $\wedge$ ($\exists$ $t2$. then_onhook $t2$ E) $\Rightarrow$
                  ($\exists$ $t3$. then_alerting $t3$ E)

The other option (which is the one used by POTS) is to treat it as unavailable until it goes onhook. In this case we would have the requirement:

PR6' = $\forall E$ t. (droop t E $\vee$ drooping_then t E) $\Rightarrow$ $\neg$then_talking t E

To cover the option where drooping phones are treated the same as requesting phones, we will say that a phone is asking if it is either requesting or drooping. There is one last requirement that we have for the system, namely that it be fair to the callers by treating them on a first come, first served basis. Assuming drooping telephones are handled the same as requesting phones, this yields:

PR7 = $\forall E1$ $t1$ $t2$.(asking_then $t1$ $E1$ $\wedge$
            (ask $t2$ $E1$ $\vee$
              (asking_then $t2$ $E1$ $\wedge$
                $\exists E2$. throughout (asking_then $t1$) $E2$ $E1$ $\wedge$
                    $\neg$throughout (asking_then $t2$) $E2$ $E1$))) $\Rightarrow$
          (then_talking $t2$ $E1$ $\Rightarrow$ then_talking $t1$ $E1$)

For the case where drooping telephones are treated as unavailable, PR7' is derived from PR7 by replacing all occurrences of asking_then by requesting_then. In the specifications given later in this paper we have focused on the case where drooping phones are treated the same as requesting phones. Therefore our requirements are

R = B $\wedge$ PR6 $\wedge$ PR7

We see no inherent difficulty with deriving specifications for the alternate system which treats drooping phones as unavailable.

Note that there is a great deal of non-determinism in our requirements. For example, none of our requirements directly stipulates a choice of caller-callee pairings. Nor do we stipulate that there should, or should not, ever be more than one phone alerting. Some of this non-determinism will be restricted by the choice of specification, but much will be passed on for the program to decide.

5 Domain Knowledge

Our domain knowledge for the VTS is a collection of facts about the environment as we choose to model it for the purposes of our system. Remember that domain knowledge gives us facts we may assume about the environment, whereas the requirements will have to be proved. First of all, we assert that types of arguments in some of our predicates are as expected:

K0 = ($\forall E1$ $E2$. earlier($E1, E2$) $\Rightarrow$ event $E1$ $\wedge$ event $E2$) $\wedge$
          ($\forall t$ E. on t E $\Rightarrow$ tel t $\wedge$ event E) $\wedge$ $\cdots$ $\wedge$
          ($\forall t1$ $t2$ E. then_connected ($t1, t2$) E $\Rightarrow$
              tel $t1$ $\wedge$ tel $t2$ $\wedge$ event E)

More significantly, the designated relation earlier is a nondense total order over 'events', there is an initial event, and an induction principle. Using the mathematical foundations we can state this as

K1 = inductive_sequence(earlier, event)

Additionally, off and on events are in disjoint classes and are not initial events. At any telephone, off and on events alternate strictly, beginning with an off event so we wish to model telephones as toggles:

K2 = ∀ t. tel t ⇒ toggle(off t, on t)

(The constant toggle actually takes (earlier, event) as an additional argument, but we have omitted it here for the sake of conciseness.)

At most one telephone is going offhook or onhook at any given time:

K3 = ∀E $t1$ $t2$. (off $t1$ E ∨ on $t1$ E) ∧ (off $t2$ E ∨ on $t2$ E) ⇒
($t1$ = $t2$)

Another expectation is that then_connected is an irreflexive relation, that is, no telephone is ever connected to itself, and connections are symmetric (perhaps because of the hardware that has been previously agreed upon).

K4 = ∀E t. ¬then_connected (t, t) E
K5 = ∀E $t1$ $t2$. then_connected$(t1, t2)$ E = then_connected$(t2, t1)$ E

Moreover, connections are in pairs:

K6 = ∀E $t1$ $t2$ $t3$. then_connected$(t1, t2)$ E ∧
then_connected$(t1, t3)$ E ⇒ ($t2$ = $t3$)

Some telephone services have connections called 'conference bridges' that allow three or more parties to be connected, but the village doesn't have this.

The rest of the domain knowledge is about people, sounds and their relation to telephones. First, people are toggles with respect to going near and going away from telephones:

K7 = ∀p t. person p ⇒ toggle(go_near_phone t, go_away_from_phone t)

If a person is near a phone $p1$ which is offhook and connected to a phone $p2$ which is also offhook, and the person makes a sound, then that sound is transmitted from $p1$ to $p2$.

K8 = ∀E p $t1$ $t2$ s. near_phone_then $(p, t1)$ E ∧ is_offhook_then $t1$ E ∧
connected_then $(t1, t2)$ E ∧ is_offhook_then $t2$ E ∧
make_sound (p, s) E ⇒ transmit_sound $(t1, t2, s)$ E

If a person is near a phone and a sound is transmitted to that phone, then it is conveyed to that person.[1]

---

[1] This can be considered analogous to conveying a packet to an application-level program by placing it in a buffer that is accessible by the application. There may be no guarantee that the application will "make use" of the packet, just as VTS makes no guarantee that a person will listen to a sound.

K9 = $\forall E\ p\ t\ s.$ near_phone_then $(p,t)\ E\ \land$
$(\exists\ t1.$ transmit_sound $(t1,t,s)\ E)\ \Rightarrow$ hear_sound $(p,t)\ E$

Lastly, we assert that if a sound is transmitted from one phone to another, they must be connected.

K10 = $\forall E\ t1\ t2\ s.$ transmit_sound $(t1,t2,s)\ E\ \Rightarrow$
connected_then$(t1,t2)\ E$

Note that K8 and K9 are sufficient to prove the requirement PR0. It is not true that all the requirements follow from the domain knowledge (PR1 does not, for example), but it is not unreasonable to expect it to happen some of the time.

6 Specifications

The principle attribute of a specification is that it lies in the common vocabulary of the environment and system but still has enough information to entail the requirement, given the domain knowledge. Viewed as a progression from user-level requirements to the development of a machine to satisfy those requirements, it can be viewed as a reduction of the requirements to observable properties of the machine. In the VTS this entails the reduction of requirements that speak of people and sounds to ones that speak of off-hook and on-hook events (which the machine detects but does not control) and telephones in alerting and connected states (which the machine can control). It also may entail reductions in the range of available solutions as it narrows possibilities by stipulating particular approaches. We describe two specifications, the first is done with HOL and uses an anycast solution, while the second is done in Mocha and uses a broadcast solution.

Up to this point, HOL has been our sole platform for formalizing aspects of the VTS. At this point, we are expanding to make use of a second system, Mocha. The question arises, what is the relation between a specification given in Mocha and one given in HOL. The answer is that the Mocha specification is directly translatable into HOL because the underlying semantics of time in Mocha, that of a *round*, coincides with that of an event in an inductive sequence in HOL, and the module variables map directly to the designated terminology. We actually studied different specifications with the two different systems, but the Mocha specification is readily expressible in HOL.

6.1 Specifications in HOL

There are essentially two cases because a phone can only do two things: go offhook and go onhook. Within each of these, there are essentially two cases again. Going offhook can happen when the phone is alerting (in which case it is a *answer* event) or it can happen when phone is not alerting (in which case it is a *request* event). Going onhook can happen when the phone is connected (a *disconnect* event), or when it is not (a *withdraw* event). We therefore organize the specification into five formulas: Initial, Answer, Request, Disconnect, and

Withdraw. For each of these we provide an abbreviated English explanation that relies on certain invariants the system satisfies. In developing the specification in HOL, we gave two versions, a "fat" version that included clauses for many cases which (one can prove in retrospect) cannot occur, and the other being a "lean" version which we describe below. We were able to prove that in the presence of domain knowledge the two specifications are logically equivalent.

The Initial Event: Immediately after the initial event no telephones are alerting or connected.

Answer Events: Assume telephone $t1$ answers at event E. Then there is a phone $t2$ which is asking and which is the unique phone connected to $t1$ after E, and any other pair of phones is connected after E iff it was connected before E. That is, $t1$ connects to some asking phone $t2$, and all standing connections are unaffected. After E the phone $t1$ is no longer alerting and, except for $t1$, a phone is alerting after E iff it was alerting before E.

The "fat" formula for answer events is more complicated because it covers all cases, such as what happens when a phone other than $t2$ is also asking: "if there is another phone besides $t2$ that is asking and $t1$ was the only phone alerting before E, then there is a phone t3 that was onhook before E and starts to alert after E". However, the "fat" set of specification formulae can be used to show that at most one phone can be asking at any one time: the greedy connection rule would connect any pair of simultaneously asking phones. Another point of interest: the "fat" specification implies that there is at most one alerting phone, so, in fact, after E there are *no* alerting phones.

Request Events: Suppose $t1$ is a phone that was not alerting when it goes offhook at E; that is, $t1$ requests a connection at E. If there is another phone $t2$ that is asking, then $t1$ is connected to $t2$, all other standing connections are unaffected, and there are no alerting phones after E. If no other phone is asking, then the standing connections are the same as before E, and some phone that is onhook at E begins to alert, if there is any onhook phone.

Again, this phrasing is based on a variety of invariants like the fact that at most one phone can be alerting at any time and the fact that if no phone is asking then no phone is alerting.

Disconnect Events: Suppose $t1$ goes onhook at event E, where $t1$ was connected to $t2$ immediately before E. Then, after E the connection between $t1$ and $t2$ ends and there are two possibilities for what happens to $t2$. Either another phone was asking and then $t2$ is connected to it and all alerting phones stop alerting, or no other phone was asking, so no new connection is made, and an onhook phone begins to alert. In either case all other connections are unaffected.

Withdraw: Suppose $t1$ goes onhook at event E, but where $t1$ was not connected immediately before E. Then, the set of standing connections is left unaffected, and all phones stop alerting.

In HOL, we have proved a collection of invariants of this specification, such as those mentioned above, and we have proved the equivalence of the two specifications. We have also proved that the specification which covers all cases, including those that cannot arise, satisfies the reduction theorem given by formulae (4) and (5) in Table 1. Using the equivalence of the specification under domain knowledge, we then showed the simplified specification also satisfied formulae (4) and (5). Therefore, either of the specifications may be passed on to developers to build a program to satisfy it. The developers need not know anything about the original requirements or the domain knowledge; if a program is supplied that satisfies formula (6), then we are guaranteed (from a theorem in HOL) that the desired formula (3) will hold.

6.2 Specification in Mocha

Mocha [2] is a model-checking verification system, which uses reactive modules [1] as a modelling language and state invariants for specifications. We specify the VTS using reactive modules.

Reactive Modules. A reactive module is a collection of synchronously updated variables. A key concept is that of a round, which is the time-step at which a variable may be updated. There is an initial round when the variables are initialized. Subsequent rounds are called update rounds. The semantics of rounds is the same as the semantics of events in an inductive sequence. Therefore, it is legitimate to identify these two notions, and we shall refer to rounds and events interchangeably from here on.

Formally, a module consists of *external* variables (ev), which are inputs to the module; *private* variables (sh), which are updated locally but are invisible outside the module; *interface* variables (sv), which are updated locally and are visible outside the module. Updated variable values can depend on the current and previous values of any of the variables in the module as long as there are no circular dependencies. Thus each variable is actually a function from rounds to values. The module expresses a set of predicates on the values of the variables in any round.

A specification for the variables in a module can be expressed by writing an invariant for it. An invariant is a condition on the variable values that is expected to hold in all rounds. Very often, the invariant mechanism is not expressive enough for temporal specifications for the module because it does not allow predicates over rounds. In such cases, we use another module to *monitor* the relevant variables. The monitor module sets a flag whenever any condition is violated. Then the specification can be expressed as an invariant of the flag value.

Specifying the VTS. In the VTS, the system and the environment are reactive systems which respond to conditions at each event. All the variables are predicated over events. Consequently, we can naturally model the VTS and its specification using reactive modules.

The specification for the VTS is expressed by defining a monitor module with a flag variable which is initially true and goes false if any of the following rules are violated in a round:

Consistency: At any round, no phone is connected to itself, connections are symmetric, and no phone is connected to two phones.

Initial: After the initial round, no telephones are alerting or connected

Answer: At any update round, if a phone is answered, then it stops alerting, there is exactly one asking phone, it is connected to every asking phone, and no standing connections are affected.

Request: At any update round, if a phone requests, then no other phone is asking, and all on-hook phones start alerting.

On-Hook: At any update round, if a talking phone goes on-hook, all its connections are broken; if a talking phone goes on-hook, the phone's partner gets connected to an asking phone if there is one, and otherwise all non-alerting on-hook phones start alerting; and if a non-talking phone goes on-hook, all alerting phones stop alerting.

The specification is then expressed as an invariant that the flag is always (in all rounds) true.

This specification differs from the HOL specification in exactly one aspect. Here the system is expected to alert all on-hook phones (broadcast) when a connection is requested, as opposed to exactly one on-hook phone (anycast) in the HOL case. We assert that this assumption does not violate the requirements. We have not formally proved that (4) and (5) hold for this specification, but in light of the proof of (4) and (5) for the HOL specification and the close relation between the two specifications, we believe that it can be proved for the reactive module specification as well.

7 Implementations

As was with the case with the specifications, we have given two implementations: one in SML satisfying the simplified HOL specification, and one in Mocha, satisfying the Mocha specification.

7.1 Implementation in SML

The HOL specification reads as a large case statement relating an onhook or offhook event (or initial event) to the set of connections and the set of alerting telephones after the event, given enough history to know which phones are already onhook, offhook, alerting, or connected (and to whom). The SML implementation consists of a state variable containing the current set of connections, a state variable containing the current set of alerting phones, and a recursive program over a stream of onhook and offhook events, yielding state changes to the set of connections and the set of alerting phones. The loop of the recursive program takes as arguments the current set of onhook phones as well the current event. It generates the changes to the state of the connections and alerting phones, and returns the new set of onhook phones. This internal record of the the set of phones onhook is a machine-controlled, world-hidden variable that mirrors the defined term onhook_then. The loop mirrors the case statement of the simplified specification very closely. We did not perform a formal proof that the program satisified the specification (i.e., formula (6) from Table 1), but we did do an informal proof. A formal proof should be possible, given the semantics of SML encoded in HOL, but since the similarity of the program and the specification was so great, there seemed diminished value in doing so.

7.2   Implementation in Mocha

In Mocha we implemented VTS as a reactive module with environment controlled variables on(t), off(t) as external (input) variables and then_alerting(t), then_connected($t1, t2$) as interface (output) variables. These variables are implicitly predicated over rounds (events) so they are just expressed as predicates over telephones. The implementation makes use of the fact that there can be at most one asking phone. Also, whenever any connection is requested, all onhook phones need to be alerted. So the system module just keeps track of the connections and the identity of the asking phone. Modeling the updates of these variables presents no challenges and is directly derivable from the specification. The value of then_connected($t1, t2$) follows simply from the connections for $t1$, $t2$ and then_alerting(t) is true for any on-hook phone t whenever there is an asking phone.

To verify the implementation we need to prove (6) from Table 1 for our system (M, P) and specification (S). In reactive modules, every module variable must have a value in each round, regardless of input. So the consistency of the system

$$\exists \; sv \; sh. \; \mathsf{M} \wedge \mathsf{P}$$

is implicitly guaranteed by the programming platform. What remains is to prove that for all values of ev that do not falsify S, the following holds true:

$$(\forall sv \; sh.(\mathsf{M} \wedge \mathsf{P}) \Rightarrow \mathsf{S})$$

We write an module that generates a superset of the values of ev that do not falsify S and supply the generated ev as input to the system module. Then we prove the above property by composing the system module in parallel with the specification and checking that the invariant holds for all possible states.

We use the enumerative model-checker in the Mocha system for the proof. Since the model checker will only work for a finite state space, we need to fix the number of telephones. Most of the non-trivial conditions of the VTS become visible when we have more than four telephones. We verify the system for a village with up to 9 telephones.

We ran the enumerative model-checker in Mocha-1.0 on a 167MHz Sun UltraSPARC with 96MB memory, running SunOS 5.5.1. For a village with 6 telephones, the system has 233 reachable states and is verified in 80 seconds. At 9 telephones, it has 9497 reachable states and the verification takes 233 minutes. The model-checking breaks at 10 telephones for lack of memory. This suggests that Mocha is probably useful as a debugging aid, allowing non-trivial tests, but cannot handle the number of states involved in checking any but the smallest villages. Clearly it would be of interest to find "saturation" principles that allow us to conclude properties of villages of all sizes from those of a fixed size, or techniques for allowing the checker to be used in conjunction with infinitary proof techniques like induction.

8   Conclusions and Acknowledgements

We have shown how to carry out an "end-to-end" formal development of an illustrative software system. This process included modelling parts of the process that are not usually treated formally, such as the user-level requirements. By a systematic approach to refinement we have shown how these requirements can be reduced to a specification that a programmer can implement. Formal proofs were developed for each of the refinements involved except for a gap between our SML implementation and its (extremely similar) HOL specification, and a gap between our Mocha specification and a corresponding HOL specification. The benefit of closing the first gap is probably not worth the trouble in this case, but better integration between Mocha and HOL could yield interesting benefits.

We would like to express thanks to Rajeev Alur, Trevor Jim, and Insup Lee for their input to this work.

References

1. R. Alur and T.A. Henzinger. Reactive modules. In *Proceedings of the 11th IEEE Symposium on Logic in Computer Science*, pages 207–218, 1996.
2. R. Alur, T.A. Henzinger, F. Mang, S. Qadeer, S. Rajamani, and S. Tasiran. Mocha: Modularity in Model Checking. To appear in the Conference on Computer Aided Verification, 1998.
3. Marco Defillers, David Griffioen, and Olaf Müller. Possibly infinite sequences in theorem provers: A comparative study. In *Lecture Notes in Computer Science 1275: Proceedings of the 10th International Conference, TPHOLs '97*. Springer, 1997.
4. Carl A. Gunter, Elsa L. Gunter, Michael Jackson, and Pamela Zave. A reference model for requirements and specifications. Available by request, 1998.
5. Michael Jackson and Pamela Zave. Domain descriptions. In *Proceedings of the IEEE International Symposium on Requirements Engineering*, pages 56–64. IEEE Computer Society Press, 1992.
6. Michael Jackson and Pamela Zave. Deriving specifications from requirements: An example. In *Proceedings of the Seventeenth International Conference on Software Engineering*, pages 15–24. IEEE Computer Society Press, 1995.
7. Pamela Zave and Michael Jackson. Four dark corners of requirements engineering. ACM Transactions on Software Engineering and Methodology, 6(1):1–30, January 1997.

Generating Embeddings from Denotational Descriptions*

Richard J. Boulton

Department of Artificial Intelligence, University of Edinburgh
80 South Bridge, Edinburgh EH1 1HN, Scotland
rjb@dai.ed.ac.uk

Abstract. This paper describes a tool for generating embeddings of computer languages from denotational-style specifications of semantics. The language used to specify the semantics is based on ML with extra features for succinctly handling environments/states. The tool generates input for the HOL theorem prover in the form of files containing ML code. Three files are generated: one for defining the semantics as recursive functions, one containing proof rules that 'evaluate' the semantics, and one containing ML functions that simulate the semantics (if it is executable). The definitions allow reasoning about computer languages and specific language texts. The simulation functions provide a means of rapidly testing the semantics and/or the behaviour of language texts. The proof rules can be used for more rigorous simulation when that is appropriate. In this case the evaluation can be symbolic, i.e., parts of a language text can be replaced by logical variables. The proof rules are also useful when proving properties. The embedding generator exploits the notion of a monad (from work on functional programming languages and semantics) to handle environments in a regular way.

1 Introduction

In recent years, theorem provers, and the HOL system in particular, have been used to reason about computer languages by defining the semantics of the languages in the logic of the theorem prover. Proof tools specific to the language have then been built to support verification, etc. The meta-language, ML, of the LCF prover and its descendants makes these systems well-suited to this process, which is known as *embedding*.

Construction of embeddings is becoming a routine activity but the effort required to construct and maintain an embedding for a realistically sized language remains considerable. Types for abstract syntax, logical definitions for the semantics, proof rules, and tools for supporting concrete syntax all have to be written and kept consistent as changes to the language are made. (The syntax may change if only a sublanguage is being supported and the formalization of

---

* Research supported by the Engineering and Physical Sciences Research Council of Great Britain under grants GR/J42236 and GR/L14381. Much of this work was done while the author was at the University of Cambridge Computer Laboratory.

the semantics may vary as problems with it are discovered.) Furthermore, the embedding cannot easily be changed to work with a different theorem prover, even one that supports the same logic as the original prover.

A solution is to separate the essential information about the syntax and semantics of the language from the implementation details of an embedding in a particular theorem proving system. High-level specifications of syntax and semantics can be written from which the implementations can be generated automatically, much as a compiler generates low-level machine-dependent code from programs in a high-level language. Having only one specification of the syntax and one of the semantics enables the various parts of the implementation to be kept consistent automatically.

A tool already exists to generate an embedding in the HOL system from semantics defined as rules over an attributed abstract syntax tree [13, 12]. In this paper we describe a tool for generating an embedding from a denotational-style specification of semantics. The tool is part of the CLaReT system [5] which includes the facility to generate abstract syntax tree (AST) representations, parsers and pretty-printers from a single specification of syntax [4].

The denotational descriptions are in the style of those often used in papers on semantics. A rule is given for each possible form of the abstract syntax. An ML-like language is used to define the meaning of each form. The intention is for the specifications to be sufficiently abstract to be compilable to both definitions of recursive functions in HOL and to ML functions. Furthermore, the use of environments in the specifications is made implicit wherever possible, with the aim of increasing readability.

2   Use of Monads

When the semantics of a non-trivial language is expressed using recursive functions over abstract syntax trees (as is the case in this work) it is usually necessary to pass around additional information. Sometimes this information may simply be passed down to the recursive calls on subtrees but more often information is also passed back. This information is in addition to the actual denotation of the language constructs. Examples of this kind of information are environments that keep track of declarations, and states.

So, for an imperative programming language with a sequencing construct between two statements, the state s_0 may be passed to the recursive function call that computes the denotation of the first statement. The result will include a new state s_1 that is in turn passed to the function call for the second statement. The result of this call includes a state s_2 that is returned along with the denotation of the entire sequencing construct. In ML the function might look like this:

```
fun sem_of_statement (Seq (stat1,stat2)) s0 =
    let val (den1,s1) = sem_of_statement stat1 s0
        val (den2,s2) = sem_of_statement stat2 s1
    in  (... den1 ... den2 ...,s2)
    end ...
```

This use of `let` expressions to thread the state through the computation can be expressed more cleanly as a state monad. A monad [17] is a mathematical object that can be used to capture many features of programming languages such as state, exceptions, and input/output. Monads have been used both in formal semantics and by the pure functional programming community. There is more than one (equivalent) formulation of a monad. Here, the formulation using the functions unit and bind is used. In this formulation a monad is a triple consisting of a polymorphic type constructor monad and the two functions just mentioned. In their most general form the functions have the following types:

$$\text{unit} : \alpha \to (\alpha)\text{monad}$$
$$\text{bind} : (\alpha)\text{monad} \to (\alpha \to (\beta)\text{monad}) \to (\beta)\text{monad}$$

In addition the functions must satisfy the following three equations:

$$\text{bind (unit } a) \; k = k \; a \tag{1}$$
$$\text{bind } m \text{ unit} = m \tag{2}$$
$$\text{bind } m \; (\lambda a. \text{ bind } (k \; a) \; h) = \text{bind (bind } m \; (\lambda a. \; k \; a)) \; h \tag{3}$$

For a state monad, the type (α)monad corresponds to state $\to \alpha \times$ state and unit and bind are defined as follows:

$$\text{unit } x = \lambda s_0. \; (x, s_0)$$
$$\text{bind } m \; f = \lambda s_0. \; (\lambda(x, s_1). \; f \; x \; s_1) \; (m \; s_0)$$

The semantic specifications in this paper are implemented using a variant of the state monad that also has a component for information that is only passed down to the recursive calls, i.e., is not threaded. The monad type then has three type parameters α, ρ and τ, and corresponds to $\rho \times \tau \to \alpha \times \tau$. The parameters ρ and τ are the non-threaded and threaded environment components, respectively. They may each be instantiated to a record structure or a tuple so that there can be multiple non-threaded components and multiple threaded components. An individual component will be referred to as a *field*. Call this monad a *denotation monad* and the monad functions unitD and bindD. Their definitions are:

$$\text{unitD } x = \lambda(p, t_0). \; (x, t_0)$$
$$\text{bindD } m \; f = \lambda(p, t_0). \; (\lambda(x, t_1). \; f \; x \; (p, t_1)) \; (m \; (p, t_0))$$

The proofs that unitD and bindD satisfy the monad equations are straightforward.

In addition to unitD and bindD a derived function bindD_map is used:

$$\text{bind\_list } m f \text{ nil} = \text{unitD nil}$$
$$\text{bind\_list } m f \; (mx :: mxs) = \text{bindD } (mf \; mx) \; (\lambda y.$$
$$\text{bindD (bind\_list } m f \; mxs) \; (\lambda ys.$$
$$\text{unitD } (y :: ys)))$$
$$\text{bindD\_map } m f \; mxs \; f = \text{bindD (bind\_list } m f \; mxs) \; f$$

This function threads the environment through the computation involved in mapping a function over a list.

Given that the intention is to generate HOL definitions and ML functions from a specially designed specification language, one might ask, "Why bother to use monads at all? Why not translate directly into `let` expressions or the like?" There are a number of motivations for using monads:

Uniformity The two monad functions provide a succinct uniform target for translation, in contrast to *ad hoc* translations to `let` expressions, etc.

Optimisability A corollary of uniformity is that the target code can readily be optimised. The monad laws, especially (2), are used for this.

Extensibility Looking to the future, use of monads will facilitate extension of the semantic specification language with features such as input/output. One might even envisage users specifying the monad themselves. The user's monad might be automatically combined with the built-in monad.

3   An Example

To give a flavour of the semantic specification language here is an example. The object language is a very simple structural hardware description language (HDL) similar in style to Verilog HDL. The language consists of a sequence of modules such as:

```
module AND (a,b,c);
    input a;
    input b;
    output c;
    wire d;
    NAND (a,b,d);
    INV (d,c);
endmodule
```

The syntax of the language as an extended BNF grammar is:

> *description* ::= *module*+
>
> *module* ::= "module" *id* "(" ((*id* ",")* *id*)? ")" ";" (*statement* ";")+
>   "endmodule"
>
> *statement* ::= "input" *id* | "output" *id* | "wire" *id*
> | *id* "(" ((*id* ",")* *id*)? ")"

Terminals are in quotes. '?', '*', and '+' denote an optional item, zero or more occurrences of an item, and one or more occurrences, respectively. Parentheses are used for grouping.

Fig. 1 shows a static semantics for the HDL expressed in the semantic specification language. Other examples have been used in developing the tools but this HDL example has the merit of illustrating many of the interesting features of the semantic specification language in a small amount of space. Note in particular that the specification language is not restricted to static semantics of languages; dynamic semantics may be expressed too. The text 'Static' appearing in the specification after the name of the language is itself simply a name. It allows multiple semantics to be specified for a language but the tools place no interpretation on the name used.

```
HDL (Static):

#import Boolean List
#pass_down Ports
#thread Modules Inputs Outputs Wires

!description
|[ Description(<<[modules]>>) ]| == foldr and true |[<<modules>>]|;

!module
|[ Module(<<id>>,<<[ids]>>,<<[statements]>>) ]| ==
   (().#Modules <- insert <<id>> #Modules.;
    foldr and true |[<<statements>>]|.#Ports <- <<ids>>.);

!statement
|[ Input(<<id>>) ]| ==
   (().#Inputs <- insert <<id>> #Inputs.; member <<id>> #Ports);
|[ Output(<<id>>) ]| ==
   (().#Outputs <- insert <<id>> #Outputs.; member <<id>> #Ports);
|[ Wire(<<id>>) ]| == (().#Wires <- insert <<id>> #Wires.; true);
|[ Component(<<id>>,<<[ids]>>) ]| ==
   and (member <<id>> #Modules,
        subset <<ids>> (union (union (#Inputs) #Outputs) #Wires));
```

Fig. 1. Static semantics of a simple hardware description language

The specification begins by declaring modules of functions to be imported from the library (see Sect. 8). Then various fields (environment components) are declared. A list of port names for a module will simply be passed down to the functions that handle the body of the module. The other fields, which keep track of the names used for modules and various kinds of connections within modules, have to be passed back by the semantic functions in addition to being received as arguments. In the implementation all the fields are handled using the denotation monad described in Sect. 2.

The body of the specification consists of rules, one for each abstract syntax form. The rules are grouped by syntactic category. Within a rule the ASCII notation |[and]| represent the Strachey (emphasized) brackets [and] commonly used in denotational semantics. The notation <<...>> is used for identifiers that are bound to abstract syntax tree (AST) fragments. On the left-hand side of rules the form <<[...]>> is also used to indicate that the identifier is actually bound to a list of ASTs. If the AST is simply an identifier (or some other terminal category of the object language) it may be used directly on the right-hand side of the rule. Otherwise it must appear in Strachey brackets indicating that a semantic function will be applied to it.

So, for example, the rule for a whole module is:

```
|[ Module(<<id>>,<<[ids]>>,<<[statements]>>) ]| ==
    (().#Modules <- insert <<id>> #Modules.;
     foldr and true |[<<statements>>]|.#Ports <- <<ids>>.);
```

The subtrees of the AST are the name of the module, a list of names of ports, and a list of statements. The body of the rule is a sequence of two expressions. The first of these produces a unit value, i.e., '()' but has the side effect of adding the name of the module to the Modules field. The notation #Modules <- ... means, "Replace the Modules field with the value of the expression ...", and within the expression #Modules means "the current value of the Modules field".

The second expression in the sequence produces the value to be returned by the whole rule. It computes the denotation of the statements with the Ports field set to the list of port names for the module. Note that because Ports is only passed down it could not be set in an earlier expression of the sequence (as Modules is) because such a change would simply be thrown away and the value of Ports on entry to the rule would be used instead when processing the statements. (This is a consequence of the definition of bindD.) The denotation of the statements is a list of boolean values. These are combined by iterating an 'and' operator over the list using foldr, with true as the identity element for and.

The intended meaning of the body of the rule may be seen in the following expression that uses the denotation monad functions:

$$\text{bindD } (\lambda e. \ (\text{unitD } () \ \circ \ \text{apply\_to\_Modules } (\lambda\_. \ \text{insert } id \ (\text{Modules } e))) \ e)$$
$$(\lambda z_1. \ \text{bindD } (\text{bind\_list } [\cdot] \ statements \ \circ \ \text{apply\_to\_Ports } (\lambda\_. \ ids))$$
$$(\lambda z_2. \ \text{unitD } (\text{foldr and true } z_2)))$$

The function Modules extracts the modules field from an environment and apply_to_Modules applies a function (its first argument) to the modules field leaving the other fields unchanged. The infix symbol 'o' is function composition. The outermost bindD implements the sequencing. The value of the first expression in the sequence is thrown away because the bound variable z_1 is not used anywhere. Notice how the environment is implicit except where some value is extracted from it.

The static semantics simply returns true or false according to whether the HDL text is well-formed. It could be more rigorous. For example, it allows an identifier to be declared as both an input and an output, an output to be driven by more than one component, and does not check whether the arguments of a component are of the correct type according to the corresponding module declaration. More details of the constructs used in the specification language are given in subsequent sections.

4 Syntax of the Semantic Specification Language

The semantic specification language is based on the syntax of ML (see the Definition of Standard ML [8]). In addition, the language includes special constructs not found in ML related to defining a semantics and handling environments. An extended BNF grammar for the syntax is given in Fig. 2. The notation used is as in Sect. 3.

$$
\begin{aligned}
specification ::=\ & id\ ("("\ id\ ")")?\ ":"\ header*\ category+ \\
header ::=\ & "\#import"\ id+\ |\ "\#pass\_down"\ field+\ |\ "\#thread"\ field+ \\
field ::=\ & field\_id\ (":"\ typ)? \\
category ::=\ & "!"\ cat\_id\ (rule\ ";")+ \\
rule ::=\ & denotation\ "=="\ exp \\
env\_exp ::=\ & env\_component\ "<-"\ exp \\
env\_component ::=\ & "\#"\ field\_id\ |\ "\#"\ field\_id\ "!"\ exp \\
atexp ::=\ & number\ |\ string\ |\ identifier\ |\ "\#"\ field\_id\ |\ metavar \\
|\ & denotation\ ("."\ (env\_exp\ ".")+)?\ |\ "()"\ "."\ (env\_exp\ ".")+ \\
|\ & "()"\ |\ "("\ exp\ ","\ exp\ ")"\ |\ "fst"\ atexp\ |\ "snd"\ atexp \\
|\ & "["\ ((exp\ ",")*\ exp)?\ "]" \\
|\ & "("\ (exp\ ";")+\ exp\ ")" \\
|\ & "let"\ "val"\ pat\ "="\ exp\ "in"\ exp\ "end" \\
|\ & "("\ exp\ ")" \\
exp ::=\ & "\#"\ field\_id\ "!"\ exp\ |\ "\#"\ field\_id\ "?"\ exp \\
|\ & atexp+ \\
|\ & "if"\ exp\ "then"\ exp\ "else"\ exp \\
|\ & "fn"\ pat\ "=>"\ exp \\
pat ::=\ & id\ |\ "\_" \\
typ ::=\ & vartyp\_id \\
|\ & typ\_id\ |\ typ\ typ\_id\ |\ "("\ (typ\ ",")*\ typ\ ")"\ typ\_id \\
|\ & typ\ "*"\ typ\ |\ typ\ "+"\ typ\ |\ typ\ "->"\ typ\ |\ "("\ typ\ ")"
\end{aligned}
$$

Fig. 2. Extended BNF grammar for the semantic specification language

The syntactic category *denotation* has the form |[...]| where the '...' is a representation of the abstract syntax for which the semantics is being given. Eventually it will be possible to use concrete syntax instead. Subtrees of the abstract syntax are represented by meta-variables that have the form <<...>>. These meta-variables may be used in the body of the semantic definition as indicated by the occurrence of the syntactic category *metavar*.

There are various forms of identifier. All the syntactic categories whose names end in 'id', except for *vartyp_id*, are ML-style alphanumeric identifiers. A *vartyp_id* is similar but begins with a single forward quotation mark. An *identifier* may be either alphanumeric or symbolic.

The fields may be given a type. This type information may be required for some target languages. An *env_component* is either a whole field, or if the field is an association list (finite map), some entry in the list ("#" *field_id* "!" *exp*). In the former case an *env_exp* changes the whole field. In the latter case, only the entry for the key (*exp*) specified in the *env_component* is changed. The value of a whole field or of an entry in the field may be obtained by the analogous constructs in the syntactic categories for ordinary expressions. Thus, if the value '1' is bound to the name 'x' in the field 'vars', then '#vars!"x"' evaluates to 1, and '#vars!"x" <- 2' rebinds x to the value '2'. In addition, the form "#" *field_id* "?" *exp* allows a finite map field to be tested for the presence of a key. Environment expressions are enclosed in dots ('.') and are usually used within a sequence expression ('(...; ...; ...)'). While sequences provide for sequential updates to the environment, multiple environment expressions separated by dots are interpreted as simultaneous parallel updates, i.e, they all read the environment as it was before any of the updates.

5   An Intermediate Form

Before generating actual logical definitions or ML programs from the semantic specifications they are translated into an intermediate form, as illustrated in Fig. 3. The advantages of using a generic intermediate form include avoiding duplicated code in the tools, obtaining consistency between the targets (especially the HOL definitions and the programs (conversions) that symbolically evaluate them), and ease of extension to other theorem provers and target languages.

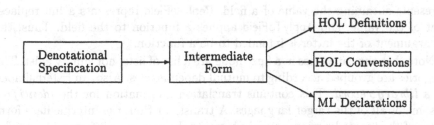

Fig. 3. Translation via an intermediate form

The abstract syntax of the intermediate form is given in Fig. 4. The occurrences of (*field**, *field**) record all the fields in the original specification, split into the two kinds. This information is included in the Field, ReplaceField and ApplyToField forms because some target languages may need to know the position of the field being processed in, say, a tuple containing all the fields. Field

$$specification ::= \text{Spec}(id, (field*, field*), (category+)+)$$
$$category ::= \text{Category}(id, rule+)$$
$$rule ::= \text{Rule}(ast\_node, parameter*, exp)$$
$$exp ::= \text{Num}(number) \mid \text{String}(string) \mid \text{LocalVar}(id)$$
$$\mid \text{External}(identifier, library\_record)$$
$$\mid \text{App}(exp, exp) \mid \text{Abs}(pat, exp) \mid \text{Let}(pat, exp, exp)$$
$$\mid \text{If}(exp, exp, exp)$$
$$\mid \text{Null} \mid \text{Pair}(exp, exp) \mid \text{Fst}(exp) \mid \text{Snd}(exp)$$
$$\mid \text{List}(exp*) \mid \text{Seq}(exp+)$$
$$\mid \text{Field}((field*, field*), field, exp)$$
$$\mid \text{ReplaceField}((field*, field*), field, exp)$$
$$\mid \text{ApplyToField}((field*, field*), field, exp)$$
$$\mid \text{Call}(id, exp) \mid \text{ListCall}(id, exp)$$
$$\mid \text{Compose}(exp, exp)$$
$$\mid \text{Unit}(exp) \mid \text{Bind}(exp, exp) \mid \text{BindMap}(exp, exp, exp)$$
$$\mid \text{Set}(exp, exp) \mid \text{Get}(exp) \mid \text{CanGet}(exp)$$
$$pat ::= \text{VarPat}(id) \mid \text{WildPat}$$
$$parameter ::= \text{Param}(id) \mid \text{OptParam}(id) \mid \text{NoParam}(id) \mid \text{SomeParam}(id)$$
$$\mid \text{ListParam}(id)$$
$$typ ::= \text{VarTyp}(vartyp\_id) \mid \text{ConTyp}(id, typ*)$$
$$\mid \text{ProdTyp}(typ, typ) \mid \text{SumTyp}(typ, typ) \mid \text{FunTyp}(typ, typ)$$

Fig. 4. Abstract syntax of the intermediate form

represents obtaining the value of a field, ReplaceField represents a full replacement of the value, and ApplyToField applies a function to the field. Thus, the *exp* argument of the latter is intended to be a function.

Note that the categories in a Spec node are a list of lists, not simply a list. The categories are grouped according to mutual dependencies. Also, an External node has a *library_record*. This contains translation information for the *identifier* for some or all of the target languages. A translator from the intermediate form to one of the target languages simply extracts the pertinent information, or if it is not present, reports an error.

The Call and ListCall nodes are for recursive calls to denotation functions, the latter being for arguments that are lists. Compose represents function composition, and Set, Get and CanGet represent functions for operating on finite map fields. There are also nodes for the three monad functions.

A rule consists of the name of the node used in the abstract syntax, parameters (subtrees) of the node, and a body. The parameters may be single-valued, list-valued, or (though not illustrated by the example in Sect. 3) option-valued. An option may also be explicitly either present (SomeParam) or absent (NoneParam). Consider, for example, the node labelled 'Module' in the following:

```
|[ Module(<<id>>,<<[ids]>>,<<[statements]>>) ]| == ...
```

The parameters are `<<id>>`, `<<[ids]>>` and `<<[statements]>>`. The first is single-valued and the other two are list-valued.

6   Translation to the Intermediate Form

This section describes the translation from the semantic specification language to the intermediate form. Readers who are not interested in the details of the translation can skip to Sect. 6.2. The translation is shown in Fig. 5. This description omits static checks such as ensuring that field names that are used have actually been declared. Monadic functions are used in the figure to succinctly express the translation. Although Fig. 5 looks like a semantic specification, it is *not* intended as an example of one. The similarity does, however, illustrate that the semantic specification language is realistic.

6.1   Commentary

In the description None and Some are constructors of a polymorphic option type and the following functions are defined over this type:

$$\text{case\_opt None } z \ f = z$$
$$\text{case\_opt (Some } x) \ z \ f = f \ x$$
$$\text{map\_opt } f \ \text{None} = \text{None}$$
$$\text{map\_opt } f \ (\text{Some } x) = \text{Some } (f \ x)$$

An explicit list is represented by [...], nil is the empty list, and '::' is the infix list constructor. The function map is the usual second-order function for applying a function to all the elements of a list, rev reverses a list, foldr iterates a function over a list, and assoc finds an item in an association list. A special function for filtering lists is also used:

$$\text{extract } c \ \text{nil} = \text{nil}$$
$$\text{extract } c \ (y :: ys) = \begin{cases} x :: \text{extract } c \ ys & \text{if } y = c(x) \\ \text{extract } c \ ys & \text{otherwise} \end{cases}$$

Concatenation of two lists is represented by the infix operator '@', and concatenation of character strings by the infix '⌢'. The empty string is "". The components of a pair are extracted using the projection functions π_1 and π_2. The function swap is defined by swap $f \ (x, y) = f \ (y, x)$.

A number of functions make use of external information:

groups uses the syntax of the language being specified to gather dependent syntactic categories into groups. This is required because dependent categories give rise to mutually recursive functions.

$[id_1 \; ((\; id_2 \;))? : h_1 \ldots h_m \; c_1 \ldots c_n]_S =$
  let $hs = [h_1]_H @ \ldots @ [h_m]_H$ and $[g_1, \ldots, g_k] = \text{groups}([c_1, \ldots, c_n])$
  in let $ps = \text{extract PassDown } hs$ and $ts = \text{extract Thread } hs$
    in $(\mathcal{L} \leftarrow \text{lookup (extract Import } hs); \; \mathcal{F} \leftarrow (\text{map } \pi_1 \; ps, \text{map } \pi_1 \; ts);$
      $\text{Spec}(id_1 \frown \text{case\_opt } id_2 \; "" \; (\lambda s. \; s), (ps, ts), [[g_1]_G, \ldots, [g_k]_G]))$
$[\#\text{import } id_1 \ldots id_n]_H \doteq [\text{Import}(id_1), \ldots, \text{Import}(id_n)]$
$[\#\text{pass\_down } f_1 \ldots f_n]_H \doteq [\text{PassDown}([f_1]_F), \ldots, \text{PassDown}([f_n]_F)]$
$[\#\text{thread } f_1 \ldots f_n]_H \doteq [\text{Thread}([f_1]_F), \ldots, \text{Thread}([f_n]_F)]$
$[fid \; (: t)?]_F \doteq (fid, \text{map\_opt } [\cdot]_T \; t)$
$[[c_1, \ldots, c_n]]_G \doteq (\mathcal{G} \leftarrow [c_1, \ldots, c_n]; \; [[c_1]_C, \ldots, [c_n]_C])$
$[!id \; r_1; \; \ldots; \; r_n;]_C \doteq$
  $(\mathcal{C} \leftarrow id; \; \mathcal{A} \leftarrow \text{alternatives}(id); \; \text{Category}(id, [[r_1]_R, \ldots, [r_n]_R]))$
$[| \; [c(args)] \; | \; == e]_R \doteq (\mathcal{T} \leftarrow \text{arg\_types } \mathcal{A} \; c \; args; \; \mathcal{E} \leftarrow "e";$
                 $\text{Rule}(c, \text{map (rename } \mathcal{T}) \; args, \text{wrap } [e]_E \; ((0, \text{nil}), \text{false})))$

$[ec <- e]_{EE} \doteq \text{bind } [ec]_{EC} \; (\lambda f. \; \text{bind } [e]_E \; (\lambda x. \; \text{unit } (f \; x)))$
$[\# \; fid]_{EC} \doteq \text{unit } (\lambda x. \; \text{ReplaceField}(\mathcal{F}, fid, x))$
$[\# \; fid \; ! \; e]_{EC} \doteq \text{bind } [e]_E \; (\lambda e'. \; \text{unit } (\lambda x. \; \text{ApplyToField}(\mathcal{F}, fid, \text{Set}(e', x))))$

$[number]_{AE} \doteq \text{unit } (\text{Num}(number))$
$[string]_{AE} \doteq \text{unit } (\text{String}(string))$
$[id]_{AE} \doteq \text{unit } (\text{External}(id, \mathcal{L}(id)))$
$[\# \; fid]_{AE} \doteq \text{used } (\text{Field}(\mathcal{F}, fid, \text{LocalVar}(\mathcal{E})))$
$[<<id>>]_{AE} \doteq \text{unit } (\text{LocalVar}(id))$
$[| \; [<<id>>] \; | . ee_1. \; \ldots \; . ee_n.]_{AE} =$
  let $(name, ty) = \text{assoc } id \; \mathcal{T}$
  in let $call = (\text{if is\_a\_list } ty \text{ then ListCall else Call}) \; (\text{base\_type } ty, \text{LocalVar}(name))$
  in local (bind_map $[\cdot]_{EE} \; [ee_1, \ldots, ee_n] \; (\lambda es. \; \text{replace (foldr (swap Compose)} \; call \; es)))$
$[() . ee_1. \; \ldots \; . ee_n.]_{AE} \doteq \text{local (bind\_map } [\cdot]_{EE} \; [ee_1, \ldots, ee_n]$
                        $(\lambda es. \; \text{replace (foldr(swap Compose)(Unit(Null))} \; es)))$
$[()]_{AE} \doteq \text{unit Null}$
$[(e_1, e_2)]_{AE} \doteq \text{bind } [e_1]_E \; (\lambda e_1'. \; \text{bind } [e_2]_E \; (\lambda e_2'. \; \text{unit } (\text{Pair}(e_1', e_2'))))$
$[\text{fst } ae]_{AE} \doteq \text{bind } [ae]_{AE} \; (\lambda e. \; \text{unit}(\text{Fst}(e)))$
$[\text{snd } ae]_{AE} \doteq \text{bind } [ae]_{AE} \; (\lambda e. \; \text{unit}(\text{Snd}(e)))$
$[[e_1, \; \ldots, \; e_n]]_{AE} \doteq \text{bind\_map } [\cdot]_E \; [e_1, \ldots, e_n] \; (\lambda es. \; \text{unit } (\text{List}(es)))$
$[(e_1; \; \ldots; \; e_n)]_{AE} \doteq \text{bind\_map } [\cdot]_E \; [e_1, \ldots, e_n] \; (\lambda es. \; \text{unit } (\text{Seq}(es)))$
$[\text{let val } p = e_1 \text{ in } e_2 \text{ end}]_{AE} \doteq$
  $\text{bind } [e_1]_E \; (\lambda e_1'. \; \text{bind } [e_2]_E \; (\lambda e_2'. \; \text{unit } (\text{Let}([p]_P, e_1', e_2'))))$
$[(e)]_{AE} \doteq [e]_E$
$[\# \; fid \; ! \; e]_E \doteq \text{bind } [e]_E \; (\lambda e'. \; \text{used } (\text{App}(\text{Get}(e'), \text{Field}(\mathcal{F}, fid, \text{LocalVar}(\mathcal{E})))))$
$[\# \; fid \; ? \; e]_E \doteq \text{bind } [e]_E \; (\lambda e'. \; \text{used } (\text{App}(\text{CanGet}(e'), \text{Field}(\mathcal{F}, fid, \text{LocalVar}(\mathcal{E})))))$
$[ae_1 \ldots ae_n]_E \doteq$
  $\text{bind\_map } [\cdot]_{AE} \; [ae_1, \ldots, ae_n] \; (\lambda [ae_1', \ldots, ae_n']. \; \text{unit } (\text{App}(\ldots \text{App}(ae_1', ae_2') \ldots ae_n')))$
$[\text{if } e_1 \text{ then } e_2 \text{ else } e_3]_E \doteq \text{bind } [e_1]_E \; (\lambda e_1'. \; \text{bind (wrap } [e_2]_E)$
                        $(\lambda e_2'. \; \text{bind (wrap } [e_3]_E) \; (\lambda e_3'. \; \text{replace } (\text{If}(e_1', e_2', e_3')))))$
$[\text{fn } p => e]_E \doteq \text{bind } [e]_E \; (\lambda e'. \; \text{unit } (\text{Abs}([p]_P, e')))$

Fig. 5. Translation to intermediate form

alternatives uses the syntax to find the possible syntactic forms of a category.

arg_types uses the syntactic forms to compute the name and type of each of the arguments of an abstract syntax tree node.

is_a_list is a predicate that returns true if the argument of an AST node is a list of items.

base_type returns the syntactic category to which an AST node argument belongs.

rename computes suitable names for AST node arguments.

lookup accesses the library modules included in the list it takes as its first argument in order to find information about its second argument (an identifier).

Patterns and types are translated in the obvious way. The translations are denoted by $[\cdot]_P$ and $[\cdot]_T$ respectively. The only non-trivial feature is the translation of a lone *typ_id* to ConTyp with an empty list of argument types and *typ typ_id* to ConTyp with a singleton list.

The translation of rules and expressions uses several pieces of information obtained from other parts of the specification:

$\mathcal{L}$ A function that maps an identifier to data about the identifier in the library (see Sect. 8).

$\mathcal{F}$ The names of the fields in the environment. This is a pair of lists, one for the non-threaded fields and one for the threaded fields.

$\mathcal{G}$ A list of the syntactic categories in the group to which the category being processed belongs.

$\mathcal{C}$ The name of the category being processed.

$\mathcal{A}$ A list of the possible syntactic forms of the category.

$\mathcal{T}$ The arguments of the abstract syntax tree node and their types.

$\mathcal{E}$ The name being used for the environment in the target languages.[1]

The passing around of this data is left implicit in the translation in Fig. 5. Only the initialisation of and changes to these values are recorded explicitly. The '←' notation is used to denote such a change. For example, the result of an expression $(\mathcal{L} \leftarrow f; [e])$ is for e to be translated in a context in which $\mathcal{L}$ has value f. The result of the translation becomes the result of the entire expression.

The denotations of expressions, atomic expressions, environment expressions, and environment components are functions. The argument of these functions[2] is of the form $((n, r), b)$ where n is a counter used for generating new variable names, r is a list of replacements, and b is a boolean value indicating whether or not the environment has been used (e.g., to read one of the fields). If the environment is not used there is no need to represent it explicitly in the target code. The list r records expressions that must be replaced by a new variable and a usage of bindD because they may have an effect on the environment, e.g., **f | [<<cat>>] |** is translated to:

---

[1] Something ought to be done to ensure its uniqueness.

[2] The denotation of an environment component takes a further argument.

```
bindD (den_of_cat cat) (λc1. unitD (f c1))
```

Here c1 is the new variable. Its name is constructed from the replaced expression and the value of n. So r is a list of pairs where each pair is a replaced expression and the name of the variable that replaces it.

A $((n, r), b)$ value is also returned as part of the result of computing the denotation. A state monad is used to pass this information around, hence the use of the functions unit and bind in Fig. 5. In addition to these two functions, a function bind_map is used that is defined in an analogous way to the function bindD_map of Sect. 2, and also some special purpose monad functions:

$$\text{explicit } b \ e = \text{if } b \text{ then } \text{Abs}(\text{VarPat}(\mathcal{E}), \text{App}(e, \text{LocalVar}(\mathcal{E}))) \text{ else } e$$

$$\text{replace } e \ ((n, r), b) = \text{let } v = \text{newvar } e \ n$$
$$\text{in } (\text{LocalVar}(v), ((n + 1, (\text{explicit } b \ e, v)::r), b))$$

$$\text{wrap\_one } ((e_1, v), e_2) = \text{Bind}(e_1, \text{Abs}(\text{VarPat}(v), e_2))$$

$$\text{wrap\_all } old \ e \ ((\_, r), b) = (\text{foldr wrap\_one } (\text{explicit } b \ e) \ (\text{rev } r), old)$$

$$\text{wrap } m \ old = \text{bind } m \ (\lambda e. \ \text{wrap\_all } old \ (\text{Unit}(e))) \ ((0, \text{nil}), \text{false})$$

$$\text{used } e \ ((n, r), \_) = \text{unit } e \ ((n, r), \text{true})$$

$$\text{restore } b \ e \ ((n, r), \_) = \text{unit } e \ ((n, r), b)$$

$$\text{local } m \ ((n, r), b) = \text{bind } m \ (\text{restore } b) \ ((n, r), \text{false})$$

The function **replace** implements the replace operation described above and **wrap** constructs the application of bindD. The environment is made explicit where necessary. The function **used** records the fact that the environment has been accessed, **restore** restores b to a previous value, and **local** sets up a local context for b. Note that **wrap** has to be used around the branches of an **if** expression because only one of them will be evaluated. It would be incorrect to move any effects that occur in a branch to a point higher up in the expression.

6.2 Optimisation

Before the target languages are generated from the intermediate form the following transformations are applied wherever possible:

$$\text{Bind}(e, \text{Abs}(\text{VarPat}(s), \text{Unit}(\text{LocalVar}(s')))) = e \quad \text{if } s = s'$$
$$\text{Let}(\text{WildPat}, \_, e) = e$$
$$\text{If}(e_1, e_2, e_3) = e_2 \quad \text{if } e_2 = e_3$$
$$\text{Seq}([e_1, \ldots, e_n]) = e_n$$

The first transformation is an extension of monad law (2). The last transformation is valid because once all the effects have been moved out of a sequence of expressions only the last one contributes to the sequence's value.

6.3 A Simple Example

Fig. 6 shows the result of translating the following expression:

```
(().#Inputs <- insert <<id>> #Inputs.; member <<id>> #Ports)
```

The application of Seq is later removed during the optimisation phase.

```
Bind(Abs(VarPat("e"),
         App(Compose
             (Unit(Null),
              ReplaceField
              (...,"Inputs",
               App(App(External("insert",...),LocalVar("id")),
                   Field(...,"Inputs",LocalVar("e"))))),
              LocalVar("e"))),
     Abs(VarPat("z1"),
         Abs(VarPat("e"),
             App(Unit(Seq([LocalVar("z1"),
                           App(App(External("member",...),LocalVar("id")),
                               Field(...,"Ports",LocalVar("e")))])),
                 LocalVar("e"))))),
```

Fig. 6. Example intermediate form

6.4   Extensions

The specification language does not currently cater for more sophisticated environment manipulations such as restoring an earlier environment. This could be rectified by allowing identifiers to be bound to intermediate environments and for environments to be named explicitly in accesses to fields. Other extensions may include subscripts on the denotations to allow an item to be given multiple meanings in different contexts, and multiple simultaneous updates to finite map fields.

7   Generating Definitions and Programs

7.1   Generating ML Code

Generating ML from the intermediate form is straightforward though there is some detail involved in generating suitable concrete syntax. Each group of categories becomes a mutually recursive ML function declaration, and each rule within a category becomes a clause in one of the function declarations. Some of the intermediate expression forms require ML functions (such as the monad functions) to be available in the environment. These are obtained either from built-in ML structures or from user-defined structures.

One area of interest is the handling of the separate fields of the environment. The obvious way to represent these in ML is with a record type. The environment fields then become fields in the record and can be accessed using the # notation in ML. However, to disambiguate the record type, explicit type assertions may have to be added. Instead, local functions for reading and updating components of the environment are defined. The same approach is used in generating HOL definitions (see below).

It may not always be possible to generate ML code. This relies on the semantics being executable, i.e., on there being executable versions of all the external functions defined in the library. For example, logical quantifiers could be used which are not, in general, executable. When the semantics is executable the ML code acts as an interpreter for the language. This provides a means of rapidly simulating the semantics to either test the semantics itself or to investigate the correctness of a program or HDL description before attempting a rigorous proof. It would be interesting to see if partial evaluation [3] could be applied to the generated code to yield a compiler.

7.2 Generating HOL Definitions

For the HOL embedding the abstract syntax is represented as recursive types in the logic. The types may be mutually recursive or nested under list or option constructors. Hence Gunter's nested recursive types package [7] is used. This package also provides for making mutually recursive function definitions over the types. The intermediate form is translated to such definitions.

The translator creates a file of commands as input for HOL. The commands begin by creating a new HOL theory for the semantic definitions. Other theories containing definitions of the external functions are then made parents of this theory. Functions are defined for accessing the environment. For the example from Sect. 3 some definitions are shown below. The texts of the form `''...''` are HOL quotations. These texts are in the concrete syntax of the HOL logic and are parsed to yield logical terms. The remaining code below is ML which is used as the meta-language of the HOL system.

```
val HDLStatic_Inputs =
  new_definition
    ("HDLStatic_Inputs",
     ''HDLStatic_Inputs
        (env:'Ports # ('Modules # ('Inputs # ('Outputs # 'Wires)))) =
        FST (SND (SND (env:...)))'');

val Apply_to_HDLStatic_Inputs =
  new_definition
    ("Apply_to_HDLStatic_Inputs",
     ''Apply_to_HDLStatic_Inputs f
          ((Ports,(Modules,(Inputs,(Outputs,Wires)))):...) =
          ((Ports,(Modules,(f Inputs,(Outputs,Wires)))):...)'');
```

The type of the environment is shown just once and then elided at other occurrences. The type is a Cartesian product, denoted by '#' in HOL's logic. In this example, the components of the type are polymorphic (indicated by their names beginning with a quotation mark). If the types had been specified in the original specification, constant types could have been used instead. Having defined these functions and analogous ones for the other fields of the environment, they can be used in the recursive definitions generated from the semantic rules.

The example intermediate form given in Sect. 6.3 yields the following HOL term:

```
''BIND_D (λe. (UNIT_D one o
                Apply_to_HDLStatic_Inputs
                  (λx. INSERT id (HDLStatic_Inputs e))) e)
         (λz1. λe. UNIT_D (MEMBER id (HDLStatic_Ports e)) e)''
```

The argument of `Apply_to_HDLStatic_Inputs` discards the old value of the field (but uses it anyway by explicitly referencing the environment).

The bulk of the complexity in the translation to HOL input is in keeping track of names, ensuring their uniqueness, etc. In addition, the recursive definition mechanism is more fussy about the form of its input than ML is. In fact, the intermediate form is pre-processed to coalesce rules that have optional parameters into single rules in which the split on the option occurs inside the body. Also, auxiliary functions have to be defined for the meaning of lists of items and optional items; second-order functions like `MAP` cannot be used because the recursion is then not of an acceptable form.

To generate the HOL terms, the intermediate form is translated into a representation of the HOL term structure and a pretty-printer is used to generate the concrete syntax.

Currently association lists are being used to implement the `Set`, `Get` and `CanGet` forms. For the logical definitions it might be better to use finite maps [6] instead. For the ML code a more efficient implementation, e.g., trees, might be used.

7.3   Generating HOL Conversions

The translation from intermediate form to HOL conversions is less straightforward. Conversions were invented by Paulson [10] for Cambridge LCF and have been inherited by HOL. They map a term t to a theorem stating that $t = t'$ for some t', or they fail (raise an exception in ML).

The translation declares new conversions in ML for each case of the recursive function definitions. These conversions rewrite with the equation from the definition. They are used by recursive conversions that follow the syntactic structure of the object language. There is a conversion for each syntactic category. Each conversion analyses the term it is given, assuming it to be an application of a denotation function to some abstract syntax and a fully explicit environment[3].

---

[3] Parts of the environment may be symbolic but there is then no guarantee that the evaluation will go full course.

A case split is performed on the top node of the abstract syntax. Each case corresponds to one of the syntactic forms of the category. The appropriate rewriting conversion is applied and then further simplification is attempted based on the form of the body of the definition.

Generating the conversions requires more manipulation of the intermediate form than for generating HOL definitions but can still be done methodically. The current implementation is a prototype and may require some tuning to obtain reliable evaluators. Some parts are flexible anyway; once the translator encounters an expression that it has no special knowledge of, it resorts to using a strict evaluation with conversions for the library functions that occur in the expression. It is the presence of conversions for each library function that gives this system its power; without them evaluation would not proceed very far.

Just as partial evaluation might be applicable to the ML code generated from a semantic specification, it may also be applicable here. Welinder has suggested using partial evaluation to construct an efficient symbolic evaluation conversion from the equations of a large definition [18].

8 Libraries of Functions

The library functions are grouped together in modules, e.g. for standard types like the integers. For each module the library contains a specification file and implementation files. The specification file is used to map names occurring in the semantic specification language to names to be used in the generated code. In some cases the target names will be built-in functions of ML or HOL. In other cases the definitions are stored in the implementation files. The header and a typical entry in the specification file look like this:

```
List: ML(Structure,Name,Fixity,Precedence)
      HOL(Theory,Name,Fixity,Precedence) HOLConv(Structure,Name):
   :
"member"(List,member,Prefix,0)
      (more_list,MEMBER,Prefix,0)(ListConv,MEMBER_CONV);
```

The header specifies the contents of the library and gives names for accessing the data. The name in quotes at the beginning of the entry is the name used in the semantic specifications.

With the library mechanism it would be easy to add implementation files for theorem provers other than HOL. It is also possible for a specialist user to implement modules for a particular application area, such as semantics of structural hardware description languages, which can then be used by someone unfamiliar with the intricacies of the theorem prover in order to specify the semantics of a language. Since the libraries include proof procedures for the functions, it may be possible in this way to provide a high degree of proof automation without the language specifier needing to know how to implement proof procedures.

9   Related Work

As mentioned above, Reetz and Kropf [13,12] have produced a system that generates an embedding in the HOL theorem prover from specifications of the grammar of the language and attributation and translation rules for attributed abstract syntax trees (derivation trees). The semantic information is stored in the attributes rather than in the environment argument used in the denotational style.

This work also owes a lot to the field of semantics based compiler generation. See, for example, the work of Pettersson and Fritzson [11]. In that field the intention is to generate a compiler rather than a proof tool but many of the techniques are similar. As noted in Sect. 7.1, the ML code generated by our tool acts as an interpreter. Compiler generation often uses so-called continuation passing style (CPS) which is closely related to the use of monads. CPS was invented for use with denotational semantics and the use of monads for structuring denotational semantics was proposed by Moggi [9].

The Programming System Generator (PSG) [1] generates interactive programming environments from specifications of syntax, context conditions, and dynamic semantics. The dynamic semantics of a language is defined in a denotational style using a functional language based on the lambda calculus, which is very similar to the approach taken here. However, our primary concern is to support formal proof using the semantics, whereas in PSG the semantics is used only to execute program fragments.

Structured operational semantics and natural semantics can readily be formalized as inductive relations over recursive datatypes, and most higher-order logic theorem provers have support for defining inductive relations. In COQ it is one of the primary features and there has been some work on compiling formal specifications into both definitions in COQ and executable code [2].

A more detailed discussion of related work can be found in the overview paper of CLaReT [5].

10   Conclusions

This paper has described a high-level way of making definitions for computer language semantics in higher-order logic and automatically generating some proof procedures for those definitions. The system exploits the similarity between ML and higher-order logic. The definitions and programs are generated using a pretty-printer, so they can easily be read (or even edited) by a human.

The design of the specification language was motivated by a hand-written embedding for an industrial hardware description language and has been tested on several small languages. Nevertheless, the expressiveness of the specification language and the correctness of the generators must be assessed with lots more examples before any solid conclusions can be reached. For example, are the specifications too imperative? Would it be better to make the monad operations more explicit and possibly use some kind of infix notation to make them more readable?

11   Future Work

Future work could include:

- extensions to the semantic specification language to allow an item to be given different meanings in different contexts;
- allowing local well-founded recursive functions to be defined in the specifications, with Slind's TFL system [16] being used to define them in HOL;
- allowing transformations on language fragments to be specified and semi-automatically justified as HOL theorems with the aid of a proof planner;
- a type checker for the specification language (The tools currently rely on type checking in ML and HOL.);
- support for specifications given over concrete syntax;
- providing code generators for other higher-order logic theorem provers.

The last item would be simplest for systems built using Standard ML, in particular Isabelle. A reviewer of this work suggested linking CLaReT to Regensburger's HOLCF instantiation [14] of Isabelle which has good support for denotational semantics of programming languages.

Acknowledgements

Thanks to Andrew Gordon (now at Microsoft Research, Cambridge), Mike Gordon (Cambridge), Peter Homeier (Pennsylvania), Matthias Mutz (Passau), and Daryl Stewart (Cambridge) for discussions about various aspects of this work, and to Konrad Slind (Cambridge) and the anonymous referees for comments on a draft of this paper.

References

1. R. Bahlke and G. Snelting. The PSG system: From formal language definitions to interactive programming environments. *ACM Transactions on Programming Languages and Systems*, 8(4):547–576, October 1986.
2. Y. Bertot and R. Fraer. Reasoning with executable specifications. In P. D. Mosses, M. Nielsen, and M. I. Schwartzbach, editors, *Proceedings of the 6th International Joint Conference on Theory and Practice of Software Development (TAPSOFT'95)*, volume 915 of *Lecture Notes in Computer Science*, pages 531–545, Aarhus, Denmark, May 1995. Springer-Verlag.
3. L. Birkedal and M. Welinder. Partial evaluation of Standard ML. DIKU-report 93/22, DIKU, Department of Computer Science, University of Copenhagen, October 1993.
4. R. J. Boulton. Syn: A single language for specifying abstract syntax trees, lexical analysis, parsing and pretty-printing. Technical Report 390, University of Cambridge Computer Laboratory, March 1996.
5. R. J. Boulton. A tool to support formal reasoning about computer languages. In E. Brinksma, editor, *Proceedings of the Third International Workshop on Tools and Algorithms for the Construction and Analysis of Systems (TACAS'97)*, volume 1217 of *Lecture Notes in Computer Science*, pages 81–95, Enschede, The Netherlands, April 1997. Springer.

6. G. Collins and D. Syme. A theory of finite maps. In Schubert et al. [15], pages 122–137.
7. E. L. Gunter. A broader class of trees for recursive type definitions for HOL. In J. J. Joyce and C.-J. H. Seger, editors, *Proceedings of the 6th International Workshop on Higher Order Logic Theorem Proving and its Applications (HUG'93)*, volume 780 of *Lecture Notes in Computer Science*, pages 141–154, Vancouver, B.C., Canada, August 1993. Springer-Verlag, 1994.
8. R. Milner, M. Tofte, R. Harper, and D. MacQueen. *The Definition of Standard ML (Revised)*. MIT Press, 1997.
9. E. Moggi. Notions of computation and monads. *Information and Computation*, 93(1):55–92, July 1991.
10. L. Paulson. A higher-order implementation of rewriting. *Science of Computer Programming*, 3:119–149, 1983.
11. M. Pettersson and P. Fritzson. DML – a meta-language and system for the generation of practical and efficient compilers from denotational specifications. In *Proceedings of the 4th International Conference on Computer Languages (ICCL'92)*, pages 127–136. IEEE, April 1992.
12. R. Reetz. Deep embedding VHDL. In Schubert et al. [15], pages 277–292.
13. R. Reetz and T. Kropf. Simplifying deep embedding: A formalised code generator. In T. F. Melham and J. Camilleri, editors, *Proceedings of the 7th International Workshop on Higher Order Logic Theorem Proving and Its Applications*, volume 859 of *Lecture Notes in Computer Science*, pages 378–390, Valletta, Malta, September 1994. Springer-Verlag.
14. F. Regensburger. HOLCF: Higher order logic of computable functions. In Schubert et al. [15], pages 293–307.
15. E. T. Schubert, P. J. Windley, and J. Alves-Foss, editors. *Proceedings of the 8th International Workshop on Higher Order Logic Theorem Proving and Its Applications*, volume 971 of *Lecture Notes in Computer Science*, Aspen Grove, UT, USA, September 1995. Springer-Verlag.
16. K. Slind. Function definition in higher-order logic. In J. von Wright, J. Grundy, and J. Harrison, editors, *Proceedings of the 9th International Conference on Theorem Proving in Higher Order Logics (TPHOLs'96)*, volume 1125 of *Lecture Notes in Computer Science*, pages 381–397, Turku, Finland, August 1996. Springer.
17. P. Wadler. The essence of functional programming. In *Conference Record of the Nineteenth Annual ACM SIGPLAN-SIGACT Symposium on Principles of Programming Languages*, pages 1–14, Albuquerque, New Mexico, USA, January 1992.
18. M. Welinder. Very efficient conversions. In Schubert et al. [15], pages 340–352.

An Interface between CLᴬM and HOL*

Richard Boulton[1], Konrad Slind[2], Alan Bundy[1], and Mike Gordon[2]

[1] Department of Artificial Intelligence, University of Edinburgh
80 South Bridge, Edinburgh EH1 1HN, Scotland
{rjb,bundy}@dai.ed.ac.uk
[2] University of Cambridge Computer Laboratory
New Museums Site, Cambridge CB2 3QG, England
{kxs,mjcg}@cl.cam.ac.uk

Abstract. This paper describes an interface between the CLᴬM proof planner and the HOL interactive theorem prover. The interface sends HOL goals to CLᴬM for planning, and translates plans back into HOL tactics that solve the initial goals. The combined system is able to automatically prove a number of theorems involving recursively defined functions.

1 Introduction

HOL [10] is a general-purpose proof system for classical, higher-order predicate calculus; it has been used to formalize many areas of interest to computer scientists and mathematicians. The HOL system provides powerful simplifiers, automatic first order provers (both tableaux and model elimination), a semi-decision procedure for a useful fragment of arithmetic, and a co-operating decision procedure mechanism [2]. However, HOL lacks automation for many important areas, and moreover, there is always more that can be done to automate the proof process. A good case in point is *induction*. Induction is certainly a central proof method, but in HOL, as in many other systems, the user must interactively control the application of induction.

CLᴬM is a proof planning system for Oyster [5], a tactic-based implementation of the constructive type theory of Martin-Löf. Both Oyster and CLᴬM are implemented in Prolog. CLᴬM works by using formalized pre- and post-conditions of Oyster tactics as the basis of plan search. These high-level specifications of tactics are called *methods*. When a plan for a goal is found, the expectation is that the resulting tactic will solve the goal. Experience shows that the search space for plans is often small enough to allow a plan to be found automatically in a practical amount of time. One emphasis on research with CLᴬM has been the automation of inductive proofs [7, 6].

Our main goal in combining these two systems is to investigate the practical utility for hardware and software verification of artificial intelligence planning

---

* Research supported by the Engineering and Physical Sciences Research Council of Great Britain under grants GR/L03071 and GR/L14381.

techniques. We aim to simplify the interaction between the user and the theorem prover and hence reduce the time it takes HOL users to verify systems. Eventually, we plan to test the combined system on industrially significant verification problems.

The system design treats CLᴬM as a black box and thus avoids the need to modify the CLᴬM implementation to suit the classical higher-order logic used by the HOL system. Instead, correspondences between syntactic features of HOL's logic and the constructive type theory of Oyster/CLᴬM are exploited. This allows a beneficial partition of concerns: the consistency of HOL is unaffected by interaction with CLᴬM; furthermore, advances in the theory and practice of proof planning in CLᴬM can be pursued without regard to impact on HOL. The only changes to CLᴬM involve bypassing its library mechanism and the well-formedness checks applied to formulas. The latter are avoided because the formulas generated by HOL may involve constants that may not have been defined in Oyster. Thus far, none of CLᴬM's methods have been changed.

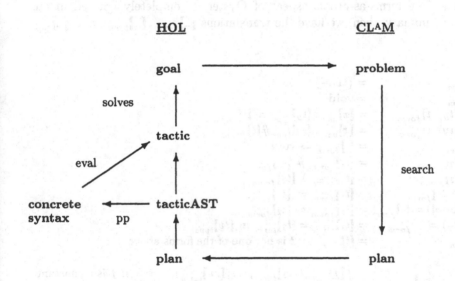

Fig. 1. System structure

A diagram for the system is Fig. 1. The data flow is represented by arrows. The HOL formula (goal) to be proved is translated into the abstract syntax of Oyster's logic and, together with supporting definitions and induction schemes, is passed to the CLᴬM process. CLᴬM then attempts to plan the goal. If a plan is found, it is passed back to the HOL process. The plan is then translated to an intermediate form (**tacticAST**) from which both tactics and (equivalent) concrete syntax (by prettyprinting via **pp**) can be generated. Finally, the tactic is applied to the HOL goal. The combined system can be understood by examining the following interfaces:

- The translation from the HOL object language to Type Theory.
- The translation of plans to tactics.
- The static and dynamic correspondences that are maintained between the two systems.
- The interprocess communication scheme.

2 Translation of the Object Language

Fig. 2 shows the translations from the HOL logic to Oyster syntax. Emphasized brackets [and] are used to denote the translation functions. The main syntactic distinction between the two systems is that types in HOL serve to categorize terms, and HOL formulae are just terms with boolean type. (In spite of this, we distinguish the two kinds of HOL term in our translation.) In contrast, Type Theory identifies types and formulae, using lambda terms to denote proofs of formulae. The terms-as-proofs aspect of Oyster is completely ignored in our work. In summary, then, we have the translations $[\_]_{form}$, $[\_]_{term}$, and $[\_]_{type}$

$$
\begin{aligned}
[T]_{form} &= \{true\} \\
[F]_{form} &= void \\
[\forall (x:ty).\, t]_{form} &= [x]_{var} : [ty]_{type} \Rightarrow [t]_{form} \\
[\exists (x:ty).\, t]_{form} &= [x]_{var} : [ty]_{type} \# [t]_{form} \\
[\neg t]_{form} &= [t]_{form} \Rightarrow void \\
[t_1 \wedge t_2]_{form} &= [t_1]_{form} \# [t_2]_{form} \\
[t_1 \vee t_2]_{form} &= [t_1]_{form} \setminus [t_2]_{form} \\
[t_1 \implies t_2]_{form} &= [t_1]_{form} \Rightarrow [t_2]_{form} \\
[(t_1 : \mathbf{bool}) = t_2]_{form} &= [t_1]_{form} \Leftrightarrow [t_2]_{form} \\
[(t_1 : ty) = t_2]_{form} &= [t_1]_{term} = [t_2]_{term} \text{ in } [ty]_{type} \\
[t]_{form} &= [t]_{term} \quad \text{if } t \text{ is not one of the forms above}
\end{aligned}
$$

$$
\begin{aligned}
[f\ x_1\ \dots\ x_n]_{term} &= \begin{cases} [f]_{const}([x_1]_{term}, \dots, [x_n]_{term}) & \text{if } f \text{ is a constant} \\ [f]_{term} \text{ of } [x_1]_{term} \text{ of } \dots \text{ of } [x_n]_{term} & \text{otherwise} \end{cases} \\
[\lambda x.\, t]_{term} &= lambda([x]_{var}, [t]_{term}) \\
[x]_{term} &= [x]_{var} \\
[c]_{term} &= [c]_{const}
\end{aligned}
$$

$$
\begin{aligned}
[tyv]_{type} &= [tyv]_{vartype} \\
[tyc]_{type} &= [tyc]_{consttype} \\
[ty_1 \to ty_2]_{type} &= [ty_1]_{type} \Rightarrow [ty_2]_{type} \\
[(ty_1, \dots, ty_n)tyc]_{type} &= [tyc]_{consttype}([ty_1]_{type}, \dots, [ty_n]_{type})
\end{aligned}
$$

Fig. 2. Translating HOL terms and types to Oyster syntax

for formulae, terms, and types. The translation of plans to tactics will need to map from Oyster terms to HOL terms; this will be denoted by $[\_]_{term}^{-1}$. The translation of (term) constants, $[\_]_{const}$, and of (term) variables, $[\_]_{var}$, along with the translation of type constants $[\_]_{consttype}$, and type variables $[\_]_{vartype}$ map HOL names to names that are suitable for use in Prolog. We defer the discussion to Sect. 5.

False (F) is translated to the empty type and true (T) to the special type used to represent truth in Oyster. Conjunction is translated to a product type, disjunction to a disjoint union type, implication to a function type, and negation to a function type from the argument of the negation to the empty type. Universal quantification becomes a dependent function and existential quantification a dependent product. Equality between booleans is translated to if-and-only-if and other HOL equalities to equalities in CLAM. Decidability issues for the latter create some problems in planning. For example, CLAM's simplification (elementary) method only simplifies equalities over types it knows to have a decidable equality. The types communicated by HOL are all unknown to CLAM, so it knows nothing about their decidability, and sometimes fails to solve simple goals. Other HOL terms are translated almost directly into the corresponding type-theoretic constructs.

Certain kinds of formula (Boolean-valued terms) exist in HOL that are not explicitly handled by the translation in Fig. 2, e.g., unique existence formulas ($\exists!x.\,P$), which can be handled simply by expanding out occurrences with the definition. Another problematic construct is HOL's indefinite description operator; this embodies a form of the Axiom of Choice, which is known to distinguish classical and constructive systems. For example, an intuitionistic logic plus the full Axiom of Choice allows the derivation of the Law of the Excluded Middle. There is no direct equivalent of the choice operator in Oyster's type theory. For these reasons we don't translate HOL choice terms. Another point is that many of the syntactic forms shown in the translation are derived forms. In fact, HOL terms have only four basic syntactic forms: variables, constants, function application and λ-abstraction.

The ML-style polymorphism of HOL terms is handled by translating HOL type variables to Oyster type variables. However, this is not sufficient. In HOL, type variables are implicitly universally quantified. In Oyster they have to be bound. So, at the top level, the variables introduced for HOL type variables are quantified by assuming that they inhabit the first type universe, $u(1)$. As Felty and Howe point out [8], the domain should really be restricted to the inhabited types of $u(1)$ since HOL types have to be non-empty. However, for the kinds of proof under consideration this will be of no consequence and, as described in Sect. 3.3, cannot lead to inconsistency in HOL.

3   Translation of Plans to Tactics

In this section, we will first give brief introductions to plans and tactics before proceeding to discuss the basis tactics that had to be written to match the methods of CLᴬM. The section finishes with the translation from plans to tactics.

3.1   Plans

As mentioned previously, CLᴬM computes proof plans (which are currently represented by Prolog terms). Notionally, a plan is a hierarchy of method applications, with the high-level methods representing steps in a proof that a human mathematician might use, e.g., induction, while low-level methods correspond to more detailed (and directed) syntactic manipulations. CLᴬM uses a wide variety of methods as it searches for solutions, among them being induction, generalization, rippling, and fertilization.

In the induction method, for example, automatically inserted annotations serve to mark differences between the induction conclusion and the induction hypothesis in each clause of the induction scheme. The aim of the rippling method is to move differences in the conclusion (e.g., by moving them to the outside of the term or into positions that correspond to universally quantified variables in the hypothesis) until the induction hypothesis can be applied. Wave-rules provide the means of moving the annotations. They are themselves annotated and the annotations in the wave-rules must match the annotations in the induction conclusion for the rules to be applicable. Annotations include a direction of movement for the differences, which ensures that rippling will terminate.

3.2   Tactics

Tactics are a well-known method for backward proof. The original conception of Milner [11], which is that of tactics in HOL, is that a tactic can be represented by the type

$$goal \longrightarrow goal\ list * justification,$$

i.e., a tactic decomposes a goal into subgoals plus a justification function. The justification function takes the theorems resulting from the solved subgoals and performs inference with them to return a new theorem that *achieves* the original goal. Thus the justification has type

$$thm\ list \longrightarrow thm.$$

A theorem $\Gamma \vdash M$ achieves a goal (Δ, N) when $M =_\alpha N$ and also each element of Γ is equal, modulo α convertibility, to an element of Δ. A tactic t *solves* a goal g when $t\ g$ creates an empty list of subgoals and a justification function f such that $f[\ ]$ achieves g. *Tacticals* are used to compose tactics: our translation makes use of THEN and THENL. The compound tactic tac_1 THEN tac_2 applies tac_1 to the goal, and tac_2 to all remaining subgoals (the composition of justifications for tac_1 and tac_2 must also be done). The tactic tac THENL $[tac_1, \ldots, tac_k]$ applies tac to the goal, and then applies tac_i to subgoal i.

Before describing the basis tactics in our translation, we must discuss some terminology.

- *Director strings*, *i.e.*, lists of numbers, are used to index subterms, usually for a rewriting tactic. The director strings of CLAM are intended to handle a first order syntax, where functions are n-ary, hence the translation of plans to tactics employs a translation of director strings to suit the higher-order syntax of HOL. Note: director strings are processed from right to left: for example, [1,2] is interpreted with respect to a term M as 'take the first subterm of the second subterm of M'.
- *Fertilization* is the name given to the use of the induction hypothesis after the goal has been manipulated into a form in which the hypothesis can be used. When the hypothesis immediately solves the goal, the fertilization is said to be *strong*. If not, the method is known as *weak fertilization*. An example of this is when the hypothesis and goal are equations and one side of the hypothesis appears as a subterm of the goal but the other side does not. The hypothesis can be used (by rewriting the subterm) but further work is required to prove the goal.

Basis Tactics

$ELEM\_TAC$: *tactic*. Finishes off a branch in the proof. A series of basic reasoners are invoked, in order of (roughly) increasing cost. First, the goal is checked to see whether it is an instance of reflexivity; then whether it becomes true by use of various simple rewrite rules; then whether it is a tautology of classical propositional logic; and finally, whether it is an instance of a theorem of linear arithmetic. (Actually the last two steps are integrated, by calling Boulton's HOL implementation of Nelson and Oppen's co-operating decision procedure mechanism [2].) The elementary method in CLAM to which this tactic corresponds does intuitionistic reasoning and is incomplete in a number of respects. We anticipate that $ELEM\_TAC$ will be able to prove any goals that the elementary method accepts.

OCC_RW_TAC : *string* $\longrightarrow$ *int list* $\longrightarrow$ *direction* $\longrightarrow$ *tactic*. Provides rewriting (by a perhaps conditional equality) at a specified subterm in the goal. The first argument is the name of the rewrite rule in a rewrite rule database. The second singles out the subterm to be rewritten; the third is the direction (left-to-right or *vice versa*) of use for the equality. This tactic is required for CLAM's symbolic evaluation, rippling [6], and weak fertilization methods.

ANT_RW_TAC : *string* $\longrightarrow$ *int list* $\longrightarrow$ *direction* $\longrightarrow$ *tactic*. Provides *implicational replacement* at a specified subterm in the goal. As in OCC_RW_TAC, a director string indexes the subterm to be rewritten and the first argument is the name of the rewrite rule in a rewrite rule database. This tactic is required for CLAM's symbolic evaluation, rippling, and weak fertilization methods. In an implicational replacement, suppose the theorem

$\vdash M \supset N$ is given: there are two cases. When the direction is RIGHT, a match θ is found between the subterm and N (thus the subterm is identical to $\theta(N)$). Then the subterm is replaced by $\theta(M)$. When the direction is LEFT, things are reversed: the subterm is matched with M and $\theta(M)$ is replaced by $\theta(N)$.

$WFERT\_EQ\_TAC$: *direction* * *int list* $\longrightarrow$ *tactic*. Implements weak fertilization [6] of equality goals. The *direction* is either RIGHT or LEFT. The other argument is a director string, which is used to locate the subterm in the goal to rewrite with the induction hypothesis. If the direction is RIGHT, the induction hypothesis $M = N$ is swapped around so that the goal is rewritten by $N = M$ at the occurrence; otherwise, the direction is LEFT and the induction hypothesis is not switched around.

$WFERT\_IMP\_TAC$: *direction* * *int list* $\longrightarrow$ *tactic*. Implements weak fertilization of implicational goals, essentially by calling ANT_RW_TAC with assumptions of the goal until a replacement succeeds. This approach is too non-deterministic to work in complex settings, but it will have to suffice until more complete information about how CLᴬM names hypotheses can be extracted from proof plans.

$SFERT\_TAC$: *tactic*. Implements strong fertilization: the first assumption that solves the goal is taken.

$SPEC\_TAC$: *term* * *term* $\longrightarrow$ *tactic*. Generalizes the goal, by replacing the first term by the second (a variable), and then universally quantifying the variable in the goal. If the term to be generalized has some occurrences in the goal that are not free, then some outermost universal quantifications will be eliminated so that the generalization will work. In HOL it is conventional to name tactics after the inference rules they "invert". So, $SPEC\_TAC$ is so named because it inverts a specialization rule.

ASM_EQ_TAC : *tactic*. All equational assumptions involving a variable on at least one side (such that the variable does not also occur on the opposite side) are eliminated by substituting for the variable throughout the goal.

$CASE\_SPLIT\_TAC$: *term* $\longrightarrow$ *tactic*. Performs a case split on the specified term.

IND_TAC : *string* $\longrightarrow$ (*term* * *term*) *list* $\longrightarrow$ *tactic*. The first argument is used to get the induction scheme from the database. The second argument is a list of pairs $(v_1, M_1), \ldots, (v_n, M_n)$; these are used to identify the induction variables and to control the names used in the inductive cases of the proof. The following are the steps that IND_TAC takes:

1. The list $v_1, \ldots, v_n$ designates the induction variables. We use it to manipulate the universal prefix of the goal so that it matches the binding structure of the scheme. That is, if the goal is

$$\Delta, \forall w_1 \ldots w_k. \ Q$$

and $\{u_1, \ldots, u_j\} = \{w_1, \ldots, w_k\} - \{v_1, \ldots, v_n\}$, then the result of this step will be

$$\Delta, \forall v_1 \ldots v_n. \ \forall u_1 \ldots u_j. \ Q.$$

2. Rename variables in the selected induction scheme into those that CLAM used in planning. The list $M_1 \ldots M_n$ enumerates *templates* used by CLAM in the induction cases. These are used to obtain, for each case in the induction, a list of quantification prefixes that CLAM used. For example, if we have, by the previous step, manipulated a goal into the form

$$\Delta, \forall l\, u_1 \ldots u_j.\ Q\, l\, u_1 \ldots u_j$$

and the method used by CLAM was

        Induction("listInduct", [(l, v0::v1)])

where listInduct denotes

$$\forall P.\ P[\,]\ \wedge (\forall h\, t.\ P\, t \supset P(h :: t)) \supset \forall l.\ P\, l,$$

the instantiated and renamed induction scheme will be

$$(\forall u_1 \ldots u_j.\ Q\, [\,]\, u_1 \ldots u_j)\ \wedge$$
$$(\forall v_0\, v_1\, u_1 \ldots u_j.\ Q\, v_1\, u_1 \ldots u_j\ \supset Q\, (v_0 :: v_1)\, u_1 \ldots u_j)$$
$$\supset \forall l\, u_1 \ldots u_j.\ Q\, l\, u_1 \ldots u_j.$$

   Only now can the induction scheme be applied in HOL.

Notice that *bound variable names matter* in our combination: the precise names used by CLAM must be tracked in HOL, because of generalization. When CLAM generalizes a goal, it does so with an explicit term, which can have occurrences of variables from previously applied induction schemes. For HOL to make the same generalization step, its goal must have corresponding occurrences of the corresponding term, with corresponding occurrences of variables. In the current system combination, only the application of an induction rule can introduce new variables into a proof, so it suffices to closely track the instantiations of the induction scheme, as above.

3.3   Translation of Plans to Tactics

Plans get turned into tactics in two stages; there is first a mapping from the type of plans into a type of tactic abstract syntax (tacticAST). Then there are translations from tacticAST into tactics and into concrete syntax (via pretty-printing). Translation into tactics (*i.e.*, their internal representations) allows the plan to be applied to the goal without parsing and evaluating ML code. The generation of concrete syntax allows the tactic to be inserted in ML scripts and used in other HOL sessions (e.g., ones where CLAM may not be present). If the translation from plans to tactics is successful (as it normally is) the tactic is applied to the original HOL goal. Since CLAM uses heuristics, the tactic application may be unsuccessful; however, in practice it is very rare for CLAM to return an inappropriate plan. Most importantly, an inappropriate plan cannot lead to a non-theorem being 'proved' in HOL because HOL invokes its own tactics (guided by the plan) in checking the proof.

   The abstract syntax of tactics can be defined as follows:

$$[m_1 \text{ then } [m]] = THEN([m_1], [m])$$
$$[m \text{ then } [m_1, \ldots, m_n]] = THENL([m], [[m_1], \ldots, [m_n]])$$
$$[\text{casesplit}[\text{Disjunction}[\neg M, M]]] = CASE\_SPLIT\_TAC([M]^{-1}_{term})$$

$$\left[\!\!\left[\begin{array}{l} \text{ind\_strat(induction}(id, \\ \quad [(v_1, M_1), \ldots, (v_n, M_n)]), [m_1, \ldots, m_k]) \end{array} \right]\!\!\right] = \begin{array}{l} THENL(IND\_TAC(id, \\ \quad [(v_1, [M_1]^{-1}_{term}), \ldots, (v_n, [M_n]^{-1}_{term})]), \\ \quad [[m_1], \ldots, [m_k]]) \end{array}$$

$$[\text{generalise}(tm, id, ty)] = SPEC\_TAC([tm]^{-1}_{term}, [id : ty]^{-1}_{term})$$
$$[\text{reduction } (=, [path, [s, (style, lr)]])] = OCC\_RW\_TAC \; s \; path \; lr$$
$$[\text{reduction } (\equiv, [path, [s, (style, lr)]])] = OCC\_RW\_TAC \; s \; path \; lr$$
$$[\text{reduction } (imp, [path, [s, (style, lr)]])] = ANT\_RW\_TAC \; s \; path \; lr$$
$$[\text{wave } [dir, path, [s, (=, lr), \_]]] = OCC\_RW\_TAC \; s \; path \; lr$$
$$[\text{wave } [dir, path, [s, (\equiv, lr), \_]]] = OCC\_RW\_TAC \; s \; path \; lr$$
$$[\text{wave } [dir, path, [s, (imp, lr), \_]]] = ANT\_RW\_TAC \; s \; path \; lr$$
$$[\text{unblock}(wave\_front, path, s, \equiv, lr)] = OCC\_RW\_TAC \; s \; path \; lr$$
$$[\text{weak\_fertilize } [\text{RIGHT}, in, path, \_]] = WFERT\_EQ\_TAC(path@[2, 1], \text{RIGHT})$$
$$[\text{weak\_fertilize } [\text{LEFT}, in, path, \_]] = WFERT\_EQ\_TAC(path@[1, 1], \text{LEFT})$$
$$[\text{weak\_fertilize } [\text{LEFT}, \Rightarrow, path, \_]] = WFERT\_IMP\_TAC(path@[1], \text{LEFT})$$
$$[\text{weak\_fertilize } [\text{RIGHT}, \Rightarrow, path, \_]] = WFERT\_IMP\_TAC(path@[2], \text{RIGHT})$$
$$[\text{fertilize } (\text{strong})] = SFERT\_TAC$$
$$[\text{normal}(univ\_intro, \_)] = GEN\_TAC$$
$$[\text{normal}(imply\_intro, \_)] = DISCH\_TAC$$
$$[\text{normal}(conjunct\_elim, \_)] = ASM\_CONJ\_TAC$$
$$[\text{equal } \_] = ASM\_EQ\_TAC$$
$$[\text{elementary } m] = ELEM\_TAC$$
$$[\text{base\_case}(L)] = [L]^{\bullet}$$
$$[\text{step\_case}(m)] = [m]$$
$$[\text{sym\_eval}(L)] = [L]^{\bullet}$$
$$[\text{intro}(L)] = [L]^{\bullet}$$
$$[\text{normalize}(L)] = [L]^{\bullet}$$
$$[\text{normalize\_term}(L)] = [L]^{\bullet}$$
$$[\text{ripple}[dir, m]] = [m]$$
$$[\text{ripple\_and\_cancel}(L)] = [L]^{\bullet}$$
$$[\text{unblock\_then\_fertilize}[str, m]] = [m]$$
$$[\text{unblock\_fertilize\_lazy}(m)] = ALL\_TAC$$
$$[\text{fertilize}[str, m]] = [m]$$
$$[\text{fertilize\_then\_ripple } L] = [L]^{\bullet}$$
$$[\text{fertilize\_left\_or\_right}[dir, m]] = [m]$$
$$[L] = [L]^{\bullet}$$

Fig. 3. Translation from methods to tactics

```
datatype tacticAST = NO_TAC
                   | ALL_TAC
                   | PRIM of pprinter * tactic
                   | THEN of tacticAST * tacticAST
```

| THENL of tacticAST * tacticAST list

An item of type tacticAST can be seen as carrying a pretty-printer and a tactic at each leaf node, so that compound concrete syntax and tactics can be generated easily.

The translation from methods to tacticAST – denoted by [_] – is given in Fig. 3. The notation $[L]^*$ (where L is expected to be a non-empty list $[m_1, \ldots, m_n]$) equals

$$THEN([m_1], \ldots, THEN([m_{n-1}], [m_n]) \ldots).$$

A sample tactic generated from a proof plan – along with an explication of the steps in the proof – is given in the Appendix.

4   Examples

The following theorems give some idea of the kind of theorems which are currently proved fully automatically in the combined system. Some are known to be difficult to automate. In others, CLAM is working in an impoverished setting and must overcome this by recursively planning the lemmas it needs. In such cases, the focus is not primarily the theorem, which may be rather simple, but in how CLAM found the plan – by making multiple and nested inductions and generalizations – and in that the translation of plans to tactics manages to follow the twists and turns of the automatic planner. For example, the proof of the commutativity of multiplication (given only the defining equations for multiplication and addition in Peano arithmetic) takes seven inductions and two generalizations.

$\forall m\ n\ p.\ m * (n * p) = (m * n) * p$

$\forall m\ n.\ m * n = n * m$

$\forall l_1\ l_2\ l_3.\ \text{APPEND } l_1 \text{ (APPEND } l_2\ l_3) = \text{APPEND (APPEND } l_1\ l_2)\ l_3$

$\forall l_1\ l_2.\ \text{LENGTH (APPEND } l_1\ l_2) = \text{LENGTH } l_1 + \text{LENGTH } l_2$

$\forall f\ l_1\ l_2.\ \text{MAP } f \text{ (APPEND } l_1\ l_2) = \text{APPEND (MAP } f\ l_1) \text{ (MAP } f\ l_2)$

$\forall x\ y.\ \text{REV (APPEND } x\ y) = \text{APPEND (REV } y) \text{ (REV } x)$

$\forall x\ m\ n.\ \text{APPEND (REPLICATE } x\ m) \text{ (REPLICATE } x\ n) = \text{REPLICATE } x\ (m+n)$

$\forall x\ m\ n.\ \text{FLAT (REPLICATE (REPLICATE } x\ n)\ m) = \text{REPLICATE } x\ (m*n)$

The functions here are curried. LENGTH computes the length of a list, APPEND concatenates two lists, MAP applies a function to every element of a list, REV reverses a list, FLAT flattens a list of lists into one list (by iterated concatenation), and REPLICATE x n generates a list of n copies of x.

The following are some implicational theorems that can be proved in the system:

$\forall x\ y.\ (x * y = 0) \supset (x = 0) \lor (y = 0)$

$\forall x\ y\ z.\ \neg(\text{LESS } z\ x) \land \neg(\text{LESS } x\ y) \supset \neg(\text{LESS } z\ y)$

$\forall x\ y\ z.\ \text{LESS } x\ y \supset \text{LESS } x\ (y + z)$

$\forall x\ l.\ \text{MEMBER } x \text{ (SORT } l) \supset \text{MEMBER } x\ l$

$\forall x\ l.\ \text{MEMBER } x\ l \supset \text{MEMBER } x \text{ (SORT } l)$

These examples use the following definitions/rules:

$$\forall x.\ \text{LESS } x\ 0 = \text{F}$$
$$\forall y.\ \text{LESS } 0\ (\text{SUC } y) = \text{T}$$
$$\forall x\ y.\ \text{LESS } (\text{SUC } x)\ (\text{SUC } y) = \text{LESS } x\ y$$
$$\forall m.\ \text{MEMBER } m\ [\,] = \text{F}$$
$$\forall el\ h\ l.\ (el = h) \supset (\text{MEMBER } el\ (\text{CONS } h\ l) = \text{T})$$
$$\forall el\ h\ l.\ \neg(el = h) \supset (\text{MEMBER } el\ (\text{CONS } h\ l) = \text{MEMBER } el\ l)$$
$$\forall n.\ \text{INSERT } n\ [\,] = [n]$$
$$\forall n\ h\ t.\ \text{LESS } n\ h \supset (\text{INSERT } n\ (\text{CONS } h\ t) = \text{CONS } n\ (\text{CONS } h\ t))$$
$$\forall n\ h\ t.\ \neg(\text{LESS } n\ h) \supset (\text{INSERT } n\ (\text{CONS } h\ t) = \text{CONS } h\ (\text{INSERT } n\ t))$$
$$\text{SORT } [\,] = [\,]$$
$$\text{SORT}(\text{CONS } h\ t) = \text{INSERT } h\ (\text{SORT } t)$$

and the induction scheme

$$\forall P.$$
$$(\forall y.\ P\ 0\ y) \supset (\forall x.\ P\ x\ 0) \supset (\forall x\ y.\ P\ x\ y \supset P\ (\text{SUC } x)\ (\text{SUC } y))$$
$$\supset \forall x\ y.\ P\ x\ y$$

has been added to the usual set of induction schemes that CLᴬM is allowed to use (which includes the induction theorems for lists and natural numbers).

5   Correspondences

Identifying the correspondences needed between the two systems – and how they should be maintained – is an important matter. The following is a summary of the information that needs to be maintained.

1. The two systems need to agree on which definitions, wave rules, and induction schemes are used. The design currently uses a database in HOL indexed by names. The naming scheme is independent of whatever internal bindings are used in either system. For example, suppose HOL sends CLᴬM a wave rule, which is subsequently used in a plan. When the plan is returned to HOL, the name appearing in the plan is used to index into the database; the effect is that neither CLᴬM nor HOL has to know about the location of objects in the other system.

2. The object language *lexi* of the two systems must be respected. Constant names in HOL's logic may begin with either an upper-case or lower-case letter and be followed by any number of letters, digits, underscores, and primes ('). Since primes are not allowed in CLᴬM names they are replaced by underscores. Symbolic names are also permitted in HOL. These are replaced by alphanumeric representations, e.g., '+' becomes 'PLUS'. CLᴬM names must begin with a lower-case letter. So, if after replacement the name begins with

an upper case letter or a digit, the name is prefixed with 'hol'. Under this mapping two HOL names could be translated to the same CLAM name but this is unlikely to arise in practice. The names of HOL type constants are translated in a similar way but for them the 'hol' prefix is always used. If HOL names are used according to the conventions of the built-in theories, this leads to CLAM terms in which the names of constants begin with 'hol' and the names of variables are as they appear in the original HOL term.

3. The CLAM name used for each HOL name is stored and used by $[\![-]\!]^{-1}_{term}$ when translating CLAM plans to HOL tactics.

4. Type variables in HOL have a different lexical form than term variables. It seems sufficient to replace their initial prime character with 't_'. As an example, the HOL formula expressing the associativity of the function for appending two lists is:

$$\forall l_1\, l_2\, l_3.\ \text{APPEND}\ l_1\ (\text{APPEND}\ l_2\ l_3) = \text{APPEND}\ (\text{APPEND}\ l_1\ l_2)\ l_3.$$

It is translated to:

```
t_a:u(1) =>
    l1:hollist(t_a) => l2:hollist(t_a) => l3:hollist(t_a) =>
        holAPPEND(l1,holAPPEND(l2,l3)) =
        holAPPEND(holAPPEND(l1,l2),l3) in hollist(t_a)
```

5. The CLAM implementation we use has been modified to provide some independence from Oyster and the built-in types and induction schemes of the CLAM library. Before using CLAM in a proof attempt, supporting definitions and induction schemes are sent from HOL. These are translated as for the goals. Additional rewrite rules may also be sent. CLAM processes these according to their structure (relative to the definitions it knows about) and records them for further use. They may be used as reduction rules, wave-rules, etc. Thus one can – from HOL – control the setting (wave rules, definitions, and induction schemes) in which CLAM works. Each goal can be planned in an independent setting, which makes some aspects of correspondence maintenance easy to handle.

6   Interprocess Communication

In the current system, the HOL user starts a CLAM process (or connects to one that is already running) from within a HOL session. The output from the CLAM process either appears as output in the HOL session or in a separate window, depending on how the CLAM process was invoked. Once the CLAM process has initialized, communication between the CLAM and HOL processes is via *sockets*. (Sockets are an inter-process communication mechanism provided by many versions of the Unix operating system. A socket behaves much like a bidirectional Unix pipe would.) In our current set-up, the socket may be either a local file-system socket or a socket connection over the Internet. An important benefit of using such an inter-process communication scheme is that the CLAM process is left running between proof attempts, so definitions, induction schemes, etc., have to be communicated only once.

Recapitulating the control flow from Fig. 1, first the HOL formula (goal) to be proved is translated into the abstract syntax of Oyster's logic and the result is written to the socket (in concrete syntax) as a Prolog goal. The CLᴬM process waits for a message from HOL and, on receiving one it recognizes, executes it and either returns the result back down the socket or sends a handshaking message. After the goal has been sent, the CLᴬM process is instructed to plan a proof for it. If a plan is found, it is returned to the HOL process via the socket. The HOL process then regains control and parses the plan into an ML data structure. Then the translation into tactics from Sect. 3.3 is performed, and finally the tactic is applied to the goal.

7   Interfacing CLᴬM with Other Systems

One might envisage generalizing our system interface so that CLᴬM could be connected to other theorem proving systems than HOL. A step towards this would be to equip CLᴬM with a more neutral concrete syntax for terms, in particular to avoid the use of infix operators with a precedence that is assumed by CLᴬM. A Lisp-like syntax would be much easier to deal with. This would simplify the task of interfacing other systems to CLᴬM. A more radical solution would be to parameterize CLᴬM over the object logic but this would involve major re-implementation work.

Regarding the semantic aspects, our work suggests that many of CLᴬM's methods are suitable for a wide range of logics. Some methods, however, such as those for propositional reasoning, are logic-dependent. These methods could be replaced by ones suitable for the prover being interfaced. An alternative would be to have CLᴬM ask the object-level prover to handle propositional reasoning and the like. This requires extended dialogues between the two systems, which is a subject of our current research.

Another issue is the form of plans. By good fortune (or possibly due to HOL and CLᴬM having a common heritage in LCF [11], via Nuprl and Oyster in the case of CLᴬM), the structure of CLᴬM's methods closely matches the structure of HOL tactics. The behaviours of the sequencing operations (then for CLᴬM methods and THEN and THENL for HOL tactics) are similar enough to ease the translation of sequencing operations from plans to tactics. Translation might be significantly more difficult for a theorem prover in which the sequencing operations for tactics have a different behaviour, e.g., Isabelle [13].

8   Related Work

Felty and Howe [8] have made principled use of HOL theories as part of a proof within the Nuprl theorem prover. Since CLᴬM was designed to work with Oyster which is essentially a re-implementation of Nuprl, some of the issues they encountered are relevant to our work, in particular the translation between logics.

However, thus far we have not had to be concerned with most of these semantic issues, thanks to the high-level nature of CL^AM's methods.

The Open Mechanized Reasoning Systems (OMRS) project [9] aims to provide a general framework in which mechanized reasoning systems can be connected. The intention is to specify the logical services of the systems, the specification being structured as a logical component, a control component, and an interaction component. The case studies so far include Nqthm (the Boyer-Moore theorem prover) [4], which like CL^AM focuses on proof by mathematical induction. Parts of Nqthm have been specified as an OMRS, in particular the connection between the main part of the prover and a linear arithmetic decision procedure. It would be interesting to try to specify our interface in the OMRS framework.

The ΩMEGA system [1] is intended to provide theorem proving support for mathematics. It includes a proof planner together with various other theorem proving components and proof presentation tools. Most of these components appear to have been designed to be part of ΩMEGA rather than being existing systems, but there has been some work on integrating provers such as Otter, TPS, constraint solvers, and also computer algebra systems.

The PVS [16] proof system is augmented with various tightly-integrated decision procedures, for example BDD-based propositional simplification and model checking, equality, and linear arithmetic. In contrast to this and many other systems with specialized reasoning components, our combination system is loosely integrated.

9   Summary

This experiment has resulted in a combination of HOL and CL^AM that allows some HOL goals to be planned by CL^AM and the resulting plan to be returned and applied in the HOL session. We think our work is of interest because of the following points:

- In our examples the nature of the underlying logic (constructive or classical) has not mattered. This can be explained by examining the translation of plans to tactics: the generated inference steps (chiefly induction, generalization, and various forms of rewriting) behave identically in both constructive and classical settings. It seems that the plans generated by CL^AM do not make reference to the proof terms used to justify Type Theory propositions. Thus, instead of an interesting (but difficult) interpretation of Type Theory in the HOL logic, we can have a simple yet still secure design. However, notice that it can happen that CL^AM may not find a plan for a simple HOL theorem because of the constructive character of Oyster.
- The system must maintain correspondences between the names of (term and type) constants, wave rules, definitions, and induction schemes in both systems. These correspondences are essentially *static*, since they do not change during the course of plan search. *Dynamic* correspondences also need to

be maintained between variables and other terms created or otherwise introduced by CLᴬM in the course of planning, and the variables and terms appearing in the resulting tactic.

- The pernickety details of the translations and lexical requirements can be re-used by other logic mechanizations wishing to employ CLᴬM's proof planning resources.
- The interprocess communication infrastructure we have built seems to be usable in a variety of other systems.
- The mappings both to and from CLᴬM have largely been automatically generated from a single source document, in which the syntax of Oyster/CLᴬM formulas and the syntax of CLᴬM proof plans have been specified as extended BNF grammars. (The extensions include layout information for pretty-printing.) ML code for parsers and pretty-printers is generated from this specification using the ML-Syn tool [3]. Clearly, this technology will be of use to others attempting work similar to ours.

We see the following as future work.

- CLᴬM's handling of induction schemes ought to be generalized to allow more induction schemes. One opportunity is to extend the representation to the schemes returned when the TFL package is used to define functions by well-founded recursion [15, 14].
- The current design allows only one chance for CLᴬM to plan a proof, and it seems obvious that a more complicated protocol between the proof systems may be useful, so that a kind of 'dialogue' occurs between the two systems. We have designed such a protocol and have built an initial prototype, with encouraging results.

References

1. C. Benzmüller, L. Cheikhrouhou, D. Fehrer, A. Fiedler, X. Huang, M. Kerber, M. Kohlhase, K. Konrad, E. Melis, A. Meier, W. Schaarschmidt, J. Siekmann, and V. Sorge. ΩMEGA: Towards a mathematical assistant. In McCune [12], pages 252–255.
2. R. J. Boulton. Combining decision procedures in the HOL system. In *Proceedings of the 8th International Workshop on Higher Order Logic Theorem Proving and Its Applications*, volume 971 of *Lecture Notes in Computer Science*, Aspen Grove, Utah, USA, September 1995. Springer-Verlag.
3. R. J. Boulton. Syn: A single language for specifying abstract syntax trees, lexical analysis, parsing and pretty-printing. Technical Report 390, University of Cambridge Computer Laboratory, New Museums Site, Pembroke Street, Cambridge CB2 3QG, UK, March 1996.
4. R. S. Boyer and J S. Moore. *A Computational Logic Handbook*, volume 23 of *Perspectives in Computing*. Academic Press, San Diego, 1988.
5. A. Bundy, F. van Harmelen, C. Horn, and A. Smaill. The OYSTER-CLAM system. In M. E. Stickel, editor, *Proceedings of the 10th International Conference on Automated Deduction*, volume 449 of *Lecture Notes in Artificial Intelligence*, pages 647–648, Kaiserslautern, FRG, July 1990. Springer-Verlag.

6. A. Bundy, A. Stevens, F. van Harmelen, A. Ireland, and A. Smaill. Rippling: A heuristic for guiding inductive proofs. *Artificial Intelligence*, 62:185–253, 1993.
7. A. Bundy, F. van Harmelen, J. Hesketh, and A. Smaill. Experiments with proof plans for induction. *Journal of Automated Reasoning*, 7(3):303–324, September 1991.
8. A. P. Felty and D. J. Howe. Hybrid interactive theorem proving using Nuprl and HOL. In McCune [12], pages 351–365.
9. F. Giunchiglia, P. Pecchiari, and C. Talcott. Reasoning theories – towards an architecture for open mechanized reasoning systems. In F. Baader and K. U. Schulz, editors, *Proceedings of the First International Workshop on Frontiers of Combining Systems (FroCoS'96)*, volume 3 of *Applied Logic Series*, pages 157–174, Munich, Germany, March 1996. Kluwer Academic Publishers.
10. M. J. C. Gordon and T. F. Melham, editors. *Introduction to HOL: A theorem proving environment for higher order logic.* Cambridge University Press, 1993.
11. M. J. Gordon, A. J. Milner, and C. P. Wadsworth. *Edinburgh LCF: A Mechanised Logic of Computation*, volume 78 of *Lecture Notes in Computer Science*. Springer-Verlag, 1979.
12. W. McCune, editor. *Proceedings of the 14th International Conference on Automated Deduction (CADE-14)*, volume 1249 of *Lecture Notes in Artificial Intelligence*, Townsville, North Queensland, Australia, July 1997. Springer.
13. L. C. Paulson. *Isabelle: A Generic Theorem Prover*, volume 828 of *Lecture Notes in Computer Science*. Springer-Verlag, 1994.
14. K. Slind. Function Definition in Higher Order Logic. In *Proceedings of the 9th International Conference on Theorem Proving in Higher Order Logics (TPHOLs'96)*, volume 1125 of *Lecture Notes in Computer Science*, Turku, Finland, August 1996. Springer-Verlag.
15. K. Slind. Derivation and Use of Induction Schemes in Higher-Order Logic. In *Proceedings of the 10th International Conference on Theorem Proving in Higher Order Logics (TPHOLs'97)*, volume 1275 of *Lecture Notes in Computer Science*, Murray Hill, New Jersey, USA, August 1997. Springer-Verlag.
16. N. Shankar PVS: Combining Specification, Proof Checking, and Model Checking. In *Proceedings of the International Conference on Formal Methods in Computer-Aided Design (FMCAD'96)*, volume 1166 of *Lecture Notes in Computer Science*, Palo Alto, CA, USA, November 1996, pages 257–264. Springer-Verlag.

Appendix

A good example of the power of proof planning is the proof of

$$\forall l. \ \text{REV} \ (\text{REV} \ l) = l,$$

since it is short and because CL^{A}M finds an interesting alternative to the natural hand proof, which requires the lemma

$$\forall l_1 l_2. \ \text{REV} \ (\text{APPEND} \ l_1 \ l_2) = \text{APPEND} \ (\text{REV} \ l_2) \ (\text{REV} \ l_1)$$

to be identified by the user and then proved. The tactic (slightly re-typeset) generated from the plan found by CL^{A}M is

```
QIND_TAC (RENAME (scheme"hol_list_INDUCTION")
                  [["v1","v0"]]) ['L:'a list']
THENL [OCC_RW_TAC "hol_REV1" [1,1,1] LEFT
        THEN OCC_RW_TAC "hol_REV1" [1,1] LEFT THEN ELEM_TAC,
      OCC_RW_TAC "hol_REV2" [1,1,1] LEFT
        THEN ALL_TAC THEN WFERT_EQ_TAC([2, 2, 1],RIGHT)]
THEN QSPEC_TAC('(REV:'a list -> 'a list) v0','(v3 :'a list)')
THEN QIND_TAC (RENAME (scheme "hol_list_INDUCTION")
                  [["v5", "v4"]]) ['v3:'a list']
THENL
  [OCC_RW_TAC "hol_APPEND1" [1,1,1] LEFT
    THEN OCC_RW_TAC "hol_REV2" [1,1] LEFT
    THEN OCC_RW_TAC "hol_REV1" [1,1,1] LEFT
    THEN OCC_RW_TAC "hol_APPEND1" [1,1] LEFT
    THEN OCC_RW_TAC "hol_REV1" [2,2,1] LEFT THEN ELEM_TAC,
  OCC_RW_TAC "hol_REV2" [2,2,1] LEFT
    THEN OCC_RW_TAC "hol_APPEND2" [2,1] RIGHT
    THEN OCC_RW_TAC "hol_APPEND2" [1,1,1] LEFT
    THEN OCC_RW_TAC "hol_REV2" [1,1] LEFT THEN ALL_TAC
    THEN WFERT_EQ_TAC([1, 2, 1],RIGHT) THEN ELEM_TAC]
```

Tracing this through, applying list induction and solving the base case leaves us with the goal.[1]

```
REV (REV (CONS v1 v0)) = CONS v1 v0
-------------------------------------
REV (REV v0) = v0
```

Simplification and use of the inductive hypothesis from right to left gives the goal (the i.h. is discarded after use)

```
REV (APPEND (REV v0) [v1]) = CONS v1 (REV (REV v0)).
```

Notice that this fertilization is one that a human would probably avoid, since the goal seemingly gets more complex. However, CL^AM has set itself up for a generalization of the subterm REV v0, replacing it by the variable v3, after which we are confronted with the goal

```
REV (APPEND v3 [v1]) = CONS v1 (REV v3).
```

Now we use list induction on v3 to get the base case

```
REV (APPEND [] [v1]) = CONS v1 (REV [])
```

and the inductive case

---
[1] HOL goals are written with the goal formula above the line and the assumptions below.

$$\frac{\text{REV (APPEND (CONS v5 v4) [v1]) = CONS v1 (REV (CONS v5 v4))}}{\text{REV (APPEND v4 [v1]) = CONS v1 (REV v4)}}$$

The base case gets solved by a few rewriting steps. The inductive case simplifies to

$$\frac{\text{APPEND(REV(APPEND v4 [v1])) [v5] = APPEND(CONS v1 (REV v4)) [v5]}}{\text{REV (APPEND v4 [v1]) = CONS v1 (REV v4)}}$$

This reduction is noteworthy because it uses the recursive clause of the definition of APPEND twice: once from right-to-left and once from left-to-right; in an ordinary rewriting system such free use of rules would lead to an infinite loop, however in CLᴬM, the wellfoundedness of the rippling rewrite relation means that such equations can be used in both directions without fear of looping. Finally, the inductive hypothesis can be used to finish the proof.

Classical Propositional Decidability via Nuprl Proof Extraction

James L. Caldwell*

Department of Computer Science
Cornell University, Ithaca, NY 14853-7501, USA
caldwell@cs.cornell.edu

Abstract. This paper highlights a methodology of Nuprl proof that results in efficient programs that are more readable than those produced by other established methods for extracting programs from proofs. We describe a formal constructive proof of the decidability of a sequent calculus for classical propositional logic. The proof is implemented in the Nuprl system and the resulting proof object yields a "correct-by-construction" program for deciding propositional sequents. If the sequent is valid, the program reports that fact; otherwise, the program returns a counter-example in the form of a falsifying assignment. We employ Kleene's strong three-valued logic to give more informative counter-examples, it is also shown how this semantics agrees with the standard two-valued presentation.

1   Introduction

Nuprl is both a constructive type theory and an implementation of the type theory in the form of a proof development system. As a result of the constructivity, and by design, Nuprl proofs yield programs in the form of terms of an untyped lambda calculus.

This paper presents a Nuprl proof of decidability for a classical propositional logic along with the resulting programs. Nuprl is used here as a formal metatheory for a deep embedding of the syntax and semantics of the logic in Nuprl. Decidability for this embedded formal system is proved within the Nuprl system and the program extracted from the proof is a "correct-by-construction" propositional decider.

The idea of verifying of decision procedures is not a new one; proposals to extend theorem provers by adding formally verified decision procedures were made as as early as 1977 [7]. Harrison provides a detailed survey of two approaches to the disciplined extension of prover capabilities in [9]. Actual formal verifications of decision procedures are less common. One example that has been repeated a number of times is Boyer and Moore's propositional tautology checker in the form of an IF-THEN-ELSE normalization procedure [2, 14, 16, 12, 15]. Both Shankar [17]

---

* Part of this work was performed while the author was a member of the Formal Methods Group at NASA Langley Research Center in Hampton VA.

and Hayashi [11] verify deciders for implicational fragments of propositional logic presented in sequent forms. Paulin-Mohring and Werner's work [15] is the closest in spirit to the work presented here in that they extract the program for the Boyer and Moore tautology checker from a constructive proof. In their development they address issues related to the efficiency of the extracted program.

1.1   Overview of the Approach

The development presented in this paper is based on the informal account given by Constable and Howe in [5]. The program extracted from the formal proof corresponds to the algorithm which searches for a sequent calculus proof via repeated (backward) application of the sequent rules until all propositional operators have been eliminated. The leaves of the resulting derivation tree form a collection of atomic sequents (sequents composed strictly of variables) which are easily checked for validity by determining if they are axioms. If they are all axioms, then the derivation tree is a proof and that fact is reported. If there is a leaf that is not axiomatic, it is used to construct a falsifying assignment which serves as a counter-example to the original goal. The core of the algorithm is the recursive procedure extracted from a normalization lemma proved via a well-founded (inverse image) induction on the rank of a sequent. This procedure collects the leaves of the derivation tree implicit in its recursion, i.e. the tree is not explicitly constructed but is implicit in the recursion.

The presentation given here is unique in that the semantics are defined via Kleene's strong three valued logic which is the natural partial evaluation semantics for classical propositional logic. Under a "fullness" condition defined for three-valued assignments, three-valued validity coincides with the standard Boolean semantics. As developed here, a formula is valid under the Kleene semantics when every assignment that contains enough information (assigns values to enough variables) to determine truth or falsity of the formula asserts it's truth. This notion of validity is lifted to sequents in the natural way. The Kleene semantics account for partial assignments in a particularly clean way and allow for tighter counter-examples by allowing "don't care" conditions in assignments.

The proof presented here is a version of the one presented by the author in [3] that has been optimized to produce more efficient and readable computational content. The Nuprl proofs for the earlier development are available on the web at the site noted in reference [3].

2   An Overview of the Nuprl System

The Nuprl type theory is a sequent presentation of a constructive type theory via type assignment rules. The underlying programming language is untyped and the objective of a proof is to either prove a type is inhabited, i.e. to show that some term (program) is a member of the type, or to show that a term inhabits a particular type. A complete presentation of the type theory can be found in the Nuprl book [6].

The Nuprl system, as distinguished from the type theory, implements a rich environment to support reasoning about and computing with the Nuprl type theory. The system implementing the type theory has evolved since publication of the book but (with a few extensions) the type theory presented there is faithfully implemented by the Nuprl system. Complete documentation is included in the Nuprl V4.2 distribution.[1]

2.1 The Computation System

Nuprl's *terms* include the constructs of its untyped functional programming language with additional constructs for denoting types and propositions. Terms are printed here in typewriter font. The Nuprl computation system provides reduction rules for a left-most outermost (lazy) evaluation strategy.

For terms t and t' we will write t ▷ t' to indicate that t evaluates to t' under the reduction rules. The computation system can be extended via the rewrite facility. For terms t and t' we will write t▷$_R$ t' to indicate that t reduces to t' in the extended system.

As usual, the notation t[t'/x] denotes the term resulting from the substitution of t' for free occurrences of x in t. Similarly, t[t$_1$,···,t$_n$/x$_1$,···,x$_n$] denotes the simultaneous substitution of each t$_i$ for each x$_i$ in t. We will sometimes write $\bar{t}$ to denote a vector of terms or variables.

2.2 The Type Theory

A *Nuprl type* is a term T of the computation system together with a transitive and symmetric relation denoted by x=y∈T. This relation is known as *equality on T*. The term x∈T, meaning x is a member of T, is an abbreviation of x=x∈T. Equality on T is an equivalence relation when restricted to members of T, it is nonsense otherwise. Interpreting the type membership equality relation and type membership as types is made sensible via the propositions-as-types interpretation [6, pg.29–31].

In addition to the type membership equality provided with each type, there is an equality between types. Equality of types is intensional i.e. type equality in Nuprl is a structural equality modulo the direct computation rules. This means that, unlike sets which enjoy extensional equality, two types may contain the same elements and share an equality relation but not be equal types. For example, although T and {x:T | True} have the same members and equality relations, they are not equal types in Nuprl.

Nuprl's type theory is predicative, supporting an unbounded cumulative hierarchy of type universes. Every universe is itself a type and every type is an element of some universe.

---

[1] The Nuprl system is available from Cornell at
http://www.cs.cornell.edu/Info/Projects/Nuprl/nuprl.html or by anonymous ftp from ftp.cs.cornell.edu.

U{i} denotes the type *universe* where i is a polymorphic specification of universe level. The members of the universe U{i} are types and other universes U{j} for j<i. When the level is ''i'', U{i} is displayed simply as U. The statement that T is a type is formally written T∈U.

P{i} is a synonym for U{i} and is sometimes used to emphasize the propositional side of the propositions-as-types interpretation.

Nuprl includes the following types:

Void is the *empty* type of which there are no members. Given a declaration x:Void (absurdly declaring the existence of an element of the empty type) the constant any(x) is an element of all types T, i.e. any(x)∈T.

Z is the type *integer* whose members are denoted by the numerals $\cdots, -1, 0, 1, 2, \cdots$.

Atom is the type whose elements are denoted by *strings* of the form ''$\cdots$'' where $\cdots$ is any character string. Atoms are equal when they are the same character string.

T list is the type of *lists* of elements of type T. The elements of T list include the empty list, denoted [] and conses of the form a::t where a∈T and t∈T list. Lists are equal either when they are both the empty list or when they have equal heads and their tails are equal.

y:A→B[y] is the *dependent function* type containing functions with domain of type A and where B[y] is a term and y is a variable possibly occurring free in B. When a∈A, B[a/y] is a type, and M[a/x]∈B[a/y], a lambda abstraction of the form λx.M is an element of the type y:A→B[y]. These are the functions whose range may depend on the element of the domain applied to. Function equality is extensional.

A→B is the *function* type which is an abbreviation for the term y:A→B when y does not occur free in B.

x:A×B[x] is the *dependent product* type consisting of pairs <a,b> where a∈A and b∈B[a/x]. Two pairs <a,b> and <a',b'> are equal in x:A×B[x] when a=a'∈A and b=b'∈B[a/x].

A×B is the *product* type and is an abbreviation for the term x:A×B where x does not occur free in B.

A | B denotes the *disjoint union* of types A and B, elements of this type are tagged elements of the form inl(a) for a∈A and inr(b) for b∈B. Two elements of the disjoint union are equal when their tagged elements are equal in the underlying type A (if the tag is inl) or B (if the tag is inr).

rec(x.T[x]) is the Nuprl *inductive type* constructor where x is a variable and T[x] is a term possibly containing a x free. Free occurrences of x in T denote inductively smaller elements of the type, thus its members are the members of T[rec(x.T)/x]. There are some technical constraints on the form of T but we do not include them here. Whenever rec(x.T) is a type, members a and b are equal if a=b∈T[rec(x.T)/x].

{y∈T|P[y]} denotes a *set type* when T is a type and P[y] is a proposition possibly containing free occurrences of the variable y. Elements x of this type are elements of T such that P[x/y] is true. Equality for set types is just the equality of T restricted to those elements in the set type.

$\cap$x:T.P[x] denotes the *intersection* type. It is a type whenever T is a type and P[z/x] can be shown to be a type under the condition that z is a hidden variable of type T. Two members a and b are equal in type $\cap$x:T.P[x] if T is a type and a=b$\in$P[z/x] for z an arbitrary element of T.

x,y:A//E[x,y] denotes a *quotient* which is a type whenever A is a type, and E[x,y] is an equivalence on A. Its members are elements of A and it identifies elements a and b whenever the equivalence E[a,b/x,y] is inhabited.

2.3   Logic via Propositions-as-types

A constructive logic is encoded within the Nuprl type theory. The following definitions in the Nuprl V4 core_1 system library encode the logic.

$$\text{True} \overset{def}{=} 0 \in \mathbb{Z} \qquad\qquad \text{False} \overset{def}{=} \text{Void}$$

$$P \wedge Q \overset{def}{=} P \times Q \qquad\qquad P \vee Q \overset{def}{=} P \mid Q$$

$$P \Rightarrow Q \overset{def}{=} P \rightarrow Q \qquad\qquad \neg A \overset{def}{=} A \Rightarrow \text{False}$$

$$\exists x\text{:}A.\ B[x] \overset{def}{=} x\text{:}A \times B[x] \qquad \forall x\text{:}A.\ B[x] \overset{def}{=} x\text{:}A \rightarrow B[x]$$

The Nuprl tactics have been built to manipulate both propositions and types uniformly.

2.4   Judgements

Nuprl judgements are the assertions one proves in the system. Nuprl judgements take the following form:

$$x_1\text{:}T_1,\cdots,x_n\text{:}T_n \gg S\ [\text{ext } s]$$

where $x_1,\cdots,x_n$ are distinct variables and $T_1,\cdots,T_n$, S, and s are terms (n may be 0), every free variable of T_i is one of $x_1,\cdots,x_{i-1}$ and every free variable of S or of s is one of $x_1,\cdots,x_n$. The list $x_1\text{:}T_1,\cdots,x_n\text{:}T_n$ is called the *hypothesis list*, each $x_i\text{:}T_i$ a declaration (of x_i), each T_i is a *hypothesis*, S is the *consequent* or *conclusion*, the term following the keyword ext is the *extract*, and the entire form is a Nuprl *sequent*. The extract component of judgements are not displayed as part of the implementation of the proof editor. A judgement of the form

$$x_1\text{:}T_1,\cdots,x_n\text{:}T_n \gg s \in S$$

is called a *well-formedness goal*. Since s$\in$S is simply shorthand for s=s$\in$S by the propositions-as-types interpretation for type equality, the extract of a well-formedness goal is the constant Axiom.

Somewhat informally, a judgement asserts that, assuming the hypotheses are well-formed types, then the term S is an inhabited type and the extract s is an inhabitant [6, pg.141]. That the extract term s inhabits S is an artifact of the proof that S is inhabited. If S is inhabited there may be more than one inhabitant and different proofs may yield different inhabitants.

A Nuprl proof is a decorated tree of sequents, its root being the main goal of the proof and where the children of each node are sequents justifying the parent according to the rules of the type theory. A proof of a sequent shows that its main goal is both well-formed and inhabited. Given terms inhabiting the hypotheses of a rule, a proof specifies how to construct a term inhabiting the type in the conclusion of the rule; thus, proofs contain instructions for the construction of witness terms. *Extraction* is the process of constructing a witness term as specified by proof.

2.5   The Nuprl System

The Nuprl system supports construction of proofs by top-down refinement. The prover is implemented as a tactic based prover in the style of HOL [8]. Nuprl differs from HOL in that each tactic invocation defines more of the structure of an explicitly represented proof tree which is directly manipulated in the editor, stored in the Nuprl library, and retrieved for later editing. The tactic language is ML. In Nuprl the proposition-as-types interpretation allows for presentations to be cloaked in either logical or more purely type-theoretic terms.

The Nuprl system supports a powerful display mechanism. Nuprl terms are edited using a structure editor; however, the structure of a term is independent of its display. The display form is specified by the user and can be changed without changing the structure of the term. Thus, the displayed form of a Nuprl term is never parsed, the editor displays the terms to the user as specified, but manipulates the actual underlying structure. All Nuprl terms occurring in this paper appear on the page as they do in the Nuprl editor and library. In [1] Allen gives an example of a non-trivial application of the display mechanism.

2.6   Decidability, Stability, the Squash Type, and Squash Stability

Being constructive, Nuprl does not assume all propositions are decidable, i.e. in general the so-called law of excluded middle is not provable; that is, $\forall P : \mathbb{P}.\, P \vee \neg P$ is not a theorem of Nuprl. Even though decidability for an arbitrary proposition P is not assumed, for many P it is uniformly decidable (i.e. there is an algorithm to decide) which of P or $\neg P$ holds. That is precisely the definition of the decidability abstraction Dec{P}.

```
*ABS decidable      Dec{P} ≝ P ∨¬P
*THM decidable_wf   ∀P:ℙ{i}. (Dec{P} ∈ ℙ{i})
```

Note that the well-formedness theorem `decidable_wf` asserts the fact that the term Dec{P} is a type for all propositions P, but it does not prove it is inhabited for arbitrary propositions P.

A related notion is that of *stability* which is constructively weaker than, but classically equivalent to, decidability (i.e. they're both tautologies). Stability is also not constructively valid.

```
*ABS stable      Stable{P} ≝ ¬¬P⇒P
*THM stable_wf   ∀P:ℙ{i}. (Stable{P}∈ℙ{i})
```

A **squashed type** (or proposition) is one whose computational content has been discarded. The squash operator is defined in Nuprl by a set type as follows:

*ABS squash $\downarrow(T) \overset{\text{def}}{=} \{True| T\}$

Thus for any type (proposition) T, $\downarrow(T)$ is inhabited if and only if T is, and furthermore, has as its only inhabitant the term Axiom (the sole inhabitant of the proposition True.) The operator is called **squash** because it identifies all inhabitants of T with the single constant Axiom.

If we can reconstruct an inhabitant of a type P simply from knowing $\downarrow(P)$ is inhabited we say P is *squash stable*.

*ABS sq_stable $SqStable\{P\} \overset{\text{def}}{=} \downarrow(P) \rightarrow P$

*THM sq_stable_wf $\forall P: \mathbb{P}\{i\}. (SqStable\{P\} \in \mathbb{P}\{i\})$

Squash stability is weaker even that stability and is related to stability in that they are equivalent for decidable propositions.

2.7   Existential VS Set Type

A method of generating efficient and readable extracts by the use of the set type (as opposed to the existential) was presented by the author in [4]. Earlier work by Hayashi [10] stressed a similar approach. We reiterate the main points here.

Inhabitants of the existential $\exists x: T.P[x]$ are pairs <a,b> where $a \in T$ and $b \in P[a/x]$. The term b inhabiting $P[a/x]$ specifies, as far as the proofs-as-programs interpretation goes, how to prove $P[a/x]$. When an existential type of the form above occurs as a hypothesis it can be decomposed into two hypotheses, one of the form a:T and another asserting $b:P[a/x]$. If v is the name of the variable denoting the existential hypothesis, occurrences of a in the final extract will appear as $\pi_1(v)$, and occurrences of b appear as $\pi_2(v)$.

Alternatively, consider the Nuprl set type $\{y \in T | P[y]\}$. Its inhabitants are elements of T, say a, such that $P[a/y]$ holds. Thus, a set type does not carry the computational content associated with the logical part $P[a/y]$. Since the computational content is not available, the fact that the a has the property $P[a/x]$ is not freely available in parts of a proof where it might find its way into an extract. When a set type of this form, occurring as a hypothesis, is decomposed it results in two new hypotheses: one of the form a:T; and the other, a "hidden" hypothesis, of the form $b:P[a/x]$. Recall that every hypothesis declares a variable. The proof rules prevent the variable of a hidden hypothesis from appearing free in the extract of a proof.

Nuprl system manages hidden hypotheses by "unhiding" them when appropriate and by preventing their inadvertent use. Hidden hypotheses become unhidden and are freely available in the parts of a proof where they do not contribute to computational content; these parts include proofs of well-formedness (membership) subgoals, equality subgoals, when the computational content on a branch of the proof has already been fully determined, or when the conclusion is decidable, stable, or squash stable. Hidden hypotheses may be "unhidden" when their computational content can be effectively decided; typically when they themselves can be shown to be decidable, stable, or squash stable.

3   Syntax and Semantics of Formulas and Sequents

In this section the Nuprl definitions supporting the statement and proof of the decidability theorem are presented.

3.1   Formulas

In the Nuprl formalization, formulas are modeled by a recursive type.

*ABS Formula $\overset{\text{def}}{=}$ rec(F.Var | F | (F × F) | (F × F) | (F × F))

The Formula type abstraction is defined to be the recursive type whose members are a disjoint union of five elements. The first element of the disjoint union is the type Var of propositional variables. These form the basis of the recursive type. The second component of the disjoint union is an instance of the bound variable F denoting a recursively smaller element of the formula type. These elements of the disjoint union will denote negations and will be displayed as ($\ulcorner\sim\urcorner$x). The third, fourth, and fifth elements of the disjoint union are the products of two recursively smaller formulas. When the semantics of propositional formulas is defined below it becomes clear that the pairs of formula in the third, fourth, and fifth disjuncts denote the operators for conjunction (p$\ulcorner\wedge\urcorner$q), disjunction (p$\ulcorner\vee\urcorner$q), and implication (p$\ulcorner\Rightarrow\urcorner$q).

A formula of the form $\ulcorner$x$\urcorner$, where x denotes an element of type Var, will be called an *atomic formula*.

The destructor for the Formula type is given by a formula_case operator defined by nested case analysis on the disjoint union type. A measure on formulas is defined as the number of operators occurring in it. It is defined recursively as follows.

```
*ABS formula_rank
ρ ≝ letrec measure(f) =
        case f:
        ⌜x⌝ → 0;
        ⌜∼⌝p → measure(p) + 1;
        p⌜∧⌝q → measure(p) + measure(q) + 1;
        p⌜∨⌝q → measure(p) + measure(q) + 1;
        p⌜⇒⌝q → measure(p) + measure(q) + 1;
```

The well-formedness theorem for the formula_rank function certifies it is a function from formulas to natural numbers.

3.2   Three Valued Semantics of Propositional Logic

We define a semantics of classical propositional logic in terms of Kleene's strong three-valued logic [13]. A Kleene valuation reflects the classical interpretations of the standard propositional connectives under fully determined assignments (those assigning true or false to every variable in the formula). For example, if either p or q is *false* under the Kleene valuation induced by a partial assignment

a, then $p \wedge_K q$ is *false* under the valuation too. It does not matter what value the other conjunct has, or even if it is defined. Clearly, exhibiting a partial assignment that falsifies a formula is gives more information than a falsifying total assignment does.

N_3 is the three valued type containing elements displayed as 0_3, 1_3, and 2_3 denoting *False*, *undefined*, and *True* respectively. The operators of Kleene's three valued logic [13] are defined over N_3 as follows.

$\sim_K$	
0	2
1	1
2	0

$\wedge_K$	0	1	2
0	0	0	0
1	0	1	1
2	0	1	2

$\vee_K$	0	1	2
0	0	1	2
1	1	1	2
2	2	2	2

$\Rightarrow_K$	0	1	2
0	2	2	2
1	1	1	2
2	0	1	2

Inspection of their matrices reveals that on inputs restricted to 0_3 and 2_3 the operators behave exactly as the familiar boolean operators of the same names. Thus, these operators are uniquely determined as the strongest possible regular extensions of the classical 2-valued operators. These operators are formalized in Nuprl using **case** analysis over N_3.

Three valued assignments are functions of type $Var \rightarrow N_3$. The Kleene valuation of a formula F under the partial assignment a (displayed as (F under a)) is defined as follows.

*ABS valuation

```
(F under a)  ≝  (letrec val(f) =
                  case f:
                    ⌈x⌉ → a(x);
                    ⌈∼⌉p → ∼_K val(p);
                    p⌈∧⌉q → val(p) ∧_K val(q);
                    p⌈∨⌉q → val(p) ∨_K val(q);
                    p⌈⇒⌉q → val(p) ⇒_K val(q);
                ) F
```

Using the Kleene valuation we define the semantic notion of a formula being satisfied (falsified) by an assignment a.

*ABS formula_sat $a \models F \overset{\text{def}}{=} ((F \text{ under } a) = 2_3) \in N_3$

*ABS formula_falsifiable $a \not\models F \overset{\text{def}}{=} ((F \text{ under } a) = 0_3) \in N_3$

Thus, a formula F is satisfied by assignment a (written $a \models F$) when (F under a) evaluates to 2_3. Similarly, a formula F is falsified by assignment a (written $a \not\models F$ when (F under a) evaluates to 0_3.

The satisfaction of a formula by an assignment is clearly a decidable property; to decide if a formula is satisfied by a, evaluate (F under a) and check whether the result is equal to 2_3. Falsification is similar. This property is captured by the following theorems.

*THM decidable_formula_sat:
  $\forall a: \text{Assignment}. \ \forall F: \text{Formula}. \ \text{Dec}\{a \models F\}$

*THM decidable_formula_falsifiable:
  $\forall a: \text{Assignment}. \ \forall F: \text{Formula}. \ \text{Dec}\{a \not\models F\}$

3.3 Sequents

Sequents are formalized as pairs of lists of formulas:

*ABS Sequent: Sequent $\stackrel{\text{def}}{=}$ Formula list $\times$ Formula list

We define a measure function on sequents (ρ) as the sum of the ranks of their hypothesis and conclusion lists. Note that we have not distinguished the display form for rank of a formulas from the display form for rank of a sequent. Their terms are distinguished in the system, but we have chosen to display them in the same way.

We call sequents having rank 0 *atomic* sequents. They contain only variables.

In this section the semantics of sequents is given. First the meaning of a sequent is given in informal mathematical terms and then this definition is translated into the three-valued model being developed here.

A sequent is true when the conjunction of the hypotheses implies the disjunction of the conclusions.

$$(H_1 \wedge \cdots \wedge H_n) \Rightarrow (C_1 \vee \cdots \vee C_m)$$

Adopting the convention that an empty conjunction denotes truth and the empty disjunction denotes falsity, $\langle [H_1, \ldots, H_n], [] \rangle$ evidently means $\neg H_1 \vee \cdots \vee \neg H_n$, $\langle [], [C_1, \ldots, C_m] \rangle$ means $C_1 \vee \cdots \vee C_m$, and the empty sequent, $\langle [], [] \rangle$, denotes an unsatisfiable sequent.

We are interested in the notion of satisfaction under a Kleene valuation induced by a partial assignment. A convenient definition is based on the observation that a sequent is satisfied by a partial assignment either, when it falsifies some hypothesis, or when there is some formula in the conclusion that it satisfies. This suggests the following definition.

*ABS sequent_satisfiable

a |= <hyp,concl> $\stackrel{\text{def}}{=}$ ∃F∈hyp. a |≠ F ∨ ∃F∈concl. a |= F

Similarly, a sequent is falsified by an assignment if it satisfies every hypotheses and falsifies every conclusion.

*ABS sequent_falsifiable

a |≠ <hyp,concl> $\stackrel{\text{def}}{=}$ ∀F∈hyp. a |= F ∧ ∀F∈concl. a |≠ F

These definitions exhibit the first use here of list quantification. The term ∃x∈L. P[x] is inhabited (true) if, for some member x of the list L, the predicate P[x] is non-void. Thus, for empty lists it is false. Similarly, the term ∀x∈L. P[x] is true if every x in L satisfies P[x]. For the empty list, the quantifier is vacuously true.

Note that it can effectively be decided whether a sequent is satisfied or falsified by an assignment; this follows from the decidability of the same properties for formulas. These facts are formalized in two decidability lemmas.

A *full assignment for a formula* F is a partial assignment that either satisfies or falsifies F, i.e. it contains enough information to determine a value for F.

*ABS full_sequent_assignment

Full(S) $\stackrel{\text{def}}{=}$ {a:Assignment| (a |= S ∨ a |≠ S)}

Validity is defined with respect to full assignments.

*ABS sequent_valid $\models S \overset{\text{def}}{=} \forall a{:}\text{Full(S)}. \; a \models S$

The author has shown elsewhere [3] that partial assignments are monotone with respect to satisfaction and falsification as defined here, thereby showing that the definition of validity just given agrees with the standard notion of validity over total Boolean assignments.

4   Decidability

The most natural formalization of the decidability theorem would simply say a sequent is either valid or not. A logically equivalent (and computationally stronger) form of falsifiability gives the following theorem.

$\forall S{:}\text{Sequent}. \; \models S \; \lor \; \exists a{:}\text{Assignment}. \; a \not\models S$

A constructive proof of this theorem [3] results in a function accepting a sequent S as its argument and returning one of inl(t) or inr(⟨a,e⟩). We are interested here in the computational content of the theorem. The term t under the injection inl has no computational interest, and so we squash it. The first element of the pair ⟨a,e⟩ under the inr injection is the counter-example, but the second element of the pair, the witness for the falsifiability of the sequent is not interesting. Thus, we modify the existential to be set type. This gives the final statement of the theorem proved here.

*THM propositional_decidability
$\forall S{:}\text{Sequent}. \; \downarrow(\models S) \; \lor \; \{a{:}\text{Assignment} \mid \; a \not\models S\}$

4.1   A Strategy for the Proof

Consider the following propositional sequent proof system.

$$\overline{M, q, N \vdash M', q, N'}$$

$$\frac{M, N \vdash p, \text{concl}}{M, \lceil{\sim}\rceil p, N \vdash \text{concl}} \qquad \frac{p, \text{hyp} \vdash M, N}{\text{hyp} \vdash M, \lceil{\sim}\rceil p, N}$$

$$\frac{q, r, M, N \vdash \text{concl}}{M, q\lceil\land\rceil r, N \vdash \text{concl}} \qquad \frac{\text{hyp} \vdash q, M, N \quad \text{hyp} \vdash r, M, N}{\text{hyp} \vdash M, q\lceil\land\rceil r, N}$$

$$\frac{q, M, N \vdash \text{concl} \quad r, M, N \vdash \text{concl}}{M, q\lceil\lor\rceil r, N \vdash \text{concl}} \qquad \frac{\text{hyp} \vdash q, r, M, N}{\text{hyp} \vdash M, q\lceil\lor\rceil r, N}$$

$$\frac{M, N \vdash q, \text{concl} \quad r, M, N \vdash \text{concl}}{M, q\lceil\Rightarrow\rceil r, N \vdash \text{concl}} \qquad \frac{q, \text{hyp} \vdash r, M, N}{\text{hyp} \vdash M, q\lceil\Rightarrow\rceil r, N}$$

A sound rule preserves validity, i.e. if the validity of its hypotheses implies the validity of its conclusion. A proof rule is said to be *invertible* when every assignment satisfying the conclusion also satisfies all the hypotheses. Thus if any hypothesis of an invertible rule is falsified by a given assignment, then the conclusion is falsified by the same assignment. Each of these rules has been shown to be both sound and invertible [3].

These facts coupled with the observation that the backwards application of each rule results in one or two sequents having smaller rank suggests a recursive procedure for eliminating propositional operators, resulting in a collection of sequents having the following properties:

i.) the induced sequents are all atomic,

ii.) if all the induced sequents are valid then so is the original sequent (by soundness), and

iii.) if any of the induced sequents is falsified by an assignment then that assignment falsifies the original sequent too (by invertibility).

This is formalized by the following lemma.

```
* THM normalization_lemma
 ∀G:Sequent
    {L:Sequent List|
     ↓((∀s∈L. ρ(s) = 0)
       ∧ ((∀s∈L. |= s ) ⇒ |= G )
       ∧ (∀a:Assignment. (∃s∈L. a |≠ s) ⇒ a |≠ G))}
```

It should be remarked here that the propositional proof rules given are the ordinary rules. The reader might suspect that since we are using Kleene semantics the logic is somehow special, but the Kleene semantics simply allows for the construction of tighter counter-examples. Above the layer of abstraction provided by the definitions of satisfaction, falsification, and validity, the effect of the Kleene semantics on the decidability proof and the extracted program is isolated to one point. That point occurs in the proof of the following lemma which asserts that every sequent in a collection of atomic sequents is either valid or there is an assignment falsifying it.

```
* THM zero_rank_valid_or_falsifiable
∀L:{L:Sequent List| ∀s∈L.(ρ(s) = 0)}
     ↓(∀s:Sequent. s∈L ⇒ |= s ) ∨
     {a:Assignment| ∃s:{s:Sequent| s∈L} . a |≠ s}
```

In the proof of this lemma, a decision must be made as to the values to assign to variables not occurring in an atomic sequent. Rather than arbitrarily choosing *True* or *False*, as we would have to do in a two valued semantics, using Kleene's semantics, we assign the "undefined" value 1_3.

4.2   Decidability Proof

We present highlights of the Nuprl proof of decidability to show how the potentially troublesome hidden hypotheses generated by the set type are handled.

⊢ ∀S:Sequent. ↓(|= S) ∨ {a:Assignment| a |≠ S}

Decomposing the universal and instantiating the normalization lemma with S as the goal results in the following Nuprl sequent.

```
1. S: Sequent
2. L: Sequent list
[3.] ↓((∀s∈L.ρ(s) = 0) ∧
        (∀s∈L.|= s) ⇒ |= S ∧
        ∀a:Assignment. (∃s∈L.a |≠ s) ⇒ a |≠ S)
 ⊢ ↓(|= S) ∨ {a:Assignment| a |≠ S}
```

Instantiating the lemma zero_rank_valid_or_falsifiable with L leaves a disjunction asserting that either all elements of L are valid or some element of L is falsifiable. Decomposing this disjunction leaves two subgoals. In the first case we know all sequents in L are valid and so choose to prove the first disjunct of the conclusion. In the second case we have an assignment that falsifies some sequent in L and so choose to prove the second disjunct of the main goal in that case.

Consider the first case.

```
4. ↓(∀s:Sequent. s∈L ⇒ |= s)
 ⊢ ↓(|= S)
```

Because the conclusion is squashed, the hidden hypothesis (3) can be freely unhidden. Eliminating the squash operators and then decomposing the conjuncts in 3 results in the following:

```
3. ∀s∈L.ρ(s) = 0
4. (∀s∈L.|= s) ⇒ |= S
5. ∀a:Assignment. (∃s∈L.a |≠ s) ⇒ a |≠ S
6. ∀s:Sequent. s∈L ⇒ |= s
 ⊢ |= S
```

Backchaining through Hypothesis 4 combined with the fact stated in 6 completes the proof of this branch.

Now consider the second case.

```
4. {a:Assignment| ∃s:{s:Sequent| s∈L} . a |≠ s}
 ⊢ {a:Assignment| a |≠ S}
```

After decomposing the conjunction in Hypothesis 3 (see above) and then decomposing the set type in Hypothesis 4 we provide the resulting assignment as the witness for the set type in the conclusion. This yields the following subgoal.

```
3. ∀s∈L.ρ(s) = 0
4. (∀s∈L.|= s)  ⇒ |= S
5. ∀a:Assignment. (∃s∈L.a |≠ s) ⇒ a |≠ S
6. a:Assignment
7. ∃s:{s:Sequent| s∈L} . a |≠ s
 ⊢ a |≠ S
```

The hidden hypotheses have been unhidden by the system because the computational content of the proof is completed. The remaining goal is proved by appeal to facts in Hypotheses 5 and 7. This completes the proof.

The program extracted from this proof (after one step of reduction) is the following term.

```
λS.decide ext{valid_or_falsifiable}(ext{normalize}(S))
    of inl(%3) => inl(Axiom)
     | inr(%4) => inr(%4)
```

It accepts a sequent S as input and applies the normalization procedure to it. The result is a list of zero rank sequents which serve as input to valid_or_falsifiable. This returns a term of the form inl(Ax) or inr(a) where a is a partial assignment falsifying some element of L (and by extension which falsifies S.) A case split is made on the form of this term which is then packaged up and returned as the final result of the procedure. Thus, we see that this program is nearly the natural one to write given the procedures ext{valid_or_falsifiable} and ext{normalize}. A simple optimization results in the following simpler program which foregoes the redundant decide.

```
λS. ext{valid_or_falsifiable}(ext{normalize}(S))
```

4.3 The Normalization Proof

The proof of this lemma provides the core of the computational procedure. The proof is by induction on the rank of a sequent. Recall the statement of the lemma.

```
⊢ ∀G:Sequent
  {L:Sequent List|
   ↓((∀s∈L. ρ(s) = 0)
   ∧ ((∀s∈L. |= s ) ⇒ |= G )
   ∧ (∀a:Assignment. (∃s∈L. a |≠ s) ⇒ a |≠ G))}
```

The measure induction tactic is invoked with sequent_rank as the measure. Decomposing G into its component formula lists, hyp and concl, results in the following subgoal.

```
1. hyp: Formula List
2. concl: Formula List
3. IH: ∀k:{k:Sequent| ρ(k) < ρ(<hyp, concl>)}
        {L:Sequent List|
          ↓((∀s∈L. ρ(s) = 0)
          ∧ ((∀s∈L. |= s ) ⇒ |= k )
          ∧ (∀a:Assignment. (∃s∈L. a |≠ s) ⇒ a |≠ k))}
⊢ {L:Sequent List|
    ↓((∀s∈L. ρ(s) = 0)
    ∧ ((∀s∈L. |= s ) ⇒ |= <hyp, concl> )
    ∧ (∀a:Assignment. (∃s∈L. a |≠ s) ⇒ a |≠ <hyp, concl>))}
```

The proof proceeds by inductively decomposing non-zero rank elements of the sequent <hyp, concl> if there are any; if not we directly argue the theorem holds. Thus, to proceed with the proof we case split on whether the list hyp contains any non-zero rank formula. In the case where all formulas in hyp are atomic we do a case split on whether concl is atomic or not. Thus, in all, we have three cases, we consider this last case first.

The Sequent is Atomic. In this case the list <hyp,concl>::[] witnesses the set type. A step of reduction leaves the following squashed conjunction to prove.

4. ¬∃f∈hyp.ρ(f) > 0
5. ¬∃f∈concl.ρ(f) > 0
⊢ ↓((∀s∈(<hyp,concl>::[]). ρ(s) = 0)
    ∧ ((∀s∈(<hyp,concl>::[]). |= s) ⇒ |= <hyp, concl>)
    ∧ (∀a:Assignment. (∃s∈(<hyp,concl>::[]). a |≠ s)
            ⇒ a |≠ <hyp, concl>))

By 4 and 5 the first conjunct holds and the remaining two conjuncts are trivial.

The Hypothesis Contains Non-atomic Formula. Now we consider the case where the formula list hyp contains a non-zero rank formula, ∃f∈hyp.(ρ(f) > 0).

Whenever property (P) is asserted to hold for some element of a list L, we use the following lemma to decompose the list, explicitly naming an element of the list having the property.

* THM list_exists_decomposition
∀T:U. ∀P:T → ℙ. ∀L:T List.
    (∃x∈L.P[x]) ⇒ ∃M:T List.∃x:T.{N:T List| L = M @ (x::N) ∧ P[x]}

Forward chaining through this lemma with hypothesis ∃f∈hyp.(ρ(f) > 0) yields

4. ∃f∈hyp.(ρ(f) > 0)
5. M: Formula List
6. f: Formula
7. N: Formula List
[8]. hyp = M @ (f::N) ∧ ρ(f) > 0
⊢ {L:Sequent List|
    ↓((∀s∈L. ρ(s) = 0)
    ∧ ((∀s∈L. |= s) ⇒ |= <hyp, concl>)
    ∧ (∀a:Assignment. (∃s∈L. a |≠ s) ⇒ a |≠ <hyp, concl>))}

We provide the following term as a witness for the set type in the conclusion.

case f:
⌜x⌝ → [];
⌜¬⌝x → (IH(<M @ N, x::concl>));
x1⌜∧⌝x2 → (IH(<x1::x2::(M @ N), concl>));
x1⌜∨⌝x2 → (IH(<x1::(M @ N), concl>) @ IH(<x2::(M @ N), concl>));
y1⌜⇒⌝y2 → (IH(<y2::(M @ N), concl>) @ IH(<M @ N, y1::concl>));

This term encodes the left rules of the sequent proof system presented above. This step results in two subgoals: the first a well-formedness goal to show that the term is in the type Sequent List and the second to show that term satisfies the three part conjunction defining the set. At this point the computational content for this branch of the proof is complete. The remaining proof goals serve to verify the logical part of the theorem and do not contribute to its computational content.

The Conclusion Contains Non-atomic Formula. This cased is similarly verified. After a second instantiation and decomposition of the the lemma list_exists_decomposition we must prove the following:

4. $\exists f \in concl.(\rho(f) > 0)$
5. M: Formula List
6. f: Formula
7. N: Formula List
[8]. concl = M @ (f::N) ∈ Formula List ∧ $\rho(f) > 0$
⊢ {L:Sequent List|
        ↓((∀s∈L. $\rho(s) = 0$)
        ∧ ((∀s∈L. |= s) ⇒ |= <hyp, concl>)
        ∧ (∀a:Assignment. (∃s∈L. a |≠ s) ⇒ a |≠ <hyp, concl>))}

In this case the set type in the conclusion is eliminated by the following term.

```
case f:
⌈x⌉ → [];
⌈¬⌉x → (IH(<x::hyp, M @ N>));
x1⌈∧⌉x2 → (IH(<hyp, x1::(M @ N)>) @ IH(<hyp, x2::(M @ N)>));
x1⌈∨⌉x2 → (IH(<hyp, x1::x2::(M @ N)>));
y1⌈⇒⌉y2 → (IH(<y1::hyp, y2::(M @ N)>));
```

This completes the computationally significant part of the proof of the normalization lemma. The remaining part of the proof verifies that the extracted term does indeed satisfy the specification.

A purer application of the proofs as programs method would have implicitly constructed the case statements and recursive calls to the computational content of the induction hypothesis. A purer proof, equivalent to the one presented here, having the same extract, proceeds in the two branches by decomposing the formula f in Hypothesis 6, resulting in five subgoals in each case. One subgoal for each class of formula. The proof then proceeds by appeal to the induction hypothesis. The proof presented here is more compact.

The Extracted Program. The extract of the proof is shown in the Fig. 1. The term in the figure is nearly, but not completely a raw extract term; it is shown after one step of computation has been performed, two definitions have been folded, and some system generated variables have been renamed for readability. The structure of the program reveals the natural structure of the recursion which reflects the structure of the inductive proof. Those familiar with programs extracted from formal proofs may be surprised at the readability and naturalness of this extract. These properties are a result of the careful use of the set and squash types in the specification

5 Conclusions

The principal aim of this paper has been to exhibit recently established methodology for generating efficient and clean programs from Nuprl proofs. This paper extends the work reported on in [4] and applies those techniques to a reasonably sized example. Propositional decidability is a well understood but non-trivial test-bed for these techniques. The formalization presented in this paper shows how the use of the Nuprl set type and squash type eliminates unnecessary and inefficient computational content from proof extracts.

Acknowledgements

The author would like to thank the anonymous referees for their helpful comments. Thanks are also due to Bob Constable and especially Stuart Allen for his careful reading and insightful comments on this paper.

```
λG.(letrec normalize(S) =
    let <hyp,concl> = S in
      case ∃f∈hyp.(ρ(f) > 0)
      of inl(%2) =>
          let M,f@0,N = (ext{list_exists_decomposition}
                          (Formula)(λ₂f.ρ(f) > 0)(hyp)(%2)) in
            case f@0:
              ⌜x⌝ → [];
              ⌜∼⌝x → (normalize(<M @ N, x::concl>));
              x1⌜∧⌝x2 → (normalize(<x1::x2::(M @ N), concl>));
              x1⌜∨⌝x2 → (normalize(<x1::(M @ N), concl>)
                                @ normalize(<x2::(M @ N), concl>));
              y1⌜⇒⌝y2 → (normalize(<y2::(M @ N), concl>)
                                @ normalize(<M @ N, y1::concl>));
        | inr(%3) =>
            case ∃f∈concl.(ρ(f) > 0)
            of inl(%5) =>
                let M,f@0,N = (ext{list_exists_decomposition}
                            (Formula)(λ₂f.ρ(f) > 0)(concl)(%5)) in
                  case f@0:
                    ⌜x⌝ → [];
                    ⌜∼⌝x → (normalize(<x::hyp, M @ N>));
                    x1⌜∧⌝x2 → (normalize(<hyp, x1::(M @ N)>)
                                      @ normalize(<hyp, x2::(M @ N)>));
                    x1⌜∨⌝x2 → (normalize(<hyp, x1::x2::(M @ N)>));
                    y1⌜⇒⌝y2 → (normalize(<y1::hyp, y2::(M @ N)>));
              | inr(%6) => <hyp, concl>::[]  )
        (G)
```

Fig. 1. Extract of the Normalization Lemma

References

1. Stuart F. Allen. From dy/dx to [ ]P: A matter of notation. In *Proceedings of User Interfaces for Theorem Provers 1998*. Eindhoven University of Technology, July 1998.
2. R. S. Boyer and J. S. Moore. *A Computational Logic*. NY:Academic Press, 1979.
3. James Caldwell. Extracting propositional decidability: A proof of propositional decidability in constructive type theory and its extract. Available at http://simon.cs.cornell.edu/Info/People/caldwell/papers.html, March 1997.
4. James Caldwell. Moving proofs-as-programs into practice. In *Proceedings, 12th IEEE International Conference Automated Software Engineering*. IEEE Computer Society, 1997.
5. R. Constable and D. Howe. Implementing metamathematics as an approach to automatic theorem proving. In R.B. Banerji, editor, *Formal Techniques in Artificial Intelligence: A Source Book*. Elsevier Science Publishers (North-Holland), 1990.
6. Robert L. Constable, et al. *Implementing Mathematics with the Nuprl Proof Development System*. Prentice-Hall, Englewood Cliffs, New Jersey, 1986.
7. M. Davis and J. Schwartz. Metamathematical extensibility for theorem verifiers and proof checkers. Technical Report 12, Courant Institute of Mathematical Sciences, New York, 1977.
8. Michael J. C. Gordon and Tom F. Melham. *Introduction to HOL*. Cambridge University Press, 1993.
9. John Harrison. Metatheory and reflection in theorem proving: A survey and critique. Technical Report CRC-053, SRI Cambridge, Millers Yard, Cambridge, UK, 1995.
10. Susumu Hayashi. Singleton, union, and intersection types for program extraction. In *Proceedings of the International Conference on Theoretical Aspects of Computer Software TACS'91*, volume 526 of *Lecture Notes in Computer Science*, pages 701–730, Berlin, 1991. Springer Verlag.
11. Susumu Hayashi and Hiroshi Nakano. *PX: A Computational Logic*. Foundations of Computing. MIT Press, Cambridge, MA, 1988.
12. M. Hedberg. Normalising the associative law: An experiment with Martin-Löf's type theory. *Formal Aspects of Computing*, 3:218–252, 1991.
13. Stephen C. Kleene. *Introduction to Metamathematics*. van Nostrand, Princeton, 1952.
14. J. Leszczylowski. An experiment with Edinburgh LCF. In W. Bibel and R. Kowalski, editors, *5th International Conference on Automated Deduction*, volume 87 of *Lecture Notes in Computer Science*, pages 170–181, New York, 1981. Springer-Verlag.
15. C. Paulin-Mohring and B. Werner. Synthesis of ML programs in the system Coq. *Journal of Symbolic Computation*, 15(5-6):607–640, 1993.
16. Lawrence Paulson. Proving termination of normalization functions for conditional expressions. *Journal of Automated Reasoning*, 2:63–74, 1986.
17. N. Shanker. Towards mechanical metamathematics. *Journal of Automated Reasoning*, 1(4):407–434, 1985.

A Comparison of PVS and Isabelle/HOL

David Griffioen[1,2]* and Marieke Huisman[2]

[1] CWI, Amsterdam, The Netherlands
[2] Computing Science Institute, Univ. Nijmegen
PO Box 9010, 6500 GL Nijmegen, The Netherlands
{marieke,davidg}@cs.kun.nl

Abstract. There is an overwhelming number of different proof tools available and it is hard to find the right one for a particular application. Manuals usually concentrate on the strong points of a proof tool, but to make a good choice, one should also know (1) which are the weak points and (2) whether the proof tool is suited for the application in hand. This paper gives an initial impetus to a consumers' report on proof tools.
The powerful higher-order logic proof tools PVS and Isabelle are compared with respect to several aspects: logic, specification language, prover, soundness, proof manager, user interface (and more). The paper concludes with a list of criteria for judging proof tools, it is applied to both PVS and Isabelle.

1 Introduction

There is an overwhelming number of different proof tools available, e.g. in the *Database of Existing Mechanised Reasoning Systems* one can find references to over 60 proof tools [7]). All have particular applications that they are especially suited for. Introductory papers on proof tools usually emphasise their strong points by impressive examples. But, if one really wishes to start using one particular proof tool, this information is usually not enough. To make the right choice, one should also know (1) which are the weak points of the proof tool and (2) whether the proof tool is suited for the application in hand. The choice of a proof tool is very important: it can easily take half a year before one fully masters a tool and is able to work on significant applications.

It would be desirable to have some assistance in choosing the appropriate proof tool. When one wishes to buy a toaster, there is also a wide choice, but one is assisted by the reports from consumers' organisations. It is desirable to have similar consumers' reports for proof tools. Such a report should not summarise the manuals, but they should be based on practical experience with these tools. It should discuss several important aspects from a users' perspective. These aspects should be both theoretical (e.g. the logic used) and practical (e.g. the user interface). It also should contain a list of criteria on which all proof tools are

* Supported by the Netherlands Organisation for Scientific Research (NWO) under contract SION 612-316-125.

judged. This consumers' report can be interesting for both new and experienced users. It can assist in selecting an appropriate proof tool, but it also can help to gain more insight in various existing proof tools, including the proof tool one is usually working with.

We are aware that proof tools change in time and that such a consumers' report only can have temporary validity. However, it would be nice if it could have some influence on the direction in which proof tools are developing.

This paper gives the initial impetus to such a report. It describes two proof tools, PVS [21] and Isabelle [17]. We have chosen PVS and Isabelle as the basis for our comparison, because both are known as powerful proof tools for higher-order logic, which have shown their capabilities in non-trivial applications. Both PVS and Isabelle are very complex tools and it is impossible to take all features into account. Therefore, our opinion on the important advantages and disadvantages of working with PVS or Isabelle, is to some extend subjective and influenced by our own histories and fields of research.

Section 1.1 briefly gives some background information on PVS and Isabelle. Next, Sect. 2 compares PVS and Isabelle/HOL. Section 3 discusses our experiences with PVS and Isabelle. Section 4 sketches what we think is the best of both tools. Finally, in Sect. 5 we apply a list of criteria to both PVS and Isabelle.

We based our experiences on PVS version 2.417 and on Isabelle versions 94-8 and 98.

Related Work. We are not the first to compare different proof tools. A comparison of ACL2, a first-order logic prover based on Lisp, and PVS – based on the verification of the Oral Message algorithm – is described in [25]. HOL is compared to PVS in the context of a floating-point standard [4]. In the first comparison, the specification language of PVS is described as too complex and sometimes confusing, while the second comparison is more enthusiastic about it. Gordon describes PVS from a HOL perspective [10]. Other comparisons have been made between HOL and Isabelle/ZF (in the field of set theory) [1], HOL and Coq [26] and Nuprl and NQTHM [3]. Three proof tool interfaces (including PVS) are compared from a human-computer interaction perspective in [14].

To the best of our knowledge, we are the first to compare PVS and Isabelle/HOL. Our comparison is not based on a particular example, but treats systematically several aspects of both tools.

1.1 Short Overview of PVS and Isabelle

The **PVS** Verification System is being developed at SRI International Computer Science Laboratory. Work on PVS started in 1990 and the first version was made available in 1993. A short overview of the history of the system can be found in [19]. PVS is written in Lisp and it is strongly integrated with (Gnu and X) Emacs. The source code is not freely available.

PVS has been applied to several serious problems. For example to specify and design fault-tolerant flight control systems, including a requirements specification for the Space Shuttle [5]. References to more applications of PVS can be found in [19].

Isabelle is being developed in Cambridge, UK, and in Munich. The first version of the system was made available in 1986. Isabelle uses several ideas of the LCF prover [9]: formulae are ML values, theorems are part of an abstract data type and backward proving is supported by tactics and tacticals. The aim of the designers of Isabelle was to develop a generic proof checker, supporting a variety of logics, with a high level of automation. Isabelle has been called the *next 700 provers* [16]. Isabelle is written in ML, and the source code is freely available.

Isabelle is used in a broad range of applications: formalising mathematics (including semantics), logical investigations, program development, specification languages, and verification of programs or systems. References to applications of Isabelle can be found in [18].

2   A Comparison of PVS and Isabelle/HOL

This section first describes several important aspects of a proof tool in general. Subsequently, the comparison of PVS and Isabelle will be structured along these lines. The division is somewhat artificial, because strong dependencies exist between the various parts, but is helpful in the comparison. The emphasis will be on aspects that are important from a users' perspective

The first aspect that we distinguish is the **logic** that is used by the tool. In this paper we will restrict ourselves to (extensions of) typed higher-order logic.

Strongly related with the logic is the **specification language**. It is very important to have a good specification language, because a significant part of a verification effort comes down to specifying what one actually wishes to verify. It is not very useful to have a fully verified statement, if it is not clear what the statement means.

The next aspect that we distinguish is the **prover**. An important issue for the prover is which proof commands (tactics) are available (i.e. which steps can be taken in a proof). Strongly related with this is the choice of a **tactical language**. Tacticals or proof strategies are functions which build new proof commands, using more basic ones. A sophisticated tactical language significantly improves the power of a prover. Another important aspect is whether **decision procedures** (such as for linear arithmetic and for abstract data types) are available.

Another aspect is the **architecture** of the tool, i.e. whether there is a small kernel which does all logical inferences. When the code of the kernel is available (and small) it is possible to convince oneself of the **soundness** of the tool.

Another component is the **proof manager**, which determines e.g. how the current subgoals are displayed, whether the proof trace is recorded and how proof commands can be undone.

Theoretically non-existent, but very important for the actual use of a tool, is the **user interface**. Of course this does not influence the "computing power" of the tool, but a good user interface can significantly increase the effectiveness and usability of a proof tool.

2.1   The Logic

PVS. PVS implements classical typed higher-order logic, extended with predicate subtypes and dependent types. PVS has many built-in types, such as booleans, lists, reals and integers; standard operations on these types are also hard-coded in the tool. Type constructors are available to build complex types e.g. function types, product types, records (labelled products) and recursively-defined abstract data types. The use of predicate subtypes and dependent types will be explained in more detail below.

Isabelle. Isabelle has a meta-logic, which is a fragment of higher-order logic. Formulae in the meta-logic are built using implication ⇒, universal quantification ⋀ and equality ≡. All other logics (the object logics) are represented in this meta-logic. Examples of object logics are first-order logic, the Barendregt cube, Zermelo-Fraenkel set theory and (typed) higher-order logic.

In this paper we will restrict attention to typed higher-order logic (HOL) as object logic. The formalisation of HOL in Isabelle relies heavily on the meta-logic. HOL uses the polymorphic type system of the meta-logic. In its turn, the type system of the meta-logic is similar to the type system of Haskell. Implication, quantification and equality are immediately defined in terms of the meta-logic. Together with some appropriate axioms, these form the basis for the higher-order logic theory. All other definitions, theorems and axioms are formulated in terms of these basic constructs.

Predicate Subtypes and Dependent Types. Predicate subtypes and dependent types can be very useful in writing down a succinct and correct specification.

In PVS a predicate subtype is a new type constructed from an existing type, by collecting all the elements in the existing type that satisfy a predicate (see also [20]). Perhaps, the most famous basic example of a predicate subtype is the type of non-zero-numbers. This type is used in the declaration of the division operator in PVS. The code below[1] is a fragment of the PVS prelude (which contains the theories that are built-in to the PVS system).

```
nonzero_real: NONEMPTY_TYPE = {r: real | r /= 0}    % /= is inequality

+, -, * : [real, real -> real]
/ : [real, nonzero_real -> real]
```

When the division operator is used in a specification, type checking will require that the denominator is nonzero. As this is not decidable in general, a so-called Type Correctness Condition (TCC) is generated, which forces the user to prove

---

[1] All examples in this paper are available at
   http://www.cs.kun.nl/~marieke/Comparison.html.

```
Ex_Array[T:TYPE]: THEORY
BEGIN
  Ex_Array: TYPE = [# length : nat,
                      val : [below(length) -> T ]
                    #]
END Ex_Array
```

Fig. 1. Dependent typing in PVS

that the denominator is indeed nonzero. A theory is not completely verified unless all of its type correctness conditions have been proven. In practice, most of the TCCs can be proven automatically by the tool. The use of predicate subtypes improves the readability of a specification and helps in detecting many semantical errors, as the user can state explicitly all the type constraints. Carreño and Miner come to the same conclusion in [4].

As mentioned, PVS offers another useful typing facility, namely dependent typing. In PVS dependent types can only be constructed using predicate subtypes, in contrast to other approaches to dependent typing, like Martin-Löf's dependent type theory [13]. In Fig. 1 a theory of arrays is depicted. The type Ex_Array is a record with two fields: length, a natural number denoting the length of the array, and val, a function denoting the values at each position in the array. The domain of val is the predicate subtype below(length) of the natural numbers less than length. The type of val thus depends on the actual length of the array.

2.2 The Specification Language

PVS. The specification language of PVS is rich, containing many different type constructors, predicate subtypes and dependent types. We will discuss some specific points.

- PVS has a **parametrised module** system. A specification is usually divided in several theories and each theory can be parametrised with both types and values. At every point in a theory (multiple) other theories can be imported, so that a value or type that has just been declared or defined can immediately be used as an actual parameter.

  Polymorphism is not available in PVS, but it is approximated by theories with type parameters. To define a polymorphic function, one can put it in a theory which is parametrised with the type variables of the function. However, this approach is not always convenient, because when a theory is imported *all* parameters should have a value. Thus when a function does not use all type parameters of a theory, the unused types should still get some instantiation.

- PVS allows non-uniform **overloading**. By this we mean that different functions can have the same name as long as they have different types. For

```
sort[T:TYPE,<=:[T,T->bool]]: THEORY % parametrised theory
BEGIN

ASSUMING                         % assuming clause
  total: ASSUMPTION total_order?(<=)    % infix operator
ENDASSUMING

l : VAR list[T]
e : VAR T

sorted(l): RECURSIVE bool =      % recursive definitions
  IF null?(l) OR null?(cdr(l))   % with measure
  THEN true
  ELSE car(l) <= car(cdr(l)) AND sorted(cdr(l))
  ENDIF
MEASURE length(l)

qsort(l): RECURSIVE list[T] =
  IF null?(l) THEN null
  ELSE LET piv = car(l)
       IN append(qsort(filter(cdr(l),(LAMBDA e: e <= piv))),
                 cons(piv,
                 qsort(filter(cdr(l),(LAMBDA e: NOT e <= piv)))))
  ENDIF
 MEASURE length(l)

qsort_sorted: LEMMA sorted(qsort(l))

END sort
```

Fig. 2. A specification of the quicksort algorithm in PVS

instance, it is allowed to have three functions f in one theory: f: nat, f: nat -> bool and f: bool -> bool. Different functions in different theories can have the same name too, even when they have the same types. The theory names can be used as a prefix to distinguish between them. Names for theorems and axioms can be reused as well, as long as they are in different theories. Again, the theory names can be used to disambiguate this.

- A theory can start with a so-called **assuming clause**, where one states assumptions, usually about the parameters of the theory. These assumptions are used as a fact in the rest of the theory. When the theory is imported, TCCs are generated, which force the user to prove that the assumptions hold for the actual parameters.

- **Recursive data types and functions** can be defined in PVS. An induction principle and several standard functions, such as map and reduce, are automatically generated from an abstract data type definition. PVS allows general recursive function definitions. All functions in PVS have to be total, therefore termination of the recursive function has to be shown, by giving a measure function which maps the arguments of the function to a type with a well-founded ordering. The tool generates TCCs that force the user to prove that this measure decreases with every recursive call.

- PVS has much fixed **syntax**. Many language constructs, such as IF... and CASES... are built-in to the language and the prover. There is a fixed set of symbols which can be used as infix operators; most common infix operators, such as + and <= are included in this set. Sometimes PVS uses syntax which is not the most common, e.g. [A,B] for a Cartesian product of types A and B and (:x,y,z:) for a list of values x, y, and z.

As an example, a PVS specification of the quicksort algorithm can be found in Fig. 2. The name of the theory (sort) is followed by the parameters of the theory, in this case a type T and a relation <= on T. In the ASSUMING clause it is stated that the relation <= is a total order; the predicate total_order? is already defined in the prelude. The VAR keyword is used to 'declare' the variables e and l to have the types list[T] and T, respectively, unless specified otherwise.

The **sorted** predicate expresses that a list is sorted, with respect to the <= order. It is defined recursively, and after the MEASURE clause an expression is given which decreases for each recursive call. The function qsort sorts a list (using the quicksort algorithm). Here the pivot piv is simply the first element of the list car(l). The tail of the list is returned by cdr(l), while null?(l) denotes whether the list is empty. The function filter(l,p) removes all elements from the list l which do not fulfil the predicate p. Finally, the lemma **qsort_sorted** expresses that the quicksort algorithm indeed sorts a list.

Isabelle. The specification language of Isabelle is inspired by functional programming languages (especially ML). We discuss some specific aspects.

- The **module system** allows importing multiple other theories, but it does not permit parametrisation. The type parameters of PVS are not necessary in Isabelle, because functions can be declared polymorphically. The value parameters of PVS can be thought of as an implicit argument for all functions in the theory. Making this argument explicit could be the way to 'mimic' the value parameters in Isabelle.
- **Axiomatic type classes** [23, 24] are comparable to the assuming clause in PVS, and type classes in functional programming [22]. In a type class polymorphic declarations for functions are given. Additionally, in *axiomatic* type classes required properties about these functions can also be stated. These properties can be used as axioms in the rest of the theory. The user can make different instantiations of these axiomatic type classes, by giving appropriate bodies for the functions and proving that the properties hold. Notice that a limited form of overloading can be realised using Isabelle's axiomatic type classes, only for functions with a single polymorphic type.
- Isabelle automatically generates induction principles for each **recursive data type**. The user can give **inductive** and **coinductive** function definitions. There is a special construct to define primitive recursive functions.

```
QSort = HOL + List + WF_Rel +      (* theory importings *)

consts                              (* infix operators *)
  "<<=" :: "['a, 'a] => bool"        (infixl 65)

axclass                             (* axiomatic type class *)
  ordclass < term
  total_ord "total (op <<=)"

consts                              (* primitive recursion *)
  sorted:: "[('a :: ordclass) list] => bool"
primrec sorted list
  sorted_nil  "sorted [] = True"
  sorted_cons "sorted (x#xs) =
                  ((case xs of [] => True | y#ys => x <<= y) &
                   sorted xs)"

consts                              (* well-founded recursion *)
  qsort :: "[('a :: ordclass) list] => ('a :: ordclass) list"
recdef
  qsort "measure size"
    "qsort [] = []"
    "qsort (x # xs) = qsort [y : xs. y <<= x] @
                          (x # qsort [y : xs. ~ y <<= x])"

end
```

Fig. 3. A specification of the quicksort algorithm in Isabelle

Well-founded recursive functions can be defined as well, together with a
measure function to show their termination.

- Isabelle **syntax** can easily be extended. In particular, Isabelle allows the user
  to define arbitrary infix and mixfix operators. There is a powerful facility to
  give priorities and to describe a preferred syntax. This allows the user to
  define that lists should be represented for input and output as e.g. [1,2,3]
  while internally this is represented as (cons 1 (cons 2 (cons 3 nil))).
  Language constructs like if...then...else are defined explicitly in terms
  of the basic operators.

In Fig. 3 the quicksort example is shown in Isabelle syntax. The theory Qsort
is the union of the theories HOL, List, WF_Rel and the constants and definitions
in this file. Type variables start with a quote, in this specification this is 'a.
The constant <<= is declared to be an infix operation with priority 65. It is a
relation on 'a. The axiomatic type class ordclass is declared as a subclass of
the general type class term. It has an axiom total_ord, which states that <<=
is a total order. In this axiom the infix symbol <<= is prefixed by op to make it
behave like an ordinary function symbol.

The constant **sorted** is a polymorphic function, where the type parameter **'a** must be in **ordclass**. It is defined as a primitive recursive function, using the special **primrec** declaration. Pattern matching is used to give rules for the definition of **sorted** on the empty list **[]** and on the nonempty list **x#xs**. Within the rule **sorted_cons** an extra case distinction on **xs** is made. The constant **qsort** also is a polymorphic function where the type parameter **'a** must be in **ordclass**, but it is defined using well-founded recursion. The **recdef** declaration requires the user to give a measure and rules to define **qsort**. Again pattern matching is used in the definition. The **@** symbol denotes list concatenation. The list comprehension **[y : xs. y <<= x]** should be read as: the list containing all elements **y** of the list **xs**, satisfying **y <<= x**.

2.3   The Prover

PVS. PVS represents theorems using the sequent calculus. Every subgoal consists of a list of assumptions $A_1, \ldots A_n$ and a list of conclusions $B_1, \ldots, B_m$. One should read this as: the conjunction of the assumptions implies the disjunction of the conclusions i.e. $A_1 \wedge \ldots \wedge A_n \Rightarrow B_1 \vee \ldots \vee B_m$.

The proof commands of PVS can be divided into three different categories.[2]

- **Creative proof commands.** These are the proof steps one also writes down explicitly when writing a proof by hand. Examples of such commands are **induct** (start to prove by induction), **inst** (instantiate a universally quantified assumption, or existentially quantified conclusion), **lemma** (use a theorem, axiom or definition) and **case** (make a case distinction). For most commands, there are variants which increase the degree of automation, e.g. the command **inst?** tries to find an appropriate instantiation itself.
- **Bureaucratic proof commands.** When writing a proof by hand, these steps usually are done implicitly. Examples are **flatten** (disjunctive simplification) **expand** (expanding a definition), **replace** (replace a term by an equivalent term) and **hide** (hide assumptions or conclusions which have become irrelevant).
- **Powerful proof commands.** These are the commands that are intended to handle all "trivial" goals. The basic commands in this category are **simplify** and **prop** (simplification and propositional reasoning). A more powerful example is **assert**. This uses the simplification command and the built-in decision procedures and does automatic (conditional) rewriting. PVS has some powerful decision procedures, dealing, among other things, with linear arithmetic. The most powerful command is **grind**, which unfolds definitions, skolemizes quantifications, lifts if-then-elses and tries to instantiate and simplify the goal.

---

[2] This division is made by the authors, not by the developers of PVS. Nevertheless it resembles the division made in [6].

Isabelle. In Isabelle, every goal consists of a list of assumptions and one conclusion. The goal $[A_1; A_2; \ldots; A_n] \Rightarrow B$ should be read as $A_1 \Rightarrow (A_2 \Rightarrow \ldots (A_n \Rightarrow B))$. Notice that $\Rightarrow$ is the implication of the meta-logic.

The basic proof method of Isabelle is resolution. The operation RS, which is used by many tactics, implements resolution with higher-order unification. It unifies the conclusion of its first argument with the first assumption of the second argument. As an example, when doing resolution with $([?P] \Rightarrow ?P \vee ?Q)$ and $([?R; ?S] \Rightarrow ?R \wedge ?S)$, this results in the theorem $[?P; ?S] \Rightarrow (?P \vee ?Q) \wedge ?S$.

Isabelle supports both forward and backward proving, although its emphasise lies on backward proving by supplying many useful tactics for it. A tactic transforms the proof goal into several subgoals and gives a justification for this transformation.

Many tactics try to find themselves a useful instantiation for unknowns in the current goal, and variables in the applied theorems. In general there are many possible instantiations, therefore tactics return a lazy list containing (almost) all possible next states of the proof (in a suitable order). When the first instantiation is not satisfactory the next instantiation can be tried with back. This possibility is mainly used by powerful tactics.

The proof commands of Isabelle can be divided in several categories as well, although these are different from the categories used earlier for PVS.

- **Resolution** is the basis for many tactics. The standard one is resolve_tac. It tries to unify the conclusion of a theorem with the conclusion of a subgoal. If this succeeds, it creates new subgoals to prove the assumptions of the theorem (after substitution).
- Another basic tactic is assume_tac, which tries to unify the conclusion with one of the assumptions.
- **Induction** is done by induct_tac, which does resolution with an appropriate induction rule.
- **Use an axiom or theorem** by adding it to the assumption list. There are several variants: with and without instantiation, in combination with resolution etc.
- **Simplification** tactics for (conditional) rewriting. For every theory a so-called simplification set can be built. This set contains theorems, axioms and definitions, which can be used to rewrite a goal. It is possible to extend the simplification set (temporarily or permanently).
  Isabelle's simplifier uses a special strategy to handle permutative rewrite rules, i.e rules where the left and right hand side are the same, up to renaming of variables. A standard lexical order on terms is defined and a permutative rewrite rule only is applied if this decreases the term, according to this order. The most common example of a permutative rewrite rule is commutativity $(x \oplus y = y \oplus x)$. With normal rewriting (as in PVS) this rule will loop, but ordered rewriting avoids this.
- **Classical reasoning** is another powerful proof facility of Isabelle. There are various tactics for classical reasoning. One of them, blast_tac, uses a tableau prover, coded directly in ML. The proof that is generated is then reconstructed in Isabelle.

- **Bureaucratic** tactics are also available, such as rotate_tac, which changes the order of the assumptions. This can be necessary for rewriting with the assumptions, because this is done from top to bottom.

A theorem can contain so-called meta-variables, which can be bound while proving it. As an example, consider the specification of quicksort (Fig. 3). Suppose that we instantiated the axiomatic type class with the natural numbers (defining <<= as ≤) and that the definition of quicksort is automatically rewritten. Now we can state for example the following goal

```
goal QSort.thy "qsort[4, 2, 3] = ?x";
```

where ?x is a meta-variable. When simplifying this goal, the meta-variable is bound to [2,3,4] (and the theorem is proven). The theorem is stored as qsort[4, 2, 3] = [2, 3, 4]. This feature makes Isabelle well-suited for transformational programming [2] and writing a Prolog interpreter [17].

Tactical Language. A tactical (or proof strategy) is a function to build complex tactics (or proof commands) using more basic ones. A well-known example is the tactical **then**. This tactical gets two tactics as arguments and applies them sequentially to the goal.

PVS has a limited proof strategy language; containing constructs for sequencing, backtracking, branching, let-binding and recursion. When one wishes to go beyond this, for example to write a strategy which inspects the goal, this should be done in Lisp. The Lisp data structure that contains the proof goal is not officially documented; some accessor functions are known to work but the developers explicitly allow themselves to change PVS at this level of implementation. Probably it is possible to change the goal in Lisp without a logical justification.

In Isabelle the tactical language is ML, so a complete functional language is available. All logical inferences on terms of type thm (the theorems) are performed by a limited set of functions. In ML a type can be 'closed', which means that a programmer can express that no other functions than a number of 'trusted' functions are allowed to manipulate values of this type (in this case: theorems). In this way the full power of ML can be used to program proof strategies, and soundness is guaranteed via the interface.

Proving with Powerful Proof Commands. Both PVS and Isabelle can do simple calculations quite fast. For instance the theorem below is proven in (almost) zero time in PVS by (ASSERT), using the built-in integer arithmetic.

```
calc: LEMMA 700 * 400 * 11 = 2 * 7 * 22 * 10000
```

In Isabelle/HOL we have a similar result. After loading the theories defining the integers we can prove the following goal in (almost) zero time using simplification. Note that, for technical reasons, integers have a sharp-sign # as prefix. Operations on integers are defined using their binary representation, so in contrast to PVS, arithmetic is not part of the kernel, but defined in the logic.

```
goal Bin.thy "#700 * #400 * #11 = #2 * #7 * #22 * #10000";
```

Linear (and some non-linear) arithmetic has standard support in PVS and the next theorem is also proven with a single command.

```
arith: LEMMA 7 + x < 8 + x  AND 2 * x * x <= 3 * x * x
```

In Isabelle a package to cancel out common summands (and factors) is available. It is loaded standardly for the naturals, but not for the integers. The following goal is proven in one step, using simplification.

```
goal Arith.thy "1 + x < 2 + x";
```

A well-known [6] example of the simplification procedures of PVS is the proof of the characterisation of the summation function. The theorem below is proven by a single command (induct-and-simplify "k")

```
sum(k:nat): RECURSIVE nat =
  IF k = 0 THEN 0 ELSE k + sum(k-1) ENDIF
MEASURE k

sum_char: LEMMA sum(k) = k*(k+1)/2
```

An impressive example of the classical reasoner of Isabelle is the following theorem, problem 41 of Pelletier. Isabelle proves this automatically using the classical reasoner (Blast_tac).

```
(ALL z. EX y. ALL x. J x y = (J x z & (~ J x x))) -->
~(EX z. ALL x. J x z)
```

2.4   System Architecture and Soundness

PVS. The developers of PVS designed their prover to be useful for real world problems. Therefore the specification language should be rich and the prover fast with a high degree of automation. To achieve this, powerful decision procedures were added to PVS. However, these decision procedures sometimes cause soundness problems, thus the procedures can be considered to be part of the kernel, which makes the kernel large and complex. Further, PVS once was considered to be a prototype for a new SRI prover. Perhaps for these reasons PVS still seems to contain a lot of bugs and frequently new bugs show up. An overview of the known bugs at the moment can be seen on the PVS bug list [15]. It would be desirable that the bugs in PVS would only influence completeness and not soundness. Unfortunately, this is not the case, as some recent proofs of true=false have shown [15, bug numbers 71, 82, 113 and 160]. Most bugs do not influence soundness, but they can be very annoying.

Because of the soundness bugs in the past, it is reasonable to assume that PVS will continue to contain soundness bugs. The obvious question thus arises, why use a proof tool that probably contains soundness bugs? Our answer is threefold:

PVS is still a very critical reader of proofs. PVS lets fewer mistakes slip through than many of our human colleagues (and PVS is much more patient), thus in comparing PVS to an average logician/mathematician PVS is much more precise and sceptic.

Furthermore, history tells us that the fixed soundness bugs are hardly ever unintentionally explored, we know of only a single case.

Thirdly, most mistakes in a system that is to be verified are detected in the process of making a formal specification. Thus economically spoken, the specification is very important, and PVS has a expressive and human friendly specification language. Therefore when we specify a system in the language of PVS this gives extra confidence that the specification expresses what is 'meant'.

A lot of effort has been put into the development of PVS. For this reason SRI does not make the code of PVS freely available. As a consequence, to most users the structure of the tool is unknown and making extensions or bug fixes is impossible, although sometimes users go to SRI to implement a feature.

Isabelle. Isabelle was developed from quite a different perspective. The main objective was to develop a flexible and sound prover, and next to develop powerful tactics, so that large proof steps could be taken at once. Isabelle seems to be much more stable than PVS. It does not show unpredictable behaviour. Isabelle is an open system, which means that everybody can easily add extensions to it. Recently a new Isabelle version was released.[3] To our surprise some tactics (especially Auto_tac) were changed, so that our old proofs really had to be adapted, and not all of these changes were clearly documented.

2.5   The Proof Manager

PVS. All proofs in PVS are done in a special proof mode. The tool manages which subgoals still have to be proven and which steps are taken to construct a proof, so it is not the users responsibility to maintain the proof trace. Proofs are represented as trees. There is an Tcl/Tk interface which gives a picture of the proof tree (see Fig. 4). It helps the user to see which branches of the proof are not proven yet. One can click on a turnstile to see a particular subgoal, also the proof commands can be displayed in full detail.

When using a proof tool most of the time the theorems and specification are under construction, as the processes of specifying and proving are usually intermingled. The notion of "unproved theorem" allows to concentrate on the crucial theorems first and prove the auxiliary theorems later. PVS keeps track of the status of proofs, e.g. whether it uses unproved theorems.

Line numbers can be used in PVS to specify that a command should work only on some of the assumptions/conclusions, e.g. (expand "f" 2) expands f in the second conclusion. When a specification or theorem is slightly changed (*e.g.* a conjunct is added), the line numbers in the goal often change. It would be more

---

[3] Isabelle98

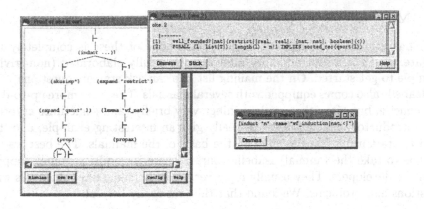

Fig. 4. Example of a Tcl/Tk proof tree

robust, if one could use commands expressing things like: expand all fs with zero as first argument, and only expand f in the assumptions where function g occurs. This has an additional advantage, namely that the intentions of the proof steps become more clear. The authors have made their own Lisp functions to calculate a list of line numbers that satisfy a simple regular expression. This is already helpful (especially in strategies), but many extensions are possible. For example, in the presence of overloading it would be useful to expand fs of a specific type.

Isabelle. Isabelle does not give elaborate proof support. The user has to keep track of everything him/herself (including the undos). The proofs are structured linearly, there is just a list of all subgoals. This stimulates the use of tacticals such as ALLGOALS, but it is not so easy to see how "deep" or in which branch one is in a proof. On the other hand, in Isabelle it is possible to undo an undo (or actually: a choplev, which steps back an arbitrary number of levels, or to a particular level). And even more, it is also possible to look at the subgoals at an earlier level, without undoing the proof.

2.6   User Interface

PVS's standard user interface is better developed than Isabelle's. It is strongly integrated with Emacs. Recently, a batch mode was added to PVS. The *de facto* interface for Isabelle is Isamode (also based on Emacs). There are some more advanced user interfaces based on Tcl/Tk, but they only work for particular versions of Isabelle.

2.7   Manuals and Support

PVS has a number of different manuals, but none of these is completely up-to-date. There is an introductory manual with a fully elaborated (non-trivial) example to get started. On the mailing list one can ask starters questions.

Isabelle also comes equipped with several manuals. These are more up-to-date and concise, but often they explain things very briefly (and sometimes cryptic). The introductory manual does not really give an interesting example, and it is hard to start using Isabelle, only on the basis of the manuals. The best way to start is to take the (annual) Isabelle course. There is good (personal) support from the developers. They usually reply very quickly (same day) on emails with questions and problems. We found that this was really helpful.

2.8   Runtime Speed

We did not compare the speed of the tools because we think the game is not to "run" a proof, but to construct it. This construction consists of building a specification of a problem and proving appropriate theorems. This is hard and depends heavily on the user, his/her experience with the proof tool etc. We do mention though that the "experienced speed" of the two tools is comparable. By this we mean the time it takes to type check a specification or to execute a smart tactic. Both for PVS and Isabelle, the execution of a single command – on a Pentium II 300Mhz – often takes less then a second and hardly ever more than ten seconds.

3   Our Experiences

In this section we wish to discuss in some detail our own, more personal, experiences. After using PVS for several years we became increasingly unhappy with it, because so many bugs appeared. Sometimes we felt that we would spend more time on working around small bugs, than on proving serious properties. In this period the first author visited Munich and became enthusiastic about Isabelle. However, reading the Isabelle manuals did not provide enough background to get really started with it. Therefore, in September 1997 the second author visited the Isabelle course in Cambridge. After this course, it seemed relatively easy to start working seriously with Isabelle.

To start with a well-understood, but non-trivial example, the *Tree Identification Phase (TIP)* [8] of the 1394 protocol was selected, as the first author had already worked extensively on it using PVS. The first challenge was to transform the PVS specification into Isabelle, because Isabelle's specification language lacks e.g. records and function updates.

After transforming the specification, the next step was to start proving. We are used to PVS's proof manager, which records all the steps we take in a proof. Isabelle only provides a so-called *listener*, which records everything the user types in (including the typos and steps that were undone later), so the proof has to be filtered out. We experienced that it works faster to copy the steps immediately than to use the listener.

When we then really started proving, we noticed a big difference in the handling of conditional expressions (i.e. `if...then...else...`). In PVS, conditionals are built-in and the prover knows how to deal with them. In Isabelle conditional expressions are explicitly defined and the prover does not have special facilities for them. We discussed this with Larry Paulson and Tobias Nipkow, which resulted in a solution for Isabelle94-8. In Isabelle98 more tactics to deal with conditional expressions are available by default.

Despite these differences, we managed to prove the "same" invariants as in PVS. The lengths of the proofs (in number of commands/tactics) were comparable to the lengths of the proofs in PVS.

We also studied whether a translation of object-oriented specifications into higher-order logic (part of a different project [12]) could be adapted to Isabelle. In the translation to PVS we made extensive use of overloading and this caused serious difficulties in Isabelle. In discussions with the Isabelle developers we tried several solutions, but none of these were satisfactory. Isabelle98 has the possibility to define different name spaces and this might help. Due to time constraints and lack of documentation we did not investigate this option.

4   The Best of Both Worlds

When comparing PVS and Isabelle we realised that both tools had their advantages and disadvantages. Our ideal proof tool would combine the best of both worlds.

The Logic. Predicate subtyping and dependent typing give so much extra expressiveness and protection against semantical errors, that this should be supported. The loss of decidability of type checking is easily (and elegantly) overcome by the generation of TCCs and the availability of a proof checker.

The meta-logic of Isabelle gives the flexibility to use different logics, even in a single proof. However, in our applications, we did not feel the need to use a logic other than HOL and the interference with the meta-logic sometimes complicated matters.

The Specification Language. The specification language should be readable, expressive and easily extendible. For function application, we have a slight preference for the bracketless syntax of Isabelle.

It should be possible to parametrise theories with values. We have a preference for type parametrised theories, because polymorphism is hard to combine with non-uniform overloading. A disadvantage of type inference, in combination with implicitly (universally) quantified variables, is that typos introduce new variables, and do not produce an error. As an example, suppose that one has declared a function myFunction :: nat => nat, but that by accident the following goal is typed in: "myFunction x < myFuntion (x+1)". This is internally equivalent to: "ALL myFuntion. myFunction x < myFuntion (x+1)". This error can be detected by asking explicitly for the list of variables (and their types) in the goal.

The Prover. The ideal prover has powerful proof commands for classical reasoning and rewriting, including ordered rewriting. A tactic should return a lazy list of possible next states, as this is useful to try (almost) all possible instantiations. Also, decision procedures (for example for linear arithmetic) should be available. Preferably, these decision procedures are not built-in to the kernel, but written in the tactical language, so that they can not cause soundness problems. The style of the interactive proof commands of PVS is preferred over that of Isabelle, because this is more intuitive. It is important to have a structured tactical language, which allows the user to access the goal. For this purpose, the structure of the goal should be well-documented.

System Architecture. To ensure soundness of the proof tool, the system should have a small kernel. The tool should be an open system, of which the code is freely available, so that users can easily extend it for their own purposes and (if necessary) implement bug fixes.

The Proof Manager and User Interface. The tool should keep track of the proof trace. Proofs are best represented as trees, because this is more natural, compared to a linear structure. The tree representation also allows easy navigation through the proof, supported by a visual representation of the tree. When replaying the proof, after changing the specification, the tool can detect for which branches the proof fails, thanks to the tree representation.

5 Conclusions and Future Work

We tried to describe some important aspects of PVS and Isabelle which are not in the 'advertising of the tool', but are important in making a decision about which tool to use. To conclude, Table. 1 gives a list of criteria for judging a proof tool, filled in for PVS and Isabelle. This list is not complete and based on the available features of PVS and Isabelle and our work done with these proof tools. We hope that in the future users of other proof tools will produce a similar consumers' test on "their" proof tool too, so that a broad overview of users' experiences with different proof tools will be available.

Maybe such comparisons will lead to a proof tool which combines the best of all available proof tools. Looking only at PVS and Isabelle, it would be desirable to have a proof tool with the specification language, proof manager and user interface of PVS, but the soundness, flexibility and well-structuredness of Isabelle.

Table 1. A consumer report of PVS and Isabelle

	PVS 2.417	Isabelle98/HOL
logic	typed HOL	typed HOL
predicate subtypes	++	not available
dependent predicate subtypes	++	not available
standard syntax	++/+	+
flexible syntax	-	++
module system	++/+	+
polymorphism	-	++
overloading	++	-
abstract data types	++/+	++/+
recursive functions	++/+	++/+
proof command language	+	+/-
tactical language	-	++
automation	+	+
arithmetic decision procedures	++	+/-
libraries	+	++/+
proof manager	++	+/-
interface	++	+
soundness	-	++
upwards compatible	+/-	+/-
easy to start using	+	-
manuals	+/-	+/-
support	+	++
time it takes to fix a bug	-	?
ease of installation	++	++

Acknowledgements

We thank Bart Jacobs and Frits Vaandrager for their comments on earlier drafts of this paper.

References

1. Sten Agerholm and Mike Gordon. Experiments with ZF set theory in HOL and Isabelle. In E. Thomas Schubert, Philip J. Windley, and James Alves-Foss, editors, *Proceedings of the 8th International Workshop on Higher Order Logic Theorem Proving and Its Applications*, Aspen Grove, UT, USA, volume 971 of *LNCS*. Springer-Verlag, September 1995.
2. Abdelwaheb Ayari and David A. Basin. Generic system support for deductive program development. In T. Margaria and B. Steffen, editors, *Proceedings of the Workshop on Tools and Algorithms for the Construction and Analysis of Systems*, Passau, Germany, volume 1055 of *LNCS*. Springer-Verlag, April 1996.
3. David Basin and Matt Kaufmann. The Boyer-Moore prover and Nuprl: An experimental comparison. In Gérard Huet and Gordon Plotkin, editors, *Logical Frameworks*, pages 90 – 119. Cambridge University Press, 1991.

4. Victor A. Carreño and Paul S. Miner.   Specification of the IEEE-854 floating-point standard in HOL and PVS.   In *HOL95: Eighth International Workshop on Higher-Order Logic Theorem Proving and Its Applications*, Aspen Grove, UT, September 1995.   Category B proceedings, available at http://lal.cs.byu.edu/lal/hol95/Bprocs/indexB.html.

5. Judith Crow and Ben L. Di Vito. Formalizing Space Shuttle software requirements. In *First Workshop on Formal Methods in Software Practice (FMSP '96)*, pages 40–48, San Diego, CA, January 1996. Association for Computing Machinery.

6. Judy Crow, Sam Owre, John Rushby, Natarajan Shankar, and Mandayam Srivas. A tutorial introduction to PVS. Presented at WIFT '95: Workshop on Industrial-Strength Formal Specification Techniques, Boca Raton, Florida, April 1995. Available, with specification files, at http://www.csl.sri.com/wift-tutorial.html.

7. Database of existing mechanized reasoning systems. http://www-formal.stanford.edu/clt/ARS/systems.html.

8. Marco Devillers, David Griffioen, Judi Romijn, and Frits Vaandrager. Verification of a leader election protocol formal methods applied to IEEE 1394. Technical Report CSI-R9728, Computing Science Institute, Catholic University of Nijmegen, 1997.

9. Michael J.C. Gordon, Robin Milner, and Cristopher P. Wadsworth. *Edinburgh LCF: A Mechanised Logic of Computation*, volume 78 of *LNCS*. Springer-Verlag, 1979.

10. Mike Gordon.   Notes on PVS from a HOL perspective.   Available at http://www.cl.cam.ac.uk/users/mjcg/PVS.html, August 1995.

11. Elsa L. Gunter and Amy Felty, editors. *Proceedings of the 10th International Workshop on Theorem Proving in Higher Order Logics*, Murray Hill, NJ, USA, volume 1275 of *LNCS*. Springer-Verlag, August 1997.

12. Ulrich Hensel, Marieke Huisman, Bart Jacobs, and Hendrik Tews. Reasoning about classes in object-oriented languages: Logical models and tools. In *Proceedings of ESOP at ETAPS '98*, LNCS. Springer-Verlag, 1998. To appear.

13. Per Martin-Löf. Constructive mathematics and computer programming. In *Sixth International Congress for Logic, Methodology, and Philosophy of Science*, pages 153–175. North Holland, Amsterdam, 1982.

14. Nicholas A. Merriam and Michael D. Harrison. Evaluating the interfaces of three theorem proving assistants. In F. Bodart and J. Vanderdonckt, editors, *Proceedings of the 3rd International Eurographics Workshop on Design, Specification, and Verification of Interactive Systems*, Eurographics Series, Namur, Belgium, June 1996. Springer-Verlag.

15. Sam Owre. http://www.csl.sri.com/htbin/pvs/pvs-bug-list.

16. Lawrence C. Paulson. Isabelle: The next 700 theorem provers. In P. Odifreddi, editor, *Logic and Computer Science*, pages 361–386. Academic Press, 1990.

17. Lawrence C. Paulson. *Isabelle: A Generic Theorem Prover*, volume 828 of *LNCS*. Springer-Verlag, 1994.

18. Frank Pfenning. Isabelle bibliography. http://www.cl.cam.ac.uk/Research/HVG/Isabelle/biblio.html.

19. John Rushby. PVS bibliography. http://www.csl.sri.com/pvs-bib.html.

20. John Rushby, Sam Owre, and N. Shankar. Subtypes for specifications: Predicate subtyping in PVS. *IEEE Transactions on Software Engineering*, 24, 1998. To appear.

21. N. Shankar. PVS: Combining specification, proof checking, and model checking. In Mandayam Srivas and Albert Camilleri, editors, *Formal Methods in Computer-*

Aided Design (FMCAD '96), volume 1166 of *LNCS*, pages 257–264, Palo Alto, CA, November 1996. Springer-Verlag.

22. Philip Wadler and Stephen Blott. How to make ad-hoc polymorphism less ad hoc. In *16'th ACM Symposium on Principles of Programming Languages*, Austin, Texas, January 1989.
23. Markus Wenzel. Using axiomatic type classes in Isabelle, a tutorial, 1995. http://www4.informatik.tu-muenchen.de/~wenzelm/papers.html.
24. Markus Wenzel. Type classes and overloading in higher-order logic. In Gunter and Felty [11].
25. William D. Young. Comparing verification systems: Interactive Consistency in ACL2. *IEEE Transactions on Software Engineering*, 23(4):214–223, April 1997.
26. Vincent Zammit. A comparative study of Coq and HOL. In Gunter and Felty [11].

Adding External Decision Procedures to HOL90 Securely

Elsa L. Gunter

Bell Laboratories, 600 Mountain Ave.
Murray Hill, NJ 07974, USA
elsa@research.bell-labs.com

Abstract. This paper describes a modest conservative extension of HOL90 that allows the results from external decision procedures to be used within HOL90 without compromising its logical consistency.

1 Introduction

Theorem provers such as HOL90 place a great deal of emphasis on being expressive and on being secure. As a result, they are inherently interactive, sometimes to the annoyance of the user. On the other hand, decision procedures, such as BBD's and model checkers [5, 6], place a great deal of emphasis on being totally automatic and fast. However, they work on restricted languages and their security is usually checked by hand proof at most. Therefore, the level of trust that is reasonably put in their results may be somewhat less than the level of trust reasonably put in the results of theorem provers. To improve the level of automation of a theorem prover, it is sometimes desirable to call an appropriate decision procedure from within the theorem prover when the problem being worked on has been reduced to the appropriate subset. PVS [7] is an example of a theorem prover that makes use of such a link to model-checkers.

The problem arises, however, of how to incorporate the results of an arbitrary decision procedure within a theorem prover without compromising the security of the theorem prover. One solution to incorporating decision procedures in a fully expansive theorem prover, such as HOL90, is to write them as tactics, conversions, etc. This solution provides the highest security, but often leads to much less efficient procedures, since they must actually build a proof, not just decide whether one exists. Also, it doesn't allow us to directly take advantage of existing external decision procedures.

In this paper we will describe a mechanism for using external decision procedures from within HOL90 while maintaining HOL90's high standard of security. This method should be applicable to any of the family of HOL theorem provers, and most likely to a much broader class than that. The basic idea is that each theorem will carry with it a tag indicating that an external result was used. This tag is internal to the logic; it is not an external annotation on theorems. There are two variants of tagging possible; one just documents the fact that an external procedure was called, and the other records in addition which results were accepted and used.

The version that records the results that were accepted provides the greatest documentation, and allows for the subsequent elimination of dependency on external results should they be proved within the theorem prover. The usefulness of this method will depend on the number of results from external decision procedures being relatively small. For those instances when the number of results from external decision procedures is quite large, we provided a more limited, but equally secure method for incorporation. Again the theorems using external results are in essence tagged, but only with that fact that an external procedure was used, and not with the result itself. In this second method, it will not be possible to eliminate the tag because the precise result assumed is not recorded.

2 The Library add_dec_proc

We have added to HOL90 a contributed library named add_dec_proc which supports two methods for allowing HOL90 to accept as theorems results from external decision procedures while maintaining the logical consistency of HOL90. This library consists of a theory dec_proc_tokens introducing a type and some constants used for tagging, and functions implementing two new primitive inference rules, corresponding tactics, and a modified version of the goalstack manipulation functions expand and e. We also include a trivial example defining the "decision procedure" clearly, used by humans when they don't wish to give the details of a proof, and a more substantive example using the method in conjunction with Peter Homeier's Verification Condition Generator [4].

To support the tagging in both methods, we introduce a type : dec_proc_token. The type : dec_proc_token is defined to be isomorphic to an arbitrary non-empty subset of the infinite type : ind. (We use the Hilbert choice operator here to select such a subset.) Elements of this type are treated as the names of the external decision procedures. They will be used as arguments to constants that yield boolean results that will become hypotheses of theorems using the external procedures in their proofs. Both of the methods we describe work basically the same way, and we shall describe them in sequence here.

The first of the two methods for accepting external results is somewhat simpler to understand, and more concise, but it is also of less utility. Let proc be the name of a decision procedure external to the HOL90. To be able to use the library with either of the two methods, the user must supply a procedure for calling proc and for notifying the HOL90 of the result. For the first method, we shall assume that we have an SML procedure call_proc : term → unit which returns () : unit if proc was able to verify the goal, and raises an HOL_ERR exception otherwise. By raising an exception, it can be used as a component of tactics that try various options depending upon which options succeed or raise an exception. Using new_constant, we may introduce a constant proc : dec_proc_token to represent the procedure within HOL90. (If the user does not wish to introduce their own constant, the library supplies the constant default_token : dec_proc_token which may be used instead.) With these two pieces, we may make use of the supplied SML function

```
trust_proc_result {token = (--'proc'--),
                   dec_proc = call_proc} : term -> thm
```

which implements the new primitive inference rule

$$\frac{}{[\text{trusted\_token proc}] \vdash tm}$$

assuming call_proc *tm* completes without raising an exception. The hypothesis trusted_token proc intentionally may be thought of as an oracle saying whether proc always proves correct results. If it does, then the hypothesis is true and we have the desired theorem; if it does not always give correct results, then the theorem is still valid since the hypothesis is false – it is just meaningless. Extensionally, trusted_token is a constant introduced via constant specification to be of HOL90 type : dec_proc_token $\rightarrow$ bool, and the result of an application is either T or F, but we cannot in general know which. On the other hand, the primitive inference rule trust_proc_result is a proper logical extension to HOL90 and will require proof that it is a conservative one.

We now have the basic machinery for incorporating external results, at least for the simple method. However, typically we do not want to use trust_proc_result directly, but rather we would prefer to use a version that works as a tactic on goals on the goalstack. The corresponding tactic

```
trust_proc_result_TAC : {token = (--'proc'--),
                         dec_proc = call_proc} : tactic
```

calls trust_proc_result on the current goal rendered as a term. If the goal is $[a_1, \ldots, a_n] \vdash tm$ with free variables $x_1, \ldots, x_m$, then the term to which trust_proc_result will be applied is $\forall x_1 \ldots x_m. \, a_1 \wedge \cdots \wedge a_n \Rightarrow tm$.

The tactic trust_proc_result_TAC resolves the theorem resulting from the call to trust_proc_result (if there is one) with the assumptions of the goal, and attempts to derive the goal as a theorem. However, the theorem returned has a hypothesis not occurring (at least not usually) among the assumptions of the goal, namely trusted_token proc. The standard functions expand and e for applying tactics to the goalstack perform a validity check which assures that all the hypotheses of the theorem returned by the validation computed by the tactic are among the assumptions of the current goal. Therefore, the tactic trust_proc_result_TAC will be rejected by these standard goalstack manipulation functions. To address this, we have included a modified version of these functions. The modified version of these two functions performs almost the same validity checks as before; the one difference is that now they ignore tagged hypotheses (from either method) among the hypotheses of the validation theorem. With this modification, trust_proc_result_TAC can be used the same way as other tactics. This pretty much completes the story (accept for proof of consistency) for the simple method.

The second method has the same components as the simple method, but in a more complicated, and informative manner. There are also some additional functions to make use of some of the added flexibility of this second method. The tokens generated to name external procedures for the simple method may be reused for the second method. However, this time the user is expected to supply an SML function for calling the procedure that returns a term stating the theorem to be accepted, if there is one. Thus, in our case, we will assume we have `consult_proc` : `term → term`. As before, we may now create

```
use_proc_result {token = (--'proc'--),
                 dec_proc = consult_proc} : term -> thm
```

which, when applied to the input term *in_term*, implements the primitive inference rule

$$\frac{}{[\text{used\_token proc } tm] \vdash tm} \quad \text{where } \texttt{consult\_proc } in\_term = tm$$

provided the term *tm* returned by `consult_proc` is a closed term, i.e. contains no free variables. This inference rule is not only more informative (by putting the result accepted from and external procedure in the hypotheses), but it is also more broadly applicable than the one given by `trust_proc_result`. The rule can be used to couple HOL90 with calculators (such as computer algebra systems), as well as decision procedures. For example, it could be used to couple HOL90 with the Unix utility `dc`. In that case, the term to which it would be applied would be a complex numeric expression and the result would be a term stating that the expression was equal to its numeric value.

It will oftentimes be the case that we do not want to make use of this extra flexibility. Then we would like to have just one method for calling a given external procedure. To facilitate using one kind of calling function where the other is required, we supply two coercion functions: `trust_use` and `use_trust`. Given `call_proc` used with the simple method, we could define `consult_proc` by:

```
val consult_proc = trust_use call_proc
```

The term that will be returned is the universal closure of the term to which `consult_proc` is applied. Similarly, if we have `consult_proc` and we wish to define `call_proc`, we could use

```
val call_proc = use_trust consult_proc
```

This function will only succeed if the term returned by `consult_proc` is the universal closure of the term to which `call_proc`, and hence `consult_proc`, is applied.

As in the first method, the way we expect `trust_proc_result` to be most commonly used is not directly, but through a tactic. In this situation, however, it makes sense to apply the tactic only to calling functions that return the (universal closure of) the term to which they are applied. This is reflected by the type of the decision procedure calling function argument being the same as it is for the tactic `trust_proc_result_TAC`. The new tactic we get is:

```
use_proc_result_TAC {token = (--'proc'--),
                     dec_proc = use_trust consult_proc} : tactic
```

which calls use_proc_result on the current goal. It, too, resolves the resulting theorem (if there is one) with the assumptions of the goal and attempts to derive the goal as a theorem.

The inference rule given by use_proc_result introduces a hypothesis, much as trust_proc_result does. The nature of this hypothesis is different, however, in that it contains the theorem statement, tm, as a subterm. This causes some difficulty with the interaction with tactics. We restricted the decision procedure calling functions to ones that return closed terms because it makes the tactic use_proc_result_TAC operate more robustly in conjunction with other tactics. Without this restriction, proofs built with use_proc_result_TAC and tactics such as GEN_TAC which introduce scoped free variables would fail when the final theorem was being built because there would be free variables in the hypotheses introduced by use_proc_result_TAC that would need to escape their scope. There is a similar concern with type variables, but without the ability to quantify propositions by type variables, we are limited in our ability to protect against it. Whenever use_proc_result_TAC is used on a goal where the validating theorem generated by use_proc_result contains type variables, a warning message is printed.

As we have seen above, the fact that use_proc_result introduces a hypothesis with the theorem statement causes some difficulty with tactic style theorem proving. Therefore, the question arises of why we would want this version over what the simple method gives us. There are two answers to this question: documentation and future elimination. The hypotheses serve as documentation, recording for each theorem all the results that depended on theorems from use_proc_result. Moreover, since the result accepted from external procedures are carried along with the theorems they go into proving, if we were to prove those results in HOL90, then roughly by Modus Ponens we ought to be able to eliminate them from the hypotheses of any theorem. And in fact we can. This is given to us by the way used_token is introduced. The constant used_token is specified to satisfy

$$\vdash \forall tok\ p\ q.\ p \wedge ((\text{used\_token}\ tok\ p) \Rightarrow q) \Rightarrow q.$$

Constant specification requires us to show that there exists a value that satisfies the given property. In this case, we can use the function $\lambda\ tok\ p\ .\ p$ as our witness. This specification gives us the desired elimination property.

We have the specification of used_token, but how are we to think of it? Intentionally, we would like to think of it as telling for each proposition to which it is applied whether it was correctly verified by the associated external procedure. Unfortunately, that doesn't really match with the extensional view. Extensionally, each proposition is either equal to T or F. Therefore, if used_token proc returns T for any true proposition, then it must return T for all true propositions. Thus, probably the best intentional understanding of used_token proc is that it is the identity function. There is one other extensional possibility for used_token proc which we shall discuss in Sect. 4.

In this second method we saw that we can use use_proc_result in conjunction with various calculators to generate theorems simplifying expressions or perhaps solving for unknowns. It seems unnecessarily confining to require all theorems that make use of such calculations to carry the results of the calculations with them as hypotheses, as opposed to carrying the simpler tag of the first method. Space considerations may render such record-keeping impractical. In which case, we would like to have the same functionality, but with the simpler tagging. This is given to us by the property used for the constant specification of trusted_token, which we failed to give earlier. That specification is

$$\vdash \forall tok\ p\ q.((\text{used\_token } tok\ p) \Rightarrow q) \Rightarrow ((\text{trusted\_token } tok) \Rightarrow q).$$

The witness that makes this a legitimate constant specification of trusted_token is $\lambda\ tok$. F. This specification allows us to replace any hypothesis of the form used_token $tok\ p$ by ones of the form trusted_token tok. To automate this we have the SML function used_hyp_to_trusted_hyp : term -> thm -> thm which implements the derived rule of inference:

$$\frac{[\text{used\_token } tok\ p, a_2, \ldots, a_n] \vdash q}{[\text{trusted\_token } tok, a_2, \ldots, a_n] \vdash q}$$

3 Examples

To illustrate the usefulness of the library add_dec_proc, we have created two examples of its application. As a simple example of how these pieces fit together, we have written a trivial example "decision procedure" called clearly. Given a term tm, clearly will return the term $\forall x_1 \ldots x_m.tm$ where $x_1 \ldots x_m$ are all the free variables in the term. Naturally, this procedure decides nothing. It is used only when the person proving a theorem wants to quit at some level. This can be a useful thing to do in some cases. In addition, we have introduced a token clearly to represent this procedure in HOL90. Given clearly we can then define the rule

```
val clearly_RULE =
    use_proc_result {token = (--'clearly'--),
                     dec_proc = clearly} : term -> thm
```

which is in essence mk_thm but on closed terms instead of sequents, and the tactic

```
val clearly_TAC =
    use_proc_result_TAC {token = (--'clearly'--),
                         dec_proc = use_trust clearly} : tactic
```

which solves any goal. In this form, clearly_TAC can be a quite useful tactic, allowing one to postpone the completion of certain proof obligations indefinitely, while still retaining the ability to discharge them at any time should one happen to actually prove them. We feel that clearly_RULE and clearly_TAC are general enough and useful enough that they have been included as part of the library add_dec_proc.

The second example is a modification of Peter Homeier's Verification Condition Generator for the Sunrise system [4], as included in the contrib library vcg for HOL90. This example is included as a separate file, and depends upon both the add_dec_proc library and the vcg library. The library vcg gives a verification condition generator for a small imperative programming language, Sunrise, with mutually recursive procedures, proving total correctness. This is implemented two ways, one where the verification condition generator has been implemented as conversions and tactics within HOL90, and the other where the basic programs for checking well-formedness and for generating the verification conditions are written in SML, with their results accepted into HOL90 by the use of mk_thm. We shall refer to the second approach as the "fast" approach and the first as the "secure" approach. The second approach is considered unsound in principle, but the algorithms for these two functions were verified as part of the project, and thus in this instance it would be reasonable to assume that the second method is roughly as secure as the method that does all the proof in HOL90. We have rewritten the conversions FAST_WFp_CONV and FAST_vcg_CONV from the fast version so that instead of calling mk_thm, they use use_proc_result. We have then added a derived rule of inference VCG_SIMPLIFY that uses the conversions WFp_CONV and vcg_CONV from the secure version to eliminate the tagged hypotheses giving well-formedness and stating what the verification conditions are (or rather, that they are sufficient). By modifying this work in this manner we make it possible for proofs of program correctness to be done interactively using the fast version, when the human user doesn't want to wait, and then later to clean up to totally verified proofs by doing the well-formedness and vcg results totally automatically after the fact. While this division may not be especially useful for proofs in the Sunrise system, where the verification condition generator has actually been verified, it does illustrate a methodology that can be applied to similar projects where security is critical, but where there is not the time to carry out such a system verification. While in this method the user must still incur the cost of actually proving the well-formedness and vcg results generated by the fast version, it is done so at minimum cost with no reproving required, and it can be done after all interactive parts have been completed, off-line as it were.

It is worth noting that this example also takes full advantage of the additional flexibility of use_proc_result over trust_proc_result. The conversion FAST_WFp_CONV is in essence a decision procedure, and as such could have been implemented using trust_proc_result had we not been interested in eliminating our dependence on its results. However, FAST_vcg_CONV is really a calculation of the verification conditions, which are not known in advance. Therefore, we need use_proc_result to hand back a term telling us what those conditions are.

4 Consistency with the Existing System

The library add_dec_proc is a proper extension of HOL90; it adds two new primitive inference rules trust_proc_result and use_proc_result. The question arises: Why is this a logically sound thing to do? The rules trust_proc_result and use_proc_result may be seen as introducing a family of axioms, all of the form

$$\frac{}{[\text{trusted\_token tok}] \vdash P} \quad \text{or} \quad \frac{}{[\text{used\_token proc } tok] \vdash P}$$

for some constant *tok* and some proposition P. These may all be seen as specific instances of the propositions

$$\forall tok\ P.\text{trusted\_token } tok \Rightarrow P \tag{1}$$
$$\forall tok\ P.\text{used\_token } tok\ P \Rightarrow P. \tag{2}$$

The only other axioms we have about trusted_token and used_token are their specifications:

$$\vdash \forall tok\ p\ q.\ p \wedge ((\text{trusted\_token } tok\ p) \Rightarrow q) \Rightarrow q \tag{3}$$
$$\vdash \forall tok\ p\ q.((\text{used\_token } tok\ p) \Rightarrow q) \Rightarrow ((\text{trusted\_token } tok) \Rightarrow q). \tag{4}$$

The propositions (1), (2), (3) and (4) are all satisfied if trusted_token is defined to be λ *tok* . F and used_token is defined to be $\lambda tok\ prop.\ prop$, i.e., essentially the identity function. We can make these as definitions in HOL90 without any new extensions, and derive the propositions (1), (2), (3) and (4) as theorems. Since any definitional extension to HOL90 is known to be conservative, to see that the extension given in this paper is a conservative extension, it suffices to show that any theorem of the new system is also a theorem in the system given by the definitional extension. A rigorous proof of this is done by induction on the height of the proof tree (given as a sequent style encoding of natural deduction proofs) of a theorem in the new extension. The only cases of interest are the base cases. If we make use of one of the new primitive rules of inference or one of the axioms of constant specification in the new extension, they must be replaced by the derived results in the definitional extension. From here all applications of inference rules translate directly without modification.

Let us consider the possible semantics in HOL90 of trusted_token and used_token. Because of their types, for each token *tok*, there are two possible values for trusted_token *tok* and four possible functions for used_token *tok*. As indicated above, it is consistent with the extended system to interpret trusted_token as λ *tok* . F and used_token as $\lambda tok\ prop.\ prop$. For each token *tok* for which only true results have been returned, it is also possible to interpret trusted_token *tok* as the value T. As soon as a given procedure proc accepts a false result (for either trust_proc_result or use_proc_result), from that point on the only valid interpretation of trusted_token proc is F. Also as indicated above, it is consistent to interpret trusted_token as λ *tok* . T. The other three possibilities are that it maps everything to T, that it maps everything to F, or that it is negation. However, because we have the axiom

$$\vdash \forall tok\ p\ q.\ p \wedge ((\text{used\_token}\ tok\ p) \Rightarrow q) \Rightarrow q$$

we must have that used_token tok T = T. Thus trusted_token tok could be the identity function, or it could map both T and F to T. As long as use_proc_result only returns theorems with conclusions which are true, it is also consistent to interpret it as either of these functions. However, for each procedure proc for which mk_trusted_thm has returned a theorem

$$[\text{used\_tokenproc}\ P] \vdash P$$

where P is provably equal to F, we must have that trusted_tokenproc is the identity function. As long as our decision procedures never return false results, there will remain multiple interpretations (two for each token) of both trusted_token and used_token.

5   Future Work

The library described in the paper is largely untested. The next step is to build a class of decision procedures in SML and hooks through SML to other independent procedures to be used with this library and to carry out realistic examples using them. One way in which we will create the decision procedures in SML will be to choose an existing implementation of some decision procedure, such as a model checker, translate HOL90 terms into the syntax accepted by that implementation, pipe the appropriate string into it, and collect the response. After creating a few such procedures, it may become clear whether there is additional common infrastructure that is desired.

6   Related Work

The methods described in the paper allow results from external sources to be incorporated in HOL90 as theorems, but with tagged hypotheses. In his 1992 HOL conference paper [1], Richard Boulton presented a method of achieving much the same effect by creating and additional datatype of lazy_thm. This was a method external to the logic and required a fair amount of duplication of functions for theorems as functions for lazy theorems. John Harrison went on to use this method in his work coupling HOL with computer algebra systems [3]. The advantage of Richard Boulton's work is that it requires no change to the logic. Our work does require a change to the logic, but is it provably consistent and we feel is actually much more light-weight. It also provides many of the advantages of his system; implementing John Harrison's work should be entirely straightforward in this new method, for example.

In a recent release of Konrad Slind's system HOL98, the core data structure for theorems has been changed to carry tags to support the inclusion of results from external procedures. Once a result is obtained from an external source it will be tagged and the tag will appear in all theorems subsequently derived from the result. This method provides essentially the same functionality as the first method described in this paper. And it suffers the same limitation in its inability to eliminate tags once they have been introduced. Moreover, it carries a greater overhead with it than our first method does, since every theorem must have a tag field, and every step of inference must merge the tag fields of the input theorems, even when those fields are empty. In both versions of our method, no additional overhead is incurred for those theorems whose proofs are done entirely within the system.

In the most recent release of Isabelle, oracles have been added. It appears to use a mechanism quite similar to that of HOL98. We believe that the PVS system has some mechanism, possibly similar to lazy theorems, but we have not seen it formally described in the literature.

Acknowledgements

I would like to thank Amy Felty, Carl Gunter and Davor Obradovic for their helpful discussions on this topic.

References

1. R. J. Boulton. A Lazy Approach to Fully-Expansive Theorem Proving. In *Higher Order Logic Theorem Proving and Its Applications*. North-Holland, 1992.
2. M. J. C. Gordon and T. Melham, *Introduction to HOL*. Cambridge University Press, 1993.
3. J. Harrison and L. Théry. Extending the HOL theorem prover with a Computer Algebra System to Reason about the Reals. In *Higher Order Logic Theorem Proving and Its Applications*. Springer-Verlag, 1993.
4. P. V. Homeier and D. F. Martin. A Mechanically Verified Verification Condition Generator. In *The Computer Journal*, Vol. 38, No. 2, July 1995, pages 131-141.
5. G. J. Holzmann. *Design and Validation of Computer Protocols*. Prentice-Hall Software Series, 1991.
6. K. L. McMillan. *Symbolic Model Checking*. Kluwer Academic Publishers, 1993.
7. S. Owre, S. Rajan, J. Rushby, N. Shankar, and M. Srivas. PVS: Combining specification, proof checking, and model checking. In *Proceedings of CAV'96*, Lecture Notes in Computer Science. Springer Verlag, 1996.
8. L. C. Paulson. The Isabelle Reference Manual. http://www.cl.cam.ac.uk/ Research/HVG/Isabelle/dist/Isabelle98/doc/ref.dvi
9. K. Schneider, R. Kuma, and T. Kropf. Integrating a first-order automatic prover in the HOL environment. In *Proceedings of the 1991 International Tutorial and Workshop on the HOL Theorem Proving System and Its Applications*. IEEE Computer Society Press, 1992.

Formalizing Basic First Order Model Theory

John Harrison

Intel Corporation, EY2-03
5200 NE Elam Young Parkway, Hillsboro, OR 97124, USA
johnh@ichips.intel.com

Abstract. We define the syntax of unsorted first order logic as a HOL datatype and define the semantics of terms and formulas, and hence notions such as validity and satisfiability. We prove formally in HOL some elementary metatheorems such as Compactness, Löwenheim-Skolem and Uniformity, via canonical term models. The proofs are based on those in Kreisel and Krivine's book on model theory, but the HOL formalization raises several interesting issues. Because of the limited nature of type quantification in HOL, many of the theorems are awkard to state or prove in their standard form. Moreover, simple and elegant though the proofs seem, there are surprising difficulties formalizing Skolemization, one of the more intuitively obvious parts. On the other hand, we significantly improve on the original textbook versions of the arguments, proving two of the main theorems together rather than by separate arguments.

1 Introduction

This paper deals with the formalization, in the HOL Light theorem prover, of the basic model theory of first order logic. Our original motivation was that we were writing a textbook on mathematical logic, and wanted to make sure that when presenting some of the major results, we didn't make any slips – hence the desire for machine checking. We took as our model for this part of logic the textbook of Kreisel and Krivine [6], hereinafter referred to as K&K. However, as we shall see, in the process of formalizing the proofs we made some significant improvements to their presentation.

In view of the considerable amount of mathematics that has been formalized, mainly in Mizar [14, 11], it is perhaps hardly noteworthy to formalize yet another fragment. However, we believe that the present work does at least raise a few interesting general points.

- Formalization of syntax constructions involving bound variables has inspired a slew of research; see e.g. Chap. 3 of Pollack [9], or Gordon and Melham [3]. We offer an unusual angle, in that for us, syntax is subordinate to semantics.
- The apparent intuitive difficulty of parts of the proof does not correlate well with the difficulty of the HOL formalization: an apparently straightforward part turns out to be the most difficult. This raises interesting questions over whether the textbook or HOL is at fault.

- As part of the task of formalization, we found improvements to the textbook proof. Though this was an indirect consequence of formalization, resulting from the necessary close reading of the text, it serves as a good example of possible auxiliary benefits.
- We provide a good illustration of how HOL's simplistic type system can be a hindrance in stating results in the most natural way. In particular, care is needed because quantification of type variables happens implicitly at the sequent level, rather than via explicit binding constructs.

HOL Light is our own version of HOL, and while its logical axiomatization, proof tools and even implementation language are somewhat different from other versions, the underlying logic is exactly equivalent to the one described by Gordon and Melham [4]. This is a version of simply typed lambda calculus used as a foundation for classical higher order logic.

2 Syntactic Definitions

We define first order terms in HOL as a free recursive type: a term is either a variable, identified by a numeric code, or else a function symbol, also identified by a number, followed by a possibly empty list of arguments. (We regard nullary functions as individual constants.)

```
term = V num
     | Fn num (term list)
```

Here we have already made two significant choices. First of all, we have restricted ourselves to countable languages, since the function symbols are indexed by N. This restriction is inessential, however; everything that follows extends to any infinite HOL type, given a theorem that for an infinite type α there is an injection $\alpha \times \alpha \to \alpha$, a fairly easy consequence of Zorn's Lemma. The restriction to countable languages was made entirely for convenience, to avoid having to specify types everywhere.

Secondly, we have not made any restrictions on the arities of functions, e.g. that function 6 can only be applied to two arguments. Rather, we really consider a function symbol as identified by a pair consisting of its numerical code and its arity, so in $f_3(x)$ and $f_3(x, y)$, the two functions are different, identified by the pairs $(3, 1)$ and $(3, 2)$ respectively. In fact, we define a function that returns the set of functions, in this sense, that occur in a term:

```
|- (∀v. functions_term (V v) = {}) ∧
   (∀f l. functions_term (Fn f l) =
          (f,LENGTH l) INSERT (LIST_UNION (MAP functions_term l)))
```

where:

```
|- (LIST_UNION [] = {}) ∧
   (LIST_UNION (CONS h t) = h UNION (LIST_UNION t))
```

Next we define formulas; there is a wide choice over which connectives to take as primitive and which as defined. We differ a bit from our textbook model by taking falsity, atoms, implications and universal quantifications as primitive.

```
form = False
     | Atom num (term list)
     | --> form form
     | !! num form
```

Once again, identically-numbered predicates used with different arities are considered different. We now define functions to return the set of functions and predicates in this sense occurring in a formula:

```
|- (functions_form False = {}) ∧
   (functions_form (Atom a l) = LIST_UNION (MAP functions_term l)) ∧
   (functions_form (p --> q) =
       (functions_form p) UNION (functions_form q)) ∧
   (functions_form (!! x p) = functions_form p)

|- (predicates_form False = {}) ∧
   (predicates_form (Atom a l) = {(a,LENGTH l)}) ∧
   (predicates_form (p --> q) =
       (predicates_form p) UNION (predicates_form q)) ∧
   (predicates_form (!! x p) = predicates_form p)
```

It's more convenient to lift these up to the level of sets of formulas, and we pair up the sets of functions and predicates as the so-called *language* of a set of formulas.

```
|- functions fms = UNIONS {functions_form f | f IN fms}

|- predicates fms = UNIONS {predicates_form f | f IN fms}

|- language fms = functions fms, predicates fms
```

Trivially we have then, for a singleton set of formulas:

```
|- language {p} = functions_form p,predicates_form p
```

Other logical constants are defined in a fairly standard way; it doesn't really matter for what follows exactly how this is done. These are respectively negation, truth, disjunction (or), conjunction (and), bi-implication (iff) and existential quantification.

```
|- Not p = p --> False

|- True = Not False

|- p || q = (p --> q) --> q

|- p && q = Not (Not p || Not q)

|- p <-> q = (p --> q) && (q --> p)

|- ?? x p = Not(!!x (Not p))
```

The set of free variables in a term and formula are now defined:

```
|- (∀x. FVT (V x) = {x}) ∧
   (∀f 1. FVT (Fn f 1) = LIST_UNION (MAP FVT 1))

|- (FV False = {}) ∧
   (∀a 1. FV (Atom a 1) = LIST_UNION (MAP FVT 1)) ∧
   (∀p q. FV (p --> q) = FV p UNION FV q) ∧
   (∀x p. FV (!! x p) = FV p DELETE x)
```

We prove various simple consequences of the definition, most importantly, by induction over the syntax of terms and formulas, that these always give finite sets, e.g.

```
|- ∀p. FINITE(FV p)
```

The most complex syntactic definition is of substitution. We have chosen a 'name-carrying' formalization of syntax, rather than indexing bound variables using some scheme following de Bruijn [1]. The latter is usually preferred when formalizing logical syntax precisely because substitution is simpler to define correctly. (Indeed, it is foreshadowed in the tradition – see Prawitz [10] for example – of distinguishing between [bound] variables and [free] parameters.) Our decision to stick with name-carrying terms was partly in order to stay closer to intuition, and as we shall see, defining substitution so that it renames variables appropriately is not too difficult. In some sense, things are easier for us since we always have semantics (to be defined later) as a check. By contrast, in formalizing, say, beta reduction in lambda-calculus, the syntax is the primary object of investigation and substitution must be defined in a way that is correct and intuitively clear or the whole exercise loses its point.

In order to define renaming substitution as a clean structural recursion over terms, it's necessary to define multiple substitutions rather than single ones [13]. This is because for something like $(\forall x.\ P(x) \Rightarrow P(y))[x/y]$ we need recursively to perform two substitutions on the body of the quantifier, one to substitute for y and one to rename the variable x. Therefore we take multiple parallel substitution as primitive. (Multiple serial substitution would also be acceptable, since by construction the substitutions in renaming clauses never interfere, but this seems less intuitive.) We represent substitutions simply as functions : `num->term`, mapping each variable index to the term to be substituted for that variable. (The identity substitution is therefore the type constructor for variable terms, V.) Although in practice we only need substitutions that are nontrivial (i.e. differ from V) only for finitely many arguments, nothing seems to be gained by imposing this restriction generally. Substitution at the term level is simple:

```
|- (∀x. termsubst v (V x) = v(x)) ∧
   (∀f l. termsubst v (Fn f l) = Fn f (MAP (termsubst v) l))
```

It's when we come to formulas that the complexities of renaming arise. We need to see if a variable in the substituted body would become captured by the bound variable in a universal quantifier, and if so, rename the bound variable appropriately.

```
|- (formsubst v False = False) ∧
   (formsubst v (Atom p l) = Atom p (MAP (termsubst v) l)) ∧
   (formsubst v (q --> r) = (formsubst v q --> formsubst v r)) ∧
   (formsubst v (!!x q) =
        let v' = valmod (x,V x) v in
        let z = if ∃y. y IN FV(!!x q) ∧ x IN FVT(v'(y))
                then VARIANT(FV(formsubst v' q)) else x in
        !!z (formsubst (valmod (x,V(z)) v) q))
```

Here the function valmod modifies a substitution, or more generally any function, as follows:

```
|- valmod (x,a) v = λy. if y = x then a else v y
```

while VARIANT picks a variable not in a given set. It is defined constructively over finite sets to find the maximum free variable in the set and add one to it. An important theorem gives the free variables in a substituted formula.

```
|- FV(formsubst i p) = {x | ∃y. y IN FV(p) ∧ x IN FVT(i y)}
```

while another states that only variables free in the formula are relevant to the outcome of performing a substitution.

```
|- (∀x. x IN (FV p) ⇒ (v'(x) = v(x)))
   ⇒ (formsubst v' p = formsubst v p)
```

3   Semantic Definitions

The above syntactic definitions are really only a tool; we are primarily interested in semantics. The first step is to define the notion of an interpretation in HOL:

it is simply a triple consisting of a domain, interpretations for the function symbols and interpretations for the relation symbols. The three parts of a triple are selected by the HOL functions Dom, Fun and Pred respectively. The truth or falsity of a formula, or more generally the element of an interpretation's domain selected by a term, depends in general not just on the interpretation M but also on a valuation of free variables v. Only at the top level, so to speak, if the formula has no free variables, does the valuation cease to play a role. Accordingly the valuations of terms and formulas are defined w.r.t. an interpretation and a valuation:

```
|- (∀x. termval M v (V x) = v(x)) ∧
   (∀f l. termval M v (Fn f l) = Fun(M) f (MAP (termval M v) l))

|- (holds M v False = F) ∧
   (∀a l. holds M v (Atom a l) = Pred(M) a (MAP (termval M v) l)) ∧
   (∀p q. holds M v (p --> q) = holds M v p ⇒ holds M v q) ∧
   (∀x p. holds M v (!! x p) =
                  ∀a. a IN Dom(M) ⇒ holds M (valmod (x,a) v) p)
```

Once again, whether a formula holds depends only on the valuation of the free variables:

```
|- (∀x. x IN (FV p) ⇒ (v'(x) = v(x))) ⇒ (holds M v' p = holds M v p)
```

and so in particular for a formula with no free variables, v plays no role. Analogously, the interpretation of function symbols given by the interpretation is only important for the language of the formula concerned:

```
|- (Dom(M) = Dom(M')) ∧
   (∀P zs. Pred(M) P zs = Pred(M') P zs) ∧
   (∀f zs. (f,LENGTH zs) IN functions_form p
           ⇒ (Fun(M) f zs = Fun(M') f zs))
   ⇒ ∀v. holds M v p = holds M' v p
```

One of the main theorems relates substitution and holding in an interpretation. The proof is quite straightforward, though involves a slightly messy case analysis. Its intuitive plausibility is good evidence that our definition of substitution is satisfactory, and, indeed, its later usefulness means that from now on we can largely forget the details of how substitution was defined.

```
|- holds M v (formsubst i p) = holds M (termval M v o i) p
```

We have not yet imposed any restrictions on interpretations. For some purposes, like the above theorems, they are not needed, and it seems appropriate not to restrict their generality. But we often need to assume that the domain of an interpretation is nonempty; this is generally done in the logical literature, though a few authors like Johnstone [5] try to avoid it. More importantly, the interpretations of functions must indeed be functions back into the appropriate domain. We abbreviate this by saying that a triple is an interpretation of a particular language, and define it in HOL as follows:

```
|- interpretation (fns,preds) M =
    ∀f l. (f,LENGTH l) IN fns ∧ FORALL (λx. x IN Dom(M)) l
        ⇒ (Fun(M) f l) IN Dom(M)
```

Similarly, we are only really interested in valuations that map into the domain of an interpretation, and so we define:

```
|- valuation(M) v = ∀x. v(x) IN Dom(M)
```

We also define what it means for an interpretation to satisfy (be a model of) a set of formulas:

```
|- M satisfies fms = ∀v p. valuation(M) v ∧ p IN fms ⇒ holds M v p
```

We might wish to define satisfiability as:

```
satisfiable fms = ∃M. M satisfies fms
```

However such a definition cannot be made with the appropriate type variable on the right-hand side; one can only define a notion of being satisfiable in models of a certain type. This is ultimately unimportant because we will prove in what follows that a formula is satisfiable iff it is satisfiable over the natural numbers (the Löwenheim-Skolem theorem). In any case, even in systems like ZF set theory which allow us to state the required quantification directly, we must in general take care that it corresponds to the intuitive notion. For second order logic, the identification of validity in a ZF-like cumulative set theory with a more general notion ('Kreisel's principle') is known to be a strong assumption, entailing higher order reflection principles [12].

4   Proofs of the Metatheorems

The proofs of the metatheorems given by K&K are based on several steps:

- Compactness for the propositional subsystem
- Prenex normal form and Skolem normal form.
- Use of canonical models

We will consider each of these steps separately.

4.1 Propositional Logic

We define the class of quantifier-free formulas by recursion over the structure of formulas.

```
|- (qfree False = T) ∧
   (qfree (Atom n l) = T) ∧
   (qfree (p --> q) = qfree p ∧ qfree q) ∧
   (qfree (!!x p) = F)
```

If a formula is quantifier-free, we can look at it not as a first order formula based on the appropriate language, but rather as a formula of propositional logic based on atomic first order formulas. In this case, we have a separate notion of holding in a valuation, which in this context is a function of type `term->bool` indicating whether each atom is considered true or false.

```
|- (pholds v False = F) ∧
   (pholds v (Atom p l) = v (Atom p l)) ∧
   (pholds v (q --> r) = pholds v q ⇒ pholds v r) ∧
   (pholds v (!!x q) = v (!!x q))
```

The last clause turns out to be irrelevant to the later proofs, since the function `pholds` is only used for quantifier-free formulas. We chose to define it this way, treating quantified formulas as atoms, with the vague idea of later formalizing a first order proof system given by Enderton [2], which has the nice feature that a formula is valid iff it follows propositionally from the (infinite) set of axioms, interpreting quantified formulas as atomic. However at time of writing we haven't tackled this.

The key theorem for the propositional subsystem is compactness, which states that if all finite subsets of a set of (quantifier-free) formulas are propositionally satisfiable, then so is the set as a whole.

```
|- (∀p. p IN A ⇒ qfree p) ∧
   (∀B. FINITE(B) ∧ B SUBSET A ⇒ ∃d. ∀r. r IN B ⇒ pholds(d) r)
   ⇒ ∃d. ∀r. r IN A ⇒ pholds(d) r
```

The proof is a fairly routine application of Zorn's Lemma, already proved in HOL from the primitive form of the Axiom of Choice. We start by defining the notions of propositional satisfiability and finite satisfiability:

```
|- psatisfiable s = ∃v. ∀p. p IN s ⇒ pholds v p

|- finsat s = ∀t. t SUBSET s ∧ FINITE(t) ⇒ psatisfiable t
```

We can now rephrase compactness as: if a set is finitely propositionally satisfiable, and contains only quantifier-free formulas, then it is propositionally satisfiable. We use Zorn's Lemma to show that every finitely satisfiable set can be extended to a maximal one:

```
|- finsat(A) ⇒ ∃B. A SUBSET B ∧ finsat(B) ∧
              ∀C. B SUBSET C ∧ finsat(C) ⇒ (C = B)
```

The use of Zorn's Lemma is unnecessary here; since the set of primitive propositions is countable, we can construct the maximal set by recursion: just enumerate the formulas (ψ_n) and then add either ψ_n or $\neg\psi_n$ to the starting set at each stage; it's easy to see this preserves finite satisfiability. However we chose to use a proof that would also work if we lifted the restriction to countable languages. K&K assert that this sort of step-by-step proof also works for any wellordered set of primitive propositions, but it requires nontrivial changes to work over a non-discrete order.

Now we can define a valuation based on the maximal finitely satisfiable set. This works because the set has the following closure properties:

```
|- finsat(B) ∧ (∀C. B SUBSET C ∧ finsat(C) ⇒ (C = B))
   ⇒ ¬(False IN B)

|- finsat(B) ∧ (∀C. B SUBSET C ∧ finsat(C) ⇒ (C = B))
   ⇒ ∀p q. (p --> q) IN B = p IN B ⇒ q IN B
```

Because of the HOL identification of sets and predicates, the maximal finitely consistent set is a satisfying valuation for itself, and *a fortiori*, for the starting set. Hence the compactness theorem is established.

4.2 Normal Forms

The next stage is to show that each formula has a prenex normal form and a (purely universal) Skolem normal form. We first define, inductively, the appropriate syntactic classes:

```
|- (∀p. qfree p ⇒ prenex p) ∧
   (∀x p. prenex p ⇒ prenex (!!x p)) ∧
   (∀x p. prenex p ⇒ prenex (??x p))

|- (∀p. qfree p ⇒ universal p) ∧
   (∀x p. universal p ⇒ universal (!!x p))
```

The goal is to prove that every formula has a logically equivalent prenex form, and also a purely universal Skolem normal form that, while not logically equivalent, is satisfiable iff the original formula is. We define constructive procedures for calculating these forms, that can be executed by conditional rewriting. This is not so much because such concreteness seems useful – though it can hardly be bad – but because otherwise we get tripped up by type quantification. Logical equivalence involves a quantification over all models with arbitrary domain types, so if we express these theorems as existence assertions:

$$\forall p.\, \exists q.\, \forall M : (\alpha) interpretation.\ E[M, p, q]$$

we have the problem that we have really stated:

$$\forall \alpha. \forall p. \exists q. \forall M : (\alpha)interpretation.\ E[M, p, q]$$

rather than

$$\forall p. \exists q. \forall \alpha. \forall M : (\alpha)interpretation.\ E[M, p, q]$$

This means that according to the theorem, the prenex form q might depend on the type α! This problem no longer arises if instead we prove:

$$\forall p. \forall M : (\alpha)interpretation.\ E[M, p, Prenex(p)]$$

Prenexing and Skolemization can't quite be defined as primitive recursions over the structure of formulas. For example it can happen that we need to rename variables, so we define a function on a formula in terms of *a substitution instance of* one of its parts. It's easier, then, to argue by wellfounded induction on the size of a formula (as do K&K), which we define as:

```
|- (size False = 1) ∧
   (size (Atom p l) = 1) ∧
   (size (q --> r) = size q + size r) ∧
   (size (!!x q) = 1 + size q)
```

We can define the recursive functions we want by using this, together with the fact that the formulas !!x p and ??y q are always distinct. (This needs to be proved since the latter is not a primitive notion – for example it isn't true that Not p and ??y q are always distinct.) We use the fact that substitution doesn't change the size of a formula, an easy structural induction:

```
|- size (formsubst i p) = size p
```

To prenex an arbitrary formula, we need to be able to prenex falsity, atoms, implications and universal quantifications, for then the prenexability of an arbitrary formula follows by structural induction. Falsity and atoms are trivial; they are already prenex. Universal quantifiers are also easy: just prenex the body. This leaves implication as the only nontrivial case, with the overall definition of the prenexing procedure being:

```
|- (Prenex False = False) ∧
   (Prenex (Atom a l) = Atom a l) ∧
   (Prenex (p --> q) = Prenex_left (Prenex p) (Prenex q)) ∧
   (Prenex (!!x p) = !!x (Prenex p))
```

This requires the function Prenex_left, which is supposed to prenex an implication assuming that its antecedent and consequent are already prenex. This is its turn is defined by the following recursion equations, shown to be admissible as indicated above:

```
|- (∀p x q. Prenex_left (!!x q) p =
              let y = VARIANT(FV(!!x q) UNION FV(p)) in
              ??y (Prenex_left (formsubst (valmod (x,V y) V) q) p)) ∧
   (∀p x q. Prenex_left (??x q) p =
              let y = VARIANT(FV(??x q) UNION FV(p)) in
              !!y (Prenex_left (formsubst (valmod (x,V y) V) q) p)) ∧
   (∀p q. qfree q ⇒ (Prenex_left q p = Prenex_right q p))
```

Note that the intimidating-looking formsubst (valmod (x,V y) V) simply substitutes variable y for variable x, leaving other variables unchanged. (Perhaps it would be worth defining a shorter form for this special case.) Apart from performing variable renaming, this simply pulls the quantifiers in the consequent outwards one by one. When the consequent is quantifier-free, an analogous function Prenex_right is called to do likewise for the antecedent: It is now straightforward to prove successively that the three prenexing functions Prenex_right, Prenex_left and Prenex do the right thing in the appropriate situation, most notably:

```
|- prenex(Prenex p) ∧
   (FV(Prenex p) = FV(p)) ∧
   (language {Prenex p} = language {p}) ∧
   ∀M v. ¬(Dom M = EMPTY) ⇒ (holds M v (Prenex p) = holds M v p)
```

This says that the result of applying Prenex to a formula p is indeed prenex, has the same language and free variables as p and is logically equivalent to it. Note that for the last part we need to assume nonemptiness of the domain. Prenex normal forms do not in general exist without this restriction, since any prenex formula containing quantifiers is either trivially true or false in an empty domain, regardless of the valuation.

Next we come to Skolem normal forms. The idea here is to replace a formula $\exists y. P[x_1, \ldots, x_n, y]$ with free variables $x_1, \ldots, x_n$ by $P[x_1, \ldots, x_n, f(x_1, \ldots, x_n)]$ where f is a fresh function symbol, not originally appearing in P. While not logically equivalent in general, the Skolemized form implies the original, while any model of the original can be extended to a model of the Skolemized form by picking the appropriate interpretation of f, or more precisely in our framework, of (f, n). The starting point is a HOL definition of just this procedure:

```
|- Skolem1 f x p =
      formsubst (valmod (x,Fn f (MAP V (list_of_set(FV(??x p))))) V) p
```

Here list_of_set, not surprisingly, converts a finite set to a list. It's defined as an inverse of the operation of converting a list to a set:

```
|- (set_of_list [] = {}) ∧
   (set_of_list (CONS h t) = h INSERT (set_of_list t))

|- list_of_set s = εl. (set_of_list l = s) ∧ (LENGTH l = CARD s)
```

We're mainly interested in Skolemizing a formula already in prenex form, so in the main theorem about Skolem1, we make this assumption. The derivation of the main theorem is a bit lengthy, with lots of details to get right, but intuitively obvious. The most difficult part is showing how to extend a model of the existing formula to a model of the Skolemized form. We pick an appropriate denotation of the new function symbol, namely:

```
λg zs. if (g = f) ∧ (LENGTH zs = CARD(FV(??x p)))
       then εa. a IN Dom(M) ∧
                holds M
                 (valmod (x,a)
                   (ITLIST valmod
                     (MAP2 (λx a. (x,a)) (list_of_set(FV(??x p))) zs)
                     (λz. εc. c IN Dom(M)))) p
       else Fun(M) g zs
```

where:

```
|- (MAP2 f [] [] = []) ∧
   (MAP2 f (CONS h1 t1) (CONS h2 t2) = CONS (f h1 h2) (MAP2 f t1 t2))

|- (ITLIST f [] b = b) ∧
   (ITLIST f (CONS h t) b = f h (ITLIST f t b))
```

The definition looks complicated, but corresponds to intuition. We are defining the interpretation of function g on argument (list) zs. If it isn't the new function, f with the right arity, then we just take the denotation given by M, i.e. we don't change the interpretation of other functions. Otherwise, we have that there exists some a satisfying (the interpretation of) p; we make the above definition to correspond to unfolding the definition of validity in this case. The valuation constructed maps each free variable – which is an argument of the Skolem function – to the appropriate object of the model.

However, we want to apply Skolemization repeatedly to get rid of all existential quantifiers, and moreover, for later use we need to be able to apply it to a set of formulas 'in parallel'. K&K (p. 23) say 'we assume that the function letters added to $\mathcal{L}(\mathcal{E})$ for different formulas F are different'. However it takes quite a bit of work to make sure of this. Roughly speaking, starting from a set S of formulas, we just need to take an additional set of distinct function symbols with size equal to the number of existential quantifiers in S. In something like ZF set theory this presents no serious difficulties. It's more awkward in HOL since we can only add function symbols from the same underlying type that was used originally, at present :num. It's perfectly possible that the original set of formulas included every possible function symbol, leaving us no more to add. So we can't literally start with exactly the same set of function symbols. First we need to map them into a type with room for additions. In fact we use the same type :num starting with the following injective pairing function (we'll write $< x, y >$ informally instead of NUMPAIR x y)

```
|- NUMPAIR x y = (2 EXP x) * (2 * y + 1)
```

and the corresponding destructors

```
|- NUMFST(NUMPAIR x y) = x

|- NUMSND(NUMPAIR x y) = y
```

A similar approach works for any infinite type since one can define an injective pairing. Now we take a formula p and shift up all the function symbols from (k, n) to $(< 0, k >, n)$.

```
|- (bumpterm (V x) = V x) ∧
   (bumpterm (Fn k l) = Fn (NUMPAIR 0 k) (MAP bumpterm l))

|- (bumpform False = False) ∧
   (bumpform (Atom p l) = Atom p (MAP bumpterm l)) ∧
   (bumpform (q --> r) = bumpform q --> bumpform r) ∧
   (bumpform (!!x r) = !!x (bumpform r))
```

Obviously we can make a corresponding change in the interpretation:

```
|- bumpmod(M) = Dom(M),(λk zs. Fun(M) (NUMSND k) zs),Pred(M)
```

so that

```
|- holds M v (bumpform p) = holds (unbumpmod M) v p
```

Now we have all function symbols of the form $(< m + 1, k >, n)$ to use as Skolem functions. Using NUMPAIR, we define a 'Gödel numbering' of formulas, mapping a formula p to a number $\ulcorner p \urcorner$, written in HOL as num_of_form. Now we use $(< 1 + \ulcorner p \urcorner, k >, n)$ for the kth Skolem function (with arity n) used in Skolemizing a formula p. We will not show the HOL statement of the theorem (20 lines), but it says that the Skolemized version of a formula is universal, with the same free variables and a language only changed by adding the appropriate Skolem functions, that any model of a formula extends to a model of its Skolemized form, and that the Skolemized form logically implies the original. From this we distil the key fact needed later: a set of formulas is satisfiable iff the Skolemized form is. We add a final pass to strip off all the universal variables:

```
|- (specialize False = False) ∧
   (specialize (Atom p l) = Atom p l) ∧
   (specialize (q --> r) = q --> r) ∧
   (specialize (!!x r) = specialize r)

|- SKOLEM p = specialize(SKOLEMIZE p)
```

and the theorem looks like this:

```
|- (∃M. ¬(Dom M :A->bool = EMPTY) ∧
        interpretation (language s) M ∧ M satisfies s) =
   (∃M. ¬(Dom M :A->bool = EMPTY) ∧
        interpretation (language {SKOLEM p | p IN s}) M ∧
        M satisfies {SKOLEM p | p IN s})
```

4.3   Canonical Models

Thanks to Skolemization, we can for many purposes restrict ourselves to considering quantifier-free formulas. In this case, they can also be treated as formulas of propositional logic, and the relation between these two views is central to what follows. First of all, given an interpretation M and valuation v we can choose a corresponding propositional valuation:

```
|- prop_of_model M v (Atom p l) = holds M v (Atom p l)
```

'corresponding' in the following precise sense:

```
|- qfree(p) ⇒ (pholds (prop of model M v) p = holds M v p)
```

That is, a quantifier-free formula holds in a given M and v iff it holds as a formula of propositional logic under valuation prop_of_model M v. Conversely, given a propositional valuation, we can find a corresponding first order interpretation and valuation. We are at liberty to interpret the atomic formulas to match the required propositional valuation, provided that the interpretation of function symbols is such that the interpretation cannot map distinct terms to identical objects of the domain. There are plenty of ways of avoiding this, the simplest being to take as the domain (a suitable subset of) the set of terms, and interpret function symbols 'as themselves', i.e.

```
|- canon_of_prop L = terms(FST L),Fn,λp l. d(Atom p l)
```

There is some freedom over how to choose the domain of the model. We take the set of all terms restricted to a certain first order language L, which is defined inductively by:

```
|- (∀x. terms fns (V x)) ∧
   (∀f l. (f,LENGTH l) IN fns ∧ FORALL (terms fns) l
          ⇒ terms fns (Fn f l))
```

In general we say that an interpretation is a *canonical* interpretation of a language if the domain and interpretations of function symbols are defined as in the above particular case:

```
|- canonical L M = (Dom M = terms (FST L)) ∧ (∀f. Fun(M) f = Fn f)
```

Under the identity valuation V, terms are literally interpreted as themselves, and so canon_of_prop does indeed work as hoped, i.e.

```
|- qfree p ⇒ (holds (canon_of_prop L d) V p = pholds d p)
```

In particular, the theorem about prop_of_model tells us that a propositional tautology is first order valid in all interpretations, while this one tells us that if a formula holds in all (or even just all canonical) interpretations, then it is a propositional tautology.

```
|- qfree(p) ∧ (∀d. pholds d p) ⇒ ∀M v. holds M v p

|- qfree(p) ∧ (∀C v. canonical(language {p}) C ⇒ holds C v p)
   ⇒ ∀d. pholds d p
```

This extends to an arbitrary set of formulas. However none of this works if we consider not validity, but satisfiability. If a formula is first order satisfiable it is propositionally satisfiable:

```
|- (∀p. p IN s ⇒ qfree p) ∧ M satisfies s ∧ valuation(M) v
   ⇒ (prop_of_model M v) psatisfies s
```

But if it's propositionally satisfiable, we only know that it is satisfiable *under the identity valuation*, not more generally. For example, the formula $P(x) \land \neg P(y)$ is propositionally satisfiable but not first order satisfiable. However, it's easy to prove a slight variant of the second theorem:

```
|- qfree p
   ⇒ (holds (canon_of_prop L d) v p = pholds d (formsubst v p))
```

This tells us that a formula is first order satisfiable iff all its substitution instances (in the appropriate language) are propositionally satisfiable:

```
|- (∀p. p IN s ⇒ qfree p) ∧
   d psatisfies {formsubst v p | p IN s ∧ ∀x. v x IN terms(FST L)}
   ⇒ (canon_of_prop L d) satisfies s
```

Moreover, note that we actually have something a bit stronger: if all substitution instances are propositionally satisfiable, then it has a *canonical* first order model. This fact, not isolated by K&K but hinted at in their proof of the Compactness theorem, is the key to getting the main metatheorems. First let us note that an interpretation satisfies all substitution instances of a set of formulas w.r.t. an arbitrary language iff it satisfies the set itself.

```
|- interpretation(language t) M ∧
   ⇒ (M satisfies
       {formsubst i p | p IN s ∧ ∀x. i x IN terms(FST(language t))} =
       M satisfies s)
```

Now we get a simple proof of the Compactness and Löwenheim-Skolem theorems together, whereas K&K establish them by separate arguments. If all finite subsets of a set of quantifier-free formulas have a model then the set as a whole has a (canonical) model:

```
|- (∀p. p IN s ⇒ qfree p) ∧
   (∀t. FINITE t ∧ t SUBSET s
        ⇒ ∃M. interpretation(language ss) M ∧
              ¬(Dom(M) = EMPTY) ∧ M satisfies t)
   ⇒ ∃C. interpretation (language ss) C ∧
         canonical (language ss) C ∧ C satisfies s
```

Once again we have a certain liberty over the language ss. Note that all the models of finite subsets are based on a particular type – HOL forces us to make such a restriction. However, precisely because we have as a corollary that every set of formulas that has a model has a canonical model, this doesn't amount to a genuine weakening of the theorem as normally stated. Now we can use Skolemization to lift this theorem to the class of all formulas, not just quantifier-free ones. We reason as follows. If all finite subsets T of S are satisfiable, then so are the Skolemized forms T^*, and so all finite subsets of S^*, which must be contained in such a set. By the above theorem, S^* has a canonical model, and this is also a model of S. This last step isn't quite true in our formalization; it's really a model of the modified form of S with the function symbols shifted. So when we reverse the transition, the model isn't actually canonical. We could have modified the construction of the canonical model appropriately to make this work, but it doesn't seem worth it: the interesting thing about the model is really that it's countable.

We separate out the fact that every set of formulas that has a model has a model with domain a subset of the set of terms, simply using the fact that if a set is satisfiable, so are all finite subsets of it. By applying the Gödel numbering on terms used earlier, we can map the model into the natural numbers and obtain the usual form of the Löwenheim-Skolem theorem.

```
|- interpretation (language s) M ∧
   ¬(Dom M :A->bool = EMPTY) ∧
   M satisfies s
   ⇒ ∃N. interpretation (language s) N ∧
         ¬(Dom N :num->bool = EMPTY) ∧ N satisfies s
```

Finally, using the same lemmas about substitution instances, we easily obtain the Uniformity (aka Skolem-Gödel-Herbrand) theorem, i.e. that if an purely existential term is provable, some disjunction of substitution instances of the body is also provable, or equivalently, is a propositional tautology. The reasoning is straightforward; we'll sketch it with one variable for clarity. If $\exists x.\ p$ is valid then $\forall x.\ \neg p$ is unsatisfiable. Hence the set of all substitution instances $\neg p[t/x]$ is propositionally unsatisfiable; by propositional compactness, so is some finite subset, and hence a finite conjunction $\neg p[t_1/x] \wedge \cdots \wedge \neg p[t_n/x]$. But this means that the negation $p[t_1/x] \vee \cdots \vee p[t_n/x]$ is a propositional tautology and first order valid. In HOL we prove the full theorem in this form:

```
|- qfree p ∧ (∀C v. ¬(Dom C = EMPTY) ∧ valuation C v
                ⇒ holds C v (ITLIST ?? xs p))
   ⇒ ∃is. (∀i x. MEM i is ⇒ terms (FST (language {p})) (i x)) ∧
          (∀d. pholds d
                (ITLIST (||) (MAP (λi. formsubst i p) is) False))
```

The iterated uses of quantifiers and disjunctions are expressed using the standard list operation ITLIST defined earlier.

5 Related Work

Most related work in theorem provers is more heavily syntactic, dealing with proof theory. However, Persson [8] formalizes in the ALF prover a constructive completeness proof for intuitionistic logic w.r.t. models based on formal topology.

6 Conclusions

Our original goal has been achieved: we have machine-checked the proofs of the theorems given here, and have significantly improved the original proofs. While applications weren't at the front of our mind, we have since used the above work as the basis of a construction of the hyperreals. First we extended the Compactness theorem to first logic with equality (once more following K&K). This means restricting ourselves to *normal* models where binary predicate 0 is interpreted as equality. Then we used this to show that there is a model of the set of all first order statements true in the reals which also has infinite elements. This could be used to give a foundation for theorem proving in nonstandard analysis, though we haven't pursued that.

Our paper can be read as strong support for adding first-class type quantifiers to HOL, as proposed by Melham [7]. More generally, though, types make little positive contributions in this area, bearing out the commonplace feeling that types tend to become a hindrance in more abstract parts of mathematics.

Just whether the awkwardness of choosing Skolem functions indicates a failure in HOL (logic or system) or a genuine gap in K&K is a matter of opinion. Certainly, it's quite intuitive that one can pick the Skolem functions independently, but it's interesting that the reasoning we did almost duplicates the kind of constructions in Henkin-style completeness proofs [2]. These tend to look ugly because one needs to add constants to the language (to act as 'witnesses' for existential assertions), but this yields new existential formulas so the procedure needs to be iterated. The K&K proofs avoid this nicely by Skolemizing once and for all. Yet when doing this, we still need to pay attention to the same kinds of issues.

References

1. N. G. de Bruijn. Lambda calculus notation with nameless dummies, a tool for automatic formula manipulation, with application to the Church-Rosser theorem. *Indagationes Mathematicae*, **34**, 381–392, 1972.
2. H. B. Enderton. *A Mathematical Introduction to Logic*. Academic Press, 1972.
3. A. D. Gordon and T. Melham. Five axioms of alpha-conversion. In J. von Wright, J. Grundy, and J. Harrison (eds.), *Theorem Proving in Higher Order Logics: 9th International Conference, TPHOLs'96*, Volume 1125 of *Lecture Notes in Computer Science*, Turku, Finland, pp. 173–190. Springer-Verlag, 1996.
4. M. J. C. Gordon and T. F. Melham. *Introduction to HOL: A theorem proving environment for higher order logic*. Cambridge University Press, 1993.
5. P. T. Johnstone. *Notes on Logic and Set Theory*. Cambridge University Press, 1987.
6. G. Kreisel and J.-L. Krivine. *Elements of mathematical logic: model theory* (Revised second ed.). Studies in Logic and the Foundations of Mathematics. North-Holland, 1971. First edition 1967. Translation of the French 'Eléments de logique mathématique, théorie des modeles' published by Dunod, Paris in 1964.
7. T. F. Melham. The HOL logic extended with quantification over type variables. In L. J. M. Claesen. and M. J. C. Gordon. (eds.), *Proceedings of the IFIP TC10/WG10.2 International Workshop on Higher Order Logic Theorem Proving and its Applications*, Volume A-20 of *IFIP Transactions A: Computer Science and Technology*, IMEC, Leuven, Belgium, pp. 3–18. North-Holland, 1992.
8. H. Persson. *Constructive Completeness of Intuitionistic Predicate Logic: A Formalisation in Type Theory*. Licentiate thesis, Department of Computing Science, Chalmers University of Technology and University of Göteborg, Sweden, 1996.
9. R. Pollack. *The theory of LEGO: A Proof Checker for the Extended Calculus of Constructions*. Ph. D. thesis, University of Edinburgh, 1994.
10. D. Prawitz. *Natural deduction; a proof-theoretical study*, Volume 3 of *Stockholm Studies in Philosophy*. Almqvist and Wiksells, 1965.
11. P. Rudnicki. An overview of the MIZAR project, 1992. Available by anonymous FTP from menaik.cs.ualberta.ca as pub/Mizar/Mizar_Over.tar.Z.
12. S. Shapiro. *Foundations without Foundationalism: A case for second-order logic*. Number 17 in Oxford Logic Guides. Clarendon Press, 1991.
13. A. Stoughton. Substitution revisited. *Theoretical Computer Science*, **17**, 317–325, 1988.
14. A. Trybulec. The Mizar-QC/6000 logic information language. *ALLC Bulletin (Association for Literary and Linguistic Computing)*, **6**, 136–140, 1978.

Formalizing Dijkstra

John Harrison

Intel Corporation, EY2-03
5200 NE Elam Young Parkway, Hillsboro, OR 97124, USA
johnh@ichips.intel.com

Abstract. We present a HOL formalization of the foundational parts of Dijkstra's classic monograph "A Discipline of Programming". While embedding programming language semantics in theorem provers is hardly new, this particular undertaking raises several interesting questions, and perhaps makes an interesting supplement to the monograph. Moreover, the failure of HOL's first order proof tactic to prove one 'theorem' indicates a technical error in the book.

0   A Discipline of Programming

Dijkstra's "A Discipline of Programming" [4] is widely, and we think rightly, regarded as a classic. As he describes it, the original intention was to present some algorithms, emphasizing the process of discovery leading to them rather than giving them as cut-and-dried results. However, Dijkstra also wished to present the programs using more mathematical rigour than is the norm. The book emphasizes a view of a program as an abstract mathematical object, whose runnability on a machine is, so to speak, a fortunate accident:

> Historically speaking ... the fact that programming languages could be used as a vehicle for instructing existing automatic computers ... has for a long time been regarded as their most important property. ... I view a programming language primarily as a vehicle for the description of (potentially highly sophisticated) abstract mechanisms. [pp. 8–9]

Dijkstra's main technical innovation, covered in depth for the first time in this book, is the use of predicate transformers to give the semantics of programs. Predicate transformer semantics is quite convenient for formal correctness proofs, since it has a direct relationship with the satisfaction of appropriate input-output conditions. Moreover, it turned out [1] that one could introduce predicate transformers not implementable as code, and use these as stepping stones in formal program derivations, giving a natural formalization of informal top-down design methods.

Dijkstra was one of the earliest and strongest advocates of formal correctness proofs of programs rather than extensive testing. Nowadays this point of view is increasingly having a practical impact, with major hardware companies pursuing formal verification. But for a long time Dijkstra must have felt like a prophet crying in the wilderness.

As I have now said many times and written in many places: program testing can be quite effective for showing the presence of bugs, but is hopelessly inadequate for showing their absence. [p. 20]

These points of view must lie behind flourishes such as:

None of the programs in this monograph, needless to say, has been tested on a machine. [p. xvi]

In the light of this comment, it seemed interesting to check his proofs by machine! While Dijkstra [7] attacked the anti-verification polemic of DeMillo, Lipton, and Perlis [2] as a 'political pamphlet from the Middle Ages', he accepted that long tedious proofs are inadequate, and that 'communication between mathematicians is an essential part of our culture'. Moreover Dijkstra [5] elsewhere seems to oppose the idea of checking proofs by computer:

To the idea that proofs are so boring that we cannot rely upon them unless they are checked mechanically I have philosophical objections, for I consider mathematical proofs as a reflection of my understanding and 'understanding' is something we cannot delegate, either to another person or to a machine.

Formalizing programming languages inside theorem provers has become a major research topic. Our work largely follows the classic paper by Gordon [9], and doesn't pretend to offer any major technical advances, but we think that in combination with an analysis of Dijkstra's book it raises a few interesting issues.

1   Formalization of States

A fundamental concept throughout the book, and imperative programming generally, is the notion of a *state*. Dijkstra devotes all of Chap. 2 to a gentle and rather non-operational introduction to the concept. To fall short of his ideal somewhat, we may briefly describe the state as a mapping that given a particular point during execution returns the values of all the program variables at that point.

For the moment, we will not concern ourselves with how states are represented and how variables as rvalues or lvalues consult or modify the state, nor how variables are declared or scoped – this is discussed much later, as in Dijkstra's monograph where it is delayed until Chap. 10. For all the basic semantics and program command definitions, we can think of the state as simply some arbitrary type, and we normally use the HOL type variable : S.

In what follows, predicates over states, or equivalently sets of states, are used incessantly.[1] One often wants to say that for example 'P and Q both hold in state s'. This isn't the same as $P \wedge Q$, but rather $P(s) \wedge Q(s)$. It's often attractive –

---

[1] Dijkstra [p14] talks about predicates 'corresponding' to sets; in the HOL formalization they actually are sets.

and in any case Dijkstra does it this way – to 'hide' the state in such assertions. The easiest way, already used in many programming language embeddings, is to define analogs of all the logical operations but lifted up to the level of predicates:

```
|- False = (λx. F)

|- True = (λx. T)

|- Not p = (λx. ¬p x)

|- p And q = (λx. p x ∧ q x)

|- p Or q = (λx. p x ∨ q x)

|- p Imp q = (λx. p x ⇒ q x)

|- (!!) q = (λx. ∀k. q k x)

|- (??) q = (λx. ∃k. q k x)
```

These correspond to Dijkstra's F, T, non, and, or, ⇒, A and E respectively. (It would be possible, and consistent with our later approach to operators in the programming language, to overload the standard logical symbols for this level too, but on balance that is probably too confusing.) We also use the following variant, which doesn't give a function on states, but rather says that the implication holds for all states:

```
|- p Implies q = ∀x p x ⇒ q x
```

Dijkstra doesn't define this explicitly, but rather says sometimes in words 'for all states'. Some writers use a special triple-lined implication sign for this purpose. Dijkstra and his followers also sometimes enclose an expression in square brackets to indicate universal quantification over all free variables, though that isn't quite the same thing.

2   The Characterization of Semantics

Chapter 3 of Dijkstra's book discusses the behaviour of 'mechanisms', viewing them as systems that when started in an initial state, will end up in a final state (or else fail to terminate). Dijkstra distinguishes between deterministic and nondeterministic machines (in the former, 'the happening that will take place upon activation of the mechanism is fully determined by its initial state' [p. 15]), but doesn't describe mechanisms with great formality. There is not much controversy over how to formalize this in HOL: essentially, a mechanism is formalized as a relation between possible initial and final states.

Gordon [9] actually used relations $\Sigma \times \Sigma \to bool$. But as he pointed out, this formalization can only indicate the nontermination of R on a state s by the absence of any state s' with $R(s, s')$. So while it allows us to consider nondeterministic machines, there is no obvious way to indicate *possible nontermination* rather than *certain nontermination*. Indeed, Grundy [10] shows how there is no really satisfactory way of doing so based on this formalization. Instead, therefore, we consider relations $\Sigma \to \Sigma_\perp \to bool$, where $\Sigma_\perp$ augments the state space with an additional element denoting nontermination. We refer to $\Sigma_\perp$ as the set of *outcomes*; it is defined in HOL as a type:

```
(A) outcome = Loops | Terminates A
```

However, our formalization still has one peculiar feature that should be commented on. It does not automatically follow that the relation associates each state s with some outcome. How are we to interpret a relation where this is not the case – some abnormal condition such as arithmetic overflow or division by zero? We don't do this here; as we shall see below, its interpretation in terms of program correctness is quite the reverse! In any case we define a notion of *totality* and include it as a condition in theorems where needed.

Dijkstra introduces in Chap. 3 the key notions of the weakest precondition and weakest liberal precondition. The weakest precondition of a command[2] c with respect to a postcondition q is the set of initial states such that c, when started in one of those states, is guaranteed to terminate in a state satisfying q. The weakest *liberal* precondition is the set of initial states such that *if* the command terminates it does so in a state satisfying q, but nontermination is allowed as an alternative. The HOL formalization follows Dijkstra except that we use a curried rather than paired wp function. This is mainly a matter of taste, but as we will see shortly, our version makes sequencing of commands correspond exactly to function composition of the weakest preconditions.

```
|- terminates c s = ¬c s Loops

|- wlp c q s = ∀s'. c s (Terminates s') ⇒ q s'

|- wp c q s = terminates c s ∧ wlp c q s
```

A feature of non-total commands is that they trivially satisfy every pre/postcondition relationship! Hesselink [11] regards this as a virtue, using them as an 'miracles'. We, however, regard non-total commands as a blemish, and rule them out where needed.

Dijkstra then gives informal derivations of some important conditions that the predicate transformer must obey if it is to arise as $wp\ c$ for some 'mechanism' c. In our formalization, the first of these only follows from an assumption of totality, and is in fact equivalent to it:

---

[2] Dijkstra unusually bows to the masses and refers to *statements*, but we will stick to *commands*. Dijkstra admits himself [p. 25] that this is better.

```
|- total c = ∀s. ∃t. c s t

|- (wp c False = False) = total c
```

Dually, we have:

```
|- terminating c = ∀s. terminates c s

|- (wp c True = True) = terminating c
```

The other 'healthiness conditions' (2–4) are rendered in HOL very easily, and the proofs are essentially automatic using a tactic for first order reasoning by model elimination:

```
|- q Implies r ⇒ wp c q Implies wp c r

|- wp c q And wp c r = wp c (q And r)

|- wp c q Or wp c r Implies wp c (q Or r)
```

A stronger form of the last is predicated on an assumption of determinacy:

```
|- deterministic c = ∀s t1 t2. c s t1 ∧ c s t2 ⇒ (t1 = t2)

|- deterministic c ⇒ (wp c p Or wp c q = wp c (p Or q))
```

Conversely, it's straightforward to recover (the relational semantics of) a command *c* from *wp c* and *wlp c*. This topic is not discussed explicitly by Dijkstra, who keeps operational details informal, though Hesselink [11] does mention it [p. 105]. Once again, the HOL proof is essentially automatic:

```
|- (c s Loops = ¬wp c True s) ∧
   (c s (Terminates s') = Not (wlp c (λx. ¬(x = s'))) s)
```

For a deterministic command, *wp c* alone suffices:

```
|- deterministic c
   ⇒ (c s (Terminates s') = ¬wp c False s ∧ wp c (λx. x = s') s) ∧
     (c s Loops = ¬wp c True s)
```

Indeed, on the assumption of totality, determinism implies a simple relation between *wp c* and *wlp c*; as Hesselink [11] mentions [p. 111] we can split this up into two strong equivalences:

```
|- total c = ∀p. wp c p Implies Not (wlp c (Not p))

|- deterministic c = ∀p. Not (wlp c (Not p)) Implies wp c p

|- ∀c. total c ∧ deterministic c = ∀p. wp c p = Not (wlp c (Not p))
```

However, for nondeterministic commands, *wp c* alone isn't enough – as with a relation on $\Sigma \times \Sigma$, the weakest precondition semantics cannot distinguish between possible and certain nontermination. Dijkstra only introduces *wlp c* on p. 21, some time after *wp c*, probably precisely because it is necessary to give a satisfactory account in predicate transformer terms of the behaviour of a nondeterministic machine. On pp. 21–2 Dijkstra enumerates 7 'mutually exclusive' possibilities when a nondeterministic command *c* is started in a given state with a postcondition *r* in mind:

- (a) *c* will terminate and establish *r*
- (b) *c* will terminate and establish $\overline{r}$
- (c) *c* will not terminate
- (ab) *c* will terminate and may or may not satisfy *r*
- (ac) *c* may or may not terminate, but if it does will satisfy *r*
- (bc) *c* may or may not terminate, but if it does will satisfy $\overline{r}$
- (abc) *c* may or may not terminate, and if it does may or may not satisfy *r*

Unfortunately, Dijkstra's rendering of some of these in formal terms is wrong, a fact we noticed only when one of HOL's automatic tactics failed to prove 3 out of the 15 mutual exclusions between the above. (In the precise terms of Dijkstra's description, far from all being mutually exclusive, area (c) is contained in areas (ac) and (bc).) Dijkstra uses Not (wp c True) to indicate possible nontermination, but this wrongly includes the third case of *certain* nontermination. There is a confusion here of levels of certainty: we need to be *uncertain whether we are certain* that a command will not terminate. We can express this correctly by saying we are not certain it will terminate, and not certain that it will fail to terminate. Using instead Not (wp c True Or wlp c False), we find that all the cases are indeed distinct:

```
|- total c
  ⇒ (wp c r And wp c (Not r) = False) ∧
     (wp c r And wlp c False = False) ∧
     ....
```

and still enumerate all the possibilities:

```
|- total c
  ⇒ (wp c r Or
       wp c (Not r) Or
       wlp c False Or
       wp c True And Not (wlp c r) And Not (wlp c (Not r)) Or
       wlp c r And Not (wp c True Or wlp c False) Or
       wlp c (Not r) And Not (wp c True Or wlp c False) Or
       Not (wlp c r Or wlp c (Not r) Or wp c True)
     = True)
```

That Dijkstra should make such an elementary error is perhaps indicative of something slightly unintuitive about nondeterministic machines, despite his confident pronouncements:

> Eventually I came to regard nondeterminacy as the normal situation, determinacy being reduced to a –not even very interesting – special case. [p. xv]
> Once the mathematical equipment needed for the design of nondeterministic mechanisms achieving a purpose has been developed, the nondeterministic machine is no longer frightening. On the contrary! We shall learn to appreciate it, even as a valuable stepping stone in the design of an ultimately fully deterministic mechanism. [p. 20]

3 The Semantic Characterization of a Programming Language

Up to now we have considered a fairly abstract notion of mechanism; now we specialize this by considering how to build them up from a fixed repertoire of constructs. It must be made clear that Dijkstra defines the weakest preconditions axiomatically, and often stresses the primacy of this view:

> We take the point of view that we know the possible performance of the mechanism S sufficiently well, provided that we can derive for any postcondition R the corresponding weakest precondition $wp(S, R)$, because then we have captured what the mechanism can do for us; and in the jargon the latter is called "its semantics". [p. 17]

We sometimes have freedom to choose a particular operational definition that yields the same notion of weakest precondition; see for example the discussion of **abort** below. The commands or command-building constructs are all defined as HOL constants. We don't give any HOL version of the concrete syntax at this stage, but we indicate the concrete syntax for the sake of familiarity, and to allow easy comparison with Dijkstra's book.

The simplest command is **skip** which 'does nothing', rather like a no-op in machine codes. This is defined in HOL as the identity relation between initial states and final outcomes.

```
|- Skip s z = (z = Terminates s)
```

It's easy to see that this gives the identity as its weakest precondition:

```
|- ∀q. wp Skip q = q
```

More interesting is the **abort** command, which always fails to establish any postcondition. Our operational definition is that it always loops indefinitely:

```
|- Abort s z = z = Loops
```

This gives the appropriate weakest precondition:

```
|- ∀q. wp Abort q = False
```

On the other hand, we have the following, for which Dijkstra offers no particular support:

```
|- ∀q. wlp Abort q = True
```

Obeying Dijkstra's mantra that the weakest precondition is all we are interested in, we need not consider whether the operational definition is reasonable. It has some support in the literature, e.g. in Hesselink [11] [p. 17]. But the name rather suggests the immediate erroneous termination of the computation, and this conception is borne out by some of Dijkstra's later comments. For example at the end of Chap. 7 [p. 50], he comments on a program's "pleasant property that attempted activation outside its domain will lead to immediate abortion", something that can hardly be called pleasant if abortion is an infinite loop. It's interesting that occasionally Dijkstra's mask slips and operational thinking can be glimpsed.

Next comes the assignment statement. This is written concretely using the assignment symbol :=, but at this level, we abstract away from variables and so on, treating an assignment simply as a functional state transition:

```
|- Assign f s z = (z = Terminates (f s))
```

and we find simply:

```
|- ∀f q. wp (Assign f) q = q o f
```

These are all the 'atomic' commands, and next come the ways in which compound commands can be built up from other commands. The simplest and most conventional is sequencing, where two commands are executed one after the other. This is defined by an infix constant Seq, corresponding to a semicolon in the concrete syntax:

```
|- (c1 Seq c2) s z =
      c1 s Loops ∧ (z = Loops) ∨
      (∃s'. c1 s (Terminates s') ∧ c2 s' z)
```

This operational definition is a bit involved, because we need to consider separately whether the first command loops or not. However the weakest precondition version could hardly be simpler. Two equivalent forms of it are:

```
|- ∀c1 c2 q. wp (c1 Seq c2) q = wp c1 (wp c2 q)

|- ∀c1 c2. wp (c1 Seq c2) = wp c1 o wp c2
```

Dijkstra's other composite constructs involve 'guarded commands', and are more complicated than the usual if-then-else and while-do forms. It's clear he considers them a significant innovation, for he starts Chap. 15 [p. 117] with 'When the guarded commands had emerged and the word got around . . . '. He doesn't really offer any detailed justification for not taking conventional forms, and we can scarcely dare to ask for some when we read elsewhere [3]:

> I do not know whether . . . it is a Swiss national trait to be "solid" first and only "adventurous" as far as then allowed (and that is not very far). Part of my talk dealt with guarded commands. Now, for anyone with some understanding it is clear that as sequencing tools they are much more attractive to use than the traditional while-do and if-then-else, and if, fifteen years ago, someone had thought of them, while-do and if-then-else would perhaps never have become established the way they are now. While at other places – Albuquerque and Toronto, for instance – it sufficed to show the difference, I felt this time more or less pressed to quantify the improvement.

We start with the notion of a guarded command; this is simply a pair of a predicate (the 'guard') and a command, written $b \longrightarrow c$, with the approximate meaning 'only execute the command c if the guard b is true'. However this doesn't tell us what to do if the guard is false, and in fact it depends on context, so we can't really consider these as independent commands (and Dijkstra doesn't try to). Rather, they are building-blocks for the alternative and repetitive constructs, each of which takes a finite number of guarded commands. We take as the HOL formalization of a such a set of guarded commands a list of predicate-command pairs. Using lists means that first, there can be zero guarded commands; Dijkstra doesn't rule this out, but remarks [p. 34, p. 36] that in this case the if and do constructs reduce to abort and skip respectively. Also, we are introducing an order, but this seems quite reasonable at the level of abstract syntax: the semantics is, as we shall see shortly, independent of this order.

Using lists means that many of the theorems require quantification over lists, which we do both at the boolean and state level:

```
|- (EX P [] = F) ∧ (EX P (CONS h t) = P h ∨ EX P t)

|- (FORALL P [] = T) ∧ (FORALL P (CONS h t) = P h ∧ FORALL P t)

|- (Exists P [] = False) ∧ (Exists P (CONS h t) = P h Or Exists P t)

|- (Forall P [] = True) ∧ (Forall P (CONS h t) = P h And Forall P t)
```

Dijkstra instead uses an indexing function, so it could be argued that we would stay closer to his treatment by doing the same, but then we would need to include an indication of the domain, i.e. the number of guarded commands.

Dijkstra's conditional statement is written as follows:

$$\text{if } g_0 \longrightarrow c_0$$
$$\square \quad g_1 \longrightarrow c_1$$
$$\ldots$$
$$\square \quad g_n \longrightarrow c_n$$
$$\text{fi}$$

The intuitive meaning is: if one of the guards is true, execute one of the commands with a true guard; otherwise abort. This permits nondeterminism since more than one guard can be true. The HOL translation of the intuitive semantics is as follows:

```
|- If gcs s t =
     EX (λ(g,c). g s ∧ c s t) gcs V
     ¬EX (λ(g,c). g s) gcs ∧ (t = Loops)
```

We can derive the weakest precondition effectively as Dijkstra gives it:

```
|- ∀gcs q.
     wp (If gcs) q =
         Exists (λ(g,c). g) gcs And Forall (λ(g,c). g Imp wp c q) gcs
```

The repetitive construct is constructed syntactically just like the conditional:

$$\text{do } g_0 \longrightarrow c_0$$
$$\square \quad g_1 \longrightarrow c_1$$
$$\ldots$$
$$\square \quad g_n \longrightarrow c_n$$
$$\text{od}$$

The intended semantics is: while some guard is true, execute one of the commands with a true guard then repeat. If no guard is true, terminate immediately. Dijkstra pointedly defines the semantics at the level of weakest preconditions in terms of k-fold iteration. Although our definitions are at the operational level, we try to follow his style, rather than use an inductive definition. First, we define a relation between initial and final states meaning that this input-output relation can hold after executing the loop a given number of times.

```
|- (Do_step 0 gcs s s' = s' = s) ∧
   (Do_step (SUC k) gcs s s' =
      (∃s''. If gcs s (Terminates s'') ∧ Do_step k gcs s'' s'))
```

This is then used to define the semantics of the do-loop as a whole. Note that we need to ensure that looping is possible if the body can be executed indefinitely.

```
|- (Do gcs s Loops =
      (∃k s'. Do_step k gcs s s' ∧
              EX (λ(g,c). g s' ∧ c s' Loops) gcs) ∨
      (∃ss. (ss 0 = s) ∧
              (∀k. EX (λ(g,c). g (ss k) ∧
                      c (ss k) (Terminates (ss (SUC k))))
                      gcs))) ∧
     (Do gcs s (Terminates s') =
      (∃k. Do_step k gcs s s' ∧ ¬EX (λ(g,c). g s') gcs))
```

This definition is rather messy, but it's easy to get fixpoint characterizations, which are useful later:

```
|- Do gcs s Loops =
    EX (λ(g,c). g s ∧ c s Loops) gcs ∨
    (∃s'. EX (λ(g,c). g s ∧ c s (Terminates s')) gcs ∧
          Do gcs s' Loops)

|- Do gcs s (Terminates s') =
    ¬EX (λ(g,c). g s) gcs ∧ (s' = s) ∨
    (∃s''. EX (λ(g,c). g s ∧ c s (Terminates s'')) gcs ∧
          Do gcs s'' (Terminates s'))
```

We can't actually derive Dijkstra's (axiomatic) weakest precondition semantics for loops, which somewhat hampers our ability to copy his later proofs. The reason is that his axiomatic definition is based on the assumption that if a loop is guaranteed to terminate, there is some maximum number of iterations after which it is guaranteed to terminate. This follows from an assumption of 'bounded nondeterminacy', i.e. that a command guaranteed to terminate cannot have infinitely many possible successor states. Presumably Dijkstra hoped to sneak this assumption past his readers till he was ready to discuss it.

It is in fact the case that all commands constructed so far have only bounded nondeterminism, as Dijkstra proves in Chap. 9, where he finally discusses the notion. Here he belatedly admits [p. 77] that in the presence of unbounded non-determinacy, the 'semantics of the repetitive construct would have been subject to doubt, to say the least'. Actually, the idea of bounded nondeterminacy is only meaningful from an operational point of view, and he proves a property of continuity that is the appropriate concept at the level of weakest preconditions. Of course Dijkstra's proof presupposes the semantics of do-loops, so while perfectly sound from his axiomatic viewpoint, it is useless (circular) as a justification of the semantics. To be fair to Dijkstra, he doesn't explicitly claim otherwise, though this has often been misunderstood [6]. This impression is heightened by the fact that he remarks in this chapter [p. 77] that unbounded nondeterminism cannot be implemented, but doesn't give a serious discussion of why it isn't a useful abstraction any more than the assumption of unbounded execution time or unlimited storage.

One thing we can easily prove without further assumptions is a fixpoint equation for the weakest preconditions of do-loops:

```
|- wp (Do gcs) q =
        q And Not (Exists (λ(g,c). g) gcs) Or wp (If gcs) (wp (Do gcs) q)
```

We could in fact prove that Do gcs is the *least* fixpoint, i.e. the smallest (w.r.t. inclusion) solution of the above equation. It is customary in programming language semantics to define the semantics of loops as least fixpoints. Dijkstra seems to dislike this trend [p. xvii], and in some ways we agree that an iterative version is more intuitive. However fixpoints are very nice to work with, and as we shall see, the leastness is not normally needed.

4   Theorems about Commands

Dijkstra devotes Chap. 5 to proving some useful theorems about if and do commands, that are more useful than the raw weakest preconditions for performing correctness proofs of programs. First of all, we have the following theorem for the conditional:

```
|- (∀s. (q Imp Exists (λ(g,c). g) gcs) s) ∧
   (∀s. Forall (λ(g,c). q And g Imp wp c r) gcs s)
   ⇒ (∀s. (q Imp wp (If gcs) r) s)
```

This is more or less a direct translation of Dijkstra's statement. In fact, we can strengthen it to hold pointwise. (Dijkstra normally specifies 'for all states', though occasionally forgets to even when it is clearly intended.)

```
|- (q Imp Exists (λ(g,c). g) gcs) And
   Forall (λ(g,c). q And g Imp wp c r) gcs Implies
   q Imp wp (If gcs) r
```

These are really versions of the traditional Hoare rule: if q implies that one of the guards holds, and if q together with the ith guard is enough to ensure that the ith command terminates in a state satisfying r, then the whole conditional always leads from a state satisfying q to one satisfying r.

Next we have the theorem for the do-loop. Once again, this is close to the traditional Hoare rule, with p acting as a loop invariant, and the assumption wp (Do gcs) True included because we want to guarantee termination, not just partial correctness.

```
|- p And Exists (λ(g,c). g) gcs Implies wp (If gcs) p
   ⇒ p And wp (Do gcs) True Implies
         wp (Do gcs) (p And Not (Exists (λ(g,c). g) gcs))
```

Because our semantics of loops is different from Dijkstra's, we can't use his proof, but the above is easy to prove by induction on the number of steps as seen by Do_step.

The above theorem simply includes an assumption of termination, with no indication as to how it might be proved. In Chap. 6, this difficulty is addressed, and versions of the above theorems are proved with the assumption of a non-negative 'variant' that decreases with each iteration of the loop. We actually generalize Dijkstra's version somewhat by allowing any wellfounded ordering on the state, not just those defined by measure functions:

```
|- WF (<<) ∧
    (∀X. p And Exists (λ(g,c). g) gcs And (λs. s = X) Implies
        wp (If gcs) (p And (λs. s << X)))
  ⇒ p Implies wp (Do gcs) (p And Not (Exists (λ(g,c). g) gcs))
```

where wellfoundedness is defined in the usual way:

```
|- WF (<<) = ∀P. (∃x. P x) ⇒ (∃x. P x ∧ (∀y. y << x ⇒ ¬P y))
```

We then specialize this general version to Dijkstra's theorem based on an integer (sic) measure function f. This just uses the fact that the order $x << y =_{def} 0 < f(x) \land f(x) < f(y)$ is wellfounded, where $f : \Sigma \to \mathbb{Z}$. We use the auxiliary notion:

```
|- wdec c t s = wp c (λs'. t(s') < t(s)) s
```

and so derive the exact theorem he gives:

```
|- ∀t. p And Exists (λ(g,c). g) gcs Implies (λs. t s > & 0) ∧
        FORALL (λ(g,c). p And g Implies wp c p And wdec c t) gcs
    ⇒ p Implies wp (Do gcs) (p And Not (Exists (λ(g,c). g) gcs))
```

There is an interesting feature of these theorems using a wellfounded ordering or measure function. The proofs only rely on the fixpoint property of the do-loop, not leastness or any equivalent property. Even if one dislikes inductive definitions, the fixpoint is highly intuitive, for in the context of an ordinary while-loop it just amounts to the admissibility of a one-step loop unrolling of 'while e do c' to 'if e then (c; while e do c) else skip'. That the above theorems – the ones actually used in proving programs – should only depend on this seems worth noting.

Note that the first theorem about do-loops, with a raw assumption of termination, doesn't follow from the fixpoint property alone. For example

```
do x > 0 -> x := x + 1 od
```

has a fixpoint of guaranteed termination with x = 0, which plainly doesn't satisfy the constraints of that theorem. We actually prove this in HOL:

```
|- ¬(∀D gcs p.
         (∀q. D q = q And Not (Exists (λ(g,c). g) gcs) Or
                wp (If gcs) (D q)) ∧
         p And Exists (λ(g,c). g) gcs Implies wp (If gcs) p
      ⇒ p And D True
         Implies D (p And Not (Exists (λ(g,c). g) gcs)))
```

5   Program Variables

So far, we have used a completely indeterminate type for the state. Though this is fine for the general theory, particular programs manipulate the state by referencing and assigning to program variables. We now need to decide how to represent program variables in the HOL formalization. Perhaps the simplest approach, used by von Wright, Hekanaho, Luostarinen, and Långbacka [15] for example, is to regard the state space as a large tuple, and implicitly abstract expressions involving variables over this tuple. For example, if the state consists of variables x, y and z, the expression $x + y$ is translated by the parser into $\lambda(x, y, z).x + y$, while the assignment $z := x + y$ is translated into a state mapping $\lambda(x, y, z). (x, y, x + y)$. With this approach, operations on the data values can be inherited directly from HOL's theories and used in programs, and there is no problem using arbitrary different types for the variables. Moreover, HOL's typechecking and type inference apply automatically. Some parsing and printing support is needed to maintain these transformations, but it isn't really difficult. The main defect is, however, that variable names have no first-class existence. From a HOL point of view $\lambda(x, y, z). x + y$ is the same as $\lambda(y, x, z). y + x$; this means that the intuitive meaning of programs is sensitive to the choice of bound variable names. Compositionality is poor: one can only plug together program fragments in the obvious way if they have exactly the same state, even with the variables in the same order.

A simple alternative, originally used by Gordon [9], that gives variables a first-class existence is to represent the state as a function from names to values. In a simply typed system like HOL, however, this presents some problems because the state function can have only a single type `string -> X` for some particular X. If used in a straightforward way, this would require all the variables in a program to have the same type, rather an irksome restriction. A first way of avoiding this is to declare an enumerated type containing all the possible types one might want to use. However even in simple imperative languages the range of types is potentially unlimited, e.g. assuming one allows arrays of arrays of arrays .... But there is a reasonable alternative, which we adopt: we can use instead of an enumerated type a properly *recursive* type.[3] This has already been used [13, 14] for languages with rather richer type systems. The idea is that we can allow in this recursive type certain ways of constructing new types, e.g. 'array of', 'pointer to' etc:

---

[3] We are grateful to Tanja Vos for pointing out this possibility.

```
value = Bool bool
      | Int int
      | Array ((value)array)
      | Pointer value
      | ...
```

Then we still have an unlimited range of types constructed using this fixed repertoire of constructors. At present, we only allow booleans, integers and arrays. Arrays, with various operations as defined in Chap. 11 of Dijkstra's book, are represented as a pair consisting of a starting index and a list of elements, the size and upper bound of the array being calculated from these. HOL's nested type definition package is able to define this type automatically. We can immediately define appropriate type discrimination and destructor functions, e.g.

```
|- Intval (Int x) = x
```

We take the view that program expressions are functions from state to values. This means that various transformations are required by the parser and printer. Actually, we shift a lot of the transformations away from this level and down to the logical level, by defining new operations on program expressions, e.g.

```
|- x + y = λs. Int (Intval (x s) + Intval (y s))
```

Thanks to operator overloading (available in the HOL Light version of HOL), we can use the standard addition symbol here, and similarly for all the other operators. (Excluding completely polymorphic ones such as equality; at present we use a C-like operator ==.) This is done for addition by the following directive, which tells HOL Light that instances of + with the appropriate type map down to the constant value_add.

```
overload_interface("+",
   '(value_add):((string->value)->value)->((string->value)->value)
                ->((string->value)->value)');;
```

Of course, this requires us to set up versions of every operation we want to use. This seems acceptable since typical programming languages only offer a fairly small range. However it stands in sharp contrast to von Wright's approach, where all the standard operators can be used 'as is'. At present it should be regarded as experimental, and we will see how it performs when we consider more particular programs. We still need to perform parser transformations for constants and variables. Variables are translated using the function that looks up the appropriate name (a HOL string) in the state:

```
|- lookup x s = s x
```

Assignments are built up in several stages. The modification of the state s caused by assignment of a single variable x the value a is as follows:

```
|- update (x,a) s = λy. if y = x then a else s(y)
```

However, following Dijkstra, we allow concurrent assignments of the form x1,...,xn := E1,...,En, where the xi can be assumed distinct. To implement this we need to evaluate all the Ei in the starting state, then iteratively apply the function update. This is done by the following function:

```
|- Assignment asl s = ITLIST update (MAP (λ(x,e). (x,e s)) asl) s
```

This relies on two standard list combinators:

```
|- (MAP f [] = []) ∧ (MAP f (CONS h t) = CONS (f h) (MAP f t))

|- (ITLIST f [] b = b) ∧ (ITLIST f (CONS h t) b = f h (ITLIST f t b))
```

We still need to deal with the declarations of variables and scoping rules. Dijkstra's system, given in Chap. 10, is somewhat unusual. He uses blocks as in Algol-like languages generally, but the usual distinctions between local and global variables are ramified. First, blocks are not allowed to inherit global values implicitly: all global variables used in the body must be explicitly declared. This means that as well as the usual declarations of local variables (which Dijkstra calls **pri** for private), blocks contain declarations of the imported ones. These imported variables are further divided into initialized (**glo** for global) and uninitialized (**vir** for virgin). Finally, all 'variables' are split into true variables (**var**) and constants **con**. The latter might simply be considered non-program variables, but we follow Dijkstra in considering them as program variables that aren't allowed to be assigned to. Hence it's permissible for a variable to be treated as a constant in an inner block and a variable outside. This means there are no fewer than six different classes of variable declaration: **privar**, **pricon**, **glovar**, **glocon**, **virvar** and **vircon**. Finally, all variables must be initialized before being referenced, using a statement similar to an assignment but with a type declaration. There are quite strong syntactic restrictions on variable initialization so that this condition can easily be checked statically.

Formalizing the above looks quite intimidating. But we elect to treat most of it extra-logically, as a series of static checks much like type checking that are performed before the parser even accepts a program and parses it into its HOL form. (And in fact at present we haven't bothered to implement any static checks at all, partly because it's not very interesting, partly because we assume Dijkstra will manage to stick to his own rules.) This means that distinctions between constants and variables, and between global and virgin variables, need have no semantic interpretation. These variable declarations are all represented as separate constants, to keep the representation of program texts invertible, but most of them mean the same semantically. All of them are represented not as individual commands, but rather as functions building a command from a declaration and a command, which is the remainder of the block, possibly including other declarations. This makes it easy to restore the value of a temporarily-overridden global variable. The main distinction is between imports of global names, which are semantically null, e.g.

```
|- Glovar x c = c

|- Vircon x c = c
```

and introduction of local names, which temporarily hide outer parts of the state, e.g.

```
|- (Privar x c s Loops = (∃a. c (update (x,a) s) Loops)) ∧
   (Privar x c s (Terminates s') =
   (∃a s''.
        c (update (x,a) s) (Terminates s'') ∧
        (s' = update (x,lookup x s) s'')))
```

Here we express the undefinedness of the initial value a for the new variable by making the semantics nondeterministic. In practice, this never matters since one always has an initialization before the variable is referenced. Initializing assignments are represented by a constants semantically equivalent to the usual assignment, but with an extra argument for the type; this is only retained for invertibility. Finally, we have another semantically null tagging constant to indicate the start of a block; without this we would have no means of deciding whether a series of declarations belong to the same block or several nested ones.

6   Conclusions and Future Work

Our formalization has almost covered all the 'foundational' parts of Dijkstra's monograph. The gaps that remain are (i) the parser does not perform any static checks like typechecking, making sure variables are initialized and that parallel assignments do not include repeated variables, etc., and (ii) the theory of arrays has not been fully developed. Once the latter at least is finished, we will be ready to try verifying some of the examples given later in the book. Doing so will reveal how successful the formalization we have chosen is in practice.

References

1. R. Back. *Correctness Preserving Program Transformations: Proof Theory and Applications*, Volume 131 of *Mathematical Centre Tracts*. Mathematical Centre, Amsterdam, 1980.
2. R. DeMillo, R. Lipton, and A. Perlis. Social processes and proofs of theorems and programs. *Communications of the ACM*, **22**, 271–280, 1979.
3. E. W. Dijkstra. Trip report visit ETH Zurich, EWD474, 3-4 February 1975. See [8], pp. 95–98.
4. E. E. Dijkstra. *A Discipline of Programming*. Prentice-Hall, 1976.
5. E. W. Dijkstra. Formal techniques and sizeable programs, EWD563. See [8], pp. 205–214, 1976. Paper prepared for Symposium on the Mathematical Foundations of Computing Science, Gdansk 1976.

188   John Harrison

6. E. W. Dijkstra. A somewhat open letter to EAA or: Why I proved the boundedness of the nondeterminacy in the way I did, EWD614, 1977. See [8], pp. 284–287.
7. E. W. Dijkstra. On a political pamphlet from the middle ages. *ACM SIGSOFT, Software Engineering Notes*, **3**, 14, 1978.
8. E. W. Dijkstra (ed.). *Selected Writings on Computing: A Personal Perspective*. Springer-Verlag, 1982.
9. M. J. C. Gordon. Mechanizing programming logics in higher order logic. In G. Birtwistle and P. A. Subrahmanyam (eds.), *Current Trends in Hardware Verification and Automated Theorem Proving*, pp. 387–439. Springer-Verlag, 1989.
10. J. Grundy. Predicative programming – a survey. In D. Bjørner, M. Broy, and I. V. Pottosin (eds.), *Formal Methods in Programming and Their Applications: Proceedings of the International Conference*, Volume 735 of *Lecture Notes in Computer Science*, Academgorodok, Novosibirsk, Russia, pp. 8–25. Springer-Verlag, 1993.
11. W. H. Hesselink. *Programs, Recursion and Unbounded Choice*, Volume 27 of *Cambridge Tracts in Theoretical Computer Science*. Cambridge University Press, 1992.
12. J. J. Joyce and C. Seger (eds.). *Proceedings of the 1993 International Workshop on the HOL theorem proving system and its applications*, Volume 780 of *Lecture Notes in Computer Science*, UBC, Vancouver, Canada. Springer-Verlag, 1993.
13. D. Syme. Reasoning with the formal definition of Standard ML in HOL. See [12], pp. 43–60.
14. M. VanInwegen and E. Gunter. HOL-ML. See [12], pp. 61–74.
15. J. von Wright, J. Hekanaho, P. Luostarinen, and T. Långbacka. Mechanizing some advanced refinement concepts. *Formal Methods in System Design*, **3**, 49–82, 1993.

Mechanical Verification of Total Correctness through Diversion Verification Conditions

Peter V. Homeier[1] and David F. Martin[2]

[1] Computer and Information Science Department
University of Pennsylvania, Philadelphia, PA 19104-6389, USA
homeier@saul.cis.upenn.edu
[2] Computer Science Department, UCLA, Los Angeles, CA 90095, USA

Abstract. The total correctness of programs with mutually recursive procedures is significantly more complex than their partial correctness. Past methods of proving termination have suffered from being rigid, not general, non-intuitive, and *ad hoc* in structure, not suitable for mechanization.We have devised a new method for proving termination and mechanized it within an automatic tool called a Verification Condition Generator. This tool analyzes not only the program's syntax but also, uniquely, its procedure call graph, to produce verification conditions sufficient to ensure the program's total correctness. *Diversion verification conditions* reduce the labor involved in proving termination from infinite to finite. The VCG tool has itself been deeply embedded and proven sound within the HOL theorem prover with respect to the underlying structural operational semantics. Now proofs of total correctness of individual programs may be significantly automated with complete security.

1 Introduction

If a program is partially correct but not proven to terminate, then its correct answers may not ever be provided. Thus, the termination of programs is an essential element of their proper function. Even for programs which are not intended to terminate, such as operating systems or embedded reactive programs, significant portions *are* expected to terminate, such as a response to an external event. But assuring this termination is a complex task. Previous methods have required considerable work and skill to create proofs of termination, and each such proof has depended greatly on the *ad hoc* structure of the particular problem. What is needed is automation of the proof process; but these prior methods are not sufficiently regular to support mechanization.

In this paper we investigate the semi-automatic verification of the total correctness of programs with mutually recursive procedures, including termination. The automation is performed by a tool called a *Verification Condition Generator*, or VCG, which constructs the proof of a program's correctness, modulo a set of *verification conditions*, which are logical formulae left to the user to prove. This twice simplifies the programmer's task, as it reduces both the volume and the level of the proof. These verification conditions do not contain any references to programming language constructs or concepts, such as assignment or recursion, but only involve relationships among the values used in the program.

In the past, VCG tools in general were not themselves verified [8]. This meant that the soundness of a proof of a program's correctness rested upon the soundness of an unverified tool. Most VCGs are based on an axiomatic semantics, and in particular for procedures, there is a history of axiomatic semantics proposed in the literature which were later found to be unsound [1]. The VCG tool we present is itself verified to be sound. This means that for any program and specification, if the verification conditions are proven, then the program must be totally correct with respect to its specification. The proof of soundness was conducted within and checked by the HOL mechanical theorem prover [3], based on the structural operational semantics for the programming language. The theorem of the soundness of the VCG forms the basis for practical, effective proofs of total correctness for individual programs, with complete security. We have previously verified a VCG for partial correctness [7]; the requirement of proving termination has added at least as much complexity as all of partial correctness.

In this investigation, we have discovered a more powerful method for verifying the termination of programs with mutually recursive procedures than those previously proposed in the literature, called the *diversion verification condition* method. Though counterintuitive at first glance, these diversion verification conditions reduce the labor involved in proving termination from infinite to finite. This method is both more general and more natural than prior ones, and is also suitable for mechanization in a VCG. The VCG we exhibit here implements this new method for proving termination and hence total correctness.

The organization of this paper is as follows. Section 2 discusses approaches to proving termination. In Sect. 3 we give the syntax of the language used, and in Sect. 4 its semantics. Section 5 defines the automatic VCG tool. Section 6 applies the VCG to an example with an interesting termination argument. Section 7 focuses on the graph analysis, and in Sect. 8 we conclude.

2 Termination

For normal while loops, termination can be assured through the specification of a "variant" expression, with values in a well-founded set, that can be shown to strictly decrease for each iteration of the loop. For programs with mutually recursive procedures, a new form of nontermination arises, where a procedure calls itself recursively, either directly or through a chain of intermediate procedures, where each recursive invocation continues calling itself deeper and deeper, without ever returning from any of these calls. This is known as "infinite recursive descent," and it must be eliminated for total correctness.

Originating with Sokołowski [11], and continuing with Apt [2], America and de Boer [1], and Pandya and Joseph [10], rules have been presented based on Hoare's rule for partial correctness [4]; but these have suffered from *ad hoc* organization, lack of generality and awkwardness for many real programs. The essential idea of these methods is the introduction of a recursion depth counter, an integer-valued expression which is required to decrease by exactly one upon each deeper procedure call. Since the expression is required to be non-negative, it cannot continue decreasing forever, and hence no infinite descent is possible.

This is effective for proving the termination of many programs whose code naturally matches this structure, but many real programs, like recursive descent parsers, do not easily fit within the rigor of requiring the recursion depth counter to decrease by exactly one upon each new call. A fast multiplication example was given by Pandya and Joseph [10]. They ameliorated the problem by reducing the number of procedures for which the depth counter needed to decrease, but retained the rigidity of the recursion depth counter for the remainder.

We have designed a more general and flexible approach, where we require progress not across a single procedure call, but around a *cycle* in the procedure call graph. Each procedure which is intended to recurse is given a well-founded expression which is expected to decrease between recursive calls of *that* procedure, irrespective of the number of other procedures called along the way. This decrease around each cycle can be demonstrated if the progress along each single arc of the cycle is known. This allows individual arcs to contribute no forward progress, or even to step backwards, as long as in the end, when the cycle is completely traversed, the accumulation of all the progress along the cycle suffices to ensure the well-founded decrease. Thus we free the termination argument from being artificially attached to the number of procedure calls, and return it to the actual problem of instances of recursion. Also, different procedures may use different well-founded expressions, according to the reason why each terminates.

We establish the decrease of a procedure's well-founded expression across every path of nested calls that leads to a recursive call in two parts. First, the progress of each individual procedure across a single call is specified and proven by analysis of the program's syntax. Then in the second part, the procedure call graph is analyzed, where the progress of all the procedures around a cycle in the procedure call graph is "added together." If the progress around each cycle implies the recursive progress, then termination of the procedure is assured.

Most programs which contain mutually recursive procedures will have an infinite number of possible paths of recursion, all of which need to be verified for the necessary recursive progress. This would be impossible, but we have discovered a counter-intuitive but effective means to simplify this task to a finite one, through *diversion verification conditions*. This is discussed in Sect 7.

Our new method is more general and flexible than previous proposals. It supports more natural proofs and also may enable proofs of programs otherwise impractical. In addition, the proofs are more stable under program evolution, such as breaking out an interior code block into a new procedure, because this method is based on essential progress between recursive calls, rather than the fragile rigidity of the exact number of procedure calls involved, an artifact of the code rather than the problem being solved. Of ultimate practical value, the regular structure of this proof method supports mechanization in a VCG.

3   Programming and Assertion Languages Syntax

We deeply embed a simple imperative programming language called Sunrise in the HOL logic to illustrate the VCG with the new termination methodology. The syntax of the Sunrise programming and assertion languages is given in Fig. 1.

---

exp: $e ::= n \mid x \mid {++}x \mid e_1 + e_2 \mid e_1 - e_2 \mid e_1 * e_2$

bexp: $b ::= e_1 = e_2 \mid e_1 < e_2 \mid es_1 \ll es_2 \mid b_1 \wedge b_2 \mid b_1 \vee b_2 \mid {\sim}b$

cmd: $c ::=$ **skip** $\mid$ **abort** $\mid x := e \mid c_1 \, ; \, c_2 \mid$ **if** b **then** c_1 **else** c_2 **fi** $\mid$
          assert a **with** a_{pr} **while** b **do** c **od** $\mid p(x_1, \ldots, x_n \, ; \, e_1, \ldots, e_n)$

decl: $d ::=$ **procedure** $p(\mathbf{var}\, x_1, \ldots, x_n \, ; \, \mathbf{val}\, y_1, \ldots, y_m);$
             global $z_1, \ldots, z_k \, ;$
             pre $a_{pre};$ (this will be represented later as
             post $a_{post};$ **proc** $p\, vars\, vals\, glbs\, pre\, post\, enters\, rec\, c$)
             enters p_1 **with** $a_1;$
             $\vdots$
             enters p_j **with** $a_j;$
             recurses with $a_{rec};$
             c
             end procedure $\mid$
             $d_1 \, ; \, d_2 \mid$
             empty

prog: $\pi ::=$ **program** $d \, ; \, c$ **end program**

---

vexp: $v ::= n \mid x \mid v_1 + v_2 \mid v_1 - v_2 \mid v_1 * v_2$

aexp: $a ::=$ **true** $\mid$ **false** $\mid v_1 = v_2 \mid v_1 < v_2 \mid vs_1 \ll vs_2 \mid a_1 \wedge a_2 \mid a_1 \vee a_2 \mid$
        ${\sim}a \mid a_1 \Rightarrow a_2 \mid a_1 = a_2 \mid a_1 \Rightarrow a_2 \mid a_3 \mid$ **close** $a \mid \forall x . a \mid \exists x . a$

Fig. 1: Programming and assertion language syntax

The notation $f[e/x]$ indicates the function f overridden so that

$$(f[e/x])(x) = e, \text{ and for } y \neq x, \ (f[e/x])(y) = f(y)$$

We will also use $f[es/xs]$ where es and xs are lists, to indicate a multiple override in order from right to left across the lists, so the right-most elements of es and xs make the first override, and the others are added on top of this.

Most of these constructs are standard. n is an unsigned integer ≥ 0 (num). x is a program variable, required to not begin with the single quote character (') ; such names are reserved as "logical" variables. ++ is the increment operator, with a side effect as in C. $es_1 \ll es_2$ is the lexicographic ordering between two lists. **abort** causes an immediate abnormal termination. The **while** loop requires an invariant assertion a and a variant expression v (in $a_{pr} = (v < x)$) to be supplied. In the procedure call $p(xs; es)$, p is a string, xs is a list of variables, denoting the actual variable parameters (passed by call-by-name), and es is a list of **exp** expressions, denoting actual value parameters (call-by-value).

The procedure declaration specifies the procedure's name p, formal variable parameter names $x_1, \ldots, x_n$, formal value parameter names $y_1, \ldots, y_m$, global variables used in p (or any procedure p calls) $z_1, \ldots, z_k$, precondition a_{pre}, postcondition a_{post}, entrance progress expressions a_1 for p_1 through a_j for p_j, recursive progress expression a_{rec}, and body c. All parameter types are **num**. The *entrance* of a procedure is within its scope, just before the body. We refer to a typical procedure declaration as **proc** p *vars vals glbs pre post enters rec c*, instead of the longer version in Fig. 1. Here *enters* collects all the entrance progress clauses together, as an *entrance progress environment*, of type **prog_env** = **string** -> **aexp**, defined as $enters = (\lambda p.\textbf{false})[a_1/p_1] \ldots [a_j/p_j]$. Procedures are mutually recursive, and may call each other irrespective of declaration order.

The syntax of the associated assertion language is also given in Fig. 1. Most of these constructs are standard. Note that $v_1 - v_2$ terminates at zero, e.g., $3 - 5 = 0$. $vs_1 \ll vs_2$ is the lexicographic ordering between two lists. $a_1 \Rightarrow a_2 \mid a_3$ is a conditional expression, yielding the value of a_2 or a_3 depending on the value of a_1. **close** a forms the universal closure of a, quantifying all free variables.

The functions FV_a a and FV_v v yield the sets of all free variables in a and v.

Variables contain two parts, a string and a variant number (of type **num**), assembled into a variable by the constructor function VAR s n. The function *variant* x s produces a variable which is a variant of x, but which is guaranteed not to be within the set s. In addition, the closest possible variant is produced, so if x itself is not within s, then *variant* x $s = x$. More generally,

$$variant \; x \; s \; = \; (x \in s \Rightarrow variant \; (mk\_variant \; x \; 1) \; s \mid x)$$

where $mk\_variant \; (VAR \; s \; n) \; k = VAR \; s \; (n + k)$.

The function *variants* xs s applies *variant* repeatedly to each of the elements of the list xs to produce variants distinct from the set s and from each other.

$$\begin{aligned}
&variants \; [\,] \; s &&= [\,] \\
&variants \; (\textbf{cons} \; x \; xs) \; s &&= \textbf{let} \; x' = variant \; x \; s \; \textbf{in} \\
& && \quad \textbf{cons} \; x' \; (variants \; xs \; (\{x'\} \cup s))
\end{aligned}$$

Variables are separated into two classes, program variables and logical variables, where logical variables are distinguished by beginning with a quote character (′). A program variable may be converted to a corresponding logical variable by prepending a quote; this is done by the function *logical* x. This is naturally extended to lists of variables by the function *logicals* xs. The variant functions above may be applied to either program or logical variables.

A simultaneous substitution of expressions for variables is considered an object, apart from applying the substitution to an expression. The substitution is represented by a function from variables to expressions; all but a finite number of variables map to themselves. Such a substitution is created by $[ys/xs]$, where ys and xs are lists of variables. (Note this overloads the notation for function override.) Then $a \lhd ss$ explicitly applies a substitution ss to an expression a, automatically renaming bound variables in a as necessary to avoid capture.

Because the programming and assertion languages are distinct, functions are provided to translate from the programming language to the assertion language: VE for numeric expressions, VES for lists of numeric expressions, and AB for boolean expressions. Since in this language expressions may have side effects, functions are also provided to yield the substitutions that represent those side effects: VE_state for numeric expressions, VES_state for lists of numeric expressions, and AB_state for boolean expressions.

As a product, we may now define the simultaneous substitution that corresponds to a single or multiple assignment statement, overriding the expression's state change with the change of the assignment:

$$[x := e] = (VE\_state\ e)[(VE\ e)\ /\ x]$$
$$[xs := es] = (VES\_state\ es)[(VES\ es)\ /\ xs]$$

Also, we define the function ab_pre, which given a boolean expression b and a desired postcondition q, yields an appropriate precondition which if true, ensures that after executing b that the postcondition q holds.

$$ab\_pre\ b\ q\ =\ q \lhd (AB\_state\ b)$$

This brief description of the translation functions is detailed more in [6], [7].

4   Operational Semantics

This language is almost exactly the same as that given by Homeier and Martin [7], except for the additional annotations for termination. That paper presents a structural operational semantics for the programming language and a denotational semantics for the assertion language, which apply here almost without modification. In that paper, tables 2 and 3 give the structural operational semantics of the Sunrise programming language, as rules inductively defining the six relations E, B, ES, C, D, and P. These relations (except for ES) are defined within HOL using Tom Melham's excellent rule induction package [9].

For example, the relation $C\ c\ \rho\ s_1\ s_2$ expresses how a command c may operate on a state s_1 of type `state = var->num` (binding non-negative integer values to variables), in the presence of an environment ρ (containing all information about all declared procedures), to produce a resulting state s_2. The procedure environment ρ is represented as a function from procedure names to tuples; we define the type `env` as

```
string -> (var list # var list # var list # aexp # aexp
          # prog_env # aexp # cmd),
```

The tuple contains, in order, the variable parameter list, value parameter list, global variables list, the precondition, the postcondition, the entrance progress environment, the recursive progress expression, and the body.

The semantics is changed from that described in [7] as follows. The multiplication operator is added, analogous to the addition operator. The lexicographic ordering operator is added, analogous to the less-than operator, where the two arguments are evaluated using the relation ES instead of E. The empty declaration is added, with the semantics of not producing any modification in the environment ρ. Other than these, where loops or declarations have additional annotations, consider the semantics rules to be adapted without any new effect.

For defining P, we use the empty environment $\rho_0 = \lambda p.\langle\,[\,],\,[\,],\,[\,],\,\textbf{false},$ $\textbf{true},\,(\lambda p.\,\textbf{false}),\,\textbf{false},\,\textbf{abort}\rangle$, and the initial state $s_0 = \lambda x.\,0$. We may construct an environment ρ from a declaration d as $\rho = mkenv\,d\,\rho_0$, where

$$mkenv\,(\textbf{proc}\ p\ vars\ vals\ glbs\ pre\ post\ enters\ rec\ c)\ \rho$$
$$= \rho[\langle vars, vals, glbs, pre, post, enters, rec, c\rangle\,/\,p]$$
$$mkenv\,(d_1;\,d_2)\,\rho\ = mkenv\,d_2\,(mkenv\,d_1\,\rho)$$
$$mkenv\,(\textbf{empty})\,\rho = \rho$$

The semantics of the assertion language is almost the same as that given in Table 4 of [7] by recursive functions V, VS, and A defined on the structure of assertion-language expressions, in a denotational fashion. The only change is the addition of the lexicographic relation. For example, the function $A\,a\,s$ evaluates the boolean expression a in the state s, yielding a boolean value. Similarly, V and VS evaluate numeric expressions and lists of numeric expressions, respectively.

The Hoare-style total correctness of programs ($\pi[q]$) can now be defined as

$$\pi[q]\ =\ (\forall s.\ P\ \pi\ s \Rightarrow A\ q\ s) \wedge (\exists s.\ P\ \pi\ s)$$

5   Verification Condition Generator

In this section we give the definition of the Verification Condition Generator as new functions within the HOL logic for proving the total correctness of Sunrise programs. There are two general classes of functions, those which analyze the structure of the program's syntax, and those which analyze the structure of the program's procedure call graph.

5.1   Verification of Commands and Declarations

We begin with the analysis of commands. The VCG functions for this are $vcgc$, the main function, and $vcg1$, which does most of the work. These are presented in Fig. 2. In the definitions of these functions, comma (,) makes a pair of two items, square brackets ([]) delimit lists, semicolon (;) within a list separates elements, and ampersand (&) appends two lists. In addition, the function $dest_<$ is a destructor function, breaking an assertion language expression of the form $v_0 < v_1$ into a pair of its constituent subexpressions, v_0 and v_1.

$vcg1$ **(skip)** $enters\ q\ \rho\ =\ q,\ []$
$vcg1$ **(abort)** $enters\ q\ \rho\ =\ false,\ []$
$vcg1\ (x := e)\ enters\ q\ \rho\ =\ q \lhd [x := e],\ []$
$vcg1\ (c_1\ ;\ c_2)\ enters\ q\ \rho\ =$
$\qquad\qquad\qquad\quad$ **let** $(s, h_2) = vcg1\ c_2\ enters\ q\ \rho$ **in**
$\qquad\qquad\qquad\quad$ **let** $(p, h_1) = vcg1\ c_1\ enters\ s\ \rho$ **in**
$\qquad\qquad\qquad\qquad\qquad p,\ h_1\ \&\ h_2$
$vcg1$ **(if** b **then** c_1 **else** c_2 **fi)** $enters\ q\ \rho\ =$
$\qquad\qquad\qquad\quad$ **let** $(r_1, h_1) = vcg1\ c_1\ enters\ q\ \rho$ **in**
$\qquad\qquad\qquad\quad$ **let** $(r_2, h_2) = vcg1\ c_2\ enters\ q\ \rho$ **in**
$\qquad\qquad\qquad\qquad (AB\ b => ab\_pre\ b\ r_1\ |\ ab\_pre\ b\ r_2),\ h_1\ \&\ h_2$
$vcg1$ **(assert** a **with** a_{pr} **while** b **do** c **od)** $enters\ q\ \rho\ =$
$\qquad\qquad\qquad\quad$ **let** $(v_0, v_1) = dest_<\ a_{pr}$ **in**
$\qquad\qquad\qquad\quad$ **let** $(p, h) = vcg1\ c\ enters\ (a \wedge a_{pr})\ \rho$ **in**
$\qquad\qquad\qquad\qquad a,\ [\ a \wedge AB\ b \wedge (v_0 = v_1) \Rightarrow ab\_pre\ b\ p\ ;$
$\qquad\qquad\qquad\qquad\qquad a \wedge \sim(AB\ b) \Rightarrow ab\_pre\ b\ q\ ]\ \&\ h$
$vcg1$ **(call** $p\ (xs\ ;\ es))\ enters\ q\ \rho\ =$
$\qquad\qquad\qquad\quad$ **let** $(vars, vals, glbs, pre, post, enters', rec, c) = \rho\ p$ **in**
$\qquad\qquad\qquad\quad$ **let** $vals' = variants\ vals\ (FV_a\ q \cup sl(xs\ \&\ glbs))$ **in**
$\qquad\qquad\qquad\quad$ **let** $u = xs\ \&\ vals'$ **in**
$\qquad\qquad\qquad\quad$ **let** $v = vars\ \&\ vals$ **in**
$\qquad\qquad\qquad\quad$ **let** $x = u\ \&\ glbs$ **in**
$\qquad\qquad\qquad\quad$ **let** $y = v\ \&\ glbs$ **in**
$\qquad\qquad\qquad\quad$ **let** $x_0 = logicals\ x$ **in**
$\qquad\qquad\qquad\quad$ **let** $y_0 = logicals\ y$ **in**
$\qquad\qquad\qquad\quad$ **let** $x_0' = variants\ x_0\ (FV_a\ q)$ **in**
$\qquad\qquad\qquad\qquad (\ (\ ((pre \wedge enters\ p) \lhd [u/v]\ ) \wedge$
$\qquad\qquad\qquad\qquad\ (\ (\forall x.\ (post \lhd [u\ \&\ x_0'/v\ \&\ y_0]) \Rightarrow q) \lhd [x/x_0']\ )$
$\qquad\qquad\qquad\qquad) \lhd [vals' := es],\ []$

$vcgc\ p\ c\ enters\ q\ \rho = $ **let** $(a, h) = vcg1\ c\ enters\ q\ \rho$ **in**
$\qquad\qquad\qquad\qquad\qquad [\ p \Rightarrow a\ ]\ \&\ h$

$vcgd$ **(proc** $p\ vars\ vals\ glbs\ pre\ post\ enters\ rec\ c)\ \rho\ =$
$\qquad\qquad\qquad\quad$ **let** $x = vars\ \&\ vals\ \&\ glbs$ **in**
$\qquad\qquad\qquad\quad$ **let** $x_0 = logicals\ x$ **in**
$\qquad\qquad\qquad\qquad vcgc\ (x_0 = x\ \wedge\ pre)\ c\ enters\ post\ \rho$
$vcgd\ (d_1\ ;\ d_2)\ \rho = $ **let** $h_1 = vcgd\ d_1\ \rho$ **in**
$\qquad\qquad\qquad\quad$ **let** $h_2 = vcgd\ d_2\ \rho$ **in**
$\qquad\qquad\qquad\qquad h_1\ \&\ h_2$
$vcgd$ **(empty)** $\rho = []$

Fig. 2: Definition of VCG functions for commands and declarations

The *vcg*1 function has type cmd → prog_env → aexp → env → (aexp × aexp list). *vcg*1 takes a command, an entrance progress environment, a postcondition, and a procedure environment, and returns a pair, consisting of a precondition and a list of verification conditions that must be proved in order to verify that command with respect to the precondition, postcondition, and environments. *vcg*1 is defined recursively, based on the structure of the command. Note that the procedure call clause includes the expression *enters p*; this strengthens the precondition generated to verify not only the partial correctness of the command, but also the entrance progress claims in *enters*.

The *vcgc* function is similar to *vcg*1, but takes an additional parameter, a precondition of type aexp, and returns only a list of verification conditions.

The verification condition generator function to analyze declarations is *vcgd*. The *vcgd* function is also presented in Fig. 2. This function has type decl → env → aexp list. *vcgd* takes a declaration and a procedure environment, and returns a list of verification conditions that must be proved in order to verify that declaration with respect to the procedure environment.

5.2   Verification of Recursion

The next several functions analyze the structure of the procedure call graph. We will begin with the lowest level functions, and build up to the main VCG function for the procedure call graph, *vcgg*.

The purpose of the graph analysis is to verify that the progress specified in the **recurses with** clause for each procedure is achieved for every possible recursive call of the procedure. This key process is justified in Sect. 7.

The fundamental building block for the graph analysis is the *call_progress* function. Just as weakest precondition functions compute the appropriate precondition to establish a given postcondition for a partial correctness specification, *call_progress* computes the appropriate precondition when starting execution from the entrance of procedure p_1 to establish a given entrance condition q at the entrance of procedure p_2, using the entrance progress declared in p_1 for p_2.

There are two mutually recursive functions at the core of the algorithm to analyze the procedure call graph, *extend_graph_vcs* and *fan_out_graph_vcs*. They are presented together in Fig. 3. Each yields a list of verification conditions to verify recursive progress across parts of the graph. In the definitions, **sl** converts a list to a set, and **cons** adds an element to a list. **length** simply returns the length of the list. **map** applies a function to each element of a list, and gathers the results of all applications into a new list which is the value yielded. **flat** takes a list of lists and appends them together, to "flatten" the structure into a single list of elements from all the lists.

extend_graph_vcs performs the task of tracing backwards across a particular arc of the procedure call graph. *fan_out_graph_vcs* traces backwards across all incoming arcs of a particular node in the graph. The types and meanings of the arguments to these functions are given at the bottom of Fig. 3.

The depth counter n was a necessary artifact to be able to define these functions in HOL. Originally, the function *fan_out_graph_vcs* was defined as

$call\_progress\ p_1\ p_2\ q\ \rho\ =$
$\quad$ let $\langle vars, vals, glbs, pre, post, enters, rec, c \rangle = \rho\ p_1$ in
$\quad$ let $x = vars\ \&\ vals\ \&\ glbs$ in
$\quad$ let $x_0 = logicals\ x$ in
$\quad$ let $x_0' = variants\ x_0\ (FV_a\ q)$ in
$\quad$ let $\langle vars', vals', glbs', pre', post', enters', rec', c' \rangle = \rho\ p_2$ in
$\quad$ let $y = vars'\ \&\ vals'\ \&\ glbs'$ in
$\quad$ let $a = enters\ p_2$ in
$\quad$ ($a = \mathbf{false}$ $=>$ $\mathbf{true}$
$\qquad\qquad$ | $(\forall y.\ (a \lhd [x_0'/x_0]) \Rightarrow q) \lhd [x/x_0']$)

$induct\_pre\ \mathbf{false}\ =\ \mathbf{true}$
$induct\_pre\ (v < x)\ =\ (v = x)$

$extend\_graph\_vcs\ p\ ps\ p_0\ q\ pcs\ \rho\ all\_ps\ n\ p'\ =$
$\quad$ let $q_1 = call\_progress\ p'\ p\ q\ \rho$ in
$\quad$ ($q_1 = \mathbf{true}$ $=>$ []
$\quad$ | $p' = p_0$ $=>$
$\qquad\qquad$ let $(vars, vals, glbs, pre, post, enters, rec, c) = \rho\ p_0$ in
$\qquad\qquad$ [$pre \wedge induct\_pre\ rec \Rightarrow q_1$]
$\quad$ | $p' \in \mathrm{sl}(\mathbf{cons}\ p\ ps)$ $=>$ [$pcs\ p' \Rightarrow q_1$]
$\quad$ | $fan\_out\_graph\_vcs\ p'\ (\mathbf{cons}\ p\ ps)\ p_0\ q_1\ (pcs[q_1/p'])\ \rho\ all\_ps\ n$
$)$

$fan\_out\_graph\_vcs\ p\ ps\ p_0\ q\ pcs\ \rho\ all\_ps\ (n+1)\ =$
$\quad$ $\mathbf{flat}\ (\mathbf{map}\ (extend\_graph\_vcs\ p\ ps\ p_0\ q\ pcs\ \rho\ all\_ps\ n)\ all\_ps)$

$fan\_out\_graph\_vcs\ p\ ps\ p_0\ q\ pcs\ \rho\ all\_ps\ 0\ =\ []$

Types and meanings of arguments:

p	: **string**	: current node (procedure name)
ps	: **string list**	: path (list of procedure names)
p_0	: **string**	: starting node (procedure name)
q	: **aexp**	: current path condition
pcs	: **string** $\rightarrow$ **aexp**	: prior path conditions
ρ	: **env**	: procedure environment
all_ps	: **string list**	: all declared procedures (list of names)
n	: **num**	: depth counter
p'	: **string**	: source node of arc being explored

Fig. 3: Definition of core VCG functions for graph analysis

$graph\_vcs\ all\_ps\ \rho\ p\ =$
    let $(vars, vals, glbs, pre, post, enters, rec, c) = \rho\ p$ **in**
    $fan\_out\_graph\_vcs\ p\ []\ p\ rec\ (\lambda p'.\ \mathbf{true})\ \rho\ all\_ps\ (\mathbf{length}\ all\_ps)$

$vcgg\ all\_ps\ \rho\ =\ \mathbf{flat}\ (\mathbf{map}\ (graph\_vcs\ all\_ps\ \rho)\ all\_ps)$

Fig. 4: Definition of top-level VCG functions for graph analysis

a single primitive recursive function on n combining the definitions of both *fan_out_graph_vcs* and *extend_graph_vcs*. Then *extend_graph_vcs* was defined as a part of *fan_out_graph_vcs*, and *fan_out_graph_vcs* resolved to the remainder. For calls of *extend_graph_vcs*, n should be **length** all_ps − **length** ps − 1. For calls of *fan_out_graph_vcs*, the argument should be **length** all_ps − **length** ps.

The definition of *fan_out_graph_vcs* maps *extend_graph_vcs* across all defined procedures, in *all_ps*. This leads to exponential time complexity. To minimize this, it is important for the application of *extend_graph_vcs* to terminate quickly for arcs which do not exist. These are indicated by the lack of an **enters ... with** clause in the header of the procedure which is the source of the arc, leading to the default value for the progress expression, **false**. If the call of *call_progress* (from *extend_graph_vcs*) retrieves **false** for the arc, then it returns **true** immediately to *extend_graph_vcs*, which in turn immediately returns the empty list of no verification conditions. This rapid dismissal limits the exponential growth to a factor depending more on the average number of incoming arcs for nodes in the graph, than on the total number of declared procedures.

The *fan_out_graph_vcs* function is called initially by the function *graph_vcs*, given in Fig. 4. *graph_vcs* analyzes the procedure call graph beginning at a particular node, and generates verification conditions for paths in the graph to that node to verify its recursive progress, as declared for the procedure.

The *graph_vcs* function is called by the function *vcgg*, given in Fig. 4. *vcgg* analyzes the entire procedure call graph, beginning at each node in turn, and generates verification conditions for paths in the graph, to verify the recursive progress declared for each procedure in *all_ps*.

5.3 Verification of Programs

The main VCG function is *vcg*, presented in Fig. 5. *vcg* calls *vcgd* to analyze the declarations, *vcgg* to analyze the call graph, and *vcgc* to analyze the main body of the program. *vcg* takes a program and a postcondition as arguments, analyzes the entire program, and generates verification conditions which are sufficient to prove the program totally correct with respect to the given postcondition. In the definition of *vcg*, *proc_names* returns the list of procedure names declared in a declaration, and g_0 is the "empty" call progress environment $\lambda p.\ \mathbf{true}$.

$$vcg \ (\textbf{program } d; c \textbf{ end program}) \ q \ =$$
$$\textbf{let } \rho = mkenv \ d \ \rho_0 \textbf{ in}$$
$$\textbf{let } h_1 = vcgd \ d \ \rho \textbf{ in}$$
$$\textbf{let } h_2 = vcgg \ (proc\_names \ d) \ \rho \textbf{ in}$$
$$\textbf{let } h_3 = vcgc \textbf{ true } c \ g_0 \ q \ \rho \textbf{ in}$$
$$h_1 \ \& \ h_2 \ \& \ h_3$$

Fig. 5: Definition of vcg, the main VCG function

$$\text{vcg\_THM} : \ \vdash \ \forall \pi q. \ WF_p \ \pi \ \wedge \ \textbf{every close} \ (vcg \ \pi \ q) \ \Rightarrow \ \pi[q]$$

Fig. 6: Verification condition generator verification theorem

The VCG has been verified within the Higher Order Logic (HOL) mechanical theorem prover [3], based on the given structural operational semantics. The ultimate theorem of the verification of the VCG is given in Fig. 6. This theorem states that for any program π and postcondition q, if the program is well-formed ($WF_p \ \pi$) and if all of the verification conditions yielded by the VCG ($vcg \ \pi \ q$) are true, then the program must be totally correct with respect to the postcondition ($\pi[q]$). For the vital definition of program well-formedness, please see [5].

The proof of this theorem involved 8 new types, 217 definitions, and 906 major theorems proved within HOL, using over 57,000 lines of proof. These types, definitions, and theorems were organized into 22 HOL theories, on subjects including syntax, structural operational semantics, axiomatic semantics, recursive progress, termination, and the VCG. This proof shows that the VCG is sound, that the correctness of the verification conditions it produces suffice to establish the total correctness of the annotated program. This soundness result is quite useful, as we may directly apply the verification theorem in proving individual programs totally correct within HOL, with the amount of work involved reduced significantly by the VCG while maintaining complete security, and with the full power of HOL available to the user to prove the verification conditions.

Unfortunately, space precludes giving many interesting details of the proof of this theorem, which can be found in the first author's dissertation [5]. However, Fig. 7 displays the overall structure of this proof. Each box indicates a property about the entire program, with the arrows indicating logical consequence. The boxes are numbered in the order the properties are proven. The preceeding paper [7] described the proof of partial correctness; this is accomplished by the proofs of boxes 1–4. The addition in this paper of the proof of termination is accomplished by the proofs of boxes 5–9. Then the partial correctness and termination properties are combined to prove total correctness in boxes 10–12. Despite the altitude of this proof structure, it does reasonably depict the increase in conceptual difficulty in adding termination, as a factor between 2 and 3.

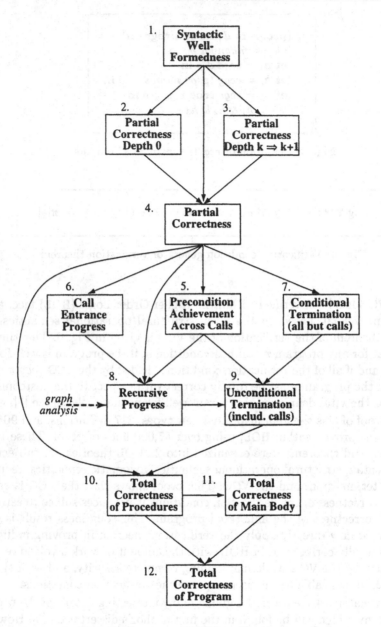

Fig. 7: Structure of VCG verification proof

Fig. 8: Bicycling Example Call Graph.

```
program

    procedure pedal(; val n, m);
        global a, b, c;
        pre     n * m + c = a * b;
        post    c = a * b;
        enters pedal with n < 'n ∧ m = 'm;
        enters coast with n < 'n ∧ m < 'm;
        recurses    with n < 'n;

        if n = 0 ∨ m = 0 then
                skip
        else
                c := c + m;
                if n < m then
                        coast(; n − 1, m − 1)
                else
                        pedal(; n − 1, m)
                fi
        fi
    end procedure;

    procedure coast(; val n, m);
        global a, b, c;
        pre     n * (m + 1) + c = a * b;
        post    c = a * b;
        enters pedal with n = 'n ∧ m = 'm;
        enters coast with n = 'n ∧ m < 'm;
        recurses    with m < 'm;

        c := c + n;
        if n < m then
                coast(; n, m − 1)
        else
                pedal(; n, m)
        fi
    end procedure;

    a := 7;  b := 12;  c := 0;
    pedal(; a, b)
end program

[ c = 7 * 12 ]
```

Fig. 9: Bicycling example program

6   Example

We consider an artificial but simple example, the Bicycling program in Fig. 9. Its procedure call graph is given in Fig. 8. The effect of this program is to multiply two numbers $(a * b)$ by repeated additions, and leave the result in c. Despite the surprising nature of the partial correctness of this program, however, our primary interest is in its termination.

We call this example "Bicycling" because the structure of the call graph reminds us of a bicycle, with its two wheels and the chain that transfers power from the pedals to the rear wheel. Imagine a bicycle with one pedal damaged so that it could not support any pressure. When pedaling such a bicycle, one would need to thrust hard when the good pedal was moving downward, but while it was moving upwards would exert no force, and would coast, depending solely on the momentum generated by the other phase to propel one to the goal.[1] This corresponds to the entrance progress achieved across the arcs of the call graph.

We believe that it is difficult to prove termination for the Bicycling program using either Sokołowski's or Pandya and Joseph's methods. Sokołowski's does not easily apply, since for the call from *coast* to *pedal*, neither n nor m change, and if $n = 0$, not even c changes. Pandya and Joseph's method relies on finding a smaller set of procedures, but since both procedures are self-recursive, neither can be eliminated, devolving to Sokołowski's method, with the difficulties above. Nevertheless there is a very natural and simple argument that this program terminates, namely that the variable n decreases in any recursion involving *pedal*, and m decreases in any recursion involving *coast*. This argument suggests the arc labels in Fig. 8, and the progress annotations in Fig. 9.

The VCG has been implemented as a secure HOL tactic. In the Bicycling example, applying *vcgd* to the two procedure declarations generates two VC's:

VC1: Partial correctness and entrance progress for *pedal*:

$$('n = n \ \wedge \ 'm = m \ \wedge \ n * m + c = a * b) \Rightarrow$$
$$((n = 0 \ \vee \ m = 0 \ =>$$
$$c = a * b$$
$$| \ (n < m \ =>$$
$$(n - 1) * ((m - 1) + 1) + c + m = a * b \ \wedge$$
$$n - 1 < 'n \ \wedge \ m - 1 < 'm$$
$$| \ (n - 1) * m + c + m = a * b \ \wedge \ n - 1 < 'n \ \wedge \ m = 'm)))$$

VC2: Partial correctness and entrance progress for *coast*:

$$('n = n \ \wedge \ 'm = m \ \wedge \ n * (m + 1) + c = a * b) \Rightarrow$$
$$((n < m \ =>$$
$$n * ((m - 1) + 1) + c + n = a * b \ \wedge \ n = 'n \ \wedge \ m - 1 < 'm$$
$$| \ n * m + c + n = a * b \ \wedge \ n = 'n \ \wedge \ m = 'm))$$

Then applying *vcgg* to the procedure call graph generates six VC's:

VC3: Undiverted recursion verification condition for the path
pedal $\rightarrow$ *pedal*:
$$n * m + c = a * b \ \wedge \ n = 'n \ \Rightarrow \ (\forall n_1 m_1. \ n_1 < n \ \wedge \ m_1 = m \ \Rightarrow \ n_1 < 'n)$$

---

[1] We are grateful to Prof. D. Stott Parker for his recollection of such a damaged bicycle.

VC4: Undiverted recursion verification condition for the path $pedal \rightarrow coast \rightarrow pedal$:

$n * m + c = a * b \wedge n = 'n \Rightarrow$

$(\forall n_1 m_1. \; n_1 < n \wedge m_1 < m \Rightarrow (\forall n_2 m_2. \; n_2 = n_1 \wedge m_2 = m_1 \Rightarrow n_2 < 'n))$

VC5: Diversion verification condition for the path $coast \rightarrow coast \rightarrow pedal$:

$(\forall n_1 m_1. \; n_1 = n \wedge m_1 = m \Rightarrow n_1 < 'n) \Rightarrow$

$(\forall n_1 m_1. \; n_1 = n \wedge m_1 < m \Rightarrow (\forall n_2 m_2. \; n_2 = n_1 \wedge m_2 = m_1 \Rightarrow n_2 < 'n))$

VC6: Diversion verification condition for the path $pedal \rightarrow pedal \rightarrow coast$:

$(\forall n_1 m_1. \; n_1 < n \wedge m_1 < m \Rightarrow m_1 < 'm) \Rightarrow$

$(\forall n_1 m_1. \; n_1 < n \wedge m_1 = m \Rightarrow (\forall n_2 m_2. \; n_2 < n_1 \wedge m_2 < m_1 \Rightarrow m_2 < 'm))$

VC7: Undiverted recursion verification condition for the path
$coast \rightarrow pedal \rightarrow coast$:

$n * (m + 1) + c = a * b \wedge m = 'm \Rightarrow$

$(\forall n_1 m_1. \; n_1 = n \wedge m_1 = m \Rightarrow (\forall n_2 m_2. \; n_2 < n_1 \wedge m_2 < m_1 \Rightarrow m_2 < 'm))$

VC8: Undiverted recursion verification condition for the path $coast \rightarrow coast$:

$n * (m + 1) + c = a * b \wedge m = 'm \Rightarrow (\forall n_1 m_1. \; n_1 = n \wedge m_1 < m \Rightarrow m_1 < 'm)$

Finally, applying *vcgc* to the main body of the program generates one VC:

VC9: Total correctness for main body:

$\textbf{true} \Rightarrow (7 * 12 + 0 = 7 * 12)$

The reader is invited to verify that these verification conditions are true. We have applied the VCG to this example, proved the resulting VC's in HOL, and hence proven the total correctness of the Bicycling example as an HOL theorem.

7   Graph Analysis

To justify the recursive progress claims, we must prove that the recursive decrease is implied by the cumulative progress across *every* possible path in the procedure call graph that is an instance of recursion. A path is an instance of recursion if it begins and ends with the same procedure (the "root"). There is a potentially infinite number of such paths, but the task may be simplified by a series of steps.

First, if an instance of recursion includes another instance of the root interior to the path, then we call this an instance of *multiple recursion*; otherwise we call this *single recursion*. Fortunately, to prove the progress claims for instances of multiple recursion, it suffices to prove them for instances of single recursion.

This simplifies the task, but it may still involve an infinite number of paths due to the presence of other cycles in the call graph. This is because a path which is an instance of single recursion may contain duplicate nodes other than the root. We call such an occurrence of duplicate nodes other than the root a *diversion*, as it seems to temporarily divert the path from its goal of the root procedure. To simplify the task further, we can collapse the cases for paths which differ only in how many times the diversion is traversed, if we can prove that traversing the diversion does not "lose ground" logically.

Every node in every path must be annotated with it's "path condition." This is computed using the *call_progress* function backwards across each arc, starting from the end of the path, which is initially annotated with the recursion expression for the root procedure. Paths with the same root procedure at the end may be collected into a *call tree* (see Fig. 10 for *coast*), since they share some of the same path conditions. For each path, if it is an instance of recursion, the path condition at the beginning is the precondition for satisfying the recursion progress at the end. If this precondition is implied by the *induct_pre* value of the recursion expression of that procedure, this path shows the needed progress. We call such an implication a *undiverted recursion verification condition*.

Consider such a path marked with path conditions that contains a diversion. Let the earlier node of the diversion have path condition pc_1, and the later node pc_2 (see Fig. 10). The similar but shorter path with the diversion removed is verified above. This verification can apply to the current path if traversing the diversion "loses no ground" logically. Surprisingly, this is assured if $pc_2 \Rightarrow pc_1$. This may seem counterintuitive, since pc_1 is earlier in time than pc_2. But in fact this guarantees that traversing the diversion continues to ensure achieving the desired recursive progress. We call $pc_2 \Rightarrow pc_1$ a *diversion verification condition*.

Proving such diversion verification conditions allows us to collapse the set of paths we must consider to a finite number, because any path with a diversion can then be reduced to a path without the diversion, and any path of single recursion without any diversions can include all non-root procedures at most once. With a finite number of declared procedures, each such path must be finite, and even with a completely connected procedure call graph, the number of possible such paths must be finite. The diversion verification condition method for proving total correctness is currently U.S. Patent Pending.

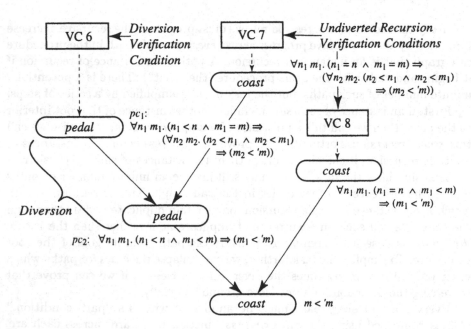

Fig. 10: Call tree for *coast*, with path conditions and verification conditions

8   Summary and Conclusions

We have defined concisely and verified within HOL a verification condition generator which effectively implements the diversion verification condition method. This new method is more general and flexible than prior proposals, and more powerful while remaining intuitive. It is compositional and readily mechanized.

The real security of this work is in the mechanical verification of the VCG. In such subtle areas as mutual recursion and graph analysis, our personal intuition was insufficient to guarantee soundness. HOL made this security possible.

This VCG substantially decreases the difficulty of proving programs totally correct, and does so with a very high level of security. A VCG itself must be trustworthy for the proofs to be trustworthy. This level of trustworthiness is now demonstrated to be feasible, by the example of this mechanically verified VCG.

For more information on the Sunrise system, please see

> http://www.cis.upenn.edu/~hol/sunrise.

Soli Deo Gloria.

References

1. P. America and F. de Boer. Proving Total Correctness of Recursive Procedures. *Information and Computation*, 84(2):129–162, 1990.
2. K. R. Apt. Ten Years of Hoare logic: A Survey – Part 1. *ACM TOPLAS*, 3(4):431–483, 1981.
3. M. Gordon and T. Melham. *Introduction to HOL, A Theorem Proving Environment for Higher Order Logic*. Cambridge University Press, Cambridge, 1993.
4. C. A. R. Hoare. Procedures and Parameters: an axiomatic approach. In: *Proceedings of Symposium on Semantics of Algorithmic Languages*, ed. E. Engeler, volume 188 of *Lecture Notes in Mathematics*, pages 102–116, 1971.
5. P. Homeier. *Trustworthy Tools for Trustworthy Programs: A Mechanically Verified Verification Condition Generator for the Total Correctness of Procedures*. Ph.D. Dissertation, UCLA Computer Science Department, 1995.
6. P. Homeier and D. Martin. A Mechanically Verified Verification Condition Generator. *The Computer Journal*, 38(2):131–141, 1995.
7. P. Homeier and D. Martin. Mechanical Verification of Mutually Recursive Procedures. In M. A. McRobbie and J. K. Slaney (eds.), *Proceedings of the 13th International Conference on Automated Deduction (CADE-13)*, volume 1104 of *Lecture Notes in Artificial Intelligence*, pages 201–215, Springer-Verlag, 1996.
8. S. Igarashi, R. L. London, and C. Luckham. Automatic program verification: A logical basis and its implementation. *Acta Informatica*, 4:145–182, 1975.
9. T. Melham. A Package for Inductive Relation Definitions in HOL. In M. Archer, J. Joyce, K. Levitt, and Windley (eds.), *Proceedings of the 1991 International Workshop on the HOL Theorem Proving System and its Applications*, Davis, August 1991. IEEE Computer Society Press, pages 350–357, 1992.
10. P. Pandya and M. Joseph. A Structure-directed Total Correctness Proof Rule for Recursive Procedure Calls. *The Computer Journal*, 29(6):531–537, 1986.
11. S. Sokolowski. Total Correctness for Procedures, In J. Gruska (ed), *Proceedings, 6th Symposium on the Mathematical Foundations of Computer Science*, volume 53 of *Lecture Notes in Computer Science*, pages 475–483, Springer-Verlag, 1977.

A Type Annotation Scheme for Nuprl

Douglas J. Howe

Bell Labs, 700 Mountain Ave., Murray Hill, NJ 07974, USA
howe@research.bell-labs.com

Abstract. Nuprl's constructive type theory, like conventional set theory, buys much of its expressive power and flexibility at the cost of giving up the more manageable kind of type system found in other logics. Many of the benefits and costs of Nuprl's approach to type theory are related to the fact that terms are *untyped* in the sense that there is no algorithm to determine from the syntax of an expression what type, if any, it is a member of. We have designed and implemented an annotation scheme where terms are decorated with types in such a way that types can (almost always) be efficiently maintained during inference. These type annotations in a term are obtained using Nuprl's existing type checking and type inference machinery, which use contextual information in the term to determine types for subterms.

Our implementation still needs some tuning for performance, but the current working prototype already gives roughly a factor of 10 speedup in term rewriting (the main workhorse in Nuprl proofs). In addition, tactics such as conditional rewriting are now more effective because they can quickly and more reliably obtain the types of terms.

1 Introduction

Nuprl [2] is an interactive theorem-proving system in the lineage of LCF. One of its main distinguishing characteristics is its highly expressive formal logic, a constructive type theory whose classical variant has expressive power equivalent to conventional set theory (ZFC) [9, 5].

Nuprl has been extensively applied, and its expressive power has been shown to be a substantial advantage in a variety of domains (see [7] for a recent example), but little work has been specifically directed toward effectiveness for the kind of large-scale practical applications, such as protocol verification, where a great deal of the formal mathematics is highly complicated, but shallow and representationally simple. In applications such as this, there will be parts, such as reasoning about abstraction and refinement methods (see [1] for an example), where expressive power can be a great advantage. There will be other parts, such as verifying that the atomic state transitions of a system satisfy an invariant, where expressive power is less important and where the speed and effectiveness of basic inference mechanisms, such as term rewriting, is crucial. The goal of the work in this paper is to enhance the second kind of reasoning without imposing restrictions that affect the first kind.

Many of the benefits and costs of Nuprl's approach to type theory are related to the fact that terms are *untyped* in the sense that one cannot determine from the syntax of an expression what type, if any, it is a member of. This is a problem for automation for two reasons. First, it is often important to have terms come with their types; for example, in term rewriting, type information can be used to implement a useful form of conditional rewriting. Second, typing properties require proof, so, for example, every time a lemma is instantiated, the instantiating objects must be proved to have the right types. While these typing proofs can almost always be done automatically, the large number of such proof obligations arising in practice causes a serious performance problem. This problem is at its worst in term rewriting, where a lemma is instantiated (resulting in type-checking subgoals) every time a rewrite rule is applied and every time rewriting descends through an operator to rewrite subterms.

We have designed and implemented an annotation scheme for Nuprl where terms are decorated with types in such a way that types can (almost always) be efficiently maintained during inference, but without placing any new syntactic restrictions on the logic. The implementation needs some recoding in spots for efficiency, but our current prototype already gives roughly a factor of 10 speedup in term rewriting.

An important point is that the annotations do not restrict the kinds of types that can be assigned to terms. In particular, any type generated by Nuprl's existing type inference machinery can be use in annotations.

The scheme relies on the following observation. Although type inference (and checking) is undecidable in Nuprl, and although typeable terms may have untypeable subterms, we can compute a type for virtually all terms occurring in proofs arising in practice. In fact, each occurrence of an operator (i.e. term constructor) can be assigned a result type and also expected types for its operands. In our annotation scheme, we place a restriction on how a result type relates to an expected type of a surrounding operator, but this restriction is a minimal semantic one just sufficient to support term rewriting. What the annotation scheme amounts to is a way of retaining, in the term structure itself, the types found for subterms of a term. The types are kept around during inference, so they can be reused when, for example, a lemma is instantiated.

Another important point about the scheme is that almost all existing Nuprl tactics work, without change, when terms are annotated. A few of the tactics, such as the rewriting machinery, have been updated to take advantage of annotations. Some of the old tactics are now more effective because the basic function that attempts to find a type for a term is now more effective since the procedure which annotates terms takes advantage of context that is often missing when tactics ask for the type of a term.

In addition, our scheme has the following properties. First, annotations are optional. Not every subterm of a term needs to be annotated. Second, there are no heuristics in the scheme *per se*. Although type inference and checking are highly heuristic in Nuprl, this is independent of the annotation scheme. Annotations for terms are generated by applying Nuprl's existing type inference machinery. Third, we retain the tree-structuring of proofs, with independence of proof branches, that allows us, among other things, to do dependency-directed backtracking, and selective replay of subproofs. Fourth, soundness depends only on a fixed set of primitive inference rules that all proofs must reduce to. Finally, the scheme is (almost) completely invisible to users.

Because the modifications made to Nuprl in order to account for annotations are largely made on a rule-by-rule basis, there is a high degree of modularity in the implementation. Nevertheless, the modifications add about 4,000 lines of Lisp code to the refinement engine, making Nuprl's inference system substantially more complicated, and this is a serious negative aspect of our work. We have made a choice to give up some confidence in the correctness of the implementation in order to gain the practical benefits described above.

The work should be viewed as experimental. Our results are quite encouraging, and it may be worthwhile to redesign Nuprl's logic to directly support some kind of type annotations. This could make the annotation scheme much simpler as well as more efficient. The main cost would be extensive modifications to Nuprl's tactic machinery and compatibility problems with existing libraries of mathematics. It would be interesting to see if an annotation scheme similar to ours would be useful for another logic with an untyped syntax, for example some formalization of set theory (ZFC).

The type theory of the PVS system [8] has some similarities to Nuprl, such as subtypes, a limited form of dependent type, and undecidable type checking. PVS uses a typing discipline that achieves most of the goals above, but it would only be applicable to an insufficiently small subtheory of Nuprl. Some complicating aspects of Nuprl, which aren't present in PVS, are: type universes; type-indexed equality, so that two terms may both be in two types, but be equal in one type and not in the other; contravariant subtyping, where a function type is enlarged when its domain is shrunk; and general dependent types. Of course, one can argue about whether the extra expressive power is worth the trouble for practical applications, but this is beyond the scope of the paper.

In our paper [3], which describes a project to verify the SCI cache coherence protocol, there is a 2-page summary of a prototype of this annotation scheme.

2 Nuprl: Syntax and Semantics

This section gives a description of Nuprl, focusing on the syntax and semantics of the type theory. The semantics we use is the set-theoretic one we developed in [6]. The main advantage of this semantics for our purposes here is that it has a much simpler account of "hypothetical judgments" than other semantics, in particular the one given in [2]. A *hypothetical judgment* in our context is essentially a typing judgment, where a term is asserted to have a type under assumption that some variables have certain types.

Before proceeding to the syntax and semantics, we give a brief overview of Nuprl. Formal mathematics in Nuprl is organized in a single library, which is broken into files simulating a theory structure. Library objects can be definitions, display forms, theorems, comments or objects containing ML code. Definitions define new operators, possibly with binding structure, in terms of existing Nuprl terms and previously defined operators. Display forms provide notations for defined and primitive operators. These notations need not be parsable since Nuprl uses structure editors. Theorems have tree structured proofs, possibly incomplete. Each node has a sequent, and represents an inference step. The step is justified either by a primitive rule, or by a *tactic*. Nuprl's notion of tactic is derived from that of LCF, as is HOL's [4].

Nuprl's type theory has a rich set of type constructors. The following are some example types: $\Pi n \in N . B^n \rightarrow B^n$, $\{ x \in N \; list \mid x \neq nil \}$, $\Sigma n \in N . B^n$ and $(x, y) : Z \times N^+ // (x_1 y_2 = y_1 x_2)$. This first of these can be thought of as the type of functions mapping an n and an n-ary bit-vector to an n-ary bit-vector. The second is the type of nonempty lists of natural numbers, the third is the collection of pairs (n, b) such that b is an n-ary bit-vector, and the last is a quotient type representing the rational numbers represented as pairs of integers with the usual equivalence relation.

Although Nuprl is a type theory, its term language is untyped in a fundamental way. For example, we can prove $(\lambda x. \; 17)(3 + true) = 17 \in Z$. This is because Nuprl has lazy function application and so we can compute the left-hand side to 17. The fact that no commitment is made to a conventional kind of static typing discipline for terms is what gives Nuprl much of its expressive power.

The details of most of the particular type constructors in Nuprl will be irrelevant for the bulk of the paper. The semantic account we give of our annotation scheme is abstract with respect to the set of constructors in the theory. It is only in the discussion of how Nuprl's inference rules are modified to account for annotations that we will be concerned with specific type constructors.

Nuprl terms have the form $\theta(\overline{x}_1. \; e_1; \ldots; \overline{x}_n. \; e_n)$ where θ is an *operator* and in each *operand* $\overline{x}_i. \; e_i$, each of the variables in the sequence $\overline{x}_i$ binds in e_i. We assume that the variables in $\overline{x}_i$ are all distinct. Nuprl also allows members of $\overline{x}_i$ to be a fixed "invisible" variable which can never occur free – these is handled in our annotation scheme, but we ignore it in the paper since dealing with it is nothing more than an annoyance.

For example, in Nuprl syntax a lambda term $\lambda x. \; b$ could be written as $lam \; (x. \, b)$, and a universally quantified expression $\forall x : A. \; B$ could be written as $all \, (A; x. B)$. Note that in the latter expression for universal quantification, there is no syntactic relationship between A and x; the syntax does not specify that A is a type to be associated with x. At the level of syntax, there is no distinction between types and terms. There are only terms, and types will be those terms that can be proved to be types using Nuprl's inference rules.

In the semantics for Nuprl given in [6], we augment the set the of terms with an infinite collection of constants representing objects from a universe of set-theoretic objects, and extend the operational semantics to deal with these new objects. This allows us to give set theoretic meaning to types and members of types in the type theory, even though the semantics is based on a term model and an evaluation relation over terms.

We omit all details of the semantics, and assume as given a subset of the set of closed terms, whose elements we will call *types*, and a mapping that associates with each type T a partial equivalence relation σ_T over closed terms. (A partial equivalence relation over a set X is an equivalence relation over a subset of X.) We write $e = e' \in T$ to mean that T is a type and $(e, e') \in \sigma_T$. We use $e \in T$ as shorthand for $e = e \in T$, and we will call the terms $e \in T$ the *members* of T. We will say that a closed term T is *true* if it is a type and there exists e such that $e \in T$. This definition of truth corresponds to Nuprl's use of the proposition-as-types principle, where types and propositions are identified and the truth of a proposition is taken to be non-emptiness of the type.

We assume two particular type constructors at this stage: equality and conjunction. An expression $e = e' \doteq T$ is a type if and only if $e, e' \in T$. If $e = e' \in T$, then $e = e' \doteq T$ is a non-empty type (there is no need to specify its members here), and if $e \neq e' \in T$, then $e = e' \doteq T$ is an empty type. We write $e \doteq T$ as shorthand for $e = e \doteq T$. Note that by our definition of truth of expressions, $t \doteq T$ is true if and only if $t \in T$. We assume conjunction has the usual properties, in particular $T \& T'$ is true if and only if both T and T' are.

Nuprl's inference rules involve *sequents*, which have the form

$$x_1 : A_1, \ldots, x_n : A_n \vdash T \ [t]$$

where $t, T, A_1, \ldots, A_n$ are terms and for all i, $1 \leq i \leq n$, all of the free variables of t and T are among $x_1, \ldots, x_n$, and all of the free variables of each A_i are among $x_1, \ldots, x_{i-1}$. A *closing substitution* for the sequent is a substitution which has domain $x_1, \ldots, x_n$ and whose values are all closed terms.

Definition 1. *The sequent* $x_1 : A_1, \ldots, x_n : A_n \vdash T \ [t]$ *is true if* $\sigma(t) \in \sigma(T)$ *for all closing substitutions* σ *such that for all* i, $1 \leq i \leq n$, $\sigma(x_i) \in \sigma(A_i)$.

3 Semantic Type Annotations

Before giving a precise specification of the annotation scheme, we give a rough description along with examples and some comments about choices that were made.

Roughly speaking, an annotated term is a term decorated with type expressions. A type annotation may be attached to a subterm, or to a binding occurrence of a variable. The meaning of the annotations in a term e is partly the obvious one. For example, let t be some subterm occurrence in e, and suppose that t has an annotation, T say. Suppose also t is in the scope of exactly one binding variable in e, and that the binding occurrence of x has an annotation A attached to it. Then the annotation on t is sound if for all closed terms a, if $a \in A$ then $e[a/x] \in T[a/x]$.

We need more out of type annotations than just the fact that subterms are members of their annotated types. Consider the following example. Suppose *fact* is a defined operator for the factorial function over natural numbers. We might have proved a typing property for *fact*: $\forall x : N. \ fact \ (x) \in N$.

Consider the term $fact(e)$, where e is some arithmetic expression over the integers. Arithmetic expressions in Nuprl are usually given type Z, the type of integers. The example, for $x, y \in Z$, $x + y \in Z$. Assume, then, that the "result type" of e is Z. From the typing property for $fact$, the result type of $fact(e)$ is N. Thus, if we label subterms with their result types, $fact(e)$ would be annotated as $fact(e : Z) : N$. This means that the subterm e has annotation Z and the whole term has annotation N. Assume that the annotations are sound. Thus we know $e \in Z$ and $fact(e) \in N$. Suppose we now apply a lemma $\forall x : N.\ fact(x) > 0$ to the annotated term. We have to prove $e \in N$, and the annotations don't help us. We have lost information, since presumably we had to show $e \in N$ in order to establish $fact(e) \in N$.

Instead of using the result type for a subterm as its annotation, we could use the type that is "expected" from the context. In the example, N is the expected type of e. But now we have a problem with term rewriting, since rewriting e using arithmetic equalities could result in a term e' such that $e = e' \in Z$. Here the type over which the equality holds is not the same as the annotation type. In this simple case we know that the rewrite is justified anyways, but in general if terms e and e' satisfy $e, e' \in T$, $e, e' \in T'$ and $e = e' \in T$, then it is not necessarily true that $e = e' \in T'$. For example, if $f, f' \in Z \to Z$ differ on negative numbers but agree on N, then $f = f' \in N \to Z$ but $f \neq f' \in Z \to Z$. This example is an instance of *contravariant subtyping* in Nuprl: if A' is a subtype of A, and B is a subtype of B', then $A \to B$ is a subtype of $A' \to B'$.

Because of these considerations, we keep both "expected" and "result" types around. One can think of annotations in a term as being associated with the operators used to build the term. With each operator occurrence, there is a *result* type for the whole expression headed by the operator, and also *expected types* for the operands. Since the operands may have binding variables, the expected types may have assumptions associated with them. The assumptions give types for the binding variables.

Before giving the precise definition of the syntax of annotated terms, we give a few examples. A fully annotated term involving $fact$ is $fact((3 : Z) : [true]N) : N$. Here we see that 3 has result type Z and expected type N under assumption $true$. We will usually write $[]$ in place of $[true]$. One way of thinking of the expression $[true]N$ is as a "guarded type": the type $[\phi]A$ has as members all terms e such that if ϕ is true then $e \in A$. Note that if ϕ is false then every term is a member of $[\phi]A$.

An annotated form of a universally quantified expression is $all\ (A : []U; x.B : [x \in A]P) : P$ where U is one of Nuprl's universes of types, and P is a universe of propositions. In this example, B has expected type P under assumption $x \in A$. Here we have given only the annotation associated with the operator all, including its expected types; the terms A and B may also have annotations. As a final example, we can annotate a conditional expression as follows: $if(b : B;\ e_1 : [b]A;\ e_2 : [\neg b]A) : A$, where B is the type of booleans. Thus e_1 is only required to have the expected type A under the condition that the boolean b is true.

Since we do not want a fixed, decidable restriction to Nuprl's type theory, we must allow for proof of soundness of annotations. This leads us to introduce two modes for annotations, which we will call *polarities*. *Positive* annotations are those which are not known to be sound and thus require proof. A sequent with positive annotations will be provable only if all the positive annotations are provable. *Negative* annotations are assumed true. In proving a sequent, we may assume that all the negative annotations are true.

This may all seem a bit complicated, but keep in mind that it is invisible to the user. Positive annotations are introduced by certain tactics behind the scenes, but are always handled by a tactic and are never left around for the user to see. Sometimes proving the annotations may involve subgoals, but these are essentially the same subgoals that would arise in proving the expression well-typed in Nuprl without the annotation scheme. Users never enter annotated terms directly. Negative annotations are not displayed by the proof editor (unless one sets a special switch).

To illustrate the ideas introduced so far, consider the following simple example. Suppose we are proving a goal $\vdash even(4)$, and that we want to start by annotating it. We first use Nuprl's "cut" rule to introduce the formula $even((4 :^? Z) :^? [true]N) :^? P$, where P is a type of propositions and $:^?$ indicates a positive annotation. Let *pos* be this cut formula, and let *neg* be the same formula but with annotations negated, so *neg* is $even((4:Z):[true]N):P$. Applying the rule results in two subgoals: $\vdash pos \dot\in P$ and $neg \dot\in P \vdash even(4)$. Note that since the first subgoal requires proving that the annotations are correct, we may assume them in the second subgoal, and so the cut rule has been modified to do this negation.

To prove the second subgoal, we use the cut rule with the formula *neg*, getting subgoals $neg \dot\in P \vdash neg$ and $neg \dot\in P, neg \vdash even(4)$. The second of these is trivial, and the first gives us the annotated version of the original goal (after we remove the unwanted hypothesis using the "thinning" rule). Note that we are allowed to introduce *neg* in this step without any annotation-related proof-obligations because *neg* already occurs is the goal and hence the annotations in it may be assumed sound.

To prove the the goal $\vdash pos \dot\in P$, we use a new primitive rule to refine it to three subgoals. The first is to show that *even* respects equality:

$$x:N, \ x = 4 \dot\in N \ \vdash \ even(x) = even(4) \dot\in P.$$

The second subgoal, $\vdash (4 :^? Z) \dot\in Z$, is to show the annotation on 4 is correct, and the third, $\vdash Z \subseteq_4 N$, is to show that the result type of 4 "matches", in a sense to be explained later, the expected type N. All of the above steps are handled automatically and invisibly in the implementation.

To formalize annotated terms it is convenient to quantify over polarities. We will let p range over the set $\{-, +\}$, and will use these values as "superscripts" on annotations. An annotation with a superscript of $-$ is taken to be negative, and one with a superscript of $+$ is positive. The *unannotated terms* are the terms of Nuprl as defined earlier.

For convenience, we place restrictions on the form of assumptions for expected types. Suppose a is a term, and write a as a_1 & ... & a_n, $1 \leq n$, such that each a_i is not a conjunction. Let $(x_1 \in A_1), \ldots, (x_m \in A_m)$ be the sequence obtained by removing from the sequence $a_1, \ldots, a_n$ all elements that are not of the form $x \in A$ for some variable x and some term A. If $x_1, \ldots, x_m$ are all distinct, then we say that a *covers* the sequence $x_1, \ldots, x_m$, and for each i $(1 \leq i \leq m)$, the *type for x_i in a is A_i*.

Definition 2. *The annotated and subannotated terms are inductively defined as follows.*

1. *If e is a subannotated term or an unannotated term, then e is an annotated term.*
2. *If e is not a variable and is either a subannotated term or an unannotated term, and if t is an unannotated term, then $ann^p(e; t)$ is an annotated term.*
3. *Let θ be an operator, and for $i = 1, \ldots, n$ suppose e_i is an annotated term, $\overline{x}_i$ is a sequence of distinct variables, a_i, t_i are unannotated terms, and a_i covers $\overline{x}_i$. Then $\theta(\overline{x}_1.subann(e_1; a_1; t_1); \ldots; \overline{x}_n.subann(e_n; a_n; t_n))$ is a subannotated term, and in each operand the variables in $\overline{x}_i$ bind in e_i, a_i and t_i.*

When annotations are viewed in the Nuprl, $ann^-(e; t)$ appears as $e : t$, $ann^+(e; t)$ appears as $e :^? t$, and $subann(e; a; t)$ appears as $e : [a]t$. We extend the substitution to annotated terms in the obvious way, treating the type and assumption parts of annotations as components of the term. Note that $subann$ above does not have a parity superscript. Essentially, this is because we think of its parity as determined by the annotation of the surrounding term (and in the case when there is no annotation, the parity will not matter). The assumptions a_i give types for the bound variables, which are needed for annotations of either parity in e_i.

We say that e is an annotated subterm of e' if either:

1. $e = e'$,
2. $e' = ann^p(e''; t)$ and e is an annotated subterm of e'', or
3. $e' = \theta(\overline{x}_1. subann(e_1; a_1; t_1); \ldots; \overline{x}_n. subann(e_n; a_n; t_n))$ and for some i, e is an annotated subterm of e_i and $a_i = true$ (where $true$ is taken to be the empty conjunction).

The "typical" annotated term is of the form $ann^p(e; t)$ where e is a subannotated term. The other cases in the definition are present because it is not always convenient, or even possible, to give annotations for every subterm of a term. For example, clause 1 allows for the possibility that a term is missing some annotations at the top, but the subannotations give the assumptions on variable-binding occurrences that are required to make sense of annotations on subterms. These extra cases do not complicate the semantics.

Define the erasure $\epsilon(e)$ of an annotated term as follows.

− $\epsilon(e) = e$ if e is unannotated
− $\epsilon(ann^p(e; t)) = \epsilon(e)$, and

$$- \; \epsilon(\theta(\overline{x}_1 \, subann(e_1; a_1; t_1); \ldots; \overline{x}_n \, subann(e_n; a_n; t_n))) = \theta(\overline{x}_1 \epsilon(e_1); \ldots; \overline{x}_n \epsilon(e_n)).$$

We extend the semantic judgments to annotated terms via erasure. For closed annotated terms t, t is a type if $\epsilon(t)$ is a type, and for closed annotated terms e, e', define $e = e' \in t$ if $\epsilon(e) = \epsilon(e') \in \epsilon(t)$.

We now define the semantics of annotations. We define predicates ψ^p on closed annotated terms. Intuitively, $\psi^p(e)$ is true exactly if all the p-annotated subterms of e are sound in the sense described at the beginning of this section. There are two complications, both of which are related to the goal of having annotations support term rewriting. First, we must specify *operator functionality*. This is the property that if the operands of a term are replaced by terms that are equal relative to their expected types, then the new term is equal to the old in the result type of the term.

The second complication is the relationship between the result type of a subterm and the expected type associated with its context. We want equality in the result type to imply equality in the expected type. For this we will choose the minimal guarantee, using the following definition. If T, T' are types and t is a closed annotated term, then T is a *local subtype of T' at t*, written $T \subseteq_t T'$, if for all $x \in T$ such that $x = t \in T$, $x = t \in T'$. Thus, if $T \subseteq_t T'$ and $t = t' \in T$, then in the annotated term $\theta((t : T) : []T') : A$, we may rewrite t to t', getting $\theta(t) = \theta(t') \in A$.

In the following definition we will need to quantify over closed substitution instances of operands. To make the following definition more compact, we adopt a notational convention. If we have an operand $x_1, \ldots, x_n . e$, then by $e[\overline{a}]$, for $\overline{a}$ a sequence of terms of the length n, we mean $e[a_1, \ldots, a_n / x_1, \ldots, x_n]$. We also extend this substitution notation to subexpressions of e, relying on the context to specify the variables to be substituted for, and we will be sloppy about specifying the lengths of term sequences.

Definition 3. *We define $\psi^p(e)$, for closed e, by structural induction.*

1. *If e is unannotated then $\psi^p(e)$ is true.*
2. *If e is unannotated then $\psi^p(ann^p(e; t))$ if and only if $e \in t$.*
3. *If $p \neq p'$ then $\psi^p(ann^{p'}(e; t))$ if and only if $\psi^p(e)$.*
4. *Let e be a subannotated term $\theta(\overline{s})$ where $\overline{s}$ is a sequence of n operands such that for all i, operand s_i has the form $\overline{x}_i . \, subann(e_i; a_i; t_i)$. Then $\psi^p(e)$ if and only if for all i $(1 \leq i \leq n)$ and for all closed $\overline{u}$, if $a_i[\overline{u}]$ is true then $\psi^p(e_i[\overline{u}])$.*
5. *Let e be as in 4 above. Then $\psi^p(ann^p(e; t))$ if and only if the following hold.*
   (a) *$\psi^p(e)$,*
   (b) *for each i such that e_i has the form $ann^{p'}(e_i'; t_i')$: for all closed $\overline{u}$, if $a_i[\overline{u}]$ is true then $t_i'[\overline{u}] \subseteq_{e_i'[\overline{u}]} t_i[\overline{u}]$,*
   (c) *for each i such that e_i does not have the form $ann^{p'}(e_i'; t_i')$: for all $\overline{u}$, if $a_i[\overline{u}]$ is true then $e_i[\overline{u}] \in t_i[\overline{u}]$, and*
   (d) *for all $e_1', \ldots, e_n'$, if for all i and for all $\overline{u}$ we have $a_i[\overline{u}]$ true implies $e_i[\overline{u}] = e_i'[\overline{u}] \in t[\overline{u}]$, then $e = \theta(\overline{x}_1 . \, e_1'; \ldots; \overline{x}_n . \, e_n') \in t$.*

Note that in clause 4, the expected type t_i is irrelevant. It only matters when the subannotated term also has a top-level annotation (clause 5). The "typical case", which is a fully annotated term, corresponds to 5a, b and c. Clause 5a, together with 4, corresponds to the recursive case, of soundness of annotations in subterms. Clause 5b says that operand result types match expected types, and 5c says that θ respects equality.

We now extend the semantics of sequents to annotated terms. Intuitively, a sequent is now true if whenever the hypotheses are true, if all the negative annotations in the sequent are sound, then the conclusion of the sequent is true and all the positive annotations are sound. For practical reasons, in sequents over annotated terms all positive annotations must occur in the conclusion of the sequent. Also, in the conclusion T [t] of a sequent, t is restricted to be unannotated. This last restriction is of no practical import since the term t is actually the "extract" field, synthesized only when a proof is completed, and so any annotations in it would be of no use in the proof.

Definition 4. *Let* $x_1 : A_1, \ldots, x_n : A_n \vdash T$ [t] *be a sequent over annotated terms. It is true if for all closing substitutions* σ: *if* $\psi^-(\sigma(T))$, *and if for all* i *(1 $\leq i \leq n$)* $\sigma(x_i) \in \sigma(A_i)$ *and* $\psi^-(\sigma(A_i))$, *then* $\sigma(t) \in \sigma(T)$ *and* $\psi^+(\sigma(T))$.

Note that in this semantics, we assume soundness of the negative annotations in the conclusion as well as the hypotheses.

Many inference rules in Nuprl are parameterized by terms. Almost always, these terms are computed by tactics, and are usually derived from the input goal. For example, the rule for instantiating a universal quantifier requires the instantiating term, and this is usually calculated by matching against some part of the sequent. If the sequent is annotated, such terms will carry annotations, and we would like these to be preserved when the term is used in the inference rule. A term with negative annotations can be accepted only if the annotations are sound, and for this we use the following sufficient condition (terms not meeting it will have their annotations stripped).

Definition 5. *An annotated term* e *is* soundly annotated according to *the sequent* $\Gamma \vdash T$ *if for every subterm* e' *of* e *such that* e' *is of the form* ann$^-$($u; t$) *and such that* e' *is not properly contained in another subterm of* e *of the form* ann$^-$($u; t$) *nor is in the scope of a binding variable in* e, e' *is an annotated subterm of* T *or of some hypothesis in* Γ.

One alternative to our type annotation scheme would be to memoize proofs. When a term t is proven to have a certain type, we could enter the proof in a hash table with key t. The main problem with this approach is that these typing proofs quickly become "out-of-date". The problem is typified by Nuprl's thinning rule, which is extensively employed by Nuprl's tactics to keep hypothesis lists manageably small. The rule is

$$\frac{x_1 : A_1, \ldots, x_{i-1} : A_{i-1}, x_{i+1} : A_{i+1}, \ldots, x_n : A_n \vdash t \in T}{x_1 : A_1, \ldots, x_n : A_n \vdash t \in T}$$

It is straightforward to check that this rule is sound for annotated terms. However, consider its use in a tactic proof system, where proofs are constructed a top-down, or goal-directed, fashion. If we have memoized a collection of typing proofs whose root sequents are based on the hypothesis list in the conclusion of the above rule, then after we apply the rule the memoized proofs are probably useless, since new typing goals that arise could involve the smaller hypothesis list. One can try to improve on this by attempting, when proving a typing for a term, to find a minimal hypothesis list for the proof, but this is impossible in principle in Nuprl, and seems to be very difficult to adequately approximate in practice.

4   Inference Rules

In this section we describe the modifications that must be made to Nuprl's set of inference rules to support annotations. There are two new rules for dealing with positive annotations, and some new rules specifically for term rewriting. In addition, many of the existing rules have been modified to account for annotation propagation and to have extra checks on parameters.

Sequents, as defined in the previous section, have as conclusion a judgment of the form $t \in T$. As discussed earlier, t is the "extract" field. As this will not concern us in what follows, we suppress it from now on, writing only T for the conclusion. In understanding the explanations of the rules and their modifications, it is best to think in terms of goal-directed proof, i.e. to think of refining a goal by matching it with the conclusion of a a rule and proceeding to the premises.

4.1   New Rules

The main rule for positive annotations essentially implements a "step" in the inductive definition of ψ^p in Definition 3. This rule is somewhat complex, so instead of giving a detailed syntactic specification, we just describe how it relates to Definition 3. The rule has a conclusion of the form $\Gamma \vdash ann^+(e; T) \mathrel{\dot\in} T$ and has premises that depend on the form of e. We omit the degenerate case corresponding to clause 2 of Definition 3 and consider only the case corresponding to 5. In this case, if m is the number of e_i that have the form $ann^{p'}(e'_i; t')$, there are $m + n + 1$ premises in the rule. The premises correspond to parts a to d of clause 5 of Definition 3.

There are m premises corresponding to part b. The formalization is direct, using $\bar{x}_i$ in place of $\bar{u}$, since we can directly define the local subtype relation inside Nuprl, and the assumption a_i becomes a sequence of sequent hypotheses, with each conjunction becoming a hypothesis.[1] (Recall that a_i must cover $\bar{x}_i$.)

There are $n - m$ premises corresponding to part c. These are also direct formalizations.

---

[1] Some of the $\bar{x}_i$ may have to be renamed to avoid clashes with sequent eigenvariables.

For part a, we need premises implying the soundness of any positive annotations in the e_i. If e_i has the form the form $ann^{p'}(e'_i; t')$, then we include a premise with conclusion $e_i \in t'$. Otherwise, we do not include a premise, since it would be redundant with a premise added for part c.

The premise for part d is not as direct a formalization as the other cases. The problem is that we cannot directly quantify over all e'_i satisfying the specified conditions. What we want to express with this premise is that if we replace the operands $\overline{x}_i$. e_i in e by equal operands, the result is equal to e. The problem is to express "equal operands". To do this, we view an operand as a function, and quantify over functions f_i that, when applied to $\overline{x}_i$, are equal to e_i under the assumption a_i. The assumptions for the subannotations give us the domain types for the functions. A complication here is that the assumption may contain conjuncts not of the form $x \in A$, as in, for example, $if(b:B;\ e_1:[b]A;\ e_2:[\neg b]A)\colon A$. The details are omitted.

The rule we just described applies to a "top-level" positive annotation. We also need a rule for dealing with positive annotations that are buried under negatively annotated or unannotated terms. The rule is

$$\frac{\Gamma \vdash T[\tilde{t}/x]}{\Gamma \vdash T[t/x]}$$

where t is an annotated term, $\tilde{t}$ is the result of replacing in t all subterms of the form $e\colon^? T$ by $e\colon T$, and where $\tilde{t}$ is soundly annotated according to the conclusion sequent. This rule is used in conjunction with the "cut" rule, described below.

The remaining new rules have to do with term rewriting. These rules are never explicitly invoked by the user, and are used only by the basic rewriting machinery. Because of the intimate connection with rewriting, we postpone presenting the rules until we discuss the extension to rewriting.

4.2   Modifications to Existing Rules

There are number of different kinds of modifications that had to be made to the existing primitive inference rules of Nuprl. These modifications are, unfortunately, mostly not easily expressible using some simple form of rule schema. The fact that the changes necessary to Nuprl's proof system can be isolated in the rules is an advantage, but the changes are still somewhat daunting because of the complexity of the changes and the unusually large number of primitive inference rules in Nuprl.

An important point here is that the modifications only come into play when terms are annotated – all instances of rules in the version of Nuprl without annotations are rule instances in the annotated setting.

Parameter checking. There are a number of rules that are parameterized by terms. Because of the semantics of sequents over annotated terms, parameters which are soundly annotated according to the conclusion of the rule will be soundly annotated according to the premises, at least for the existing Nuprl rules. Thus for each such rule we add a side condition: if the parameter term is annotated, then the term is soundly annotated according to the conclusion of the rule. The implementation of this rule will erase annotations in a parameter if they do not satisfy the side condition.

Removal of unsound premise annotations. There are a few rules where some annotations must be removed from premises in order to maintain soundness. The most extreme example of this is the induction rules. Consider the following (derived) rule for induction over the natural numbers.

$$\frac{\Gamma \vdash T[0/x] \quad \Gamma,\, n\!:\!N,\, T[n/x] \vdash T[n+1/x]}{\Gamma,\, n\!:\!N \vdash T[n/x]}$$

This rule is unsound if T has annotations, since the soundness of (negative) annotations in $T[n]$ in the conclusion sequent, for a specific n, does not imply the soundness of annotations in $T[0/x]$ or $T[n+1/x]$. Thus we modify the rule, replacing the terms $T[0/x]$, $T[n/x]$ and $T[n+1/x]$ in the premises by their erasures. Note that this kind of erasure only applies to the primitive inductive rules. For induction schemes expressed as lemmas, no erasures typically occur when the scheme is applied.

Addition of premise annotations. Some inference rules introduce new term structure in premises, and sometimes annotations can be added. It is not clear how useful this is, since these rules tend not to be used much, and the addition of annotations is rather ad hoc. Nevertheless, we have implemented it for two rules. Since the interest is marginal, we omit further discussion.

Removal of well-formedness premises. Many rules have "well-formedness" premises. A typical example is the first premise in the following rule.

$$\frac{\Gamma,\, \forall x\!:\!A.\ B \vdash t \in A \quad \Gamma,\, \forall x\!:\!A.\ B,\, B[t/x] \vdash T}{\Gamma,\, \forall x\!:\!A.\ B \vdash T.}$$

If t has the form $ann^-(e; A)$, then the first premise is immediately justified. We could introduce an axiom scheme so that such premises are proved in one step, but this alone would not allow us to take full advantage of the annotations in the conclusion of the rule. For example, if $t = (3 : Z)$, $A = N$, and the conclusion contains as a subterm $fact((3 : Z) : []N) : N$, then the annotations validate the first premise. So, we make a generic modification to all inference rules: well-formedness premises are omitted if they are "entailed" by the conclusion's annotations. The notion of "entailed" here is a sufficient condition for semantic soundness, and the details are uninteresting. Essentially, a well-formedness premise $\Gamma \vdash t \in T$ is omitted if t occurs in the conclusion with T as either its result type or its expected type.

Side conditions for positive annotations. In order to minimize the complexity of the annotation scheme, we have chosen to drastically limit the rules that apply to positive annotations. Almost all rules have a side condition that the conclusion sequent may not contain any positive annotations. This saves us the trouble of worrying about how positive annotations get pushed around during inference. The exceptions are the new rules for rewriting, the two new rules specifically for positive annotations, a couple of rules that are used for lemma instantiation, and the cut rule.

5 Tactics

The new rules and the modifications to old rules have been implemented in Common Lisp, the implementation language of Nuprl. Tactics are written in ML. In this section we describe how the annotation scheme is viewed in ML, and discuss some of the changes that have been made to the tactic collection to take advantage of annotations.

5.1 The View from ML

Terms in Nuprl are Lisp data structures that are lifted to ML as an abstract data type. We want old tactics to behave as before when we add negative annotations, but we want annotations to be accessible in ML. Essentially, annotations are viewed as extra components of terms. Perhaps the easiest way of explaining this is to consider the single function for destructing terms:

```
dest_term: term -> ((tok # parm list) # bterm list)
```

This returns an operator (which is a token and a parameter list) and a list of "bound terms". The type bterm is defined as var list # term. When given a term of the form $ann^+(\theta(\overline{x}_1.\ subann(e_1; a_1; t_1); \ldots; \overline{x}_n.\ subann(e_n; a_n; t_n)); t)$ it returns θ together with a list whose elements are $\overline{x}_1.\ e_1, \ldots, \overline{x}_n.\ e_n$.

The usual constructor functions for terms work as before. Thus, if the destructor and constructors are used in ML to copy a term, then the copied term will not have any annotations. This behavior is undesirable in some cases. For example, term rewriting uses a substitution function implemented in ML to compute the result of applying a rewrite rule, and the existing implementation of substitution would erase most of the annotations in the right-hand-side of the rule. To account for this, we simply reimplemented 4 of the basic term-walking combinators to preserve annotations when reconstructing a term.

There are ML functions for extracting the components of the top-level annotation of a term and the subannotations associated with the operands. There are also functions for adding annotations.

5.2 Rewriting

Nuprl's approach to rewriting is similar to what is used in other tactic-based systems. Rewrites need to be mapped down to applications of primitive rules for lemma instantiation, substitution and so on. In Nuprl, a rewrite is a function that takes as input a term t and a typing environment and returns a new term t', a binary relation r, and a "justification" for $t\ r\ t'$. The justification is used to build a proof of $t\ r\ t'$. There are several kinds of justification. For example, one kind of justification is simply a tactic that will prove a goal whose conclusion is $t\ r\ t'$. There are several basic combinators for composing rewrites, and each of these builds appropriate justifications.

To extend rewriting to take advantage of annotations, we have added a new form of justification, and modified the basic combinators to handle it. To support this, we have added some new rules to Nuprl. An important point is that these rules are only used in a few combinators at the base of the rewriting package, and thus average tactic writers need not be aware of them. Also, the new form of justification meshes with the old, so that rewrites using all the kinds of justifications can be freely mixed as before.

When a rewrite is given a term with negative annotations, it will produce the rewritten term as before, but with positive annotations. The justification is like the old tactic justification, except the tactic must in addition prove the positive annotations. Partly because of the design of the new rules, establishing the positive annotations does not require any extra work. Nor is any work required to justify rewriting of subterms – is the system without annotations, functionality lemmas are invoked every time rewriting descends under a defined operator.

It is possible to get by with only one new rule for rewriting. However, for expediency we took another approach, involving 5 new rules and a modified form of sequent. The new form of sequent is syntactically simulated by wrapping the conclusion of an ordinary sequent with a special operator. The only rules for this new form of judgment are the 5 new ones for rewriting. We will not describe these rules and form of judgment since we will soon be eliminating them in favor of the single rule. Instead, we will describe a somewhat simplified version of the single rule that will replace them, which is similar to the main rule of the 5 currently implemented.

This rule is used in the combinator that maps a rewrite onto the immediate subterms of a term. The conclusion of the rule has the form

$$\Gamma \vdash \theta(\bar{s}) : A = \theta(\bar{s}') :^? A' \in T$$

where for $1 \leq i \leq n$, s_i is $\bar{x}.\ e_i : [a_i]t_i$ and s_i' is $\bar{x}.\ e_i' : [a_i]t_i$. For each i, the rule has a premise $\Gamma, \Gamma_i \vdash e_i = e_i' \in t_i$ where Γ_i is formed from a_i as in the rule discussed earlier for refining positive annotations.

This rule is not complete as described. For one thing, the premises, together with the negative annotation on the left-hand side of the equality in the conclusion sequent, imply $\theta(\bar{s}) = \theta(\bar{s}') \in A$, but we need equality over T. It turns out that this usually follows from an annotation in a preceding (in a top-down proof construction order) proof step. Our special form of judgment allows us to "remember" this information. As was mentioned earlier, there is a way to do this in tactics, without the support of a new judgment.

The "base case" of rewriting is direct application of rewrite rules. Rewrite rules in Nuprl come from theorems. After finishing a proof of a rewrite theorem (or any other kind of theorem) in Nuprl, one can invoke a program that creates a positively annotated version of the theorem. This is automatic to the extent the proof of well-formedness of the goal of the theorem is. In the case of a rewrite rule, in proving $\Gamma \vdash t : A = t' :^? A' \in T$ we can apply a negatively annotated version of the rewrite rule theorem, which will immediately justify the positive annotations.

5.3   Other Tactics

The main new tactic is the one that replaces the conclusion of a sequent by an annotated version of it. Given a goal $\Gamma \vdash T$, it uses the components of Nuprl's type inference machinery to compute annotation types in a top-down fashion, mimicking what Nuprl's typechecking tactic would do when given a goal $\Gamma \vdash T \dot{\in} P_i$, where P_i is a universe of propositions. This annotated form is used to replace T in the original goal (using the cut rule), and we are left with a proof obligation to show that the annotations are correct. This is tackled by a tactic that repeatedly applies one of the new rules for positive annotations, and other special purpose tactics that handle some of the resulting subgoals. As mentioned before, this is automatic to the extent the proof of $\Gamma \vdash T \in U$ is.

There are a few other new tactics and modifications to old ones. The basic tactics for lemma instantiation have been updated to apply the annotated version of the lemma if it exists. There is a tactic (called invisibly within the Nuprl's "autotactic", which is run after every top level refinement) for proving goals of the form $\Gamma \vdash T \subseteq_e T'$. Finally, tactics which need to compute types for terms now use annotations if they exist.

6   Discussion

The preceding account omitted a number of features and details which, while important to the practicality of the annotation scheme, are not so significant conceptually. We discuss some of these below, as well as a limitation of the work that will be addressed in the near future.

Negative annotations in new rules. In the new rule for refining goals of the form $\Gamma \vdash e :^? t \in T$, as an "optimization", some occurrences of the subterms of e in the premises have their annotations negated. This is sound because we only need each positive annotation in e to appear once in the premises.

Annotation constraints for specific operators. Consider the rule for dependent function types (view these as universal quantifiers if you like).

$$\frac{\Gamma, x : A \to B \vdash t \in A \quad \Gamma, B[t/x] \vdash T}{\Gamma, x : A \to B \vdash T}$$

The object $x : A \to B$ is just a display form for $function\,(A; x.\ B)$. According to the annotation scheme as described so far, a permissable annotation is $function\,(A : U; x.\ B : [x \in A']U) : U$ where A' need not have any particular relationship to A. In order for $B[t/x]$ to be a soundly annotated term, we need to know that t's annotation type is a local subtype of A'. In practice, what is likely is that the annotations in the conclusion entail this if we know $A = A'$. We thus impose restrictions on certain operators. For example, we require the above annotation of $function\,(A; x.\ B)$ to have $A = A'$. This kind of constraint is practically valuable only for a few of primitive operators. The constraints are checked when positively-annotated parameters are supplied to rules.

Assorted hacks. In order to simplify the implementation and to speed up certain checks, there are restrictions on where positive annotations can occur. They are only allowed to occur in the conclusion of a sequent, and if they do, they must occur "near" the top-level (where the definition of near is determined by several implementation concerns). They may not occur under negative annotations.

We discussed earlier how we modified existing rules to remove typing premises that were justified by annotations in the conclusion of the rule. We actually do not remove them, but instead replace them by a fixed trivial typing goal. This is because some tactics expect rule applications to produce a particular number of subgoals.

There is one "hack" which is somewhat gross and will be fixed soon. In Nuprl, definitions are essentially a form of hygienic macro. Nuprl's "direct computation" rule can be used to expand in-place an instance of a definition. This is a problem for annotations, since definitions have no annotations, and a scheme to add them would be a major change to the system. For most definitions, this can be avoided. Defined terms are usually reasoned about abstractly, via lemmas (which are annotated). In addition, one can unfold definitions, keeping terms annotated, by first proving unfolding rewrite rules that equate a definition to its right-hand side. However, the Nuprl tactic collection regards a few particular definitions as "soft abstractions". These are mostly the definitions of the logical connectives in terms of type constructors. They also include definitions for simulating second-order substitution. They are "soft" because they are not reasoned about abstractly – they are unfolded whenever any analysis is required. For these connectives (only), we have hacked the direct computation rule to propagate annotations.

Searching for annotated terms. When a term t with negative annotations is supplied as a parameter to a rule, the system must search the current goal to check that the annotations are sound according to the goal. For each maximal subterm u of t whose top annotation is negative, we search for it in the goal. Since typical proofs involve many rule parameters, it is vital that this check be fast. Because of this, the search for u is via Lisp's "eq", which means that the occurrence of u found must be pointer-identical to u. This is not much of a restriction in practice, since a parameter with negative annotations almost certainly originated in the goal. To further speed up the search, tactics are allowed to supply "hints", in the form of sequent addresses, specifying where to start searching. Only a few tactics do this at this point. In the absence of hints, searching starts with the conclusion of the sequent, and within the conclusion and each hypothesis, the search is breadth-first.

Since the negatively annotated term u being searched for may be within the scope of binding variables in t, we must also check contexts. The types for these bound variables, and any other subannotation assumptions (i.e., "guard" assumptions) affecting u, must be identical to those for the occurrence found for u in the goal. Definition 5 can be extended to account for this kind of annotation entailment.

Rewriting over propositional equivalence. So far, the only rewriting we have discussed has been with respect to equality. If Nuprl used boolean-valued logical connectives, as in HOL and PVS, this would be enough for our purposes. However, because of the representation of propositions as types, equality of propositions is finer than if-and-only-if. We have modified the semantics of annotations to include propositional equivalence. In particular, in 5d of Definition 3, we replace equality in a type A by $\Leftrightarrow$ if A is a type of propositions. It requires the "classical mode" of proof discussed in [6].

Type dependencies. A serious drawback of our scheme is that it does not adequately account for type dependency. Suppose that $\{1..n\}$ is the type of all integers i such that $1 \le i \le n$, suppose that $f \in n : N \to \{1..n\}$, and consider the annotated expression $f(m+n):\{1..m+n\}$. If we rewrite $m+n$ to $n+m$, the annotated result will be $f(m+n):\{1..n+m\}$. This is still a sound annotation, but it is not the most "natural" type, and may prevent the annotation from being useful in subsequent rewriting. One could imagine applying rewriting to the types in annotations, but this might be expensive and would involve duplicated work. The right way to deal with dependency is to store operator typings in a form where the expected and result types are abstracted with respect to the operands. This would amount to associating a sort of function type with each operator occurrence in a term. This was not done because it was judged much harder to implement in Nuprl, and the simpler scheme is adequate for the SCI effort.

References

1. C.-T. Chou and D. Peled. Verifying a model-checking algorithm. In *Tools and Algorithms for the Construction and Analysis of Systems*, number 1055 in LNCS, pages 241–257, Passau, Germany, 1996. Springer-Verlag.
2. R. L. Constable, et al. *Implementing Mathematics with the Nuprl Proof Development System*. Prentice-Hall, Englewood Cliffs, New Jersey, 1986.
3. A. Felty, D. Howe, and F. Stomp. Protocol verification in nuprl. In *CAV'98*, Lecture Notes in Computer Science. Springer-Verlag, 1998.
4. M. J. C. Gordon and T. F. Melham. *Introduction to HOL: A Theorem Proving Environment for Higher Order Logic*. Cambridge University Press, Cambridge, UK, 1993.
5. D. J. Howe. On computational open-endedness in Martin-Löf's type theory. In *Proceedings of the Sixth Annual Symposium on Logic in Computer Science*, pages 162–172. IEEE Computer Society, 1991.
6. D. J. Howe. Semantics foundations for embedding HOL in Nuprl. In M. Wirsing and M. Nivat, editors, *Algebraic Methodology and Software Technology*, volume 1101 of *Lecture Notes in Computer Science*, pages 85–101, Berlin, 1996. Springer-Verlag.
7. P. B. Jackson. Exploring abstract algebra in constructive type theory. In A. Bundy, editor, *12th Conference on Automated Deduction*, Lecture Notes in Artifical Intelligence. Springer, June 1994.
8. S. Owre and N. Shankar. The formal semantics of PVS. Technical report, SRI, August 1997.
9. B. Werner. Sets in types, types in sets. In *International Symposium on Theoretical Aspects of Computer Software*.

Verifying a Garbage Collection Algorithm[*]

Paul B. Jackson

Department of Computer Science, University of Edinburgh
King's Buildings, Edinburgh EH9 3JZ, UK
pbj@dcs.ed.ac.uk

Abstract. We present a case study in using the PVS interactive theorem prover to formally model and verify properties of a tricolour garbage collection algorithm. We model the algorithm using state transition systems and verify safety and liveness properties in linear temporal logic. We set up two systems, each of which models the algorithm itself, object allocation, and the behaviour of user programs. The models differ in how concretely they model the heap. We verify the properties of the more abstract system, and then, once a refinement relation is exhibited between the systems, we show the more concrete system to have corresponding properties.

We discuss the linear temporal logic framework we set up, commenting in particular on how we handle fairness and how we use a 'leads-to-via' predicate to reason about the propagation of properties that are stable in specified regions of system state spaces. We also describe strategies (tactics) we wrote to improve the quality of interaction and increase the degree of automation.

1 Introduction

This case study is part of larger project at the University of Edinburgh to develop and assess formal models and verification techniques for garbage collection algorithms. This project is being carried out in consultation with the memory management group of the software house Harlequin[1] which, amongst other things, produces compilers for Lisp, ML and Dylan. One of the primary goals of our project is to demonstrate that formal techniques can have a positive impact on this group's software development process.

In this case study, we treat a garbage collector as a component of a reactive system that also includes a heap object allocator and an abstraction of the user program. We use state transition system models and linear temporal logic for providing a specification and verification framework. Similar approaches have been successfully used in previous work on mechanically verifying garbage collectors (see Sect. 10). We introduce two systems at different levels of abstraction

---

[*] This work was supported by the UK Engineering and Physical Sciences Research Council under grant GR/J85509 and, while the author was a Visiting Fellow in the Computer Science Laboratory of SRI International in Menlo Park, California USA, by the US National Science Foundation under contract CCR-9509931.

[1] http://www.harlequin.com/

that we show to be related by a refinement relation. The more abstract system is simpler to verify, and the more concrete system is a more faithful model of an actual memory management system.

We chose to look at an algorithm that is relatively straightforward to analyse, so that we could quickly gain experience with the styles of proofs needed for reasoning about garbage collectors in linear temporal logic. In future work we will be studying the verification of successively more complicated algorithms.

Much of the literature on verifying garbage collection algorithms has focussed on abstract concurrent algorithms that have particularly subtle behaviours because of the fine-grain of the concurrency. Our interest at the moment is primarily in sequential algorithms, since few algorithms in use today are truly concurrent. At an abstract level, sequential garbage collection algorithms have simpler behaviours, but there are still plenty of challenges to be faced in verifying them, especially when considering implementation details. The techniques we are using for reactive systems are designed for reasoning with concurrency, and it would be easy to adapt our work to both concurrent and distributed settings.

We carry out our formalization using the PVS theorem prover [17]. The PVS specification language is a classical higher-order logic with subtyping by arbitrary predicates. Proofs are carried out interactively by users repeatedly applying *strategies*, PVS's version of tactics. PVS has strategies for such operations as case splitting, expanding definitions, instantiating quantifiers, rewriting and simplifying. It also has strategies which invoke decision procedures that integrate congruence closure with linear arithmetic.

To accurately model garbage collection algorithms, we want to consider arbitrarily large and complex heap data structures. There is no obvious way to abstract these structures to produce finite state models suitable for model checking. Work so far in model checking garbage collection algorithms has had to use small fixed values (4 heap objects, for example) for heap parameters [3, 9]. However, PVS has interfaces to several model checkers, and we hope in future to look at using model checking to assist in parts of our interactive proofs.

The rest of this paper is organized as follows: we present our formalization of linear temporal logic in Sect. 2 and then Sects. 3, 4, and 5 describe the more abstract model we set up and show the safety and liveness proofs we carried out. Sect. 6 introduces our more concrete model, Sect. 7 summarises our framework for reasoning about refinement, and Sect. 8 covers the proof of refinement and the transfer of properties from the more abstract model to the more concrete. Sect. 9 discusses issues raised by the case study that are not covered elsewhere and a comparison with related work is made in Sect. 10. Finally we give our conclusions in Sect. 11.

We present definitions and lemmas in syntax that is very close to the actual syntax of PVS. The main change is that we replace certain keywords, operators and identifiers with non-ASCII logical and mathematical symbols.

2   Linear Temporal Logic

In Sect. 2.1 we define a notion of transition system and introduce a shallow embedding of linear temporal logic operators into the Pvs specification language. We then go on in Sect. 2.2 and Sect. 2.3 to describe the most important rules we used in our proofs. Our approach is most similar to that of Manna and Pnueli [13, 14]. Much is standard, but, as far as we know, the emphasis in Sect. 2.3 on the use of leads-to-via constructs for reasoning about liveness is novel. See also Sect. 9.1 and Sect. 9.2 for a discussion of some more subtle issues we had to address in order to produce an embedding that was practically useful and well-suited to our particular needs.

2.1   Basics

We consider a transition system to be characterized by a type State of states, a type TxLab of labels for transition kinds, a collection of binary relations on states tx, indexed by labels in TxLab, a set of initial states init, and a subset fair of TxLab being those transitions on which a fairness requirement is imposed.

Pvs doesn't permit us to form tuples or records including types, so instead we define the record type

```
TxSys : TYPE = [# tx : [TxLab→pred[[State,State]]],
                  init : pred[State],
                  fair : set[TxLab] #]
```

for the non-type components of transition systems that is implicitly parameterized by types State and TxLab. The notations $[S→T]$ and $[S,T]$ are for function and product types respectively. pred$[T]$ and set$[T]$ are both definitions for the type $[T→$bool$]$. Square brackets in Pvs syntax are used both for the syntax of type constructors and for explicitly specifying instantiating expressions for parameters. Definitions and lemmas in Pvs are grouped into modules called *theories* which can take parameters. Definitions of types and constants in Pvs are parameterised by the parameters of the theory they are defined in. When those types and constants are used, the parameters can either be left implicit for the Pvs type checker to infer or can be explicitly supplied, as with, for example, set[TxLab] above. All the constants defined below are implicitly parameterised by a type State of some transition system, and most are also implicitly parameterized by a type TxLab and an element of type TxSys.

State formulas are predicates on states. The type of state formulas is

```
SFmla : TYPE = pred[State]
```

Let A,B,C,D,E and I be state formulas. Temporal formulas are predicates on pairs of form (σ,i) where σ is a sequence of states and i a natural number indicating a distinguished position in σ.

```
TFmla : TYPE = pred[[sequence[State],nat]]
```

Here `sequence[T]` is a definition for `[nat→T]`. This characterization of temporal formulas permits the definition of past-looking temporal operators. Let P and Q be temporal formulas. The function `tfm` defined by

`tfm(A)(σ,i) : bool = A(σ(i))`

coerces a state formula to a temporal formula. We declare `tfm` to be a Pvs *conversion*. The Pvs type checker automatically inserts conversions as necessary, so we usually omit explicit mention of `tfm`.

The □ (for every future time) and ◇ (at some future time) temporal operators are defined as

`□ (P)(σ,i) : bool = ∀(j : {i...}) : P(σ,j)`
`◇ (P)(σ,i) : bool = ∀(j : {i...}) : P(σ,j)`

and an *until* operator is defined as

`𝒰(P,Q)(σ,i) : bool =`
  `∃(j : {i...}) : Q(σ,j) ∧ ∀ (k : {i..j-1}) : P(σ,k)`

The integer subrange types `{i...}` and `{i..j-1}` are definitions from standard theories in Pvs that are always loaded. We lift Pvs's quantifiers and logical connectives pointwise to the SFmla and TFmla types, and overload identifiers. For example:

`P ⊃ Q  ≡  λ(σ,i) : P(σ,i) ⊃ Q(σ,i)`

The lifted quantifiers take lambda terms as arguments. For presentation purposes, we suppress the lambda symbol: we present ∀(λn : P) as ∀n : P, for example. We abbreviate □ (P ⊃ Q) by P ⇒ Q.

Let `sys` be some element of the `TxSys` type. We define several binary relations based on `sys`.

`step(s,t) : bool = ∃a : tx(sys)(a)(s,t)`
`possible_step : pred[[State,State]] = refl_cl(step)`
`fair_step(s,t) : bool = ∃a : fair(sys)(a) ∧ tx(sys)(a)(s,t)`

Here a is of type `TxLab`, and `refl_cl` is a reflexive closure operator. Pvs uses prefix function application notation rather than the common postfix 'dot' notation for record projection operators (`tx(sys)` rather than `sys.tx`, for example).

A *run* is an infinite sequence of states generated by following transitions of `sys` from some initial state.

`run : TFmla = tfm(init(sys)) ∧ □ taken(possible_step)`

where

`taken(tx)(σ,i) : bool = tx(σ(i),σ(i+1))`

We allow for the system to take idling transitions; these simplify proving refinement relations between systems and also free us from needing to separately consider finite runs. A *computation* is a run in which fairness conditions are obeyed.

```
computation : TFmla = run ∧ fairseq
```

Here we have

```
fairseq : TFmla =
   □ ¬ □ (tfm(enabled(fair_step)) ∧ ¬ taken(fair_step))
```

```
enabled(tx)(s) : bool = ∃t : tx(s,t)
```

A computation is a run in which it is never the case that a fair step is always enabled but never taken. See Sect. 9.1 for a discussion of our choice of what constitutes a fair run.

A temporal formula is *temporally valid* if it holds for all sequences of states. Frequently, we are concerned only with whether a formula holds for all computations of a given transition system. In this case we say a temporal formula is *temporally program valid*. A state formula is *state program valid* if it holds in all states of all computations of some system.

```
tv(P) : bool = ∀σ : P(σ,0)
tpv(P) : bool = tv(computation ⊃ P)
spv(A) : bool = tpv(□ (tfm(A)))
```

2.2 Safety Reasoning

We say a state formula is *invariant* if it is true in all accessible states. Since the fairness conditions we consider constrain only infinite runs, not finite initial segments of runs, a state formula is invariant just when it is state program valid. We say a state formula is *inductive* if it is invariant and, furthermore, its validity can be established by induction on the transition relation of the system. The induction rule we establish is

```
ind_rule_1 : LEMMA
   (∀ (s: (init(sys))) : I(s))  ∧  leadsto(step)(I,I)
   ⊃ spv(I)
```

where

```
leadsto(T)(A, B): bool = ∀s,t : A(s) ∧ T(s, t) ⊃ B(t)
```

and (init(sys)) is an abbreviation for the type {s:State | init(sys)(s)}. As with any shallow embedding of a logic, we express rules of linear temporal logic as lemmas.

Inductive invariants I are commonly conjunctions $I_1 \wedge \ldots \wedge I_n$ of invariant formulas I_j that are not themselves inductive. Conveniently, we can divide proofs of the induction rule premise leadsto(step)(I,I) into separate proofs of leadsto(step)(I,I_j) for each j. Initial conjectures of invariants being inductive are often false and one needs to go through several iterations of adding conjuncts until one finds an invariant that is indeed inductive. As in the safety proofs that Havelund carried out [9], we carefully set up definitions so that new conjuncts can be added to a conjectured inductive invariant without having to modify any existing proofs of conjuncts being preserved by step.

2.3 Liveness Reasoning

Temporal formulas of form A $\Rightarrow$ (B $\mathcal{U}$ C) are ubiquitous in our liveness proofs. Such a formula can be read as "if the system is in a state satisfying A, it will remain in states satisfying B until eventually a state satisfying C is reached". More concisely, the formula can be read as "A leads to C via B", and we refer to such a formula as a *leads-to-via* formula. We usually omit the parentheses in leads-to-via formulas, since the operator $\mathcal{U}$ binds more tightly than $\Rightarrow$.

Leads-to-via properties for states related by a single transition are established using the rule

```
one_step_leadsto : LEMMA
  (∀s : A(s) ⊃ enabled(fair_step)(s))
  ∧ leadsto(step)(A, B)
  ⊃ tpv(A ⇒ A 𝒰 B)
```

We have numerous rules for chaining together the flows of control described by leads-to-via formulas. For example,

```
leadsto_tx_1_or : LEMMA
  tv( (A ⇒ B 𝒰 C) ∧ (C ⇒ D 𝒰 E)
      ⊃ ((A ∨ C) ⇒ (B ∨ D) 𝒰 E) )
```

A particularly useful rule is the following induction rule used for proving termination of transition loops:

```
wf_leadsto_rule : LEMMA
  tv( (∀t : (A ∧ λs : ρ(s) = t)
            ⇒ B 𝒰 ((A ∧ λs : ρ(s) < t) ∨ C))
      ⊃ (A ⇒ B 𝒰 C) )
```

Here < is some well-founded order relation (always the usual < ordering on naturals in our case), and ρ is a rank function mapping states to the type the well-founded order relation is over.

We prefer working with leads-to-via formulas rather than the more common but less informative *leads-to* formulas of form A $\Rightarrow$ $\Diamond$B which is equivalent to A $\Rightarrow$ True $\mathcal{U}$ B. The reason is that they allow us to factor reasoning about flow of control and about how certain properties remain unchanged in specified regions of the system. The relevant rule is:

```
leadsto_stable_augmentation: LEMMA
  stable?(D, B)
  ⊃ tpv( (A ⇒ B 𝒰 C) ⊃ ((A ∧ D) ⇒ B 𝒰 (C ∧ D)) )
```

where

```
stable?(D,B) : bool = leadsto(step)(D ∧ B,D)
```

If we know that control state A always leads to control state C via control states specified by B, and a property of data D is stable in region B and established in control state A, then we can conclude that property D will still hold when we reach control state C. We haven't seen this factorization benefit of leads-to-via formulas pointed out in the literature (in [16, 14] or [4], for example).

3   More Abstract Transition System Model

We describe in this section a model of a stop-and-collect, non-copying algorithm. We assume a single thread of control (no concurrency). We use the tricolour marking scheme first introduced for a concurrent algorithm [6]. The extra complication of the tricolour marking scheme might seem unnecessary for our immediate needs. However the scheme is useful for incremental collectors working in a sequential single-process setting, and we intend to look at such collectors in the near future. The scheme can also be viewed as an abstraction of most copying algorithms. See [11] for further details on this marking scheme and on garbage collection algorithms in general.

The idea behind most garbage collection algorithms in use is to first mark all heap objects accessible from certain root objects. Then objects not marked are considered garbage and can be collected. With tricolour marking, the roots start off marked grey and the rest of the heap is white. Marking proceeds by greying the white children of grey objects and blackening objects which have no white children. (We consider an object A to be the child of an object B if some field of B contains a pointer to A.) Marking is complete when there are no grey objects left. In the setting we consider here, where there is no interleaving of marking and user program activity, it is easy to see that the garbage objects are just those that are left white.

The model is parameterized by a finite non-empty type Node of heap nodes. One node rt is distinguished as being the *root* node of the heap. We think of nodes as representing objects in the heap.

We model pointers between objects using a directed graph. We consider an edge from node m to n as indicating that there are one or more pointers between the objects m and n.

```
Heap : TYPE = pred[[Node,Node]]
```

We are assuming here that the heap memory is divided up into object-sized chunks rather than being a continuous sequence of addresses and are not considering such issues as fragmentation. Each object is either i) free (available for allocation) or ii) allocated and marked with a certain colour. There is no need to record colours for free objects.

```
Color : TYPE = {free, black, grey, white}
Marking : TYPE = [Node→Color]
```

Our linear temporal logic framework assumes that the control state of a system is simply one component of the complete state. We use four control states

```
Control : TYPE = {mutate, alloc1, alloc2, trace}
```

and the type of system states is defined as

```
State : TYPE = [# heap: Heap,
                  marking : Marking,
                  control : Control #]
```

In what follows, variables d and e are of type State.

We define eight kinds of transitions divided into three categories. They are described informally in Table 1. The 'From' column indicates the control state in which each transition is enabled and the 'To' column the value that the control state is changed to if each transition is taken.

Table 1. Transitions for More Abstract Model

Name	From	To	Description
mutator transitions:			
add_edge	mutate	mutate	Pick nodes m and n reachable from the root and add an edge from m to n if one isn't there already.
remove_edge	mutate	mutate	Pick nodes m and n reachable from the root and remove any edge from m to n.
allocator transitions:			
alloc_call	mutate	alloc1	Always enabled.
alloc_ok	alloc1	alloc2	Enabled if at least one free node.
alloc_sat	alloc2	mutate	Pick free node n, remove any out edges of n, add edge from root to n and make n black.
collector transitions:			
gc_init	alloc1	trace	Make root grey and every black node white.
trace_node	trace	trace	Pick grey node n, grey any white children of n and make n black.
gc_end	trace	alloc2	If no grey nodes, free every white node.

The mutator transitions provide an abstract model of the user program, the allocator transitions model the allocation procedure of the memory management system and the collector transitions the garbage collection procedure. We have the collector invoked from the allocation routine, since this is the most common practice. For generality's sake, we don't insist that collection wait for the heap to be exhausted. We place the fairness requirement on the last five of the transitions, since these are internal to the memory manager and are not considered to be initiated by the user program.

Formally, each transition is defined as a binary relation on states. For example, the formal definition for the gc_init step is

```
gc_init(d,e) : bool =
  at(alloc1)(d) AND
  e = d WITH [(control) := trace,
              (marking) := init_marking_for_gc(marking(d))]
```

where

```
init_marking_for_gc(s : Marking) : Marking =
  λn : IF n = rt THEN grey
```

```
       ELSIF black?(s(n)) THEN white
       ELSE s(n) ENDIF
```

The WITH construct is convenient syntax for the non-destructive update of fields of records and points in the domains of functions. In this case, the control and marking fields of the record d are being updated.

We consider the initial state of the system to be one in which control is in the mutate state, the root is black, the rest of the nodes are free and there are no edges between nodes.

4 Proof of Safety of More Abstract Model

The safety property we prove is that the garbage collection algorithm only collects unreachable objects in the heap. Formally, we assert that all white nodes are unreachable whenever the next transition might be the collector transition gc_end which frees all white nodes.

```
safety : SFmla =
  enabled(gc_end) ⊃ ∀n : white(n) ⊃ ¬ reachable(n)
```

```
safety_lemma : LEMMA spv(safety)
```

where

```
reachable?(d)(m) : bool = star(heap(d))(rt,m)
reachable(m)(d) : bool = reachable?(d)(m)
white(m)(d) : bool = white?(marking(d)(m))
```

and star is reflexive transitive closure.

We prove safety_lemma using the induction rule ind_rule_1 introduced in Sect. 2.2. The invariant safety is not inductive, so we show it to be true as a consequence of the stronger invariant inv that is inductive. inv is the conjunction of the properties:

1. the root node is grey or black,
2. there is no edge from a black node to a white node
3. there is no edge from a non-free node to a free node
4. no node is coloured grey when control is not in the trace state.

The proofs showing that this conjunction is inductive draw on a couple of auxiliary lemmas:

```
reachable_not_free : LEMMA
  inv(d) ∧ reachable?(d)(n) ⊃ ¬ free?(marking(d)(n))
```

```
reachable_black_if_no_greys : LEMMA
  inv(d) ∧ reachable?(d)(n) ∧ ¬ (∃m : grey?(marking(d)(m)))
    ⊃ black?(marking(d)(n))
```

The proofs of these auxiliary lemmas involve applying general properties of `star`. In particular, the induction lemma

```
narrowing_of_change : LEMMA
  star(R)(x,y) ∧ P(x) ∧ ¬P(y) ⊃ ∃u,v : R(u,v) ∧ P(u) ∧ ¬P(v)
```

is helpful.

The proof of `inv` being inductive splits naturally into 32 cases, one for each choice of conjunct and transition. The `grind` strategy automatically solves 25 of these. `grind` combines all the strategies mentioned in Sect. 1 and is often used to completely prove simpler goals and subgoals. Of these 25 cases, 10 are very straightforward because the selected conjunct refers only to parts of the state unchanged by the selected transition. `grind` solves these by rewriting with the state change equation contained in the transition definition and simplifying the resulting expressions. The other 15 automatic cases are more interesting. `grind` generates case splits, some based on update expressions, and guesses instantiations of quantifiers. The PVS simplifier knows of the distinctness of elements of the `Color` and `Control` datatypes and uses congruence closure to simplify equalities involving expressions of type `Color` and `Control` to true or false. The remaining 7 cases involve an average of about 7 steps of manual proof guidance (excluding work involved in proving the auxiliary lemmas).

5   Proof of Liveness of More Abstract Model

The liveness condition we prove is that garbage nodes always eventually become free. The formal statement is

```
liveness : TFmla =
  allocs_keep_coming
  ⊃ ∀m : (at(mutate) ∧ garbage(m)) ⇒ ◇ free(m)

garbage_eventually_freed_a : LEMMA tpv(liveness)
```

where

```
allocs_keep_coming : TFmla =
  at(mutate) ⇒ at(mutate) U at(alloc1)
free(m)(s) : bool = free?(marking(s)(m))
garbage(m) : SFmla = ¬ free(m) ∧ ¬ reachable(m)
```

and `m` is of type `Node`.

The `allocs_keep_coming` precondition expresses the need to assume that the user program allocates new storage with sufficient regularity. If the user program doesn't keep calling the allocator, then there is no guarantee that garbage collection will ever take place. The restriction that we only consider garbage when in the `mutate` state is a minor one. It simplifies the proofs. With a little more work we could relax it.

The main stages of the proof are as follows. The first two have to do with flow of control. They establish that if we start in the mutate state, we eventually call the collector, and then eventually complete tracing of the reachable objects in the heap.

```
mutate_to_trace : LEMMA
  tpv( allocs_keep_coming
       ⊃ ( at(mutate)
             ⇒ at((:alloc1,alloc2,mutate:)) U at(trace) ) )
```

```
eventually_no_greys_in_trace : LEMMA
  tpv( (at(trace) AND exist_greys)
       ⇒ (at(trace) ∧ exist_greys)
       U (at(trace) ∧ ¬ exist_greys) )
```

where

```
exist_greys(d) : bool =  ∃m : grey?(marking(d)(m))
```

Each of these lemmas is proved using the wf_leadsto_rule introduced in Sect. 2.3. In the first lemma, the rank of the state is the number of free nodes, in the second, the number of non-black nodes.

We note that, if making a transition starting in any state except one in which gc_end is enabled, garbage always remains garbage.

```
garbage_stable : LEMMA
  stable?(garbage(m), at((:alloc1,alloc2,mutate:))
                        ∨ (at(trace) ∧ exist_greys) )
```

Using the leadsto_stable_augmentation lemma discussed in Sect. 2.3 and the above lemmas about flow of control and stability of garbage, we deduce that, if we start at a point in a trace where we are in a mutate state and node m is garbage, we will always eventually reach a state in which the gc_end transition is enabled and m is still garbage.

We prove an additional invariant

```
garbage_in_trace_is_white : LEMMA
  spv(garbage(m) ∧ at(trace) ⊃ white(m))
```

and a characterization of the effect of the gc_end transition

```
freeing_of_whites: LEMMA
  leadsto(step)(at(trace) ∧ ¬ exist_greys ∧ white(m)
                ,free(m))
```

from which we easily derive tpv(liveness).

6   More Concrete Transition System Model

This model is close in spirit to some that we at Edinburgh discussed with the memory management group at Harlequin when learning about the systems that they develop. The main difference between it and the more abstract model is that here we consider the edges between heap nodes as being labelled with elements of a type Label. Multiple edges are allowed between two given nodes, providing they have distinct labels. We model the heap by a function of type

Heap : TYPE = [Node,Label→Lift[Node]]

where $[S,T{\rightarrow}U]$ is an abbreviation for the type $[[S,T]{\rightarrow}U]$ and Lift[T] is a PVS datatype with elements bot and lift(t), t being an element of type T. The labels on edges from the root node rt can be thought of as the names of heap roots, for example, the names of CPU registers or static variables or the addresses of stack locations. The labels on edges from a non-root node can be thought of as the names or addresses of pointer-containing fields of the heap object represented by the node. If the value of the heap function on node m and label r is lift(n), then we consider there to be a pointer labelled r from m to n; if the value is bot, we consider the pointer r from m to be null.

The control and marking components of the state have the same definitions as in the more abstract model. In particular, every node has one of the four same colours. We add a new component label_arg of type Label which we explain below.

Table 2 shows the transitions. The read, write, drop, and del transitions replace the add_edge and remove_edge transitions of the more abstract model, and the gc_init, trace_node, gc_end and alloc_ok transitions have virtually the same definitions. We think of the read transition as the reading into CPU register s of the pointer in the field u of the object pointed to by CPU register r. We think of the write transition as the writing of a pointer to the object n into field u of object m. The conditions under which read, write, drop, and del are enabled are perhaps more restrictive than might be desired. If we were to relax them, we would need to add a transition in the more abstract model that simultaneously adds and remove edges. This would involve a little extra work, but would be straightforward. We think of the label_arg component of the state as holding the address on the stack for the return value of an allocation function: the the alloc_call transition sets this address and the alloc_sat transition sets the value to a fresh object.

As an example, the transition relation for the read transition is formalized as ∃r,u,s : read(r,u,s)(d,e), where

read(r,u,s)(d,e) : bool =
    at(mutate)(d) ∧ val?(d(r)) ∧ val?(d(val(d(r)),u)) ∧ bot?(d(s))
    ∧ e = d WITH [(heap)(rt,s) := d(val(d(r)),u)]

Conversions are used here to abbreviate expressions: when conversions are inserted, d(n,u) becomes heap(d)(n,u) and d(r) becomes heap(d)(rt,u).

Table 2. Transitions for More Concrete Model

Name	From	To	Description
mutator transitions:			
read	mutate	mutate	If there are heap pointers $rt \xrightarrow{r} m$, $m \xrightarrow{u} n$ and $rt \xrightarrow{s} \emptyset$ (pointer s from root is null), then update the heap so that $rt \xrightarrow{s} n$.
write	mutate	mutate	If there are heap pointers $rt \xrightarrow{r} m$, $rt \xrightarrow{s} n$ and $m \xrightarrow{s} \emptyset$, then update the heap so that $m \xrightarrow{s} n$.
drop	mutate	mutate	If there is a pointer $rt \xrightarrow{r} m$, then make it null.
del	mutate	mutate	If there are pointers $rt \xrightarrow{r} m$ and $m \xrightarrow{u} n$, then null the pointer u.
allocator transitions:			
alloc_call	mutate	alloc1	If $rt \xrightarrow{r} \emptyset$, then store the label r in a component of the state called label_arg.
alloc_ok	alloc1	alloc2	Enabled if at least one free node.
alloc_sat	alloc2	mutate	If there is some free node n, then null all pointers out of n, add a pointer $rt \xrightarrow{r} n$ where r is the value of label_arg and make n black.
collector transitions:			
gc_init	alloc1	trace	Make root grey and every black node white.
trace_node	trace	trace	Pick grey node n, grey any white children of n and make n black.
gc_end	trace	alloc2	If no grey nodes, free every white node.

7   Framework for Refinement

We consider a transition system B to be a refinement of a system A when we can exhibit an abstraction mapping ϕ (sometimes called a *refinement mapping* [12]) mapping states of B to states of A, that when applied to any computation of B yields a computation of A. In a theory parameterized by systems A and B, we make the definition

```
refinement?(φ) : bool =
   ∀σb : b.computation(σb,0) ⊃ a.computation(map(φ,σb),0)
```

where ϕ has type [StateB→StateA] and σb has type sequence[StateB].

   Identifiers in Pvs can take prefixes that specify which theory they are from and how the parameters to that theory are instantiated. Local abbreviations can be introduced for these prefixes. The prefixes a. and b. in this section specify parameters appropriate for systems A and B. Later on, we use prefix abbreviations to distinguish between identifiers with the same name but from different theories. To improve readability, we use prefixes more than is strictly necessary: Pvs's type checker can often resolve ambiguities when prefixes are left out. For simplicity, we deviate slightly here from exact PVS syntax in that we use the same prefix for identifiers from closely-related theories.

Because we consider computations rather than runs in the definition of refinement?, system B can inherit all temporally program valid properties proven of system A.

```
tpv_refinement : LEMMA
  refinement?(φ) ∧ a.tpv(PA) ⊃ b.tpv(treify(φ,PA))


spv_refinement : LEMMA
  refinement?(φ) ∧ a.spv(AA) ⊃ b.spv(sreify(φ,AA))
```

where PA and AA are, respectively, temporal and state formulas of system A, and the reification functions have definitions:

```
sreify(φ,AA) : SFmla[StateB] = λsb :  AA(φ(sb))
treify(φ,PA) : TFmla[StateB] = λσb,i : PA(map(φ,σb),i)
```

We establish that an abstraction mapping ϕ characterizes a refinement in two stages:

1. we show that ϕ maps runs of B to runs of A by showing that ϕ is a *simulation*:

   ```
   simulation?(φ) : bool =
     (∀sb : b.init(tsb)(sb) ⊃ a.init(tsa)(φ(sb)))
     ∧ (∀sb,tb : b.accessible?(sb) ∧ b.step(sb,tb)
                 ⊃ a.possible_step(φ(sb),φ(tb)) )
   ```

2. we show that the abstraction of every computation of B satisfies the 'fair sequence' property of A (see the definition of fairseq in Sect. 2.1). A simple case when this is true is when
   (a) a fair step of A being enabled implies that a fair step of B is enabled, and
   (b) if a fair step is taken between two adjacent states in a run of system B, then a fair step can also be taken in system A between the abstractions of these states.
   These conditions are fulfilled by refinements such as the one we consider in Sect. 8, where the refinement involves a change of data representation, but no significant change of control structure.

Our definition of refinement is similar to that of Chou [5]. In particular, Chou identifies the same simple case of when a simulation is a refinement.

8   Verification of More Concrete Model

Let us refer to the more abstract transition system model introduced in Sect. 3 as sys1 and the more concrete in Sect. 6 as sys2. We show that sys2 is a refinement of sys1, considering a sys1 that has the same type Node and same node rt as sys2. We define an abstraction mapping rmap that forgets the label_arg component of the sys2 state, and is the identity function on the control and marking components. A heap component h2 of the sys2 state is mapped to the sys1 heap edge?(h2) where

edge?(h)(m,n) : bool = ∃u : h(m,u) = lift(n)

Showing that rmap defines a simulation relation between sys2 and sys1 is straightforward. At one point we need to exploit the fact that the simulation only quantifies over all accessible states of the concrete system, not all states. The relevant lemma is

```
alloc_sat_simulation_a : LEMMA
  sys2.accessible?(d2) ∧ sys2.alloc_sat(d2,e2)
  ⊃ sys1.alloc_sat(rmap(d2),rmap(e2))
```

We need the accessible? precondition to know that, when alloc_sat is enabled, the pointer from rt named by the value of label_arg is null. If it isn't, the sys2 alloc_sat operation might also remove an edge from root in the heap graph, a behaviour that isn't simulated by the sys1 alloc_sat operation. To establish that this pointer is null when alloc_sat is enabled, we prove by induction the stronger invariant that this pointer is null whenever control is not in the mutate state.

Establishing the relationships between the fair steps being taken and enabled is also straightforward. For the relationship between the fair steps being taken, we can reuse the specific facts about transitions simulating each other such as the one cited above.

We therefore have

rmap_is_refinement : LEMMA refinement?(rmap)

and consequently

```
sys2_safety_a : LEMMA sys2.spv(sreify(rmap, sys1.safety))
sys2_liveness_a : LEMMA sys2.tpv(treify(rmap, sys1.liveness))
```

These formulations of the safety and liveness results for sys2 are not satisfactory because they refer to the sys1 characterizations. We therefore apply lemmas such as

```
treify_until : LEMMA
  treify(φ, PA U QA) = treify(φ,PA) U treify(φ,QA)
```

to push the reification operators down the definitions of sys1.safety and sys1-.liveness, and lemmas about reification of atomic predicates to arrive at

```
sys2_safety_b : LEMMA sys2.spv(sys2.safety)
sys2_liveness_b : LEMMA  sys2.tpv(sys2.liveness)
```

where the definitions of safety and liveness are similar to those for sys1, but only refer to components of the state and transitions of sys2.

9   Discussion

9.1   Fairness

We discuss here our choice of fairness condition introduced in Sect. 2.1.

Since our primary interest for the moment is in sequential rather than concurrent algorithms, we don't need fairness conditions to account for a scheduler being fair to different processes. Rather, the only need for fairness conditions is to rule out runs where the system idles indefinitely with control at some internal point of a memory management procedure and with some transition of that procedure enabled.

The fairness condition we use is often called weak fairness [12] or justice [14]. More precisely, using terminology from Manna and Pnueli's book [14, pp132–134], the condition we use is *process justice*. Manna and Pnueli use for their own transition systems a different weak fairness condition they call *transition justice*. In our notation, this is

```
tj_fairseq : TFmla =
  ∀(a:TxLab): □ ¬ □ (enabled(tx(sys)(a)) ∧ ¬ taken(tx(sys)(a)))
```

Manna and Pnueli give an example of a run of a system that exhibits livelock and is transition just but not process just. They argue that a more detailed implementation of this system would also exhibit livelock and so, if process justice were to be adopted, this system would erroneously be shown to be livelock free.

However, there are also scenarios in which a run that exhibits livelock can be process just, but not transition just. For example, consider a system with two states S and T and two fair transitions $S \to S$ and $S \to T$ belonging to one process that are always enabled in state S. A run in which the system always stays in state S is process just, but not transition just for the transition $S \to T$. Manna and Pnueli in [14] miss this point because they claim that process justice is a more restrictive than transition justice.

A key feature of this example is the single-step looping transition $S \to S$. Such transitions are not uncommon in the sequential models we consider in which multiple program steps are represented by single transitions (consider trace_node in Sect. 3). It also seems that scenarios like the one that Manna and Pnueli cite rely on their being more than one process. We therefore prefer to use process justice rather than transition justice.

9.2   Working with Temporal Logic Judgements

One problem with linear temporal logic is the failure of equivalence of implication at the temporal logic level and the metalogic level (Pvs's boolean logic level): the assertion $\mathtt{tv}(P \supset Q)$ is strictly stronger than the assertion $\mathtt{tv}(P) \supset \mathtt{tv}(Q)$. We find that we get strong enough rules only if we link the premises and conclusions at the temporal level rather than the boolean level. For example, the lemma:

```
weak_leadsto_tx : LEMMA
  tv(A ⇒ B 𝒰 C)  ∧  tv(C ⇒ D 𝒰 E)
  ⊃ tv(A ⇒ (B ∨ D) 𝒰 E)
```

is true, but not useful. Instead, we need:

```
leadsto_tx : LEMMA
  tv( (A ⇒ B 𝒰 C)  ∧  (C ⇒ D 𝒰 E)
       ⊃ (A ⇒ (B ∨ D) 𝒰 E) )
```

It is awkward to directly use standard strategies to apply rules phrased in this way. The solution we adopt is to preprocess such lemmas by unfolding the semantic definitions for tv, ∧ and ⊃ in the top-level temporal structure. This exposes boolean-level structure that standard strategies can work with. We also apply similar preprocessing to goals such as garbage_eventually_freed_a in Sect. 5. For convenience, we integrate this preprocessing into other strategies we have for applying lemmas and breaking down goals.

This solution might seem unaesthetic and ad-hoc, but it is similar in practice to an approach being explored for TLA [12] by Merz [15]. There, the judgement w ⊨ P of a temporal formula P being true at *world* w is introduced. A world corresponds in our case to a pair (σ, i) of a state sequence σ and a position i and the judgement to the application $P(\sigma, i)$. The difference is that in Merz's approach the type of worlds is not concretely specified. More generally, proof systems for temporal and modal logics that use such judgements are increasingly attracting interest in both the computer science and the logic communities. See Gabbay's book on labelled deduction systems [7], for example.

9.3 PVS Strategies

We found the automation provided by Pvs's strategies to be of significant help. In Sect. 4 we give a brief analysis of which kinds of automation are used where in a few of the safety proofs.

In the course of the work, we added several extra strategies to those that are supplied by default. Some are general purpose and involve simply sequencing existing strategies, providing alternative default arguments, or providing slightly different functionality. Others are specific to our formulation of transition systems and to this particular model. Most of these others are for expanding certain sets of definitions. A few combine definition expansion with application of particular lemmas, carrying out case splits, and simplifying.

We found the strategy collection for the current version of Pvs[2] to be weakest when it comes to quantifier instantiation. Quantifier instantiation is handled by the inst? strategy. inst? searches for instantiations by matching parts of quantified formula bodies against expressions found in the formulas of the current goal sequent. Unfortunately, it often guesses unhelpful instantiations. The grind strategy calls on inst?, and inst? is the most common cause of grind failing

---

[2] V2.1, released April 1997

to completely prove a goal. PVS users consequently often run `grind` twice, first with `inst?` disabled. This improves matters a bit, but there's still a significant problem. The PVS developers at SRI are well aware of this problem and are experimenting with tracking the polarities of formulas involved in matches to increase the likelihood that `inst?` guesses useful instantiations.

In the course of our work on the case study described in this paper, we have been experimenting with our own variations on `inst?`. We have done this partly to improve `grind`'s behaviour, but also to improve `inst?`'s usefulness when used for single or multiple step chaining. For example, we modified `inst?` to seek instantiations from matching multiple parts of quantified formula bodies. This is important for applying transitivity lemmas, since PVS doesn't have logic variables.

There is certainly much further to go in this direction. For example, the Isabelle and HOL communities have found model elimination tactics of great use. Such tactics effectively do multiple step of chaining in constrained ways.

10   Comparison with Related Work

The tricolour algorithm we use for this case study was first put forward as a concurrent algorithm [6]. Ben-Ari considered this algorithm to be one of most difficult concurrent algorithms ever studied and proposed a two colour algorithm with similar properties, but with what he considered to be a significantly simpler proofs of safety and liveness [2]. Later pencil-and-paper proofs pointed out flaws with Ben-Ari's proofs, but these too contained flaws, and there were no fully correct proofs until Russinoff did a mechanical formalization in NQTHM [18]. More recently, Havelund redid the formalization of the safety proof in PVS [9], and Havelund and Shankar [10] looked at how the safety proof could be better organised using refinement techniques.

The models in all the work cited above abstract away the notion of objects being free. Object allocation is not modelled as a separate activity from the mutator updating the heap and object collection is modelled as some operation that makes the object accessible from root. Effectively, free list management is lumped in with the mutator. This abstraction improves the tractability of the proofs but results in models where the collector has the pathological behaviour of marking 'free' objects during the tracing phase. There is a loss in clarity here of the connection between the models and any real implementation of them. In contrast, we have set up more concrete models that do have free objects and that are close in spirit to abstract descriptions of garbage collection systems used by software engineers at Harlequin.

In two other ways our models are more abstract than those of the two colour and tricolour concurrent algorithms. Firstly our models are significantly more non-deterministic: we leave open many details of the memory management algorithm that are unimportant for reasoning about its correctness, for example, the order in which the collectors considers nodes for greying and blacking. Secondly, since we don't have to model interleavings of atomic operations of different processes, we can create abstract models with single transitions that represent many atomic operations (consider for instance the trace_node transition described in Sect. 3).

Having to model atomic operations doesn't always place a ceiling on how abstract a transition system one can consider. For example, Havelund and Shankar in [10] started with an abstract initial system with just two transitions. However, their approach is tailored for safety reasoning; there is no way in their approach that liveness properties can be inherited down the chain of refinements of models.

Gonthier formally verified the safety of a much more detailed concurrent garbage collection algorithm that was used in an experimental concurrent version of Caml-light [8]. The state-transition system model involved 63 transitions and the safety proof 46 invariants. Gonthier argued many subtleties in the algorithm only came to light because of the realistic detail included in the model. Gonthier used the TLP system, a Larch-based theorem prover for TLA. The TLP script for the proof was 22,000 lines long. Few would want to repeat Gonthier's achievement without much better proof automation.

11 Conclusions

We successfully verified safety and liveness properties of a tricolour garbage collection algorithm that is close in spirit to abstract descriptions of garbage collection systems used by software engineers at Harlequin. We found it necessary and useful to adapt the presentations of transition systems and linear temporal logic we found in the literature. Most notably, we chose a slightly different notion of fairness and we had to develop a calculus for liveness reasoning based on a refinement of the common 'leadsto' operator.

We found Pvs to be a suitable and effective tool for carrying out this formalization. We appreciated the automation provided by its decision procedures and supplied strategies, and were able to develop both general purpose and domain specific strategies that significantly simplified proofs.

We plan in the future on tackling successively more complicated garbage collection algorithms. For example, we intend to look at incremental read-barrier collectors and generational collectors.

Acknowledgements

The models presented in Sect. 3 and Sect. 6 are closely related to models that were developed in collaboration with, most notably, Healf Goguen and Rod Burstall at Edinburgh and Richard Brooksby, formerly at Harlequin.

The author wishes to thank Shmuel Katz and N. Shankar for their advice on linear temporal logic and Stephen Bevan, Rod Burstall, Healf Goguen, Cliff Jones, Pekka Pirinen, Gavin Matthews, Brian Monahan and the anonymous referees for their helpful comments on earlier drafts of this paper.

References

1. Rajeev Alur and Thomas A. Henzinger, editors. *Computer Aided Verification : 8th International Conference*, volume 1102 of *Lecture Notes in Computer Science*. Springer, July 1996.
2. Mordechai Ben-Ari. Algorithms for on-the-fly garbage collection. *ACM Transactions on Programming Languages and Systems*, 6(3):333–344, July 1984.
3. Glenn Bruns. *Distributed Systems Analysis with CCS*. Prentice Hall Europe, 1997.
4. K. Mani Chandy and Jayadev Misra. *Parallel Program Design: A Foundation*. Addison Wesley, 1988.
5. Ching-Tsun Chou. Predicates, temporal logic, and simulations. In Jeffrey J. Joyce and Carl-Johan H. Seger, editors, *Higher Order Logic Theorem Proving and Its Applications: 6th International Workshop, HUG '93.*, volume 780 of *Lecture Notes in Computer Science*, pages 310–323. Springer-Verlag, August 1993.
6. Edsger W. Dijkstra, Leslie Lamport, A. J. Martin, C. S. Scholten, and E. F. M. Steffens. On-the-fly garbage collection: An exercise in cooperation. *Communications of the ACM*, 21(11):966–975, November 1978.
7. Dov M. Gabbay. *Labelled deductive systems*, volume 1 of *Oxford Logic Guides*. Oxford University Press (Imprint: Clarendon Press), 1996.
8. Georges Gonthier. Verifying the safety of a practical concurrent garbage collector. In Alur and Henzinger [1].
9. Klaus Havelund. Mechanical verification of a garbage collector. Available from http://www.cs.auc.dk/~havelund/, May 1996.
10. Klaus Havelund and Natarajan Shankar. A mechanized refinement proof for a garbage collector. Available from http://www.cs.auc.dk/~havelund/, December 1996.
11. Richard Jones and Rafael Lins. *Garbage Collection: Algorithms for Automatic Dynamic memory Management*. John Wiley & Sons, 1996.
12. Leslie Lamport. The temporal logic of actions. *ACM Transactions on Programming Languages and Systems*, 16(3):872–923, May 1994.
13. Zohar Manna and Amir Pnueli. Completing the temporal picture. *Theoretical Computer Science*, 83:97–130, 1991.
14. Zohar Manna and Amir Pnueli. *Temporal Logic of Reactive and Concurrent Systems: Specification*. Springer, 1991.
15. Stephan Merz. Yet another encoding of TLA in Isabelle. Available from http://www4.informatik.tu-muenchen.de/~merz/isabelle/. The encoding described by this note accompanies the Isabelle98 release.
16. Susan Owicki and Leslie Lamport. Proving liveness properties of concurrent programs. *ACM Transactions on Programming Languages and Systems*, 4(3):455–495, July 1982.
17. S. Owre, J.M. Rushby, and N. Shankar. PVS: A prototype verification system. In D. Kapur, editor, *11th Conference on Automated Deduction*, volume 607 of *Lecture Notes in Artificial Intelligence*, pages 748–752. Springer-Verlag, 1992. See http://www.csl.sri.com/pvs.html for up-to-date information on PVS.
18. David M. Russinoff. A mechanically verified garbage collector. *Formal Aspects of Computing*, 6:359–390, 1994.

HOT: A Concurrent Automated Theorem Prover Based on Higher-Order Tableaux

Karsten Konrad

Universität des Saarlandes, Fachbereich Informatik
D-66141 Saarbrücken, Germany
konrad@ags.uni-sb.de

Abstract. HOT is an automated higher-order theorem prover based on $\mathcal{HTE}$, an extensional higher-order tableaux calculus. The first part of this paper introduces an improved variant of the calculus which closely corresponds to the proof procedure implemented in HOT. The second part discusses HOT's design that can be characterized as a concurrent blackboard architecture. We show the usefulness of the implementation by including benchmark results for over one hundred solved problems from logic and set theory.

1 Introduction

It is a well known result of Gödel's Incompleteness Theorem [15] that completeness for consistent higher-order logics can not be achieved for standard model semantics. On the other hand, complete higher-order calculi can be obtained for weaker notions of semantics such as **Henkin models** [17]. M. Kohlhase's article *Higher-Order Tableaux* [20] presents a free variable tableau calculus for classical higher-order logic which includes substitutivity of equivalence. Kohlhase's $\mathcal{HTE}$ calculus is able to prove for instance tautologies with embedded equivalent formulas like $c(a) \vee \neg c(\neg\neg a)$. The $\mathcal{HTE}$ calculus removes a source of incompleteness that all earlier higher-order machine-oriented calculi exhibited.

However, $\mathcal{HTE}$ in its original form is not Henkin complete. For instance, it can not be used to prove the tautology:

$$(p_{(\alpha\to\beta)\to o}(f_{\alpha\to\beta}) \Rightarrow p_{(\alpha\to\beta)\to o}(g_{\alpha\to\beta})) \Rightarrow f = g$$

which states that two functions f and g must be equal if $p(g)$ follows from $p(f)$ for arbitrary predicates p. This is a direct result of extensionality in Henkin models.

By using two additional inference rules first introduced for the higher-order theorem prover LEO [6], $\mathcal{HTE}$ becomes complete relative to Henkin models (see Sect. 2.3). The resulting improved $\mathcal{HTE}$ calculus is the theoretical backbone of our higher-order automated theorem prover HOT.

This paper is divided into two parts. In the first part (Sect. 2), we will introduce $\mathcal{ETAB}$, a variant of the extended $\mathcal{HTE}$ calculus which closely corresponds to

HOT's actual implementation. In the second part, we will discuss HOT's architecture that can be described as a blackboard system implemented in a concurrent logic programming language (see Sect. 3).

We demonstrate the usefulness of our implementation by including benchmark results for over one hundred solved problems from logic and set theory.

2   Theoretical Background

2.1   Preliminaries

We consider a higher-order logic based on Church's simply typed lambda calculus [10] and choose the set of **basetypes** $\mathcal{BT}$ to consist of the types ι and o, where o denotes the set of truth values and ι the set of individuals. The set of all **types** $\mathcal{T}$ is inductively defined over $\mathcal{BT}$ and the right-associative type constructor $\rightarrow$. We assume that our signature Σ contains a countably infinite set of variables and constants for every type.

We have the **standard logical connectives** $\neg_{o\rightarrow o}$, $\vee_{o\rightarrow o\rightarrow o}$, $\wedge_{o\rightarrow o\rightarrow o}$, $\Rightarrow_{o\rightarrow o\rightarrow o}$, and $\equiv_{o\rightarrow o\rightarrow o}$ and the **quantifier constants** $\forall_{(\alpha\rightarrow o)\rightarrow o}$ and $\exists_{(\alpha\rightarrow o)\rightarrow o}$. Furthermore, we postulate constants for **unification constraints** $\neq^?_{\alpha\rightarrow\alpha\rightarrow o}$ for all types α.

If the type of a symbol is determined by the given context we avoid its explicit mention. To ease readability, we follow the usual conventions for logical expressions and λ-terms, leaving out brackets where the construction of an expression is uniquely determined. Also, we will use infix notation whenever constants denote traditional infix connectives.

We distinguish **bound variables** such as x in $\lambda x.\ x$ from **free** variables. Free variables are written in upper-case letters X, Y, V etc., while constants and bound variables appear as lower-case letters.

Terms and formulas are denoted by bold capital letters like e.g., $\mathbf{A}_\alpha$ or $\mathbf{F}$. We will sometimes write $h\overline{\mathbf{U}^n}$ to abbreviate $(hU^1,\ldots,U^n)$, where function application is considered to be left-associative. We abbreviate formulas of the form $(\forall(\lambda x.\ \mathbf{F}))$ by $\forall x.\ \mathbf{F}$ and $(\exists(\lambda x.\ \mathbf{F}))$ by $\exists x.\ \mathbf{F}$.

The notions of α-, β- and η-**conversion**, **substitutions** and the **application of substitutions** are as usual, see e.g., [3].

We use the **uniform notation** for higher-order inference systems analogous to the notational system presented for first-order logics in [13]. The idea behind uniform notation is to classify formulas as implicitly conjunctive (α), disjunctive (β), existentially quantified (δ) or universally quantified (γ). Using this notation, inference systems can be specified in a compact way regardless of the actual number of logical connectives or quantifiers.

Tableaux calculi usually decompose α- and β-formulas into their **components** while **instantiating** δ- and γ-formulas. Table 1 shows the components of α- and β-formulas, and Table 2 shows the relation between higher-order γ- and δ-formulas and their instantiations. Note that the notion of α and β-formulas here is neither related to the α- and β-conversion of higher-order terms nor the use of α and β as type variables.

Table 1. α- and β-formulas and components

α	α_1	α_2	β	β_1	β_2
$A \wedge B$	A	B	$\neg(A \wedge B)$	$\neg A$	$\neg B$
$\neg(A \vee B)$	$\neg A$	$\neg B$	$A \vee B$	A	B
$\neg(A \Rightarrow B)$	A	$\neg B$	$A \Rightarrow B$	$\neg A$	B
$A \equiv B$	$A \Rightarrow B$	$B \Rightarrow A$	$\neg(A \equiv B)$	$\neg A \wedge B$	$A \wedge \neg B$

Table 2. γ- and δ-formulas and instantiations

γ	$\gamma(A)$	δ	$\delta(A)$
$\forall x.\ F$	$[A/x]F$	$\neg \forall x.\ F$	$[A/x]\neg F$
$\neg \exists x.\ F$	$[A/x]\neg F$	$\exists x.\ F$	$[A/x]F$

2.2 A Higher-Order Tableau Calculus

The $\mathcal{ETAB}$ calculus presented in this section is an extended variant of $\mathcal{HTE}$. $\mathcal{ETAB}$ uses the "naive" Skolemization known from first-order calculi. Strictly speaking, this form of Skolemization is not sound for classical higher-order logic: it would permit us to prove an instance of the Axiom of Choice which is known to be independent from higher-order logic [2]. A solution due to [23] is to associate with each Skolem constant the minimum number of arguments the constant has to be applied to.

We will now follow Kohlhase's approach and first introduce a calculus without extensionality. We begin with a set of rules that decompose the logical structure of the formulas in the tableau:

$$\frac{\alpha}{\begin{array}{c}\alpha_1\\\alpha_2\end{array}}\ alpha \qquad \frac{\beta}{\beta_1 \mid \beta_2}\ beta \qquad \frac{\neg\neg F}{F}\ not$$

$$\frac{\delta}{\delta((sk^n X_1,\ldots,X_n))}\ delta \qquad \frac{\gamma}{\gamma(V)}\ gamma$$

In these rules, V is a new variable and $(sk^n X_1,\ldots,X_n)$ is a Skolem term with a new Skolem function sk^n requiring a minimum of n arguments. We utilize the sound Skolemization method presented in [23]. $X_1,\ldots,X_n$ are all free variables of δ.

The rules above recursively build up the tableau tree by decomposing the logical structure of formulas and adding new nodes and branches. Before we can close a tableau branch, we have to select a **linked pair** of formulas $\mathbf{F}_1$ and $\mathbf{F}_2$ in this branch from which we can construct a contradiction. The two link rules below correspond to the *cut*-rule of $\mathcal{HTE}$. They introduce unification constraints for a linked pair:

$$\frac{\begin{array}{c} \mathbf{A}_o \\ \mathbf{B}_o \end{array}}{\neg \mathbf{A} \neq^? \mathbf{B}} \; link_1 \qquad \frac{\begin{array}{c} \mathbf{A}_o \\ \mathbf{B}_o \end{array}}{\mathbf{A} \neq^? \neg \mathbf{B}} \; link_2$$

The next group of rules solve the unification constraints[1] that are introduced by the *link* rules:

$$\frac{(\lambda x_\alpha.\ \mathbf{T}_1) \neq^? (\lambda y_\alpha.\ \mathbf{T}_2)}{[(sk^n X_1,\dots,X_n)/x]\mathbf{T}_1 \neq^? [(sk^n X_1,\dots,X_n)/y]\mathbf{T}_2} \; lam_1$$

$$\frac{(\lambda x_\alpha.\ \mathbf{T}_1) \neq^? \mathbf{T}_2}{[(sk^n X_1,\dots,X_n)/x]\mathbf{T}_1 \neq^? \mathbf{T}_2(sk^n X_1,\dots,X_n)} \; lam_2$$

$$\frac{h\overline{\mathbf{U}^n} \neq^? h\overline{\mathbf{V}^n}}{\mathbf{U}^1 \neq^? \mathbf{V}^1 \Big| \dots \Big| \mathbf{U}^n \neq^? \mathbf{V}^n} \; dec$$

$$\frac{F\overline{\mathbf{U}} \neq^? h\overline{\mathbf{V}}}{F \neq^? \mathbf{G} \Big| F\overline{\mathbf{U}} \neq^? h\overline{\mathbf{V}}} \; gb$$

In each of these rules, $(sk^n x_1,\dots,X_n)$ is a Skolem term for the rule's antecedent and $\mathbf{G}$ is a **general binding** that approximates the head h.

For both $\mathcal{HTE}$ and $\mathcal{ETAB}$ there is the **tableau substitution rule** *subst* that instantiates the whole tableau with an elementary substitution $[\mathbf{T}/X]$, iff some path ends in a formula of the form $X \neq^? \mathbf{T}$ such that the X is not free in $\mathbf{T}$. $\mathcal{ETAB}$ also inherits from $\mathcal{HTE}$ the **primitive substitution rule** *prim* that instantiates a flexible literal with a general binding that approximates some logical constant in $\{\neg, \vee\} \cup \{\forall_{(\alpha\to o)\to o}|\alpha \in \mathcal{T}\}$.

We call a branch Θ in a higher-order tableau **closed**, iff Θ ends in a flex/flex pair[2] or a formula of the form $\mathbf{A} \neq^? \mathbf{A}$. Note that the *subst* rule immediately closes the branch Θ that ends in a solved pair. A tableau is called **closed**, iff each branch of it is closed. A formula $\mathbf{A}$ is called a $\mathcal{ETAB}$ **theorem** iff there exists a closed higher-order tableau which can be constructed from $\neg\mathbf{A}$.

---

[1] For a general introduction to higher-order unification and especially for the definition of a set of *general bindings* $\mathbf{G}_\alpha$ for a type α and a (head-)constant h, we refer to [16].

[2] A flex/flex pair is a unification problem with variable heads, e.g., $P_{\iota\to\iota}a \neq^? Q_{\iota\to\iota}b$. A flex/flex pair has infinitely many incomparable solutions, e.g., $P = Q = \lambda x.\ c_\iota$ for all constants c_ι.

2.3   Extensionality

The **Leibniz definition** of equality defines two terms to be equal if they have the same properties. We will use $=$ as defined by

$$=_{\alpha \to \alpha \to o} := \lambda x \lambda y. \ \forall p_{\alpha \to o}. \ px \Rightarrow py$$

The following tableau construction rules complement $\mathcal{ETAB}$ with regard to extensionality in Henkin model semantics:

$$\frac{A_o \neq^? B_o}{\neg(A \equiv B)} ext_o \qquad \frac{A_\alpha \neq^? B_\alpha}{\neg(A = B)} ext_\alpha \qquad \frac{A_{\alpha \to \beta} \neq^? B_{\alpha \to \beta}}{\neg \forall p_\alpha. \ (Ap = Bp)} ext_{\alpha \to \beta}$$

The three rules specify that *unification* constraints $A \neq^? B$ can be replaced by negated *equality* constraints using either equivalence, Leibniz equality or functional extensionality depending on the type of the constrained terms. Functional extensionality can be formalized as $\lambda x. \ \lambda y. \ \forall p(xp = yp)$. In other words, we consider two functions A and B to be equal if they map identical arguments p of their domain to equal values.

Both $ext_{\alpha \to \beta}$ and ext_α have no counterpart in the original $\mathcal{HTE}$ specification. The three rules together correspond to the extensionality rules of the higher-order resolution calculus $\mathcal{ERES}$ as implemented in LEO [6].

2.4   Soundness and Completeness

Soundness and completeness proofs for extensional higher-order calculi can be found in [8] and [21]. $\mathcal{ETAB}$-like calculi with a different Skolemization are investigated in [20] and [21].

The soundness of Skolemization as used in $\mathcal{ETAB}$ is discussed in [23]. In [8], this Skolemization technique is used in order to form a sound higher-order resolution calculus $\mathcal{ERES}$. Benzmüller and Kohlhase show that $\mathcal{ERES}$ is Henkin complete by using the technique of abstract consistency classes. Considering the strong relationship between $\mathcal{ETAB}$, $\mathcal{HTE}$ and $\mathcal{ERES}$, we conjecture that there is a straightforward proof for soundness and completeness of $\mathcal{ETAB}$ following the same approach.

2.5   Examples

As an example, we discuss the theorem $(\exists p_o. \ p) \wedge (\exists p_o. \ \neg p)$, i.e., there exists a true and a false statement. The negation of this is equivalent to the formula at the root of the following tableau:

$$(\forall p_o. \ \neg p) \vee (\forall p_o. \ p)$$

$$
\begin{array}{c|c}
\forall p_o. \ \neg p & \\
\neg P_1 & \forall p_o. \ p \\
\neg P_2 & P_3 \\
\neg\neg P_1 \neq^? \neg P_2 & P_4 \\
*[\neg P_1 \neq^? P_2] & *[\neg P_3 \neq^? P_4]
\end{array}
$$

The negated theorem is a disjunction, and the *beta* rule splits the formula into two branches, each one holding a γ-formula. The *gamma* rule instantiates the γ-formula in each branch twice, creating the literals $\neg P_1$ and $\neg P_2$ for the first branch and P_3 and P_4 for the second branch. All newly introduced variables P_i are of type o. The *link* selects linked pairs for both branches by introducing the unification constraints $\neg\neg P_1 \neq^? \neg P_2$ and $\neg P_3 \neq^? P_4$. While the left branch becomes a candidate for decomposition (we remove the leading negation sign), the right branch can directly be closed using the *subst* rule. In the end, P_2 gets bound to $\neg P_1$ and P_4 to $\neg P_3$. Both branches now end in solved pairs and the tableau is closed.

The formula $p_{o\to o}(a_o \wedge b_o) \Rightarrow p(b \wedge a)$ is a theorem that requires extensionality of equivalence. The theorem is proved by the following $\mathcal{ET\!AB}$ tableau:

$$p(a \wedge b) \wedge \neg p(b \wedge a)$$
$$p(a \wedge b)$$
$$\neg p(b \wedge a)$$
$$\neg p(a \wedge b) \neq^? \neg p(b \wedge a)$$
$$p(a \wedge b) \neq^? p(b \wedge a)$$
$$(a \wedge b) \neq^? (b \wedge a)$$
$$\neg((a \wedge b) \equiv (b \wedge a))$$

$\neg(a \wedge b) \wedge (b \wedge a)$		$(a \wedge b) \wedge \neg(b \wedge a)$	
$\neg a$	$\neg b$	a	
$(b \wedge a)$	$(b \wedge a)$	b	
b	b	$\neg(b \wedge a)$	
a	a	$\neg b$	$\neg a$
$\neg a \neq^? \neg a$	$\neg b \neq^? \neg b$	$\neg b \neq^? \neg b$	$\neg a \neq^? \neg a$
$*[a \neq^? a]$	$*[b \neq^? b]$	$*[b \neq^? b]$	$*[a \neq^? a]$

Here again, we start with the negated theorem at the root of the tableau. We decompose its logical structure using the α-rule and create a linked pair $p(a \wedge b) \neq^? p(b \wedge a)$. We decompose using rule *dec* and obtain the unification problem $a \wedge b \neq^? b \wedge a$. The interesting step here is the transition from this unification problem which is unsolvable to the refutation proof of the equivalence $a \wedge b \equiv b \wedge a$ using the extensionality rule ext_o. From this point on, we have a plain propositional problem, and it becomes a trivial task to close the tableau.

3   The Theorem Prover HOT

Theorem provers can be characterized by many different features, for instance by their underlying logical system, programming language, heuristics, and so forth. The first part of this paper deals with the arguably most important characterization, namely the prover's underlying logic and the inference rules it employs. The $\mathcal{ET\!AB}$ calculus outlines a proof procedure, but only on a very abstract level. In the following we describe how this abstract proof procedure has been realized as an actual theorem proving system. We will also discuss some important design decisions, especially those that affect completeness.

We conceptualize tableaux implementations as **blackboard systems** [12] where tableau agents, equipped with abilities that implement parts of their underlying calculus, manipulate a blackboard-like data structure. The blackboard contains all globally accessible data such as the tableau itself and all variable assignments. The proof search space is defined by each agent's nondeterministic decisions.

Existing tableaux provers, for instance the first-order implementation presented in [13], construct proofs using only one single tableau agent. We propose an alternative approach where this task is distributed among multiple concurrent agents, all working together in order to create a proof on the blackboard (see Sect. 3.2). Blackboard systems are considered a basic form of a quasi-parallel system architecture, and we propose this concept as a natural and simple implementation of parallel theorem proving[3] in tableaux calculi. The construction of each branch in a free-variable tableaux is an isolated task except for the global variable substitutions which are derived from choosing unifiers and linked pairs when closing a branch.

Blackboard systems employ advanced concepts to control search, for instance so-called referee agents and ambassadors [22] that evaluate actions of other agents if there is any conflict between their decisions. For the current implementation, we have chosen a simple control strategy that favors short branches and simple unifiers. Basically, each agent tries to close its branch as fast as possible. The first agent that computes a linked pair and a unifier decides on the global variable substitution that has to be respected by all other agents, while a complete search strategy, iterative deepening, ensures that all linked pairs and all possible unifiers up to a certain complexity will be considered eventually.

3.1 Basic Design

HOT is basically a first-order theorem prover using extended Higher-Order Unification (HOU) instead of first-order unification. Theorem proving and HOU interact: while HOU is used to close tableau branches in the theorem proving part, extensionality is implemented by calling the theorem prover within unification (see Sect. 2.3).

HOT's theorem proving part has been inspired by the LEANTAP tableau theorem prover [9] that implements a complete and sound theorem prover for classical first-order logic.

Figure 1 schematically shows HOT's tableau construction. Theorem proving starts with a pre-processing step (called `read-problem`) that constructs an initial tableau. This initial tableau is the input for the initial tableau agent that tries to extend and contract branches using a search strategy based on iterative deepening.

Pre-processing Problems. Proof problems in HOT are defined as a triple $\langle D, A, T \rangle$ where D is a set of higher-order definitions, A is a set of assumptions

---

[3] For an overview to different approaches to parallel deduction, we refer to [7].

and T is a conjecture (theorem) to be proved. The pre-processing step expands all defined expressions while simultaneously checking for type errors. Definitions may be polymorph. For instance, the operator *intersection* for sets can be defined as $\lambda x_{\alpha \to o}.\ \lambda y_{\alpha \to o}.\ \lambda z_\alpha.\ xz \wedge yz$ with α being an arbitrary type.

Next, the theorem is negated and added to the set of assumptions to form the initial tableau. A simplification procedure removes all double negations and creates normal forms in each part of the tableau. The basic simplified tableau is the input for the initial tableau agent.

Tableau Agents. A tableau agent consists of three parts, `prove`, `extend`, and `contract` (see Fig. 1). The `extend` part performs extension on the examined branch of the tableau and includes extensionality rules, decomposition rules and HOU. The `contract` part tries to close branches by systematically applying the *link* rules to the last member of the branch and all its literal predecessors. `prove` chooses between extending and closing a branch, calculating suitable candidates for `contract` by a simple filter and indexing mechanism.

The rules *alpha*, *beta*, *delta* and *gamma* in $\mathcal{ETAB}$ have direct counterparts in the implementation of `extend`. The *not*-rule is replaced by the preprocessing done in the `read-problem` step and a local formula simplification whenever a proof step introduces a new negation. Whenever HOU is applied, the agent chooses between actually unifying or applying an extensionality step *ext* if the selected term pair is not $\alpha\beta\eta$-equal. The number of *ext* applications is restricted for each branch by an extensionality depth limit.

Proof Search. Tableau expansion is possibly infinite even for refutable conjectures. Hence, a naive depth-first strategy for tableau expansion would result in an incomplete search. In order to circumvent this, HOT performs **iterative deepening** depending on the γ-**depth** of branches: it first searches for all proofs which can be found with only one application of the γ-rule per branch, then for all proofs with two applications and so forth.

In the first-order case, for instance when proving theorems with LEANTAP, this search strategy is sound and complete as long as the choice of γ-formulas is fair. We can only have finitely many first-order tableau proofs for a given γ-depth, and when we make sure that eventually each γ-formulas can be used as often as needed, each possible tableau proof can be constructed. A fair choice of γ-formulas can be realized for instance by keeping all γ-formulas in a queue.

A complete proof search is harder to obtain in the higher-order case. In contrast to first-order unification, HOU is undecidable, so we can not simply use it as a procedure to decide unifiability. Instead, HOT restricts the number of general bindings for each unification attempt. This leads to a finite HOU search space. HOU is not unitary, i.e., a given unification problem may yield several solutions. HOT must consider all pre-unifiers that can be found within the unification depth limit. By gradually increasing both the unification limit

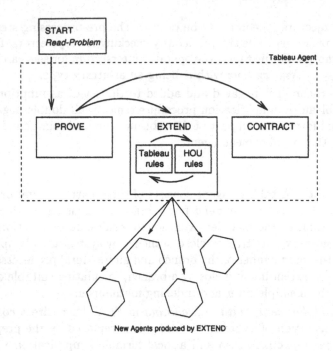

Fig. 1. HOT's schematized proof procedure

and the γ-depth for each iteration, we can make sure that all unifiers will be used eventually.[4]

3.2   Concurrency and the Blackboard Architecture

HOT has been implemented in Oz [24], a constraint programming language based on a new computation model providing a uniform foundation for higher-order functional programming, constraint logic programming, and concurrent objects with multiple inheritance [25]. Oz is a concurrent programming language, i.e., a procedure may start sub-processes, called **threads** which are executed concurrently in a fair way. HOT makes use of this feature when descending a branching tableau and when solving flex/flex pairs.

Extending Disjunctive Branches. A generally useful heuristic for first-order tableaux is to extend those branches first that have a simpler, less disjunctive structure. Otherwise, a tableau agent may construct a large tree before it can detect that the variable substitutions computed so far do not allow to close the simpler parts of the tableau. In this case, the proof search must backtrack, and most of the previous work may be lost. In order to circumvent this problem,

---

[4] This has not been implemented yet. Section 3.3 comments on this and other possible sources of incompleteness in the current implementation.

LEANTAP for instance orders formulas in a pre-processing step while moving sub-formulas in front which have a smaller, less branching structure.

For higher-order tableaux, this pre-processing can not be fully performed. Flexible heads may be instantiated either by primitive substitution or unification and change their propositional structure during proof search. HOT implements an alternative optimization of branch extension using concurrent tableau agents.

A tableau agent that encounters a disjunctive formula β will start a new thread that extends the β_1 component while the original agent continues to extend the β_2 branch (see Fig. 2). Also, we split expansion between distinct agents when decomposing unification problems. Instead of a single agent that has to decide on the order of branches to visit, we analyze separate branches by separate agents, each one working autonomously on its own part of the tableau. Agents communicate with each other by manipulating the global variable assignments that are part of the blackboard. The first agent which is able to close its branch by applying a substitution decides on the important choice of the next unifier to explore. An agent closing a flat, less branching branch will hopefully inhibit unnecessary unification attempts in other, more complex parts of the tableau. The search strategy backtracks and considers other possibilities to close a branch if a unifier found in this way can not be used to construct a refutation.

As long as the concurrent execution of the agents is fair in a small enough time segmentation, this technique implements a weak form of breadth-first tableau expansion. It is not unusual for a proof search to create several hundred tableau agents.

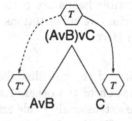

Fig. 2. An agent T splitting up into a concurrent copy T' and an original T when analyzing a disjunction

Solving Flex/Flex Constraints. HOT's concurrent implementation gives us an efficient treatment of flex/flex pairs. $\mathcal{ETAB}$ considers all branches ending in flex/flex pairs as closed, but an instantiation of one of the flexible heads will open the branch again. Each unification problem is part of the tableau, and therefore a unique agent deals with it. In the case of a branch ending in a flex/flex pair, the agent related to the branch simply suspends and waits for one of the flexible heads to become determined. An instantiation will reactivate the agent, and the extension/contraction cycle of the branch continues.

The blackboard design leads to a nondeterministic behavior of the whole system. Since we do not synchronize agents in any way, a proof search is not guaranteed to follow the same route every time. An instantiation of a flexible head can reactivate several agents at the same time, and all of these will try to apply general bindings immediately. For a few proof problems with flexible heads, for instance Cantor's theorem (see Appendix A), it is a matter of luck for the right agent to "win the race". The difference between a good and a bad choice for a unifier results in a difference of more than two orders of magnitude in the case of Cantor's theorem.

3.3   Completeness of the Implementation

Implementations of automated theorem provers always feature some trade-offs between the theoretical concept of completeness and the intended problem solving power. For instance, completeness relative to a calculus can not be maintained if the rules of a proof procedure span a search space which is too large for practical purposes. In the following, we will discuss some design decisions that affect HOT's completeness relative to $\mathcal{ETAB}$ and Henkin model semantics.

Primitive Substitutions. In the case of higher-order theorem proving, the *prim* rule is a case where a single inference rule creates a much larger search space without producing more solutions except for some few examples where primitive substitutions are clearly necessary. The only flexible heads that are quite common are those introduced by Leibniz equality when unifying individual constants. As a rule, these flexible heads are better treated in a goal-oriented way by literal links than by primitive substitutions. Therefore, we have left out an implementation of *prim* in HOT.

Literal Links. The *link* rules of the calculus allow to link arbitrary formulas, as long as one is the negation of the other. Experiments have shown that this feature, together with the extensionality rule ext_o, creates an overwhelming number of unification problems. We therefore restricted the *link* rules to literals, which produces deeper proofs on the one hand and less unification attempts on the other. This approach alone does not lead to incompleteness [21], but as a result of the missing *prim* rule, more proofs may become unobtainable. In some way, linking non-literal formulas can have an identical effect as a sequence of *prim* applications. Instead of guessing the right substitutions for a flexible head in order to create a linked pair, the HOU will directly instantiate the flexible head with the appropriate substitution.

Extensionality. The number of applications of the extensionality rule in each tableau branch as well as the number of general bindings for each unification attempt is restricted because both are (a) a potential source of infinite loops and (b) can not be simply linked to the increasing γ-depth. Especially extensionality is critical since most proofs are unobtainable if the extensionality depth limit is too high. Note that HOT can apply *ext* whenever unification is attempted. An extensionality depth of 5 or higher usually is devastating.

HOT furthermore implements a possibly incomplete heuristic choice of the extensionality rule. Basically, we will apply ext_α exclusively to unification constraints of the form $\mathbf{A}_\iota \neq^? \mathbf{B}_\iota$. Leibniz equality is the potentially most expensive form of equality since it introduces new flexible heads that can be freely instantiated by unification. We therefore restrict Leibniz equality to individuals and treat boolean values and functions only by ext_o and $ext_{\alpha \rightarrow \beta}$. Following the same idea, the equality constant $=$ will be substituted by equivalence or functional extensionality whenever possible.

Indexing. Indexing is a source of incompleteness because the `prove` procedure will not use terms $\mathbf{F}_1$ and $\neg \mathbf{F}_2$ for contraction if $\mathbf{F}_1$ and $\mathbf{F}_2$ have incompatible constant heads. Such pairs can not be solved alone by unification, but extensionality may nevertheless lead to a proof. On the other hand, removing indexing increases the number of unification attempts even more. With the help of the extensionality rule, this again makes proof search hopeless for all except simple examples. The question whether indexing can be implemented at all as a useful and complete heuristic for extensional higher-order proof procedures such as higher-order resolution or higher-order tableaux remains open.

4   Conclusion and Future Work

We have presented a calculus and a concurrent implementation for an automated theorem prover based on an extensional higher-order tableaux calculus. While the theorem prover's design is still quite simple, we can demonstrate that extensional higher-order tableaux is a worthwhile contribution to machine-oriented reasoning (see appendix). Some implementation-related questions that are raised in this paper are usually neglected in purely theoretical research. For instance, the problematic interaction of indexing and extensionality discussed in Sect. 3.3 is important to all automated higher-order theorem proving systems that are based on full extensionality. HOT helped us to identify these problems and allowed us to experiment with possible solutions. For instance, HOT's concurrent architecture evolved from the observation that many proof problems can not be solved using a standard depth-first expansion of the tableaux.

HOT's intended application is the construction of natural language semantics. [19] describes how HOT tableaux can be used to analyze a certain class of natural language utterances (corrections). So far, there exists no theorem prover that is optimized for inferences in natural language processing. Full-scale automated theorem proving systems like TPS [1] are optimized for mathematical theorems that may require long and deeply nested proofs. Inferences in natural language processing tend to be shallow, but require answer-complete or even abductive reasoning techniques that are not as common in mathematical theorem proving. The author is especially interested in proof techniques and heuristics for semantics construction. One of these techniques is higher-order **coloured** unification (HOCU) [18] which can be used to guide the search for unifiers in natural language semantics [14]. Hot's concurrent HOU module developed by Martin Müller and the author already includes the constraint propagation needed for computing coloured unifiers.

The author would like to link Hot to the ΩMEGA proof development system [4]. ΩMEGA features a database of mathematical knowledge (e.g., definitions in higher-order formalization), a large selection of examples, proof-checking and human-readable proof representation. Hot itself only uses a simple preprocessing mechanism for definition expansion and does not produce compact and easily verifiable proofs.

5 Acknowledgements

The work reported in this paper was funded by the Deutsche Forschungsgemeinschaft (DFG) in Sonderforschungsbereich SFB-378, Project C2 (LISA). The results reported here owe to stimulating and clarifying discussions with Christoph Benzmüller, Volker Sorge, Martin Müller, Michael Kohlhase and Jörg Siekmann. I would like to thank Martin Müller for the original concurrent HOU implementation and Christian Schulte for his technical assistance regarding search engines and timer routines. Furthermore, I appreciate the various helpful comments and suggestions made by the anonymous referees.

References

1. Peter B. Andrews, Matthew Bishop, Sunil Issar, Dan Nesmith, Frank Pfenning, and Hongwei Xi. TPS: A theorem proving system for classical type theory. *Journal of Automated Reasoning*, 16(3):321–353, 1996.
2. Peter B. Andrews, 1973. letter to Roger Hindley dated January 22, 1973.
3. H. P. Barendregt. *The Lambda Calculus*. North Holland, 1984.
4. C. Benzmüller, L. Cheikhrouhou, D. Fehrer, A. Fiedler, X. Huang, M. Kerber, M. Kohlhase, K. Konrad, E. Melis, A. Meier, W. Schaarschmidt, J. Siekmann, and V. Sorge. ΩMEGA: Towards a mathematical assistant. In William McCune, editor, *Proceedings of the 14th Conference on Automated Deduction*, number 1249 in LNAI, pages 252–255, Townsville, Australia, 1997. Springer Verlag.
5. Christoph Benzmüller, 1997. LEO benchmarks
   http://www.ags.uni-sb.de/projects/deduktion/projects/hot/mizar/.
6. Christoph Benzmüller. A Calculus and a System Architecture for Extensional Higher-Order Resolution. Research Report 97-198, Department of Mathematical Sciences, Carnegie Mellon University, Pittsburgh,USA, June 1997.
7. Maria Paola Bonacina and Jieh Hsiang. Parallelization of Deduction Strategies: An Analytical Study. *Journal of Automated Reasoning*, (13):1–33, 1994.
8. Christoph Benzmüller and Michael Kohlhase. Resolution for henkin models. SEKI-Report SR-97-10, Universität des Saarlandes, 1997.
9. Bernhard Beckert and Joachim Posegga. Lean, Tableau-based Deduction. *Journal of Automated Reasoning*, 15(3):339–358, 1995.

10. Alonzo Church. A formulation of the simple theory of types. *Journal of Symbolic Logic*, 5:56–68, 1940.
11. Ingo Dahn, 1997. Statistics for Problems from the Mizar Library.
    http://www-irm.mathematik.hu-berlin.de/~ilf/miz2atp/mizstat.html.
12. R. Engelmore and T. Morgan, editors. *Blackboard Systems*. Addison-Wesley, 1988.
13. Melvin Fitting. *First-Order Logic and Automated Theorem Proving*. Springer Verlag, 1990.
14. Claire Gardent, Michael Kohlhase, and Karsten Konrad. Higher-order coloured unification: a linguistic application. Submitted for publication, 1997.
15. Kurt Gödel. Über formal unentscheidbare Sätze der Principia Mathematica und verwandter Systeme I. *Monatshefte der Mathematischen Physik*, 38:173–198, 1931. English Version in [27].
16. Jean H. Gallier and Wayne Snyder. Complete sets of transformations for general *E*-unification. *Theoretical Computer Science*, 1(67):203–260, 1989.
17. Leon Henkin. Completeness in the theory of types. *Journal of Symbolic Logic*, 15(2):81–91, 1950.
18. Dieter Hutter and Michael Kohlhase. A coloured version of the λ-calculus. SEKI-Report SR-95-05, Universität des Saarlandes, 1995.
19. Michael Kohlhase and Karsten Konrad. Higher-order automated theorem proving for natural language semantics. Seki Report SR-98-04, Fachbereich Informatik, Universität Saarbrücken, 1998.
20. Michael Kohlhase. Higher-order tableaux. In *Proceedings of the Tableau Workshop*, pages 294–309, Koblenz, Germany, 1995.
21. Michael Kohlhase. Higher-order automated theorem proving. In Wolfgang Bibel and Peter Schmitt, editors, *Automated Deduction – A Basis for Applications*, volume 2. Kluwer, 1998. forthcoming.
22. Luiz V. Leao and Sarosh N. Talukdar. COPS: A System for Constructing Multiple Blackboards. In Alan H. Bond and Les Gasser, editors, *Readings in Distributed Artificial Intelligence*, page 547ff. Morgan Kaufmann, 1988.
23. Dale Miller. *Proofs in Higher-Order Logic*. PhD thesis, Carnegie-Mellon University, 1983.
24. Programming Systems Lab Saarbrücken, 1998. The Oz Webpage:
    http://www.ps.uni-sb.de/oz/.
25. Gert Smolka. The oz programming model. In Jan van Leeuwen, editor, *Computer Science Today*, volume 1000 of *LNCS*, pages 324–343. Springer Verlag, 1995.
26. Z. Trybulec and H. Swieczkowska. Boolean properties of sets. *Journal of Formalized Mathematics*, 1, 1989.
27. Jean van Heijenoort, editor. *From Frege to Gödel A Source Book in Mathematical Logic, 1879-1931*. Source Books in the History of the Sciences. Harvard University Press, 1967.

A   Performance

Table 3 shows the performance of HOT for some selected problems. The runtime has been measured on a Pentium Pro 200 using Oz 3.0.2 [24].

The first theorem is a variant of Cantor's theorem. We prove that the set of functions $f_{\alpha \to \beta}$ is not enumerable if there exists at least one fix-point free function.

Table 3. Benchmark results for some selected problems

Nr.	Theorem	msec
1	*Cantor*	1100
2	$\exists p_o.\ p$	10
3	*Counting*	660
4	$s_1 \subseteq s_2 \Rightarrow \neg \exists x.\ x \in s_1 \wedge x \notin s_2$	20
5	$a \in \wp a$	20
6	$s_1 \subseteq s_2 \Rightarrow \wp s_1 \subseteq \wp s_2$	340
7	$c \in \wp(a \backslash b) \Rightarrow c \subseteq a \wedge c \cap b = \emptyset$	130
8	$c \in \wp(a \backslash b) \equiv c \subseteq a \wedge c \cap b = \emptyset$	460
9	$\emptyset \in \wp a$	10
10	$\{x\} \subseteq \wp a \equiv x \in a$	620
11	$(a \cap b) \cap (a \backslash b) = \emptyset$	20
12	$p(a \wedge b) \Rightarrow p(b \wedge a)$	70
13	$p(a) \wedge p(b) \Rightarrow p(a \wedge b)$	260
14	$p(c \vee (a \wedge b)) \Rightarrow p((b \wedge a) \vee c)$	120
15	$(c_1 \equiv c_2) \Rightarrow p(c_1) \vee \neg p(c_2)$	150
16	$(c_1 \equiv c_2) \wedge (f = g) \Rightarrow p(fc_1) \vee \neg p(gc_2)$	490
17	$(c_1 = c_2) \Rightarrow (pc_1) \vee \neg(pc_2)$	1870
18	$(f = g) \wedge (c_1 = c_2) \Rightarrow p(fc_1) \vee \neg p(gc_2)$	15170
19	$\neg \forall x_o.\ \forall y_o.\ x = y$	20
20	$(f = g) \Rightarrow (g = f)$	160
21	$f = f$	0
22	$(f = g) \Rightarrow (fc = gc)$	2780
23	$(\forall c.\ fc = gc) \Rightarrow (pf = pg)$	3020
24	$(f = g) \wedge (g = h) \Rightarrow (f = h)$	12100
25	*Santa*	10780

A restricted version of Cantor's theorem states that the set of functions $f_{\alpha \to o}$ is not enumerable. In this case, we do not need an additional axiom for the existence of fix-point free functions, because the existence of such functions can be inferred from the properties of type o. This version of Cantor's theorem is one of the few examples where proof search is really unstable: it is possible to prove the theorem very quickly – in about 70msecs – when HOT's tableau agents hit upon a favorable choice of unifiers and linked pairs. In the worst case, it can take over 25 seconds!

Theorem (3) is a plain benchmark that makes the theorem prover count to 6 using a unary encoding of numbers.

Theorems (5)–(10) state some properties of power-sets. Theorem (11) is proposition (111) from [26]. This problem is trivial for higher-order theorem provers like LEO, TPS or HOT, while prominent first-order theorem provers are not able to solve it in less than 15 seconds (see Appendix B).

All theorems so far do not require extensionality and all proofs were found with an extensionality depth limit of 0. Theorems (12) to (25) have been proved using extensionality with a depth limit of 4. The last theorem is a complicated variant of (13). Its formulation is

$$believes(peter, \exists x.\ santa(x)) \land$$
$$believes(peter, \exists x.\ toothfairy(x)) \Rightarrow$$
$$believes(peter, (\exists x.\ santa(x)) \land (\exists x.\ toothfairy(x)))$$

This proposition is quite hard to prove without concurrent branch expansion. An extensionality depth of 4 for this proposition will not lead to a solution because of the high branching factor of the proof search, while an extensionality limit of less than 3 makes it impossible to close some branches.

B   Boolean Properties of Sets

Table 4 shows benchmark results for propositions from [26], again measured on a Pentium Pro 200. For comparing these results with those achieved by LEO, we refer to [5].

Each entry documents the plain runtime (Run), the time spend for copying data (Copy) and the total time for finding the proof (Total), including garbage collection. All values are given in msec. The table is divided into three parts. The first part are those theorems which can be found with a γ-depth ranging from 2 to 5. The rest are "harder" theorems that require a γ-depth of at least 5 (problems 50, 59, 99, 100, 110, 115, 119 and 120) and those that require a γ-depth of at least 8 (51, 55, 114 and 121) in order to be solvable in less than 15 seconds. All proofs where found with an extensionality depth of 0.

Note that both LEO and HOT outperform prominent high-speed first-order theorem provers on this class of examples [11]. Like LEO, HOT can not solve the problems (56) and (57) that still have a complex first-order structure after definition expansion.

Table 4. Benchmark results for set theoretical problems from [26]

Nr.	Run	Copy	Total	Nr.	Run	Copy	Total
8	30	30	80	9	40	30	70
10	40	30	70	12	30	0	30
13	10	10	20	15	20	0	20
17	20	10	40	18	90	410	700
19	180	450	810	20	150	410	780
23	110	310	640	24	30	0	30
25	800	4620	8210	27	10	0	10
28	1200	1410	3080	29	210	160	370
30	20	10	30	31	10	0	10
32	410	540	1130	33	40	30	80
34	590	620	1440	35	70	80	150
37	10	0	10	38	20	0	20
39	260	260	610	40	50	20	70
41	310	260	660	42	40	120	160
44	130	400	710	45	80	70	150
46	50	20	70	47	40	30	70
48	350	340	790	49	20	0	20
52	100	150	250	53	230	590	980
54	90	90	180	58	30	0	30
60	30	0	30	61	10	10	20
62	30	20	50	64	80	40	120
65	20	10	40	67	100	70	170
68	40	20	60	69	40	40	80
70	100	170	450	71	70	120	190
72	290	1320	2380	73	20	0	20
74	20	10	30	75	20	0	20
76	20	20	40	77	60	50	110
78	40	30	70	79	50	50	100
80	60	100	170	81	70	220	480
82	50	50	100	83	70	80	150
84	70	220	480	85	110	90	200
86	110	160	460	87	100	200	480
88	110	50	170	89	150	200	550
90	640	1810	2960	91	110	200	500
92	90	90	190	93	30	60	100
95	100	120	240	96	110	240	530
97	320	760	1890	98	250	670	1090
101	30	0	30	102	40	0	40
104	10	0	10	111	10	0	10
112	30	0	30	113	30	0	30
116	60	110	170	117	90	130	220
118	70	80	150				
50	50	20	70	59	130	140	480
99	390	2270	3440	100	310	1110	2120
110	130	240	520	115	330	1380	2410
119	160	410	750	120	130	160	420
51	180	250	590	55	200	270	630
114	160	290	640	121	130	110	250

Free Variables and Subexpressions in Higher-Order Meta Logic

Chuck Liang

Department of Computer Science, Trinity College
300 Summit Street, Hartford, CT 06106-3100, USA
chuck.liang@mail.trincoll.edu

Abstract. This paper addresses the problem of how to represent free variables and subexpressions involving λ-bindings. The aim is to apply what is known as higher-order abstract syntax to higher-order term rewriting systems. Directly applying β-reduction for the purpose of subterm-replacement is incompatible with the requirements of term-rewriting. A new meta-level representation of subterms is developed that will allow term-rewriting systems to be formulated in a higher-order meta logic.

1 Introduction

Higher-order logic, and specifically the technique of *higher-order abstract syntax* has been shown to be a useful paradigm in the formulation of object-level systems.[1] These range from automated theorem proving to polymorphic type inferencing and to program transformation. Compared to first-order systems, higher-order logic based on the λ-Calculus can represent variables and abstractions in the object theory in a more natural manner. Issues such as the renaming of bound variables are eliminated by α-equivalence classes of the meta logic. Many techniques have been developed on this basis.

The existing techniques, however, are still insufficient for using higher-order logic as a generic framework (and meta-programming language) for dealing with the wide range of problems encountered in representing object-level systems. Many operations required by these systems are seemingly inconsistent with characteristics of the meta logic. In many object-level systems, extracting a subexpression or *subterm* from an expression is a common procedure. In term-rewriting systems in particular, we need to be able to substitute some occurrence of a subterm in an expression with another term. In the λ-calculus, substitution is synonymous with β-reduction. β-reduction alone, however, does not suffice to formulate all aspects of term replacement required in implementing and reasoning about term-rewriting systems. This is especially true when the *object-level* rewriting system is itself higher-order. Higher-order rewriting requires substitution to be regarded in the broadest sense, one in which the scopes of bound

---

[1] See [17, 4, 10, 5] for background and sample work on higher-order abstract syntax.

variables are not necessarily respected. We are required to consider x as, in some sense, a *subterm* of $\lambda x.x$. This is the central problem we shall address here.

This paper also complements the work of Felty [3], which showed how higher-order term rewriting can be implemented in a logic programming language supporting higher-order abstract syntax. The techniques presented in this previous work does not address the problem of subterms with free variables directly, and are therefore limited in their capacity as a *meta-theory* for reasoning about various aspects of higher-order writing systems (Nipkow's higher-order critical pairs [15] in particular). We shall develop a technique that is compatible with those of [3], but which allows for full flexibility in reasoning about individual subterms.

2   Substitutions and Contexts in Higher-Order Rewriting

In the λ-calculus, β-reduction alone is incompatible with substitution required in term-rewriting. First of all, β-reduction will universally replace all occurrences of a variable, whereas in term rewriting we may only wish to replace a particular occurrence. This can be solved by using λ-abstraction to represent a *context* that identifies the precise location in the term structure where the substitution is to take place.

Definition 1. *A context is a term of the form $\lambda c.D$ where c appears free exactly once in D.*

For example, given a term $(f\ a\ (f\ a\ b))$, the "context" $C = \lambda c.(f\ a\ (f\ c\ b))$ identifies the second occurrence of a as the one to be replaced, so that the β-reduction of $(C\ S)$ will replace that occurrence of a with the term S. The replacement of subterms using this higher-order representation is therefore a three-place relation involving a context in addition to the original and final terms.

There remains, however, many problems with such a formulation. The first of which is control and computational feasibility. Consider again term-rewriting. Given an arbitrary term T and a rewrite rule of the form $lhs \longrightarrow rhs$, we need to be able to determine what, if any subterms of T, along with their contexts, can be rewritten using this rule. That is, what context C and subterm S exist such that S is an instance of lhs and $(C\ S) = T$. One may be tempted to specify this relation using Huet's formulation of higher-order unification [7]. Such a specification, however, is computationally unacceptable since higher-order unification is undecidable and the set of unifiers for a problem is generally too large. That is, only a few of the multitude of unifiers are acceptable as correct solutions for S and C, because we require C to be a context.

An even more serious problem occurs when the object-theory itself may involve λ-terms, and this forms the major focus of this paper. In [15], Nipkow extended the critical pair formulation used in the well-known Knuth-Bendix Completion procedure to a rewriting system involving (a restricted class of) λ-terms. In this system, subterms that are subject to rewrite rules may contain bound variables. For example, assume that g is an (object-level) unary operator and f some binary operator. Given a sample term $T = \lambda x.(f\ (\lambda x.x)\ \lambda y.(g\ x))$, we would like to consider $(g\ x)$ as a subterm of T. This is because it is valid to apply a rewrite rule, such as $(g\ Z) \longrightarrow (h\ Z)$, to $(g\ x)$, yielding the term $(h\ x)$. We also need to graft $(h\ x)$ *back* into the context for $(g\ x)$ in T to form the final term $\lambda x.(f\ (\lambda x.x)\ \lambda y.(h\ x))$. But in both $(h\ x)$ and $(g\ x)$ x is a free variable. This process therefore requires the *recapturing* of the free variable x by λ-abstraction. But capturing a *free* variable under λ-abstraction is in direct opposition to substitution as β-reduction. Furthermore, we also must ensure that x is captured under the original abstraction that bound it in T, namely the outermost λx, and not the inner λy. The names of bound variables in T are now critical. It may therefore appear that α-equivalence classes, as well as β-reduction, are both inconsistent with higher-order term-rewriting systems. Yet $\alpha\beta$-equivalence forms the basis of higher-order abstract syntax. This apparent inconsistency induces the abandonment of higher-order logic as meta-language. We would need to use an essentially *first* order theory as the meta logic of a *higher* order system. This approach was in fact adopted by Nipkow in his formulation of higher-order critical pairs.

The inconsistency described above is only one of many which may arise in meta-programming. Related to the problem of substitution is the issue of how to represent object-level variables in the meta-logic. The naive approach of using free variables in the meta-logic to represent free variables in the object-logic, known as the "non-ground representation", is insufficient for all but the most trivial systems.[2] In order for a meta-logic to properly represent the object-theory, it can be enriched with new features that will allow it to address certain issues directly. Alternatively, we can try to preserve the meta-logic and address the same issue by *changing the representation of the object-theory* in the meta-logic. In [9] for example, it was shown how meta-level bound variables can be used to represent free type variables in an object-level typing system. The problem of determining subterms is similar in that meta-level substitution (i.e, β-reduction) must not be used to represent subterm replacement at the object-level. In order to preserve the λ-calculus as meta-theory, we must first adopt a different representation of a "subterm" of an expression in the λ-calculus, and then redefine the subterm-replacement relation using this new representation. α-equivalence classes can be preserved (with all the benefits of adopting them) using this new representation. β-reduction will still be used to implement term-replacement, but in a restricted and indirect manner.

3   Term Trees with λ-expressions

Term-rewriting requires the notion of "subterm" to be regarded in the widest possible sense. In [15], Nipkow showed that the traditional treatment of first-order term trees can be extended to λ-terms by simply treating each occurrence of λx as a unary first-order term constructor. Each subterm of an expression or

---

[2] This is well documented (see [6]).

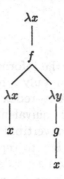

Fig. 1. Term tree for $\lambda x.(f\ (\lambda x.x)\ \lambda y.(g\ x))$

term is associated with a unique sequence representing the *position* of the subterm in the tree. The empty sequence ϵ represents the position of the "root" of the
tree, or the term itself. Each member of the sequence is an integer starting from 1
to the maximum branching factor (or the maximum arity of the constructors) of
the expression. We will use $T_@p$ to represent the subterm at position p in T. Inductively, $T_@\epsilon = T$ and for any n-ary operator op, $(op\ X_1,\dots,X_n)_@i.p = X_{i@}p$.
For example, position 1 represents the leftmost subtree of the root. Position
1.3 represents the third descendent of the first subtree of the root, and so on.
The notation $T[S]/_@p$ is used to represent T with S replacing the subterm at
position p. Each λ-binding λx represents one node in the term tree (the x is
not a separate node). If we confine ourselves to pure λ-terms with only application and abstraction, then positions are sequences over $\{1,2\}$. The term tree for
$\lambda x.(f\ (\lambda x.x)\ \lambda y.(g\ x))$ is given in Fig. 1. The subterm $\lambda x.x$ is at position 1.1.

Under this formulation, subexpressions with bound variables can be extracted
by "pruning" off a subtree. Expressions with free variables can be inserted or
"grafted" into a tree – *allowing* for the capture of free variables under λ-bindings.
α-equivalence is therefore not preserved under such an interpretation. In particular, x can be considered a subterm of (for example) $\lambda x\lambda y.(f\ y\ x)$ because
$x = (\lambda x\lambda y.(f\ y\ x))_@1.1.2$. We shall call x a *free subterm* when considered in this
manner.

Definition 2. S *is a* **free subterm** *of* T *if for some sequence* p, $T_@p = S$.

We emphasize that x is a free subterm of $\lambda x.x$ but *not* of $\lambda y.y$ although
the two λ-expressions are α-equivalent. Nipkow used free subterms and term
trees in formulating higher-order critical pairs. The clarity of this formulation
suffers from the need to explicitly maintain consistent names for free and bound
variables – something that a higher-order meta logic should provide for automatically. A reformulation of the representation of subterms and substitution
is required - one that preserves α-equivalence classes and yet respects the first-
order notion of replacing subterms in a term tree. This formulation is necessarily
different from traditional β-reduction because of reasons stated above.

4   Subterm Redefined

The meta-language we shall use in the reformulation is the λ-Calculus with α-equivalence. Concerning β-reduction, only a restricted form is required. This is the "β_0" reduction of Miller [12]. A β_0-redex is a β-redex of the form $(\lambda x.A)y$ where y is a λ-bound variable - or equivalently, an arbitrary variable not appearing free elsewhere.[3] Given α-convertibility, β_0-reduction can be simplified to $(\lambda x.A)x =_{\beta_0} A$. We shall write E^{β_0} to represent the β_0-reduced form of E. β_0-reduction is terminating since no new redeces can be introduced. The meta language need not involve types (though our result will usually be applied to object-level $\beta\eta$-long normal forms in practice).

Our general approach can be summarized by the following:

The free variables in a free subterm should be represented by bound variables at the meta-level.

If α-equivalence is to be preserved, some mechanism must be applied to associate the free variables in a free subterm with the bound variables in the parent term. Consider the term represented by the tree in Fig.1. The free occurrence of x in the free subterm $(g\ x)$ must be associated with the outermost λ-abstraction, and not with either of the two other λ-abstractions occurring in the parent term. This relationship between variables in free subterms and the scopes of λ-abstractions they fall under can be cleanly represented by λ-abstraction itself (at the meta-level). For each λ-bound variable in the parent term, we *include* the λ-abstraction in representing the free subterm. The free subterm $(g\ x)$ of the term in Fig.1 will be represented by (the α-equivalence class of) $\lambda x \lambda y.(g\ x)$.

We shall call $\lambda x \lambda y.(g\ x)$ a Λ-*subterm* of its parent term. The ordering of the λ-abstraction prefix of a Λ-subterm, *not* the names of bound variables, preserves the relationship between variables in the subterm and λ-bindings in the parent term.

In the following definition of Λ-subterms we do *not* distinguish meta-level λ-abstraction from object-level λ-abstraction. Although in practice this distinction is usually made, the result we prove is more general without the distinction. We show how to add the distinction in discussing the implementation of this technique in Sect. 6.

Definition 3.   *(Λ-subterms)*
The three-place relation $\Lambda_{subterm}$ is inductively defined over the third argument (representing the context) on all terms A, B, D, X and $X_1, \ldots, X_n$ as follows:

1. $\Lambda_{subterm}\ X\ X\ \lambda c.c$.

2. $\Lambda_{subterm}\ A\ (op\ X_1 \ldots X_i \ldots X_n)\ \lambda c.(op\ X_1 \ldots (D\ c)^{\beta_0} \ldots X_n)$ *if and only if* $\Lambda_{subterm}\ A\ X_i\ D$, *where op is any n-ary operator symbol (including applica-*

---

[3] See [13] for the formulation of this equivalence.

tion) that is not of the form λx.[4]

3. $\Lambda_{subterm}\ A\ B\ \lambda c.\lambda x.(D\ x\ c)^{\beta_0}$ *if and only if* $\Lambda_{subterm}\ (A\ x)^{\beta_0}(B\ x)^{\beta_0}(D\ x)^{\beta_0}$ *where x is an arbitrary variable not appearing free in A, B or $\lambda x.(D\ x)^{\beta_0}$.*

The intuitive meaning of $\Lambda_{subterm}\ S\ T\ C$ is that S is a Λ-subterm of T under the context C. The context replaces the position sequence in first order term trees. We say that S *is a Λ-subterm of* T if $\Lambda_{subterm}\ S\ T\ C$ holds for some context C.[5]

4.1   Examples

Some sample derivations of Λ-subterms are provided below:

1. The first example does not involve λ-bindings:

$$\Lambda_{subterm}\ a\ (f\ (g\ a)\ b)\ \lambda c.(f\ (g\ c)\ b)$$

holds if, by the second clause of the definition of $\Lambda_{subterm}$, with $i = 1$,

$$\Lambda_{subterm}\ a\ (g\ a)\ \lambda c.(g\ c)$$

holds. Again using clause two, this holds if

$$\Lambda_{subterm}\ a\ a\ \lambda c.c$$

holds. But $\Lambda_{subterm}\ a\ a\ \lambda c.c$ holds by clause one.

2. For the second example,

$$\Lambda_{subterm}\ \lambda x\lambda y.(g\ x)\ \lambda x.(f\ (\lambda x.x)\ \lambda y.(g\ x))\ \lambda c.\lambda x.(f\ (\lambda x.x)\ \lambda y.c)$$

holds since (by clause three with $D = \lambda x\lambda c.(f\ (\lambda x.x)\ \lambda y.c)$ and arbitrary z)

$$\Lambda_{subterm}\ \lambda y.(g\ z)\ (f\ (\lambda x.x)\ \lambda y.(g\ z))\ \lambda c.(f\ (\lambda x.x)\ \lambda y.c)$$

holds since (by clause two)

$$\Lambda_{subterm}\ \lambda y.(g\ z)\ \lambda y.(g\ z)\ \lambda c.\lambda y.c$$

holds since (by clause three with $D = \lambda y\lambda c.c$ and arbitrary variable x)

$$\Lambda_{subterm}\ (g\ z)\ (g\ z)\ \lambda c.c$$

holds by clause one. The reader is invited to verify that $\lambda y\lambda x.(g\ x)$ would be a Λ-subterm of $\lambda x.(f\ (\lambda x.x)\ \lambda y.(g\ y))$, but *not* of $\lambda x.(f\ (\lambda x.x)\ \lambda y.(g\ x))$.

---

[4] For pure λ-terms, *op* would just be application and this case would be for $(X_1\ X_2)$. We generalize this case to arbitrary operators in order to better connect the definition with arbitrary term trees.

[5] $\Lambda_{subterm}$ is defined so that C must be a context if $\Lambda_{subterm}\ S\ T\ C$ holds (see Theorem 1).

3. The final example demonstrates the generality of the $\Lambda_{subterm}$ relation. It is possible to consider y as a free subterm of $\lambda x\lambda y.(y\ x)$ by treating op implicitly as the application (app) operation of the λ-calculus. $(y\ x)$ can then be read as $(app\ y\ x)$. As a Λ-subterm, y becomes $\lambda x\lambda y.y$:

$$\Lambda_{subterm}\ \lambda x\lambda y.y\quad \lambda x\lambda y.(y\ x)\quad \lambda c.\lambda x\lambda y.(c\ x)$$

holds since (by clause three with $D = \lambda x\lambda c\lambda y.(c\ x)$ and arbitrary variable u)

$$\Lambda_{subterm}\ \lambda y.y\quad \lambda y.(y\ u)\quad \lambda c.\lambda y.(c\ u)$$

holds since (by clause three with $D = \lambda y\lambda c.(c\ u)$ and arbitrary variable v)

$$\Lambda_{subterm}\ v\quad (v\ u)\quad \lambda c.(c\ u)$$

holds since (by clause two)

$$\Lambda_{subterm}\ v\quad v\quad \lambda c.c$$

holds by clause one.

It is worthwhile to note that, as in the second example, the $\Lambda_{subterm}$ relation will also hold under different contexts. Specifically, $\lambda x\lambda y.(g\ x)$ is also a Λ-subterm of $\lambda x.(f\ (\lambda x.x)\ \lambda y.(g\ x))$ under the context $\lambda c.\lambda x.(f\ (\lambda x.x)\ c)$. In this case, $\lambda x\lambda y.(g\ x)$ would correspond to the free subterm $\lambda y.(g\ x)$ and not $(g\ x)$. This ambiguity as to how to interpret the λ-bindings is resolved by attaching the precise context to the $\Lambda_{subterm}$ relation. It can also be resolved by separating meta-level λ-abstraction from object-level λ-abstraction, which we do in Sect. 6.

4.2 Rewriting with Λ-subterms

The $\Lambda_{subterm}$ relation can be used for term-rewriting because we can now safely extract the subterm to be replaced. A rewrite rule can be applied by "looking inside" the λ-bindings for the subterm to be replaced. That is, we can define the application of rewrite rules in higher-order abstract syntax as follows:

Definition 4. *Given a rewrite rule $R = lhs \longrightarrow rhs$, we say that B **replaces** A under R if either*

1. *$A \longrightarrow B$ is an instance of $lhs \longrightarrow rhs$, or*
2. *$(B\ x)^{\beta_0}$ replaces $(A\ x)^{\beta_0}$ under R for an arbitrary variable x not appearing free in A, B or R.*

Thus $\lambda u\lambda v.(h\ u)$ replaces $\lambda x\lambda y.(g\ x)$ under the rule $(g\ Z) \longrightarrow (h\ Z)$ (where Z is a free variable). That is, the "replaces" relation rewrites a Λ-subterm to a term that preserves the λ-abstraction prefix. The rewritten term can be grafted into a context to form a new term. We can define rewriting for general λ-terms as follows:

Definition 5. *A* **rewrites** *to B under rule R if:*

1. *for some term S_a, $\Lambda_{subterm}$ S_a A C holds for some (context) C.*
2. *for some term S_b, S_b replaces S_a under R.*
3. *$\Lambda_{subterm}$ S_b B C holds.*

That is, if S_a is a Λ-subterm of A and S_b is a Λ-subterm of B under the same context, and such that S_b replaces S_a under R, then A rewrites to B under R. Thus $\lambda x.(f\ (\lambda x.x)\ \lambda y.(g\ x))$ rewrites to $\lambda u.(f\ (\lambda x.x)\ \lambda v.(h\ u))$ under the rule $(g\ Z) \longrightarrow (h\ Z)$ because:

1. $\Lambda_{subterm}$ $\lambda u \lambda v.(g\ u)$ $\lambda x.(f\ (\lambda x.x)\ \lambda y.(g\ x))$ $\lambda c.\lambda x.(f\ (\lambda x.x)\ \lambda y.c)$ holds
2. $\lambda u \lambda v.(h\ u)$ replaces $\lambda x \lambda y.(g\ x)$ under $(g\ Z) \longrightarrow (h\ Z)$.
3. $\Lambda_{subterm}$ $\lambda u \lambda v.(h\ u)$ $\lambda u.(f\ (\lambda x.x)\ \lambda v.(h\ u))$ $\lambda c.\lambda x.(f\ (\lambda x.x)\ \lambda y.c)$ holds.

The reader is invited to verify that this example is preserved under α-equivalent classes of terms.

The technique used in Definition 4 of looking inside λ-bindings to find a matching instance of a rewrite rule is similar to how higher-order rewriting is formulated by Felty in [3]. Instead of extracting a subterm together with its context explicitly, Felty's method essentially *combines* the stripping away of λ-bindings with the finding of a subterm that can be rewritten. While this approach suffices for the *implementation* of a higher-order rewriting system, it can not be used for the meta-level *reasoning* about properties of such systems. Nipkow's higher-order critical pairs provide the best example, for it requires a greater degree of flexibility in reasoning about individual subterms and their contexts. Consider the rewrite rules $\lambda y.(h\ (g\ (f\ y))) \longrightarrow a$ and $(g\ X) \longrightarrow (b\ X)$. A critical pair is formed by the terms a and $\lambda y.(h\ (b\ (f\ y)))$. By Nipkow's definitions this pair is formed by *extracting* the free subterm $(g\ (f\ y))$ together with its position and *grafting* the term $(b\ (f\ y))$ into the same position. Notice that the variable y becomes *recaptured* under the original λ-binding. This process can not be formulated using only the "tacticals" of [3]. The subterm and context must be extracted explicitly, but in a way that preserves α-equivalence classes. As shown above, both the extracting and grafting of subterms can be formulated using the $\Lambda_{subterm}$ relation.

5   Correctness Theorem

In this section we show that this higher-order formulation of subterms is correct in the sense that it is consistent with the term-tree representation.

Theorem 1. *For any terms S, T, and C, $\Lambda_{subterm}$ S T C holds if and only if:*

1. *$S =_\alpha \lambda x_1 \ldots \lambda x_n.S'$ for some $n \geq 0$ (if $n = 0$ then $S =_\alpha S'$), such that*
2. *for some position p, $T_@p = S'$ where*
3. *$x_1, \ldots, x_n$ are all the λ-bound variables in T that includes $T_@p$ in their scope, and such that if $i < j$ then λx_i includes λx_j in its scope, and*

4. C is a context, and $(C\ x)^{\beta_0} =_\alpha T[x]/@p$ for an arbitrary variable x not occurring in S, T or C.

Proof: both the forward and reverse directions are proved by induction on the structure of the context C:

Forward Direction:

Base Case: if $C = \lambda c.c$: assume $\Lambda_{subterm}\ S\ S\ \lambda c.c$ holds. Here, let $S' = S$, $p = \epsilon$ and so the first and third conditions holds vacuously. If $p = \epsilon$ then $S_{@}\epsilon = S = S'$ and the second condition is satisfied. Finally, for an arbitrary x, $(\lambda c.c)x =_{\beta_0} x$, and $S[x]/@\epsilon = x$ and so the fourth condition is also satisfied.

Inductive Case for $C = \lambda c.op\ X_1 \ldots (D\ c)^{\beta_0} \ldots X_n$: T must have the form

$$op\ X_1 \ldots X_i \ldots X_n$$

By definition of $\Lambda_{subterm}$, $\Lambda_{subterm}\ S\ X_i\ D$ holds, which by inductive hypotheses yields:

1. $S =_\alpha \lambda x_1 \ldots \lambda x_n.S'$
2. there's a sequence p such that $X_{i@}p = S'$
3. $x_1, \ldots, x_n$ are all bound variables in X_i that contain S' in their scopes are for $i < j\ \lambda x_j$ is in the scope of λx_i.
4. D is a context, and for an arbitrary x, $(D\ x)^{\beta_0} =_\alpha X_i[x]/@p$

Now we need to show that each condition holds for the larger context:

1. S remain the same and $S =_\alpha \lambda x_1 \ldots \lambda x_n.S'$
2. Let $p' = i.p$. Then since $T_{@}i = X_i$, $T_{@}p' = X_{i@}p = S'$.
3. Since $x_1, \ldots, x_n$ satisfies the third condition with respect to S' in X_i, then $x_1, \ldots, x_n$ also satisfies the condition with respect to S' in T.
4. for an arbitrary x,

$$(\lambda c.op\ X_1 \ldots (D\ c)^{\beta_0} \ldots X_n)x =_{\beta_0} op\ X_1 \ldots (D\ x)^{\beta_0} \ldots X_n$$

By part 4 of the inductive hypothesis,

$$op\ X_1 \ldots (D\ x)^{\beta_0} \ldots X_n = op\ X_1 \ldots X_i[x]/@p \ldots X_n = T[x]_{@}i.p$$

Finally, C is a context since D is a context.

Inductive Case for $C = \lambda c.\lambda x.(D\ x\ c)$: assume that $\Lambda_{subterm}\ S\ T\ C$ holds. Then by definition of $\Lambda_{subterm}$,

$$\Lambda_{subterm}\ (S\ x)^{\beta_0}\ (T\ x)^{\beta_0}\ (D\ x)^{\beta_0}$$

holds. Application of the inductive hypothesis yields:

1. $(S\ x)^{\beta_0} =_\alpha \lambda x_1 \ldots \lambda x_n.S'$

2. for some sequence p, $(T\ x)^{\beta_0}{}_{@}p = S'$
3. $x_1, \ldots, x_n$ are all bound variables in $(T\ x)^{\beta_0}$ that contain S' in their scopes are for $i < j$ λx_j is in the scope of λx_i.
4. $(D\ x)^{\beta_0}$ is a context and for an arbitrary y, $(D\ x\ y)^{\beta_0} =_\alpha (T\ x)^{\beta_0}[y]/{_{@}p}$

Again we need to show that these four conditions are preserved:

1. Since $(S\ x)^{\beta_0} =_\alpha \lambda x_1 \ldots \lambda x_n.S'$, $S =_\alpha \lambda x \lambda x_1 \ldots \lambda x_n.S'$
2. Let $p' = 1.p$. T can be written as $\lambda x.(T\ x)^{\beta_0}$. Since $(T\ x)^{\beta_0}{}_{@}p = S'$, we have

$$\lambda x.(T\ x)^{\beta_0}{}_{@}p' = S'.$$

3. Since $x_1, \ldots, x_n$ satisfies the third condition with respect to S' in $(T\ x)^{\beta_0}$, $x, x_1, \ldots, x_n$ satisfies the condition with respect to S' in $\lambda x.(T\ x)^{\beta_0}$.
4. For an arbitrary y, $(\lambda c.\lambda x.(D\ x\ c)^{\beta_0})y =_{\beta_0} \lambda x.(D\ x\ y)^{\beta_0}$. By inductive hypothesis, $(D\ x\ y)^{\beta_0} =_\alpha (T\ x)^{\beta_0}[y]/{_{@}p}$, so $\lambda x.(D\ x\ y)^{\beta_0} =_\alpha \lambda x.[(T\ x)^{\beta_0}[y]/{_{@}p}]$. But $\lambda x.[(T\ x)^{\beta_0}[y]/{_{@}p}] = \lambda x.(T\ x)^{\beta_0}[y]/{_{@}p'}$. Finally, $\lambda c.\lambda x.(D\ x\ c)^{\beta_0}$ is a context since $(D\ x)^{\beta_0}$ is a context implies that c occurs exactly once in $\lambda x.(D\ x\ c)^{\beta_0}$.

Reverse Direction:

Base Case: assuming $C =_\alpha \lambda c.c$ (since C must be a context) and the four conditions of the theorem holds for C. By the fourth condition, $T[x]\_{@}p = (C\ x)^{\beta_0} = x$. We can derive from this that $p = \epsilon$. Now by the second condition, $T_{@}p = T = S'$ where (by condition one) $S =_\alpha \lambda x_1 \ldots \lambda x_n.S'$. Now by condition three, $n = 0$ ($x_1, \ldots, x_n$ is an empty sequence) since $x_1, \ldots, x_n$ are variables in T that contain T, which is equal ot $T_{@}p$, in their scopes. Thus we have $S = S' = T$, and

$$\Lambda_{subterm}\ S\ S\ C$$

holds by definition.

Inductive Case for $C = \lambda c.op\ X_1 \ldots X_m$: since by the fourth condition c is a context, c appears in exactly one X_i among $X_1, \ldots, X_m$. Let $D = \lambda c.X_i$. D is therefore also a context. We need to show that all four conditions holds for D in order to apply the inductive hypothesis. We can write

$$C = \lambda c.op\ X_1 \ldots (D\ c)^{\beta_0} \ldots X_m.$$

Condition four also yields

$$T[x]/{_{@}p} =_\alpha (C\ x)^{\beta_0} = op\ X_1 \ldots (D\ x)^{\beta_0} \ldots X_m$$

for some arbitrary variable x. Since x can occur only in $(D\ x)^{\beta_0}$, $p = i.p_2$ for some sequence p_2. Let $T_2 = T_{@}i$. Then $T[x]/{_{@}p} = op\ X_1 \ldots T_2[x]/{_{@}p_2} \ldots X_m$. Now we have $(D\ x)^{\beta_0} =_\alpha T_2[x]/{_{@}p_2}$ (condition four is satisfied for D). Since by condition two $T_{@}p = S'$, $T_{2@}p_2 = S'$. Conditions one and three gives us that

$S =_\alpha \lambda x_1 \ldots \lambda x_n.S'$ where $x_1, \ldots, x_n$ are all bound variables in T containing S' in their scope. But this also means that $x_1, \ldots, x_n$ are all bound variables in T_2 containing S' in their scope (there are no more λ-abstractions outside of T_2). Now we are read to apply the inductive hypothesis, which yields that

$$\Lambda_{subterm} \ S \ T_2 \ D$$

holds. Then by definition of the $\Lambda_{subterm}$ relation, $\Lambda_{subterm} \ S \ T \ C$ also holds.

Inductive Case for $C = \lambda c.\lambda x.D'$: let $D = \lambda x.\lambda c.D'$. Then $C = \lambda c.\lambda x.(D \ x \ c)^{\beta_0}$ We are allowed to assume that the four conditions hold for S, T and C. We need to show that they also hold for $(S \ x)^{\beta_0}$ $(T \ x)^{\beta_0}$ and $(D \ x)^{\beta_0}$ in order to apply the inductive hypothesis. Since C is a context, $(D \ x)^{\beta_0}$ must be a context. Condition four also yields $T[y]/@p =_\alpha (C \ y)^{\beta_0} = \lambda x.(D \ x \ y)^{\beta_0}$ for some arbitrary variable y. This implies $p = 1.p_2$ for some p_2. Since $T[y]/@p =_\alpha \lambda x.(D \ x \ y)^{\beta_0}$. T is an abstraction of the form $\lambda x.T@1$, and in particular $(T \ x)^{\beta_0} = T@1$. But then

$$\lambda x.(D \ x \ y)^{\beta_0} =_\alpha T[y]/@p = \lambda x.T@1[y]/@p_2.$$

This implies that

$$(D \ x \ y)^{\beta_0} =_\alpha T@1[y]/@p_2 = (T \ x)^{\beta_0}[y]/@p_2$$

And so the fourth condition is satisfied for $(T \ x)^{\beta_0}$. By condition two on $T@p$,

$$(T \ x)^{\beta_0}@p_2 = T@1@p_2 = T@p = S'$$

so condition two is also satisfied for $(T \ x)^{\beta_0}$. If $S =_\alpha \lambda x_1 \ldots \lambda x_n.S'$ and $x_1, \ldots, x_n$ satisfies condition three, then $x_1 = x$ since $T = \lambda x.T@1$. This means

$$(S \ x)^{\beta_0} =_\alpha \lambda x_2 \ldots \lambda x_n.S'$$

and $x_2, \ldots x_n$ satisfies condition three with respect to $(T \ x)^{\beta_0}$ since $T@1 = (T \ x)^{\beta_0}$. We can now apply the inductive hypothesis on $(S \ x)^{\beta_0}$, $(T \ x)^{\beta_0}$ and $(D \ x)^{\beta_0}$ so that

$$\Lambda_{subterm} \ (S \ x)^{\beta_0} \ (T \ x)^{\beta_0} \ (D \ x)^{\beta_0}$$

holds. So by definition of the $\Lambda_{subterm}$ relation we have that the following holds:

$$\Lambda_{subterm} \ S \ T \ C$$

$\square$

We summarize the result of this theorem in corollary 1, which is directly derivable. It formalizes the relationship between Λ-subterms and free subterms:

Corollary 1. *For all terms S and T:*

1. *if S is a Λ-subterm of T then (for some $n \geq 0$) $S =_\alpha \lambda x_1 \ldots \lambda x_n.S'$ such that S' is a free subterm of T.*

2. *if S is a free subterm of T and $x_1, \ldots, x_n$ are all the bound variables in T that contain a common occurrence of S in their scope, and such that for $i < j$ λx_j is in the scope of λx_i, then $\lambda x_1 \ldots \lambda x_n.S$ is a Λ-subterm of T.*

6 Declarative Implementation

The inductive definition of $\Lambda_{subterm}$ suggests that, in addition to the λ-calculus, the meta-logic must support some form of logical inference, such as natural-deduction style theorem proving. Many systems, such as Coq [1,2] and Isabelle [16], meet this criteria. Furthermore, to use the $\Lambda_{subterm}$ relation as a *meta-programming* device requires a system that involves a form of automated *proof search*. A higher-order logic programming interpreter in the sense of [14] meets this criteria. In particular, the $\Lambda_{subterm}$ relation has a direct formulation in the logic programming language L_λ [12], which is the subset of the better known λProlog language [11] that involves only *higher-order patterns*. A higher-order pattern is a term in β-normal form where in every occurrence of subterms of the form $(F\ X_1 \ldots X_n)$ with F a free variable, $X_1, \ldots, X_n$ must be a distinct list of bound variables. In other words, solutions to higher-order patterns can only involve β_0-redeces. Unification of higher-order patterns is decidable and yields most-general unifiers. Furthermore, L_λ supports negative occurrences of universal quantifiers. The operational interpretation of a logic programming query of the form $\forall x A$ is to prove A with a fresh variable x not occurring elsewhere. L_λ is the simplest known language capable of supporting meta-programming in higher-order abstract syntax. A formulation in L_λ is therefore also a formulation in a wide variety of systems in which L_λ is embedded.

It is appropriate in describing the implementation of $\Lambda_{subterm}$ in L_λ to separate the meta-language from the object-language. Object-level application and λ-abstraction can be represented at the meta-level with a pair of higher order constants *app* and *abs* respectively. Although the meta-language need not be typed, it is helpful to think of *app* as having type $\tau \to \tau \to \tau$ and *abs* as having type $(\tau \to \tau) \to \tau$, where τ is the type of object-level expressions. The object-level term $\lambda x.(x\ y)$ is represented as $(abs\ \lambda x.(app\ x\ y))$ at the meta-level. We also need another constant in order to eliminate the ambiguity mentioned in Sect. 4.1. The outermost λ-bound variables of Λ-subterms intuitively represent *free* variables at the object level. We therefore introduce the constant fv (of type $(\tau \to \tau) \to \tau$) to "label" a meta-level λ-bound variable as representing an object-level free variable. Λ-subterms can be modified to use fv-abstractions. A Λ-subterm such as $(fv\ \lambda x.x)$ is a Λ-subterm of $(abs\ \lambda x.x)$ under *only* the context $\lambda c.(abs\ \lambda x.c)$, and not $\lambda c.c$.

Figure 2 contains the logic programming concrete-syntax[6] reformulation of the $\Lambda_{subterm}$ relation for object-level λ-terms (*app* and *abs* terms). The symbol pi represents universal quantification and x\e represents $\lambda x.e$. As is common in logic programming, upper-case letters represent universally quantified variables over the entire clause.

The closure under the lsubterm clauses represents the $\Lambda_{subterm}$ relation with separated meta- and object-language. As a logic program, these clauses can be used to implement a higher-order term rewriting system. Given a term τ, the query lsubterm S τ C (where S and C are free logic variables) will return a

---

[6] This syntax is actually for λProlog, which directly embeds L_λ.

```
lsubterm X X (c\c).
lsubterm S (app A B) (c\(app (D c) B) :- lsubterm S A D.
lsubterm S (app A B) (c\(app A (D c)) :- lsubterm S B D.
lsubterm (fv S) (abs T) (c\(abs x\(D x c))) :-
                 pi x\(lsubterm (S x) (T x) (D x)).
```

Fig. 2. $\Lambda_{subterm}$ as logic program clauses

solution instantiating S and C such that S is a Λ-subterm of τ under context C. Conversely, given a context γ and a term σ, solving lsubterm σ T γ will, if possible, instantiate T as the term with σ "grafted" into the position indicated by context γ. Finally, given σ and τ and with C as a free logic variable, the query lsubterm σ τ C will succeed if and only if σ is *some* Λ-subterm of τ.

A slightly modified form of the lsubterm clauses (among other techniques out of scope here) was used in giving a declarative implementation of Nipkow's formulation of higher-order critical pairs. This implementation is described in [8].

7 Conclusion

Higher-order term rewriting systems require a degree of flexibility in reasoning about free variables and subterms. This flexibility, however, is seemingly incompatible with substitution as β-reduction in the λ-calculus, which forms the basis of many meta-theoretic frameworks such as theorem provers and logic programming languages. Term trees provide an unsatisfactory meta-level representation of λ-terms because α-equivalence classes are lost.

We have shown that the λ-calculus can be preserved as the basis of a meta-theory for reasoning about higher-order term rewriting systems. Substitution can be reformulated by replacing β-reduction with the simpler β_0-reduction combined with the ability to deduce $\Lambda_{subterm}$ relations. This combination exists in many systems. The simplified logic programming language L_λ in particular can give a direct implementation of Λ-subterms.

For future work, we hope to apply the Λ-subterm concept to more generic problems than higher-order term rewriting systems.

Acknowledgments

The author wishes to thank Dale Miller and Amy Felty for helpful discussions.

References

1. Thierry Coquand and Gérard Huet. The calculus of constructions. *Information and Computation*, 76(2/3):95–120, February/March 1988.

2. Joëlle Despeyroux, Amy Felty, and André Hirschowitz. Higher-order abstract syntax in Coq. In *Second International Conference on Typed Lambda Calculi and Applications*, pages 124–138. Springer-Verlag Lecture Notes in Computer Science, April 1995.
3. Amy Felty. A logic programming approach to implementing higher-order term rewriting. In Lars-Henrik Eriksson, Lars Hallnäs, and Peter Schroeder-Heister, editors, *Proceedings of the January 1991 Workshop on Extensions to Logic Programming*, volume 596 of *Lecture Notes in Artificial Intelligence*, pages 135–161. Springer-Verlag, 1992.
4. Amy Felty. Implementing tactics and tacticals in a higher-order logic programming language. *Journal of Automated Reasoning*, 11(1):43–81, August 1993.
5. John Hannan. Extended natural semantics. *Journal of Functional Programming*, 3(2):123–152, April 1993.
6. P. M. Hill and J. G. Gallagher. Meta-programming in logic programming. Technical Report Report 94.22, University of Leeds, hill@scs.leeds.ac.uk, August 1994. To appear in Vol. 5 of the *Handbook of Logic in Artificial Intelligence and Logic Programming*, Oxford University Press.
7. Gérard Huet. A unification algorithm for typed λ-calculus. *Theoretical Computer Science*, 1:27–57, 1975.
8. Chuck Liang. *Substitution, Unification and Generalization in Meta-Logic*. PhD thesis, University of Pennsylvania, September 1995.
9. Chuck Liang. Let-polymorphism and eager type schemes. In *TAPSOFT '97: Theory and Practice of Software Development*, pages 490–501. Springer Verlag LNCS Vol. 1214, 1997.
10. R. McDowell and D. Miller. A logic for reasoning with higher-order abstract syntax. In *Symposium on Logic in Computer Science*. IEEE, 1997.
11. Dale Miller. Abstractions in logic programming. In Piergiorgio Odifreddi, editor, *Logic and Computer Science*, pages 329–359. Academic Press, 1990.
12. Dale Miller. A logic programming language with lambda-abstraction, function variables, and simple unification. *Journal of Logic and Computation*, 1(4):497–536, 1991.
13. Dale Miller. Unification under a mixed prefix. *Journal of Symbolic Computation*, pages 321–358, 1992.
14. Dale Miller, Gopalan Nadathur, Frank Pfenning, and Andre Scedrov. Uniform proofs as a foundation for logic programming. *Annals of Pure and Applied Logic*, 51:125–157, 1991.
15. Tobias Nipkow. Higher-order critical pairs. In G. Kahn, editor, *Sixth Annual Symposium on Logic in Computer Science*, pages 342–349. IEEE, July 1991.
16. Lawrence C. Paulson. The foundation of a generic theorem prover. *Journal of Automated Reasoning*, 5:363–397, September 1989.
17. Frank Pfenning and Conal Elliot. Higher-order abstract syntax. In *Proceedings of the ACM-SIGPLAN Conference on Programming Language Design and Implementation*, pages 199–208. ACM Press, June 1988.

An LPO-based Termination Ordering for Higher-Order Terms without λ-abstraction

Maxim Lifantsev and Leo Bachmair

Department of Computer Science, SUNY at Stony Brook
Stony Brook, NY 11794, USA
{maxim,leo}@cs.sunysb.edu

Abstract. We present a new precedence-based termination ordering for (polymorphic) higher-order terms without λ-abstraction. The ordering has been designed to strictly generalize the lexicographic path ordering (on first-order terms). It is relatively simple, but can be used to prove termination of many higher-order rewrite systems, especially those corresponding to typical functional programs. We establish the relevant properties of the ordering, include a number of examples, and also discuss certain limitations of the ordering and possible extensions.

1 Introduction

Specification and interactive reasoning systems, such as HOL [10], Isabelle [12], or PVS [11], typically employ some expressive, higher-order logic as their basis specification formalism. Rewrite techniques, in this context, provide a computational mechanism for the simplification or evaluation of expressions and form an essential part of the (equational) reasoning component of such systems. Termination is one of the key properties of rewrite systems, and various methods have been proposed recently for proving termination properties of higher-order rewrite systems. Two directions have been pursued in the development of higher-order termination orderings: some orderings are based on (semantic) interpretations, whereas others extend (syntactic) precedence relations. This classification roughly reflects the situation with first-order termination orderings, in that the most widely used rewrite orderings are either based on interpretation functions (e.g., on polynomial interpretations) or else extend precedence relations (as the recursive and lexicographic path orderings); see [2] for basic results and further references.

Interpretation-based orderings usually provide a more general framework for proving termination and are applicable to a larger class of rewrite systems, but also require substantial user assistance, as one not only has to specify a suitable interpretation in the first place, but must also prove the requisite (and often nontrivial) properties that ensure the correctness of the corresponding termination proofs. For examples of such orderings see Van de Pol [14, 13] and Kahrs [6]. Precedence-based orderings (which were first attempted for higher-order terms by Loria-Saenz and Steinbach [8]) are usually much easier to apply, but are not as widely applicable as interpretation-based orderings. Orderings of this kind have been proposed by Jouannaud and Rubio [4,5], and Lysne and Piris [9].

In the present paper we propose a new precedence-based termination ordering for (polymorphic) higher-order terms without λ-abstraction. The ordering is a comparatively simple generalization of the lexicographic path ordering to higher-order terms without λ-abstraction. Although it does not deal with λ-abstraction, the ordering can be applied to most of the rewrite systems arising from typical (polymorphic) functional program-like specifications, with variables of arbitrary degree of functionality. The ordering is defined in terms of a precedence on function symbols and presumes only some relatively weak conditions on typing of terms that are satisfied for a variety of typing systems.

The paper is organized as follows: In the next section we define the class of simply-typed higher-order terms to which we will apply our ordering (issues pertaining to polymorphism are discussed in Sect. 5.2). The ordering itself is introduced in Sect. 3, while its main properties are described in Sect. 4. In Sect. 5 we illustrate certain aspects of the application of the ordering to termination proofs and, in Sect. 6, compare it with other higher-order termination orderings.

2   Higher-Order Terms and Rewrite Rules

This section introduces basic notions of simply-typed higher-order terms without λ-abstraction, which generalize corresponding concepts for first-order terms [2].

Let S be a set of sorts. The set of types Θ_S is generated from sorts by constructors for ordered pairs and functions:

$$\Theta_S := S \mid (\Theta_S, \Theta_S) \mid (\Theta_S \to \Theta_S)$$

We use the symbols α and β to denote sorts, and τ, ω, and ψ, to denote types. We follow the terminological convention that the type constructors are associated to the right and that the function constructor binds tighter than the pair constructor. Therefore, $\tau, \omega, \psi = \tau, (\omega, \psi)$; $\tau \to \omega \to \psi = \tau \to (\omega \to \psi)$; $\tau, \omega \to \psi = \tau, (\omega \to \psi)$; and $\tau \to \omega, \psi = (\tau \to \omega), \psi$.

A signature $\mathcal{F} = \cup_{\tau \in \Theta_S} \mathcal{F}_\tau$ is a set of typed higher-order constants such that $\mathcal{F}_\tau \cap \mathcal{F}_\omega = \emptyset$ if $\tau \neq \omega$. Constants are denoted by a, b, and c. We also assume that $\mathcal{X} = \cup_{\tau \in \Theta_S} \mathcal{X}_\tau$ is a set of typed higher-oder variables such that $\mathcal{F} \cap \mathcal{X} = \mathcal{X}_\tau \cap \mathcal{X}_\omega = \emptyset$ if $\tau \neq \omega$. The letters x, y, and z denote variables.

Simply-typed higher-order terms are generated from a signature and a set of variables by application and pairing:

$$\mathcal{T}_\tau := \mathcal{F}_\tau \mid \mathcal{X}_\tau \mid (\mathcal{T}_{\omega \to \tau} \mathcal{T}_\omega) \mid (\mathcal{T}_{\omega_1}, \mathcal{T}_{\omega_2})$$

where a pairing is legal only if $\tau = (\omega_1, \omega_2)$. The letters t, s, u, v, l, and r are used to denoted terms. (We assume that all terms used below are well-typed if not stated otherwise.) We denote by $\Theta(t)$ the type of a term t. Terms of the form $(t\ s)$ and (t, s) are called applications and pairs, respectively; with immediate subterms t and s. The following conventions are used for terms: $t, s, u = t, (s, u)$; $t\ s\ u = (t\ s)\ u$; $t, s\ u = t, (s\ u)$; and $t\ s, u = (t\ s), u$.

All subterms of a term can be specified by **positions** which are sequences over $\{1, 2\}$. We use the letters p, q, and o to denote positions; and Λ to denote the empty sequence. By $t|_p$ we denote the subterm of t at position p. We denote by $\mathcal{P}os(t)$ and $\mathcal{V}ar(t)$ the set of positions in a term t and the set of **variables** occurring in t, respectively. We write $t[s]$ to indicate that s is a (not necessarily proper) subterm of t and denote by $t[s]_p$ the term obtained from t by replacing the subterm at position p by s.

A **substitution** is a type-preserving mapping σ from variables to terms, such that $x\sigma \neq x$ for only finitely many variables x. Substitutions are denoted by σ and ρ. The result of the application of a substitution σ to a term t is the term $t\sigma$ which is called an **instance** of t. Composition of two substitutions σ and ρ is denoted by juxtaposition, that is, $t\rho\sigma = (t\rho)\sigma$ for all terms t.

First-order terms can be represented in our language by an application with a constant from $\mathcal{F}$ as the first argument and a sequence of right-associated pairs as the second argument. For example, $(f(t_1, (t_2, t_3)))$ represents the first-order term $f(t_1, t_2, t_3)$. (According to our notational conventions the latter expression is actually an abbreviation of the former, fully parenthesized expression.)

A motivation for a special treatment of pairs in the context of orderings for higher-order termination is that pairs, or more generally tuples, allow one to compare the arguments of different functions with greater flexibility. For instance, the arguments of one function may be compared lexicographically, whereas in other cases comparison may be based on the multisets of arguments. This is a useful and common feature of precedence-based first-order termination orderings. But since function symbols are much more decoupled from their arguments in a higher-order setting than in a first-order setting, the information needed for different argument-comparison methods would be lost if one, say, just curried all functions.

On the other hand, if we uncurry everything (and eliminate nontrivial uses of applications), then there is no way of knowing, given just one term, which (instances of) variables are functions (and of which order) without typing information or explicit λ-expressions in η-long form of terms (which is a representation of some typing information); though this "function-order" information is crucial in proving termination of higher-order rewriting. We did not want to depend on a specific type system and typing information, but believe that enough structural information can be extracted from terms to obtain a useful termination ordering.[1] We also did not want to employ λ-expressions and η-long terms at this stage so as to keep the definition of the ordering simple and avoid having to impose additional conditions that may be necessary in a more general framework.

An **equation** is an expression $l \approx r$ where l and r are terms of the same type. A **rewrite rule** is an expression $l \longrightarrow r$ where l and r are terms of the same type and $\mathcal{V}ar(r) \subset \mathcal{V}ar(l)$; a **rewrite system** $\mathcal{R}$ is a set of rewrite rules. Term t rewrites

---

[1] Since this structural information is only a reflection of some part of the typing information, it may also be possible to reformulate the proposed ordering directly in terms of typing information.

to term s by $l \longrightarrow r \in \mathcal{R}$ at position p with substitution σ (written as $t \longrightarrow_{\mathcal{R}} s$) if $t|_p = l\sigma$ and $s = t[r\sigma]_p$. It is obvious that the relation $\longrightarrow_{\mathcal{R}}$ is type-preserving.

Since unification and matching for the above class of higher-order terms without λ-abstraction are very similar to first-order unification and matching, one can relatively easily extend many standard first-order rewrite techniques, such as critical pairs, Knuth-Bendix completion, or constrained and ordered rewriting, to this higher-order setting. Suitable higher-order termination orderings are required in many cases, though.

3   Termination Ordering

The termination ordering we propose for higher-order terms may be viewed as an extension of a lexicographic path ordering, where pairing and application are treated in a special way.

If $\succ$ is an ordering, we write $t \succeq s$ to indicate that $t \succ s$ or $t = s$. Let $\succ_{\mathcal{F}}$ be a strict (partial) ordering (called a **precedence**) on the signature $\mathcal{F}$.

We define a relation $\succ$ based on $\succ_{\mathcal{F}}$ as follows:

1. $x \succ s$ is   false
2. $t \succ y$ if $y \in Var(t)$ and $t \neq y$
3. if t is an application $(t_1\ t_2)$ and s is a constant;
   or if t is a pair (t_1, t_2) and s is a constant or an application, then
   $t \succ s$ if $t_1 \succeq s$ or $t_2 \succeq s$
4. if s is an application $(s_1\ s_2)$ and t is a constant;
   or if s is a pair (s_1, s_2) and t is a constant or an application, then
   $t \succ s$ if $t \succ s_1$ and $t \succ s_2$
5. (a) $t = a \succ b = s$ if $a \succ_{\mathcal{F}} b$
   (b) $t = (t_1, t_2) \succ (s_1, s_2) = s$ if
   $$\left((t_1 \succ_{\text{lex}} s_1\ \lor\ (t_1 = s_1\ \land\ t_2 \succ_{\text{lex}} s_2))\ \land\ t \succ s_1\ \land\ t \succ s_2 \right)$$
   $$\lor\ t_1 \succeq s\ \lor\ t_2 \succeq s$$
   (c) $t = (t_1\ t_2) \succ (s_1\ s_2) = s$ if
   $$\left((t_1 \succ s_1\ \lor\ (t_1 = s_1\ \land\ t_2 \succ_{\text{lex}} s_2))\ \land\ t \succ s_2 \right)\ \lor\ t_2 \succeq s$$

where the relation $\succ_{\text{lex}}$ is defined as follows: $t \succ_{\text{lex}} s$ is

1. $t \succ s$ if   neither t nor s is a pair
2. $t_1 \succ_{\text{lex}} y$ if $t = (t_1, t_2)$ and $s = y$
3. $t[1] \succ_{\text{lex}} s[1]\ \lor\ (t[1] = s[1]\ \land\ t[2] \succ_{\text{lex}} s[2])$ otherwise

where $t[i] = t_i$ if $t = (t_1, t_2)$, and $t[i] = t$ otherwise.

We distinguish case 2 above from case 3 to ensure that $\succ_{\text{lex}}$ is stable under instantiation when a pair is substituted for y. For example, suppose we dropped case 2 and extended case 3 to be used also for $(t_1, t_2) \succ_{\text{lex}} y$. Then $(y, f(y)) \succ_{\text{lex}} y$ would be true, which would imply $((a, b), f(a, b)) \succ_{\text{lex}} (a, b)$ if the ordering $\succ_{\text{lex}}$ were desired to be stable. But this would require $(a, b) \succ_{\text{lex}} a$ and hence $b \succ_{\mathcal{F}} a$, which of course can not be assumed in general.

We use the condition $t_2 \succ_{\text{lex}} s_2$ in case 5c of the definition of $\succ$ rather than, say, $t_2 \succ s_2$, so that the arguments of an application are compared lexicographically. This ensures that the ordering $\succ$, when restricted to (representations of) first-order terms, behaves like a standard lexicographic recursive path ordering.

Lemma 1. *If t and s are first-order terms such that $t \succ_{\text{lpo}} s$, then $\hat{t} \succ \hat{s}$, where $\hat{t}$ and $\hat{s}$ are the expressions encoding t and s, respectively, in our language.*

Example 1 (First-order terms). If $\mathcal{F} = \{f, g, h, a, b, c\}$, $\mathcal{X} = \{x, y\}$, $f \succ_{\mathcal{F}} \{g, h\}$,[2] and $a \succ_{\mathcal{F}} c$, then we have, for instance,

$$f(x, g(a, x), y) \quad \succ_{\text{lpo}} \quad f(x, g(c, x), h(y))$$

and, correspondingly,

$$(f(x, ((g(a, x)), y))) \quad \succ \quad (f(x, ((g(c, x)), (h y))))$$

by case 5c because we have $(x, ((g(a, x), y))) \succ_{\text{lex}} (x, ((g(c, x)), (h y)))$ and $(f(x, ((g(a, x)), y))) \succ (x, ((g(c, x)), (h y)))$. The last inequality follows from term-subterm comparisons, the first one reduces to $(g(a, x)) \succ (g(c, x))$, which is true because $a \succ c$.

Note. Multiset orderings or variants of the above "left-to-right" lexicographic ordering can be accommodated by introducing tuples with associated flags as new term constructors, and modifying the comparison $t_2 \succ_{\text{lex}} s_2$ in case 5c of the definition of $\succ$ so that it depends on the flags associated with t_2 and s_2 (with according adjustments in other parts of the definition).

Example 2 (Primitive recursion [14]). If $\mathcal{S} = \{\text{Nat}\}$, $\mathcal{F}_{\text{Nat}} = \{0\}$, $\mathcal{F}_{\text{Nat} \to \text{Nat}} = \{\text{s}\}$, $\mathcal{F}_{((\text{Nat,Nat}) \to \text{Nat}) \to (\text{Nat,Nat}) \to \text{Nat}} = \{\text{Rec}\}$, $\mathcal{X}_{(\text{Nat,Nat}) \to \text{Nat}} = \{h\}$, and $\mathcal{X}_{\text{Nat}} = \{x, g\}$, then the rules

$$
\begin{aligned}
\text{Rec}(h)(g, 0) &\longrightarrow g \\
\text{Rec}(h)(g, \text{s}(x)) &\longrightarrow h(x, \text{Rec}(h)(g, x))
\end{aligned}
$$

are orientable from left to right by $\succ$. The first rule expresses a subterm relationship. For the second rule observe that we have $\text{Rec}(h) \succ h$ and $\text{Rec}(h)(g, \text{s}(x)) \succ (x, \text{Rec}(h)(g, x))$. The latter inequality follows from $(g, \text{s}(x)) \succ_{\text{lex}} (g, x)$.

Example 3 (Lists [14]). Suppose $\mathcal{S} = \{\text{Nat}, \text{List}\}$, $\mathcal{F}_{(\text{Nat,List}) \to \text{List}} = \{\text{cons}\}$, $\mathcal{F}_{\text{List}} = \{\text{nil}\}$, $\mathcal{F}_{(\text{List,List}) \to \text{List}} = \{\text{append}\}$, $\mathcal{F}_{(\text{Nat} \to \text{Nat}) \to \text{List} \to \text{List}} = \{\text{map}\}$, $\mathcal{X}_{\text{Nat}} = \{h\}$, $\mathcal{X}_{\text{List}} = \{l, t, l_1, l_2, l_3\}$, and $\mathcal{X}_{\text{Nat} \to \text{Nat}} = \{f\}$. If we choose map $\succ_{\mathcal{F}}$ append $\succ_{\mathcal{F}}$ cons, then the following rules are orientable from left to right:

$$
\begin{aligned}
\text{append}(\text{nil}, l) &\longrightarrow l \\
\text{append}(\text{cons}(h, t), l) &\longrightarrow \text{cons}(h, \text{append}(t, l)) \\
\text{map}(f)(\text{nil}) &\longrightarrow \text{nil} \\
\text{map}(f)(\text{cons}(h, t)) &\longrightarrow \text{cons}(f(h), \text{map}(f)(t)) \\
\text{append}(\text{append}(l_1, l_2), l_3) &\longrightarrow \text{append}(l_1, \text{append}(l_2, l_3)) \\
\text{map}(f)(\text{append}(l_1, l_2)) &\longrightarrow \text{append}(\text{map}(f)(l_1), \text{map}(f)(l_2))
\end{aligned}
$$

---

[2] $\{a_i\} \succ_{\mathcal{F}} \{b_j\}$ means that $a_i \succ_{\mathcal{F}} b_j$ for any i and j.

For example, the rule map (f) (cons (h, t)) $\longrightarrow$ cons $(f(h), \text{map}(f)(t))$ is orientable because map $(f) \succ$ cons, map (f) (cons (h, t)) $\succ f(h)$ (due to the fact that map $(f) \succ f$), and cons $(h, t) \succ t$; the last rule is orientable because map $(f) \succ$ append, append $(l_1, l_2) \succ l_1$, and append $(l_1, l_2) \succ l_2$.

Note that the arguments of the binary relations $\succ$, $\succ_{\text{lex}}$, $=$, and $\succeq$ in general need not be of the same type or even be well-formed according to the given typing schema.

4   Termination Properties

Let us next state the main properties of our proposed termination ordering.[3]

Proposition 1 (Irreflexivity). *We have (1) $s \nsucc t[s]$ for all subterms s of t and (2) $t \nsucc_{\text{lex}} t$ for all terms t.*

Proof. By simultaneous structural induction on t and s, using the fact that $\succ_{\mathcal{F}}$ is irreflexive and distinguishing different subcases according to the syntactic form of the term t (some subcases of part 1 are needed for part 2 and vice versa).

Lemma 2. *We have*

1. *$a \succ t$ if and only if $a \succ_{\mathcal{F}} b$ for all constants b occurring in t and t contains no variables, and*
2. *$t \succ a$ if and only if either t contains a constant b such that $b \succ_{\mathcal{F}} a$ or else it contains a as a proper subterm.*

Proof. By structural induction on t.

Proposition 2 (Transitivity).

1. *If $t \succ u$ and $u \succ s$, then $t \succ s$.*
2. *If $t \succ_{\text{lex}} u$ and $u \succ_{\text{lex}} s$, then $t \succ_{\text{lex}} s$.*

Proof. By simultaneous structural induction on t, u, and s, using Lemma 2 and the fact that $\succ_{\mathcal{F}}$ is transitive.

Lemma 3. *If t is a pair (t_1, t_2) or an application $(t_1 \, t_2)$ and s is a subterm of t_1 or t_2, then $t \succ s$.*

Proof. By induction on the combined heights of t and s.

Since only pairs and applications can have proper subterms, we obtain:

Proposition 3 (Subterm property). *If s is a proper subterm of t, then $t \succ s$.*

---

[3] Full proofs of these properties, as well as full typing information for all examples, can be found in a longer version of the present paper available at http://www.cs.sunysb.edu/~maxim/papers/HOTermin.html.

Proposition 4 (Asymmetry).

1. *If* $t \succ s$, *then* $s \not\succ t$.
2. *If* $t \succ_{\text{lex}} s$, *then* $s \not\succ_{\text{lex}} t$.

Proof. By simultaneous structural induction on t and s, using irreflexivity, transitivity, the subterm property, and the fact that the precedence $\succ_{\mathcal{F}}$ is asymmetric.

We have now established that the relations $\succ$ and $\succ_{\text{lex}}$ are irreflexive, transitive, and asymmetric, that is, they are (strict) partial orderings. We next prove that these orderings also satisfy various compatibility properties (with respect to instantiation and subterm replacement).

Proposition 5 (Stability).

1. *If* $t \succ s$, *then* $t\sigma \succ s\sigma$.
2. *If* $t \succ_{\text{lex}} s$, *then* $t\sigma \succ_{\text{lex}} s\sigma$.

Proof. By simultaneous structural induction on t and s, using the subterm property and transitivity.

Proposition 6 (Monotonicity). *If t is not a pair and $t \succ s$, then*
(1) $u[t]_p \succ u[s]_p$ and (2) $u[t]_p \succ_{\text{lex}} u[s]_p$ for all terms u and positions p.

Proof. By simultaneous structural induction on u and s, using the subterm property and transitivity.

The condition, that t should not be a pair, is needed for part 2 of the proposition when $p = \Lambda$: we have $(a, t) \succ (b, s)$ if $t \succeq (b, s)$, but $(a, t) \not\succ_{\text{lex}} (b, s)$ if $b \succ_{\text{lex}} a$. But part 2 is needed for part 1: $t \succ_{\text{lex}} s$ should follow from $t \succ s$ to infer $(t, u') \succ (s, u')$ from $t \succ s$. This condition is not overly restrictive: When one proves termination of rewrite systems, one needs the monotonicity property if t is the left-hand side of a rewrite rule. If the rewrite rules represent definitions of data types or functional programs, then pairs will not occur as left-hand sides.

We have now essentially proved that $\succ$ and $\succ_{\text{lex}}$ are (partially) monotonic and stable orderings, or weak (because of partial monotonicity) rewrite orderings.

Lemma 4. *Let t_1, t_2, ... be an infinite sequence of terms. If there is no infinite decreasing sequence with respect to $\succ$ from any subterm of t_i, then there is also no infinite decreasing sequence with respect to $\succ_{\text{lex}}$ from any subterm of t_i.*

Proof. By contradiction using induction on the maximal "pair depth" of all terms in the sequence, where the pair depth of (t_1, t_2) is 1 plus the maximal pair depth of t_1 and t_2; otherwise, the pair depth of a term is 0.

Theorem 1 (Termination). *There is no infinite decreasing sequence of terms $t = t_0 \succ t_1 \succ t_2 \succ \ldots$ from any term t.*

Proof. Using a modified argument of the termination proof from [1].

Summarizing the above results, we obtain:

Theorem 2. *The relation* $\succ$ *is a terminating strict ordering for higher-order terms without λ-abstraction. It is a 'weak' reduction ordering (in the sense that it is monotonic for non-pair terms and stable).*

Proposition 7 (Trichotomy). *Suppose the precedence* $\succ_{\mathcal{F}}$ *is total. If* t *and* s *are well-typed ground terms and not both of them are pairs, then*

1. $t \succ s$ *or* $s \succ t$ *or* $t = s$
2. $t \succ_{\text{lex}} s$ *or* $s \succ_{\text{lex}} t$ *or* $t = s$, *provided*
   (a) $\Theta(t) = \Theta(s)$ *or*
   (b) *one of the two terms* t *and* s *is a pair* u *and the other term is a non-pair* v, *such that* $u \neq (v,v)$ *and* u *does not contain* (v,v) *as a subterm nested only within repeated pairings.*

Proof. By simultaneous structural induction on t and s, using asymmetry.

Trichotomy is a useful condition in applications to ordered or constrained rewriting. In most situations trichotomy is needed when $t \approx s$ is an equation in which at least one side is not a pair and where both sides are well-typed.

Note. Trichotomy holds not only for simply-typed terms. The only requirement on a typing scheme is that whenever two applications $(t\ s)$ and $(t\ s')$ are well-typed, then the term (s,s) can not be obtained from s' by repeatedly selecting either the first or second item of a pair zero or more times. This may rule out some cases of ad-hoc polymorphism, but the property will hold for many extensions of the simple typing system.

It is an open question whether a rewrite system without λ-expressions, that can be shown to be terminating with our ordering, is also terminating if one allows general rewrite steps over all (simply-)typed higher-order terms.

5   Termination Proofs

We next discuss various aspects of using our ordering for proving termination of specific rewrite systems. We used the Larch Prover [3] to specify the orderings and verify that all rules in the given examples can be oriented as indicated.[4]

---

[4] This requires no higher-order capabilities from LP.

5.1   Examples

Example 4 (MapList [4]). The rewrite rules[5]

$$
\begin{aligned}
\text{fmap}\,(\text{fnil})\,(x) &\longrightarrow \text{nil} \\
\text{fmap}\,(\text{fcons}\,(f,t))\,(x) &\longrightarrow \text{cons}\,(f\,(x),\text{fmap}\,(t)\,(x))
\end{aligned}
$$

are orientable from left to right by $\succ$ if we choose a precedence with fnil $\succeq_{\mathcal{F}}$ nil and fcons $\succeq_{\mathcal{F}}$ cons.

For the first rule note that we have fmap (fnil) (x) $\succ$ fnil by the subterm property, and fnil $\succeq$ nil as a consequence of our choice of precedence. By transitivity, we obtain fmap (fnil) (x) $\succ$ nil. For the second rule we have (i) fmap (fcons (f,t)) $\succ$ cons (because fcons $\succeq$ cons), (ii) fmap (fcons (f,t)) $\succ$ f (because f occurs in fcons (f,t)), and (iii) fmap (fcons (f,t)) $\succ$ fmap (t) (because fcons (f,t) $\succ$ t). From this we may infer that the left-hand side is larger than the right-hand side in our ordering.

But note that we do *not* have fmap (fcons $(f,t),x$) $\succ$ cons $(f\,(x),\text{fmap}\,(t,x))$ (assuming an appropriate typing) because fmap $\succ$ f is not true.

Example 5 (Sorting [4]). If we choose a precedence with $\{\max, \min\}$ $\succ_{\mathcal{F}}$ s, sort $\succ_{\mathcal{F}}$ insert $\succ_{\mathcal{F}}$ cons, and $\{\text{ascending\_sort}, \text{descending\_sort}\}$ $\succ_{\mathcal{F}}$ $\{\min, \max, \text{sort}\}$, then the following rewrite rules are orientable by $\succ$ from left to right:

$$
\begin{aligned}
\max\,(0,x) &\longrightarrow x \\
\max\,(x,0) &\longrightarrow x \\
\max\,(\text{s}\,(x),\text{s}\,(y)) &\longrightarrow \text{s}\,(\max\,(x,y)) \\
\min\,(0,x) &\longrightarrow 0 \\
\min\,(x,0) &\longrightarrow 0 \\
\min\,(\text{s}\,(x),\text{s}\,(y)) &\longrightarrow \text{s}\,(\min\,(x,y)) \\
\text{insert}\,(f,g)\,(\text{nil},x) &\longrightarrow \text{cons}\,(x,\text{nil}) \\
\text{insert}\,(f,g)\,(\text{cons}\,(h,t),x) &\longrightarrow \text{cons}\,(f\,(x,h),\text{insert}\,(f,g)\,(t,g\,(x,h))) \\
\text{sort}\,(f,g)\,(\text{nil}) &\longrightarrow \text{nil} \\
\text{sort}\,(f,g)\,(\text{cons}\,(h,t)) &\longrightarrow \text{insert}\,(f,g)\,(\text{sort}\,(f,g)\,(t),h) \\
\text{ascending\_sort}\,(l) &\longrightarrow \text{sort}\,(\min,\max)\,(l) \\
\text{descending\_sort}\,(l) &\longrightarrow \text{sort}\,(\max,\min)\,(l)
\end{aligned}
$$

(Here x, y, h, l, t, f, and g are variables.) The second rule for insert, for instance, is orientable by case 5c of the definition of $\succ$ because insert (f,g) $\succ$ cons, $(\text{cons}\,(h,t),x)$ $\succ_{\text{lex}}$ $(t,g\,(x,h))$, insert (f,g) $\succ$ f, and insert (f,g) $\succ$ g. It is essential (for this and also the other rules for insert and sort) that the higher-order variables f and g occur at appropriate levels of nested applications in the rules defining insert and sort, so that they may be instantiated by arbitrary functions (of a suitable type).

---

[5] The sorts are Nat, List, and FList, and the functions are typed as follows: $\mathcal{F}_{\text{List}} = \{\text{nil}\}$, $\mathcal{F}_{\text{FList}} = \{\text{fnil}\}$, $\mathcal{F}_{(\text{Nat,List}) \to \text{List}} = \{\text{cons}\}$, $\mathcal{F}_{((\text{Nat} \to \text{Nat}),\text{FList}) \to \text{FList}} = \{\text{fcons}\}$, $\mathcal{F}_{\text{FList} \to \text{Nat} \to \text{List}} = \{\text{fmap}\}$, $\mathcal{X}_{\text{Nat}} = \{x\}$, $\mathcal{X}_{\text{FList}} = \{t\}$, and $\mathcal{X}_{\text{Nat} \to \text{Nat}} = \{f\}$. Typing information is usually easily derivable, and is omitted in subsequent examples.

Let us next formulate a necessary condition for the applicability of our termination ordering. We define the order $\mathcal{O}_\Theta(\tau)$ of a type τ as follows:

- $\mathcal{O}_\Theta(\alpha) = 0$
- $\mathcal{O}_\Theta((\omega, \psi)) = \max\{\mathcal{O}_\Theta(\omega), \mathcal{O}_\Theta(\psi)\}$
- $\mathcal{O}_\Theta((\omega \to \psi)) = 1 + \mathcal{O}_\Theta(\psi)$

Intuitively the order of a type measures the nesting depth of applications in that it provides a bound on the number of successive applications needed to get from a term of that type to a base (i.e., non-function) term.

The order $\mathcal{O}_P(t, p)$ of the subterm of t at position p is defined as follows:

- $\mathcal{O}_P(t, p) = 1 + \mathcal{O}_P(t', p')$ if $t = (t'\ s)$ and $p = 1 \cdot p'$
- $\mathcal{O}_P(t, p) = 0$ otherwise

Consider Example 4. We have

$$
\begin{aligned}
\mathcal{O}_\Theta(\text{Nat}) &= 0 \\
\mathcal{O}_\Theta(\text{Nat} \to \text{Nat}) &= 1 \\
\mathcal{O}_\Theta(((\text{Nat} \to \text{Nat}), \text{FList}) \to \text{FList}) &= 1 \\
\mathcal{O}_\Theta(\text{FList} \to \text{Nat} \to \text{List}) &= 2 \\
\mathcal{O}_P(\text{fmap}(\text{fcons}(f, t))(x), 1 \cdot 2 \cdot 1) &= 1
\end{aligned}
$$

For instance, $\mathcal{O}_\Theta(\text{FList} \to \text{Nat} \to \text{List}) = 1 + \mathcal{O}_\Theta(\text{Nat} \to \text{List}) = 1 + (1 + \mathcal{O}_\Theta(\text{List})) = 1 + (1 + 0) = 2$.

Note that if we nest a term t (in particular a variable) of a type of order n within enough applications so as to get a term s of a type of order 0, then the order of t as a subterm of s must be n. Take Example 4 again. The type of fmap is of order 2 and fmap has order 2 as a subterm of $\text{fmap}(t)(x)$, which type is of order 0.

We define the order $\mathcal{O}_T(t, s)$ of a term s in term t as follows: $\mathcal{O}_T(t, s) = 0$ if s is not a subterm of t; otherwise $\mathcal{O}_T(t, s)$ is the maximal order $\mathcal{O}_P(t', p)$, where t' is a subterm of t and $t'|_p = s$, i.e. $\mathcal{O}_T(t, s) = \max_{t[t'] \wedge t'|_p = s} \mathcal{O}_P(t', p)$.

Lemma 5. *If $t \succ s$, then for all variables x, $\mathcal{O}_T(s, x)$ must not exceed $\mathcal{O}_T(t, x)$.*

Proof. (By structural induction on t and by contradiction.) Suppose $t \succ s$ and let s' be a least (w.r.t. subterm relation) subterm of s such that $\mathcal{O}_T(s', x) > \mathcal{O}_T(t, x)$. This implies that $\mathcal{O}_T(s', x) = \max_{s'|_p = x} \mathcal{O}_P(s', p)$.

Then $\mathcal{O}_T(s', x)$ must be at least one, and hence s' must be an application $(s'_1[x]\ s'_2)$, implying that $\mathcal{O}_T(s', x) = 1 + \mathcal{O}_T(s'_1, x)$. By the subterm property and transitivity we have $t \succ s'$.

Case $t = (t_1, t_2)$ Then $t_1 \succeq s' \vee t_2 \succeq s'$ (case 3 of the definition of $\succ$).
If $t_1 = s' \vee t_2 = s'$, then clearly $\mathcal{O}_T(s', x) \leq \mathcal{O}_T(t, x)$ by the definition of $\mathcal{O}_T$.
If $t_1 \succ s' \vee t_2 \succ s'$, then either $\mathcal{O}_T(s', x) \leq \mathcal{O}_T(t_1, x)$ or $\mathcal{O}_T(s', x) \leq \mathcal{O}_T(t_2, x)$ by the induction hypothesis, that is, $\mathcal{O}_T(s', x) \leq \mathcal{O}_T(t, x) = \max(\mathcal{O}_T(t_1, x), \mathcal{O}_T(t_2, x))$.

Case $t = (t_1\, t_2)$ Then $((t_1 \succ s_1' \ \lor\ (t_1 = s_1' \ \land\ t_2 \succ_{\mathrm{lex}} s_2')) \ \land\ t \succ s_2') \ \lor$
$t_2 \succeq s'$ (case 5c of the definition of $\succ$).
If $t_2 \succeq s'$, then the proof is similar to the previous case.
Otherwise we have $t_1 \succeq s_1'[x]$. If t_1 does not have x in it, than $t_1 \succeq s_1'[x]$ can
not be true because of the case 2 of the definition of $\succ$. Hence t_1 has x as a
subterm, which implies that $\mathcal{O}_T(t, x) > 0$. We have $\mathcal{O}_T(t, x) \geq 1 + \mathcal{O}_T(t_1, x)$;
$\mathcal{O}_T(s', x) = 1 + \mathcal{O}_T(s_1', x)$ as noted above; and $\mathcal{O}_T(t_1, x) \geq \mathcal{O}_T(s_1', x)$ by
the induction hypothesis because $t_1 \succeq s_1'$. This means that $\mathcal{O}_T(t, x) \geq$
$\mathcal{O}_T(s', x)$.

□

This lemma gives very strict guidelines regarding the applicative structure
of terms needed for the ordering to work.

Example 6 (Folding [9]). If we have sum $\succ_{\mathcal{F}} \{\mathrm{fold}, \mathrm{add}, 0\}$ and fold $\succ_{\mathcal{F}}$ prod,
then the following rules are orientable from left to right:

$$
\begin{aligned}
\mathrm{fold}\,(f)\,(\mathrm{nil}, x) &\longrightarrow x \\
\mathrm{fold}\,(f)\,(\mathrm{cons}\,(h, t), x) &\longrightarrow \mathrm{fold}\,(f)\,(t, f\,(x, h)) \\
\mathrm{sum}\,(l) &\longrightarrow \mathrm{fold}\,(\mathrm{add})\,(l, 0) \\
\mathrm{fold}\,(\mathrm{mul})\,(l, 1) &\longrightarrow \mathrm{prod}\,(l)
\end{aligned}
$$

The order of the variable f[6] as a subterm of the left-hand side of the second rule
is 1; as is its order as subterm of $\mathrm{fold}\,(f)\,(t, f\,(x, h))$ (in its first occurrence) and
of $f\,(x, h)$.

The following example, which appeared in a preliminary version of [4], illustrates the limitation of our ordering implied by Lemma 5.

Example 7 (Ordinal recursion).

$$
\begin{aligned}
\mathrm{rec}\,(t, u, v, 0) &\longrightarrow t \\
\mathrm{rec}\,(t, u, v, \mathrm{s}\,(x)) &\longrightarrow u\,(x, \mathrm{rec}\,(t, u, v, x)) \\
\mathrm{rec}\,(t, u, v, \lim\,(f)) &\longrightarrow v\,(f, \lambda n.\mathrm{rec}\,(t, u, v, f\,(n)))
\end{aligned}
$$

The constants 0 and s are constructors of a type of order 1, and lim is a constructor of a type of order 2. The variable x is of type of order 0, and f is of type
of order 1. These variables occur as arguments of the constructors in the rules
defining the function rec. Hence, the fourth argument position of function rec
above should be made a subterm of application of rec in our language of both order 0 and 1, which is impossible to satisfy simultaneously. It should be a subterm
of order 0 (and not greater) to be able to use x as an argument of an arbitrary
function u and supply 0 and s (x) as arguments of rec from a rewrite rule using
function rec. It should be a subterm of order 1 (and not less) to be able to use f
as a function in the last rule for rec and supply $\lim\,(f)$ as an argument of rec
for an arbitrary f.[7]

---

[6] x, h, l, and t are also variables here.

[7] This argument does not take into account the issue of eliminating λn in the last rule,
and applies if the last rule were, say rec $(t, u, v, \lim\,(f)) \longrightarrow v\,(f, \mathrm{rec}\,(t, u, v, f\,(t)))$.

5.2 Polymorphism

Let us outline informally how to extend our typing scheme to include type-polymorphism. Let $\alpha[\tau_1, \ldots, \tau_n]$ be a new sort constructor, where each τ_i is either a type or a type variable. We extend the definition of type order so that $\mathcal{O}_\Theta\left(\alpha[\tau_1, \ldots, \tau_n]\right) = \max\{\mathcal{O}_\Theta(\tau_1), \ldots, \mathcal{O}_\Theta(\tau_n)\}$. It is easy to see that the ordering will work for a polymorphic type system where all type specializations are of the same type order as the original types because the ordering is not affected by such a change. The following example informally shows that the ordering also works when type specializations increase the type order.

Example 8 (Polymorphic). The rewrite rules(x, h, t, t_f and f are variables):

$$
\begin{aligned}
\text{twice}\,(f)\,(x) &\longrightarrow f\,(f\,(x)) \\
\text{map}\,(f)\,(\text{nil}) &\longrightarrow \text{nil} \\
\text{map}\,(f)\,(\text{cons}\,(h,t)) &\longrightarrow \text{cons}\,(f\,(h), \text{map}\,(f)\,(t)) \\
\text{fmap}\,(\text{nil})\,(x) &\longrightarrow \text{nil} \\
\text{fmap}\,(\text{cons}\,(f, t_f))\,(x) &\longrightarrow \text{cons}\,(f\,(x), \text{fmap}\,(t_f)\,(x))
\end{aligned}
$$

are orientable from left to right by $\succ$ if map $\succ_{\mathcal{F}}$ cons. These rules can be used to reduce, for example, both

$$
\text{map}\,(\text{inc})\,(\text{cons}\,(1, \text{cons}\,(2, \text{nil})))
$$
$$
\text{to} \quad \text{cons}\,(2, \text{cons}\,(3, \text{nil})) ; \quad \text{and}
$$
$$
\text{fmap}\left(\text{map}\,(\text{twice})\,(\text{cons}\,(\text{inc}, \text{cons}\,(\text{twice}\,(\text{inc}), \text{nil})))\right)(1)
$$
$$
\text{to} \quad \text{cons}\,(3, \text{cons}\,(5, \text{nil})).
$$

The first term instantiates f in map by a function of type of order 1 (inc), whereas the second one, by a function of type of order 2 (twice).

Note that typing information is only needed to prove trichotomy. But the corresponding requirements are not very restrictive and still hold for order increasing type-specializations (see the note after Proposition 7). Also note that Lemma 5 is not affected by the introduction of polymorphism and by order increasing type-specializations.

5.3 Elimination of λ-abstraction

We can apply our ordering only to terms without λ-expressions. It is often possible to convert a higher-order rewrite system with terms containing λ-abstractions into our language by naming certain λ-abstractions by new constants and adding equations defining these new constants. We illustrate this by an example.

Example 9 (Maps). Assume we are translating a set of rewrite rules containing the following ones into a set of rules to be handled by our ordering (r, h, t, f, g, l, x, y, z, g_1, g_2, g_3, g_4, and c are all variables in this example):

$$
\begin{aligned}
\text{map}\,(\lambda r.f\,(r), \text{cons}\,(h, t)) &\longrightarrow \text{cons}\,(f\,(h), \text{map}\,(\lambda r.f\,(r), t)) \\
t_1 &\longrightarrow \text{map}\,(\lambda x.g_1\,(x), l) \\
t_2 &\longrightarrow \text{map}\,(\lambda x.g_2\,(x, y), l) \\
t_3 &\longrightarrow \text{map}\,(\lambda x.g_3\,(\lambda z.g_4\,(z), x, y), l)
\end{aligned}
$$

where x, y, and z are of types of the same order as h.

We will transform the above rules into the following rules (all map_i rules are orientable from left to right by $\succ$):

$$
\begin{aligned}
\text{map}_1\,(f)\,(\text{cons}\,(h,t)) &\longrightarrow \text{cons}\,(f\,(h),\text{map}_1\,(f)\,(t)) \\
t_1' &\longrightarrow \text{map}_1\,(g_1)\,(l) \\
\text{map}_2\,(f)\,(c,\text{cons}\,(h,t)) &\longrightarrow \text{cons}\,(f\,(h,c),\text{map}_2\,(f)\,(c,t)) \\
t_2' &\longrightarrow \text{map}_2\,(g_2)\,(y,l) \\
\text{map}_3\,(f)\,(g)\,(c,\text{cons}\,(h,t)) &\longrightarrow \text{cons}\,(f\,(g)\,(h,c),\text{map}_3\,(f)\,(g)\,(c,t)) \\
t_3' &\longrightarrow \text{map}_3\,(g_3)\,(g_4)\,(y,l)
\end{aligned}
$$

accordingly duplicating other rules defining function map and modifying the rest of the system.

This example illustrates how one can split λ-abstractions involving variables (or terms in general) of types of different orders into suitable expressions of the same order, which results in modified versions of the original rules in which the terms have an applicative structure that can in principle be handled by our ordering.

The next example illustrates how we can specify different (type-polymorphic) higher-order functions and orient their defining equations in our framework.

Example 10 (Functional). Consider the rewrite system:

$$
\begin{aligned}
\text{apply}\,(f_1)\,(x) &\longrightarrow f_1\,(x) \\
\text{id}\,(x) &\longrightarrow x \\
\text{uncurry}\,(f_2)\,(x)\,(y) &\longrightarrow f_2\,(x,y) \\
\text{swap}\,(f_2)\,(y,x) &\longrightarrow f_2\,(x,y) \\
\text{compose}\,(g_1,f_1)\,(x) &\longrightarrow g_1\,(f_1\,(x)) \\
\text{const}\,(x)\,(y) &\longrightarrow x \\
\text{listify}\,(x) &\longrightarrow \text{cons}\,(x,\text{nil}) \\
\text{fold}\,(f_3,g_2)\,(x,\text{nil}) &\longrightarrow x \\
\text{fold}\,(f_3,g_2)\,(x,\text{cons}\,(z,t)) &\longrightarrow f_3\,(g_2\,(z),\text{fold}\,(f_3,g_2)\,(x,t)) \\
\text{sum}\,(l) &\longrightarrow \text{fold}\,(\text{add},\text{id})\,(0,l) \\
\text{append} &\longrightarrow \text{compose}\,(\text{swap},\text{fold})\,(\text{cons},\text{id}) \\
\text{reverse} &\longrightarrow \text{uncurry}(\text{fold}\,(\text{swap}\,(\text{append}),\text{listify}))\,(\text{nil}) \\
\text{uncurry}\,(\text{fold}\,(\text{cons},\text{id}))\,(\text{nil}) &\longrightarrow \text{id} \\
\text{length} &\longrightarrow \text{uncurry}\,(\text{fold}\,(\text{add},\text{const}\,(1)))\,(0)
\end{aligned}
$$

All rules are orientable by $\succ$ from left to right, provided $\text{listify} \succ_{\mathcal{F}} \{\text{cons},\text{nil}\}$, $\text{sum} \succ_{\mathcal{F}} \{\text{fold},\text{add},\text{id},0\}$, $\text{append} \succ_{\mathcal{F}} \{\text{compose},\text{cons},\text{fold},\text{id},\text{swap}\}$, $\text{reverse} \succ_{\mathcal{F}} \{\text{append},\text{uncurry},\text{listify}\}$, and $\text{length} \succ_{\mathcal{F}} \{0,\text{add},\text{const},\text{uncurry},\text{fold},1\}$.

Termination of higher-order equational specifications where the use of λ-abstraction is essential can not be established with our ordering. Here are some examples of such rewrite rules:

Example 11.

1. $\forall(\lambda x.(P(x) \wedge Q(x))) \longrightarrow \forall(P) \wedge \forall(Q)$
   $\forall(\lambda x.(P(x) \wedge Q)) \longrightarrow \forall(P) \wedge Q$ (from [13])
2. $case(u, \lambda x.f(inl(x)), \lambda x.f(inr(x))) \longrightarrow f(u)$ (from [13])
3. $(\lambda x.(\lambda y.u)) v \longrightarrow \lambda y.((\lambda x.u) v)$ (from a preliminary version of [4])
4. $P \wedge \forall(\lambda x.Q(x)) \longrightarrow \forall(\lambda x.(P \wedge Q(x)))$ (from [5])

6   Related Work

Our aim has been to design a natural extension of a standard precedence-based ordering, the lexicographic path ordering, that is (comparatively) easy to apply, yet covers the higher-order features of many common examples, in particular rewrite-based formulations of (functional) programs. There is a trade-off between the simplicity of an ordering and the expressiveness of the term language to which it can be applied. A direct comparison of our ordering with other methods is difficult in that all the other approaches we know about allow λ-expressions. Thus, other precedence-based orderings can deal with some examples that can not be adequately described in the language for which our ordering has been designed. But the differences are more subtle and there are also examples that can be handled with our ordering, but are not within the scope of other precedence-based orderings.

For example, Jouannaud and Rubio [4, 5] mention *primitive recursion* (Example 2) as one example that is not within the scope of their method. On the other hand their method (as extended in [5]) does apply to, say, Rule 4 in Example 11 (which can not be oriented in our ordering). We should also point out that the orderings in [4, 5] are not purely based on a precedence on function symbols, but in addition require a (quasi-)ordering on types. It appears that these orderings can be extended to handle polymorphism (the main issues seems to be that the ordering compares only η-long terms and that the ordering on types needs to be extended in the polymorphic case), though this is not discussed in [4, 5].

Quantifier manipulations, as expressed by rewrite Rules 1 and 4 in Example 11, can also be handled by the syntactical method proposed by Lysne and Piris [9]. But this method only works if all higher-order variables are of a type of order 0 or 1, whereas in our approach we can handle higher-order variables of arbitrary order (see Examples 8 and 9), even though we have to restrict the "applicative structure" of terms with higher-order variables. The method in [9] might scale up to the polymorphic case, though the type order constraints may present some difficulties.

Interpretation-based termination orderings are more general altogether and it is conceivable that suitable interpretations can be found for all the rewrite systems for which we have outlined termination proofs above. The difficulty is often in finding the interpretations, and proving that they are suitable, which is considerably more complicated than specifying a precedence on function symbols. In other words, interpretation-based termination proofs for these examples might serve to illustrate the basic trade-off between simplicity and generality mentioned above.

It is actually possible to emulate many rewrite systems orientable by our ordering via first-order rewrite systems, termination of which can then possibly be proved by standard first-order termination orderings. This can be done by introducing new function symbols for the application of a functional variable to arguments, as well as adding new function symbols to represent all the instances of the functional variables used in the specification, and supplying corresponding defining equations.

Example 12 (First-order Folding). We can translate Example 6 into the following first-order rewrite system:

$$
\begin{aligned}
\text{fold}\,(f, \text{nil}, x) &\longrightarrow x \\
\text{fold}\,(f, \text{cons}\,(h, t), x) &\longrightarrow \text{fold}\,(f, t, \text{apply}(f, x, h)) \\
\text{sum}\,(l) &\longrightarrow \text{fold}\,(\text{ADD}, l, 0) \\
\text{fold}\,(\text{MUL}, l, 1) &\longrightarrow \text{prod}\,(l) \\
\text{apply}\,(\text{MUL}, x, y) &\longrightarrow \text{mul}\,(x, y) \\
\text{apply}\,(\text{ADD}, x, y) &\longrightarrow \text{add}\,(x, y)
\end{aligned}
$$

All the rules are orientable from left to right by the lexicographic recursive path ordering, provided fold $\succ_{\mathcal{F}}$ apply, sum $\succ_{\mathcal{F}}$ {fold, ADD, 0}, fold $\succ_{\mathcal{F}}$ prod, and apply $\succ_{\mathcal{F}}$ {add, mul}.

This approach appears to be less elegant than our method and we suspect that it may also be less general and would of course also require the formulation of a general translation technique.

In short, we believe that our ordering represents a "reasonable" compromise between the conflicting demands on "practical" tools for proving termination of a sufficiently large class of higher-order rewrite systems.

7   Conclusion

We have presented a termination ordering that extends the lexicographic recursive path ordering to "well-typed" (polymorphic) higher-order terms without λ-abstraction. The ordering is simple, in that it requires only a precedence on the given (first-order) function symbols, yet is powerful enough to handle most of the rewrite systems arising from common functional programs and definitions, as we have illustrated by several examples. It can also be applied to many different extensions of the simple-typing discipline since it depends only on the precedence on the signature and requires relatively weak well-typing condition on terms only for trichotomy.

We are currently investigating how to generalize the underlying ideas to higher-order terms with λ-abstraction (under certain reasonable restrictions), by trying to derive the same kind of information about "the degree of functionality of a variable" that we currently get from the applicative structure of a term, either from the λ-structure of η-long terms, or directly from typing information.

Acknowledgements

The research described in this paper was supported in part by the National Science Foundation under grant CCR-9510072. A preliminary version of the ordering presented here is contained in the first author's Diploma thesis at the Department of Cybernetics of Moscow State Engineering-Physics Institute (Technical University) [7].

References

1. Nachum Dershowitz and Charles Hoot. Natural termination. *Theoretical Computer Science*, 142(2):179–207, May 1995.
2. Nachum Dershowitz and Jean-Pierre Jouannaud. Rewrite systems. In J. van Leeuwen, editor, *Handbook of Theoretical Computer Science*, volume B: Formal Methods and Semantics, chapter 6, pages 243–320. North-Holland, Amsterdam, 1990.
3. Stephen J. Garland and John V. Guttag. *LP, the Larch Prover: Version 3.1*. MIT Laboratory for Computer Science, January 1995. Available electronically at http://larch.lcs.mit.edu:8001/larch/LP/overview.html.
4. Jean-Pierre Jouannaud and Albert Rubio. A recursive path ordering for higher-order terms in η-long β-normal form. In Harald Ganzinger, editor, *Proceedings of the 7th International Conference on Rewriting Techniques and Applications (RTA-96)*, volume 1103 of *Lecture Notes in Computer Science*, pages 108–122, New Brunswick, NJ, USA, July 27–30 1996. Springer-Verlag.
5. Jean-Pierre Jouannaud and Albert Rubio. Rewrite orderings for higher-order terms in η-long β-normal form and the recursive path ordering. To appear in *Theoretical Computer Science*, 1998. Available also at http://www-lsi.upc.es/~albert/papers/horpo.ps.gz.
6. Stefan Kahrs. Towards a domain theory for termination proofs. In Jieh Hsiang, editor, *Proceedings of the 6th International Conference on Rewriting Techniques and Applications (RTA-95)*, volume 914 of *Lecture Notes in Computer Science*, pages 241–255, Kaiserslautern, Germany, April 5–7 1995. Springer-Verlag.
7. Maxim Lifantsev. Term rewriting systems. Diploma thesis, Moscow State Engineering-Physics Institute (Technical University), Moscow, Russia, February 1996. In Russian.
8. Carlos Loria-Saenz and Joachim Steinbach. Termination of combined (rewrite and λ-calculus) systems. In Michaël Rusinowitch and Jean-Luc Rémy, editors, *Conditional Term Rewriting Systems, Third International Workshop*, volume 656 of *Lecture Notes in Computer Science*, pages 143–147, Pont-à-Mousson, France, July 8–10, 1992. Springer-Verlag.
9. Olav Lysne and Javier Piris. A termination ordering for higher order rewrite systems. In Jieh Hsiang, editor, *Proceedings of the 6th International Conference on Rewriting Techniques and Applications (RTA-95)*, volume 914 of *Lecture Notes in Computer Science*, pages 26–40, Kaiserslautern, Germany, April 5–7 1995. Springer-Verlag.
10. M.J.C. Gordon and T.F. Melham. *Introduction to HOL: A Theorem Proving Environment for Higher Order Logic*. Cambridge University Press, 1993.

11. Sam Owre and Natarajan Shankar. The formal semantics of PVS. Technical Report SRI-CSL-97-2, Computer Science Laboratory, SRI International, Menlo Park, CA, August 1997.
12. Lawrence C. Paulson. Introduction to Isabelle. Technical Report 280, University of Cambridge, Computer Laboratory, 1993.
13. Jaco Van de Pol. Termination proofs for higher-order rewrite systems. In J. Heering, K. Meinke, B. Moeller, and T. Nipkow, editors, *Higher-Order Algebra, Logic, and Term Rewriting, First International Workshop*, volume 816 of *Lecture Notes in Computer Science*, pages 350–325, Amsterdam, The Netherlands, September 1993. Springer-Verlag.
14. Jaco Van de Pol and Helmut Schwichtenberg. Strict functionals for termination proofs. In M. Dezani-Ciancaglini and G. Plotkin, editors, *Proceedings of the International Conference on Typed Lambda Calculi and Applications*, volume 902 of *Lecture Notes in Computer Science*, pages 350–364, Edinburgh, Scotland, April 1995. Springer-Verlag.

Proving Isomorphism of First-Order Logic Proof Systems in HOL

Anna Mikhajlova and Joakim von Wright

Turku Centre for Computer Science, Åbo Akademi University
Lemminkäisenkatu 14A, Turku 20520, Finland

Abstract. We prove in HOL that three proof systems for classical first-order predicate logic, the Hilbertian axiomatization, the system of natural deduction, and a variant of sequent calculus, are isomorphic. The isomorphism is in the sense that provability of a conclusion from hypotheses in one of these proof systems is equivalent to provability of this conclusion from the same hypotheses in the others. Proving isomorphism of these three proof systems allows us to guarantee that meta-logical provability properties about one of them would also hold in relation to the others. We prove the deduction, monotonicity, and compactness theorems for Hilbertian axiomatization, and the substitution theorem for the system of natural deduction. Then we show how these properties can be translated between the proof systems. Besides, by proving a theorem which states that provability in flattened sequent calculus implies provability in standard sequent calculus, we show how some meta-logical provability results about Hilbertian axiomatization and natural deduction can be translated to sequent calculus. We use higher-order logic as the meta-logic for reasoning about first-order proof systems and formalize proofs in a theorem-proving environment, thereupon reducing susceptibility to errors and bringing up subtle issues which are usually overlooked when the reasoning is done in a natural language.

1 Introduction

We use the theorem proving system HOL [4] to prove meta-logical results about proof systems for classical first-order predicate logic. In particular, we establish isomorphism among the Hilbertian axiomatization (HA), the system of natural deduction (ND), and a variant of sequent calculus, which we call *flattened sequent calculus*.

We formalize syntactic constructs of first-order logic, terms and formulae, as well as the notions of an inference rule, an inference and a derivation. Then, for every axiomatization that we study, we define a set of its basic inference rules. Every proof system takes different sets of basic connectives. We present inference rules for expanding the defined connectives into the basic and contracting combinations of basic connectives into the defined connectives.

We define in HOL a proof-checking relation which is used to verify correctness of first-order logic proofs in all the proof systems. Using this relation, it is possible to check proofs based not only on basic inference rules, but on derived ones as well. When a particular derivation is shown to be a proof, its hypotheses and conclusion are used to construct a derived inference rule, which is given a name and used further on in derivations. In this manner we can build compositional derivations and check their correctness.

Sequent calculus (SC) represents a special case, being a proof system for sequents with several (more than one) formulae in the succedent. It is well-known [3] that the classical sequent calculus is more general than the other proof systems we consider, in the sense that to every SC proof there correspond several proofs in Hilbertian style or natural deduction. We formalize this idea by defining flattened sequent calculus (FlatSC) and proving that its every basic inference rule is provable in sequent calculus and that flattened sequent calculus is isomorphic to the Hilbertian axiomatization and the system of natural deduction.

Every proof system we consider has features which make it particularly suitable for a collection of applications. For instance, PROLOG is an implementation of a fragment of sequent calculus, and the "tableaux" used in automatic theorem-proving are just a special case of this calculus. The natural deduction technique is widely used for teaching of logic but makes the demonstration of meta-logical results somewhat difficult. On the other hand, Hilbertian axiomatization is particularly suited for meta-logical proofs but is quite cumbersome to work with. All of these proof systems, in one form or another, form the basis for various theorem-proving systems. HOL itself is based on a sequent formulation of natural deduction which is fairly close to our formalization; Isabelle is also based on a variant of natural deduction, and it allows formal meta-logical reasoning. Sequent calculus forms the basis for PVS, and the Metamath system [7] is based on a Hilbert-style axiomatization.

There are intrinsic interdependencies among all these mainstream proof systems, for instance, every deduction in the system of natural deduction is a translation of some proof in the sequent calculus. The latter is effectively a calculus of proof search for natural deductions. In this work we focus on these interdependencies and the implicit isomorphism among these proof systems, and analyze these issues formally in HOL. We use higher-order logic as the metalogic for reasoning about first-order proof systems, whereas usually this kind of reasoning is done in a natural language, e.g., [6, 3, 10]. By using a formal system as the metalogic and formalizing the proofs in a theorem-proving environment, we reduce susceptibility to errors.

The main theorem we prove here states that whenever a conclusion is provable from hypotheses in Hilbertian axiomatization, it is also provable from the same hypotheses in the system of natural deduction, and in flattened sequent calculus. Proving isomorphism of these three proof systems allows us to guarantee that meta-logical properties proved about one of them would hold for the others as well. The properties we prove about Hilbertian axiomatization are the deduction, monotonicity, and compactness theorems. The substitution theorem is proved to hold for the system of natural deduction. We show how these properties can be translated between the systems. Besides, by proving a theorem which states that provability in flattened sequent calculus implies provability in SC, we show how some meta-logical results about Hilbertian axiomatization and natural deduction can be translated to sequent calculus.

Notation. When referring to HOL objects, we use `typewriter` font. The ASCII character combinations used by HOL /\, \/, and ==> correspond to ordinary logical symbols $\land, \lor$ and $\Rightarrow$, whereas ? and ! stand for the existential and the universal quantification.

2   Representing First-Order Logic Concepts in HOL

To reason about proofs in first-order logic and the relationship among different proof systems, we need to formalize syntactic constructs of the logic. These constructs are built from the underlying alphabet.

In this alphabet, we distinguish a logical alphabet and a symbol set. The logical alphabet includes the symbols of logic used in every first-order language, namely, a set of individual variables ranging over the elements of the structure under consideration, the logical constant $\bot$, the logical connectives $\land, \lor, \Rightarrow,$ $\Leftrightarrow, \neg$, the universal quantifier $\forall$, and the existential quantifier $\exists$. We also use a symbol $=$ for expressing the equality of two elements. Another part of our first-order alphabet, the symbol set, contains special symbols used in the mathematical theory to be discussed, representing sets of constants, function symbols, and relation symbols. Out of the alphabet elements we build two kinds of expressions of the first-order language, terms and formulae.

The term and formula structures have little impact on proofs and, hence, proof systems. Being modular, our formalization of first-order logic allows us to slot in alternative representations of terms and formulae. We have chosen to formalize terms in the style most convenient for mechanized manipulation, namely that of de Bruijn [1].

2.1   Terms and Formulae

Our main motivation for the chosen representation of terms is to simplify handling of bound variables. Using the "traditional" representation leads to a very complicated definition of substitution of one term for a variable in another term and greatly complicates proofs involving term substitutions. All these problems arise from the necessity to deal with bound variables which have no individuality and only serve as place markers. Following [1], we no longer give bound variables names from the set of individual variables. Instead, they are distinguished from free variables and indexed by natural numbers, the number indicating which outer $\lambda-$binding they correspond to. For example, instead of $\lambda f\, x.\, f\, x$ we write $\lambda\, (\lambda\, (1\; 0))$, because f corresponds to two binders out. Since we number binders from the inside out, none of the numbers change when a given term becomes part of some larger term. We may, of course, have free variables, e.g., $\lambda\, x.\, f\, x$ is just $\lambda\, (f\; 0)$. Using this representation of terms not only simplifies their substitution, but also eliminates the need for side conditions in inference rules, because no free variables can be captured in substitution or quantification introduction.

We define a term as a constant, a variable, a bound variable, a lambda abstraction or an application of terms. In HOL we define a new type Sterm:

```
Sterm = Sconst of string
      | Svar of string
      | Sbvar of num
      | Sabs of Sterm
      | Scomb of Sterm => Sterm
```

Here type constructors are functions of types, e.g., Scomb is a curried function of two Sterm types returning Sterm. Notice that the formal syntax now has separate constructs for free variables and bound variables, Svar and Sbvar respectively. As opposed to the "traditional" representation, we don't have an identification of a bound variable in an abstraction. In general, the formal syntax of non-typed λ—calculus allows construction of ill-formed or meaningless terms, like an application of a variable term to itself, Scomb (Svar "x") (Svar "x"). We do not check for well-formedness of terms, but for our purposes this condition is not critical.

To manipulate terms, we define a number of functions recursing on the structure of a term. A function STermSubst is used to substitute a variable in a term with another term:

```
|- (!t x str. STermSubst t x (Sconst str) = Sconst str) /\
   (!t x str. STermSubst t x (Svar str) =
     ((str = x) => t | (Svar str))) /\
   (!t x n. STermSubst t x (Sbvar n) = Sbvar n) /\
   (!t x s. STermSubst t x (Sabs s) = Sabs (STermSubst t x s)) /\
   (!t x s r. STermSubst t x (Scomb r s) =
     Scomb (STermSubst t x r) (STermSubst t x s))
```

We also define two functions for binding and "unbinding" variables in a term. The binding function STermBind takes a variable and a term, and returns a lambda abstraction where all occurrences of the variable are bound with a corresponding Sbvar instance. The function STermBeta performs a beta-conversion on the given Scomb term.

Now, after providing the definition of Sterm, we can represent the type of first-order logic formulae. A formula over a symbol set S is a falsum $\bot$, an n-ary relation among Sterms, an equality of two Sterms, or a formula constructed from other formulae by using logical connectives and quantifiers. Following [10], we consider first-order logic with equality and, accordingly, distinguish a binary equality relation from other relations and treat it as a special case. In HOL the new type Sformula is defined as follows:

```
Sformula = False
         | Srel of string => (Sterm list)
         | Seq of Sterm => Sterm
         | Snot of Sformula
         | Sand of Sformula => Sformula
         | Sor of Sformula => Sformula
```

```
| Simp of Sformula => Sformula
| Sequiv of Sformula => Sformula
| Sforall of Sformula
| Sexists of Sformula
```

To perform substitutions in a formula, we define two functions, SFormulaTermSubst, which substitutes a term for a variable, and SubFormulaSubst, which substitutes a subformula with another formula. Functions SFUnivQuantify and SFExistQuantify are used to quantify a formula universally and existentially. Both take a variable to be quantified on and a formula, and return a respectively quantified formula. A function SFBetaReduce is used to specialize a quantified formula.

Having defined formulae and operations on them in this way, we can now build syntactic constructs based on formulae.

2.2 Sequents

A sequent is an expression $\Gamma \vdash \Delta$, where Γ and Δ are finite sets of formulae $p_1, \ldots, p_n$ and $q_1, \ldots, q_m$. We refer to Γ as the antecedent of a sequent and to Δ as its succedent. In our presentation we will simplify the notation and write p and Γ, p for $\{p\}$ and $\Gamma \cup \{p\}$ respectively. We use sequents to model derivability of Δ from Γ in all proof systems. In HOL we define the type of sequents to be

```
Ssequent = Sseq of (Sformula set) => (Sformula set)
```

In both Hilbertian axiomatization and the system of natural deduction Δ is a singleton set, and its only element is derivable from Γ. In sequent calculus the denotational interpretation is that the conjunction of the p_i implies the disjunction of the q_j. In particular, if Γ and Δ are both empty, the sequent asserts contradiction.

2.3 Inference Rules and Inferences

Inference rules are represented as named sets of pairs (premise set, conclusion), where the premises and the conclusion are sequents. Axiomatic rules have empty sets of premises. In HOL the type InfRule is defined to represent inference rules:

```
InfRule = Rule of string => ((Ssequent set) # Ssequent) set
```

Every individual rule is described using an inductive unary relation of type InfRule -> bool. For example, the conjunction introduction rule in the system of natural deduction

$$\frac{\Gamma \vdash p \qquad \Delta \vdash q}{\Gamma, \Delta \vdash p \wedge q} \; \text{ConjI}$$

is defined in HOL by the following theorem:

```
|- ConjI
    (Rule "ConjI" {hyps,concl | ?p q Gamma Delta.
      (hyps = {Sseq Gamma {p}; Sseq Delta {q}}) /\
      (concl = Sseq (Gamma UNION Delta) {p Sand q})})
```

Individual inferences are instantiated by the type Sinference as named pairs (premise set, conclusion):

```
Sinference = Sinf of string => ((Ssequent set) # Ssequent)
```

Functions InfHyps and InfConcl give respectively the hypotheses and the conclusion of an inference.

All individual inferences are supposed to be instances of certain inference rules. A function CorrectRuleInst:(InfRule set) -> Sinference -> bool is used to check whether a particular inference is an instance of the identically named inference rule in a certain set of rules.

2.4 Connective Exchange Rules

Every proof system is based on a certain set of basic logical connectives. Other connectives are defined in terms of the basic ones. The connective exchange rules pertinent to a particular proof system arise from these definitions. For example, Hilbertian axiomatization takes implication and falsum as basic; this is a functionally complete set and all other connectives, negation, conjunction, disjunction, and equivalence, can be defined in terms of these two. The connective exchange rules are symmetric, as they represent contraction and expansion of connectives of interest in terms of the others. For example, since the logical negation is defined by $\neg p \triangleq p \Rightarrow \bot$, we can formulate rules for contraction and expansion of $\neg$ as follows:

$$\frac{\Gamma \vdash \varphi[p \Rightarrow \bot]}{\Gamma \vdash \varphi[\neg p]} \ \text{NotContr} \qquad \frac{\Gamma \vdash \varphi[\neg p]}{\Gamma \vdash \varphi[p \Rightarrow \bot]} \ \text{NotExp}$$

For every connective exchange rule of such form there is a corresponding one with exchange in the antecedents of the sequents:

$$\frac{\Gamma, \varphi[p \Rightarrow \bot] \vdash \Delta}{\Gamma, \varphi[\neg p] \vdash \Delta} \ \text{NotContr} \qquad \frac{\Gamma, \varphi[\neg p] \vdash \Delta}{\Gamma, \varphi[p \Rightarrow \bot] \vdash \Delta} \ \text{NotExp}$$

In HOL we define a unary inductive relation NotExch which holds of the rules NotContr and NotExp. The definitions of these rules employ the subformula substitution function SubFormulaSubst.

The exchange rules for the other connectives arise from the definitions

$$p \wedge q \ \triangleq \ (p \Rightarrow (q \Rightarrow \bot)) \Rightarrow \bot$$
$$p \vee q \ \triangleq \ \neg(\neg p \wedge \neg q)$$
$$p \Leftrightarrow q \ \triangleq \ (p \Rightarrow q) \wedge (q \Rightarrow p)$$

and are as follows:

$$\frac{\Gamma \vdash \varphi[(p \Rightarrow (q \Rightarrow \bot)) \Rightarrow \bot]}{\Gamma \vdash \varphi[p \wedge q]} \ \text{AndContr} \qquad \frac{\Gamma \vdash \varphi[p \wedge q]}{\Gamma \vdash \varphi[(p \Rightarrow (q \Rightarrow \bot)) \Rightarrow \bot]} \ \text{AndExp}$$

$$\frac{\Gamma \vdash \varphi[\neg(\neg p \wedge \neg q)]}{\Gamma \vdash \varphi[p \vee q]} \ \text{OrContr} \qquad \frac{\Gamma \vdash \varphi[p \vee q]}{\Gamma, \vdash \varphi[\neg(\neg p \wedge \neg q)]} \ \text{OrExp}$$

$$\frac{\Gamma \vdash \varphi[(p \Rightarrow q) \wedge (q \Rightarrow p)]}{\Gamma \vdash \varphi[p \Leftrightarrow q]} \ \text{EqContr} \qquad \frac{\Gamma \vdash \varphi[p \Leftrightarrow q]}{\Gamma \vdash \varphi[(p \Rightarrow q) \wedge (q \Rightarrow p)]} \ \text{EqExp}$$

We define the set of all connective exchange rules as ConnExch:

```
|- ConnExch = {r | NotExch r \/ AndExch r \/ OrExch r \/ EqExch r}
```

2.5 Derivations and Proofs

A derivation is represented as a tree of inferences. The conclusion of the derivation appears at the root of the tree and the hypotheses appear at the leaves. In HOL derivations are of type Sinference ltree, where (*)ltree is the type of labeled trees. The theory of labeled trees in HOL defines tree constructors as

$$\text{Node} : * \rightarrow ((*)\text{ltree})\text{list} \rightarrow (*)\text{ltree}$$

A derivation is defined to be a proof if every inference in this derivation is a correct instance of a certain inference rule and all hypotheses of this inference are conclusions of some inferences appearing earlier in the proof.

We define an inductive relation IsProof which identifies those derivations that prove their conclusions from the premises with respect to a given set of inference rules. We can use IsProof to check correctness of derivations in all proof systems by supplying it with the corresponding set of inference rules. Given a derivation, a set of inference rules, and a conclusion, IsProof traverses the derivation tree and checks that every inference in this derivation is an instance of the specified inference rule. It also makes sure that the set of subderivation conclusions for a particular inference includes every premise of this inference. In HOL IsProof is a relation of type

```
(Sinference ltree) list -> InfRule set -> Ssequent set -> bool
```

The first argument is a list because at derivation levels other than the root level we need to deal with lists of derivations. A set of inference rules of the current axiomatization should be provided as the second argument. The third argument is the set of inference conclusions at the current level in the derivation tree. The following rules constitute the definition of IsProof:

```
IsProof_RULE =
|- (!rSet. IsProof [] rSet {}) /\
   (!S tlConclSet rSet tl. IsProof tl rSet tlConclSet ==>
       IsProof (CONS (Node (Sinf "hyp" ({S},S)) []) tl)
           rSet (S INSERT tlConclSet)) /\
   (!tlConclSet tl inf rSet.
       CorrectRuleInst rSet inf /\ IsProof tl rSet tlConclSet ==>
       IsProof (CONS (Node inf []) tl) rSet
           (InfConcl inf INSERT tlConclSet)) /\
   (!tlConclSet tl dList inf rSet.
       CorrectRuleInst rSet inf /\ IsProof tl rSet tlConclSet /\
       (?upConclSet. InfHyps inf SUBSET upConclSet /\
           IsProof dList rSet upConclSet) ==>
       IsProof (CONS (Node inf dList) tl) rSet
           (InfConcl inf INSERT tlConclSet))
```

In addition to the notion of correct derivation identified by the relation IsProof, we define the notion of provability. The inductive relation IsProvable specifies when a sequent is provable from a set of sequents with respect to a set of inference rules:

```
IsProvable_RULE =
|- (!h c rSet.
   (?d h'. IsProof [d] rSet {c} /\ DerHyps d h' /\ h' SUBSET h) ==>
      IsProvable rSet h c) /\
   (!h c hyps rSet. IsProvable rSet hyps c /\
      (!el. el IN hyps ==> IsProvable rSet h el) ==>
      IsProvable rSet h c) /\
   (!c h derived rSet. IsProvable (rSet UNION derived) h c /\
      (!r. r IN derived ==>
         (?inf. CorrectRuleInst {r} inf /\
               IsProvable rSet (InfHyps inf) (InfConcl inf))) ==>
      IsProvable rSet h c) /\
   (!c h rSet. IsProvable (rSet UNION ConnExch) h c ==>
      IsProvable rSet h c)
```

We distinguish four cases. First of all, a sequent c is provable from the set of sequents h in the proof system with inference rules rSet if there exist a derivation d and a set of hypotheses h' such that d is a proof of the conclusion c from the hypotheses h' and all hypotheses h' are in h. Secondly, a sequent c is provable from h in rSet if it is provable using the same set of inference rules from some set of hypotheses hyps, such that every element in this set is, in turn, provable from h. This rule encodes transitivity of provability. We choose to formalize it as a rule rather than prove it as a theorem, using the first provability rule, because of the difficulty presented by building a derivation as a tree of inferences. Namely, the proof would require splitting a derivation tree into transitive subtrees, which appears to be impractical. The third rule formalizes provability of conclusion c from the hypotheses h using the set of basic and derived rules. The rule states that whenever every derived rule, used in the proof of c from h, has itself a proof in the system with basic rules only, we can conclude that c is provable from the hypotheses h using just these basic rules. And, finally, the last rule formalizes provability using the set of connective exchange rules in addition to the logical rules. The connective exchange rules are often used implicitly, and this rule allows us to "hide" their application.

In practice derived rules are constructed in the following way. When a derivation of a certain conclusion from certain hypotheses is shown to be a proof, we define a derived rule similarly to the way basic rules have been defined. The hypotheses sequents and the conclusion sequent of the derivation are taken to be the hypotheses and the conclusion of the new inference rule. This new rule is given a name and can further on be used in derivations along with basic rules. In this manner we can construct modular derivations and prove their correctness much easier.

3   The Proof Systems of First-Order Logic and Their Isomorphism

The main theorem proving the isomorphism states that whenever a conclusion sequent c is provable from hypotheses sequents h in Hilbertian axiomatization, given by the corresponding set of basic inference rules HARules, it is also provable from the same hypotheses in the system of natural deduction, given by NDRules, and in the flattened sequent calculus, given by FlatSCRules:

```
IsomorphismThm =
|- !h c. (IsProvable NDRules h c = IsProvable HARules h c) /\
         (IsProvable FlatSCRules h c = IsProvable NDRules h c)
```

We prove this theorem by transitivity of implication, showing that provability in ND implies provability in HA, and provability in HA implies provability in flattened sequent calculus, and, finally, that provability in FlatSC implies provability in natural deduction. These proofs, in turn, reduce to proving that every basic inference rule of natural deduction has a proof of its conclusion from its hypotheses in Hilbertian axiomatization, and similarly for the other two cases.

The second main result we prove here relates provability in (standard) sequent calculus to provability in the other three proof systems. As we have already mentioned in the introduction, sequent calculus manipulates sequents with more than one formulae in the succedent, whereas the other proof systems have exactly one formula there. We define the notion of flattening a sequent so that it has a singleton succedent set, and prove that if a conclusion sequent c is provable from hypotheses sequents h in any of FlatSC, HA, and ND, then it is also provable from the same hypotheses in sequent calculus. We depict these relationships diagrammatically in Fig. 1.

3.1   Hilbertian Axiomatization

The first formal system we present is the Hilbertian axiomatization, which we formalize following [2]. This axiomatization is a good starting point for reasoning

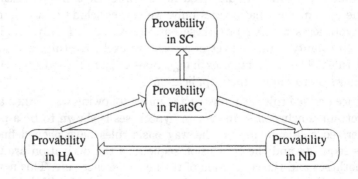

Fig. 1. Relationship among provability in different proof systems

about properties of the logic because of its formal simplicity. It is particularly convenient for proving the deduction, monotonicity, and compactness theorems which have important implications.

As we have mentioned above, Hilbertian axiomatization takes $\perp$ and $\Rightarrow$ as basic connectives. The following rules constitute the set of axioms and basic inference rules of HA:

$$\frac{}{\varGamma \vdash p} \ (p \in \varGamma) \qquad\qquad \text{IdentRule}$$

$$\frac{}{\varGamma \vdash p \Rightarrow (q \Rightarrow p)} \qquad\qquad \text{Ax1}$$

$$\frac{}{\varGamma \vdash (p \Rightarrow (q \Rightarrow r)) \Rightarrow ((p \Rightarrow q) \Rightarrow (p \Rightarrow r))} \qquad\qquad \text{Ax2}$$

$$\frac{}{\varGamma \vdash ((p \Rightarrow \perp) \Rightarrow \perp) \Rightarrow p} \qquad\qquad \text{Ax3}$$

$$\frac{\varGamma \vdash p \qquad \varDelta \vdash p \Rightarrow q}{\varGamma, \varDelta \vdash q} \qquad\qquad \text{MP}$$

$$\frac{}{\varGamma \vdash p \Rightarrow \forall x.p[x]} \qquad\qquad \text{ForallIntro}$$

$$\frac{}{\varGamma \vdash \forall x.p[x] \Rightarrow p[t]} \qquad\qquad \text{ForallElim}$$

$$\frac{}{\varGamma \vdash (\forall x.p \Rightarrow q) \Rightarrow ((\forall x.p) \Rightarrow (\forall x.q))} \qquad\qquad \text{ForallDistr}$$

Having defined for every rule a corresponding identically named unary relation, we define the set of basic inference rules as HARules:

```
|- HARules = {r | IdentRule r \/ Ax1 r \/ Ax2 r \/ Ax3 r \/ MP r \/
                  ForallIntro r \/ ForallElim r \/ ForallDistr r}
```

We also derive the corresponding provability theorems, which we call HAProvability_RULES:

```
|- !hyps Gamma p. p IN Gamma ==>
   IsProvable HARules hyps (Sseq Gamma {p}),
|- !hyps Gamma p q.
   IsProvable HARules hyps (Sseq Gamma {p Simp q Simp p}),
|- !hyps Gamma p q r. IsProvable HARules hyps
        (Sseq Gamma {(p Simp q Simp r) Simp (p Simp q) Simp p Simp r}),
|- !hyps Gamma p. IsProvable HARules hyps
        (Sseq Gamma {((p Simp False) Simp False) Simp p}),
|- !hyps Delta1 Delta2 p q.
   IsProvable HARules hyps (Sseq Delta1 {p}) /\
   IsProvable HARules hyps (Sseq Delta2 {p Simp q}) ==>
   IsProvable HARules hyps (Sseq (Delta1 UNION Delta2) {q}),
|- !hyps Gamma p x.
   IsProvable HARules hyps (Sseq Gamma {p Simp (SFUnivQuantify x p)}),
|- !hyps Gamma p tm. IsProvable HARules hyps
        (Sseq Gamma {(Sforall p) Simp (SFBetaReduce (Sforall p) tm)}),
|- !hyps Gamma p q. IsProvable HARules hyps (Sseq Gamma
        {(Sforall (p Simp q)) Simp ((Sforall p) Simp (Sforall q))})
```

The formal simplicity of Hilbertian axiomatization facilitates proving useful properties about this proof system. In what follows we prove the deduction theorem, the monotonicity theorem, and the compactness theorem.

The Deduction Theorem for Hilbertian Axiomatization. The deduction theorem states that for all formulae p and q and all sets of formulae Γ if q is provable from Γ, then $p \Rightarrow q$ is provable from Γ without p:

$$\frac{\Gamma \vdash q}{\Gamma \setminus p \vdash p \Rightarrow q} \text{ DeductRule}$$

In HOL the corresponding theorem is expressed as follows:

```
DeductionThm =
|- !Gamma p q.
   IsProvable HARules {Sseq Gamma {q}} (Sseq (Gamma DELETE p) {p Simp q})
```

A general theorem `ProvImplThm` states that a sequent `s2` is provable from a sequent `s1` if provability of `s1` from hypotheses `hyps` implies provability of `s2` from the same hypotheses:

```
ProvImplThm =
|- !rules s1 s2.
   (!h. IsProvable rules h s1 ==> IsProvable rules h s2) ==>
   IsProvable rules {s1} s2)
```

This theorem allows us to reduce the proof of `DeductionThm` to a proof of a lemma

```
|- !hyps Gamma p q. IsProvable HARules hyps (Sseq Gamma {q}) ==>
   IsProvable HARules hyps (Sseq (Gamma DELETE p) {p Simp q})
```

which we prove by induction on `HARules`. The subgoals we should prove are as follows:

```
1. q IN Gamma ==>
   IsProvable HARules hyps (Sseq (Gamma DELETE p) {p Simp q})
2. IsProvable HARules hyps (Sseq (Gamma DELETE p)
     {p' Simp q Simp p'})
3. IsProvable HARules hyps (Sseq (Gamma DELETE p)
     {p Simp ((q Simp False) Simp False) Simp q})
4. IsProvable HARules hyps (Sseq (Delta1 DELETE p) {p Simp p' Simp q}) /\
   IsProvable HARules hyps (Sseq (Delta2 DELETE p) {p Simp p'}) ==>
   IsProvable HARules hyps
     (Sseq ((Delta1 UNION Delta2) DELETE p) {p Simp q})
5. ...
```

and similarly for the axioms concerning quantification manipulation. We resolve the axiomatic subgoals by matching them with an auxiliary theorem

```
DeductAxThm =
|- !hyps p q Gamma. IsProvable HARules hyps (Sseq Gamma {q}) ==>
   IsProvable HARules hyps (Sseq Gamma {p Simp q})
```

and rewriting with the corresponding theorems in HAProvability_RULES. To resolve the subgoal based on the rule Modus Ponens, we prove a theorem

```
DeductMPThm =
|- !hyps p q r Gamma Delta.
   IsProvable HARules hyps (Sseq Gamma {p Simp q Simp r}) /\
   IsProvable HARules hyps (Sseq Delta {p Simp q}) ==>
   IsProvable HARules hyps (Sseq (Gamma UNION Delta) {p Simp r})
```

Rewriting with this theorem completes the proof of the deduction lemma, and, consequently, the proof of DeductionThm.

The Monotonicity Theorem for Hilbertian Axiomatization. The second fundamental property of our proof system states that adding formulae to the antecedent set of a sequent is monotonic, in the sense that if $\Gamma \vdash p$ then $\Gamma \cup \Delta \vdash p$, for a finite Δ. We prove this monotonicity property as a theorem in HOL:

```
MonoThm =
|- !Gamma Delta p. FINITE Delta =>
   IsProvable HARules {Sseq Gamma {p}} (Sseq (Gamma UNION Delta) {p})
```

The proof of MonoThm is performed by induction on both the set Delta and the basic inference rules of Hilbertian axiomatization, HARules. Inducting first on HARules results in the following subgoals:

```
1. p IN Gamma ==> !Delta. FINITE Delta ==>
        IsProvable HARules hyps (Sseq (Gamma UNION Delta) {p})
2. !Delta. FINITE Delta ==>
        IsProvable HARules hyps
           (Sseq (Gamma UNION Delta) {p Simp q Simp p})
3. !Delta. FINITE Delta ==> FINITE Delta2 ==>
        IsProvable HARules hyps (Sseq (Delta2 UNION Delta) {p}) /\
   !Delta. FINITE Delta ==> FINITE Delta1 ==>
        IsProvable HARules hyps (Sseq (Delta1 UNION Delta) {p Simp q}) ==>
   !Delta. FINITE Delta ==> FINITE (Delta1 UNION Delta2) ==>
        IsProvable HARules hyps
           (Sseq ((Delta1 UNION Delta2) UNION Delta) {q})
4. ...
```

To solve the first subgoal, we apply the induction principle for finite sets and resolve the case when Delta is equal to the empty set by matching it against the first of HAProvability_RULES. To resolve the induction case, we derive in HA a new rule

$$\frac{\Gamma \vdash p}{\Gamma, q \vdash p} \text{ MonoOne}$$

and prove the corresponding theorem:

```
MonoOneThm =
|- !hyps Gamma p q. IsProvable HARules hyps (Sseq Gamma {p}) ==>
   IsProvable HARules hyps (Sseq (q INSERT Gamma) {p})
```

Rewriting the first subgoal using this theorem completes its proof. All the remaining subgoals are resolved by inducting on finiteness of Delta and rewriting with the corresponding rule in HAProvability_RULES.

The Compactness Theorem for Hilbertian Axiomatization. Compactness is another fundamental property that we prove about Hilbertian axiomatization. The compactness theorem states that if a formula p is provable from a set of formulae Γ, then there exists a finite subset Δ of Γ, such that p is provable from Δ.

```
CompactThm =
|- !hyps Gamma p. IsProvable HARules hyps (Sseq Gamma {p}) ==>
   (?Delta. Delta SUBSET Gamma /\ FINITE Delta /\
        IsProvable HARules hyps (Sseq Delta {p}))
```

This theorem is also proved by induction on HARules.

Despite its formal simplicity, Hilbertian axiomatization is quite inconvenient to work with. Proofs and derivations are unintuitive and it's usually very difficult to invent them even in simple cases. In this respect the system of natural deduction is by far superior to HA. We demonstrate that higher-level modular rules of the system of natural deduction are the derived rules of HA. For this purpose, we first present ND and then derive its basic inference rules in the Hilbertian axiomatization.

3.2 System of Natural Deduction

The fundamental property of the system of natural deduction is the symmetry of its introduction and elimination rules. The only axiomatic rule that we have in our system states that from a set of assumptions containing a formula we can always conclude that the formula is true. The basic introduction and elimination rules are restricted to those for three connectives, $\wedge$, $\Rightarrow$ and $\perp$. The rules for other connectives are derived. We also have a pair of introduction and elimination rules for universal quantification. Existential quantification rules are derived from these rules.

$$\frac{}{\Gamma \vdash p}\ (p \in \Gamma)\ \text{IdRule}$$

$$\frac{\Gamma \vdash p \qquad \Delta \vdash q}{\Gamma, \Delta \vdash p \wedge q}\ \text{ConjI} \qquad\qquad \frac{\Gamma \vdash p \wedge q}{\Gamma \vdash p} \qquad \frac{\Gamma \vdash p \wedge q}{\Gamma \vdash q}\ \text{ConjE}$$

$$\frac{\Gamma, p \vdash q}{\Gamma \vdash p \Rightarrow q}\ \text{ImpI} \qquad\qquad \frac{\Gamma \vdash p \qquad \Delta \vdash p \Rightarrow q}{\Gamma, \Delta \vdash q}\ \text{ImpE}$$

$$\frac{\Gamma, p \Rightarrow \perp \vdash \perp}{\Gamma \vdash p}\ \text{RAA} \qquad\qquad \frac{\Gamma \vdash \perp}{\Gamma \vdash p}\ \text{FalseE}$$

$$\frac{\Gamma \vdash p}{\Gamma \vdash \forall x.p[x]}\ \text{ForallI} \qquad\qquad \frac{\Gamma \vdash \forall x.p[x]}{\Gamma \vdash p[t]}\ \text{ForallE}$$

The set of these inference rules is called NDRules and given as follows:

```
|- NDRules = {r | IdRule r \/ ConjI r \/ ConjE r \/ ImpI r \/
                ImpE r \/ RAA r \/ FalseE r \/ ForallI r \/ ForallE r}
```

Based on the exchange rules for the connectives $\neg$ and $\vee$, we derive the corresponding introduction and elimination rules:

$$\frac{\Gamma, p \vdash \perp}{\Gamma \vdash \neg p} \quad \texttt{NotIntro} \qquad \frac{\Gamma \vdash p \quad \Delta \vdash \neg p}{\Gamma, \Delta \vdash \perp} \quad \texttt{NotElim}$$

$$\frac{\Gamma \vdash p \quad \Gamma \vdash q}{\Gamma \vdash p \vee q} \quad \texttt{OrIntro} \qquad \frac{\Gamma \vdash p \vee q \quad \Delta, p \vdash r \quad \Theta, q \vdash r}{\Gamma, \Delta, \Theta \vdash r} \quad \texttt{OrElim}$$

The Substitution theorem for Natural Deduction. The equivalence connector $\Leftrightarrow$ is of special interest, because using equivalences we can make substitutions. Having a substitution rule of the form

$$\frac{\Gamma \vdash p \Leftrightarrow q \qquad \Delta \vdash \varphi}{\Gamma, \Delta \vdash \varphi[p \backslash q]} \quad \texttt{SubstRule}$$

significantly facilitates derivations in natural deduction. For deriving this rule we prove the substitution theorem

```
SubstThm =
|- !hyps p q phi phi_with_q.
   SubFormulaSubst phi p q phi_with_q ==>
      IsProvable NDRules hyps (Sseq {p Sequiv q} {phi Sequiv phi_with_q})
```

where `SubFormulaSubst` substitutes a subformula q for p in the formula phi to produce the formula phi_with_q. The proof of this theorem requires deriving a few intermediate rules, namely

$$\frac{}{\Gamma \vdash p \Leftrightarrow p} \quad \texttt{EqId} \qquad \frac{\Gamma \vdash p \Leftrightarrow q}{\Gamma \vdash \neg p \Leftrightarrow \neg q} \quad \texttt{EqNot}$$

and a number of rules of the form

$$\frac{\Gamma \vdash p1 \Leftrightarrow q1 \qquad \Delta \vdash p2 \Leftrightarrow q2}{\Gamma, \Delta \vdash p1 * p2 \Leftrightarrow q1 * q2} \quad \texttt{Eq*}$$

where $*$ is one of the connectives $\wedge, \vee, \Rightarrow$ and $\Leftrightarrow$.

Using the substitution rule, we can derive a number of useful connective exchange rules. The first rule allows us to introduce and eliminate double negation:

$$\frac{\Gamma \vdash \varphi[\neg\neg p]}{\Gamma \vdash \varphi[p]} \quad \texttt{DblNegContr} \qquad \frac{\Gamma \vdash \varphi[p]}{\Gamma \vdash \varphi[\neg\neg p]} \quad \texttt{DblNegExp}$$

The second rule handles exchanging the connectives $\vee$ and $\Rightarrow$:

$$\frac{\Gamma \vdash \varphi[\neg p \vee q]}{\Gamma \vdash \varphi[p \Rightarrow q]} \quad \texttt{OrToImp} \qquad \frac{\Gamma \vdash \varphi[p \Rightarrow q]}{\Gamma \vdash \varphi[\neg p \vee q]} \quad \texttt{ImpToOr}$$

For every derived connective exchange rule there is naturally a corresponding one with exchange in the antecedents of the sequents.

3.3 Sequent Calculus

Finally, let us present formalizations of the sequent calculus and its flattened version. The sequent calculus illustrates the symmetries of logic [3], and has numerous analogies with the system of natural deduction. The rules of the calculus are in fact more or less complex combinations of the rules of ND. We formalize sequent calculus without structural rules, resulting in the following set of inference rules:

$$\frac{}{\Gamma, p \vdash p, \Delta}\; \text{IdAx}$$

$$\frac{\Gamma \vdash p, \Delta \quad \Phi \vdash q, \Theta}{\Gamma, \Phi \vdash p \wedge q, \Delta, \Theta}\; \text{ConjR} \qquad \frac{\Gamma, p \vdash \Delta}{\Gamma, p \wedge q \vdash \Delta} \quad \frac{\Gamma, q \vdash \Delta}{\Gamma, p \wedge q \vdash \Delta}\; \text{ConjL}$$

$$\frac{\Gamma \vdash p, \Delta}{\Gamma \vdash p \vee q, \Delta} \quad \frac{\Gamma \vdash q, \Delta}{\Gamma \vdash p \vee q, \Delta}\; \text{DisjR} \qquad \frac{\Gamma, p \vdash \Delta \quad \Phi, q \vdash \Theta}{\Gamma, \Phi, p \vee q \vdash \Delta, \Theta}\; \text{DisjL}$$

$$\frac{\Gamma, p \vdash q, \Delta}{\Gamma \vdash p \Rightarrow q, \Delta}\; \text{ImpR} \qquad \frac{\Gamma \vdash p, \Delta \quad \Phi, q \vdash \Theta}{\Gamma, \Phi, p \Rightarrow q \vdash \Delta, \Theta}\; \text{ImpL}$$

$$\frac{\Gamma, p \vdash \Delta}{\Gamma \vdash \neg p, \Delta}\; \text{NotR} \qquad \frac{\Gamma \vdash p, \Delta}{\Gamma, \neg p \vdash \Delta}\; \text{NotL}$$

$$\frac{\Gamma \vdash p, \Delta}{\Gamma \vdash \forall x. p[x], \Delta}\; \text{ForallR} \qquad \frac{\Gamma, p \vdash \Delta}{\Gamma, \forall x. p[x] \vdash \Delta}\; \text{ForallL}$$

$$\frac{\Gamma \vdash p, \Delta \quad \Phi, p \vdash \Theta}{\Gamma, \Phi \vdash \Delta, \Theta}\; \text{Cut}$$

The set `SCRules` of these rules is defined as follows:

```
SCRules = {r | IdAx r \/ ConjR r \/ ConjL r \/ DisjR r \/
               DisjL r \/ ImpR r \/ ImpL r \/ NotR r \/
               NotL r \/ ForallR r \/ ForallL r \/ Cut r}
```

Flattening Sequents. Sequent calculus is the only axiomatization where succedents of sequents are not necessarily singleton sets. Sequents of SC are interpreted so that the conjunction of elements in the antecedent set asserts the disjunction of elements in the succedent set. When proving basic rules of sequent calculus as theorems of natural deduction, such sequents with non-singleton succedent sets create complications because the system of natural deduction cannot manipulate them using its basic rules. We resolve this problem by "flattening" sequents of sequent calculus. Namely, we map every sequent of SC to a corresponding one with a singleton succedent set whose only element is a disjunction of succedent elements of the original. Hence, a sequent $\Gamma \vdash \{\}$ is mapped to $\Gamma \vdash \{\bot\}$ and a sequent $\Gamma \vdash p, \Delta$ is mapped to $\Gamma \vdash \{p \vee \Delta'\}$, where Δ' is a disjunction of elements in Δ. By flattening `SCRules` in this manner, we define a proof system `FlatSCRules` representing flattened sequent calculus:

```
FlatSCRules = {r | FlatIdAx r \/ FlatConjR r \/ FlatConjL r \/
                   FlatDisjR r \/ FlatDisjL r \/ FlatImpR r \/
                   FlatImpL r \/ FlatNotR r \/ FlatNotL r \/
                   FlatForallR r \/ FlatForallL r \/ FlatCut r}
```

where, e.g., `FlatImpL` is given by

$$\frac{\Gamma \vdash p \vee \delta \quad \Phi, q \vdash \theta}{\Gamma, \Phi, p \Rightarrow q \vdash \delta \vee \theta}\; \text{FlatImpL}$$

and show that it is a subset of the standard sequent calculus, in the sense that anything provable in FlatSC is also provable in SC. In HOL we formulate and prove the corresponding theorem

```
Provability_of_FlatSC_in_SC =
|- !h c. IsProvable FlatSCRules h c ==> IsProvable SCRules h c
```

The proof of this theorem is reduced, using first the inference rule set monotonicity theorem

```
RuleSetMono =
|- !rSet1 rSet2 h c.
   IsProvable rSet1 h c ==> IsProvable (rSet1 UNION rSet2) h c
```

and then the third rule in the set defining IsProvable, to a theorem stating that every basic inference rule of FlatSC can be derived in sequent calculus:

```
BasicFlatSCRules_Provable_in_SC =
|- !r. r IN FlatSCRules ==> (?inf. CorrectRuleInst {r} inf /\
   IsProvable SCRules (InfHyps inf) (InfConcl inf))
```

Rewriting with the definition of FlatSCRules, we get twelve subgoals corresponding to the rules of flattened sequent calculus. For example, the subgoal corresponding to the rule FlatImpL states that

```
IsProvable SCRules
   {Sseq Gamma {p Sor delta}; Sseq (q INSERT Eta) {theta}}
   (Sseq ((p Simp q) INSERT (Gamma UNION Eta)) {delta Sor theta})
```

In the derivations corresponding to this and the other FlatSCRules we use auxiliary rules

$$\frac{\Gamma \vdash p \vee p}{\Gamma \vdash p}\ \mathrm{DisjId} \qquad \frac{\Gamma \vdash p \vee q}{\Gamma \vdash q \vee p}\ \mathrm{DisjComm} \qquad \frac{\Gamma \vdash p \vee (q \vee r)}{\Gamma \vdash (p \vee q) \vee r}\ \mathrm{DisjAssoc}$$

as well as a pair of double negation contraction rules

$$\frac{\Gamma, \neg\neg p \vdash \Delta}{\Gamma, p \vdash \Delta} \qquad \frac{\Gamma \vdash \neg\neg p \vee q}{\Gamma \vdash p \vee q}\ \mathrm{DblNeg}$$

derived is SC. The derivations of these rules are straightforward and we omit them for brevity.

The identity rule FlatIdAx is proved using the rules IdAx and DisjR as follows:

$$\frac{\dfrac{}{\Gamma, p \vdash p}\ \mathrm{IdAx}}{\Gamma, p \vdash p \vee \delta}\ \mathrm{DisjR}$$

Availability of FlatCut significantly simplifies further derivations, and so we construct its proof in sequent calculus next:

$$\frac{\Gamma \vdash p \vee \delta \qquad \dfrac{\dfrac{\Phi, p \vdash \theta}{\Phi, p \vdash \delta \vee \theta}\ \mathrm{DisjR} \qquad \dfrac{}{\delta \vdash \delta \vee \theta}\ \mathrm{FlatIdAx}}{\Phi, p \vee \delta \vdash \delta \vee \theta}\ \mathrm{DisjL}}{\Gamma, \Phi \vdash \delta \vee \theta}\ \mathrm{Cut}$$

The right disjunction rule `FlatDisjR` is derived using `DisjR`:

$$\cfrac{\cfrac{\cfrac{\Gamma \vdash p \vee \delta}{\Gamma \vdash q \vee (p \vee \delta)} \text{ DisjR}}{\Gamma \vdash (q \vee p) \vee \delta} \text{ DisjAssoc}}{\Gamma \vdash (p \vee q) \vee \delta} \text{ DisjComm} \qquad \cfrac{\cfrac{\Gamma \vdash q \vee \delta}{\Gamma \vdash p \vee (q \vee \delta)} \text{ DisjR}}{\Gamma \vdash (p \vee q) \vee \delta} \text{ DisjAssoc}$$

and the left disjunction rule `FlatDisjL` is derived using `DisjL`:

$$\cfrac{\cfrac{\Gamma, p \vdash \delta}{\Gamma, p \vdash \delta \vee \theta} \text{ DisjR} \qquad \cfrac{\Phi, q \vdash \theta}{\Phi, q \vdash \delta \vee \theta} \text{ DisjR}}{\Gamma, \Phi, p \vee q \vdash \delta \vee \theta} \text{ DisjL}$$

The rules `NotR` and `NotL` of sequent calculus are used to derive their flattened versions `FlatNotR` and `FlatNotL` as follows:

$$\cfrac{\cfrac{\cfrac{\Gamma, p \vdash \delta}{\Gamma, p \vdash \neg p \vee \delta} \text{ DisjR}}{\Gamma \vdash \neg p, \neg p \vee \delta} \text{ NotR} \qquad \neg p \vdash \neg p \vee \delta \text{ FlatIdAx}}{\Gamma \vdash \neg p \vee \delta} \text{ Cut}$$

$$\cfrac{\Gamma \vdash p \vee \delta \qquad \cfrac{\cfrac{\cfrac{\neg p \vdash \neg p, \delta}{\neg p, \neg\neg p \vdash \delta} \text{ NotL}}{\neg p, p \vdash \delta} \text{ DblNeg}}{\neg p, p \vdash \delta}}{\cfrac{\Gamma, \neg p \vdash \delta \vee \delta}{\Gamma, \neg p \vdash \delta} \text{ DisjId}} \text{ FlatCut}$$

The rules `FlatNotR` and `FlatNotL` can now be used in derivations of `FlatImpR` and `FlatImpL`:

$$\cfrac{\cfrac{\cfrac{\Gamma, p \vdash q \vee \delta}{\Gamma \vdash \neg p \vee (q \vee \delta)} \text{ FlatNotR}}{\Gamma \vdash (\neg p \vee q) \vee \delta} \text{ DisjAssoc}}{\Gamma \vdash (p \Rightarrow q) \vee \delta} \text{ OrToImp}$$

$$\cfrac{\cfrac{\cfrac{\cfrac{\Gamma \vdash p \vee \delta}{\Gamma \vdash \delta \vee p} \text{ DisjComm}}{\Gamma, \neg \delta \vdash p} \text{ FlatNotL} \qquad \Phi, q \vdash \theta}{\Gamma, \Phi, p \Rightarrow q, \neg \delta \vdash \theta} \text{ ImpL}}{\cfrac{\Gamma, \Phi, p \Rightarrow q \vdash \neg\neg\delta \vee \theta}{\Gamma, \Phi, p \Rightarrow q \vdash \delta \vee \theta} \text{ DblNeg}} \text{ FlatNotR}$$

Finally, the rules `FlatConjL` and `FlatForallL` are instances of the rules `ConjL` and `ForallL`, and the rules `FlatConjR` and `FlatForallR` are derived as follows:

$$\cfrac{\cfrac{\cfrac{\cfrac{\cfrac{\cfrac{\cfrac{\Gamma \vdash p \vee \delta}{\Gamma \vdash \delta \vee p} \text{ DisjComm}}{\Gamma, \neg\delta \vdash p} \text{ FlatNotL} \quad \cfrac{\cfrac{\Phi \vdash q \vee \theta}{\Phi \vdash \theta \vee q} \text{ DisjComm}}{\Phi, \neg\theta \vdash q} \text{ FlatNotL}}{\Gamma, \Phi, \neg\delta, \neg\theta \vdash p \wedge q} \text{ ConjR}}{\Gamma, \Phi, \neg\delta \vdash \neg\neg\theta \vee p \wedge q} \text{ FlatNotR}}{\Gamma, \Phi \vdash \neg\neg\delta \vee \neg\neg\theta \vee p \wedge q} \text{ FlatNotR}}{\Gamma, \Phi \vdash \delta \vee \theta \vee p \wedge q} \text{ DblNeg}}{\Gamma, \Phi \vdash (\delta \vee \theta) \vee p \wedge q} \text{ DisjAssoc}}{\Gamma, \Phi \vdash p \wedge q \vee \delta \vee \theta} \text{ DisjComm}$$

$$\cfrac{\cfrac{\cfrac{\cfrac{\cfrac{\cfrac{\Gamma \vdash p \vee \delta}{\Gamma \vdash \delta \vee p} \text{ DisjComm}}{\Gamma, \neg\delta \vdash p} \text{ FlatNotL}}{\Gamma, \neg\delta \vdash \forall x.p[x]} \text{ ForallR}}{\Gamma \vdash \neg\neg\delta \vee \forall x.p[x]} \text{ FlatNotR}}{\Gamma \vdash \delta \vee \forall x.p[x]} \text{ DblNeg}}{\Gamma \vdash \forall x.p[x] \vee \delta} \text{ DisjComm}$$

3.4 Proving Isomorphism of Natural Deduction, Hilbertian Axiomatization, and Flattened Sequent Calculus

As it was already mentioned above, we prove the IsomorphismThm by transitivity of implication, showing that provability in ND implies provability in HA, and provability in HA implies provability in flattened sequent calculus, and, finally, that provability in FlatSC implies provability in natural deduction. Therefore, we need to prove three theorems:

```
Provability_of_ND_in_HA =
|- !h c. IsProvable NDRules h c ==> IsProvable HARules h c

Provability_of_HA_in_FlatSC =
|- !h c. IsProvable HARules h c ==> IsProvable FlatSCRules h c

Provability_of_FlatSC_in_ND =
|- !h c. IsProvable FlatSCRules h c ==> IsProvable NDRules h c
```

As was the case with provability of FlatSC in SC, proofs of these theorems reduce to showing that every basic inference rule of ND, HA, and FlatSC has a proof of its conclusion from its hypotheses in respectively HA, FlatSC, and ND. For example, the theorem stating provability of basic inference rules of natural deduction in Hilbertian axiomatization is formulated as follows:

```
BasicNDRules_Provable_in_HA =
|- !r. r IN NDRules ==> (?inf. CorrectRuleInst {r} inf /\
   IsProvable HARules (InfHyps inf) (InfConcl inf))
```

Proving this theorem (and the others are proved similarly) amounts to showing that for every basic inference rule of the system of natural deduction there exists a proof in Hilbertian axiomatization, using only the basic rules of HA and, possibly, the derived rules of HA corresponding to the basic rules of ND derived in HA earlier. Proving, for instance, correctness of derivation of the rule RAA, which can be derived in Hilbertian axiomatization, using the rule ImpI of natural deduction

$$\frac{\dfrac{\Gamma, p \Rightarrow \bot \vdash \bot}{\Gamma \vdash (p \Rightarrow \bot) \Rightarrow \bot} \text{ ImpI} \qquad \dfrac{}{\vdash ((p \Rightarrow \bot) \Rightarrow \bot) \Rightarrow p} \text{ Ax3}}{\Gamma \vdash p} \text{ MP}$$

requires that correctness of derivation of ImpI in HA has already been proved. All derivations required for the proof of BasicHARules_Provable_in_FlatSC, BasicFlatSCRules_Provable_in_ND and BasicNDRules_Provable_in_HA can be found in [8].

The proof of isomorphism can be regarded as constructive in the sense that even though we do not show that every proof in one proof system can be translated to a proof in the others, we effectively use such a translation on a meta-level.

3.5 Translating Meta-logical Results Among the Proof Systems

The most important consequence of the theorems IsomorphismThm and Provability_of_FlatSC_in_SC is that the meta-logical properties we have proved about one proof system hold for the other systems as well. In particular, we have that the deduction, the monotonicity, and the substitution theorems hold for all the proof systems we study, including sequent calculus; the compactness theorem holds, in addition to the Hilbertian axiomatization, for the system of natural deduction, and flattened sequent calculus.

For example, compactness in natural deduction is expressed as a theorem

```
CompactThmND =
|- !hyps Gamma p. IsProvable NDRules hyps (Sseq Gamma {p}) ==>
   (?Delta. Delta SUBSET Gamma /\ FINITE Delta /\
      IsProvable NDRules hyps (Sseq Delta {p}))
```

and proved in two steps by rewriting with `IsomorphismThm` and `CompactThm`.

4 Conclusions and Related Work

We formalize first-order logic in the theorem proving system HOL and establish isomorphism among three first-order proof systems, namely, the Hilbertian axiomatization, the system of natural deduction, and flattened sequent calculus. Moreover, we prove that classical sequent calculus is more general than these proof systems, in the sense that anything provable in either of them is also provable in SC.

Formalization of mathematics, and, in particular, logic, in a theorem-proving system constitutes an area of related work. In particular, the formalization of higher-order logic proofs in HOL [11] was a starting point for this project. Formalization of sequent calculus in the logical framework LF and a structural proof of Cut elimination are reported in [9]. Finally, Harrison in [5] gives a thorough account of approaches to formalization of logic in a historical perspective.

Our interest in studying the relationship among first-order proof systems is by far not original. For example, Girard et al. [3] note that to a proof of $A \vdash B$ in sequent calculus there corresponds a deduction of B under the hypotheses A in natural deduction, and, conversely, a deduction of B from A can be represented in sequent calculus, but not uniquely. Kleene in [6] shows that provability in G4, which is a variant of sequent calculus, implies provability in a Hilbert-type formal system H. Also, he proves the deduction theorem for the system H; the latter differs from our proof system HA in taking all logical connectives as basic and, therefore, having three inference rules and 15 axiomatic rules. All the meta-logical reasoning in [3, 6] is carried out in a natural language, whereas we do it in a mechanized theorem-proving system using higher-order logic. Formal treatment brings up subtle issues that are usually omitted or overlooked when reasoning is done in a natural language. For example, finiteness restrictions on antecedents and succedents of sequents have to be dealt with explicitly. There are effectively two ways of imposing these restrictions. With the first approach, the finiteness restrictions are imposed on a proof system itself, being explicitly stated in all inference rules. The second approach employs the deduction, monotonicity, and compactness theorems, allowing inference rules to be given in terms of arbitrary sequents. We have chosen the latter approach because it simplifies proofs. All axiomatic inference rules in our formalization have an arbitrary antecedent set instead of the empty set, which reflects the intuitive meaning that from any assumptions at all one can deduce an axiom.

The data-type of parameterized proofs could be used in practice for reasoning about algorithms that handle proofs, such as decision procedures and proof checkers. For extension of this work we view several proof-theoretical directions. First of all, "classical" results such as normalization for natural deduction could be proved. The framework could be used to compare intuitionistic versions of proof systems. Also, it would be interesting to characterize proof systems which don't exactly give the same theorems, such as Mendelson's proof system, where all formulae in the antecedent of a sequent are implicitly universally quantified, and prove the precise interrelation with the other proof systems.

Acknowledgements

We would like to thank John Harrison for his encouragement to carry out this project, and practical help in formalization of concepts and proofs.

References

1. N. G. de Bruijn. Lambda-calculus notation with nameless dummies: a tool for automatic formula manipulation with application to the Church-Rosser theorem. *Indag. Math.*, 34(5):381–392, 1972.
2. H. B. Enderton. *A Mathematical Introduction to Logic*. Academic Press, Inc., Orlando, Florida, 1972.
3. J.-Y. Girard, Y. Lafont, and P. Taylor. *Proofs and Types*, volume 7 of *Cambridge Tracts in Theoretical Computer Science*. Cambridge University Press, Cambridge, 1989.
4. M. J. C. Gordon and T. F. Melham. *Introduction to HOL: A theorem proving environment for higher order logic*. Cambridge University Press, 1993.
5. J. Harrison. Formalized mathematics. Technical Report TUCS-TR-36, Turku Centre for Computer Science, Finland, Aug. 14, 1996.
6. S. C. Kleene. *Mathematical Logic*. Wiley and Sons, 1968.
7. N. Megill. Metamath: A computer language for pure mathematics. Unpublished; available from ftp://sparky.shore.net/members/ndm/metamath.tex.Z, 1996.
8. A. Mikhajlova and J. von Wright. Proving isomorphism of first-order logic proof systems in HOL. Technical Report 169, Turku Centre for Computer Science, March 1998.
9. F. Pfenning. A structural proof of cut elimination and its representation in a logical framework. Technical Report CMU-CS-94-218, Department of Computer Science, Carnegie Mellon University, Nov. 1994.
10. D. van Dalen. *Logic and Structure*. Universitext. Springer-Verlag, Berlin, 3rd edition, 1994.
11. J. von Wright. Representing higher order logic proofs in HOL. *Lecture Notes in Computer Science*, 859:456–469, 1994.

Exploiting Parallelism in Interactive Theorem Provers

Roderick Moten

Colgate University, Hamilton, NY 13224, USA
rod@cs.colgate.edu

Abstract. This paper reports on the implementation and analysis of the *MP refiner*, the first parallel interactive theorem prover. The MP refiner is a shared memory multi-processor implementation of the inference engine of *Nuprl*. The inference engine of Nuprl is called the refiner. The MP refiner is a collection of threads operating as sequential refiners running on separate processors. Concurrent tactics exploit parallelism by spawning tactics to be evaluated by other refiner threads simultaneously. Tests conducted with the MP refiner running on a four processor Sparc shared-memory multi-processor reveal that parallelism at the inference rule level can significantly decrease the elapsed time of constructing proofs interactively.

1 Introduction

An interactive theorem prover is a computer program that employs automated deduction to construct proofs with the aid of a user. Many interactive theorem provers require users to supply programs, called *tactics*, to carry out inference. Tactics usually carry out multiple steps of inference and use heuristics to determine the inferences to employ. A tactic may construct an entire proof or a portion of a proof. Tactics were first used with the LCF interactive proof system [9]. Most interactive theorem provers in existence today use tactics [5, 8, 6, 20, 7, 11].

We believe that parallelism will improve the performance of interactive theorem provers. Previous research has shown employing parallelism in automatic theorem provers has lead to significant speedups. For instance, the parallel version of Otter [14], Roo [13, 24], has near linear speedups for many of the tests reported on in [13]. The tests were conducted on a shared-memory multi-processor with 24 processors using the benchmark of theorem proving problems in [30]. Parallel versions of SETHEO [12], PARTHEO [22] and SPTHEO [26, 25], out performed SETHEO. In addition, 75% of the tests with the Parthenon parallel theorem prover [4] based on Warren's SRI model of OR-parallelism of Prolog [29] had a linear speedup over the sequential version of the prover. The speedups were obtained using an Encore Multimax with 16 processors.

Static Partitioning with slackness [27] characterizes the model of parallelism employed in the above parallel theorem provers and several other parallel theorem provers [28, 23]. Static partitioning with slackness divides the search process into three sequential phases. During the first phase, an initial segment of the search space is explored to obtain tasks that can be computed simultaneously using OR or independent AND-parallelism. During the second phase, the tasks are distributed amongst parallel processors. During the third phase, each of the parallel processors works on the tasks independently. After a processor completes a task, it reports its results to a master process that is responsible for global termination.

Interactive theorem provers that use tactics may also employ static partitioning with slackness because they construct proofs using AND-search and OR-search. AND-search and OR-search are obtained from constructing proofs using tactics created with THEN and ORELSE, respectively. Using a tactical, a new tactic can be created from one or more existing tactics. For example, given tactics t and t', the tactic $(t$ THEN $t')$ constructs a proof of the goal g by first applying t to g to produce subgoals $g_1, \ldots, g_n$. Afterwards, t' is used to construct proofs of each g_i. If t' constructs proofs of each g_i, then they are used to construct a proof of g. The proof of g obtained with the tactic $(t$ ORELSE $t')$ is the proof of g obtained with t. If t fails to produce a proof of g, then the proof of g obtained with $(t$ ORELSE $t')$ is the proof of g obtained with t'. THEN and ORELSE were first used in LCF and are implemented in many interactive theorem provers.

1.1 Exploiting Parallelism in Nuprl

To investigate the effects of parallelism in interactive theorem provers we developed the *MP refiner*. The MP refiner is a shared memory multi-processor implementation of the inference mechanism of the Nuprl Proof Development System [5]. The MP refiner provides concurrent tacticals for users to construct tactics that employ AND-parallelism and OR-parallelism. We call tactics that use parallelism *concurrent tactics*. We call the process of developing proofs using concurrent tactics *concurrent refinement*. AND-parallelism is obtained by creating tactics using the new tactical PTHEN. PTHEN is the concurrent version of the tactical THEN. Given tactics t and t', refining a goal g with the tactical $(t$ PTHEN $t')$ will first refine g using t to produce the subgoals $g_1, \ldots, g_n$. Then t' will be used to refine each g_i simultaneously. AND-search is being performed because proofs of each g_i are needed to construct a proof for g. OR-parallelism is obtained by creating tactics using the new tactical PORELSEL (pronounced p-or-else-l). PORELSEL is the concurrent version of ORELSE. Refining g with the tactic $(t_0$ PORELSEL $[t_1, \ldots t_n])$ results in refining g with each t_i simultaneously. One of the proofs is chosen deterministicly as the proof created by $(t_0$ PORELSEL $[t_1, \ldots t_n])$.

The MP refiner is implemented in Standard ML of NJ (SML/NJ) version 1.09.07 with **MP** [16]. **MP** extends the runtime system of (SML/NJ) to provide parallelism by mapping ML threads to operating system threads that execute concurrently on separate processors. The runtime system manages memory for ML programs, provides system services, such as I/O and file system routines, manages the ML state, and handles signals and traps caused during the execution of ML code [2]. We call the runtime system using **MP** the *MP runtime system*.

Although the MP runtime system deals with operating system and hardware dependent features, it is extremely portable [16]. We use the port for Sparc multi-processors.

1.2 Outline

In Sect. 2, we give a brief introduction to Standard ML and **MP**. We give an overview of tactics in Nuprl and the refiner in Sect. 3. In Sect. 4, we describe the implementation of the MP refiner. In Sect. 5 and Sect. 6, we analyze the performance of the MP refiner. Sect. 7 contains the conclusion and a discussion on future work.

2 Overview of Standard ML and MP

In this section, we acquaint the reader with Standard ML (SML) [15], a dialect of the ML functional programming language [9]. For a thorough coverage of SML, we encourage the reader to read "ML for the Working Programmer" by Larry Paulson [21].

An SML program is a collection of declarations binding names to values. Running an SML program creates an environment containing the association of names to values represented by the program. Values are obtained by evaluating expressions. An example declaration binding the variable x to the value 7 is given below.

```
val x = 4 + 3
```

Functions are declared using the keyword **fun**. For example, the declaration

```
fun fact n = if n <= 0 then 1 else n * fact(n-1)
```

binds the name **fact** to the function value that computes the factorial of an integer. Functions may be defined to take multiple arguments. For example, the function **monus** defined below takes two integer arguments.

```
fun monus x y = if x < y then 0 else x - y
```

Functions may also be declared using the **fn** keyword. The keyword **fn** works like λ in the λ-calculus. For example, we can declare **monus** using the following declaration.

```
val monus = fn x => fn y => if x < y then 0 else x - y
```

If we were writing the declaration of **monus** in the λ-calculus we would write

```
val monus = λ x. λ y . if x < y then 0 else x - y
```

Let-expressions permit programs to define bindings with limited scope. For example, the scope of the function **aux** and variable y exists only within the definition of **sqrt**:

```
fun sqrt x = let
    fun aux r =
        if r*r > x then r-1 else aux (r+1)
    val y = aux 1
in
    y
end
```

2.1 The MP Runtime System

MP [16] is a generic interface to a shared-memory multiprocessor for SML/NJ.
MP extends the runtime system of SML/NJ to multiplex ML threads on top
of threads provided by the operating system (OS threads). An ML thread is
the computation unit of an ML expression. ML threads run on a *virtual ML
processor*. A multi-threaded ML program may consist of several ML threads
that run on a virtual ML processor. To provide parallelism in SML/NJ, we use
several virtual processors. Each virtual processor is executed by an OS thread
that runs on a separate processor. We obtain parallel computation in ML with

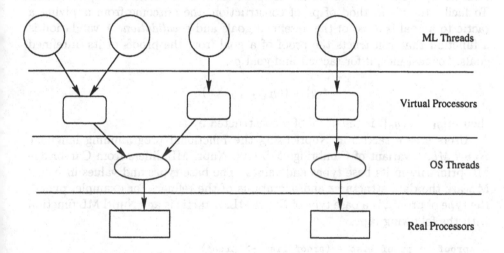

ML Threads

Virtual Processors

OS Threads

Real Processors

Fig. 1. MP diagram

multiple virtual processors each mapped to an OS thread that runs on a separate
processor (see Fig. 1).

The interface of MP provides a language level view of an OS thread as a
proc. All of the procs share the same heap. However the allocation space of
the heap is partitioned into chunks, and each proc is given a chunk to use as a
private allocation space. Although the allocation space of the heap is partitioned,
garbage collection occurs over the entire heap. In addition, garbage collection

is sequential: Only one proc performs garbage collection while the others wait. When a proc wants to perform a garbage collection it notifies the other procs to suspend themselves. After all of the other procs are suspended, the running proc performs garbage collection over the entire heap. When the garbage collection is completed, all the other procs are resumed. According to [16], the cost of synchronizing for garbage collection has little effect on performance.

3   Nuprl Tactics

In Nuprl, proofs are constructed using partial functions called tactics. A tactic constructs a proof using *primitive refinements*. A primitive refinement is a single step of primitive inference in Nuprl. Nuprl represents proofs as trees containing *unrefined* and *refined* goals. All the interior goals are refined. A leaf is either unrefined or refined. If a leaf of a proof is unrefined, then the proof is *incomplete*. On the other hand, if all the leaves of a proof are refined, then the proof is *complete* and the goal at the root of the proof has been proven. To obtain a complete proof from an incomplete proof, we apply tactics to each of the unrefined goals. Then we replace the unrefined goals with the proofs produced from the applications. We continue this process until we obtain a complete proof. To facilitate this method of proof construction, the outcome from applying a tactic to a goal is a list of the unrefined goals and a *validation*. A validation is a function that constructs the proof of a goal from the proofs of its unrefined goals. For instance, if for tactic t and goal g

$$t(g) = ([g_1, \ldots, g_n], v),$$

then $v([g_1, \ldots, g_n])$ is the proof of g constructed by t.

Users create tactics in Nuprl using the functional programming language *Nuprl ML*, a variant of Cambridge ML [19]. Nuprl ML differs from Cambridge ML primarily in its base types and values. The base types and values in Nuprl ML are the data structures and operations of the refiner. For example, `proof`, the type of proofs, is a base type of Nuprl ML. A tactic is any Nuprl ML function with the following type.

```
proof -> proof list * (proof list -> proof)
```

Goals are represented as incomplete proofs with only one node. To evaluate the application of tactics to goals, the refiner is implemented as an interactive read-eval loop for Nuprl ML.

Users often build tactics modularly [10]. First, simple tactics are created that only perform one primitive refinement. These tactics use very simple heuristics or none at all. They can be described as follows.

1. Perform some heuristic.
2. Choose a primitive refinement rule based on the result of the heuristic.
3. Refine the goal with the primitive refinement rule.

Users build sophisticated tactics using simple tactics according to the following scheme.

1. Perform some heuristic.
2. Choose a collection of tactics based on the result of the heuristic.
3. With the aid of a *tactical*, create a new tactic using the collection of tactics.
4. Refine the goal with the new tactic.

A tactical is a combinator for creating new tactics from existing tactics. Two common tacticals are THEN and ORELSE. Given two tactics, t' and t'', $(t'$ THEN $t'')$ is the tactic t such that when t is applied to g, t' is applied first to g to produce the unrefined goals $g_1, \ldots, g_n$. Then t'' is applied to each unrefined goal g_i. Given two tactics t' and t'', $(t'$ ORELSE $t'')$ is the tactic t such that $t(g) = t'(g)$ as long as t' is defined on g; otherwise $t(g) = t''(g)$. A variant of ORELSE is ORELSEL. ORELSEL is the same as ORELSE except several alternatives may be given if t' fails. Like tactics, tacticals are user-defined.

4   Implementation of the MP Refiner

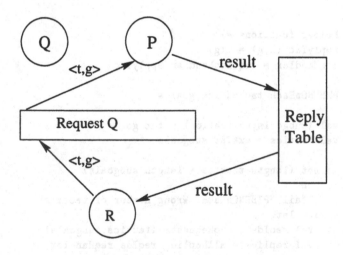

Fig. 2. MP refiner

We designed the MP refiner as a collection of refiners that share memory. Any refiner in the collection may request that another refiner evaluate an application of a tactic to a goal. In Fig. 2, for example, the refiner R *spawns* the application of the tactic t to the goal g by placing $\langle t, g \rangle$ in the *request queue*. The refiner P dequeues $\langle t, g \rangle$ from the request queue and applies t to g. Afterward, P places the result of the application in the *reply table*. R retrieves the results of the application from the reply table. The MP refiner implements parallelism by permitting a single refiner to spawn multiple tactic applications that are evaluated by multiple refiners simultaneously.

We implemented the MP refiner in version 1.09.10 of SML/NJ [3] with the **MP** runtime system for Solaris. Currently, the MP refiner runs on a Sun Sparc 670 shared memory multi-processor with 4 processors and is capable of running on any Sun Sparc multi-processor with at least 3 processors under Solaris 2.5.

Each individual refiner of the MP refiner is implemented as a ML thread. One thread behaves as a normal refiner: It is an interactive ML top-loop with primitive support for developing proofs using tactic refinement. The other threads are ML read-eval loops that only evaluate tactic applications. Each thread runs on a unique processor. We call each thread a *refinement server*.

4.1   Implementation of Concurrent Tacticals

A user creates concurrent tactics using the concurrent tacticals PTHEN and PORELSEL. PTHEN is constructed from the function PThenOnEach (see Line 19 in Fig. 3). PTHENOnEach is derived from THENOnEach for creating the various forms of THEN in the standard tactic collection of Nuprl 4.1 created by Paul Jackson [10]. We provide the code of PThenOnEach in Fig. 3.   The **else** por-

```
(* some helper functions *)
1.  fun applyTac (t,g) = t(g)
2.  val reqHandler = requestHandler applyTac
(*****)
3.  fun PTHENOnEach tac extTac goal =
4.  let
5.      val (subgoals,validation) = tac goal
6.      val tactics = extTac subgoals
7.  in
8.      if not (length tactics = length subgoals)
9.        then
10.           fail "PTHENOnEach: Wrong number of tactics"
11.       else let
12.         val reqIds = enqRequests (tactics,subgoals)
13.         val replies = allReplies reqIds reqHandler
14.         val results = processReply replies
15.       in
16.         combineResults(results, validation)
17.       end
18. end

19.  fun PTHEN (t,t') = PTHENOnEach t (map (fn _ => t'))
```

Fig. 3. Implementation of PTHEN using PTHENOnEach

```
1.    fun PFirst tactics goal = let
2.       val localTac = hd tactics
3.       val remoteTacs = tl tactics
4.       val requests = mkRequests remoteTacs goal
5.       val reqIds = enqRequests requests
6.       val (results,failedP) = applyTac (localTac(goal))
7.    in
8.       if failedP
9.          then
10.            retrieveFirstReply reqIds
11.          else
12.            (discardResults reqIds;
13.             results)
14.   end
15.   fun PORELSEL (tac, tacs) = PFirst (tac::tacs)
```

Fig. 4. Implementation of PORELSEL using PFirst

tion of the if statement in PTHENOnEach in Fig. 3 implements AND-parallelism. On Line 12, PTHENOnEach spawns each of the applications of a tactic in the list tactics to a subgoal in the list subgoals. The tactics in tactics are implicitly passed to PTHENOnEach through the function extTac (see Line 6). The goals in subgoals are the subgoals produced from the application of tac to goal on Line 5. On Line 13, PTHENOnEach polls the reply table for the results of the tactic applications it spawned. To prevent deadlock, allReplies allows a refinement server to service requests from the request queue while it retrieves replies from the reply table. Once PTHENOnEach obtains all the results, it processes the results. Processing the results will cause PTHENOnEach to generate an exceptional condition if an exceptional condition occurred during the evaluation of a spawned tactic application. On Line 16, PThenOnEach combines the results of the applications with validation to produce a list of unrefined goals and a single validation.

Notice that PTHENOnEach spawns all of the tactic applications and retains none to perform itself. Because PTHENOnEach uses allReplies to retrieve the results of the spawned applications, the refinement server may service some requests it placed in the request queue. However, this anomaly does not degrade the performance of concurrent tactics because the overhead of accessing the request queue and reply table is small, less than a millisecond.

PORELSEL implements OR-parallelism by deterministically choosing a tactic from a list of tactics to refine a goal. We implement PORELSEL using the function PFirst. The code for PFirst is given in Fig. 4. PFirst applies each tactic in the list tactics to goal. The application of the first tactic in tactics, localTac, to goal is performed on the refinement server running PFirst (see Line 6). Before applying localTac to goal, PFirst spawns the application of the other tactics to goal (see Lines 4 and 5). If the application of localTac to goal succeeds, then PFirst returns the results of the application and removes the results of the spawned applications from the reply table. If the results are not in the reply table when `PFirst` calls `discardReplies`, the reply table will not allow the results to be entered in the table. If the application of `localTac` to `goal` fails, then `retrieveFirst` is called to obtain the results of the application of the leftmost tactic in `remoteTacs` that succeeds. If none of the applications succeed then `retrieveFirstReply` generates an exceptional condition which is used to indicated that `PFirst` failed.

5   Performance

We measure the comparisons of the running times of sequential tactics and concurrent tactics as speedup. Our sample of tactics were created using THEN and ORESLEL. The tactics used as arguments to THEN and ORESLEL are listed in Table 1 and Table 2 along with the elapsed time to complete their application to a goal. The elapsed running times of each tactic in Table 1 and Table 2 is the average of 25 runs. The elapsed running times were obtained using the single processor version of the refiner implemented in SML.

We use the following naming convention for our tactics. For a tactic $taci\_j$, where i and j are integers, i is the number of primitive refinements the tactic performs and j is the number of unrefined subgoals generated. For example, `tac65_10` performs 65 primitive refinements and generates 10 subgoals.

The tactics created with THEN used each of the tactics in Table 1 as the left hand side argument of THEN. We chose these tactics based on the cost model of concurrent tactics in [17]. The tactics used on the right hand side of THEN appear in Table 2.

Table 1. Tactics on the left hand side of THEN

Tactic	Elapsed Time (Seconds)
tac1_10	0.006
tac1_50	0.022
tac1_100	0.047

We created tactics with ORELSEL for which only the last alternative succeeded.[1] We only used one tactic as the left hand side tactic, namely `tac65_10`. The tactics used as alternatives are listed in Table 2. We used each tactic in Table 2 to create lists containing 1, 5, 20, and 50 alternatives. We used each list as the right hand side argument of ORLSEL.

---

[1] In preliminary tests, tactics created with ORELSEL in which the first tactic succeeded out performed there concurrent versions. See [17] for details.

Table 2. The right hand side tactics

Tactic	Elapsed Time (Seconds)
tac1_1	0.002
tac65_10	0.01
tac400_100	0.649
tac2000_500	3.379
tac10000_100	16.567

To simplify creating tactics where only the last alternative succeeds, we used the tactical ORELSELF (pronounced or-else-l-f). ORELSELF is the same as ORELSEL except ORELSELF applies each alternative and throws aways the results of all the alternatives except the last.

For each sequential tactic, we created a concurrent tactic by replacing THEN with PTHEN, and ORELSELF with PORELSELF in the sample of sequential tactics. We obtained the elapsed times of each concurrent tactic to a goal using two, three, and four refinement servers. The MP refiner ran on a Sun Sparc 670 shared-memory multi-processor with four processors. We obtained the times using the timer supplied by SML/NJ. The timer uses gettimeofday to obtain the current time.

6 Results and Discussion

Our results show that concurrent refinement modestly improves the running times of tactics. Figure 5 depicts speedups of tactics using AND-parallelism. Figure 6 depicts speedups of tactics using OR-parallelism. None of the tactics achieve linear speedups – which we expected because of the shared memory bus between the processors. We obtained the best speedup of 2.825, from

$$\text{tac1\_100 PTHEN tac65\_10} \tag{1}$$

using four refinement servers. The speed of 2.825 indicates that (1) on four processors is almost three times as fast as

$$\text{tac1\_100 THEN tac65\_10.} \tag{2}$$

We obtained significant speedups primarily using AND parallelism and OR parallelism with tac65_10. This shows that the MP refiner works well using a fine-grain of parallelism. The running time of tac65_10 is roughly the average running time of a refinement rule in Nuprl 4.1. Performance tests conducted by Rich Eaton show that in Nuprl 4.1 the average running time of a primitive refinement is 0.012 seconds. The running time of tac65_10 is 0.1 seconds. Thus it is appears feasible to obtain significant speedups by employing parallelism at

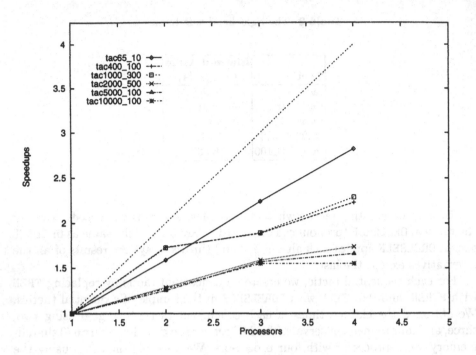

Fig. 5. AND-parallelism speedups

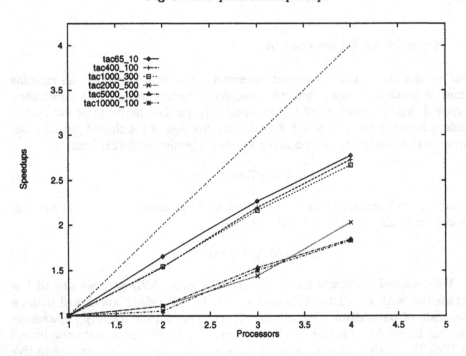

Fig. 6. OR-parallelism speedups

the primitive inference level in Nuprl. Originally we expected that parallelism would be more beneficial for tactics such as tac10000_100. However our results show that the MP refiner performed poorly on such large tactics.

We believe that memory management of Standard ML of NJ causes the MP refiner to perform poorly for large tactics. Morrisett and Tolmach [16] conjectured that contention between processors for the main-memory bus hinders performance in the MP runtime system. Morrisett and Tolmach used five benchmarks to test the performance of the MP runtime system. Of the five benchmarks, only one experienced near linear speedup.[2] This benchmark also generated the least bus traffic. We noticed in our tests that the tactics requiring the least memory had the greatest speedups: compare the speedups of (3), 2.825, and (4), 1.551.

$$tac1\_100 \; PTHEN \; tac65\_10 \tag{3}$$

$$tac1\_100 \; PTHEN \; tac10000\_100 \tag{4}$$

The application of (3) to a goal requires less memory than the application of (4) to a goal. During a tactic application, the tactic creates a proof. A refinement server needs memory to store the proof. The size of the proof depends on the number of successful primitive refinements invoked by the tactic. (3) generates $1 + 65 \times 100$ primitive refinements, and (4) generates $1 + 100 \times 10000$ primitive refinements.

The MP refiner may behave poorly for large tactics because of contention between refinement servers for the request queue and the reply table. However, we do not believe contention between refinement servers significantly hinders performance of concurrent tactics. The probability of contention is based on the number of requests and the number of refinement servers. Thus contention should equally effect (3) and (4), but their speedups differ drastically.

The overhead of suspending the refinement servers to perform garbage collection may affect the performance of large concurrent tactics. When a refinement server wants to perform garbage collection, it must wait for each of the other refinement servers to enter a write barrier. During this time, the refinement server that wants to perform the garbage collection becomes idle. Also, each refinement server that enters the write barrier becomes idle. As a result, the possibility arises for only one refinement server to be running while the others are idle. However, the amount of time for the refinement servers to synchronize for garbage collection is negligible. Based on the implementation of MP and the rate of memory allocation in SML/NJ, a refinement server will enter the write barrier within five to seven machine instructions of the request for a garbage collection.

---

[2] Actually, the benchmark had super-linear speedup.

7   Conclusion

In this paper, we described the implementation of the first parallel interactive theorem prover. Our prover, the MP refiner, uses AND-parallelism and OR-parallelism on a shared-memory multi-processor. The MP refiner is a multi-processor implementation in SML of the Nuprl refiner. The MP refiner makes significant improvement on the throughput of tactics when using a fine-grain of parallelism and only modest improvements using a coarse-grain of parallelism. Granularity is measured in the number of successful primitive refinements invoked by a tactic. We obtained the best results parallelizing tactics that have running times close to the average running time of a step of primitive inference in Nuprl. We believe the modest improvements with coarse-grain parallelism results from contention between the processors for the main-memory bus due to the memory management of SML/NJ. Concurrent tactics employing coarse-grain parallelism have higher memory requirements than concurrent tactics employing fine-grain parallelism.

7.1   Non-determinism in Concurrent Refinement

Many tactic theorem provers support *replaying* of proofs. Replaying a proof reconstructs the proof using the same tactics that created it. Replaying a proof may produce a proof different from the original proof. In other words, a user can construct two different proofs for a goal g using the exact same tactics. This is possible because the user may construct the proofs within two different states. For example, suppose a tactic t makes use of a theorem T to provide a complete proof of a goal g. If we apply t to g in a state with T present, then t will completely prove g. In a state without T, however, t will not completely prove g. As long as the state is the same, a user will construct the same proof for a goal g if he uses the same tactics (see [17]). However, with concurrent tactics, a user can construct different proofs for a goal using the same tactics with respect to a single state. The outcome of concurrent tactics, like many concurrent programs, is effected by the order of execution of its threads. For example, suppose t is the concurrent tactic (s PORELSEL $[s', s'']$). Suppose that s fails if the mutable shared variable x is 1 and succeeds otherwise. Futhermore, suppose s' changes x to 1 and s'' changes x to 0. For tactics t and t', let $t \rightarrow t'$ mean that t executes before t'. Suppose that the execution order of s', s'', and s is $s' \rightarrow s'' \rightarrow s$. Then the outcome of t is the outcome of s. However if the execution order of s', s'' and s is $s'' \rightarrow s' \rightarrow s$. Then the outcome of t is either the outcome of s' or s''. In [17], we describe a way to have determinstic concurrent tactics that have shared mutable variables.

7.2   Future Work

In the future, we intend to experiment with pipelining in the MP refiner. Pipelining is obtain by creating concurrent tactics using multiple compositions of PTHEN. To understand pipelining, consider applying the tactic (t THEN (t' THEN t'')) to the goal g. First, the tactic t is applied to g to produce the subgoals $g_1, \ldots g_n$. Afterward, t' is applied to each g_i producing the subgoals $g_{i,1}, \ldots, g_{i,m_i}$. Pipelining involves applying t'' to $g_{1,1}, \ldots, g_{1,m_1}$, for example, and t' to g_2 simultaneously. Multiple compositions of PTHEN, for example (t PTHEN (t' PTHEN t'')), implements pipelining.

Additional future work includes creating a parallel interactive theorem prover using a master-slave design. The master prover is a typical interactive theorem prover that uses one or more automatic theorem provers as slaves. The master prover spawns goals for the slaves to prove completely and automatically. The master prover only spawns goals it believes the slave can prove automatically. While the slaves are proving the goals, the master continues with its own work. This approach would probably be more favorable to interactive theorem provers such as IMPS [7] or PVS [18] that employ decision procedures as part of the inference strategy. Nuprl can also use this type of structure for proving well-formedness goals [1]. Well-formedness goals are generated by the Nuprl type theory refinement rules to validate that a term is a type. These goals usually can be proven automatically by the Auto tactic [10]. A slave prover simply refines all goals it receives using Auto.

Acknowledgements

Special thanks to Bob Constable, Stuart Allen, and Greg Morrisett for their advise and expertise. Also, I thank Karl Crary and Rich Eaton for their assistance in implementing the MP Refiner. Most of all I thank Jesus Christ for the intellect and perservance to accomplish this work.

References

1. Stuart F. Allen. *A Non-type-theoretic Semantics for a Type Theoretic Language.* PhD thesis, Cornell University, 1987.
2. Andrew W. Appel. A runtime system. *Journal of Lisp and Symbolic Compuation,* 3, 1990.
3. Andrew W. Appel and David B. MacQueen. Standard ML of New Jersey. In *Programming Language Implementation and Logic Programming: 3rd International Symposium,* pages 1–13. Springer-Verlag, 1991.
4. Soumitra Bose et al. Parthenon: A parallel theorem prover for non–horn clauses. *Journal of Automated Reasoning,* 8:153–181, 1989.
5. Robert L. Constable, Stuart F. Allen, H.M. Bromley, W.R. Cleaveland, J.F. Cremer, R.W. Harper, Douglas J. Howe, T.B. Knoblock, N.P. Mendler, P. Panangaden, James T. Sasaki, and Scott F. Smith. *Implementing Mathematics with the Nuprl Proof Development System.* Prentice Hall, Englewood Cliffs, NJ, 1986.
6. C. Cornes, J. Courant, J. Filliatre, G. Huet, P. Manoury, C. Munoz, C. Murthy, C. Parent, C. Paulin-Mohring, A. Saibi, and B. Werner. The Coq Proof Assistant Reference Manual: Version 5.10. Unpublished, 1995.
7. William M. Farmer, Joshua D. Guttman, and F. Javier Thayer. IMPS: A system description. In *Eleventh Conference on Automated Deduction (CADE),* volume 607 of Lecture Notes in Computer Science, pages 701–705. Springer–Verlag, 1990.

8. M. J. Gordon and T.F. Melham. *Introduction to HOL: A Theorem Proving Environment for Higher Order Logic.* Cambridge Univesity Press, 1993.
9. Michael Gordon, Arthur Milner, and Christopher Wadsworth. *Edinburgh LCF.* Number 78 in *Lecture Notes in Computer Science.* Springer-Verlag, New York, 1979.
10. Paul Jackson. *Enhancing the Nuprl Proof Development System and Applying it to Computational Abstract Algebra.* PhD thesis, Cornell University, 1995.
11. Matt Kaufmann. A user's manual for an interactive enhancement to the Boyer-Moore theorem prover. Technical Report 19, Computational Logic, Inc., 1988.
12. R. Letz, J. Schumann, S. Bayerl, and W. Bibel. SETHEO: A high performance theorem prover. *Journal of Automated Reasoning,* 8:183–212, 1992.
13. Ewing L. Lusk and William W. McCune. Experiments with Roo, a paralled automated deduction system. In *Parallelization in Inference Systems,* number 590 in *Lecture Notes in Artificial Intelligence,* pages 139–162. Springer-Verlag, 1990.
14. W. W. McCune. OTTER 1.0 user's guide. Technical Report ANL-88-44, Argonne National Laboratory, 1989.
15. Robin Milner, Mads Tofte, and Robert Harper. *The Definition Of Standard ML.* MIT Press, Cambridge, MA, 1990.
16. J. Gregory Morrisett and Andrew Tolmach. Procs and locks: A portable multiproceessing platform for standard ml of new jersey. In *Proceedings of the Fourth ACM SIGPLAN Symposium on Principles of Practice of Parallel Programming,* pages 198–207. ACM, 1994.
17. Roderick Moten. *Concurrent Refinement in Nuprl.* PhD thesis, Cornell University, 1997.
18. S. Owre, J. M. Rushby, and N. Shankar. PVS: A prototype verification system. In *Eleventh International Conference on Automated Deduction (CADE),* number 607 in *Lecture Notes in Artificial Intelligence,* pages 748–752. Springer Verlag, 1992.
19. Larry Paulson. *Logic and Computation: Interactive Proof with Cambridge LCF.* Cambridge University Press, Cambridge, 1987.
20. Lawrence C. Paulson. *Isabelle: A Generic Theorem Prover.* Number 828 in *Lecture Notes in Computer Science.* Springer-Verlag, Berlin, 1994.
21. Lawrence C. Paulson. *ML for the Working Programmer (Second Edition).* Cambridge University Press, Cambridge, 1996.
22. J. Schumann and R. Letz. Partheo: A high–performance parallel theorem prover. In *Tenth International Conference on Automated Deduction (CADE),* number 449 in *Lecture Notes in Artificial Intelligence,* pages 40–56. Springer-Verlag, 1990.
23. Johann M. Ph. Schumann. Parallel theorem provers: An overview. In *Parallelization in Inference Systems,* number 590 in *Lecture Notes in Artificial Intelligence,* pages 26–50. Springer-Verlag, 1990.
24. John K. Slaney and Ewing L. Lusk. Parallelizing the closure computation in automated deduction. In *Tenth International Conference on Automated Deduction (CADE),* number 449 in *Lecture Notes in Artificial Intelligence,* pages 28–39. Springer Verlag, 1990.
25. Christian B. Suttner. A parallel theorem prover with heuristic work distribution. In *Parallelization in Inference Systems,* number 590 in Lecture Notes In Computer Science, pages 243–253. Springer Verlag, 1992.
26. Christian B. Suttner. *Parallelization of Search–based Systems by Static Partitioning with Slackness.* PhD thesis, Institut für Informatik, TU München, 1995.
27. Christian B. Suttner and Manfred B Jobmann. Simulation analysis of static partitioning with slackness. In *Parallel Processing for Artificial Intelligence 2,* num-

ber 15 in Machine Intelligence and Pattern Recognition, pages 93–105. North–Holland, 1994.

28. Christian B. Suttner and Johann Schumann. Parallel automated theorem proving. In *Parallel Processing for Artificial Intelligence 1*, number 14 in Machine Intelligence and Pattern Recognition, pages 209–257. North–Holland, 1994.

29. D. H. D. Warren. The SRI model for OR-parallel execution of Prolog: Abstract design and implementation issues. In *International Symposium on Logic Programming*, pages 92–102. North–Holland, 1987.

30. G.A. Wilson and J. Minker. Resolution, refinements, and search strategies: A comparative study. *IEEE Transactions on Computers*, C-25:782–801, 1976.

I/O Automata and Beyond:
Temporal Logic and Abstraction in Isabelle

Olaf Müller*

Technische Universität München
Institut für Informatik, 80290 München, Germany
http://www4.informatik.tu-muenchen.de/~mueller/

Abstract. We describe a verification framework for I/O automata in Isabelle. It includes a temporal logic, proof support for showing implementation relations between live I/O automata, and a combination of Isabelle with model checking via a verified abstraction theory. The underlying domain-theoretic sequence model turned out to be especially adequate for these purposes. Furthermore, using a tailored combination of Isabelle's logics HOL and HOLCF we achieve two complementary goals: expressiveness for proving meta theory (HOLCF) and simplicity and efficiency for system verification (HOL).

1   Introduction

I/O automata [9, 5] are used to model reactive, distributed systems. In [15] the restricted class of safe I/O automata has been formalized in Isabelle [17]. System runs have been modeled as lazy lists using Scott's domain theory in Isabelle/HOLCF [16]. In a comparison [4] to other sequence formalizations, which all incorporated functions on natural numbers in some way, this sequence model turned out to be the most adequate.

In this paper we start with this sequence and automaton model and build an extensive framework for the verification of I/O automata in Isabelle. This framework is based on extensions to the theory of I/O automata developed in [12, 13]. These extensions comprise first of all a linear-time temporal logic, called Temporal Logic of Steps (TLS), which is similar to TLA [7], but evaluates formulas over sequences of alternating states and actions, which in addition may be finite. The applications of TLS are twofold. First, it can be used to define and reason about live I/O automata by establishing live implementation relations. Second, TLS can be employed as a property specification language for I/O automata. Furthermore, in [12] for both TLS applications abstraction rules have been developed which allow to reduce reasoning about a large or even infinite automaton to a finite and smaller automaton. Together with translations to appropriate model checkers this forms the basis for an effective combination of Isabelle with a model checker as external oracle.

---

* Research supported by BMBF, *KorSys*

In this paper we describe how all these notions have been embedded in Isabelle. The aim is to build a setting, in which the theory of I/O automata itself is verified (we only use definitional theory extensions), but that at the same time enables efficient system verification for the user. This is accomplished by combining Isabelle's object logics HOL and HOLCF in such a way, that the user employs only the simpler logic HOL, whereas the use of the more expressive, but difficult HOLCF is restricted to meta-theoretic arguments. TLS is not encoded directly, but as an instance of a generic temporal logic TL, which is evaluated over state sequences. This enables us to study the adequateness of our domain-theoretic sequence model in a more general setting, and, furthermore, reveals the connection to standard temporal logics over state sequences [10,6].

Due to lack of space we only present the main definitions and theorems and omit proofs. In particular, the translations to the model checkers STeP [3] and μcke [2] are not given formally. Instead, one translation is shown by means of a simple example. This example represents a rough simplification of an industrial case study [13] of a cockpit alarm system, which has been carried out to demonstrate the abstraction theory by combining Isabelle and STeP. For full details concerning the entire developments in Isabelle the interested reader is referred to the author's PhD thesis [13].[1]

The paper is organized as follows. Section 2 and Sect. 3 introduce HOL, HOLCF, and the models of sequences and safe I/O automata. Sect. refsec:TLisa describes the generic temporal logic TL, Sect. 5 its instance to the temporal logic of steps TLS. In Sect. 6 TLS is used to describe live I/O automata. Abstraction rules are derived in Sect. 7, which are applied to the combination of Isabelle with model checking in Sect. 8.

2 Preliminaries

Isabelle [17] is a generic theorem prover. We only use higher-order logic (HOL) and its extension to domain theory (HOLCF) [16]. We employ standard mathematical notation, which, however, differs only slightly from the syntax in Isabelle. Type abbreviations, constant declarations, definitions and theorems are introduced by the keywords **types**, **consts**, **defs**, and **thms**, respectively.

HOLCF uses Isabelle's type classes to distinguish between HOL types and domains. We write τ_C if a type τ is of class C. The default type class of HOL is *term*, the default type class of HOLCF is *pcpo*. The latter is equipped with a complete partial order $\sqsubseteq$ and a least element $\bot$. There is a special type for continuous function between *pcpos*, the type constructor is denoted by $\to_c$ in contrast to the standard HOL constructor $\to$. Abstraction and application of continuous functions is denoted by Λ (instead of λ) and $f\,{}'t$ (instead of $f\,t$). There is a tailored tactic that discharges admissibility obligations. HOLCF includes a datatype package that allows the definition of recursive domains.

---

[1] Furthermore, the theories are part of the Isabelle distribution which is available at http://www4.informatik.tu-muenchen.de/~isabelle/library/HOLCF/IOA.

3 Sequences and Safe I/O Automata

Sequences. Using the HOLCF domain package, sequences are defined by the simple recursive domain equation

> **domain** $(\alpha)\,seq = nil \mid HD\ \alpha\,\natural\,(\textbf{lazy}\ TL\,(\alpha)\,seq)$

where *nil* and the right-associative "cons"-operator $\natural$ are the constructors and *HD* and *TL* the selectors of the datatype. As $\natural$ is strict in its first argument and lazy in the second, sequences of type (α) *seq* come in three flavors: finite total (ending with *nil*), finite partial (ending with $\bot$), and infinite.

Due to the domain constructions performed by the domain package, the definition of $(\alpha)seq$ requires the argument type to be in type class *pcpo*. However, it will turn out to be crucial that elements of sequences can be handled in plain HOL. Therefore types of class *term* are lifted to flat domains by introducing a type constructor $(\alpha)\,lift$ using the HOL datatype package

> **datatype** $(\alpha_{term})\,lift = Undef \mid Def(\alpha_{term})$

and defining the least element and the approximation ordering as $\bot \equiv Undef$ and $x \sqsubseteq y \equiv (x = Undef \lor x = y)$, respectively. Note that $\bot$ and $\sqsubseteq$ are overloaded and this definition only fixes their meaning at type $(\alpha_{term})\,lift$. We define an unpacking function *the* :: $(\alpha)\,lift \to \alpha$ such that *the* $(Def\ x) = x$ and *the*$(Undef) = arbitrary$ where *arbitrary* is a fixed, but unknown value.

Now we can define a type of sequences that permits elements of type class *term* together with a corresponding "cons"-operator:

> **types** $(\alpha_{term})\,sequence = ((\alpha_{term})\,lift)\,seq$
>
> **consts** $Cons :: \alpha_{term} \to (\alpha_{term})\,sequence \to_c (\alpha_{term})\,sequence$
>
> **defs** $Cons \equiv \lambda x.\ \Lambda xs.\ (Def\ x)\,\natural\,xs$

Isabelle's syntax mechanism is used to write $x\hat{\ }xs$ instead of $Cons\,x\,{'}xs$. Finite sequences $a_1\hat{\ }\ldots\hat{\ }a_n\hat{\ }nil$ are abbreviated by $[a_1,\ldots,a_n!]$ and partial sequences $a_1\hat{\ }\ldots\hat{\ }a_n\hat{\ }\bot$ by $[a_1,\ldots,a_n?]$. The corresponding sequence flavors are characterized by the predicates *Finite* and *Partial*. From now on the default type class is assumed to be *term*, thus we will omit the explicit typing subscripts.

Recursive functions on sequences are defined as fixpoints, from which the characterizing recursive equations are derived automatically by a tactic. Thus, we will usually omit the fixpoint definition. For $\oplus$ (concatenation) the definition is given below. For *Map* and *Filter*, we merely list the interesting "cons"-case.

> **consts** $\oplus$ :: $(\alpha)\,sequence \to_c (\alpha)\,sequence \to_c (\alpha)\,sequence$
>
> Map :: $(\alpha \to \beta) \to (\alpha)\,sequence \to_c (\beta)\,sequence$
>
> $Filter$ :: $(\alpha \to bool) \to (\alpha)\,sequence \to_c (\alpha)\,sequence$
>
> **defs** $\bot \oplus y$ $= \bot$
>
> $nil \oplus y$ $= y$
>
> $(x\hat{\ }xs) \oplus y$ $= x\hat{\ }(xs \oplus y)$
>
> $Map\ f\,{'}(x\hat{\ }xs)$ $= f(x)\hat{\ }Map\ f\,{'}xs$
>
> $Filter\ P\,{'}(x\hat{\ }xs) = \textbf{if}\ P(x)\ \textbf{then}\ x\hat{\ }Filter\ P\,{'}xs$
>
> $\phantom{Filter\ P\,{'}(x\hat{\ }xs) =}\ \textbf{else}\quad Filter\ P\,{'}xs$

Boolean predicates on sequences can be defined by means of an auxiliary continuous predicate, which yields one of the truth values $\bot$, TT, or FF of the domain tr of truthvalues. As an example we present the *Forall* predicate, which uses an auxiliary $Forall_c$ predicate (and the conjunction *andalso* on tr):

consts *Forall*   :: $(\alpha \rightarrow bool) \rightarrow (\alpha)\,sequence \rightarrow bool$

  $Forall_c$ :: $(\alpha \rightarrow bool) \rightarrow (\alpha)\,sequence \rightarrow_c tr$

defs $Forall_c\ P\ `\bot$ $= \bot$

  $Forall_c\ P\ `nil$ $= TT$

  $Forall_c\ P\ `(x\hat{}xs) = Def(P\ x)\ andalso\ Forall_c\ P\ `xs$

  $Forall\ P\ xs$ $\equiv Forall_c\ P\ `xs \neq FF$

  $Forall\ P\ \bot$ $= True$

  $Forall\ P\ nil$ $= True$

  $Forall\ P\ (x\hat{}xs)$ $= P(x) \wedge Forall\ P\ xs$

The usual proof principle for sequences is *structural induction*. In contrast to finite structural induction it contains an admissibility requirement (*adm*).

thms $$\frac{adm(P)\quad P(\bot)\quad P(nil)\quad \forall x, xs.\ P(xs) \Rightarrow P(x\hat{}xs)}{\forall y.\ P(y)}\ (induct)$$

Co-inductive proof principles are available as well.

Thus, we get a sequence package, which allows powerful recursion like infinite concatenation. Furthermore, in contrast to approaches which model sequences as functions on the natural numbers operations like *Filter*, that relocate elements in an unhomogeneous way, are treated easily [4]. About 170 theorems have been derived, most of them in one step by a tailored induction tactic. Furthermore, note the advantages of *lifted* sequence elements: proof procedures tailored for two-valued logic may be employed (cf. the $\wedge$ in the last equation for *Forall*), and HOL theories and libraries may be reused.

Safe I/O Automata. In the sequel we summarize the embedding of safe I/O automata in Isabelle very briefly. For details see [13, 15].

An *action signature* models different types of actions and is described as

  types $(\alpha)\,signature = (\alpha)\,set \times (\alpha)\,set \times (\alpha)\,set$

where the components may be extracted by the selector functions *inputs*, *outputs*, and *internals*, respectively. We collectively refer to *internals* and *outputs* as *locals*, and to *outputs* and *inputs* as *externals*. The union of all three action sets, which always have to be disjoint, is denoted by *actions*.

A *safe I/O automaton* is a triple of an action signature, a set of start states, and a set of transition triples (called *steps*) described by the type

  types $(\alpha, \sigma)\,ioa = (\alpha)\,signature \times (\sigma)\,set \times (\sigma \times \alpha \times \sigma)\,set$

where the components may be extracted by the functions *sig-of*, *starts-of*, and *trans-of*, respectively. We write $s \xrightarrow{a}_A t$ for $(s, a, t) \in trans\text{-}of(A)$. Furthermore the abbreviations $act, ext, int, in, out,$ and $local$ are introduced for *actions*∘*sig-of*, *externals*∘*sig-of*, *internals*∘*sig-of*, *inputs*∘*sig-of*, *outputs*∘*sig-of*, and *locals* ∘ *sig-of*, respectively. Reachability of a state *s* for an automaton *A* is defined inductively as a predicate *reachable A s*. There are composition operators for parallel composition, hiding of internal actions, and renaming. Finally, there is a notion of invariants, for which associated proof rules have been derived.

Execution fragments of an I/O automaton *A* are (1) finite or infinite sequences of alternating states s_i and actions a_i, where (2) triples $s_i a_i s_{i+1}$ represent steps of *A*. The first condition is encoded into the type of an execution fragment, which is modeled by a pair of a start state and a sequence of action/state pairs:

types $(\alpha, \sigma)\,exec = \sigma \times (\alpha \times \sigma)\,sequence$

The second condition is captured by the predicate *is-exec-frag*, which checks recursively if all transitions are steps of *A*.

consts *is-exec-frag*   :: $(\alpha, \sigma)\,ioa \rightarrow (\alpha, \sigma)\,exec \rightarrow bool$
defs   *is-exec-frag* $A\,(s, \bot)$ $= True$
     is-exec-frag $A\,(s, nil)$ $= True$
     is-exec-frag $A\,(s, (a, t)^\frown ex) = s \xrightarrow{a}_A t \,\wedge\, is\text{-}exec\text{-}frag\,A\,(t, ex)$

The derivation of the equations for *is-exec-frag* is analogous to that for *Forall*. *Executions* are execution fragments beginning with a start state.

defs $execs(A) \equiv \{(s, ex).\ s \in starts\text{-}of(A) \wedge is\text{-}exec\text{-}frag\,A\,(s, ex)\}$

A *trace* of *A* is the subsequence of external actions of an execution of *A*. It describes the visible behaviour of *A*.

consts *mk-trace*   :: $(\alpha, \sigma)\,ioa \rightarrow (\alpha \times \sigma)\,sequence \rightarrow_c \alpha\,sequence$
defs   *mk-trace* $A \equiv \Lambda ex.\ Filter\,(\lambda a.\ a \in ext\,A)\,{}^\backprime(Map\,fst\,{}^\backprime ex)$
     $traces(A)\ \equiv \{mk\text{-}trace\,A\,{}^\backprime ex \mid_{ex}\ \exists s.\ (s, ex) \in execs(A)\}$

Safe implementation w.r.t. two I/O automata *C* and *A* is defined via trace inclusion. Furthermore, the external actions have to be the same.

defs $C \preceq_S A \equiv in(C) = in(A) \wedge out(C) = out(A)\ \wedge$
     $traces(C) \subseteq traces(A)$

Such implementation relations between *C* and *A* are shown by the use of *simulations*. In this paper we consider only specific simulations, namely *refinement mappings*. A refinement mapping *f* is a function between the state spaces of *C* and *A* that maps every start state of *C* to a start state of *A* and guarantees for every step $s \xrightarrow{a}_C t$ of *C* the existence of a corresponding *move* of *A*, i.e. a finite execution fragment with first state $f(s)$, last state $f(t)$ and external behaviour *a*. A *move* is formalized by the predicate *is-move*.

consts *is-move* :: $(\alpha, \sigma)\,ioa \rightarrow (\alpha \times \sigma)\,sequence \rightarrow (\sigma \times \alpha \times \sigma) \rightarrow bool$
defs   *is-move* $A\,ex\,(s, a, t) \equiv$
        is-exec-frag $A\,(s, ex) \wedge Finite(ex)\ \wedge$
        last-state $(s, ex) = t\ \wedge$
        mk-trace $A\,{}^\backprime ex = (\textbf{if}\ a \in ext(A)\ \textbf{then}\ [a!]\ \textbf{else}\ nil)$

where *last-state* :: $(\alpha, \sigma)exec \to \sigma$ denotes the final state of an execution, if it is finite, otherwise an unspecified value. The predicate *is-ref-map* characterizes refinement mappings.

> **consts** *is-ref-map* :: $(\sigma_1 \to \sigma_2) \to (\alpha, \sigma_1) ioa \to (\alpha, \sigma_2) ioa \to bool$
>
> **defs**   *is-ref-map* $f\ C\ A \equiv$
> $$(\forall s_0 \in starts\text{-}of(C). f(s_0) \in starts\text{-}of(A)) \land$$
> $$(\forall s\ t\ a.\ reachable\ C\ s \land s \xrightarrow{a}_C t$$
> $$\Rightarrow \exists ex.\ is\text{-}move\ A\ ex\ (f\ s, a, f\ t))$$

The correctness of refinement mappings is established by the following theorem:

> **thms** $\dfrac{is\text{-}ref\text{-}map\ f\ C\ A \quad in(C) = in(A) \land out(C) = out(A)}{C \preceq_S A}$

In [13] further meta-theoretic proofs in Isabelle are described, like soundness of the more general forward simulations, compositionality, and non-interference.

Note the following important methodological point: the correctness theorem above has been proved making heavy use of HOLCF because it involves recursively defined sequences. However, the predicate *is-ref-map* can be shown in the simpler logic HOL. Therefore actual refinement proofs in applications can be done in HOL, whereas the more powerful but at the same time more complicated domain theory is only utilized for the meta theory of I/O automata. This is a remarkable advantage of the decision to use sequences with *lifted* elements.

4   A Generic Temporal Logic

In this section we embed a generic temporal logic over finite and infinite sequences of states (called TL) into Isabelle. We use a shallow embedding, which means that we do not explicitly distinguish between syntax and semantics of temporal formulas. Instead, formulas are directly regarded as predicates and temporal operators as predicate transformers. However, Isabelle's syntax facilities permit these transformers to be denoted by the usual syntax.

We introduce a type for predicates and a corresponding notion of evaluation, which simply means function application.

> **types** $(\alpha)\,pred = \alpha \to bool$
>
> **consts** $\_ \models \_$ :: $\alpha \to (\alpha)\,pred \to bool$
>
> **defs** $x \models P \equiv P(x)$

The boolean connectives $\land$, $\lor$, $\neg$, $\Rightarrow$, and $=$ are lifted to predicates in a pointwise way.[2] As $(\alpha)\,pred$ is polymorphic, it is used to describe both state predicates and sequence predicates. The latter represent the temporal formulas of TL.

> **types** $(\alpha)\,temporal = ((\alpha)\,sequence)\,pred$

---

[2] Because it is always clear from the context whether a connective is lifted or not, we use the same symbols, although in Isabelle the syntax differs slightly.

As lifted boolean connectives already exist for this type, it suffices to define $\Box$, $\bigcirc$, and $\langle - \rangle$, where the latter means lifting a state predicate to a temporal formula.

> **consts** $\langle - \rangle$ $::$ $(\alpha)\, pred \rightarrow (\alpha)\, temporal$
> **defs** $\langle P \rangle \equiv \lambda s.\, P\,(the\,(HD\,{}^\text{'}s))$

> **consts** $\Box, \bigcirc :: (\alpha)\, temporal \rightarrow (\alpha)\, temporal$
> **defs** $\Box\, P \equiv \lambda s.\, \forall s_2.\, s_2 \leq^+_{suf} s \Rightarrow P(s_2)$
> $\bigcirc\, P \equiv \lambda s.\ \text{if } TL\,{}^\text{'}s = \bot \text{ then } P(s) \text{ else } P\,(TL\,{}^\text{'}s)$

Here suffixes and non-empty suffixes are defined as follows:

> **consts** $\leq_{suf},\ \leq^+_{suf}$ $::$ $(\alpha)\, sequence \rightarrow (\alpha)\, sequence \rightarrow bool$
> **defs** $s_2 \leq_{suf} s\ \equiv \exists s_1.\, Finite(s_1) \wedge s = s_1 \oplus s_2$
> $s_2 \leq^+_{suf} s\ \equiv s_2 \neq nil \wedge s_2 \neq \bot \wedge (s_2 \leq_{suf} s)$

Further temporal operators are defined as usual:

> **defs** $\Diamond\, P\ \ \equiv \neg\Box\neg P$
> $P \rightsquigarrow Q \equiv \Box\,(P \Rightarrow \Diamond\, Q)$

Validity of P means that it holds for all non-empty sequences:[3]

> **defs** $\models P\ \equiv \forall s.\, s \neq nil \wedge s \neq \bot \Rightarrow s \models P$

Treatment of Finite Sequences. Obviously, the empty sequence represents a pathological case in every temporal logic involving finite computations. In the definitions above this is reflected by the fact that $nil \models \langle P \rangle$ equals $P(arbitrary)$, where *arbitrary* is a fixed, but unknown value. Thus nothing reasonable can be concluded for this case. We solve the problem by circumventing the cases $s = \bot$ and $s = nil$ completely. They are excluded in the validity definition and the temporal operators are defined in such a way, that they do not introduce new statements of the form $nil \models P$ or $\bot \models P$. This is the reason why we define $\Box$ using only non-empty suffixes and use the TL operator for $\bigcirc$ only if the sequence consists of at least two elements.

Domain-Theoretic Sequence Model and Temporal Logics. The domain-theoretic sequence model in HOLCF turned out to be surprisingly adequate for defining a temporal logic. As the definition of the temporal operators shows, every theorem about TL boils down to sequence lemmas about HD, TL, and $\oplus$. Furthermore, admissibility obligations mostly cease to apply, as $\leq^+_{suf}$ needs $\oplus$ with a finite first argument only, so that finite structural induction can be applied. If admissibility obligations appear nevertheless, they can usually be discharged automatically, as HD, TL, and $\oplus$ are defined as continuous operators.

This simplicity is the result of a careful choice of the way the operators are formalized. In fact, a pointwise definition like in [10] would be infeasible in

---

[3] In Isabelle different symbols are used for validity and evaluation to avoid ambiguities.

our sequence model (indexes are awkward in our setting, see [4, 13]), the same holds for a $\square$ operator defined by some kind of drop operator motivated by the semantics of TLA [7]. A number of different attempts have already been made to definitionally embed temporal logics in higher-order logic (e.g. [8, 19]). Up to our knowledge, only infinite sequences have been considered, which are represented by functions on natural numbers. It is not obvious how these approaches should be generalized to deal with finite sequences as well. Furthermore, operators that deal with stuttering are not considered there. Take, for example, the operator that eliminates stuttering by replacing all subsequences $s \cdots s$ by s. This would be some kind of filter operation which is easily dealt with in our setting. In a functional setting, however, we face an operator which relocates elements in an unhomogeneous way, which is extremely awkward to handle according to the results of [4]. Note, however, that adding infinite stuttering is not computable and can thus not be handled in our setting.

Comparison with standard LTL. In [13] we have shown that the notions $\models_{LTL} P$ and $\models P$ coincide, where $\models_{LTL}$ denotes validity in [10] or [6] and P is restricted to the operators of TL. The proof consists of two steps: first, the temporal operators must have the same semantics, and second, it has to be equal whether formulas are evaluated over finite and infinite sequences (for $\models$) or over infinite sequences only (for $\models_{LTL}$). The second requirement essentially follows by defining an operator ∇ that adds infinite stuttering to non-infinite sequences

$$\nabla \sigma \equiv \begin{cases} arbitrary & \text{if } \sigma = nil \vee \sigma = \bot \\ \sigma s_n s_n \ldots & \text{if } \sigma = s_0 s_1 \ldots s_n \text{ is finite or partial} \\ \sigma & \text{if } \sigma \text{ is infinite} \end{cases}$$

and showing that $\sigma \models P$ equals $\nabla \sigma \models P$ under the assumption $\sigma \notin \{nil, \bot\}$.

This relation can be exploited to get a completeness result for TL simply by carrying it over from [6]. Below we prove some theorems in Isabelle, which represent a complete set of rules w.r.t. validity in TL according to [6].[4]

thms $\dfrac{\models P \Rightarrow Q \quad \models P}{\models Q}$ (mp) $\dfrac{\models P}{\models OP}$ (nex)

$\dfrac{\models P \Rightarrow Q \quad \models P \Rightarrow OP}{\models P \Rightarrow \square Q}$ (ind)

$\models O \neg P = \neg OP$ $\qquad\qquad (ax1)$
$\models O(P \Rightarrow Q) \Rightarrow (OP \Rightarrow OQ)$ $(ax2)$
$\models \square P \Rightarrow (P \wedge O \square P)$ $\qquad (ax3)$

5   A Temporal Logic of Steps

In this section we use the generic temporal logic over sequences of the previous section to embed TLS [13], i.e. a temporal logic over executions of I/O automata.

---

[4] Note that this completeness result cannot be proved within Isabelle as we use a shallow embedding.

In terms of an informal sequence model, the idea is to encode executions $\alpha = s_0 a_1 s_1 \ldots$ into a sequence of triples, where every triple (s_i, a_{i+1}, s_{i+1}) represents one step $s_i \overset{a_{i+1}}{\to}_A s_{i+1}$ of the automaton A. As finite executions are asymmetric in the sense that they contain one more state than actions, a single stuttering triple $(s_n, \sqrt{}, s_n)$ is added for the final state s_n of finite executions, where $\sqrt{}$ denotes an action disjoint from all action signatures. Intuitively, this stuttering triple ensures that finite executions may possibly be continued to infinity. In fact, it has been shown in [13] that the evaluation of TLS formulas stays the same when extending executions by infinite stuttering.

Definitions. In Isabelle, the encoding consists of two parts. First, executions, which are represented as state/sequence pairs, are transformed into triple sequences. Note that hereby redundancy is introduced, as most of the states are represented twice. Second, the action type α is extended to $(\alpha)option$, which ensures that the stuttering action, represented by *None*, is not already an element of the action type α. Both transformation tasks are performed by the function *ex-to-seq* defined below.

$$
\begin{array}{lll}
\textbf{consts} & ex\text{-}to\text{-}seq :: (\alpha, \sigma)\,exec \to (\sigma \times (\alpha)\,option \times \sigma)\,sequence \\
\textbf{defs} & ex\text{-}to\text{-}seq\,(s, ex) & \equiv ex\text{-}to\text{-}seq_c\,{}'(mk\text{-}total\ ex)\ s \\
& ex\text{-}to\text{-}seq\,(s, \bot) & = [(s, None, s)!] \\
& ex\text{-}to\text{-}seq\,(s, nil) & = [(s, None, s)!] \\
& ex\text{-}to\text{-}seq\,(s, (a, t)^\frown ex) = (s, Some(a), t)^\frown ex\text{-}to\text{-}seq\,(t, ex)
\end{array}
$$

Note that *ex-to-seq* cannot be defined via a continuous auxiliary predicate *ex-to-seq$_c$* immediately as done for *Forall*, as adding a further element to a partial sequence is not even monotone. Instead, we use a function *mk-total* which makes partial executions finite by substituting the final $\bot$ by *nil*, before the expected *ex-to-seq$_c$* is applied.

$$
\begin{array}{lll}
\textbf{consts} & mk\text{-}total & :: (\alpha)\,sequence \to (\alpha)\,sequence \\
\textbf{defs} & mk\text{-}total(s) & \equiv \textbf{if}\ Partial(s)\ \textbf{then}\ \varepsilon\,t.\ Finite(t) \wedge s = t \oplus \bot \\
& & \textbf{else}\ \ s \\
\textbf{thms} & mk\text{-}total(\bot) & = nil \\
& mk\text{-}total(nil) & = nil \\
& mk\text{-}total(a^\frown s) & = a^\frown(mk\text{-}total\ s)
\end{array}
$$

Note that *mk-total* reduces the occurring discontinuity to a generic function with the further advantage that it may be reused for other discontinuous definitions as well, e.g. for defining fair merge.

Formulas of TLS can now be defined as TL formulas, whose sequence elements are transition triples extended by an optional stuttering action *None*. Predicates over these triples are called **step predicates**.

$$
\begin{array}{lll}
\textbf{types} & (\alpha, \sigma)\,ioa\text{-}temporal = (\sigma \times (\alpha)\,option \times \sigma)\,temporal \\
& (\alpha, \sigma)\,step\text{-}pred & = (\sigma \times (\alpha)\,option \times \sigma)\,pred
\end{array}
$$

Evaluating formulas over executions boils down to evaluating formulas over sequences using *ex-to-seq*. The usual validity notions are defined accordingly.[5]

consts $\_\models_{ex}\_$ :: $(\alpha, \sigma)\,exec \rightarrow (\alpha, \sigma)\,ioa\text{-}temporal \rightarrow bool$

        $\models_{ex}\_$ :: $(\alpha, \sigma)\,ioa\text{-}temporal \rightarrow bool$

        $\_\models_A\_$ :: $(\alpha, \sigma)\,ioa \rightarrow (\alpha, \sigma)\,ioa\text{-}temporal \rightarrow bool$

defs $exec \models_{ex} P \equiv (ex\text{-}to\text{-}seq\ exec) \models P$

        $\models_{ex} P \quad\quad \equiv \forall exec.\ exec \models_{ex} P$

        $A \models_A P \quad\quad \equiv \forall exec \in execs(A).\ exec \models_{ex} P$

Note that for $\models_{ex}$ the boolean connectives have the same pointwise meaning as for $\models$, e.g. $exec \models_{ex} \neg P = exec \not\models_{ex} P$. This, however, does not hold for $\models_A$.

When talking about I/O automata it is often more convenient to use predicates on states and actions rather than step predicates, which always take the stuttering action into account. Thus, we introduce the functions ext_s and ext_a which lift state and action predicates to step predicates. Possibly occurring stuttering actions force the resulting step predicate to evaluate to *False*.

consts ext_s :: $(\sigma)\,pred \rightarrow (\alpha, \sigma)\,step\text{-}pred$

defs $ext_s(P) \equiv \lambda(s, a, t).\ P(s)$

consts ext_a :: $(\alpha)\,pred \rightarrow (\alpha, \sigma)\,step\text{-}pred$

defs $ext_a(P) \equiv \lambda(s, a', t).$ **case** a' **of**

$$None\ \Rightarrow False$$
$$|\ Some\ a \Rightarrow P(a)$$

We use the syntactical abbreviations $\langle P\rangle_s = \langle ext_s(P)\rangle$ and $\langle P\rangle_a = \langle ext_a(P)\rangle$.

Theorems. Validity in TL, i.e. on sequences, is stronger than in TLS, i.e. on executions.

thms $\models P \Rightarrow \models_{ex} P$ (*Val-Rel*)

The proof is simple: (*Val-Rel*) postulates that $ex\text{-}to\text{-}seq(exec) \models_{ex} P$ holds for every $exec$, provided that $s \models_{ex} P$ holds for every s with $s \neq \perp \wedge s \neq nil$. This is true as $ex\text{-}to\text{-}seq$ produces only non-empty sequences.[6]

Thus, the theorems $(ax1) - (ax3)$ carry over from $\models$ to $\models_{ex}$. Furthermore, the same holds for the theorems (mp), (nex), and (ind).

Note that the other direction of (*Val-Rel*) is not true, as not every transition sequence is an image under $ex\text{-}to\text{-}seq$: there may be *None* elements occurring not only after the final state of non-infinite executions, or non-identical successor states. Therefore, the completeness considerations for TL do not carry over to TLS. However, the specific form of sequences generated by $ex\text{-}to\text{-}seq$ can be

---

[5] Once more the symbol $\models_{ex}$ is overloaded in a way not supported by Isabelle.

[6] Note that the cases $s = \perp$ and $s = nil$ are the pathological cases of TL. As they are excluded by $ex\text{-}to\text{-}seq$, the stuttering action $\sqrt{}$ in TLS can, in a more abstract view, also be regarded as a remedy to rectify the insufficiency of general temporal logics involving non-infinite computations.

captured by a temporal formula for each automaton step. Having derived these step formulas, it is often sufficient to use further on only rules for $\models$ instead of $\models_{ex}$. Thus, they build some kind of interface between TL and TLS.

$$
\textbf{thms} \qquad \frac{\forall s\ t.\ P(s) \wedge s \xrightarrow{a}_A t \Rightarrow Q(t)}{A \models_A \Box(\langle P \rangle_s \wedge \langle \lambda x.\ x = a \rangle_a \Rightarrow \bigcirc \langle Q \rangle_s)}
$$

The proof of this theorem shows that these formulas indeed incorporate the fact that *ex-to-seq* adds stuttering steps at the end of finite executions only and produces always identical succeeding states. Thus, the application of these formulas yields temporal formulas, which can then be treated by standard LTL reasoning.

6   Live I/O Automata

Below, the I/O automaton model of Sect. 3 is extended to general liveness. Live I/O automata are represented by a pair of a safe I/O automaton and a TLS formula.

$$
\textbf{types}\quad (\alpha, \sigma)\ live\text{-}ioa = (\alpha, \sigma)\ ioa \times (\alpha, \sigma)\ ioa\text{-}temporal
$$

A TLS formula P is said to be *L*-valid for a live I/O automaton (A, L) if it holds for all executions of A under the further assumption L:

$$
\textbf{defs}\quad (A, L) \models_L P \equiv A \models_A (L \Rightarrow P)
$$

This reflects the intuition that liveness conditions posed on a safe I/O automaton restrict its executions [5]. Live executions, traces, and implementations generalize the corresponding safe notions in a canonical way.

$$
\begin{aligned}
\textbf{defs}\quad live\text{-}execs\ (A, L) &\equiv \{exec.\ exec \in execs(A) \wedge exec \models_{ex} L\} \\
live\text{-}traces\ (A, L) &\equiv \{mk\text{-}trace\ A\ `(snd\ ex)\ |_{ex}\ ex \in live\text{-}execs\ (A, L)\} \\
C \preceq_L A &\equiv in(C) = in(A) \wedge out(C) = out(A)\ \wedge \\
&\quad\ live\text{-}traces(C) \subseteq live\text{-}traces(A)
\end{aligned}
$$

Important cases of liveness are given by weak and strong fairness of an automaton A w.r.t. a set of actions *acts*, which are defined by the formulas *WF* and *SF*.

$$
\begin{aligned}
\textbf{consts}\quad Enabled &\ ::\ (\alpha, \sigma)\ ioa \rightarrow (\alpha)\ set \rightarrow \sigma \rightarrow bool \\
WF, SF &\ ::\ (\alpha, \sigma)\ ioa \rightarrow (\alpha)\ set \rightarrow (\alpha, \sigma)\ ioa\text{-}temporal \\
\textbf{defs}\quad Enabled\ A\ acts\ s &\equiv \exists a \in acts.\ \exists t.\ s \xrightarrow{a}_A t \\
WF\ A\ acts &\equiv \Diamond \Box \langle Enabled\ A\ acts \rangle_s \Rightarrow \Box \Diamond \langle \lambda a.\ a \in acts \rangle_a \\
SF\ A\ acts &\equiv \Box \Diamond \langle Enabled\ A\ acts \rangle_s \Rightarrow \Box \Diamond \langle \lambda a.\ a \in acts \rangle_a
\end{aligned}
$$

Note the particular meaning of *WF* and *SF* for finite executions. The formulas $\Box \Diamond P$ and $\Diamond \Box P$ express the same for finite executions, namely that P holds for the final stuttering step $(s_n, None, s_n)$. Thus, $\Box \Diamond \langle \lambda a.\ a \in acts \rangle_a$ is false, as the lifting function ext_a maps the stuttering action *None* to *False*. Therefore,

WF and *SF* express that the last state s_n is not enabled for any action in *acts*, which corresponds to the usual fairness definition using fairness sets [9].

Refinement mappings which transfer liveness from every execution of C to a corresponding one of A are called *live refinement mappings*

consts *is-live-refmap* :: $(\sigma_1 \to \sigma_2) \to (\alpha, \sigma_1)$ *live-ioa* $\to (\alpha, \sigma_2)$ *live-ioa* $\to$ *bool*
defs *is-live-refmap* $f (C, L) (A, M) \equiv$
    is-ref-map $f\ C\ A \wedge$
    $\forall exec \in exec(C).\ exec \models_{ex} L \Rightarrow (cor^{ref}\ A\ f\ exec) \models_{ex} M$

where the corresponding execution $(cor^{ref}\ A\ f\ exec)$ is given by an infinite concatenation of possible moves that correspond to the single steps of *exec*.

consts cor^{ref} :: $(\alpha, \sigma_2)\,ioa \to (\sigma_1 \to \sigma_2) \to (\alpha, \sigma_1)\,exec \to (\alpha, \sigma_2)\,exec$
defs $cor^{ref}\ A\ f\ (s, \bot)$ $= (f\ s, \bot)$
    $cor^{ref}\ A\ f\ (s, nil)$ $= (f\ s, nil)$
    $cor^{ref}\ A\ f\ (s, (a, t)\hat{\ }ex_1) = (f\ s, (\varepsilon\ ex_2.\ \textit{is-move}\ A\ ex_2\ (f\ s, a, f\ t))$
                     $\oplus\ snd\ (cor^{ref}\ A\ f\ (t, ex_1))$

Live refinement mappings are correct, i.e. they induce live implementation.

thms $\dfrac{\textit{is-live-refmap}\ f\ (C, L)\ (A, M)\quad in(C) = in(A) \wedge out(C) = out(A)}{(C, L) \preceq_L (A, M)}$

This theorem gives rise to the following proof method for showing that a live I/O automaton (C, L) implements another live I/O automaton (A, M) using temporal reasoning. First, show that f is a refinement mapping from C to A, i.e. prove the safety part. Then assume an execution $exec \in execs(C)$ with $exec \models_{ex} L$ and prove $(cor^{ref}\ A\ f\ exec) \models_{ex} M$.

In this proof method, L is evaluated over executions of C, whereas M is evaluated over executions of A. Thus, it is not sufficient to merely apply temporal tautologies for the liveness proof. Rather there have to be means to switch between properties over an execution *exec* of C and those of the corresponding execution $exec' := (cor^{ref}\ A\ f\ exec)$ of A. For refinement proofs restricted to fairness, such a switch is needed only once at the beginning of the proof: assume $exec' \models_{ex} M$ to be false, i.e. if $M = WF\ A\ acts$ then $exec' \models_{ex} \Box\Diamond\langle Enabled\ A\ acts\rangle_s$ and $exec' \models_{ex} \neg\Box\Diamond\langle \lambda a.\ a \in acts\rangle_a$. Then, both properties about $exec'$ can be reduced to properties about *exec* using the following theorems:

thms $\dfrac{exec \in execs(C)\quad ext(C) = ext(A)\quad \Lambda \subseteq ext(A)}{exec \models_{ex} \Box\Diamond\langle a \in \Lambda\rangle_a \ \Rightarrow\ (cor^{ref}\ A\ f\ exec) \models_{ex} \Box\Diamond\langle a \in \Lambda\rangle_a}$

    $\dfrac{exec \in execs(C)\quad \forall s\ t.\ reachable\ C\ s \wedge reachable\ A\ t \wedge t \models Q \Rightarrow s \models P}{(cor^{ref}\ A\ f\ exec) \models_{ex} \Diamond\Box\langle Q\rangle_s\ =\ exec \models_{ex} \Diamond\Box\langle P\rangle_s}$

For the remainder of the proof only temporal tautologies are needed.

This approach has significant advantages for our Isabelle environment. For fairness the two theorems above permit hiding HOLCF from the user, who operates only within the simpler HOL or uses standard rules of temporal logic.

7 Abstraction Rules

In this section we derive abstraction rules, which permit reducing proof obligations about large or even infinite I/O automata to corresponding proof obligations about finite and smaller automata. Rules are provided for properties expressed both as temporal formula (proof obligation $(C, L) \models_{ex} P$) and as I/O automata (proof obligation $(C, L_C) \preceq_L (P, L_P)$). In Sect. 8 we will show by means of an example how these rules can be used to combine Isabelle with model checkers.

Central are *abstraction functions* which represent specific refinement mappings, namely homomorphisms w.r.t. the transition relation.

$$
\begin{aligned}
&\textbf{consts}\ \ \textit{is-abs} \quad\quad :: (\sigma_1 \to \sigma_2) \to (\alpha, \sigma_1)\, ioa \to (\alpha, \sigma_2)\, ioa \to bool \\
&\textbf{defs}\quad\ \ \textit{is-abs } h\ C\ A \equiv (\forall s_0 \in \textit{starts-of } C.\, (h\ s_0) \in \textit{starts-of } A) \wedge \\
&\qquad\qquad\qquad\qquad (\forall s\ a.\ \textit{reachable } C\ s \wedge s \overset{a}{\to}_C t \Rightarrow (h\ s) \overset{a}{\to}_A (h\ t))
\end{aligned}
$$

The key idea of abstraction functions is that they induce a neater correspondence between executions than refinement mappings do: the corresponding execution is given as a pointwise mapping, which means that both executions always proceed within the same time raster.

$$
\begin{aligned}
&\textbf{consts}\ \ cor^{abs} :: (\sigma_1 \to \sigma_2) \to (\alpha, \sigma_1)\, exec \to (\alpha, \sigma_2)\, exec \\
&\textbf{defs}\quad\ \ cor^{abs}\ h\ (s, ex) \equiv (h\ s,\ Map\ (\lambda(a, t).\ (a, h\ t))\ {}^\backprime ex)
\end{aligned}
$$

Thus, we get as a special case of the soundness of refinement mappings that abstraction functions induce safe implementation. This result is based on the fact, that $(cor^{abs}\ h\ exec)$ is an execution of A provided that $exec$ is an execution of C. We say that A is an *automaton weakening* of C.

$$
\begin{aligned}
&\textbf{consts}\quad \textit{aut-weak} :: (\alpha, \sigma_2)\, ioa \to (\alpha, \sigma_1)\, ioa \to (\sigma_1 \to \sigma_2) \to bool \\
&\textbf{defs}\qquad \textit{aut-weak } A\ C\ h \equiv \forall exec \in execs(C).\ cor^{abs}\ h\ exec \in execs(A)
\end{aligned}
$$

$$
\textbf{thms}\qquad \frac{\textit{is-abs } h\ C\ A}{\textit{aut-weak } A\ C\ h}
$$

$$
\frac{\textit{is-abs } h\ C\ A \qquad in(C) = in(A) \wedge out(C) = out(A)}{C \preceq_S A}
$$

For the safety part, we considered until now, everything has been analogous to refinement mappings. For the liveness part, however, we get a significant improvement: whereas cor^{ref} permitted to transfer only specific patterns of fairness formulas from the corresponding execution $(cor^{ref}\ A f\ exec)$ to $exec$, the stronger cor^{abs} permits the analogous transfer for *any* kind of temporal formula, even in both directions. Such transfers are called *temporal weakenings* and *temporal strengthenings*, respectively.

$$
\begin{aligned}
&\textbf{consts}\ \ \textit{temp-strength}, \textit{temp-weak} :: \\
&\qquad (\alpha, \sigma_2)\, ioa\text{-}temporal \to (\alpha, \sigma_1)\, ioa\text{-}temporal \to (\sigma_1 \to \sigma_2) \to bool \\
&\textbf{defs}\qquad \textit{temp-strength } Q\ P\ h \equiv \forall exec.\ (cor^{abs}\ h\ exec) \models_{ex} Q) \Rightarrow exec \models_{ex} P \\
&\qquad\qquad \textit{temp-weak } Q\ P\ h \equiv \textit{temp-strength } (\neg Q)\, (\neg P)\ h
\end{aligned}
$$

Our goal is to reduce them to associated *step weakenings/strengthenings*.

consts *step-strength*, *step-weak* ::
$$(\alpha, \sigma_2) \, step\text{-}pred \rightarrow (\alpha, \sigma_1) \, step\text{-}pred \rightarrow (\sigma_1 \rightarrow \sigma_2) \rightarrow bool$$
defs *step-strength* $Q \, P \, h \equiv \forall s \, a \, t. \; Q \, (h \, s, a, h \, t) \Rightarrow P \, (s, a, t)$
step-weak $Q \, P \, h \equiv$ *step-strength* $(\neg Q) \, (\neg P) \, h$

This is accomplished by the following set of theorems, which hold as well when interchanging *temp-strength* with *temp-weak*.

thms
$$\frac{temp\text{-}strength \; P_1 \, Q_1 \, h \quad temp\text{-}strength \; P_2 \, Q_2 \, h}{temp\text{-}strength \; (P_1 \star P_2) \, (Q_1 \star Q_2) \, h} \quad \star \in \{\wedge, \vee\}$$

$$\frac{temp\text{-}weak \; P_1 \, Q_1 \, h \quad temp\text{-}strength \; P_2 \, Q_2 \, h}{temp\text{-}strength \; (P_1 \star P_2) \, (Q_1 \star Q_2) \, h} \quad \star \in \{\Rightarrow, \rightsquigarrow\}$$

$$\frac{temp\text{-}strength \; P \, Q \, h}{temp\text{-}strength \; (\star P) \, (\star Q) \, h} \quad \star \in \{\Box, \Diamond, \bigcirc\}$$

$$\frac{temp\text{-}weak \; P \, Q \, h}{temp\text{-}strength \; (\neg P) \, (\neg Q) \, h}$$

$$\frac{step\text{-}strength \; P \, Q \, h}{temp\text{-}strength \; (\langle P \rangle) \, (\langle Q \rangle) \, h}$$

These theorems form the basis for a tactic, called `abs_tac`, which automatically reduces temporal strengthenings/weakenings to step strengthenings/weakenings. This reduction represents a major advantage of our abstraction theory: the interactive theorem prover, verifying the abstraction's correctness, has to reason about steps only (which can be done in the simpler HOL), whereas reasoning about entire system runs may be left to the model checker.

Now we can define live abstractions and prove their correctness.

consts *is-live-abs* :: $(\sigma_1 \rightarrow \sigma_2) \rightarrow (\alpha, \sigma_1) \, live\text{-}ioa \rightarrow (\alpha, \sigma_2) \, live\text{-}ioa \rightarrow bool$
defs *is-live-abs* $h \, (C, L) \, (A, M) \equiv$ *is-abs* $h \, C \, A \wedge$ *temp-weak* $M \, L \, h$
thms
$$\frac{is\text{-}live\text{-}abs \; h \, (C, L) \, (A, M) \quad in(C) = in(A) \wedge out(C) = out(A)}{(C, L) \preceq_L (A, M)}$$

Finally, we can present the abstraction rules. Rules on the *lhs* treat safe I/O automata, the *rhs* considers live I/O automata. Note that after applying these rules the tactic `abs_tac` has still to be invoked.

thms

$$\frac{\begin{array}{c} is\text{-}abs \; h \, C \, A \\ temp\text{-}strength \; Q \, P \, h \\ A \models_A Q \end{array}}{C \models_A P} \qquad \frac{\begin{array}{c} is\text{-}live\text{-}abs \; h \, (C, L) \, (A, M) \\ temp\text{-}strength \; Q \, P \, h \\ (A, M) \models_L Q \end{array}}{(C, L) \models_L P}$$

$$\frac{\begin{array}{c} in(C) = in(A) \land out(C) = out(A) \\ in(Q) = in(P) \land out(Q) = out(P) \\ \textit{is-abs } h_1 \; C \; A \\ \textit{is-abs } h_2 \; Q \; P \\ A \preceq_S Q \end{array}}{C \preceq_S P} \qquad \frac{\begin{array}{c} in(C) = in(A) \land out(C) = out(A) \\ in(Q) = in(P) \land out(Q) = out(P) \\ \textit{is-live-abs } h_1 \; (C, L_C) \; (A, L_A) \\ \textit{is-live-abs } h_2 \; (Q, L_Q) \; (P, L_P) \\ (A, L_A) \preceq_L (Q, L_Q) \end{array}}{(C, L_C) \preceq_L (P, L_P)}$$

There are two further rules, which allow to strengthen the abstract model if that appears to be too weak to prove the desired property, or to weaken the concrete model, if that contains unnecessary elements which hinder the intended abstraction. They are omitted due to lack of space, see [13] or the Isabelle distribution.

8   Combining Isabelle and Model Checking

In this section we demonstrate by means of a very rough simplification of an industrial case study [13] how Isabelle can be combined with the STeP model checker [3]. We merely apply the simplest abstraction rule for a proof obligation of the form $(C, L) \models_A P$. Proof obligations of the form $(C, L_C) \preceq_L (P, L_P)$ are not considered. See [13] where such obligations are translated (in restricted versions) to the model checker μcke [2] and [14] where the example of a communication protocol is presented.

The alarm management of a cockpit control system can be described in a very abstract way by a stack. Alarms, which are initiated by the physical environment, are stored, then handled by the pilot and finally acknowledged, which means that the respective alarm is removed from the stack. When adding a new alarm to the stack, any older occurrences of this particular alarm are removed, such that only the most urgent instance of an alarm has to be treated by the pilot. There are quite a number of alarms, $Alarms = \{PonR, Fuel, Eng, \ldots\}$, which in the original specification made it impossible to verify the system via model checking. Note that the order of alarms in the stack has to be respected. However, for proving properties which concern merely a single alarm, for example the important alarm $PonR$, (Point of no Return), abstraction may be applied.

The I/O automaton $Cockpit_C$ is modeled by a list, called $stack$, which is initially empty. We present the transitions of $Cockpit_C$ in the usual informal format, which can easily be translated to our Isabelle setting.

input $Alarm(a), a \in Alarms$	**output** $Ack(a), a \in Alarms$
post: $stack := a : filter \, (\lambda x. \, x \neq a) \, stack$	**pre:** $hd(stack) = a \land stack \neq []$
	post: $stack := tl(stack)$

The properties we want to prove about $Cockpit_C$ are the following:

defs $P_1 \equiv \Box(\langle \lambda a. \, a = Alarm(PonR) \rangle_a \Rightarrow \bigcirc \langle \lambda stack. \, PonR \in stack \rangle_s)$
        "Whenever PonR arrives, it is immediately stored in the stack"

    $P_2 \equiv \Box\langle \lambda a. \, a \neq Alarm(PonR) \rangle_a \Rightarrow \Box \neg \langle \lambda stack. \, PonR \in stack \rangle_s$
        "If PonR never arrives, the system will never pretend this"

For both properties it is merely relevant whether $PonR$ is in the stack or not. Thus, we construct the abstract I/O automaton $Cockpit_A$ which replaces the alarm stack by the boolean variable $PonR\text{-}in$, initially *false*, which indicates if $PonR$ is stored.

> input $Alarm(a)$, $a \in Alarms$
> > post: if $a = PonR$ then $PonR\text{-}in := true$

> output $Ack(a)$, $a \in Alarms$
> > pre: if $a = PonR$ then $PonR\text{-}in$
> > post: if $a = PonR$ then $PonR\text{-}in := false$

The abstraction function h is obviously defined as follows:

> consts h $:: (\alpha)list \to bool$
> defs $h(stack) \equiv PonR \in stack$

As $Cockpit_A$ has been designed already with h in mind, the property *is-abs h* $Cockpit_C$ $Cockpit_A$ is easily established within Isabelle/HOL.[7] Thus, according to the first abstraction rule of the previous section, it remains to show that the corresponding abstract properties Q_i for $Cockpit_A$, defined as

> defs $Q_1 \equiv \Box((\lambda a.\ a = Alarm(PonR))_a \Rightarrow \bigcirc(\lambda PonR\text{-}in.\ PonR\text{-}in)_s)$
> $Q_2 \equiv \Box\langle\lambda a.\ a \neq Alarm(PonR)\rangle_a \Rightarrow \Box\neg\langle\lambda PonR\text{-}in.\ PonR\text{-}in\rangle_s$

are temporal strengthenings of the concrete P_i. These goals are reduced by abs_tac to the obligations $h(stack) \Rightarrow (PonR \in stack)$ and $(PonR \in stack) \Rightarrow h(stack)$, respectively, which both are trivial by definition. Therefore, the initial goals $Cockpit_C \models_A P_i$ have been reduced to the simpler goals $Cockpit_A \models_A Q_i$, which can now be verified by the STeP model checker. For this aim the I/O automaton $Cockpit_A$ is encoded into a STeP transition system. This is done by encoding explicit actions into the state space using a variable Act. Note that thereby the occurrence of an action can be observed only at the next state.

```
Transition System
    type actions = {AlarmP, AlarmNP, AckP, AckNP}
    local PonRin: bool
    local Act: actions
    Initially PonRin = false
    Transition AlarmP NoFairness:
      enable true
      assign PonRin := true, Act := AlarmP
    Transition AlarmNP NoFairness:
      enable true
      assign PonRin := PonRin, Act := AlarmNP
    Transition AckP NoFairness:
      enable PonRin
      assign PonRin := false, Act := AckP
```

---

[7] Note that the invariant that there are no duplicates in the stack is needed to show that $Ack(PonR)$ causes the transition from $PonR\text{-}in$ to $\neg PonR\text{-}in$.

```
Transition AckNP NoFairness:
   enable true
   assign PonRin := PonRin, Act := AckNP
```

The following properties represent the Q_i which are easily verified by STeP.

```
SPEC
   PROPERTY P1:   [](()Act=AlarmP --> ()PonRin)
   PROPERTY P2:   [] ()Act!=AlarmP --> []!PonRin
```

9 Conclusion

We gave a short overview of the verification framework for I/O automata in Isabelle, including temporal logics, proof support for live implementation relations, and the combination of Isabelle with model checking via abstraction. A lot of aspects had to be neglected or only glimpsed at, e.g. the extension to forward simulations, improved abstraction rules, or translations to model checkers. The entire I/O automata framework consists of 465 theorems, proved in 2332 proof steps. 81 theorems thereof concern TLS, live I/O automata and abstraction.

There are two major results. First, the domain-theoretic sequence model turned out to be especially adequate for extending meta theory to temporal logic and live I/O automata. In particular, in contrast to existing TLA embeddings [8, 19] it allows to incorporate finite sequences and to deal with certain operators that deal with stuttering. Second, a tailored combination of HOL and HOLCF allows to use the more adequate logic for meta theory and system verification, respectively. This applies to live refinements and abstractions as well.

The practical usability of this verification framework has been proven by an industrial case study of a cockpit alarm system [13].

Related Work. Further theorem proving support for I/O automata exist. However, it is either based on first order logic [18] and therefore relies on unformalized meta theory, or considers only the small fragment of invariants for safe I/O automata [1]. Instead, the works in [18, 1] consider timed systems as well. A further TLA framework in Isabelle [11], even though remarkable for its practical usability, distinguishes itself from ours by being based on an axiomatization.

References

1. M. Archer and C. Heitmeyer. Human-style theorem proving using PVS. In E. Gunter, editor, *Proc. 10th Int. Conf. on Theorem Proving in Higher Order Logics (TPHOL'97)*, volume 1275 of *Lecture Notes in Computer Science*, pages 33–48. Springer-Verlag, 1997.
2. A. Biere. μcke – Efficient μ-calculus model checking. In O. Grumberg, editor, *Proc. 9th Int. Conf. on Computer Aided Verification*, volume 1254 of *Lecture Notes in Computer Science*, pages 468–471. Springer-Verlag, 1997.

3. N. Bjørner, A. Browne, E. Chang, M. Colón, A. Kapur, Z. Manna, H. B. Sipma, and T. E. Uribe. STeP: deductive-algorithmic verification of reactive and real-time systems. In R. Alur and T. A. Henzinger, editors, *Computer Aided Verification: 8th International Conference*, volume 1102 of *Lecture Notes in Computer Science*, pages 415–418. Springer-Verlag, 1996.
4. M. Devillers, D. Griffioen, and O. Müller. Possibly infinite sequences in theorem provers: A comparative study. In E. Gunter, editor, *Proceedings of the 10th International Conference on Theorem Proving in Higher Order Logics (TPHOL'97)*, volume 1275 of *Lecture Notes in Computer Science*, pages 89–104. Springer-Verlag, 1997.
5. R. Gawlick, R. Segala, J. Sogaard-Andersen, and N. Lynch. Liveness in timed and untimed systems. Technical Report MIT/LCS/TR-587, Laboratory for Computer Science, MIT, Cambridge, MA., December 1993.
6. F. Kröger. *Temporal Logic of Programs*. Springer-Verlag, 1987.
7. L. Lamport. The Temporal Logic of Actions. *ACM Transactions on Programming Languages and Systems*, 16(3):872–923, May 1994.
8. T. Långbacka. A HOL formalisation of the Temporal Logic of Actions. In T. Melham and J. Camilleri, editors, *Proc. 7th Int. Workshop on Higher Order Logic Theorem Provers and Applications*, volume 859 of *Lecture Notes in Computer Science*, pages 332–347. Springer-Verlag, 1994.
9. N. Lynch. *Distributed Algorithms*. Morgan Kaufmann Publishers, 1996.
10. Z. Manna and A. Pnueli. *Temporal Verification of Reactive Systems: Safety*. Springer-Verlag, New York, NY, 1995.
11. S. Merz. Mechanizing TLA in Isabelle. In *Workshop Verification in New Orientations*, 1995. Technical Report, University Maribor.
12. O. Müller. Abstraction rules for I/O automata using temporal logic. 1998. in preparation.
13. O. Müller. *A Verification Environment for I/O Automata based on formalized Meta-Theory*. PhD thesis, Institut für Informatik, Technische Universität München, 1998.
14. O. Müller and T. Nipkow. Combining model checking and deduction for I/O-automata. In *Proc. 1st Workshop Tools and Algorithms for the Construction and Analysis of Systems*, volume 1019 of *Lecture Notes in Computer Science*, pages 1–16. Springer-Verlag, 1995.
15. O. Müller and T. Nipkow. Traces of I/O-automata in Isabelle/HOLCF. In *Proc. 7th Int. Joint Conf. on Theory and Practice of Software Development (TAPSOFT'97)*, volume 1214 of *Lecture Notes in Computer Science*, pages 580–595. Springer-Verlag, 1997.
16. O. Müller, T. Nipkow, D. Oheimb, and O. Slotosch. HOLCF = HOL + LCF. *J. Functional Programming*, 1998. submitted.
17. L. C. Paulson. *Isabelle: A Generic Theorem Prover*, volume 828 of *Lecture Notes in Computer Science*. Springer-Verlag, 1994.
18. J. F. Soegaard-Andersen, S. J. Garland, J. V. Guttag, N. A. Lynch, and A. Pogosyants. Computer-assisted simulation proofs. In C. Courcoubetis, editor, *Proc. 5th Int. Conf. Computer-Aided Verificatio (CAV'93)*, volume 697 of *Lecture Notes in Computer Science*, pages 305–319. Springer-Verlag, 1993.
19. J. Wright. Mechanising the Temporal Logic of Actions in HOL. In M. Archer, J. Joyce, K. Levitt, and P. Windley, editors, *Proc. 1991 Int. Workshop on the HOL Theorem Proving System and its Applications*, pages 155–159. IEEE Computer Society Press, 1992.

Object-Oriented Verification Based on Record Subtyping in Higher-Order Logic

Wolfgang Naraschewski and Markus Wenzel

Technische Universität München, Institut für Informatik
Arcisstraße 21, 80290 München, Germany
http://www4.informatik.tu-muenchen.de/~narasche/
http://www4.informatik.tu-muenchen.de/~wenzelm/

Abstract. We show how extensible records with structural subtyping can be represented directly in Higher-Order Logic (HOL). Exploiting some specific properties of HOL, this encoding turns out to be extremely simple. In particular, structural subtyping is subsumed by naive parametric polymorphism, while overridable generic functions may be based on overloading. Taking HOL plus extensible records as a starting point, we then set out to build an environment for object-oriented specification and verification (HOOL). This framework offers several well-known concepts like classes, objects, methods and late-binding. All of this is achieved by very simple means within HOL.

1 Introduction

Higher-order Logic (HOL) [2, 1, 3] is a rather simplistic typed system, Church originally even called it "Simple Theory of Types". At first sight, it might seem futile attempting to use HOL to represent extensible records with structural subtyping, or even object-oriented concepts. One might expect that this requires more advanced concepts at the level of types. The more surprising that HOL is perfectly capable of providing extensible record types. The encoding even turns out to be very simple and natural.

Extensible records in HOL give rise to applications in general mathematical modeling. We will hint at these by an example of simple abstract algebra.

Taking HOL plus extensible records as a basis we develop an object-oriented specification and verification environment (HOOL). This provides several well-known object-oriented concepts like classes, objects, methods and late-binding. On top of these basic concepts we could even achieve abstract classes and encapsulation (hiding), just by employing some mechanism of abstract theories like axiomatic type classes [13].

While this work has originated in the context of Isabelle/HOL [10], in principle its results carry over to other HOL implementations as well. Subsequently we will always refer to "HOL" in a generic sense.

A note on implementation: the latest official Isabelle release (Isabelle98) includes a prototypical package for extensible records. While demonstrating the basic ideas, it is not quite suited for real applications. You should get a more recent (probably unofficial) release for your own experiments.

This paper is structured as follows. Section 2 gives some impression on how to use extensible records in general mathematical modeling. We present a simple example of abstract algebra. Section 3 is foundational: after introducing the HOL logic to some extent, we present our particular encoding of extensible records. Section 4 introduces an environment for object-oriented specification and verification (HOOL). We demonstrate its main features by the running example of coloured points and rectangles. Section 5 explains how the HOOL concepts can be represented in HOL. Section 6 discusses object-oriented verification within the HOOL environment.

2 Basic Use of Extensible Records

2.1 What are Extensible Records Anyway?

Tuples and Records. We briefly review some basic notions and notations.

Ordinary tuples and tuple types, which are taken for granted, are written as usual in mathematics, e.g. a triple (a, b, c) of type $A \times B \times C$.

Records are a minor generalization of tuples, where components may be addressed by arbitrary labels (strings, identifiers, etc.) instead of just position. Our concrete record syntax is borrowed from ML: e.g. $\{x = a, y = b, z = c\}$ denotes an individual record of labels x, y, z and values a, b, c, respectively. The corresponding record type would be of the form $\{x :: A, y :: B, z :: C\}$. Note that the labels contribute to record identity, consequently $\{x = 3, y = 5\}$ is completely different from $\{foo = 3, bar = 5\}$.

Record Schemes. Unlike ordinary tuples, records are better suited to a property oriented view in the sense of "record r has field l". As a concise means to refer to classes of records featuring certain fields we introduce *schemes*, both on the level of records and record types. Patterns of the form $\{x = a, y = b, \ldots\}$ refer to any record having at least fields x, y of value a, b, respectively. The corresponding type scheme is written as $\{x :: A, y :: B, \ldots\}$. The dots "$\ldots$" are actually part of our notation and are pronounced "more". The more part of record schemes may be instantiated by zero or more further components. In particular, the concrete record $\{x = a, y = b\}$ is considered a (trivial) instance of the scheme $\{x = a, y = b, \ldots\}$.

As an example of relating records consider schemes $\{x = a, y = b, \ldots\}$ and $\{x = a, y = b, z = c, \ldots\}$. These are related in the sense that the latter is an extension of the former by addition of field $z = c$. On the level of types, one might say that any $\{x :: A, y :: B, z :: C, \ldots\}$ is a *structural subtype* of $\{x :: A, y :: B, \ldots\}$. Note that (in our framework) record subtyping may only hold if the parent is an *extensible* record scheme. As a counterexample, instances of $\{x :: A, y :: B, z :: C, \ldots\}$ are *not* considered extensions of the *concrete* record type $\{x :: A, y :: B\}$.

With record schemes at the term and type level we have already "extensible records" at our disposal. In particular, we can define functions that operate on whole classes of records schematically, like $f \ \{x = a, y = b, \ldots\} \equiv t$. Here the l. h. s. is supposed to bind variables a, b and "$\ldots$" by pattern matching. To improve readability, we occasionally abbreviate $\{x = x, y = y, \ldots\}$ by $\{x, y, \ldots\}$, even on the r. h. s. provided this does not cause any ambiguity.

Before discussing encodings of this general concept of extensible records in formal logical systems we demonstrate its use by an example.

2.2   Example: Abstract Algebraic Structures

Consider some bits of group theory: A *monoid* is a structure with carrier α and operations $\circ :: \alpha \to \alpha \to \alpha$ and $1 :: \alpha$ such that $\circ$ is associative and 1 is a left and right unit element (w.r.t. $\circ$). A *group* is a monoid with additional operation $inv :: \alpha \to \alpha$ such that inv is left inverse (w.r.t. $\circ$ and 1). An *agroup* (abelian group) is a group where $\circ$ is commutative.

A well-known approach to abstract theories in HOL [3] uses n-ary predicates over the structures' operations (carrier types are included implicitly via polymorphism). Then *monoid* would be a predicate on pairs and *group*, *agroup* on triples as follows (below we use fancy syntax $\circ$, 1 for variables):

defs
> *monoid* $:: (\alpha \to \alpha \to \alpha) \times \alpha \to bool$
> *monoid* $(\circ, 1) \equiv \forall x \ y \ z. \ (x \circ y) \circ z = x \circ (y \circ z) \wedge 1 \circ x = x \wedge x \circ 1 = x$
> *group* $:: (\alpha \to \alpha \to \alpha) \times \alpha \times (\alpha \to \alpha) \to bool$
> *group* $(\circ, 1, inv) \equiv monoid \ (\circ, 1) \wedge \forall x. \ (inv \ x) \circ x = 1$
> *agroup* $:: (\alpha \to \alpha \to \alpha) \times \alpha \times (\alpha \to \alpha) \to bool$
> *agroup* $(\circ, 1, inv) \equiv group \ (\circ, 1, inv) \wedge \forall x \ y. \ x \circ y = y \circ x$

Note that *monoid* and *group*, acting on different signatures, do not admit an immediate notion of inclusion. To express that any group is a monoid one has to apply an appropriate forgetful functor first, mapping $(\circ, 1, inv)$ to $(\circ, 1)$. Operations on monoids cannot be applied to groups without this coercion.

We now use extensible records instead of fixed tuples to model algebraic structures. This will eliminate above problem of incompatible signatures, as record subtyping automatically takes care of this. Monoids are defined as follows:

record α *monoid-sig* $=$
> $\circ :: \alpha \to \alpha \to \alpha$ (**infix**)
> $1 :: \alpha$

defs
> *monoid* $:: \{\circ :: \alpha \to \alpha \to \alpha, 1 :: \alpha, \ldots\} \to bool$
> *monoid* $\{\circ, 1, \ldots\} \equiv$
> $\quad \forall x \ y \ z. \ (x \circ y) \circ z = x \circ (y \circ z) \wedge 1 \circ x = x \wedge x \circ 1 = x$

The **record** declaration introduces type scheme $\{\circ :: \alpha \to \alpha \to \alpha, 1 :: \alpha, \ldots\}$ together with several basic operations like constructors, selectors and updates (with the usual properties). Selectors are functions of the same name as the corresponding fields, e. g. $1 :: \{o :: \alpha \to \alpha \to \alpha, 1 :: \alpha, \ldots\} \to \alpha$. Thus $(1\ M)$ refers to the unit element of structure M. To improve readability, we also write selector application in subscript (1_M). The update operation for any field x is called *update-x*.

Based on this abstract theory of monoids, we may now introduce derived notions and prove generic theorems. For example, consider the following definition of exponentiation (by primitive recursion), together with an obvious lemma stating that $x^{m+n} = x^m \circ x^n$ holds in monoids:

defs

> $pow :: \{o :: \alpha \to \alpha \to \alpha, 1 :: \alpha, \ldots\} \to nat \to \alpha \to \alpha$
> $pow \{o, 1, \ldots\}\ 0\ x \equiv 1$
> $pow \{o, 1, \ldots\}\ (Suc\ n)\ x \equiv x \circ (pow \{o, 1, \ldots\}\ n\ x)$

lemmas

> $monoid\ M \Rightarrow pow_M\ (m + n)\ x = (pow_M\ m\ x) \circ_M (pow_M\ n\ x)$

Next we define groups as an extension of monoids as follows:

record α *group-sig* $= \alpha$ *monoid-sig* $+$
> $inv :: \alpha \to \alpha$

defs

> $group, agroup :: \{o :: \alpha \to \alpha \to \alpha, 1 :: \alpha, inv :: \alpha \to \alpha, \ldots\} \to bool$
> $group \{o, 1, inv, \ldots\} \equiv monoid \{o, 1, inv, \ldots\} \land \forall x.\ (inv\ x) \circ x = 1$
> $agroup \{o, 1, inv, \ldots\} \equiv group \{o, 1, inv, \ldots\} \land \forall x\ y.\ x \circ y = y \circ x$

The *group-sig* type scheme has been defined as child of *monoid-sig* and directly inherits all primitive and derived operations (in particular selectors etc.). Apparently, any $\{o, 1, inv, \ldots\}$ is also an instance of $\{o, 1, \ldots\}$. Therefore, functions operating on the latter, also work on the former. For example consider the instance $pow \{o, 1, inv, \ldots\}$ for exponentiation on group structures.

By using extensible records we got for free what had to be done by explicit coercions (type casts) in other systems. Even more: apart from adapting *argument* types, *result* types are instantiated as well in our setting. As an example consider the following "functor" that reverses the binary operation of monoids:

defs

> $rev \{o, 1, \ldots\} \equiv \{o = \lambda x\ y.\ y \circ x, 1 = 1, \ldots\}$

This function generically maps objects of type *monoid-sig* to *monoid-sig* and *group-sig* to *group-sig*:

> $rev :: \{o :: \alpha \to \alpha \to \alpha, 1 :: \alpha, \ldots\} \to \{o :: \alpha \to \alpha \to \alpha, 1 :: \alpha, \ldots\}$
> $rev :: \{o :: \alpha \to \alpha \to \alpha, 1 :: \alpha, inv :: \alpha \to \alpha, \ldots\}$
> $\quad \to \{o :: \alpha \to \alpha \to \alpha, 1 :: \alpha, inv :: \alpha \to \alpha, \ldots\}$

Note that a naive approach with type casts would have yielded only *group-sig* to *monoid-sig* in the latter case.

In our setting, the type system will always take care of adapting the signatures of the mathematical structures automatically. Actual structures are restricted by additional logical properties, though, as expressed by the predicates *monoid*, *group*, *agroup*. Using simple properties of monoids and groups, like

$x \circ (inv \ x) = (inv \ x) \circ x$, we may actually prove that all three kinds of structures are logically invariant under the *rev* functor:

lemmas
  monoid M $\Rightarrow$ *monoid (rev M)*
  group G $\Rightarrow$ *group (rev G)*
  agroup G $\Rightarrow$ *agroup (rev G)*

In general, functors may not propagate that nicely down the hierarchy of algebras. If so, one might want to consider changing the meaning of such operations depending on the actual type of the argument structure. For example, some functor on monoids might be redefined on groups in order to take the additional *inv* field into account. Redefining functions this way amounts to *overriding methods* in object-oriented parlance (see Sect. 4 of how to achieve this).

3 Extensible Records with Structural Subtyping in HOL

3.1 The HOL Logic

Syntax and Semantics. The syntax of HOL is that of simply-typed λ-calculus with a first-order language of types. *Types* are either variables α, or applications $(\tau_1, \ldots, \tau_n) \ t$; we drop the parentheses for $n \in \{0, 1\}$. Binary constructors are often written infix, e. g. function types $\tau_1 \rightarrow \tau_2$ (associating right). There is no way to bind type variables or make types depend on terms in HOL.

 Terms are either typed constants c_τ or variables x_τ, applications $t \ u$ or abstractions $\lambda x. \ t$. As usual, application associates to the left and binds most tightly. An abstraction body ranges from the dot as far to the right as possible. Nested abstractions like $\lambda x. \ \lambda y. \ t$ are abbreviated to $\lambda x \ y. \ t$. Terms have to be well-typed according to a standard set of typing rules.

 HOL can be understood as a very simple version of typed set theory, with two distinct kinds of objects: terms denoting set theoretic individuals (numbers, tuples, functions etc.) and types denoting corresponding sets classifying the individuals. In ordinary untyped set theory everything is just a set, of course.

Theories. HOL theories consist of a *signature* part (declaring type constructors $(\alpha_1, \ldots, \alpha_n) \ t$ and polymorphic constant schemes $c :: \sigma$) and *axioms*. All theories are assumed to contain a certain basis, including at least types *bool* and $\alpha \rightarrow \beta$ and several constants like logical connectives $\wedge, \vee, \Rightarrow :: bool \rightarrow bool \rightarrow bool$, quantifiers $\forall, \exists :: (\alpha \rightarrow bool) \rightarrow bool$ and equality $= :: \alpha \rightarrow \alpha \rightarrow bool$.

 Any theory induces a set of derivable theorems, depending on a fixed set of deduction rules that state several "obvious" facts of classical set theory.

 Arbitrary axiomatizations are considered anathema in the HOL context. It is customary to use only *definitional extensions* (guaranteeing certain nice deductive and semantic properties) and honestly toil in deriving the desired properties from the definitions. HOL offers definition schemes for constants and types [12].

Constant Definitions. The basic mechanism only admits introducing some axiom $\vdash c \equiv t$ for a new constant c not occurring in t (and some further technical restrictions). We generalize the pure scheme to admit arguments of function definitions applied on the l. h. s. rather than abstracted on the r. h. s.: $\vdash f\,x\,y \equiv t$ instead of $\vdash f \equiv \lambda x\,y.\,t$. Furthermore, tuple abstraction, definitions by cases etc. may be written using ML-style pattern matching, e. g. $\vdash f\,(x, y) \equiv t$ (which applies the pair eliminator $split :: \alpha \times \beta \to (\alpha \to \beta \to \gamma) \to \gamma$ behind the scenes).

Later we will also use a proper extension of the HOL constant definition scheme, namely *overloading* [13]. Currently only Isabelle/HOL implements this. Here is a sample overloaded definition of some polymorphic constant $0 :: \alpha$:

defs
$$0_{nat} \equiv zero$$
$$0_{\alpha \times \beta} \equiv (0_\alpha, 0_\beta)$$
$$0_{\alpha \to \beta} \equiv \lambda x_\alpha.\, 0_\beta$$

Note that we do not have to cover all types of 0 here; additional clauses may be added later, provided overall consistency of the set of equations is preserved.

Type Definitions. New polymorphic type schemes may be introduced in HOL systematically as follows: exhibiting a non-empty representing subset A of an existing type (with further technical restrictions) one may introduce a new axiom stating that $(\alpha_1, \ldots, \alpha_n)\,t$, for a new type constructor t, is in bijection with A. This basically identifies the new type with the representing subset.

HOL type definitions are peculiar as they only state equivalence up to isomorphism. There is no way to enforce actual equality, as do type conversions in type theories. As a consequence, the HOL algebra of types can be considered as freely generated (without loss of generality), always admitting an initial model where types of different names denote different sets. This freeness property will be quite important later for distinctness of record types (Sect. 3.2). Even more fundamental, it underlies overloading [13], which is used in Sect. 4 to implement methods.

Paradoxically, more powerful logical systems like full set theory or the HOL-version underlying PVS are not quite suitable for our way of encoding extensible records, mainly because they no longer admit the freeness assumption of types.

3.2   Encoding Extensible Records

A Representation in Untyped Set Theory. Thinking in ordinary mathematics one may model extensible records as follows [6, §2.7.2]: fixing a set L of labels and a family of sets of values $(A_l)_{l \in L}$, the set of extensible records over these shall be the (dependent) partial function space $l \in L \rightharpoonup A_l$. That is, any record r is a partial function such that $r(l) \in A_l$, if $r(l)$ is defined. For example, record $\{x = 3,\, y = 5\}$ would be the function $r : x \mapsto 3, y \mapsto 5$, undefined elsewhere.

This encoding is rather "deep", labels and values are both first class individuals. We can express many notations of extensible records directly within the system as set theoretic functions or predicates. In particular, the relation "r has component l" would be "$r(l)$ is defined". Furthermore, relation "r' extends r" and operations "add component $l = x$ to r", "merge r and r'" could be expressed via set inclusion, insertion, union, respectively. Also note that these records are commutative: $\{x = 3, y = 5\}$ and $\{y = 5, x = 3\}$ are equal.

A Deep Encoding in HOL? Above encoding of records would in principle also work in HOL. We could encode partial functions as relations, or total functions to a range type with explicit *undefined* element. There is a snag, though, making this version of records very awkward to use in practice: it doesn't fit very well within the HOL type system. In particular, the sets of values A_l from above would have to be within the same type! If one wanted to have different HOL types for different fields, explicit injections were required (via disjoint sums).

A better encoding of records in HOL should try to exploit the type system as much as possible. Such a representation would be much preferable even if it lost some of the properties and expressiveness of the set theoretic version. This is yet another example of applied logic within a concrete working environment where pure expressiveness may be quite unrelated to usefulness.

Shallow Encoding of Records in HOL. To make a long story short, extensible records are basically just tuples that contain an extra "more" variable for possible extensions. Ignoring the fact that field names contribute to record identity for a while, the representation of $\{x = 3, y = 5, f = true, \ldots\}$ is just $(3, (5, (true, more)))$ where *more* is a suitable term variable. The corresponding type $\{x :: int, y :: int, f :: bool, \ldots\}$ is a nested product $(int \times (int \times (bool \times \alpha)))$, for some free type variable α.

Refining the *more* slot yields instances with additional fields, for example $\{x = 3, y = 5, f = true, z = 42, \ldots\}$ represented by $(3, (5, (true, (42, more'))))$. Containing free variables, record schemes are not basic values. Typically, they only appear in definitions of generic functions where *more* is bound by functional abstraction. On the level of types, the *more* position amounts to polymorphism.

Actual concrete record values can be achieved by instantiating the more slot to $()$, the sole element of the *unit* type, thus terminating the chain properly without affecting the semantics. For example, $\{x = 3, y = 5, f = true\}$ would be $(3, (5, (true, ())))$, and consequently its type $\{x :: int, y :: int, f :: bool\}$ would be $(int \times (int \times (bool \times unit)))$.

We now focus again on labels. These shall act as a means to distinguish records with different field names. As we have already said earlier, HOL's algebra of types is so weak that it admits a freeness assumption: types of different names can never be enforced to be actually the same within the logic. This gives rise to the following technique to make field names contribute to record identity without having to bother about labels as first-class individuals.

For any field $x :: \sigma$ we introduce an isomorphic copy of the HOL pair type $\times$ by type definition, calling it $\times_x$. We also obtain copies of the pair constructor and projections etc., with their usual properties. The copied constructor shall be $x\text{-}field :: \sigma \to \beta \to \sigma \times_x \beta$. It is declared only at an instance of the general scheme $\alpha \to \beta \to \alpha \times_x \beta$ in order to obey the type constraint for field x as specified in the record type declaration.

Using a separate pair type for any field we now get the following encoding of records: $\{x = 3,\, y = 5,\, f = true,\, \ldots\}$ is $(x\text{-}field\ 3\ (y\text{-}field\ 5\ (f\text{-}field\ true\ more)))$, its type $\{x :: int,\, y :: int,\, f :: bool,\, \ldots\}$ becomes $(int \times_x (int \times_y (bool \times_f \alpha)))$. Constructing records this way is like building inhomogeneous lists, with a separate *cons* operator for each field. The system implementation can easily provide concrete syntax for our records and do the conversion to the representation.

There are several distinguishing features of our encoding of extensible records in HOL, as compared to the set theoretic one presented earlier.

Most prominently, labels are not first class, but part of constant and type names ($x\text{-}field$ and $\times_x$). Thus we can no longer refer directly to fields within the logic, "record r has field l" is not a HOL relation in our setting. Yet this does not prevent us to write generic functions $f\ \{x = a,\, y = b,\, \ldots\}$ that expect certain fields. This is actually the way we get record subtyping for free, in the guise of ordinary polymorphism. So we gain a lot by directly employing the HOL type system for record types.

Also, our records are not commutative: $\{x = 3,\, y = 5\}$ and $\{y = 5,\, x = 3\}$ are different, even of incompatible types. So one has to ensure that records obey a canonical order of fields, which is not considered an actual limitation.

Furthermore, we do not provide a record merge operation. This would be basically concatenation of record types, requiring an associative operator. HOL with its free first-order type system cannot express this. We merely loose multiple inheritance because of this.

4   An Environment for Object-oriented Verification

We now introduce a logical environment that supports object-oriented concepts like classes, instantiation and inheritance. Our theory syntax will be similar to conventional object-oriented languages, like the one proposed in [9]. In this section we will only give some hints on how all of this can be implemented in terms of ordinary HOL declarations and definitions, see Sect. 5 for more details.

We use points, coloured points and rectangles as a running example. The root class *point* has x- and y-coordinates as fields, method *move* for moving points by a given offset and methods *reflect-X*, *reflect-Y*, *reflect-O* for reflecting them along the abscissa, ordinate, origin, respectively. Class *cpoint* adds a colour component to points. Class *rectangle* is a subclass of *cpoint* and specifies rectangles, which are determined by a reference point (bottom-left) together with the width and height. Rectangles are always in parallel to the x/y-axes. We also introduce a class *rectangle-hilite* of rectangles that set the colour to red when being moved.

4.1   Classes

To begin with the example, we define a root class *point*.

> **class** *point* =
>
> > **fields** $x, y :: int$
> >
> > **methods**
> > > $move :: \{x :: int, y :: int, ...\} \to int \to int \to \{x :: int, y :: int, ...\}$
> > > $move\ \{x, y, ...\}\ dx\ dy \equiv \{x + dx, y + dy, ...\}$
> > > $reflect\text{-}X :: \{x :: int, y :: int, ...\} \to \{x :: int, y :: int, ...\}$
> > > $reflect\text{-}X\ \{x, y, ...\} \equiv this.move\ \{x, y, ...\}\ 0\ (-2 \cdot y)$
> > > $reflect\text{-}Y :: \{x :: int, y :: int, ...\} \to \{x :: int, y :: int, ...\}$
> > > $reflect\text{-}Y\ \{x, y, ...\} \equiv this.move\ \{x, y, ...\}\ (-2 \cdot x)\ 0$
> >
> > **final methods**
> > > $reflect\text{-}O :: \{x :: int, y :: int, ...\} \to \{x :: int, y :: int, ...\}$
> > > $reflect\text{-}O \equiv this.reflect\text{-}Y \circ this.reflect\text{-}X$
> >
> > **specification**
> > > $move\ p\ 0\ 0 =^{x,y} p$ $\qquad\qquad\qquad\qquad\qquad\qquad$ (1)
> > > $x\ (move\ p\ dx\ dy) = x\ p + dx$ $\qquad\qquad\qquad\qquad$ (2)
> > > $y\ (move\ p\ dx\ dy) = y\ p + dy$ $\qquad\qquad\qquad\qquad$ (3)
> > > $this.move\ (reflect\text{-}X\ p)\ dx\ dy =^{x,y}$ $\qquad\qquad\quad$ (4)
> > > $\quad reflect\text{-}X\ (this.move\ p\ dx\ (-dy))$
> > > $reflect\text{-}Y\ (reflect\text{-}X\ p) =^{x,y} reflect\text{-}X\ (reflect\text{-}Y\ p)$
> > > $reflect\text{-}X\ (reflect\text{-}X\ p) =^{x,y} p$
> > > $reflect\text{-}Y\ (reflect\text{-}Y\ p) =^{x,y} p$
> > > $reflect\text{-}O\ (reflect\text{-}O\ p) =^{x,y} p$

We refer to methods in two ways, written with or without a prefix *this*. This distinction plays a vital rôle for inheritance, but can be ignored at the moment. Note that we use a particular equality $=^{x,y}$ which expresses that two points coincide on the coordinates, but not necessarily on the remaining fields. To improve readability, correctness proofs are not shown here. Verification issues are discussed in Sect. 6.

Since we are within a functional setting, state-modifying methods are modeled as functions mapping states to states. To be more precise, methods do not operate on particular states but on arbitrary instances of a given state scheme.

Mutual dependencies of methods are acceptable as long as they are non-circular. Recursive definition of methods is not supported as a primitive. The user has to express this using appropriate operators from the underlying logic (e. g. well-founded recursion).

4.2   Objects, Instantiation, and Method Invocation

Objects are *instantiated* from classes by specialization. Instantiating some concrete object *MyPoint* from class *point* is achieved by specializing the state-space from $\{x :: int, y :: int, ...\}$ to $\{x :: int, y :: int\}$ and determining the initial values for the coordinates. We write $MyPoint \equiv new\ point\ \{x = 3, y = 5\}$.

Method invocation is simply achieved by function application. For example, we can reset the object *MyPoint* by *move MyPoint* $(-x_{MyPoint})$ $(-y_{MyPoint})$.

4.3   Inheritance

Inheritance means being able to reuse code of superclasses in subclasses without explicit alteration. At first sight, this problem seems to be trivial just by duplicating code, but the problem is slightly more complicated. Consider, for example, the point methods, which operate on an x- and y-coordinate whereas the same methods (seen as methods of coloured points) have to operate on an extended state-space, which contains a colour field, too. Using extensible records we are able to write code for point methods generically such that the methods can operate on any state-space which contains at least x- and y-coordinates. Hence our implementation of the *point* methods can be used in a class of coloured points *cpoint* without alteration. This is what we achieve by the following definition:

> **datatype** *colour* = *Red* | *Green* | *Blue*
> **class** *cpoint* = *point* + **fields** *col* :: *colour*

As suggested by above "+" notation, class *cpoint* includes all fields and methods from *point*.

4.4   Overriding

To continue with the example, we define a new class *rectangle*, adding fields w, h and method *area*. Reflecting a rectangle cannot be achieved by simply reflecting the reference point. When reflecting the bottom-left point along the x-axis it becomes the top-left point, so we have to subtract the height of the rectangle from its y-value to fix this. An analogous correction has to be performed for the reflection along the x-axis.

> **class** *rectangle* = *cpoint* +
>
> **fields** w, h :: *nat*
>
> **methods**
>   *area* :: $\{x :: int, y :: int, col :: colour, w :: nat, h :: nat, \ldots\} \to nat$
>   *area* $\{x, y, col, w, h, \ldots\} \equiv w \cdot h$
>
> **override methods**
>   *reflect-X* $\{x, y, col, w, h, \ldots\} \equiv$
>   *this.move* (*point.reflect-X* $\{x, y, col, w, h, \ldots\}$) 0 $(-h)$
>   *reflect-Y* $\{x, y, col, w, h, \ldots\} \equiv$
>   *this.move* (*point.reflect-Y* $\{x, y, col, w, h, \ldots\}$) $(-w)$ 0
>
> **specification**
>   *area* (*move* $\{x, y, col, w, h, \ldots\}$ dx dy) = *area* $\{x, y, col, w, h, \ldots\}$

Apart from *reflect-X* and *reflect-Y* all methods and all lemmas of *cpoint* are inherited. At first sight it appears evident what we mean by saying "all other methods are inherited". But life is not as easy as it seems. Recall the definition of *reflect-O* in *point*: *reflect-O* $\equiv$ *this.reflect-Y* $\circ$ *this.reflect-X*. On the one hand we have inherited this method, on the other hand we have overridden the methods *reflect-X* and *reflect-Y* in *rectangle*. If *this.reflect-X* and *this.reflect-Y* referred statically to the methods defined in *point* the method *reflect-O* would not behave as expected for rectangles. Instead, the references to *reflect-X* and *reflect-Y* in the inherited method *reflect-O* must refer dynamically to the redefined methods. In the following section we will have a closer look at this dynamic binding of methods which sometimes is also called *late-binding*.

4.5   Late-Binding

Late-binding of methods is a powerful mechanism, making reuse of code very flexible. To back up this claim we extend rectangles by a class *rectangle-hilite*. The idea is that relocated rectangles are highlighted in red colour. Without late-binding of methods we would have to redefine *all* methods (except for *area*). The impact of these modifications on the correctness proofs would be disastrous: almost all proofs about rectangles would have to be repeated, quite redundantly though. Using late-binding of methods, the definition of *rectangle-hilite* is very simple because all methods relocating rectangles are defined directly or indirectly in terms of the generic *move*.

> **class** *rectangle-hilite* = *rectangle* +
>
> **override methods**
> > *move* ≡ (*update-colour Red*) ∘ *rectangle.move*
>
> **specification**
> > *col* (*reflect-X* $\{x, y, col, w, h, \ldots\}$) = *Red*
> > *col* (*reflect-Y* $\{x, y, col, w, h, \ldots\}$) = *Red*
> > *col* (*reflect-O* $\{x, y, col, w, h, \ldots\}$) = *Red*

The fact that we can prove these properties of *reflect-X*, *reflect-Y* and *reflect-O* is remarkable. Without having redefined any of these methods, the change of the *move* method has been propagated automatically. This demonstrates that object-oriented verification really does work in our environment.

Now we have arrived at a point where we can clarify the distinction between those methods prefixed by *this* and those which are not. Methods prefixed by *this* are late-bound and may change in subclasses whereas the others are fixed. For a better understanding of the distinction recall equation (4) from *point*:

$$this.move \ (reflect\text{-}X \ p) \ dx \ dy =^{x,y} reflect\text{-}X \ (this.move \ p \ dx \ (-dy))$$

This equation expresses that all implementations of the late-bound method *this.move* in subclasses are well behaved together with the particular implementation *reflect-X* of *point*. Expanding the definition of *reflect-X* – we cannot expand any definition of *this.move* since it is late-bound – in *point* yields:

$$this.move \ (this.move \ p \ 0 \ (-2 \cdot (y \ p))) \ dx \ dy =^{x,y}$$
$$this.move \ (this.move \ p \ dx \ (-dy)) \ 0 \ (-2 \cdot (y \ (this.move \ p \ dx \ (-dy))))$$

Of course, there are implementations of *this.move* invalidating this equation. However, it is true for all those implementations satisfying the equations for *move* given in *point*. Assuming that equations (1)–(3) hold for all implementations of *this.move* in subclasses, we can always show equation (4). This implies that (4) can be inherited in *rectangle-hilite* although method *move* has been overridden. Of course, we do not get all proofs for free. Since we have overridden *move*, we have to redo the proofs for all equations containing a particular implementation of *move* (without prefix *this*, that is).

5   Encoding of Object-Oriented Concepts in HOL

We now show that the object-oriented concepts presented in Sect. 4 are only a stone's throw away from a rigorous encoding in HOL.

States are represented as extensible records and methods as state transforming functions. As we have already seen, we can achieve inheritance simply by record subtyping. Things are getting much more complicated when taking late-binding into account. What makes it hard to model is that the semantics of late-bound methods changes relatively to the position in the inheritance hierarchy. Assuming different field types for different levels of the hierarchy, we can use *overloading* to achieve different meaning of methods in different contexts. Assuming different field types for different levels is no real restriction, since we can always enforce them by adding dummy fields.

5.1   Classes

First of all, the fields of any class definition become a record type definition:

> **record** *point* =
> x, y :: *int*

Methods are more involved. The simplest method of *point* is *move*, because it is not late-bound.

First attempt One might try to realize method *move* in HOL directly as suggested in the *point* class definition:

> **defs**
> $move :: \{x :: int, y :: int, \ldots\} \to int \to int \to \{x :: int, y :: int, \ldots\}$
> $move \{x, y, \ldots\} \; dx \; dy \equiv \{x + dx, y + dy, \ldots\}$

The problem with this definition is that it is too generic. Since *move* is defined for *all* records containing x- and y-coordinates, we cannot override this definition in subclasses any more.

Second attempt To remedy this problem one might *declare* the method generically, but *define* it on concrete records only:

> **defs**
> $move :: \{x :: int, y :: int, \ldots\} \to int \to int \to \{x :: int, y :: int, \ldots\}$
> $move \{x, y\} \; dx \; dy \equiv \{x + dx, y + dy\}$

With this definition we are able to express overriding and late-binding. Overriding is achieved simply by defining *move* on a different concrete instance of the scheme $\{x :: int, y :: int, \ldots\}$, say on $\{x :: int, y :: int, col :: colour\}$. To see, how we can achieve late-binding consider the definition of a method *reset* which sets points to the origin:

> **defs**
> $reset :: \{x :: int, y :: int, \ldots\} \rightarrow \{x :: int, y :: int, \ldots\}$
> $reset \{x, y, \ldots\} \equiv move \{x, y, \ldots\} \ (-x) \ (-y)$

Since we have given no definition of *move* on the extensible record type, its semantics and hence the semantics of *reset* is unspecified. Restricting the extensible record type to the concrete one $\{x :: int, y :: int\}$, determines a meaning as given by definition of *move*. Restricting it to a different concrete record may result in a different meaning, depending on the definition of *move* given there.

There is still a snag: we have ruled out inheritance. By defining *move* on a concrete record type we lose the ability to reuse code in subclasses.

The solution To achieve both overriding and inheritance, we define two constants *point.move* and *this.move* rather than a single constant *move*, allowing the character "." to be part of identifiers. The actual implementation of the *move* method in HOL is as follows:

> **defs**
> $point.move, this.move ::$
> $\quad \{x :: int, y :: int, \ldots\} \rightarrow int \rightarrow int \rightarrow \{x :: int, y :: int, \ldots\}$
> $point.move \{x, y, \ldots\} \ dx \ dy \equiv \{x + dx, y + dy, \ldots\}$
> $this.move \{x, y\} \equiv point.move \{x, y\}$

Apart from *reflect-O*, the remaining methods are defined analogously. Since *reflect-O* is a *final* method, we have to guarantee that it cannot be overridden. Defining it on an extensible record type achieves this:

> **defs**
> $point.reflect\text{-}O, this.reflect\text{-}O ::$
> $\quad \{x :: int, y :: int, \ldots\} \rightarrow \{x :: int, y :: int, \ldots\}$
> $point.reflect\text{-}O \equiv this.reflect\text{-}Y \circ this.reflect\text{-}X$
> $this.reflect\text{-}O \equiv point.reflect\text{-}O$

The need of two definitions for one method is no real problem for the user. These definitions can be generated automatically by some extra-logical system support.

5.2   Objects and Instantiation

Instantiation is trivial in our framework. Just let $MyPoint \equiv \{x = 3, y = 5\}$. The simplicity of instantiation stems from the fact that we generate both generic *class methods* and concrete *object methods* in classes. In a sense, we have anticipated instantiation already by the way we define classes.

5.3   Inheritance

Inheritance is just as simple as instantiation. For inheritance, all we have to do is specialize the class methods of the superclass to concrete object methods of the subclass. Class *cpoint* leads to the following definitions in HOL:

> **record** *cpoint = point* +
>   *col* :: *colour*
>
> **defs**
>   *this.move* {*x, y, col*} ≡ *point.move* {*x, y, col*}
>   *this.reflect-X* {*x, y, col*} ≡ *point.reflect-X* {*x, y, col*}
>   *this.reflect-Y* {*x, y, col*} ≡ *point.reflect-Y* {*x, y, col*}

Interestingly, we do not have to give a definition for *reflect-O* once more. Since *reflect-O* was defined for the scheme {*x* :: *int, y* :: *int, ...*} its definition works equally well on the concrete type {*x* :: *int, y* :: *int, col* :: *colour*}.

Since the methods have not been altered in *cpoint*, lemmas proved for points also hold for coloured points. Sticking to object-oriented terminology, we might say that the proofs are inherited. In a type-theoretic framework with explicit proof-terms this terminology fits perfectly well (see also [5]).

5.4   Overriding

Class *cpoint* serves as an example for inheritance, but it does not demonstrate overriding. Overriding is achieved simply by defining new methods. In case of class *rectangle* we define methods *rectangle.reflect-X* and *rectangle.reflect-Y*:

> **record** *rectangle = cpoint* +
>   *w, h* :: *nat*
>
> **defs**
>   *rectangle.reflect-X* {*x, y, col, w, h, ...*} ≡
>   *this.move* (*point.reflect-X* {*x, y, col, w, h, ...*}) 0 (−*h*)   (5)
>   *this.reflect-X* {*x, y, col, w, h*} ≡ *rectangle.reflect-X* {*x, y, col, w, h*}
>   *rectangle.reflect-Y* {*x, y, col, w, h, ...*} ≡
>   *this.move* (*point.reflect-Y* {*x, y, col, w, h, ...*}) (−*w*) 0
>   *this.reflect-Y* {*x, y, col, w, h*} ≡ *rectangle.reflect-Y* {*x, y, col, w, h*}

5.5   Late-Binding

Class *rectangle-hilite* is a good example for late-binding of methods. Apart from late-binding, class *rectangle-hilite* is interesting because it introduces no new fields. Since we have identified class membership with field types, we have to tell the field types of *rectangle-hilite* and *rectangle* apart by adding an artificial field *dummy* of type *unit*. For simplicity we omit some obvious method definitions.

> **record** *rectangle-hilite = rectangle* +
>   *dummy* :: *unit*

defs

    rectangle-hilite.move ::

      $\{x :: int, y :: int, col :: colour, w :: nat, h :: nat, dummy :: unit, \ldots\} \rightarrow$

        $\{x :: int, y :: int, col :: colour, w :: nat, h :: nat, dummy :: unit, \ldots\}$

    rectangle-hilite.move $\equiv$ (*update-col Red*) $\circ$ *rectangle.move*   (6)

    this.move $\{x, y, col, w, h, dummy\}$ $\equiv$

      rectangle-hilite.move $\{x, y, col, w, h, dummy\}$ (7)

    this.reflect-X $\{x, y, col, w, h, dummy\}$ $\equiv$

      rectangle.reflect-X $\{x, y, col, w, h, dummy\}$ (8)

In this class, method *move* additionally sets the colour to *Red*. All methods defined in terms of *move* show the same effect, as can be seen by expansion of their definitions. Take for example method *this.reflect-X* (we abbreviate the term *point.reflect-X* $\{x, y, col, w, h, dummy\}$ by Δ):

proof

    this.reflect-X $\{x, y, col, w, h, dummy\}$ $=$ by (8)

    rectangle.reflect-X $\{x, y, col, w, h, dummy\}$ $=$ by (5)

    this.move Δ 0 $(-h)$ $=$ by (7)

    rectangle-hilite.move Δ 0 $(-h)$ $=$ by (6)

    ((*update-col Red*) $\circ$ *rectangle.move*) Δ 0 $(-h)$

Be aware, that *this.reflect-X* may have a completely different meaning on different state spaces.

6   Object-Oriented Verification in HOOL

Subsequently we investigate up to what extent object-oriented concepts, developed to structure programs, provide means to structure verification, too. Since we have introduced two kinds of methods, class methods and object methods, we naturally expect two kinds of lemmas. In the end, though, we are only interested in those lemmas about object methods.

Object methods What distinguishes object methods and class methods, anyhow? There are two main characteristics for object methods: they are prefixed by *this* (which is merely a syntactic convention) and they are only defined on concrete records. Proving lemmas about object methods does not require any particular methodology. Take for example the following equation

    this.move $\{x, y\}$ 0 0 $=^{x,y}$ $\{x, y\}$

which is immediately proven by rewriting. Proving lemmas on object methods directly, though possible in principle, is not very clever: we do not exploit object-oriented structuring principles for verification. We argue now that verification of class methods entails abstract and thus structured verification.

Class methods There are both late-bound and fixed class methods. Late-bound methods are prefixed by *this* (again, this is only a syntactic convention). More importantly, they are *only predeclared*, without fixing a definition yet, e.g $this.move :: \{x :: int, y :: int, \ldots\} \to int \to int \to \{x :: int, y :: int, \ldots\}$. Fixed class methods are prefixed by class names, *declared and defined* on extensible record types and may use late-bound methods for definition. As an example consider:

defs

$$point.reflect\text{-}X :: \{x :: int, y :: int, \ldots\} \to \{x :: int, y :: int, \ldots\}$$
$$point.reflect\text{-}X \ \{x, y, \ldots\} \equiv this.move \ \{x, y, \ldots\} \ 0 \ (-2 \cdot y)$$

For fixed methods not referring to late-bound methods we can prove lemmas directly. Take for example equation (1) with every occurrence of *move* replaced by *point.move* – we write (1)[*point.move/move*]. This lemma is immediately proven by rewriting. Since the lemma expresses a property for all state-spaces which contain at least x- and y-coordinates, this lemma holds in all subclasses as long as method *point.move* is inherited. The same holds for the next three equations. By restricting the state-space to concrete records, we get the corresponding lemmas for object methods for free (by HOL type instantiation).

What happens if fixed methods refer to late-bound methods? Since late-bound methods are only declared, we cannot expect non-trivial lemmas to hold for such methods. To prove interesting lemmas we have to assume properties of the late-bound methods. For class definitions we apply the convention that the lemmas are ordered by position and (implicitly) have the preceding lemmas as assumptions. To be precise, the n-th lemma of *point* is translated to the following formula in HOL (where (i) stands for the i-th lemma of *point*, and [*this.m/m*] or [*point.m/m*] for prefixing all non-prefixed methods by *this* or *point*, respectively):

$$\bigwedge_{i=1}^{n-1} (i)[this.m/m] \Rightarrow (n)[point.m/m]$$

The question arising immediately is how to get rid of assumptions. On the one hand, we cannot discharge them in classes (which are basically abstract theories). On the other hand, assumptions can be eliminated in any concrete instance, where class methods are specialized to object methods.

Finally, we explain observational equality $=^{x,y}$ which is defined as follows:

defs

$$=^{x,y} :: \{x :: int, y :: int, \ldots\} \to \{x :: int, y :: int, \ldots\} \to bool$$
$$p =^{x,y} q \equiv (x \ p) = (x \ q) \wedge (y \ p) = (y \ q)$$

We use observational equality $=^{x,y}$ rather than ordinary equality for specification in cases when we only want to fix the meaning of methods on the coordinates. To see why this is more appropriate than actual equality, recall the definition of *move* in *rectangle-hilite*: for full equality, equation (1) would no longer hold in *rectangle-hilite* because the *col* field is manipulated there.

Let us leave our running example and see what we have achieved. We can specify non-late-bound class methods generically and thus inherit the proofs in subclasses immediately. To deal with late-bound methods we have to add assumptions to the equations to be proven. But we know that in all subclasses we can discharge the assumptions.

What happens if we override methods? Depending on which kind of method is used we get different consequences. If a method is late-bound, we cannot use any information about its implementation for the correctness proof and hence we can inherit the proof even if the method is overridden. If a method occurs non-late-bound at least once, we have to perform a new proof.

So to cut a long story short, appropriate use of late-bound methods does not only cater for flexible reuse of code, it also provides a mechanism for generic and thus reusable correctness proofs.

7   Conclusions

Stocktaking. We have seen how to obtain extensible records with structural subtyping in HOL in a very natural way. Records have been encoded as nested tuples with a special "more" slot for extension, structural subtyping turned out to be subsumed by parametric polymorphism. We also employed overloading to account for overridable methods and late-binding. Together with concrete syntax and some minimal extra-logical system support we arrived at an environment for object-oriented specification and verification (HOOL).

The only major object-oriented concept we have not dealt with explicitly in this paper is encapsulation (hiding). Due to the lack of existential types in HOL, we cannot use the standard trick [7] for data abstraction. Any abstract theory mechanism, e. g. axiomatic type classes [13], achieves abstraction from concrete implementations as well.

Note that in actual verification tasks, simple concepts like type classes are more convenient than existential types. In particular, method invocation is quite involved in encodings based on existential types [11]: the encapsulated state has to be opened and (in the case of state-modifying methods) be repacked again.

Related Work. Modeling object-oriented concepts has become a vast field of research in itself. We only give a few hints of how HOOL is related to other work in the context of theorem proving in higher-order logics.

Hensel et al. [4] define an object-oriented specification language based on co-algebra and give a translation to generic higher-order logic. This translation, though, does not fully preserve the object-oriented structure. Yet it is quite independent of the underlying logic and thus allows to do the reasoning about classes in different target theorem proving systems (e. g. PVS, Isabelle).

Hofmann et al. [5] employ type theory (ECC) for object-oriented verification. They use object-oriented concepts in a very similar way. Compared with their work, the most important contribution of HOOL is its simplicity. It does not require any advanced type theoretical concepts such as dependent types and Σ-types for the encoding. Nevertheless, HOOL can compete with their approach quite well since the resulting expressiveness is almost the same from the user's point of view. Restricting to the much simpler HOL logical framework, though, pays off by shortening the effort for correctness proofs substantially.

Naraschewski [9] proposed an environment for object-oriented verification similar to HOOL, but based on a rather different encoding of objects in ECC. Though Naraschewski sketched a translation from this environment to an encoding in LEGO, there are two drawbacks of this approach. First, translating the proposed environment to the LEGO system would require extensive extralogical support. Second, the encoding in LEGO, though feasible in principle, is not directly applicable for practical work.

Does object-oriented verification actually pay off in practice? The only case-study performed so far deals with a hierarchy of collection classes [8]. It turned out that late-binding of methods really helps to structure verification. Using the complicated encoding of [5], though, it was not possible to scale up to larger examples. With the simple encoding of object-oriented concepts in HOOL, we expect to have overcome these limitations.

References

1. P. B. Andrews. *An Introduction to Mathematical Logic and Type Theory: To Truth Through Proof.* Academic Press, 1986.
2. A. Church. A formulation of the simple theory of types. *Journal of Symbolic Logic*, pages 56–68, 1940.
3. M. J. C. Gordon and T. F. Melham (editors). *Introduction to HOL: A theorem proving environment for higher order logic.* Cambridge University Press, 1993.
4. U. Hensel, M. Huisman, B. Jacobs, and H. Tews. Reasoning about classes in object-oriented languages: Logical models and tools. In *Proceedings of ESOP/ETAPS*, volume 1381 of *Lecture Notes in Computer Science*. Springer-Verlag, 1998.
5. M. Hofmann, W. Naraschewski, M. Steffen, and T. Stroup. Inheritance of proofs. *Theory and Practice of Object Systems, Special Issue on Third Workshop on Foundations of Object-Oriented Languages (FOOL 3)*, 4(1):51–69, 1998.
6. L. Lamport and L. C. Paulson. Should your specification language be typed? Technical Report 425, University of Cambridge Computer Laboratory, 1997.
7. J. C. Mitchell and G. D. Plotkin. Abstract types have existential type. *ACM Trans. Prog. Lang. Syst.*, 10(3):470–502, July 1988.
8. W. Naraschewski. *Object-Oriented Proof Principles using the Proof-Assistant Lego.* Diplomarbeit, Universität Erlangen, 1996.
9. W. Naraschewski. Towards an object-oriented progification language. In E. L. Gunter and A. Felty, editors, *Theorem Proving in Higher Order Logics: 10th International Conference, TPHOLs'97*, volume 1275 of *Lecture Notes in Computer Science*, pages 215–230. Springer-Verlag, 1997.
10. L. C. Paulson. *Isabelle: A Generic Theorem Prover*, volume 828 of *Lecture Notes in Computer Science*. Springer-Verlag, 1994.
11. B. C. Pierce and D. N. Turner. Simple type-theoretic foundations for object-oriented programming. *Journal of Functional Programming*, 4(2):207–247, 1994.
12. A. Pitts. The HOL logic. In Gordon and Melham [3], pages 191–232.
13. M. Wenzel. Type classes and overloading in higher-order logic. In E. L. Gunter and A. Felty, editors, *Theorem Proving in Higher Order Logics: 10th International Conference, TPHOLs'97*, volume 1275 of *Lecture Notes in Computer Science*, pages 307–322. Springer-Verlag, 1997.

On the Effectiveness of Theorem Proving Guided Discovery of Formal Assertions for a Register Allocator in a High-Level Synthesis System*

Naren Narasimhan and Ranga Vemuri

Laboratory for Digital Design Environments
Department of ECECS, University of Cincinnati
PO Box 210030, Cincinnati, OH 45221, USA
{naren,ranga}@ececs.uc.edu

Abstract. This paper presents a formal specification and a proof of correctness for the register optimization task in high-level synthesis. A widely implemented register optimization algorithm is modeled in higher-order logic and verified in a theorem prover environment. A rich collection of correctness properties is systematically formulated during the theorem proving exercise. These properties constitute a detailed set of formal assertions that are identified with the invariants at various stages of the algorithm. The formal assertions are then embedded as programming assertions in the implementation of the register optimization algorithm in a production-strength high-level synthesis system. When turned on, the programming assertions (1) certify whether a specific run of the high-level synthesis system produced designs with error-free register allocation and, (2) in the event of a failure, help discover and isolate programming errors in the implementation.

We present a detailed example and supporting experimental data to demonstrate the effectiveness of these assertions in discovering and isolating errors. Based on this experience, we discuss the role of the formal theorem proving exercise in discovering a useful set of assertions for embedding in the register optimization implementation and argue that in the absence of using the mechanical proof checking effort it would have been very hard if not impossible to discover a set of assertions so useful and expressed with such precision.

1 Introduction

High-level synthesis (HLS) is the process of generating register-transfer level (RTL) designs from behavioral specifications [4, 16]. Research in this area over the past two decades has resulted in the emergence of relatively mature software tool implementations. Like any large and complex software system, HLS tools are prone to conceptual and programming errors leading to incorrect synthesis

* This work was partially supported by the DARPA and monitored by the FBI, under contract number J-FBI-93-116.

of RTL designs. Development of efficient and reliable validation methods for high-level synthesis is therefore of crucial importance.

With increase in design functionality and complexity, simulation based techniques are fast proving to be inadequate. On the other hand, scope of formal verification tools within the realm of synthesis is limited since establishing the proof of ⊢ *Implementation* ⇒ Specification is hard. Formal verification as a post-design activity is rather tedious, often resulting in a tremendous strain on the verification tool and the verification engineer. The information on how the specification was refined into an implementation is no longer available at the end of synthesis. This loss of information is a major stumbling block in large scale application of formal methods to the validation of synthesized RTL designs.

Several researchers have proposed alternatives to the post-synthesis verification effort. Formal hardware synthesis offers a solution to this verification problem by providing a methodology for formally deriving the synthesis result within some logical calculus. The idea of formal hardware synthesis was originally proposed by Johnson [19]. Since then several formal techniques have been proposed [6,8,12,20] wherein a specification could be interactively refined into an implementation employing formal logic. Another approach to formal synthesis is to tightly integrate a formal verification engine with a conventional synthesis flow so that the output of each task in synthesis is formally verified thus guaranteeing a correct hardware design. Eisenbiegler et al. [2] introduced a general scheme for formally embedding high level synthesis algorithms in HOL [11].

2   Motivation

Formal Verification of RTL designs generated in a conventional high-level synthesis environment has long been a challenge. In HLS, a behavioral specification is passed through a series of optimization and mapping stages leading finally to an RTL design. The synthesis flow is usually comprised of the following four main stages:

- The *Scheduling Stage:* This stage specifies the partial order between the operations in the input specification. Each data and control operation is bound to a time step. The operations may also be mapped to functional units in a component library during this stage.
- The *Register Allocation Stage:* Carriers in the specification, and those additionally identified during the scheduling phase are mapped to physical registers.
- The *Binding Stage:* Interconnection among the different components in the design is established.
- The *Control Generation Stage:* A controller is generated to sequence the operations in the RTL design.

Very efficient algorithms exist to realize the various stages in conventional high-level synthesis. But the algorithmic complexities involved renders the verification process in a formal proof system rather difficult. The verification approach presented in this paper attempts to bypass this problem. We propose a *Formal Assertions* based verification technique for high-level synthesis. The approach works under the premise that, if each stage in a synthesis system can be verified to perform correct modifications on its input, then we can assert that the synthesized RTL design would be equivalent to its input specification.

In this paper, we describe the formal specification and verification of a register optimization algorithm for high-level synthesis. We then apply the formalism achieved to verify an actual implementation of the algorithm in a conventional HLS system. An appealing aspect of our approach is that the verification exercise is conducted within the framework of the synthesis environment thus avoiding the complexities involved in integrating the synthesis system with a verification tool. By seamlessly integrating with conventional automatic synthesis, our approach introduces a formalism into the implementation of the synthesis sub-tasks that is transparent to the designer.

Section 3 presents an outline of our verification approach. In Sect. 4, we will introduce the verification problem and present the core set of correctness conditions. In Sect. 5, we will present a well known register optimization algorithm and formulate the conditions for our verification approach and discuss the proof strategy. Sections 6 and 7 discusses the applicability of the proof exercise within the context of a high-level synthesis environment. Results presented in Sect. 8 underscore the effectiveness of the approach. We briefly discuss the scope of our verification approach in Sect. 9. Sect. 10 presents some conclusions.

3   Formal Assertions Based Verification – An Overview

Our verification approach is based on higher-order logic theorem proving leading to formal assertions in program code. Each stage in high-level synthesis is well understood and its scope well-defined. The input specification as it passes through each stage in synthesis, undergoes a limited set of modifications that bring it closer to the final RTL design. It is thus possible to succinctly state the specification for each stage in synthesis.

3.1   Verification Outline

- *Characterization:* Identify a base specification model for each synthesis task. This model should cover all aspects of functional correctness for the particular synthesis task. With each task in synthesis being so well-defined, the base specification model is usually a tight set of correctness properties that completely characterizes the synthesis task.
- *Formalization:* The specification model is now formalized as a collection of theorems in a higher-order logic theorem proving environment: these form the base formal assertions. Next, an algorithm is chosen to realize the corresponding synthesis task and is described in the same formal environment.
- *Verification:* The formal description of the algorithm is verified against the theorems that characterize the base specification model. The proof effort is

used to verify the base specification model and enhance it with several additional formal assertions. The formally verified specification model captures the correctness issues and invariants at different stages in the algorithm.

- *Formal Assertions Embedding:* Develop a software implementation of the algorithm that was formally verified in the previous stage. Embed the entire set of formal assertions that make up the specification model of the algorithm, within this software implementation as program assertions. During synthesis, the implementation of each task is continually evaluated against the specification model specified by these assertions and any design error during synthesis can be detected. A high-level synthesis system wherein each task is embedded with its formal specification model constitutes a Formal Synthesis System that strives to generate error-free RTL designs.

In the rest of the paper, we will explain our verification approach in the context of the register allocation task in high-level synthesis.

4   Register Optimization in High-Level Synthesis

Register optimization (allocation), an important problem in high-level synthesis, deals with the minimization of the number of physical registers in synthesized designs. In a behavioral specification, carriers (variables, signals) are used to store values. During scheduling, which often precedes register optimization, additional carriers called temporary variables are introduced to preserve values across clock steps.

4.1   Base Specification Model for Register Optimization Task

Given the above statement for register optimization we will now formulate the correctness conditions for the task. Let C be the set of carriers in the specification. Let $\mathcal{R}_{bag}$ be the set of resulting registers produced by the register optimization algorithm, where each register $R \in \mathcal{R}_{bag}$ is a set of mutually compatible carriers. Any register optimization algorithm is said to be correct provided $\mathcal{R}_{bag}$ is a partition of C and each set $R \in \mathcal{R}_{bag}$ is well-formed. Formally, $\mathcal{R}_{bag}$ must satisfy the following conditions:

1. *Existence:* This condition checks for the completeness of the register allocation task. Each carrier in the specification should be mapped to a register.
   For each carrier $c \in C$, $\exists R \in \mathcal{R}_{bag}$ such that $c \in R$.
2. *Uniqueness:* A carrier in the specification should be bound to a unique register.
   For each carrier $c \in C$, if $\exists R_1, R_2 \in \mathcal{R}_{bag}$, $c \in R_1$ and $c \in R_2$ then, $R_1 = R_2$.
3. *Well-formed:* Carriers bound to the same register are mutually compatible, that is, life-spans of their instances never overlap over the entire specification.
   For each set of carriers $R \in \mathcal{R}_{bag}$, for each pair of carriers $a, b \in R$,
   $compatible(a, b) = true$.

The correctness of any register optimization algorithm can be asserted if the above three verification conditions are actually satisfied by the algorithm.We will present our verification strategy by closely looking at a register optimization algorithm used widely in high-level synthesis.

5 Theory – Formal Verification of a Register Allocation Algorithm

Register optimization techniques in high-level synthesis systems are usually based on graph partitioning or coloring. Minimization algorithms for these graph techniques are known to be either NP-hard [5,9] or NP-complete [13]. However, polynomial time heuristics have been discovered for solving these problems [1,7]. We will describe our verification approach in the context of one such popular heuristic based on compatibility graphs for carrier based register optimization.

5.1 Overview of the Clique Partitioning Algorithm for Register Allocation

Tseng et al. used a polynomial time heuristic [1] that constructs a near-minimal clique partitioning based on exploiting the graph structure. Although, it does not produce optimum results for all graph structures, Tseng's heuristic has become a classical approach widely used in the implementation of high-level synthesis systems.

After life-cycle analysis is completed on all data carriers in the input scheduled graph, a *compatibility graph* $G = (N, E)$ is built, where each node $n \in N$ has a set of carriers associated with it, represented by $C(n)$ where C is a mapping function from the domain of nodes to a range of carrier sets. Any two nodes v, w are connected by an edge $e = (v, w) \in E$ if and only if the carriers that correspond to each node are compatible in their life-cycles, that is their life-cycles do not intersect. A clique of a graph G is a set of vertices that form a complete subgraph of G, i.e., a set where every pair of distinct vertices is adjacent. The result of clique partitioning is a set $\mathcal{R}$ of sets of carriers. Each element in $\mathcal{R}$ is a set of carriers associated with the nodes of a clique. The heuristic attempts to partition the graph into minimum number of cliques i.e. minimize $|\mathcal{R}|$. Each clique corresponds to a physical register.

A slight variation of Tseng's basic clique partitioning heuristic is shown in Fig. 1. The compatibility graph (N, E) is the input to the register optimization task. At the start of the algorithm, the clique set $\mathcal{R}$ is the empty set. Also, each node in the graph has one carrier associated with it. As the algorithm proceeds, cliques are constructed and then added to $\mathcal{R}$. All nodes in the graph have an associated priority predicate that determines if a node is selected in the select_node routine. At the beginning all priorities are set to 0 so that all nodes have an equal chance of being selected. A node is selected if its priority is set to 1 or if it possesses the maximum weight. The weight of a node n is defined to be the sum of its degree and the cardinality of the carrier set, $|C(n)|$ it is

```
procedure clique_partition((N, E))
begin
  R = {}

  for n ∈ N do
      priority(n) ← 0
  end for

  while (N ≠ {})
  x ← select_node()
  Y ← {y|(x, y) ∈ E}
  if |Y| = 0
    then
        N ← N − {x}   /* x represents a clique */
        R ← R ∪ C(x) /* C(x) is a compatibility set of carriers */
    else
        for y ∈ Y do
            I_y ← {z|(y, z) ∉ E}
        end for
        min_val ← min{|I_y ∩ Y| | y ∈ Y}
        Y1 ← {y | y ∈ Y and |I_y ∩ Y| = min_val}
        max_val ← max{|I_y| | y ∈ Y1}
        Y2 ← {y | y ∈ Y1 and |I_y| = max_val}
        y ← a node arbitrarily selected from Y2

        Create a new node z /* merge nodes x and y into z*/
        C(z) ← C(x) ∪ C(y)
        priority(z) ← 1
        Delete nodes x, y and update graph.
        For every node n which is connected to both x and y,
        create an edge connecting n and z;
        Delete nodes x and y and all edges connected to them.
    end if
  end while

  return R
end
```

Fig. 1. Clique partitioning algorithm for register allocation

associated with. If more than one node has the same maximum weight, then a node that has the maximum neighbor weight is selected. Neighbor weight of a node n is defined to be the sum of the weights of its immediate neighbors. In case of a tie, a node is selected from this set of nodes. After choosing a node x using the above criterion, the algorithm proceeds into one of two flows. If the selected node x, has no edges, it is said to represent a maximal clique. The carrier set specified by the mapping $C(n)$, represents the compatibility set or the clique and is added to the register set $\mathcal{R}$. The algorithm proceeds in the other flow if node x has at least one edge incident on it and so is not a maximal clique yet. A match node y is selected from the neighbor set of x using a selection criterion described in the pseudo-code. The two nodes x and y are merged to form a new node z whose carrier set is now equal to the union of the carrier sets of x and y. The priority of the new node z is set high so that it is selected in the next iteration of the algorithm. Node z is included in the compatibility graph and nodes x and y are deleted and the edge set of the graph modified accordingly. The algorithm continues until the node set N of the input compatibility graph is empty. $\mathcal{R}$ now has the final set of near-minimal cliques that can be mapped to distinct hardware registers.

5.2   Formalization of Base Specification Model

The base specification model for the register optimization task described earlier in Sect. 4 is now formalized as theorems in higher-order logic. The formulation is done in the PVS [18] specification language environment.

We adopt the following nomenclature to describe the formulation of the base theorems or base formal assertions. The input compatibility graph CG is represented as a 3 tuple: a graph (N,E), a carrier set function cs that maps each node in N to a set of carriers and a high priority predicate HP associated with each node in CG. Let the clique partitioning algorithm be represented by cpa, a function that takes a compatibility graph CG and an initial register set IR, and generates a final register set FR.

Existence Theorem. The existence theorem shown in Fig. 2 asserts the completeness of the register optimization task. It states that, every carrier in the input compatibility graph should be mapped to some register in the final register set generated by the cpa algorithm. The existence function returns a boolean *true* if every carrier c that a node in the graph is mapped to is also present in some register in the final register set R. Otherwise it returns a *false* indicating an incomplete register allocation.

Uniqueness Theorem. The uniqueness theorem shown in Fig. 3 asserts that, every carrier in the input compatibility graph is present in exactly one register in the final register set generated by cpa. The above assertion is true for a correct register optimization algorithm, provided the following three conditions

```
existence: THEOREM
(FORALL (E: finite_set[edge], FR: registers, HP: high_priority,
        IR: registers, N: finite_set[node], cs: cset):
  FR = cpa(((N, E), cs, HP), IR) =>
                              existence(N, cs, difference(FR, IR)))

existence(N: finite_set[node], cs: cset, R: registers): bool =
FORALL (n: node, c: carrier): member(n, N) AND member(c, cs(n))
       => EXISTS(r: register): member(r, R) AND member(c, r)
```

Fig. 2. Existence theorem for register allocation

hold *true* about the initial register set and the input compatibility graph configuration: (1)The initial register set IR is unique. This is checked by the **unique**
function which returns *true* if for every two registers in its input register set,
the intersection is always the empty set. (2)The node set in the input compatibility graph is unique. This is checked by the **unique_carriers** function which
returns *true* if for two distinct nodes in the compatibility graph, the intersection of their corresponding carrier sets is always the empty set. (3)A uniqueness
property concerning the input node set and the initial register set holds. This is
checked by the **unique_init_reg_carriers** function which returns a true provided for every node in the input node set and register in its input register set,
the intersection is always the empty set.

Wellformed Theorem. The Wellformed theorem shown in Fig. 4 ensures that
only compatible carriers are mapped to the same register. Thus, for every register in the final register set FR, the intersection of the life-cycles of all carriers
belonging to that register is the empty set. Thus, this theorem ensures that carriers whose life-cycles overlap are never grouped together in the same register.
The **compatible** function performs a test on a pair of carriers and returns *true*
if one of the following two conditions is met. (1)Both carriers are associated with
the same node in the input compatibility graph. This is possible only when the
two carriers are the same. (2)The carriers are mappings of two distinct nodes in
the input compatibility graph and these nodes are neighbors (they are directly
connected by an edge).

The above three base theorems specify the functional correctness of a register
optimization algorithm. They make no assumptions about the implementation
details of the algorithm and assert properties that should be satisfied by a correct
carrier-based register optimization task. The theorems pertain to the functional
correctness of the register optimization task and do not concern themselves with
the question whether the algorithm indeed generates an optimal register allocation. If necessary, properties concerning efficiency could be easily formulated as
additional theorems and added to the above list of base theorems.

```
uniqueness: THEOREM
(FORALL (E: finite_set[edge], FR: registers, HP: high_priority,
        IR: registers, N: finite_set[node], cs: cset):
  unique(IR) AND unique_carriers(N, cs)
    AND unique_init_reg_carriers(N, cs, IR)
        AND cpa(((N, E), cs, HP), IR) = FR => unique(FR))

unique(R: registers): bool =
FORALL(r1, r2: register): member(r1, R) AND  member(r2, R)
               AND NOT(r1 = r2) => empty?(intersection(r1, r2));

unique_carriers(N, cs): bool =
FORALL (x, y): member(x, N) AND member(y, N) AND (NOT((x = y)))
                       => empty?(intersection(cs(x), cs(y)));

unique_init_reg_carriers(N, cs, IR): bool =
FORALL(n, r): member(n, N) AND member(r, IR)
                       => empty?(intersection(cs(n), r));
```

Fig. 3. Uniqueness theorem for register allocation

```
wellformed: THEOREM
(FORALL (E: finite_set[edge], FR: registers, HP: high_priority,
        IR: registers, N: finite_set[node], cs: cset):
 cpa(((N, E), cs, HP), IR) = FR
     => well_formed(((N, E), cs, HP), difference(FR, IR)))

well_formed(CG, R): bool =
FORALL(r: register, c1, c2: carrier): member(r, R) AND
   member(c1, r) AND member(c2, r) => compatible(c1, c2, CG);

compatible(c1, c2, CG): bool =
EXISTS(n: node): member(n, proj_1(proj_1(CG))) AND
        member(c1, proj_2(CG)(n)) AND member(c2, proj_2(CG)(n))
OR
EXISTS(n1, n2: node): member(n1, proj_1(proj_1(CG))) AND
 member(n2, proj_1(proj_1(CG))) AND member(c1, proj_2(CG)(n1)) AND
 member(c2, proj_2(CG)(n2)) AND neighbor(n1, n2, proj_1(CG));
```

Fig. 4. Wellformed theorem for register allocation

5.3 Formal Verification of the Clique Partitioning Algorithm for Register Allocation

A formal model of the register allocation algorithm is described in the PVS specification language environment. This model will next be verified against the three base level specifications.

As a means of illustrating our verification approach, we will look closely at the proof structure of one of the base level specification, the **wellformed** theorem. This theorem asserts that a correct register allocation task should preserve the wellformed nature of the input compatibility graph. Figure 5 shows the overall verification tree for the **wellformed** theorem. The base theorem is at the root of the tree and the branch vertices represent the lemmas and axioms used to prove the theorem correct. Each of the lemmas were verified completely. In order to prove certain lemmas, additional lemmas had to be introduced giving rise to a hierarchy of lemmas.

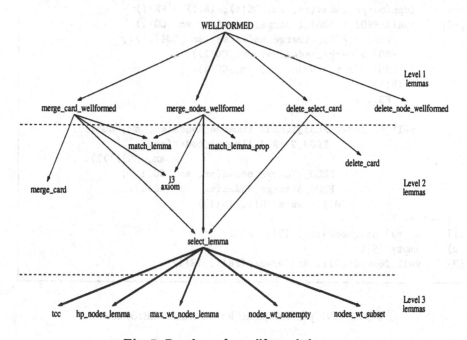

Fig. 5. Proof tree for wellformed theorem

A rich collection of additional correctness properties were then formulated, providing a deeper insight into aspects of the algorithm sensitive to the **wellformed** assertion.

Figure 6 shows a snapshot of the proof trace during the verification of the **wellformed** theorem. In the algorithm shown in Fig. 1, this corresponds to the *else* portion that selects the second node y and merges it with x and then modifies the graph accordingly. Observe how the sequent specifies all that is true about the *else* branch of the algorithm. Formulas [1] and [2] assert that the node set S!1 is nonempty and the neighbor set of the selected node **sn** is nonempty. The cardinality of the node set after merging two nodes is always less than the cardinality of the original node set and this is expressed in Formula {-4}. Formula {-5} is identical to left-hand side of the implication in Formula {-6}. The implication can be established easily by using the **extensionality** proof tactic available in PVS.

```
well_formed.2.2 :

[-1]    select_match(sn, (S!1, E!1)) = sm
[-2]    select_node(CG!1) = sn
[-3]    ((S!1, E!1), cs!1, HP!1) = CG!1
{-4}    card(PROJ_1(PROJ_1(merge_nodes(sn, sm, CG!1)))) < card(S!1)
{-5}    (cpa(merge_nodes(sn, sm, CG!1), IR!1) = FR!1)
{-6}    cpa(((PROJ_1(PROJ_1(merge_nodes(sn, sm, CG!1))),
            PROJ_2(PROJ_1(merge_nodes(sn, sm, CG!1)))),
          PROJ_2(merge_nodes(sn, sm, CG!1)),
          PROJ_3(merge_nodes(sn, sm, CG!1))),
        IR!1)
        = FR!1
        =>
        well_formed(((PROJ_1(PROJ_1(merge_nodes(sn, sm, CG!1))),
                    PROJ_2(PROJ_1(merge_nodes(sn,
                                        sm, CG!1)))),
                  PROJ_2(merge_nodes(sn, sm, CG!1)),
                  PROJ_3(merge_nodes(sn, sm, CG!1))),
                difference(FR!1, IR!1))
  |-------
[1]     empty?(neighbors(sn, (S!1, E!1)))
[2]     empty?(S!1)
[3]     well_formed(CG!1, difference(FR!1, IR!1))
```

Fig. 6. PVS proof sequent: level 1 lemma introduction

The **merge_nodes** function should not alter the compatibility relationships between nodes in the graph. Therefore, Formula [3] follows quite easily from the right-hand side of Formula {-6} provided we make the above assumption about the **merge_nodes** function. This assumption specified as a lemma in Fig. 7 can then be introduced in the proof. By making appropriate substitutions to the lemma, the proof for this particular verification branch can be quite easily discharged.

The proof of **merge_nodes_well_formed_lemma** shown in Fig. 7, in turn required the addition of several lemmas. In particular, one verification branch in

```
merge_nodes_well_formed: LEMMA
FORALL (E: finite_set[edge], HP: high_priority,
        N: finite_set[node], R: registers, cs: cset):
LET CG = ((N, E), cs, HP),
    x = select_node(CG),
    y = select_match(x, (N,E))
IN
    well_formed(merge_nodes(x, y, CG), R) => well_formed(CG, R);
```

Fig. 7. Example of level 1 lemma introduction

the proof for the merge_nodes_well_formed_lemma required us to assert that the
node selection function in the algorithm actually chooses a node from the input
compatibility graph every time it is invoked. We stated this assumption as a
Level 2 Lemma in Fig. 8. The lemma select_lemma states that, if a node set is
nonempty, the select_node function always returns a node that is a member of
this node set.

```
select_lemma: LEMMA
(FORALL (CG: cgraph, n: node):
nonempty?(proj_1(proj_1(CG))) AND select_node(CG) = n
        => member(n, proj_1(proj_1(CG))));
```

Fig. 8. Example of level 2 lemma introduction

The first level lemma select_lemma was proved correct with the introduction
of five additional lemmas (one of which was a type-check condition). These form
the Level 3 lemmas for the wellformed theorem. Figure 9 illustrates one of the
lemmas introduced to prove an assertion about high priority nodes in the input
compatibility graph.

```
hp_nodes_lemma: LEMMA
(FORALL CG):
    high_priority_nodes(CG) = N => subset?(N, proj_1(proj_1(CG)));
```

Fig. 9. Example of level 3 lemma introduction

We adopted a top-down approach to simplify the proof exercise. Theorems are proved using lemmas (Level 1 lemmas) and other appropriate inference rules provided by the proof system. The proofs of the the Level 1 lemmas sometimes require the introduction of additional lemmas (Level 2 lemmas) and sufficient care is taken to ensure that the lemmas that are introduced are consistent and relevant to the verification exercise. These lemmas are next proved and in the course of their proofs, additional lemmas are introduced. This process continues until no more lemmas need to be introduced. The top-down approach results in a well-structured proof exercise. In addition to making the overall proof effort manageable, it has the added advantage of systematically deriving a large set of formal correctness properties (lemmas).

In a large and complex task such as register allocation, it is rather difficult to identify the invariants. This makes the verification of such algorithms a hard problem. Our approach presents a systematic way to identify these invariants and generate them in a formal environment. For the Wellformed theorem alone, a total of 16 correctness properties were derived as a part of the proof exercise. This is significant since, from just one assertion specified by the wellformed theorem, we now have considerably more insight into the correctness issues. A similar proof approach was adopted to verify the other two theorems concerning existence and uniqueness. Thus, starting with three base assertion, we were able to formulate a set of 36 additional formal assertions and invariants as a consequence of the proof exercise.

6   Implementation – Formal Assertions Embedding in Program Code

We will now show how we used the formal assertions that made up the specification model of the register allocation algorithm to verify the implementation of a register optimizer in an existing high-level synthesis system, DSS [10].

The register allocation stage in DSS is implemented using a variation of the clique partitioning heuristic and is closely modeled on the algorithm described in Sect. 5.1.

The theorems and lemmas formulated during the theorem proving exercise constitute a set of formal assertions and invariants that represent the functional specification of the register allocation algorithm. *During an execution run, if the register optimizer is faithful to its formal specification model, we can assert that this would result in correct register allocation.*

Since the formal specification model is formulated in higher-order logic and the implementation (the register optimization stage in DSS) is in the C++ software domain, establishing $\vdash Imp \Rightarrow Spec$ is not a straightforward procedure. The formal assertions in the specification model are translated into C++ program assert statements and embedded in portions of the implementation that correspond to the spatial locality of the task invariants in the formal model of the algorithm. With all the programming asserts in place, we reduce the design verification problem to several, smaller, and much simpler verification problems.

The formally embedded register optimizer performs a series of these equivalence tests during each execution run and thus never permits an erroneous register allocation. Figure 10 shows a flow chart that outlines the organization of the register allocator in DSS with a small sample of the programming assert statements derived from the formal assertions described in Sects. 5.2 and 5.3.

The embedding of the formal assertions in the implementation is shown by the filled bubbles on the edges of the flow chart. Each of these bubbles represents a set of formal assertions. Two of these bubbles have been enlarged for the sake of illustration. The base formal are translated into base programming assertions and placed at the end of the actual implementation and their relative position is shown in the flow chart. They provide a high-level view of the correctness criteria and so need to have a global view of the completed register allocation before testing it for correctness. These base formal assertions behave as very effective watchpoints and detect the presence of any error in the final register allocation. The formal assertions introduced at various levels of hierarchy during the proof exercise are carefully translated into C++ programming assertions. The hierarchy is preserved in the organization of the program assertions. They are more focused and assert facts about specific portions of the register allocation algorithm. By embedding them appropriately in the implementation these facts can be continually checked against the program execution and any violations can be promptly detected. For example, the bubble that is enlarged to show the Level 1 assertions are placed such that they are checked just before the end of every iteration of the while loop. The assertions in this set, due to their spatial locality will be able to detect errors in the implementation sooner than the base theorems. As we go down the levels of hierarchy, the checks instituted by the formal assertions become more fine grained. They focus on finer details of the algorithm and check to see if these details abide by the correctness guidelines laid out by them. The verification approach can thus be extended to as many levels of hierarchy as there are in the formal assertion tree until the source of an error is isolated.

7 Error Detection and Localization – An Example

DSS, since its inception has been used to synthesize over three dozen HLS benchmarks and other large-scale specifications. These design examples were carefully chosen to test a wide range of synthesis issues and tool capabilities and ranged from straight-line arithmetic-dominated specifications to multiple process specifications with complicated synchronization protocols and various combinations of control constructs like conditionals and loops. In fact, this effort was part of a concerted attempt to systematically validate DSS using simulation and formal techniques [14, 15, 17]. During the course of this exercise, sometimes incorrect RTL designs were synthesized. Analysis of these faulty designs eventually lead to the discovery of implementation errors in the HLS system. These errors were distributed over most of the stages in the synthesis system, the register allocation stage being one of them. These errors were identified using systematic

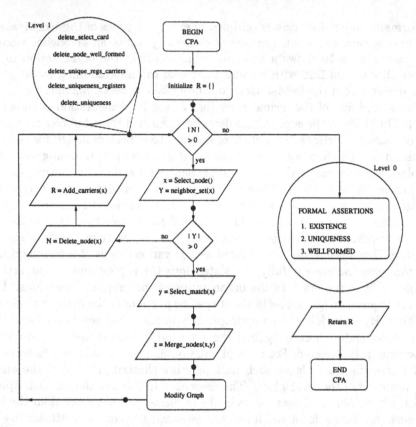

Fig. 10. Outline of register allocator with embedded formal assertions

simulation methods and traditional software debugging aids. This approach to validation presented two main problems: Simulation alone can only substantiate the presence of bugs in the design, not the absence of them. Secondly, the complexity of the synthesis system itself rendered the error trace back often quite laborious and time consuming. With the formal assertions approach, we hope to address both the above problems. In particular, since the formal specification model of the register optimizer is embedded within its implementation (as programming assertions), an incorrect register allocation is almost always guaranteed to violate this specification model. This violation is immediately flagged as an exception and the designer is notified. By systematically enabling the formally derived program assertions, the trace back to the source of the bug can be performed almost effortlessly.

We will walk through a simple error detection exercise in order to illustrate the approach. With only the base assertions enabled, the register optimizer was executed on an input compatibility graph. A bug in the implementation caused the *uniqueness* assertion to fail. Since the source of the error was not immediately evident, Level 1 assertions were enabled and the implementation was re-executed

```
this->Merge_nodes(xnode, ynode);

#ifdef PVS_WELLFORMED_1
    assert(pvs_theorems.merge_card_lemma(graph_bkp, this));
    assert(pvs_theorems.merge_nodes_well_formed(Graph_orig, partSet));
#endif

#ifdef PVS_UNIQUENESS_2
    assert(pvs_theorems.merge_preserve_nodes(this));
#endif

#ifdef PVS_UNIQUENESS_1
    assert(pvs_theorems.merge_nodes_unique_carriers(graph_bkp,this));
    assert(pvs_theorems.unique_init_reg_carriers(graph_bkp,this, partSet));
#endif
```

Fig. 11. Level 1 formal assertions in register optimizer

on the given test case. This time, one of the formal assertions in the Level 1 hierarchy failed; a snapshot of the implementation that includes this assertion is shown boldfaced in Fig. 11. This formal assertion is placed just after the merge_nodes routine and states that, if the unique_init_reg_carriers function (See Uniqueness theorem description in Sect. 4) returns *true* for a set of nodes and an initial register set, then it should return *true* for a node set where two nodes have been merged using the merge_nodes function. A failure of this lemma now gives more information on the nature of the error. On further analysis, we detected the error in the portion of the code that builds the register set and this is shown in Fig. 12. The same set of carriers were added multiple times to the register set and this lead to the violation of the uniqueness property. After selecting a node from the graph, the carriers mapped to this node are erroneously added to the register set. These carriers are later again added to the same register set after a clique is generated leading to duplication of carriers. Thus, the failure of the uniqueness theorem and its associated lemmas help trace the error back to its source.

By constraining the register allocation implementation to abide by its formal specification at every step of the execution run, we can ensure a very efficient and reliable error detection and trace mechanism. Errors can be traced back to their source using a technique of systematically enabling higher levels of formal assertions.

8   Errors Discovered by Formal Assertions Approach

In order to test the effectiveness of the formal assertions approach, the high-level synthesis system was seeded with several programming and conceptual errors in

```
/* select the first node according to neighbor weight calculations */
    xnode =  Select_node();
    partSet → insert(xnode → GetCarriers()); //BUG
#ifdef PVS_UNIQUENESS_2
    assert(pvs_theorems.select_lemma(this, xnode));
#endif
    if (xnode->getAdjacency()->getLength() == 0) //no neighbors
    {
      comGraph->remove(xnode);
      partSet->insert(xnode->GetCarriers());
```

Fig. 12. Bug detection in register optimizer

the formally embedded register optimization stage. These errors represent actual implementation errors that were discovered over a period of time through traditional validation techniques like simulation and code inspections. The purpose of this exercise was to examine the effectiveness of error discovery and show how the trace-back to the source of the program errors could be achieved with little or no intervention. We executed the synthesis system for a number of design examples in order to test our approach. The verification results are shown in Table 1. The number of variables in the examples varied from just 20 to as much as 1000.

In all the test cases, enabling the base formal assertions was sufficient to detect the presence of errors in the register assignments. Columns 3 through 8 show the extent of formal assertions enabling necessary in order to pinpoint the source of the error. For example, enabling Level 1 assertions was sufficient to detect Error 1 for all the test cases. It was observed that while processing some of the test cases, the presence of an error went unnoticed by the embedded formal assertions. The register optimizer terminated successfully in the case of these test cases even though it had errors embedded within it. These are denoted by the *no detect* entries in the table. Upon closer examination of the register allocation for these test cases, we noticed that these errors introduced in the code did not manifest themselves in the final register allocation as a result of which the register allocation for these test cases were correct.

The register optimization routine in DSS is a stable piece of software that has been thoroughly tested for errors over the past few years using traditional techniques. Discovering new errors using our technique was therefore very unlikely. Notably, using the formal assertions approach we were able to quite effortlessly and elegantly detect all errors that were seeded into the implementation, something that previously involved several days of painstaking debugging.

Table 1. Verification results using the formal assertion approach

Test No.	Size (carriers)	Errors detected					
		Error1	Error2	Error3	Error4	Error5	Error6
Test 1	20	{base,1}	no detect	{base}	no detect	{base,1,2}	{base,1}
Test2	40	{base,1}	{base,1}	{base}	{base,1}	{base,1,2}	{base,1}
Test3	120	{base,1}	{base,1}	{base}	{base,1}	{base,1,2}	no detect
Test4	200	{base,1}	{base,1}	{base}	{base,1}	{base,1,2}	{base,1}
Test5	400	{base,1}	{base,1}	no detect	{base,1}	{base,1,2}	{base,1}
Test6	800	{base,1}	{base,1}	{base}	{base,1}	{base,1,2}	{base,1}
Test7	1000	{base,1}	{base,1}	{base}	{base,1}	{base,1,2}	{base,1}

9 Scope of the Verification Effort

The formal assertions technique presented in this paper ensures the detection of an incorrect register allocation should it violate any of the base formal assertions. Therefore, the validity of the verification approach hinges on the completeness of the set of theorems that make up our base specification model. The lemmas formulated during the theorem proving exercise are usually limited to identifying errors that result in violations of any of the base theorems. The completeness of these base formal assertions cannot be formally proved but our experimental results reinforce our confidence in them.

After the completion of the proof exercise, the verified formal assertions are translated into program assertions in the synthesis system. Given the expressive differences between the logic and software domain, the translation process often could get quite complicated. Ultimately, the correctness of the formal assertions approach hinges on this translation process. Convenient data structures exist that allow us to conveniently conduct the translation process and express constructs like $\forall$, $\exists$, set operations etc. Further, the formal assertions are usually expressed in first-order logic and this considerably lowers the complexity involved in the translation process. Sometimes when a theorem cannot be translated directly in the software domain, we develop equivalent formal assertions amenable to the software domain and then formally establish the equivalence relationships to ensure the relevance between them.

For maximum leverage, the formal model of the register allocation algorithm and its software implementation should be modeled on very similar lines. This ensures a 1–1 correspondence between formal assertions and their programming counterparts in the implementation. For register optimization algorithm implementations not based on the algorithm described in Sect. 5.1, the base assertions are still applicable. Lower level formal assertions present limited portability but can be translated into the implementation with some modifications for the same class of compatibility graph algorithms. Porting the formal assertions across a different class of algorithms like conflict graph techniques is restricted and would require additional proof exercises in order to formulate appropriate formal assertions.

The formal assertions approach verifies a single execution run of the synthesis process and guarantees a correct design if the specification is not violated in the process of synthesis. It is therefore entirely feasible that the bugs in the synthesis system go undetected until they manifest themselves during an execution as shown in Table 1.

10   Conclusions

Insertion of assertions and invariants [3] in programs has been known to be an effective technique for establishing the correctness of the outcome of executing the program and for discovering and isolating errors. However, determination of an appropriate set of assertions is often a tedious and error-prone task in itself. In this paper, we made use of mechanical theorem proving to systematically discover a set of sufficiently capable assertions.

An appealing aspect of the formal assertions approach is the systematic incorporation of design verification within a traditional high-level synthesis flow. We conduct the formal verification exercise of the synthesized RTL design in the synthesis environment as the design is being synthesized, avoiding the need for functional verification of the synthesized design later using a formal verification tool or a simulator. The time taken for our "on-the-fly" verification approach scales tolerably with the size of the design being synthesized. This is in contrast with blind post-facto simulation, model checking or theorem proving based verification approaches that do not use any reasoning based on the properties of the synthesis algorithms.

One criticism of this approach may concern the care and effort involved in the the manual process of converting the formal assertions in higher-order logic into program assertions in C++. In our experience, this indeed proved to be a process requiring considerable diligence. Often, we had to express the formal assertions in several different ways in higher-order logic, each time carefully constructing the necessary data-structures in C++ to enable their implementation as program assertions. This process had to be repeated until we discovered a form for the formal assertion that lent itself to straight-forward transliteration into C++. We estimate the entire process of formalization, verification and embedding of the assertions in the implementation took about 300-350 person hours.

Another criticism of this approach concerns the sufficiency of the assertions to isolate an error. An error cannot be caught at its source, but only when it first causes an assertion violation. However, this is a problem with all assertion-based approaches for program correctness. The sufficiency of the base correctness conditions is never formally established; these conditions represent a formalization of our intuitive understanding of a correct register optimizer.

Effort is currently underway to adopt the verification strategy presented in this paper to formalize all the stages of a high-level synthesis system. This approach will allow early detection of errors in the synthesis process before the RTL design is completely generated.

References

1. C. -J Tseng and D. P. Siewiorek. Automated Synthesis of Data Paths in Digital Systems. In *IEEE Transactions on CAD*, July 1986.
2. D. Eisenbiegler, C. Blumenrohr, and R. Kumar. Implementation Issues about the Embedding of Existing High Level Synthesis Algorithms in HOL. In *TPHOL*. Springer, 1996.
3. D. Gries. *The Science of Programming*. Springer-Verlag, 1981.
4. D. D. Gajski, N. D. Dutt, A. C. Wu and S. Y. Lin. *High-Level Synthesis,Introduction to Chip and System Design*. Kluwer Academic Publishers, 1992.
5. D. L. Springer and D. E. Thomas. Exploiting the Special Structure of Conflict and Compatibility Graphs in High-Level Synthesis. In *Proceedings of ICCAD*, pages 254–157, 1990.
6. E. M. Mayger and M. P. Fourman. Integration of Formal Methods with System Design. In A. Halaax and P. B. Denyer, editor, *International Conference on VLSI*, pages 59–70. IFIP Transactions, August 1991.
7. D. E. Thomas et al. *Algorithmic and Register Transfer Level Synthesis: The System Architect's Workbench*. Kluwer Academic Publishers, 1990.
8. F. K. Hanna, M. Longley and N. Daeche. Formal Synthesis of Digital Systems. In *Workshop on Applied Formal Methods for Correct VLSI Design*, pages 532–548. IMEC-IFIP, Elsevier Science Publishers B.V., 1989.
9. M. C. Golumbic. *Algorithmic Graph Theory and Perfect Graphs*. Academic Press, 1980.
10. J. Roy, N. Kumar, R. Dutta and R. Vemuri. DSS: A Distributed High-Level Synthesis System. In *IEEE Design and Test of Computers*, June 1992.
11. M. Gordon and T. Melham, editor. *Introduction to HOL*. Cambridge Univ. Press, Cambridge, England, 1993.
12. M. Larsson. An Engineering Approach to Formal System Design. In Thomas F. Melham and Juanito Camilleri, editor, *Higher Order Logic Theorem Proving and its Applications*, pages 300–315. Springer, September 1994.
13. M. R. Garey and D. S. Johnson. *Computers and Intractability*. W. H. Freeman and Company, New York, 1979.
14. N. Narasimhan and R. Vemuri. Synchronous Controller Models for Synthesis from Communicating VHDL Processes. In *Ninth International Conference on VLSI Design*, pages 198–204, Bangalore, India, January 1996.
15. N. Narasimhan, R. Kalyanaraman, and R. Vemuri. Validation of Synthesized Register-Transfer Level Designs Using Simulation and Formal Verification. In *High Level Design Validation and Test Workshop*, November 1996.
16. R. Camposano and W. Wolf. *High-Level VLSI Synthesis*. Kluwer Academic Publishers, 1991.
17. R. Vemuri et al. Experiences in Functional Validation of a High Level Synthesis System. In *30th ACM/IEEE Design Automation Conference*, pages 194–201, 1993.
18. S. Owre, J. M. Rushby, and N. Shankar. PVS: A Prototype Verification System. In Deepak Kapur, editor, *11th International Conference on Automated Deduction (CADE)*, volume 607, pages 748–752. Springer-Verlag, June 1992.
19. S. D. Johnson. *Synthesis of Digital Designs from Recursion Equations*. MIT, 1984.
20. S. D. Johnson, R. M. Wehrmeister and Bhaskar Bose. On the Interplay of Synthesis and Verification. In *Workshop on Applied Formal Methods for Correct VLSI Design*, pages 385–404. IMEC-IFIP, Elsevier Science Publishers B.V., 1989.

Co-inductive Axiomatization of a Synchronous Language

David Nowak, Jean-René Beauvais, and Jean-Pierre Talpin

IRISA (INRIA Rennes & CNRS)
Campus de Beaulieu, F-35042 Rennes Cédex, France
{nowak,beauvais,talpin}@irisa.fr

Abstract. Over the last decade, the increasing demand for the validation of safety critical systems lead to the development of domain-specific
programming languages (e.g. synchronous languages) and automatic verification tools (e.g. model checkers). Conventionally, the verification of
a reactive system is implemented by specifying a discrete model of the
system (i.e. a finite-state machine) and then checking this model against
temporal properties (e.g. using an automata-based tool). We investigate
the use of a theorem prover, Coq, for the specification of infinite state
systems and for the verification of co-inductive properties.

1 Introduction

1.1 Motivations

In recent years, the verification of safety critical systems has become an area of
increasing importance in computer science because of the constant progression
of software developments in sensitive fields like medicine, communication, trans-
portation and (nuclear) energy. The notion of *reactive system* has emerged to
concentrate on problems related to the control of interaction and response-time
in mission-critical systems. These strong requirements lead to the development
of specific programming languages and related verification tools for reactive systems. The verification of a reactive system is done by elaborating a *discrete* model
of the system (i.e. as a finite-state machine) specified in a dedicated language
(e.g. a synchronous programming language) and then by checking a property
(e.g. liveness, dead-lock freedom, etc) against the model (i.e. model checking).
Synchronous languages (e.g. Esterel [5,4], Lustre [14], Signal [7,3,20], and Argos [17]) have proved to be well adapted to the verification of safety and liveness
properties of reactive systems. For instance, model checking has been used at an
industrial scale to Signal programs to check properties such as liveness, invari-
ance, reachability and attractivity in [15]. Whereas model checking efficiently
decides discrete properties of finite state systems, the use of formal proof systems enables to prove *hybrid properties* about *infinite state systems*. Using a
proof system, we can not only prove the safety and liveness of a reactive system
but also prove its *correctness* and its *completeness*. Such a proof, of course, cannot be done automatically: it requires human-interaction to direct the strategy.

The prover can nonetheless automate its most tedious and mechanical parts. In general, formal proofs of programs are difficult and time-consuming. We show that, in the particular case of modeling a reactive system using the synchronous language Signal, this difficulty is significantly reduced by the elegant combination between a declarative style of programming and a relational style of modeling.

1.2   Outline

We first briefly introduce Signal and co-induction in Coq. It is not the purpose of this paper to give a complete description of these subjects but just a sight on their principles in order to make the understanding of our contribution easier. Interested readers may find more in [1] about Coq, [11] about co-induction in Coq, and [3] about Signal. Our focus is the definition of a trace semantics for the synchronous language Signal in Coq. We give an example of correctness proof derived from our theorem library about Signal programs.

2   Specifying Reactive Systems with Signal

Synchronous languages like Esterel, Lustre, Signal, or Argos assume that computation takes no time. In reality, it means that computation duration is negligible in comparison with reaction time of the system. This *synchronous* hypothesis is particularly well adapted to verify safety and some forms of liveness.

Signal is a synchronous, declarative, data-flow oriented programming language. It is built around a simple paradigm: a process is a system of equations on signals; and a minimal kernel of *primitives processes*. A signal represents an infinite flow of data. At every instant, it can be absent or present with a value. The instants where values are present are determined by its associated clock.

The primitive processes are introduced in Fig. 1. The symbol := defines an equality between a signal and an expression. It is not an assignment. *Instantaneous relations* are used to specify relations between signals that must be verified at each instant. Hence, the signals involved in an instantaneous relation must be synchronous i.e. at an instant, they must either be all absent or all present. The when operator is used to select some values of a signal according to a boolean condition. x when y is the *down-sampling* of the signal x when y is present and

v	value	$P ::= R(x_1, \cdots, x_n)$	instantaneous relation
x, x_i, y, z	signal	$\mid z := x$ when y	down-sampling
P, P'	process	$\mid z := x$ default y	deterministic merge
R	relation	$\mid y := x\$ init v	delay
		$\mid P|P'$	parallel composition
		$\mid P/x$	restriction

Fig. 1. Signal-kernel

true. *Deterministic merge* of two signal is done by the default operator (with priority to the left signal). It is possible to access to the previous value (*delay*) of a signal x with $x\$$ init v (v is the initial value). The equation $y := x\$$ init v implies that x and y are synchronous. *Parallel composition* is the union of two systems of equations. *Restriction* enables to declare local signals.

The Signal compiler analyses the consistency of the system of equations. It determines whether the synchronization constraints between the signals can be satisfied or not. It determines whether the causal relations between the signals do not form a cycle (i.e. are deadlock free). The Signal compiler then automatically produces executable code in C, Fortran, Ada, or VHDL.

Table 1 illustrates each of the primitives with a trace. The symbol $\perp$ denotes the absence of a signal.

Table 1. Example of traces

x	-1 2 6 3 -5 12 7 -3 -8 13 ...
$y := x + 1$	0 3 7 4 -4 13 8 -2 -7 14 ...
$zy := y\$$ init 0	0 0 3 7 4 -4 13 8 -2 -7 ...
$py := zy$ when $zy > 0$	$\perp$ $\perp$ 3 7 4 $\perp$ 13 8 $\perp$ $\perp$ ...
$z := py$ default (0 when (event x))	0 0 3 7 4 0 13 8 0 0 ...

The rest of the language is built upon the above kernel. Derived operators are defined from the primitive operators, providing programming comfort. E.g., synchro$\{x, y\}$ constrains the signals x and y to be synchronous, i.e. their clocks to be equal. The process $y := $ event x gives the clock of y i.e. if x is present with any value then y is present and true else y is absent. The process $y := $ when x gives the clock y of occurrences of the boolean signal x at the value *true* i.e. if x is present with the value *true* then y is present and true else y is absent. The process $z := x$ cell y memorizes values of x and outputs them when y is true. Delays can be made of n instants, or on windows of n past values. Arrays of signals and of processes are available as well.

Example. We design a counter modulo n (This kind of counter is useful to design a watch [8]). This process[1] has a constant parameter n. It has two input signals top_sortie and top_incr which are respectively present when the counter value is required and when the counter value must be incremented. These two signals do not have values. We say that they are of type *event* which is a subtype of *bool* i.e. that they can only be absent or present with the value *true*. The process also has two output signals cpt (the value of the counter) and raz (the event which is present when the counter is reset to 0). In Signal, we write:

---

[1] In Signal, a reactive system can be designed modularly as a set of processes. The keyword **process** associates a name and an interface to a set of equations.

```
process mod_counter =
  {integer n}
  (? event top_sortie, top_incr
   ! integer cpt; event raz)
```

The counter must be incremented when the signal top_incr is present, or else it keeps its old value (called zcpt):

```
(| zcpt := cpt$ init 0
 | cpt := (zcpt+1) mod n when top_incr
          default zcpt
```

The counter value must be computed at each tick of top_sortie and top_incr:

```
 | synchro{cpt, top_sortie default top_incr}
```

The signal raz must be present when top_incr is present and cpt is equal to 0:

```
 | raz := when cpt=0 when top_incr |)/zcpt
```

The compiler automatically verifies these equations and produce executable code. This Signal specification is very similar to the specification in natural language.

Example. It is not always so easy to specify a reactive system in Signal. For example, the Fig. 2 is a general purpose counter which is supposed to count from an initial parameter n up to infinity. The output y is the infinite sequence of integers starting at n+1. The frequency of the output y is given as an input signal x. Each time x is present (provided from the environment), the next value of the counter is instantaneously output (signal y). This specification cannot be directly written in Signal. It is expressed saying that x and y are synchronous signals (x^=y), and output y is the previous value of y incremented by one.

```
process counter = {integer n}(? integer x ! integer y)
(|   x ^= y
 | zy := y$ init n
 |   y := zy+1 |)/zy
```

Fig. 2. A counter in Signal

How can we verify that the program Fig. 2 meets the informal specification "The infinite sequence of integers starting at n+1 up to infinity"? Obviously, this can not be done using model checking. This paper presents an axiomatization which enables to prove this kind of stream specification.

3   Using C-induction in Coq

Coq [1] is a proof assistant for higher-order logic. It allows the development of computer programs that are consistent with their formal specification. The logical language used in Coq is a variety of type theory, the *Calculus of Inductive Constructions* [23]. It has recently been extended with *co-inductive types* [11] to handle infinite objects and is thus well suited to represent signals.

3.1   Relation to Previous Work

As Signal handles infinite flows of data, we face the problem of representing and manipulating infinite objects: traces of signals. A first solution, consists of viewing signals as infinite sequences. In this setting, a signal is represented by a function which associates any instant i (a natural number) with the value v of the signal (if it is present) or with $\perp$ (if it is absent). This solution is used in [2] to handle Lustre programs in PVS and in [12] and [13] to handle Silage programs in HOL. The declarative and equational style of Signal is similar to Lustre. However, Lustre programs always have a unique reference of logical time: they are *endochronous*. Signal specifications differ from Lustre programs in that they can be *exochronous* (i.e they can have many references of logical time). For example, the process x:=1 | y:=2 does not constrain the clocks of x and y to be equal. Hence, had we used functions over infinite sequences to represent signals, we would have faced the burden of having to manipulate several, possibly unrelated, indexes of time i; but also the problem of having no higher-order unification available from Coq.

In [21], a circuit is represented as a function from the stream of inputs to the stream of outputs. By contrast, in Signal, a circuit is represented as a set of relations between the streams of inputs and the streams of outputs. We cannot define primitive processes as stream functions because Signal is a declarative language.

For the above reasons, we chose to view the infinite traces of signals as *co-inductive types* [11] and Signal programs as *co-inductive relations*. In [10] and [9], co-inductive types are used to verify reactive systems encoded in CBS (Calculus of Broadcasting Systems) [22]. Within Coq, this model allows to develop both proofs of co-inductive properties and also proofs of inductive properties of signals, as usual. The combined use of induction and co-induction enriches the expressive power of checkable properties.

4   Co-inductive Definition of Signals

A signal x is defined as a stream of $\perp$ and values v. The dot is the constructor of streams.

$$x ::= (\perp|v).x$$

In the sequel of this paper, we will need to prove stream equality co-inductively. The definitional equality of streams is not sufficient. We expect that two streams differently defined but with the same elements are equal. As in [9], we use extensional equality. The extensional equality predicate **EqSt** is the largest relation verifying the following axiom:

$$(\forall s_1)(\forall s_2)\mathsf{hd}(s_1) = \mathsf{hd}(s_2) \wedge \mathbf{EqSt}(\mathsf{tl}(s_1), \mathsf{tl}(s_2)) \Rightarrow \mathbf{EqSt}(s_1, s_2)$$

And we add the following extensionality axiom:

$$(\forall s_1)(\forall s_2)\mathbf{EqSt}(s_1, s_2) \Rightarrow s_1 = s_2$$

5   Co-inductive Definitions of Primitive Processes

Let us recall that a primitive process is not a function but only a relation between signals. This is why every primitive process is denoted by a co-inductive predicate which is the largest relation verifying a list of axioms. Practically, the difference from an inductive definition, is that it is possible to use infinitely many axioms from co-inductive definitions.

The parallel composition is denoted by the logical *and* of the underlying logic and the restriction is denoted by an existential quantifier.

Instantaneous Relation. The relation R_P^n is used to specify an instantaneous relation between n signals. At each instant, these signals verify the inductive predicate P. For all inductive predicate P, for all $n \in I\!N$, R_P^n is the largest relation verifying these axioms:

$$
\begin{array}{ll}
\mathrm{R}_1: & (\forall x_i)_{i=1,\cdots,n} \qquad\qquad R_P^n(x_1, \cdots, x_n) \Rightarrow R_P^n(\bot.x_1, \cdots, \bot.x_n) \\[2mm]
\mathrm{R}_2: & (\forall x_i)_{i=1,\cdots,n}(\forall v_i)_{i=1,\cdots,n} \left\{ \begin{array}{l} R_P^n(x_1, \cdots, x_n) \\ P(v_1, \cdots, v_n) \end{array} \right. \Rightarrow R_P^n(v_1.x_1, \cdots, v_n.x_n)
\end{array}
$$

Down-Sampling. $\mathbf{When}(x, y, z)$ means that z down-sample x when x is present and y is present with the value *true*. **When** is the largest relation verifying the following axioms:

$$
\begin{array}{lll}
\mathrm{W}_1: & (\forall x)(\forall y)(\forall z) & \mathbf{When}(x, y, z) \Rightarrow \mathbf{When}(\bot.x, \bot.y, \bot.z) \\
\mathrm{W}_2: & (\forall x)(\forall y)(\forall z)(\forall b) & \mathbf{When}(x, y, z) \Rightarrow \mathbf{When}(\bot.x, b.y, \bot.z) \\
\mathrm{W}_3: & (\forall x)(\forall y)(\forall z)(\forall v) & \mathbf{When}(x, y, z) \Rightarrow \mathbf{When}(v.x, \bot.y, \bot.z) \\
\mathrm{W}_4: & (\forall x)(\forall y)(\forall z)(\forall v) & \mathbf{When}(x, y, z) \Rightarrow \mathbf{When}(v.x, false.y, \bot.z) \\
\mathrm{W}_5: & (\forall x)(\forall y)(\forall z)(\forall v) & \mathbf{When}(x, y, z) \Rightarrow \mathbf{When}(v.x, true.y, v.z)
\end{array}
$$

Deterministic Merge. $\mathbf{Default}(x, y, z)$ means that x and y are merged in z with the priority to x. **Default** is the largest relation verifying:

$$
\begin{array}{lll}
\mathrm{D}_1: & (\forall x)(\forall y)(\forall z) & \mathbf{Default}(x, y, z) \Rightarrow \mathbf{Default}(\bot.x, \bot.y, \bot.z) \\
\mathrm{D}_2: & (\forall x)(\forall y)(\forall z)(\forall v) & \mathbf{Default}(x, y, z) \Rightarrow \mathbf{Default}(\bot.x, v.y, v.z) \\
\mathrm{D}_3: & (\forall x)(\forall y)(\forall z)(\forall v) & \mathbf{Default}(x, y, z) \Rightarrow \mathbf{Default}(v.x, \bot.y, v.z) \\
\mathrm{D}_4: & (\forall x)(\forall y)(\forall z)(\forall u)(\forall v) & \mathbf{Default}(x, y, z) \Rightarrow \mathbf{Default}(u.x, v.y, u.z)
\end{array}
$$

Delay. The co-inductive predicate **Pre** is used to access to the previous value of a signal. **Pre** is the largest relation verifying:

$$P_1: \quad (\forall x)(\forall y)(\forall v) \qquad \mathbf{Pre}(v,x,y) \Rightarrow \mathbf{Pre}(v, \bot.x, \bot.y)$$
$$P_2: \quad (\forall x)(\forall y)(\forall u)(\forall v) \quad \mathbf{Pre}(v,x,y) \Rightarrow \mathbf{Pre}(u, v.x, u.y)$$

The Table 2 shows an example of traces verifying the equation $\mathbf{Pre}(v,x,y)$. By definition, x and y must be synchronous. This is why the axiom P_1 states that a $\bot$ in x correspond to a $\bot$ in y. And, informally speaking, P_2 states that if x was present at the previous instant then its value was u and the value of y was the previous stored state v.

Table 2. example of **Pre**

x	5	0	$\bot$	9	$\bot$	$\bot$	12	...
y	v	5	$\bot$	0	$\bot$	$\bot$	9	...

Derived Operators. With the previous defined denotations of primitive processes, we derive the denotations of the derived operators of Signal. **Constant** is used to declare a constant signal. $\mathbf{Constant}(v,x)$ means that at each instant, x is absent or present with the value v. **Constant** is defined by:

$$\mathbf{Constant}(v,x) =_{\mathrm{def}} R^1_{\lambda u. u = v}(x)$$

$\mathbf{Id}(x,y)$ identifies two signals x and y. At each instant, they must be both absent or both present with the same value. **Id** is defined by:

$$\mathbf{Id}(x,y) =_{\mathrm{def}} R^2_{\lambda u. \lambda v. u = v}(x,y)$$

Op is used to apply a binary scalar function at each instant where signals are present. As it is defined with R^3_P, $\mathbf{Op}(o,x,y,z)$ implies that the signals x, y and z are present at the same instants. **Op** is defined by:

$$\mathbf{Op}(o,x,y,z) =_{\mathrm{def}} R^3_{\lambda u. \lambda v. \lambda w. w = o(u,v)}(x,y,z)$$

It is possible to manipulate the clock of a signal (i.e. the instants where it is present) with **Event**. $\mathbf{Event}(x,y)$ means that y is the clock of x. A clock is represented as a signal which can only be absent or present with $true$. **Event** is defined by:

$$\mathbf{Event}(x,y) =_{\mathrm{def}} (\mathbf{Op}(\lambda u. \lambda v. true, x, x, y)$$

It is also possible to constrain two signals to have the same clock. **Synchro** is defined by:

$$\mathbf{Synchro}(x,y) =_{\mathrm{def}} (\exists cx)(\exists cy)(\exists z)$$
$$\mathbf{Event}(x,cx) \wedge \mathbf{Event}(y,cy) \wedge \mathbf{Op}(=, cx, cy, z)$$

Example. The denotation of the process *Counter* is:

$$(\forall v)(\forall x)(\forall y)(\exists zy)(\exists one)$$
$$(\textbf{Synchro}(x,y)\wedge$$
$$\textbf{Pre}(v,y,zy)\wedge$$
$$\textbf{Constant}(1,one)\wedge$$
$$\textbf{Op}(plus,zy,one,y))$$

It is only a syntactic transformation from the Signal syntax to the Coq syntax that could be automated.

6   Clock Calculus

In order to infer the clock properties of primitive processes, we first define some clock operators co-inductively.

We define co-inductively the function $\hat{\,\cdot\,}$ which extract the clock of a signal. It is the greatest fixpoint of the following functor F:

$$F(f) = \begin{cases} \bot.x \longmapsto \bot.f(x) \\ v.x \longmapsto true.f(x) \end{cases} \qquad \hat{\,\cdot\,} = gfp(F)$$

We define co-inductively the function $[.]$ which extract the *true* instants of a boolean signal. It is the greatest fixpoint of the following functor F:

$$F(f) = \begin{cases} \bot.x \longmapsto \bot.f(x) \\ false.x \longmapsto \bot.f(x) \\ true.x \longmapsto true.f(x) \end{cases} \qquad [.] = gfp(F)$$

We define co-inductively the function $\hat{*}$ which extract the common instants of two clocks. It is the greatest fixpoint of the following functor F:

$$F(f) = \begin{cases} (\bot.x, \bot.y) \longmapsto \bot.f(x,y) \\ (\bot.x, true.y) \longmapsto \bot.f(x,y) \\ (true.x, \bot.y) \longmapsto \bot.f(x,y) \\ (true.x, true.y) \longmapsto true.f(x,y) \end{cases} \qquad \hat{*} = gfp(F)$$

We define co-inductively the function $\hat{+}$ which extract the union of the instants of two clocks. It is the greatest fixpoint of the following functor F:

$$F(f) = \begin{cases} (\bot.x, \bot.y) \longmapsto \bot.f(x,y) \\ (\bot.x, true.y) \longmapsto true.f(x,y) \\ (true.x, \bot.y) \longmapsto true.f(x,y) \\ (true.x, true.y) \longmapsto true.f(x,y) \end{cases} \qquad \hat{+} = gfp(F)$$

With these definitions we can easily prove the following clock properties of primitive processes:

Proposition 1 (Clock calculus). *For all inductive predicate P, for all n ∈ ℕ:*

$$(\forall x_i)_{i=1,\cdots,n}\; R_P^n(x_1,\cdots,x_n) \Rightarrow \widehat{x_1} = \cdots = \widehat{x_n}$$
$$(\forall x)(\forall y)(\forall v)\; \mathbf{Pre}(v,x,y) \Rightarrow \widehat{x} = \widehat{y}$$
$$(\forall x)(\forall y)(\forall z)\; \mathbf{When}(x,y,z) \Rightarrow \widehat{z} = \widehat{x} \,\widehat{*}\, [y]$$
$$(\forall x)(\forall y)(\forall z)\; \mathbf{Default}(x,y,z) \Rightarrow \widehat{z} = \widehat{x} \,\widehat{+}\, \widehat{y}$$

7 Co-inductive Properties of Signal Specifications

In the sequel of this paper, every variable is implicitly universally quantified.

7.1 Fairness of a Signal

An important hypothesis of the synchronous programming model is that a signal is assumed to have the property of being present (with a value) within a finite deadline (a set of instants). In Signal, this property is translated into the assumption that there only exists a finite number of ⊥ between two values of a signal (the so-called stuttering-robustness property). We formalize this property using the co-inductive predicate *OnlyFiniteAbsent*. This property about an infinite object obviously needs a co-inductive proof and a co-inductive definition of the predicate. To make sure that there is a finite number of ⊥ we need to mix co-induction with induction. Hence, *OnlyFiniteAbsent* is the largest relation verifying this axiom:

OFA :   *AbsentPrefix(v,x,y)* ∧ *OnlyFiniteAbsent(y)* ⇒ *OnlyFiniteAbsent(x)*

where *AbsentPrefix* is inductively defined. *AbsentPrefix(v,x,y)* states that x is of the form ⊥*.v.y. It is the smallest relation verifying the axioms:

AP₁ :   *AbsentPrefix(v,x,y)* ⇒ *AbsentPrefix(v,⊥.x,y)*
AP₂ :   *AbsentPrefix(v,v.x,x)*

In order to prove the Prop. 2 we need to prove the following lemma.

Lemma 1. OnlyFiniteAbsent($\widehat{x}$) ⇔ OnlyFiniteAbsent(x)

Proposition 2. OnlyFiniteAbsent(x) ∧ $\widehat{x} = \widehat{y}$ ⇒ OnlyFiniteAbsent(y)

7.2 Equivalence Relation Between Signals

Two signals are equivalents if they provide the same values in the same order. *EqFlot* is the largest relation verifying this axiom:

EF : *AbsentPrefix(v,x,x')*∧*AbsentPrefix(v,y,y')*∧*EqFlot(x',y')* ⇒ *EqFlot(x,y)*

Proposition 3. EqFlot *is an equivalence relation.*

7.3   Stream of a Fair Signal

It would be interesting to write a function which extract the stream of values of a signal i.e. a function which suppress the $\perp$ of a signal. Unfortunately, it is impossible to write this function in Coq. If its arguments x doesn't verify the predicate $OnlyFiniteAbsent$, this function will not terminate because it will have to extract an infinite number of $\perp$ to find the next value. It could lead to an inconsistent theory. We can only define a predicate $Stream(x, f)$ which verify that the stream f is the stream of values of x.

$Stream$ is the largest relation verifying this axiom:

$$F: \quad AbsentPrefix(v, x, y) \wedge Stream(y, f) \Rightarrow Stream(x, v.f)$$

From these definitions, we can deduce some major properties of $Stream$ and $EqFlot$ and some relations between them (Prop. 4). A stream of value is unique (s_1). If a signal has a stream of values then there only exists a finite number of $\perp$ between two values (s_2). Two signals with the same stream of values are equivalent (s_3). Two equivalent signals have the same stream of values (s_4). Two equivalent signals with the same clock are equal (s_5). Finally, we prove a fundamental property of the delay (s_6).

Proposition 4 (Stream calculus).

$$
\begin{aligned}
Stream(x, f_1) \wedge Stream(x, f_2) &\Rightarrow f_1 = f_2 & (s_1) \\
Stream(x, f) &\Rightarrow OnlyFiniteAbsent(x) & (s_2) \\
Stream(x, f) \wedge Stream(y, f) &\Rightarrow EqFlot(x, y) & (s_3) \\
Stream(x, f) \wedge EqFlot(x, y) &\Rightarrow Stream(y, f) & (s_4) \\
EqFlot(x, y) \wedge \widehat{x} = \widehat{y} &\Rightarrow x = y & (s_5) \\
\mathbf{Pre}(v, x, y) \wedge Stream(x, s) &\Rightarrow Stream(y, v.s) & (s_6)
\end{aligned}
$$

8   Properties of Derived Processes

We define co-inductively the function *constant* which compute the infinite stream of a given value. It is the greatest fixpoint of the following functor F:

$$F(f) = v \longmapsto v.f(v) \qquad constant = gfp(F)$$

To make the correctness proofs of processes easier, it is useful to prove the following properties of the derived operators. The stream of a signal x defined by $\mathbf{Constant}(v, x)$ is $constant(v)$ (d_1). Two identified signals have the same stream (d_2). If the stream of the signal x is f_1 and the stream of the signal y is f_2 then the stream of the signal z defined by $\mathbf{Op}(o, x, y, z)$ is the sequence of applications of the function o to each pair of values taken from f_1 and f_2 (d_3). Two signals x and y synchronized by $\mathbf{Synchro}(x, y)$ have the same clock (d_4).

Proposition 5 (Derived processes).

$$\text{OnlyFiniteAbsent}(x) \wedge \textbf{Constant}(v, x) \Rightarrow \text{Stream}(x, constant(v)) \qquad (d_1)$$
$$\textbf{Id}(x, y) \wedge \text{Stream}(x, s) \Rightarrow \text{Stream}(y, s) \qquad (d_2)$$
$$\textbf{Op}(o, x, y, z) \wedge \text{Stream}(x, f_1) \wedge \text{Stream}(y, f_2) \Rightarrow \text{Stream}(z, map(o, f_1, f_2)) \ (d_3)$$
$$\textbf{Synchro}(x, y) \Rightarrow \hat{x} = \hat{y} \qquad (d_4)$$

9 Correctness Proof of the Counter

An accurate (but informal) correctness property of the process `counter` (Fig. 2) is that (1) the input signal x and the output signal y are synchronous and that (2) the stream of values of y is the infinite sequence of integers starting from n+1. Using our library of definitions and theorems, we can easily formalize this informal specification (see Theorems 1 and 2).

The following theorem is an immediate application of the proposition (d_4)

Theorem 1. $Counter(n, x, y) \Rightarrow \hat{x} = \hat{y}$

To prove the second part of the specification, we need some lemmas. First we study the evolution of *Counter* from one instant to the next instant. Essentially by a case analysis, we prove the two following lemmas.

Lemma 2. $Counter(n, \perp.x, \perp.y) \Rightarrow Counter(n, x, y)$

Lemma 3. $Counter(n, v.x, (n + 1).y) \Rightarrow Counter(n + 1, x, y)$

Then we study the evolution of *Counter* from one instant to next instant where x and y are present. To prove this lemma, we need the previous lemmas.

Lemma 4. $\text{AbsentPrefix}(v, x, x') \wedge \text{AbsentPrefix}(n + 1, y, y') \wedge$
$$Counter(n, x, y) \Rightarrow Counter(n+1, x', y')$$

We define co-inductively the function *from* which computes the infinite stream of integers starting at a given number. It is the greatest fixpoint of the following functor F:

$$F(f) = n \longmapsto n.f(n + 1) \qquad from = gfp(F)$$

Finally we can prove the second part of the correctness property.

Theorem 2.
$$\text{OnlyFiniteAbsent}(x) \wedge Counter(n, x, y) \Rightarrow \text{Stream}(y, from(n + 1))$$

10 Implementation

The above theory has been implemented with Coq using co-inductive types. To prove the correctness of a Signal program, many propositions about primitive processes are needed. We cannot expose them entirely in this paper. Interested readers may find a complete Coq theory with proofs in [19].

The combined use of induction and co-induction enriches the expressive power of checkable properties. In particular, the checking might be used within Coq by simply using primitives tactics: the **Case** tactic expands all the definitions of the signals into their different possible values (e.g. *true*, *false*, ⊥ for a boolean signal) and the **Auto** tactic then checks the subgoals generated. To make co-inductive proofs, we used the **Cofix** tactic which introduces the current goal as an hypothesis in the context. The goal must be a co-inductive property and the application of this co-inductive hypothesis must be guarded. We also used intensively the inversion tactics [6].

11   Conclusion

An axiomatization of the trace semantics of Signal within a proof assistant like Coq introduces a novel approach for the validation of reactive systems. The Coq tool being continuously updated with new general-purpose proof tactics will benefit Signal program verification. We chose to use co-inductive features of Coq because we found it was the most natural and simplest way to handle infinite objects. Our practice confirmed that this was also an efficient way to prove correctness properties of reactive systems specified in Signal.

We plan to develop a reference Signal compiler in O'Caml [16] and to prove it with Coq. It will automatically translate the Signal syntax into the Coq syntax. Using our co-inductive theorem library, it will enable the interactive proof of, for instance, some clock assumptions that cannot be proved automatically by the compiler (for instance, clocks that depend on arithmetic relations).

Acknowledgements

The authors wish to thank Eduardo Giménez for the explanations he provided about the use of co-inductive types in Coq.

This work was partly funded by INRIA, "*action incitative – réécriture dans les systèmes synchrones et asynchrones*".

References

1. Bruno Barras and al. The Coq Proof Assistant Reference Manual. Technical report, INRIA, 1996.
2. Saddek Bensalem, Paul Caspi, and Catherine Parent-Vigouroux. Handling dataflow programs in PVS. Research report (draft), Verimag, May 1996.
3. Albert Benveniste, Paul Le Guernic, and Christian Jacquemot. Synchronous programming with events and relations : the Signal language and its semantics. *Science of Computer Programming*, 16:103–149, 1991.
4. G. Berry. The Constructive Semantics of Pure ESTEREL. Book in preparation, current version 2.0, http://zenon.inria.fr/meije/esterel.
5. Gerard Berry and Georges Gonthier. The ESTEREL synchronous programming language: design, semantics, implementation. *Science of Computer Programming*, 19:87–152, 1992.

6. C. Cornes and D. Terrasse. Inverting inductive predicates in Coq. In *BRA Workshop on Types for Proofs and Programs (TYPES'95)*, volume 1158 of *LNCS*, 1996.
7. Thierry Gautier, Paul Le Guernic, and François Dupont. SIGNAL v4 : manuel de référence (version préliminaire). Publication interne 832, IRISA, June 1994.
8. Thierry Gautier, Paul Le Guernic, and Olivier Maffeis. For a New Real-Time Methodology. Research report, INRIA, 1994.
9. Eduardo Giménez. An Application of Co-Inductive Types in Coq: Verification of the Alternating Bit Protocol. In *Proceedings of the 1995 Workshop on Types for Proofs and Programs*, number 1158 in LNCS, pages 135–152. Springer Verlag, 1995.
10. Eduardo Giménez. Types Co-Inductifs et Vérification de Systèmes Réactifs dans Coq. In *Proceedings of the Journées du GDR Programmation, Grenoble*, 1995.
11. Eduardo Giménez. *Un Calcul de Constructions Infinies et son Application à la Vérification des Systèmes Communicants*. PhD thesis, Laboratoire de l'Informatique du Parallélisme, Ecole Normale Supérieure de Lyon, December 1996.
12. Andrew D. Gordon. The Formal Definition of a Synchronous Hardware-Description Language in Higher Order Logic. In *Proceedings of the International Conference on Computer Design*, pages 531–534. IEEE Computer Society Press, October 1992.
13. Andrew D. Gordon. A Mechanised Definition of Silage in HOL. Research report 287, University of Cambridge Computer Laboratory, February 1993.
14. N. Halbwachs, P. Caspi, P. Raymond, and D. Pilaud. The synchronous dataflow programming language Lustre. *Proc. of the IEEE*, 79(9):1305–1320, September 1991.
15. Michel Le Borgne, Hervé Marchand, Eric Rutten, and Mazen Samaan. Formal Verification of Signal Programs: Application to a Power Transformer Station Controller. In *Proc. of the 5th Int. Conf. on Algebraic Methodology and Software Technology (AMAST'96)*, number 1101 in LNCS, pages 270–285, July 1997.
16. Xavier Leroy. The Objective Caml system, release 1.07. Documentation and users's manual, INRIA, December 1997.
17. F. Maraninchi. The Argos language: Graphical Representation of Automata and Description of Reactive Systems. In *IEEE Workshop on Visual Languages*, oct 1991.
18. Robin Milner and Mads Tofte. Co-induction in relational semantics. *Theoretical Computer Science*, 87(1):209–220, 16 September 1991.
19. David Nowak. http://www.irisa.fr/prive/nowak/signal-coq/. Coq code, IRISA, 1997.
20. David Nowak, Jean-Pierre Talpin, Thierry Gautier, and Paul Le Guernic. An ML-Like Module System for the Synchronous Language SIGNAL. In *Proceedings of European Conference on Parallel Processing (Euro-Par'97)*, number 1300 in LNCS, pages 1244–1253. Springer Verlag, August 1997.
21. Christine Paulin-Mohring. Circuits as streams in Coq : Verification of a sequential multiplier. In S. Berardi and M. Coppo, editors, *Types for Proofs and Programs, TYPES'95*, volume 1158 of *Lecture Notes in Computer Science*, 1996.
22. K. V. S. Prasad. A calculus of broadcasting systems. *Science of Computer Programming*, 25(2–3):285–327, December 1995.
23. B. Werner. *Une Théorie des Constructions Inductives*. PhD thesis, Université Paris VII, Mai. 1994.

Formal Specification and Theorem Proving Breakthroughs in Geometric Modeling*

François Puitg and Jean-François Dufourd

Laboratoire des Sciences de l'Image, de l'Informatique et de la Télédétection
LSIIT, UPRES-A 7005, Pôle API, boulevard S. Brant F-67400 Illkirch Cedex, France
{puitg,dufourd}@dpt-info.u-strasbg.fr
http://dpt-info.u-strasbg.fr/lsiit

Abstract. An innovative attempt to develop formal techniques in geometric modeling is reported through the axiomatization of the combinatorial maps in the Calculus of Inductive Constructions. A hierarchical specification of ordered sorts is presented and validated by inductive proofs of consistency and completeness in the Coq prover. Classical difficulties in theorem proving like cohabitation of objects with their generalization, smooth handling of subtyping, completion of partial relations or objects, observationality v. constructivism, and symmetry of relations, are addressed. Geometrical modeling issues are thus solved in a new and unquestionable fashion, giving a great insight on the domain and a deep understanding of the model, and so validating the methodology.

1 Introduction

The ultimate goal of the "Axiomatic Methods Group" of the computer graphics research team in Strasbourg is to get a general framework allowing construction and sound handling of geometric objects on computers, via formal methods. Algebraic specifications [23] have been intensively used, especially to design and develop from scratch *Topofil*, an interactive 3D modeler [4], and to formalize the foundations of geometric modeling [9]. But both practical and theoretical difficulties have arisen, in particular with regard to ordered sorts and preconditions, and poor proving support. We thus attempt to extend these works to the dialectics of constructive proofs, making lengthy use of induction [19]. This is a real innovative approach in geometric modeling. Though many models have been proposed, few have been really investigated in depth, except in the survey [15], but in the usual informal abstract way of mathematicians.

We want, at present, to axiomatize constructively the model of the combinatorial maps [14], set up a necessary and sufficient condition of planarity to investigate Euler's formula and the theorem of the genus, and work out a discrete Jordan's theorem (see Sect. 2.1). We do not follow Kuratowski's approach of planarity which is based on graph contraction. The theorem of the genus was

---

* This work is supported by the GDR-PRC of *Programmation*, and the GDR-PRC of *Algorithmique, Modèles et Infographie* (MENRT, CNRS, France).

proved by Jacques but from an unsafe generalization of a Serret's lemma [13]. This was corrected by Cori [7], despite the fact that several arguments are intuitive and should be clarified. One can find another proof by Tutte, but from such a general point of view that it seems impossible to get a clear idea of the variation of the genus [22]. As for Jordan's theorem, it is one of the oldest archetypal issues of geometric modeling. Exposing it in a new up-to-date fashion with adequate theories and solving it on a prover will result in a great insight and more generally will shed light on other domain of imagery – like for example digital topology [1], image processing [10] or discrete geometry [11] – and even on software development [5]. A formalization of planar graphs is proposed in [24], but with a restricted definition of graph whose proof of validity is informal, and an unusual notion of planarity hushing up theoretical and practical hot spots.

This paper thus reports an axiomatization of combinatorial planar maps in boundary representation, presented in Sect. 2, within the Calculus of Inductive Constructions, a framework for formal specifications and proofs briefly exposed in Sect. 3. Starting with free maps, we proceed with quasi-maps, then with combinatorial maps in the hierarchical specification of Sect. 4. The combinatorial characteristics are tackled in Sect. 5. Prior to the statement of a planarity criterion and the proof of Euler's formula in Sect. 7, the closure of maps is examined in Sect. 6. Section 8 concludes and opens up prospects.

2   Boundary Representation

The aim of geometric modeling is to describe geometric objects, i.e. subsets of points of $\mathbb{R}^n$, and operations. Clearly, an explicit representation is impossible since it may contain infinities of points. Though easier to set up and more suitable for calculations, an implicit representation – like for example parametric equations – is difficult to handle on a computer. A more constructive approach is preferred in Boundary Representation (B-Rep), historically investigated in order to represent solids that can be manufactured on a machine tool, i.e. solids whose boundary makes an orientable closed surface. The topology of the boundary is defined by a subdivision into cells (vertices, edges, faces) and incidence relations between them. An embedding model then associates for example vertices with points, edges with curves and faces with surfaces.

Among the numerous B-Rep mathematical models, we use the combinatorial maps. They represent the topology of polyhedra structures homeomorphic to the torus with g holes. If $g = 0$, we deal with planar maps that represent the topology of polyhedra structures homeomorphic to the sphere. Usually, a projection on the plane is used for drawings (except Fig. 2), with intersections if $g \neq 0$.

2.1   Combinatorial Maps

In the following, $\mathcal{D}$ is a finite set, and all the variables belong to $\mathcal{D}$.

Recall a *relation* $\mathcal{R}$ is a collection of ordered pairs (x, y) such that x is associated with y by $\mathcal{R}$, denoted $(\mathcal{R}\ x\ y)$. Then, y is a *successor* of x w.r.t to $\mathcal{R}$, or $\mathcal{R}$-successor of x, and x a *predecessor*, or $\mathcal{R}$-predecessor, of y.

We designate here by *total* a relation $\mathcal{R}$ for which there exists y such that $(\mathcal{R}\ x\ y)$ for all x. Otherwise, $\mathcal{R}$ is *partial*. It is *localized on* $\mathcal{D}' \subset \mathcal{D}$ if for all x, y from $\mathcal{D}$ such that $(\mathcal{R}\ x\ y)$, x and y belong to $\mathcal{D}'$. It is *involutive* if for all x, y, z such that $(\mathcal{R}\ x\ y)$ and $(\mathcal{R}\ y\ z)$, $z = x$, *injective* if for all x, x', y, such that $(\mathcal{R}\ x\ y)$ and $(\mathcal{R}\ x'\ y)$, $x' = x$, *surjective* if for all y, there exists x such that $(\mathcal{R}\ x\ y)$. It is a *function* if for all x, y, y', such that $(\mathcal{R}\ x\ y)$ and $(\mathcal{R}\ x\ y')$, $y' = y$. Then, an *application* is a total function. Reflexivity, symmetry and transitivity are defined as usual.

In this context, our functions are partial, whereas some authors take our definition of applications for functions, total then. Classically, an *involution* is an involutive application. An injective application is *one to one*, or an *injection*. A surjective application is *onto*, or a *surjection*. A *bijection* is an application one to one and onto. A bijection from $\mathcal{D}$ to $\mathcal{D}$ is also called a *permutation*.

A *combinatorial 2-map* is defined as a triple $(\mathcal{D}, \alpha_0, \alpha_1)$ where $\mathcal{D}$ is a finite set, α_0 an involution in $\mathcal{D}$ and α_1 a permutation in $\mathcal{D}$ [14]. An element of $\mathcal{D}$ is called a *dart*. For $k = 0, 1$, k-successor (resp. predecessor) stands for α_k-successor (resp. predecessor). Triple (k, x, y) such that $(\alpha_k\ x\ y)$ is called a *k-sewing*. Its darts are said *k-sewn*. Figure 1 shows the graph of a map embedded in the plane.

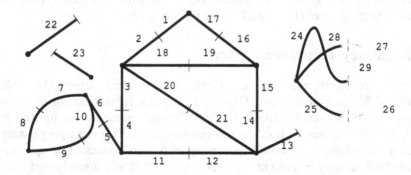

Fig. 1. A combinatorial map. $\mathcal{D} = \{1, 2, \ldots, 29\}$, and for example $(\alpha_0\ 22\ 22)$, $(\alpha_0\ 1\ 2)$, $(\alpha_0\ 2\ 1)$, $(\alpha_1\ 23\ 23)$, $(\alpha_1\ 28\ 24)$, $(\alpha_1\ 24\ 25)$, $(\alpha_1\ 25\ 28)$

Figures represent darts as half-segments of line or curve numbered by integers and symbolise α_0 with thin perpendicular dashes between the two corresponding darts and α_1 with black spots. Darts are ordered counterclockwise around dashes (resp. spots), w.r.t. to their succession in α_0 (resp. α_1).

2.2 Planar Maps

The planarity may be seen as a combinatorial concept involving the number of components and the number of the different orbits. *Components* are classically defined as equivalence classes [2], here w.r.t. α_0 and α_1. The sets of darts $\{22\}$ and $\{24, 25, 26, 27, 28, 29\}$ are two of the four components of Fig. 1.

We extend the definition of orbits – crucial in our axiomatics – to relations, from the notion of path: a *path* linking x_1 to x_n ($n \geq 1$) with respect to a relation $\mathcal{R}$ is a finite sequence $[x_1, x_2, \ldots, x_{n-1}, x_n]$ such that $(\mathcal{R}\, x_1\, x_2), \ldots, (\mathcal{R}\, x_{n-1}\, x_n)$. It is *elementary* if for all $i < j$ from $\{1, \ldots, n\}$ such that $(i, j) \neq (1, n)$, $x_i \neq x_j$, *open* if $x_1 \neq x_n$, otherwise *closed*, and *maximal* if x_n does not have $\mathcal{R}$-successors and x_1 does not have $\mathcal{R}$-predecessors.

An *orbit* $[x_1, \ldots, x_n]$ is an elementary path either maximal or closed. In the former case, $x_1 \neq x_n$, so the orbit is open, or *incomplete*. In the latter, the orbit is closed, or *complete*. Then, since the orbit is cyclic, any circular permutation of $[x_1, \ldots, x_n]$ denotes the same orbit. $< \mathcal{R} >$ is the set of the orbits of $\mathcal{R}$. Interesting orbits of a combinatorial map $(\mathcal{D}, \alpha_0, \alpha_1)$ concern respectively α_0, α_1 and $\alpha_1^{-1} \circ \alpha_0$. They contain cycles, for α_0, α_1 and $\alpha_1^{-1} \circ \alpha_0$ are bijections [2]. On the previous figure: $[22]$ and $[1, 2, 1] \in <\alpha_0>$; $[22]$ and $[28, 24, 25, 28] \in <\alpha_1>$; $[22]$, $[1, 18, 16, 1]$ and $[25, 29, 28, 26, 24, 27, 25] \in <\alpha_1^{-1} \circ \alpha_0>$. An element of $<\alpha_1>$ (resp. $<\alpha_0>$, $<\alpha_1^{-1} \circ \alpha_0>$) is a *vertex* (resp. an *edge*, a *face*). The number of edges (resp. vertices, faces) is the cardinal of $<\alpha_0>$ (resp. $<\alpha_1>$, $<\alpha_1^{-1} \circ \alpha_0>$). Figure 1 has 16 edges, 11 vertices and 8 faces, i.e. 7 plus $[2, 17, 15, 13, 12, 5, 10, 8, 6, 4, 2]$, the *external* face of the biggest component.

Let nc (resp. nd, nv, ne, nf) be the number of components (resp. darts, vertices, edges, faces). *Euler's characteristic* $\mathcal{X}$ and the *genus* g are defined by $\mathcal{X} = $ nv − (nd − ne) + nf and $g = $ nc − $\mathcal{X}/2$. Intuitively, $\mathcal{X}$ may be interpreted as the minimum number of poles necessary to mesh the corresponding surface [18]: 2 for a sphere, 0 for a torus (Fig. 2). The genus of a map gives the number of holes of the polyhedra structure whose boundary is modeled by that map: 0 for a sphere, 1 for a torus.

Fig. 2. Maps modeling the topology of a subdivision of a sphere (resp. a torus) containing 1 vertex, 1 edge and 1 face (resp. 1 vertex, 2 edges and 1 face). Vertices (resp. edges, faces) are embedded on bold crosses (resp. bold curves, meshed surfaces)

A *planar* map has a genus null and satisfies *Euler's formula*: 2nc + nd = nv + ne + nf. Figure 1 is not planar. Indeed, $g = 4 - (11 - (29 - 16) + 8)/2 = 1$. The non-planarity is introduced by the component $\{24, 25, 26, 27, 28, 29\}$. The other components are planar. The *theorem of the genus* [13, 7, 22] makes the interpretation of the genus plausible: let g be the genus of a map, then $g \in \mathbb{N}$. A discrete version of *Jordan's theorem* states that ripping a ring of sewings belonging to adjacent faces increases by one the number of components of a planar map. It will be studied in a future paper.

3   Using the Calculus of Inductive Constructions

Our axiomatizations, constructive, fit well in the *Calculus of Inductive Constructions* (CIC) [6, 17]. It is sufficiently powerful to recover our algebraic specification background into a single coherent higher order logical framework, in which our past difficulties with ordered sorts and preconditions may be solved, and our new ambitions with regard to proofs and program extraction supported. Though we cannot prejudge our future developments, higher order features are currently not absolutely necessary, but they are a very convenient and expressive mean, for instance to formalize relations and their properties, a formalization not described in this paper. In general, inductive definitions accompanied with a proof of functionality are preferred to fixpoints. We find them easier to set up and to read because of the "smallest set" property.

Our proofs are build in *Coq* [8],[1] a theorem proving assistant build on CIC. A high-level notation, the *Gallina* language, allows the declaration of axioms and parameters, the definition of abstract as well as concrete topological types and objects and a hierarchical development of our theories through sections. An interactive dialogue with the prover is achieved in a top-down manner by the application of predefined or user-programmable *tactics*.

Proofs developments in Coq are informative, so functional programs could have been associated with our proofs to perform quick prototyping, during the *program extraction* process [16]. This experiment is fully detailed in [20].

Since this paper reports a case study, we think that it is worth presenting important definitions and theorems in concrete syntax. Gallina is well suited to mechanize mathematics in higher order logic and sufficiently expressive to get a simple though unambiguous coding, close to the usual mathematical notation universally understood. The other definitions and theorems that are exposed informally have been validated by mechanical checking in Coq and prototyped by automatic extraction [20]. Likewise, every affirmation made in the following has been formally proved.

Gallina scripts are printed in `typewriter` style. Moreover, keywords are underlined, types are *italicized*, new identifiers in definitions are **boldfaced**. Cross-referred theorems names are CAPITALIZED and given according to the syntax of the theorem rather than the semantics, an easy mnemonic way to recall the hypothesis. Thus theorems are not numbered. Proof scripts, definitely too wordy, are nearly always omitted but in order to keep the clue, a few hints are sketched inside a *Proof.* □ pair.

4   A Hierarchy of Maps

As pointed out by Griffiths [12], proving often requires objects more general than the ones in play. This seems unavoidable and constitutes an underlying principle that extends beyond the scope of computer science: to better describe

---

[1] Coq is a research project common to INRIA, ENS Lyon and CNRS in France, and part of the European Esprit working group 21900 – TYPES.

and understand the evolution of a system, one has to study more general non stationary states; the constructive nature of CIC is of great help in following this rule. So, we use a hierarchy of nested abstract data types with general objects and atomic constructors at the top, and specialized objects and complex constructors at the bottom. Moreover, it is a most efficient way of getting a clear, modular, non redundant and less conceptual error-prone axiomatization.

Our hierarchy has several levels, each of these being specified with a different method. The first one is a classical specification with the constructors and selectors of what we call *free maps*. They are the most general objects, without any constraint or precondition. The second one is inhabited by *quasi-maps*. It is an explicit subset of the free maps obtained by restriction with a predicate of well-formedness. This invariant meets geometric modeling requirements, eliminating undesirable free maps. The third one houses the *combinatorial maps*. It is an implicit subset of the quasi-maps obtained by a completion operation of either a quasi-map (constructive approach) or chosen selectors on quasi-maps (observational approach [3]).

Before giving the constructors of free maps, we define some basic notions: dimension of sewing, dart and sewing.

4.1   Sewings and Darts

Since we work with 2-maps, we have two kinds of k-sewings, namely 0 or 1-sewings. So we add a new inductive type enumerating the two possibilities, as the least Set containing the constructors zero and one. Set is the built-in type of concrete sets such as booleans, natural numbers, lists, etc:

Definition 1 (dimensions). A sewing dimension, dim, is either zero or one:

```
Inductive dim : Set
   := zero : dim
    | one  : dim
```

Because some proofs bring in two or more sewing dimensions variables, the ability to distinguish between them has to be established:

Theorem. For all k, k', either k and k' are equal or they are different:

```
Theorem EQ_DIM_DEC : (k,k':dim) {k=k'} + {~k=k'}
```

Proof. Destructuration of k and k' w.r.t. their definition   □

"(:)" is the Gallina notation for universal quantification. Instead of the classical propositional connective or "\/", we use the intuitionistic disjunction "{}+{}" [8, page 101], pointing our future intention to perform program extraction out. This result, and more generally the induction principles automatically provided, are heavily used to prove statements by case analysis in proof mode.

We now focus on the notion of dart. They are just considered as distinguishable elements of some set, the so-called set of darts. Hence the declarations:

Definition 2 (dart). Let `dart` be a set whose elements are called darts. For all dart x, y, we suppose that either x and y are equal or they are different:

`Parameter dart : Set . Axiom EQ_DART_DEC : (x,y:dart) {x=y}+{~x=y}`

A sewing dimension and two darts make a sewing. But if we want to handle sewings like any other objects, we may encapsulate these three components. We thus get a more homogeneous and modular approach, as it can be seen for instance on definition 3 or 4. The corresponding type, constructed by c, is denoted `sw`. For example `(c zero x y):sw`. As for dimensions or darts, we need to distinguish sewings, this time thanks to a theorem.

4.2   Free Maps

Constructors of Free Maps. We want to be able to insert a dart or to sew two darts in order to build orbits step by step. We do not want to merge two vertices because this is a too high level operation in the sense that it can be decomposed in more atomic ones. We do not want either constraints or preconditions:

Definition 3 (free maps). This type, denoted `fmap`, is the smallest set containing the void free map (v), closed by insertion of darts (i) and sewings (l):

```
Inductive fmap : Set
  := v : fmap
   | i : dart -> fmap -> fmap
   | l : sw -> fmap -> fmap
```

Figure 3 explains how we schematize those operations.

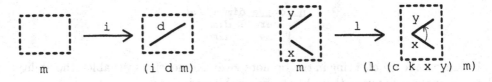

Fig. 3. Constructors of free maps. In free map m, (i d m) inserts a new dart d (left) and (l (c k x y) m) sews dart x to dart y at dimension k (right)

Selectors on Free Maps. We want to know if a dart or a sewing belongs to a free map, if a dart has successors or predecessors and which ones if it does. Though trivial, we detail the former to be terser on the latters.

Existence of darts. Let x be a dart. Its existence in a free map is a one-place predicate defined as follows: either it has just been inserted (exd_i1) or it was already in (exd_i2, exd_l):

Definition 4 (existence of darts).

```
Inductive exd [x:dart] : fmap -> Prop
:= exd_i1: (m:fmap) (exd x (i x m))
 | exd_i2: (m:fmap)(d:dart) (exd x m) -> (exd x (i d m))
 | exd_l : (m:fmap)(s:sw) (exd x m) -> (exd x (l s m))
```

Prop is the built-in type of propositions. Note the parameterization of x.

A technically very important class of results are the *inversion theorems*, because they step in as soon as we want to prove a property by induction on a recursive inductive object. They refer to the fact that its definition builds the smallest fixed point of the corresponding recursive equation. For instance, if (exd x (l s m)), then (exd x m) because exd_l is the only possible constructor. Inverting (exd x (i d m)) yields d=x (constructor exd_i1) or (exd x m) (constructor exd_i2). Statement ~(exd x v) is also an inversion theorem.

As usual, decidability is needed for already mentioned reasons, but on the existence of a dart in a free map instead of on the equality of two objects. From now on, though systematically defined and used, we will not mention decidability results and inversion theorems any more.

Existence of successors. The existence of successors of some dart is a positive information also included in the selector we define just after this one, which expresses the fact that the successor of some dart is some other dart. These two concepts overlap. We rather need a negative information stating that some dart does not have successors (resp. predecessors). So instead of overlapping we get complementarity, expressed by three theorems hereafter. The corresponding predicate, denoted nosucc (resp. nopred) and of type *dim->dart->fmap->Prop*, is inductively built, in the spirit of exd.

Successors. The idea is to specify the applications α_0 and α_1 of the mathematical definition, starting from relations. The corresponding predicate, denoted succ, is of type *dim->dart->fmap->dart->Prop*.

Properties. The refutation of the non-existence of successors and the fact that a successor can be exhibited are equivalent. Moreover, the fact that a successor can be exhibited, and the non-existence of successors are mutually exclusive. This theorem is thoroughly independent from the previous one. These results hold as well between succ – this time exhibiting an x k-successor of any y – and nopred. The whole makes the axiomatization of the concept of free maps complete and consistent. At this stage, we have not yet of course the combinatorial maps, but we do already have a generalization of the direct 2-graphs [2]. Any other property we can think of requires to move to the the quasi-map level. For instance, the functionality or the fact that succ is localized cannot be proved on free maps.

4.3   Quasi-Maps

The abstract data type of free maps defined supra is too large: some free maps are not desirable from the point of view of geometric modeling. For instance, two darts can be sewn though they have not been inserted or a dart can be inserted twice. To avoid these degenerated cases, preconditions forbidding undesirable operations should be imposed. A free map abiding by these preconditions is said to be *well-formed*, or equivalently to be a quasi-map. The corresponding predicate, of type *fmap->Prop*, is denoted wf.

The specification of quasi-maps follows, as a free map – called the *support* – and a proof of its well-formedness, thanks to the **Record** macro that stands for non recursive inductive definitions with only one constructor:

Definition 5 (quasi-maps). The type of quasi-map is the smallest set denoted qmap containing the well-formed free maps (qmap_intro):

```
Record qmap : Set
    := qmap_intro {support : fmap; wfsupport : (wf support)}
```

Note that unlike in most programming languages, a field in a record may depend on another one, as it is the case for the type of **wfsupport** which depends on **support**. Figure 4 shows an example of quasi-map. The drawing conventions are the same as before (Fig. 1). Moreover, the thin perpendicular dashes may halve and the black spots become arcs of circle when orbits are incomplete.

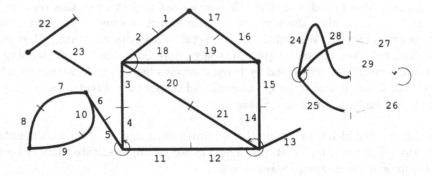

Fig. 4. A quasi-map. Dart 1 has no **zero**-predecessor and dart 2 has no **one**-successor. Dart 23 is not sewn at all

Subtyping. Making proofs part of propositions and types dependant allows a smooth and elegant subtyping both in definitions and in proofs. It is a way of getting rid of the numerous theoretical and practical problems we have encountered in algebraic specifications when defining subsorts by invariants.

Quasi-maps may be seen as a subtype of free maps. They can be used like any other type without making explicit the support and its well-formedness, as in m: *qmap*, or explicitly constructed with qmap_intro.

Structural Properties of Quasi-Maps. We are now able to prove several essential results. Note that we keep them on quasi-maps. Calling on combinatorial maps is not yet necessary. First, succ is localized. Then, it is a function, so from now on we write for quasi-maps "the" successor. Moreover, it is injective, so we write "the" predecessor. Besides, (succ zero) is involutive.

These theorems make the axiomatization of the quasi-maps complete and coherent. They constitute the smallest pool of results one can demand, and any other property we can think of requires to move to the combinatorial map level. For instance, the fact that succ is a surjection cannot be proved on quasi-maps.

4.4   Combinatorial Maps

Combinatorial maps could be inductively specified from scratch by building complete objects at each step, i.e. defining constructors adding whole orbits. This would break our hierarchy, thus denying the handling of objects and their generalization in the same framework, with all the advantages above-mentioned. So a combinatorial map is rather viewed as a quasi-map whose orbits are complete. A possible method is to complete selectors on quasi-maps in order to obtain total rather than partial relations. Another one is to complete quasi-maps adding sewings where they lack. This approach is quite heavy and difficult to set up because it requires to rip sewings. Besides, as it will be explained in Sect. 6, it relies on the ends of orbits, also needed for the lighter selectors completion method. We thus choose the former for the last stage of our hierarchy.

The existence of darts is not affected by completion: if a dart exists in a quasi-map, so does it in the same quasi-map viewed as a combinatorial map, and the converse is true. On the other hand, the existence of successors or predecessors gets a different meaning on combinatorial maps (Fig. 5).

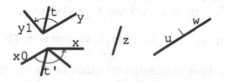

Fig. 5. Orbits with ends. If we imagine these orbits completed, the **one**-successor of x is x0, the **one**-predecessor of y is y1, z is the successor and the predecessor of itself, the **zero**-successor of u is w and the **zero**-predecessor of w is u

Thus, we must identify the ends of orbits, i.e. *heads* and *tails*. The corresponding inductive relations, of type *dim->dart->fmap->dart->Prop*, are denoted hd and tl. "Head or tail of the orbit containing dart z" is often shortened to "head or tail of z". For example, on Fig. 5, a one-head of y or t is y1, a one-tail of x or t' is x0, z is a head and a tail of itself, a zero-tail of u is w and a zero-head of w is u.

Closing orbits does not get these relations into troubles: the head of any dart is then the origin of the sewing most recently inserted in this orbit before closing it. Thus, the order of the elements of the term representing a quasi-map has an influence. This syntactic intrusion in the semantic of a relation is not a problem. On the contrary, when one wants to dismantle hd, for instance to perform historical backtracking, it guarantees the possibility of always being able to come back to the previous steps.

Completing the successor relation is now easy, thanks to tails:

Definition 6 (csuccessor). Let k be a dimension, z and z' two darts, m a free map. "z' is a k-csuccessor of z" is the smallest proposition denoted csucc holding whenever z' is a k-successor of z (csucc_succ), or z does not have k-successors and a k-tail of z is z' (csucc_tl):

```
Inductive csucc [k:dim;z:dart;m:fmap;z':dart] : Prop
 :=  csucc_succ: (succ k z m z') -> (csucc k z m z')
 |   csucc_tl: (nosucc k z m) -> (tl k z m z') -> (csucc k z m z')
```

Note that csucc is not recursive.

A better understanding of the relationships between hd and tl and of the properties of csucc requires to move to the quasi-map level, where hd is a total function, i.e. an application. Note that the existence of z is required in the proof of the latter, otherwise the theorem is not provable.

Relation hd is obviously not injective, since distinct darts may share a common head. Yet, it is if we restrict to the *bounds* of orbits. In the context of quasi-maps, the *upper* bound of an incomplete orbit is the dart of that orbit without successor, the *lower* bound being the one without predecessor. For example, on Fig. 5, the upper bound of the orbit of x is x whereas the lower bound is x0. Dart z is both an upper and lower bound.

Theorem (injectiveness of head on lower bounds). For all dimension k, quasi-map m and darts z, z', z1, if z1 is the k-head of z and z', then z and z' are equal, provided they do not have any k-predecessor.

Proof. Induction on support of m, hd, nosucc, wf inversion Th., hd is localized   □

Now, a head does not have successors on quasi-maps, unless the orbit is closed. Since we have not exactly specified what an open orbit is, we take a stronger hypothesis and suppose we are on the lower bound to prove this result. Like hd, tl is injective and does not have predecessors, on upper bounds of quasi-maps. Finally, if dart z1 is the head of dart z, then conversely z is the tail of dart z1, but only on lower (resp. upper) bound, since a head (resp. a tail) cannot have successors (resp. predecessors). A lot of the subsequent theorems use heads or tails, or both. They always take place on bounds, so these results are much used, allowing us to get a head from a tail and the converse, on quasi-maps.

Relation csucc is localized. It is a total function, i.e. an application. Moreover, it is injective and surjective. Besides, (csucc zero) is involutive.

Quasi-Maps Viewed as Maps. A quasi-map observed with succ keeps its quasi-map status. The same quasi-map observed with csucc becomes a combinatorial map, as the previous theorems on csucc show. This is the so-called *observational* approach [3]. Several quasi-maps may correspond to the same combinatorial map, "same" standing for the observational equality, i.e. any observer yields the same result.

The question of knowing if we get all the combinatorial maps this way is irrelevant, because a formal answer would be outside our theory of maps, on the meta-logic level. All we can say is that we have not be able to think of a combinatorial map not constructible with our hierarchy, whose constructors and selectors are "natural" in that they formalize the classical operations one could meet for instance in an interactive modeler.

The theorems of this section make the axiomatization of the concept of combinatorial map complete and coherent. Indeed, csucc meets the mathematical properties required for α_k presented in Sect. 2.1.

5   Combinatorial Characteristics

The main characteristics are Euler's characteristic and the genus. Since they are a linear combination of the number of darts, vertices, edges, faces and components, we must find out how to enumerate them. Counting darts is trivial:

Definition 7 (number of darts). Let nd be the recursive function from free maps to integers computing the number of darts. It is null on the void free map, incremented when inserting darts, not changed when inserting sewings:

```
Fixpoint nd [m: fmap] : Z
   := Cases m of
          v => '0'
        | (i _ mi) => '(nd mi)+1'
        | (l _ ml) => (nd ml)
     end
```

The Fixpoint construction allows the definition of a recursive function. The macro Cases performs pattern-matching on the map argument. We reuse the Coq library on integers, denoted Z, with natural syntax between quotes. Though always positive, characteristics are computed with integers instead of naturals because we want to be able to permute freely successor and predecessor, which is not always possible on whole numbers. This greatly simplifies proofs.

Computing, say the number of vertices, is more complicated. One solution is to consider the binary relation $\mathcal{R}$ on darts: "there exists a path of one-sewings from x to y" and to decrement instead of increment, as for nd. Let 0 be the number of vertices in the void free map. Inserting a dart makes that number increase by 1 because it is a potential vertex: it may constitute later on (the beginning of) a vertex. Then, sewing darts unrelated by $\mathcal{R}$ w.r.t. each other decreases it. On the contrary, sewing darts belonging to some path of one-sewings has no effect because they have already been taken into account.

This balancing process applies as well to the number of edges, faces and components with the respective relations "there exists a path of zero-sewings", "there exists a path of zero-sewing immediately followed by a one-sewing traveled through clockwise", "there exists a path, not necessarily oriented, of zero or one-sewings".

Enumerating the components of free maps is simple. Besides, we do not intend to prove complicated properties directly on these numbers. Indeed, the difficulty lies in the specification of the relations described above. So we use for once fixpoints rather than inductive definitions.

5.1   Number of j-Orbits

As vertices and edges are two specializations of the same mathematical concept – namely α_j-orbits respectively at dimension 1 and 0 – we easily generalize the corresponding relations in "there exists a path of j-sewings" by parameterizing j. An inductive relation denoted expve, of type *dim->dart->dart->fmap->Prop*, is obtained. It is reflexive and transitive, but not symmetrical. Two specializations of expve can be defined by instantiating the dimension parameter on zero or one. We thus obtain two new relations: the existence of zero-paths and the existence of one-paths, of type *dart->dart->fmap->Prop*, respectively denoted expe and expv. Following the introduction of Sect. 5, we get:

Definition 8 (number of vertices). Let nv be the recursive function from free maps to integers computing the number of vertices. It is null on the void free map, incremented when inserting darts, not changed when inserting zero-sewings, and decremented when one-sewing dart x to dart y unless there exists a one-path from y to x :

```
Fixpoint nv [m:fmap] : Z
  := Cases m of
          v => `0`
        | (i _ m0) => `(nv m0)+1`
        | (l (c zero _ _) m0) => (nv m0)
        | (l (c one x y) m0) => Cases (EXPV_DEC y x m0) of
                                       (left _) => (nv m0)
                                     | (right _) => `(nv m0)-1`
                                end
     end
```

Note the case analysis on EXPV_DEC, the decidability result for expv. For already mentioned reasons, it is stated with "{}+{}", whose constructors are left and right. Fixpoint ne, of type *fmap->Z*, is defined alike.

5.2   Number of Components

If the existence of a one-path (resp. zero-path) is able to compute the number of vertices (resp. edges), one may think the existence of a path of zero or one-sewings would allow the enumeration of the components. Such a relation is easy to define, it is a copy of expve without the dimension parameter. This feeling is correct on combinatorial maps, but wrong on quasi-maps: two darts may be in the same component without being related by the existence of a zero,one-path between them, because there is no symmetry. Thus, we symmetrize the constructors of expve to get eqc, of type *dart->dart->fmap->Prop* : "x is equivalent to y, from the point of view of the notion of component".

Like expve, eqc is reflexive and transitive. Moreover, as expected, it is symmetrical on free maps. Thus, eqc is an equivalence relation. The definition of the number of components, nc of type *fmap->Z*, ensues, built like nv.

5.3   Number of Faces

The notion of face is ticklish. It makes this section difficult, but necessary since it is the hard core of the concept of planarity. To count faces, the relation to consider is "there exists a path of zero-sewing immediately followed by a one-sewing traveled through clockwise", denoted expf. But the duality "informal specification on combinatorial maps"/"textual definition on free maps" induced by our hierarchy makes its inductive specification hairy. Indeed, in the combinatorial map of Fig. 6 (a) left, in which dart x is to be one-sewn to dart y, there exists a path along the bold face with little waves [z, x, t, y', ..., z] from dart z to dart t. When x and y are sewn (Fig. 6 (a) right), this face is split in two, and z belongs to the face with little waves, now distinct from the bold face containing t. So, unlike the last constructor of expve or eqc, we cannot claim that paths along faces are kept in the case of the insertion of sewings. In contrast, the existence of a path along a face from t to y' is not disturbed by the sewing from x to y. So in this case, we should claim that paths along faces are kept. Building an inductive definition with these two contradictory cases seems impossible.

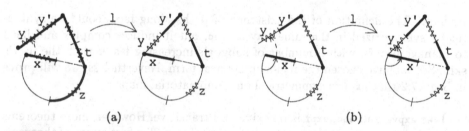

Fig. 6. Physical faces in (a) a combinatorial map, (b) a quasi-map

This contradiction disappears when we consider more general objects, namely quasi-maps (Fig. 6 (b)), because when following paths along faces, passing through x is now not allowed since there is no one-sewing starting from it. Similarly, the crossing of y is impossible because there is no one-sewing ending in it. On those maps, we can claim that paths along faces are kept (expf_1').

Sewing darts may make paths along faces grow. We just have to take into account an extra sewing. Indeed, after zero-sewing x to y (Fig. 7, left), a new path is created, from darts belonging to paths ending in x to darts belonging to paths starting with y', a one-predecessor of y (expf_1z). The same phenomenon occurs when sewing at dimension one (Fig. 7, right) (expf_1o). The insertion of darts is straightforward (expf_i1, expf_i2). So we obtain:

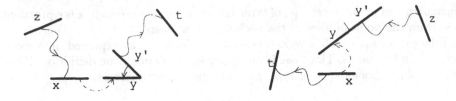

Fig. 7. Growing of paths along faces when `zero`- (left) and `one`- (right) sewing

Definition 9 (faces).

```
Inductive expf : dart -> dart -> fmap -> Prop
:= expf_i1: (d:dart)(m:fmap) (expf d d (i d m))
|  expf_i2: (z,t,d:dart)(m:fmap)
                (expf z t m) -> ~d=z -> ~d=t -> (expf z t (i d m))
|  expf_1z: (z,t,x,y,y':dart)(m:fmap)
                (expf z x m) -> (succ one y' m y) -> (expf y' t m) ->
                       (expf z t (l (c zero x y) m))
|  expf_1o: (t,z,x,y,y':dart)(m:fmap)
                (expf x t m) -> (succ zero y' m y) -> (expf z y' m) ->
                       (expf z t (l (c one x y) m))
|  expf_1': (z,t:dart)(s:sw)(m:fmap)
                (expf z t m) -> (expf z t (l s m))
```

Note that `zero`-sewing must be separated from `one`-sewing and expressed with two different constructors since paths are oriented.

Remark. The definition of the existence of paths along faces could be syntactically symmetrized in the same way as `eqc`, but it induces complex and hard to manage proofs, with a number of subgoals increasing faster than the user's skill. So, we have chosen the non-symmetrical form. Nevertheless, we will prove in Sect. 7.2 that `expf` is symmetrical on combinatorial maps.

Like `expve` and `eqc`, `expf` is reflexive and transitive. However, more theorems are needed to capture the concept of path along faces. The first bunch of theorems expresses the relationships between the existence of paths along faces and the existence of successors.

Theorem (blind alleys for paths along faces). For all darts z, t, and free map m, if z does not have `zero`-successors then there is no path along faces from z to t, provided z and t are different; idem for t.

Proof. Induction on (expf z t m), nosucc inversion Th., SUCC_NOTNOSUCC   □

The same kind of results holds when z (resp. t) does have a `zero` (resp. `one`) successor x, but x does not have `one` (resp. `zero`) predecessor. The second bunch addresses the subtraction of paths, as transitivity addresses the addition.

Theorem (subtraction of paths along faces). For all darts x, y, z and quasi-map m, if there exists a path along faces from x to z and from x to y, then there exists a path along faces from y to z or from z to y. Idem by swapping y and z.

Proof. Induction on support of m, inversion of paths, succ is one to one, reflexivity of expf   □

We are now able to enumerate faces on quasi-maps. Unfortunately, the decidability result for expf, required to make our fixpoint definition, is wrong on free maps because its proof needs the injectiveness of succ, which holds for quasi-maps. But due to a syntactic limitation of CIC, fixpointing on quasi-maps is impossible. So we fall back on an inductive construction, of type *fmap->Z->Prop*, denoted nf. It is built as usual (cf. nv), but dimensions zero and one must be treated separately because paths along faces are oriented. Moreover, since a new dart must be introduced, a new rule describes what is going on when such a dart does not exist: the count does not change. From a syntactic point of view, we get quite a tedious definition (7 constructors, 21 lines) [20], but easy to understand, thanks to the use of expf. Since it is not a fixpoint, it must be accompanied by a theorem of existence:

Theorem (existence of a number of faces). For all quasi-map m, there exists an integer n such that n is the number of faces in m

Proof. Induction on the support of m, decidability of expf   □

Whereas it is not necessary for subsequent proofs or for extraction, we prove moreover that nf is a function, in order to convince us of its legitimacy. So from now on, we write for quasi-maps "the number of faces" instead of "a number of faces".

5.4   Properties

Several properties needed later on are grouped in this section because they make the relationships between the existence of paths and the other observers clearer. The first result is obvious:

Theorem (successor and j-orbit). For all dimension k, darts x, y and quasi-map m, if y is the k-successor of x, then there exists a k-path from x to y.

Proof. Induction on (succ k x m y), well-formedness of support of m, reflexivity of expve   □

The same result holds for tails and heads. Moreover, the converse is true on bounds. Then, a successor is in the same component as its predecessor. The same result holds for faces.

5.5   Conclusion

We now know how to enumerate the number of darts, components, vertices, edges and faces on *incomplete* maps. Unfortunately, the latter has to be expressed on *combinatorial* maps in Euler's characteristic, which cannot be done directly (cf. Sect. 5.3). Besides there is no evident relation between the number of faces on quasi-maps and on combinatorial maps. Thus, next section is devoted to the definition of a relation yielding combinatorial maps.

6   Closure of Maps

Relation completion (Sect. 4.4) is not enough for our needs. We now want to add sewings where they lack to get real complete maps. We show why an inductive definition performing this addition requires sewings deletion, i.e. a new generator.

The completion of the void free map is itself. When inserting a dart d in a free map m, the completion is easily obtained by adding d and the sewings (c zero d d) and (c one d d) in the completion of m. There are two cases for the insertion of sewings. If darts x and y are in the same vertex or edge, the completion when inserting (c k x y) is straightforward. Indeed, there is nothing to do since we are precisely closing the incomplete orbit. Otherwise, the completion is impossible without ripping, as showed in Fig. 8 where we are k-sewing x, whose k-tail is x0, to y, whose k-head is y1, in m. As we want an inductive definition, we are bound to express the completion of (l (c k x y) m) w.r.t. the completion mc of m. We just have to rip (c k x x0) and (c k y1 y) in order to make the proper sewings, namely (c k y1 x0) and (c k x y).

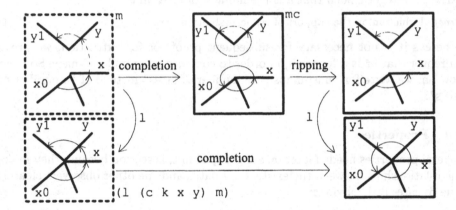

Fig. 8. Sewing insertion in free maps (dotted lines) and completion (bold lines)

There is no difficulty about ripping sewings in a free map: just build another free map, leaving out the sewing to be ripped when it occurs. Since it is that simple, we opt for a fixpoint construction [20], denoted rip and of type sw->fmap->fmap, rather than an inductive definition. Free map (rip s m) is called the "s-ripped of m".

Fixpoint rip is a free map generator. The selectors we have defined so far have to be applied to the free maps so generated. For example, for all dart d, sewing s and free map m, if d exists in m then it exists in the s-ripped of m. This leads to a first group of results – looking like constructors in inductive definitions – that state the behavior of the selectors when ripping sewings. The converse of those theorems inhabit the second group and are analogous to inversion theorems.

The proofs in the first group are usually more complicated. For example, the one w.r.t. eqc is already 117 lines long. Then, the one w.r.t. expf is twice as long

and the one with respect to nf, which heavily relies on it, exceeds 800 lines. Fortunately, a lot of intermediary cases are analogous, and more or less proved by
"copy-paste". Splitting these huge proofs in manageable chunks making lemmas
is not that easy but writing our own tactics could probably help to handle them
more or less automatically.

Thanks to ripping, the completion relation, of type *fmap->fmap->Prop*, is inductively defined and denoted clo. It is a total function, i.e. an application. Like
rip, it is a free map generator, so we have to study the behavior of our selectors.
For example: for all dimension k, dart x and quasi-map m, if x does not have
k-successors in m, then the k-successor of x in the closure of m is the k-tail of x
in m. Finally, we have the important theorem: for all quasi-map m, the closure
of m is well-formed [20].

Closing does what we expect: it makes succ total and surjective on closures,
i.e. an onto application, when it was just an injective function on quasi-maps.
Moreover, it can be proved that observational and constructive approach are
equivalent: applying completed selectors on quasi-maps or applying raw selectors on their closures is exactly the same. Through lack of time, we have not
completely worked out the proof of the latter but it does not appear to be more
difficult than that of the former. Then, the concluding remark of Sect. 4.4 applies
as well to closures.

7   Planarity of Maps and Symmetry of Paths along Faces

We want to express the conditions – or planarity criterion – under which the
construction of a map from the void free map by insertion of darts and sewings
is planar, i.e. the number of components minus half Euler's characteristic is
equal to 0. Let planar, of type *fmap->Prop*, be the corresponding non-recursive
predicate. Then, our criterion will be validated by proving Euler's formula.

7.1   Planarity Criterion

First of all, a systematic combinatorial analysis of the variation of the characteristics, exposed in [20], is undertaken. It relies heavily on expf inversion theorems, on the fact that expf is an equivalence relation on completed quasi-maps –
especially the symmetry (not yet proved) – and on the results on blind alleys.
The planarity criterion so obtained is very compact, and reads:

(expf x y' mc)

when one-sewing x to y in the same component when there is no path of one-
sewing from y to x. The closure mc of m pops up because the number of faces must
be computed on closed quasi-maps (Sect. 5.3). Dart y' is the zero-predecessor
of x in mc. The criterion is exactly the same at dimension zero, but from y' –
the one-predecessor of x – to x. When there is a path of k-sewing from y to x or
when x and y are not in the same component, the criterion is trivial. An inductive
relation of type *fmap->Prop* denoted ws ("well-sewnness") describes these various

configurations. We must now address the problem of the symmetry of `expf` on combinatorial maps since it is a key factor in the proof of Euler's formula.

7.2 Symmetry of Paths along Faces on Combinatorial Maps

Relation `expf` is definitely a nuisance, as the length of the passing of `expf` and `nf` through `rip` has testified. Proving its symmetry on combinatorial maps is far worse: there are two sewings and two rippings in a closure, so the complicated definition of `expf` must be inverted twice and the theorem of the passing of `expf` through `rip` must be used twice as well, each time with three possible choices since there are two disjunctions in its conclusion, also to be inverted, and so on. This leads to an explosion of the number of cases and to a huge proof, impossible to handle. So a direct proof of the symmetry is unacceptable.

We apply an alternate observational method we believe extremely fruitful and general. Most of the difficulties above-mentioned come from the induction variable. The idea, quite natural in mathematics, is to make an induction on another variable, namely here the length of the paths along faces [21]. The current version of `expf` does not support that notion, so we have to build another equivalent definition introducing it:

Definition 10 (observational faces). If a dart exists in a map, then the existence of a path along faces from this dart to itself can be observed: the empty path (`expf0_ref`). If the existence of a n steps long path along faces from x to t is observed, then the existence of a path from y' – a `zero`-predecessor of a one-successor y of x – to t, can be observed (Fig. 9 left, `expf0_1x`). Idem for paths ending in y' (Fig. 9 right, `expf0_1y`):

```
Inductive expf0 [m: fmap] : dart -> dart -> nat -> Prop
 := expf0_ref :  (z:dart) (exd z m) -> (expf0 m z z 0)
  | expf0_1x  :  (x,y,y',t:dart)(n:nat)
                        (succ zero y' m y) -> (succ one x m y) ->
                        ~x=y' -> (expf0 m x t n) -> (expf0 m y' t (S n))
  | expf0_1y  :  (x,y,y',z:dart)(n:nat)
                        (succ zero y' m y) -> (succ one x m y) ->
                        ~y'=x -> (expf0 m z y' n) -> (expf0 m z x (S n))
```

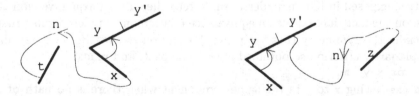

Fig. 9. Observational existence of path along faces

New paths are one step longer because we consider one step stands for two sewings, a `zero`-sewing followed by a `one`-sewing traveled through clockwise.

We have easily that expf0 implies expf. Naturally, the converse requires the reflexivity, immediate, and the transitivity, proved by double induction, of expf0. But quite unexpectedly, two lemmas expressing that the number of steps of an observational path along faces between two darts does not change when inserting darts or sewings, are needed. In fact, it is not surprising. They are the constructive counterpart of the observational constructors of expf0.

The symmetry of expf0 is now provable in a few lines by induction on the number of steps, as soon as the following unsuspected lemma holds: for all quasi-map m and darts z, t, t', if t is the one-successor of z, and t' the zero-predecessor of t in mc (the closure of m), then there exists a path along faces from z to t' in mc. Again, this is an intrusion of constructivism in our observational land. Nevertheless, it would have shown up anyway, even in a pure constructive approach. It corresponds here to a case not reachable by induction, since there is no number of steps to induce on. It illustrates the fact that two symmetrical paths do not necessarily contain the same number of steps. Its proof is long, more than 1300 lines, because of the inversions of the two sewings and the two rippings appearing in the closure. Fortunately, it is quite redundant, and large parts can be copied with just a careful renaming and a few permutations of variables. Again, user-defined tactics would probably simplify the proof. Note that an estimate and a few preliminary trials of the direct approach rejected supra have given a lot more than 1300 lines.

At last, we have the symmetry of expf0 whose a corollary is the symmetry of expf. Relation expf is thus an equivalence relation on combinatorial maps, as promised, and we can now validate our planarity criterion by proving Euler's formula.

7.3 Euler's Formula

Theorem (ws implies planar). For all quasi-map m, if m is well-sewn, then it is planar.

Proof. Induction on (ws m), most of results proved so far, mainly symmetry and blind alleys for expf   □

The proof is rather long but quite redundant, since the interesting case (sewing from x to y not in the same orbit but in the same component) is examined twice, at dimensions zero and one. Because doing formal proofs is too much time consuming, the converse – which anyway is not needed for subsequent developments of our axiomatics – has not been completely verified. We are nevertheless convinced that we can prove it. For the same reasons, the theorem of the genus has not been investigated yet. But from the proof of Euler's formula, we know very precisely the variation of the number of faces: for example, when one-sewing x to y in the same component of a free map m when there is no path of one-sewings from y to x, it is equal to +1 if there exists a path along faces from x to y', a zero-predecessor of y, −1 otherwise. In other words, and this is in itself an important and interesting result, when building a map, the genus may only increase. That is, it is either constant in the planar cases or incremented by one in the non-planar cases. The theorem of the genus is an easy corollary of this result, by induction on m. On the other hand, we have just terminated the axiomatization of rings of sewings and the proof of a discrete Jordan's theorem.

These ultimate results make the axiomatization of the notion of planarity on combinatorial maps coherent and complete, and put an end to the presentation of our axiomatics.

8   Conclusions

We have reported our innovative experiment in the proof of archetypal geometric modeling properties never constructively nor rigorously tackled before, through a hierarchical formal specification of combinatorial maps in the Coq prover. Starting with free maps without any constraint, we proceed with well-formed free maps or quasi-maps. These are partial objects. The combinatorial maps are obtained by completing either quasi-maps or relations on quasi-maps. Proofs of consistency and completeness validating our specifications have been undertaken in Coq. Then, the combinatorial characteristics have been defined, the difficult planarity criterion has been set up and a proof of Euler's formula achieved. The whole development makes a full-scale case-study with its 232 theorems, 40 definitions and more than 10000 proof lines.

Geometric modeling issues like the notion of face, the closure of quasi-maps, and the validation of a planarity criterion, as well as technical formal specification problems, like the handling of ordered sorts within a hierarchy, the cohabitation of objects with their generalization, the smooth integration of subtypes defined by invariants to both the axiomatics and the proof process, the completion of partial relations or incomplete objects and the use of observationality v. constructivism to ease proofs of symmetry, have been addressed. Tactic programming should be investigated in the future in order to improve proof management.

This has resulted in a methodology of specification, proof and extraction, opening up new prospects in formal geometric modeling such as revisiting the foundations of boundary representation with the generalized maps, a model more expressive than the combinatorial maps. This is one of the most promising and exciting long-range outlook because it could end in the classification of surfaces [12]. Also, how Kuratowski's theorem and our planarity criterion are related would worth being studied. The extension of Euler's formula to the third dimension is an open problem that could surely benefit from a systematic formalization in the spirit of this paper.

References

1. R. Aharoni, G. Herman, and M. Loebl. Jordan Graphs. *Graphical Models and Image Processing*, 58(4):345–359, July 1996.
2. C. Berge. *Graphes et Hypergraphes*. Dunod, Paris (France), 1973.
3. G. Bernot, M. Bidoit, and T. Knapik. Behavioural Approaches to Algebraic Specifications: a Comparative Study. *Acta Informatica 31(7):651–671*, 1994.

4. Y. Bertrand and J.-F. Dufourd. Algebraic Specification of a 3D-Modeler Based on Hypermaps. *Graphical Models and Image Processing*, 56(1):29–60, 1994.
5. Y. Bertrand, J.-F. Dufourd, J. Françon, and P. Lienhardt. Algebraic Specification and Development in Geometric Modeling. In *TAPSOFT*, pages 74–87, Orsay (France), 1993. Springer-Verlag, LNCS 668.
6. T. Coquand and G. Huet. Constructions: a Higher Order Proof System for Mechanizing Mathematics. In *EUROCAL*, Linz, 1985. LNCS 203.
7. R. Cori. Un Code pour les Graphes Planaires et ses Applications. *Société Math. de France, Paris*, Astérisque 27, 1975.
8. C. Cornes et al. *The Coq Proof Assistant Reference Manual V6.1*. INRIA-Rocquencourt, CNRS-ENS Lyon (France), December 1996.
9. J.-F. Dufourd. Algebras and Formal Specifications in Geometric Modeling. In *The Visual Computer*, pages 131–154. Spinger-Verlag, 1997.
10. J.-F. Dufourd and F. Puitg. Boundary Representation Specification Revisited with a New Quasi-map Concept. Submitted to *Graphical Models and Image Processing*, 1998.
11. J. Françon. Topologie Combinatoire en Imagerie. Research report 95/12, Université L. Pasteur, LSIIT, Strasbourg (France), 1995.
12. H. Griffiths. *Surfaces*. Cambridge University Press, 1981.
13. A. Jacques. Sur le Genre d'une Paire de Substitutions. *Notes des membres et correspondants*, volume 267, pages 625–627, 1968.
14. A. Jacques. Constellations et Graphes Topologiques. In *Combinatorial Theory and Applications*, pages 657–673. Budapest (Hungary), 1970.
15. P. Lienhardt. Topological Models for Boundary Representation : A Survey. In *Computer Aided Design*, volume 23(1), pages 59–81. 1991.
16. C. Parent. Synthesizing Proofs from Programs in the Calculus of Inductive Constructions. In *Mathematics of Program Construction*. LNCS 947, 1995.
17. C. Paulin-Mohring. Inductive Definitions in the System Coq – Rules and Properties. In *Typed Lambda-calculi and Applications*. LNCS 664, 1993.
18. J.-P. Petit. *Le Topologicon*. Belin, 1985.
19. F. Puitg and J.-F. Dufourd. Spécifications en Modélisation Géométrique par la Théorie des Constructions. In *Proc. Preuves et Spécifications Algébriques*, Grenoble (France), 1995. Journées du GDR de Programmation du CNRS.
20. F. Puitg and J.-F. Dufourd. Combinatorial Maps and Planarity: Formal Specifications and Proofs in the Calculus of Inductive Constructions. Tech. Rep. 98/05 (100 pages), LSIIT, Strasbourg (France).
http://dpt-info.u-strasbg.fr/~puitg/rr98/main.html, 1998.
21. J. Rouyer. *Développements d'Algorithmes dans le Calcul des Constructions*. PhD thesis, Institut National Polytechnique de Lorraine, Nancy (France), March 1994.
22. W. Tutte. Combinatorial Oriented Maps. In *Canadian Journal of Mathematics*, volume XXXI(2), pages 986–1004. 1979.
23. M. Wirsing. Algebraic Specification. In *Formal Models and Semantics*, chapter 13, pages 675–788. Elsevier, North-Holland, Amsterdam, 1990.
24. M. Yamamoto et al. Formalization of Planar Graphs. In *HOL Theorem Proving and Its Applications*, p 369, Aspen Grove (USA), 1995. Springer-Verlag, LNCS 971.

A Tool for Data Refinement

Rimvydas Rukšėnas[1,2] and Joakim von Wright[2]

[1] Turku Centre for Computer Science (TUCS)
Lemminkäisenkatu 14A, 20520 Turku, Finland
[2] Dept. of Computer Science, Åbo Akademi University
Lemminkäisenkatu 14A, 20520 Turku, Finland

Abstract. Refinement is a transformational approach to program development. Replacing data structures and adding computations over a new data structure are important steps in many formal methods of program construction. We consider the calculational approach to such transformations within the refinement calculus framework. In the calculational approach, there is no need for inventing a new program; instead, it is constructed from the old one using an abstraction relation that is to hold between the old and new data structures. We describe the foundations of a tool supporting this approach which uses the HOL theorem-proving system as an inference engine. In the tool, a refinement theorem is automatically derived as a consequence of the program calculation. We illustrate our approach with two small case studies.

1 Introduction

Refinement is a process by which specifications are transformed into executable programs. Frequently, two forms of refinement are recognised – algorithmic refinement and data refinement [11]. Algorithmic refinement is usually incremental, replacing a small subcomponent of the program at a time. In contrast, data refinement works on whole programs or on blocks that delineate the scope of a local data structure. A more elaborate form of data refinement is superposition, which not only replaces a data structure but also adds new computations over an added data structure. Data refinement and superposition can be seen as high-level transformation strategies and they are in fact used as major strategies in, e.g., VDM [14], Action Systems [3] and DisCo [13].

The *refinement calculus* [1, 18] is a formalisation of the stepwise refinement method of program construction, based on the weakest precondition calculus of Dijkstra [7]. The refinement calculus supports transformational development of programs. In each step, a new program is derived from the old one by application of a refinement rule.

Typical refinement transformations involve a considerable amount of formula manipulation. Thus, tool support is needed for application of the refinement calculus in practice. Since program refinement is a creative and open-ended activity, such tools cannot in general be fully automated. However, a good tool combines user-directed choice of transformation strategies with automated calculation and simplification of new program versions. The Refinement Calculator [5] is an environment for program development using the refinement calculus. It uses the HOL theorem-proving system [8] as an underlying inference engine and produces as the result of a refinement step a theorem in the HOL logic stating that the refinement in question holds.

In the paper we describe the foundations of a tool for data refinement and superposition. The implementation is based on the calculational approach to data refinement [19, 20, 23], which preserves the structure of an abstract program. The tool is implemented as an extension to the Refinement Calculator. Thus, data refinement and superposition steps can be carried out at any point in the program development process and interleaved with algorithmic refinement steps.

The tool is implemented in the logic of the HOL system, which is simply typed classical higher-order logic. We use lambda abstraction for functions, and application of function f to argument x is written $f\ x$.

Overview of the Paper. In Sect. 2 we give a brief introduction to the Refinement Calculator and a theory behind it. Sect. 3 describes the approach to data refinement supported by our tool. From the general rules of data refinement we also derive more specific rules for a number of special cases in Sect. 4. These rules allow our tool to produce simpler programs with less proof effort. The implementation of the tool as an extension to the Refinement Calculator is described in Sect. 5 and its use is illustrated with a small example in Sect. 6. Superposition and its implementation is described in Sect. 7. We finish with conclusions in Sect. 8.

2   The Refinement Calculator

The Refinement Calculator is a user-friendly environment supporting development of provably correct programs within the refinement calculus. It is built on top of the HOL theorem proving system [8] and uses the Window Library [10] to implement program transformations. The Window Library supports transforming a term by restricting attention to a subterm, called a *focus*, and transforming it. The rest of the term (the context) is left unchanged. The Tcl/Tk [21] programming system provides a graphical user interface to the environment. The user selects (using the mouse) objects to manipulate and chooses the desired transformation (refinement) from a menu.

2.1   The Refinement Calculus

The refinement calculus is a formalisation of the stepwise refinement method of program construction. An initial specification is given as an abstract, often nonexecutable, program. By a series of correctness-preserving steps, the specification is then refined into an executable program.

In the refinement calculus, programs are given a weakest precondition semantics [7]. The refinement relation between program statements S and S' is defined using their weakest preconditions: we say that a statement S is *refined* by S', written $S \sqsubseteq S'$, iff

$$\forall q \cdot wp(S, q) \Rightarrow wp(S', q)$$

Intuitively, refinement means that the new statement S' preserves the total correctness of S. The refinement relation is a preorder (i.e., it is reflexive and transitive). Transitivity of the relation justifies a program development by a series of refinement steps:

$$S_1 \sqsubseteq S_2 \sqsubseteq \cdots \sqsubseteq S_n$$

In data refinement, abstract data structures are replaced by concrete ones. Typically, 'concrete' means more easily or efficiently implementable. Assume that an *abstraction relation* R (i.e., a boolean expression over global variables v, abstract local variables a and concrete local variables c) is given. This relation is then encoded in an abstraction statement E, which replaces the concrete component of the program state by the abstract component but leaves the rest of the state unchanged. The abstraction statement is defined as follows:

$$wp(E, q) = (\exists a \cdot R \wedge q)$$

We then have that the algorithmic refinement of the block statement (see Sect. 2.3)

$$|[\text{ var } a \mid ini \cdot S]| \sqsubseteq |[\text{ var } c \mid ini' \cdot S']|$$

holds and models data refinement, if the two *data refinement conditions* are satisfied:

(i) $ini' \Rightarrow wp(E, ini)$,
(ii) $E; S \sqsubseteq S'; E$.

2.2   Formalization in HOL

The HOL theory of refinement [23] is a *shallow embedding*, which means that the theory manipulates semantic objects, rather than the actual syntax of programs. The type of the state space is not fixed, so we model it with a type variable 's. For any given program, this type variable is instantiated to a product with one component for each program variable. For example, if a program works on a natural number variable and a boolean variable, then the program state has type num#bool. Program variables are modeled as locally named (let-bound) projection functions.

Predicates, pred, are then functions of type 's→bool. The order relation on predicates is defined as follows:

$$\vdash \text{ p implies q } \stackrel{\text{def}}{=} \forall s. \text{ p s} \Rightarrow \text{q s}$$

A predicate transformer is a function of type pred→pred from predicates to predicates. The refinement relation ref between two predicate transformers S and S' is simply an order relation lifted from the type pred:

$$\vdash \text{ S ref S' } \stackrel{\text{def}}{=} \forall q. \text{ S q implies S' q}$$

```
Prog ::= program Name var v : Type · Com
Com ::= Com; Com
      |  skip
      |  {Pred}
      |  [Pred]
      |  v := Exp
      |  v := v' • Pred
      |  if Pred then Com else Com fi
      |  if Actionlist fi
      |  do Actionlist od
      |  (rec X · Com )
      |  |[ var v : Type | Pred · Com ]|
Actionlist ::= Action # Actionlist
   Action ::= Pred → Com
```

Fig. 1. Syntax of programs

2.3   Programming Notation

The syntax of programs (specifications) supported by the Refinement Calculator is shown in the Fig. 1. In the syntax definition, *Type* denotes data types used in programs, *Pred* is any boolean expression over program variables, and *Exp* stands for an expression of a suitable type.

The notation is an extension of Dijkstra's guarded command language. It includes *assertions* and *assumptions*, representing context information, as well as *nondeterministic assignment*, *recursive* construct and *block*. An occurrence of an assertion, $\{p\}$, in a program guarantees that condition p holds at that point in the program. Dually, an assumption, $[p]$, represents our anticipation that p holds at that point. The validity of the anticipation needs to be demonstrated at some point. This is done by propagating context information [15] and then using the following refinement rule (when $q \Rightarrow p$ holds)

$$\{q\}; [p] \sqsubseteq \text{skip}$$

to remove assumption statements. A nondeterministic assignment, $v := v' \bullet post$, is used for specification purposes. It is interpreted as an assignment to v of some value such that predicate *post* is satisfied (in *post*, v refers to initial values and v' to final values of the variable v).

Every program statement denotes a predicate transformer. For example, the meaning of the sequential composition $S_1; S_2$ is given as the predicate transformer S1 seq S2. Here, S1 and S2 are predicate transformers representing program statements S_1 and S_2, respectively, and the sequential composition seq is defined as

$$\vdash (\text{S1 seq S2}) \; q \stackrel{\text{def}}{=} \text{S1(S2 q)}$$

The nondeterministic assignment $v := v' \bullet post$ stands for the predicate transformer nondass $(\lambda v \; v'. \; post)$, where the constant nondass is defined as follows:

⊢ nondass P q $\overset{\text{def}}{=}$ λv. ∀v'. P v v' ⇒ q v'

A block (which is the target of data refinement in our approach)

|[**var** x | $ini \cdot S$]|

adds the local variable(s) x to the program state and initializes them according to the initialization predicate ini. The block is represented by the predicate transformer block (λx,v. ini) S, where S is a predicate transformer corresponding to the block body S. All local variables of the block are modelled as a tuple. The constant block is defined in HOL as

⊢ block p c q $\overset{\text{def}}{=}$ λv. (∀x. p(x,v) ⇒ c (λu. q(SND u)) (x,v))

where the predicate transformer S works on the extended program state of type 'x#'s.

2.4 Using the Refinement Calculator

User interaction with the refinement calculator follows a 'focus-transform' paradigm; the user first highlights a subterm (the focus) and then selects a transformation from a menu and supplies arguments to the transformation. The tool checks applicability, computes the new version of the program and the associated proof obligations, and proves the refinement theorem. After this, the user can try to prove (interactively, using the same tool) and discharge the nontrivial proof obligations (the trivial ones are discharged automatically). It is also possible to continue with new transformations and postpone the discharging of proof obligations.

Standard transformations included in the Refinement Calculator are, e.g., rules for introducing conditionals and loops, splitting an assignment into a sequence of two assignments, adding an initializing assignment etc.

A program variable can have any type that is known to the HOL system. Examples of available types are booleans, natural numbers, reals, and lists. The HOL logic allows new types to be defined, and we have defined a type of arrays, indexed by natural numbers. Because the logic does not support dependent types, it is impossible to have a type of the form "array of size n" with a parameter which can be instantiated to different natural numbers. Instead, the typing is of the form $a : (T)array$ where T is the element type. The size of the array is given by a function size (for simplicity, we write size a as $|a|$).

3 Data Refinement Calculators

It has been shown [19, 20] that the body S' of the concrete block can be constructed from the abstract body S and the abstraction relation. We use that approach with some adaptations and extensions owing to our programming notation. Since the abstraction statement is not a part of the syntax, programs cannot operate on both the abstract and the concrete state at the same time.

A data refinement transformation must replace all occurrences of the abstract variables in one step.

Without loss of generality we may assume that all abstract variables a of a block, $|[$ **var** $a \mid ini \cdot S]|$, are data-refined by concrete variables c while the remaining (global) variables v are left unchanged. If only some of the local variables are replaced, then the remaining variables are simply treated as (unchanged) global variables. Furthermore, we assume that the variable lists a, c, and v are disjoint. The body S of the abstract block works on the program state (a, v). Hence, a body of the concrete block will operate on the program state (c, v).

Now assume that abstract and concrete variables are related by the abstraction relation R. We then define *calculators* (syntactic transformations) of data refinement, D_R for predicates and $\mathcal{D}_R$ for statements, such that

$$|[\textbf{ var } a \mid ini \cdot S]| \sqsubseteq |[\textbf{ var } c \mid D_R(ini) \cdot \mathcal{D}_R(S)]|$$

For an abstract predicate p, D_R and its *dual calculator* D_R° are defined as follows:

$$D_R(p) = (\exists a \cdot R \wedge p)$$
$$D_R^\circ(p) = (\forall a \cdot R \Rightarrow p)$$

The calculator $\mathcal{D}_R$ for statements is defined recursively over the structure of program notation and reflects data refinement theorems for the corresponding program statements. In Sect. 5 we show how these calculators are formalised and proved sound in the HOL system.

Basic Statements. For a nondeterministic assignment of the form $b, w := b', w' \bullet post$, where b and w are some of the local variables a and v, respectively, we calculate the data refinement as follows:

$$\mathcal{D}_R(b, w := b', w' \bullet post) =$$
$$c, w := c', w' \bullet (\forall b \cdot R \;\Rightarrow\; (\exists b' \cdot R[b, c, w := b', c', w'] \wedge post))$$

Since the predicate *post* is binary (may refer to the values of variables before and after execution of the assignment), the rule is a generalization of earlier similar ones [19, 20].

An ordinary assignment statement, $v := e$, is first replaced by the equivalent nondeterministic assignment $v := v' \bullet v' = e$. Then the above rule can be applied. In general, the result is a nondeterministic assignment.

For context assertions and assumptions $\mathcal{D}_R$ is defined as follows:

$$\mathcal{D}_R(\{p\}) = \{D_R(p)\}$$
$$\mathcal{D}_R([p]) = [D_R^\circ(p)]$$

Compound Statements. The calculator of data refinement distributes over sequential composition:

$$\mathcal{D}_R(S_1; S_2) = \mathcal{D}_R(S_1); \mathcal{D}_R(S_2)$$

It can also be pushed into conditional, alternation and loop statements as follows:

$$\mathcal{D}_R(\textbf{if } g \textbf{ then } S_1 \textbf{ else } S_2 \textbf{ fi}) =$$
$$\textbf{if } D_R(g) \textbf{ then } [D_R^\circ(g)]; \mathcal{D}_R(S_1) \textbf{ else } \mathcal{D}_R(S_2) \textbf{ fi}$$

$$\mathcal{D}_R(\textbf{if } A_1 \# \dots \# A_n \textbf{ fi}) \quad = \textbf{if } \mathcal{D}_R(A_1) \# \dots \# \mathcal{D}_R(A_n) \textbf{ fi}$$
$$\mathcal{D}_R(\textbf{do } A_1 \# \dots \# A_n \textbf{ od}) = \textbf{do } \mathcal{D}_R(A_1) \# \dots \# \mathcal{D}_R(A_n) \textbf{ od}$$

Here an abstract action, $g \rightarrow S$, is data-refined using the rule:

$$\mathcal{D}_R(g \rightarrow S) = D_R(g) \rightarrow [D_R^\circ(g)]; \mathcal{D}_R(S)$$

This means that context assumptions of the form $[D_R^\circ(g)]$ can appear in the concrete statements.

Morgan and Gardiner [19] and Morris [20] give a simpler rule for data-refining actions in alternation and loop statements:

$$\mathcal{D}_R(g \rightarrow S) = D_R^\circ(g) \rightarrow \mathcal{D}_R(S)$$

However, this rule either generates the proof obligation $D_R(\vee i \cdot g_i) \Rightarrow (\vee i \cdot D_R^\circ(g_i))$ or adds the assumption $[\vee i \cdot D_R^\circ(g_i)]$ before the alternation statement [20]. In principle, it is possible in some cases that the added proof obligation is dischargeable, whereas an assumption in our version of the action rule cannot be established. At the same time, however, our rule for the loop statement is more flexible and more suitable for an automatic tool. It does not require a loop invariant to be included into the abstraction relation, which is necessary when a proof obligation is generated instead of an explicit assumption statement. This is particularly advantageous when a loop invariant refers to local variables of inner block statements or there are several loops in the program to be refined. Note that Morris' rule for the alternation statement could easily be implemented in our tool as well.

The calculator of data refinement can be pushed into inner blocks of the outermost block (the target of data refinement transformation) as follows:

$$\mathcal{D}_R(|[\textbf{ var } b \mid q \cdot T]|) = |[\textbf{ var } b \mid D_R^\circ(q) \cdot \mathcal{D}_R(T)]|$$

Note that the initialization of a concrete inner block is calculated using the dual predicate calculator instead of D_R. A similar rule in [20] uses an (explicit) assignment instead of an initialization predicate.

For the recursive statement, assume that its body S contains a free statement variable X. Note that the calculator applied to X gives just X:

$$\mathcal{D}_R(X) = X$$

Then the calculator is simply pushed into the body of the recursive construct:

$$\mathcal{D}_R((\textbf{rec } X \cdot S)) = (\textbf{rec } X \cdot \mathcal{D}_R(S))$$

This calculational rule for data refinement of the recursive statement corresponds to the theorem of distributivity of simulation in a paper by Hoare et al. [12].

Assumptions vs. Proof Obligations. We have seen that data refinement calculations of alternation and loop statements introduce assumptions of the form $[D_R^\circ(g_i)]$, where the predicate g_i is the guard of an abstract action A_i. These assumptions can be discharged automatically in many cases. Nevertheless, rules for context handling [15] may be needed to discharge more complex ones. An alternative approach would be to generate proof obligations of the form $D_R(g_i) \Rightarrow D_R^\circ(g_i)$, without adding assumptions into the program. However, we feel that our approach is advantageous since it allows more freedom. For example, context information can later be propagated (i.e., transported to a different place in the program text) to demonstrate the validity of an assumption.

4   Special Cases of Data Refinement

In general, the result of calculating a data refinement can be very complex. By considering special cases, we derive simpler rules and calculations that are easier to handle. By incorporating these rules, our tool for data refinement is capable of producing simpler programs.

Since calculated programs incorporate the abstraction relation the obvious place to start with is being more specific about it. Usually, an abstraction relation R can be written as $abs \land ci$, where the conjunct ci (the *concrete invariant*) does not refer to the local abstract variables a. The initialization of a concrete block, $D_R(ini)$, guarantees that ci holds before the execution of its body. Furthermore, the calculator of data refinement ensures that local variables may be only assigned values that satisfy the predicate ci. Thus, ci is an invariant within the concrete block, i.e. it holds before and after the execution of any statement in the block, and can be used as a context information throughout it. Therefore, ci can be dropped from the guards of concrete alternations and loops. We get the following simplified rule for calculation of a concrete action:

$$\mathcal{D}_R(g \to S) = D_{abs}(g) \to [D_R^\circ(g)]; \mathcal{D}_R(S)$$

Functional Data Refinement. Now consider the case when the above predicate abs is written as $a = f(c, v)$. An abstraction relation of the form

$$a = f(c, v) \land ci$$

is called a *functional* relation. It makes calculations of the concrete program simpler. Specialised techniques for functional relations are considered, e.g., in [19, 20]. In our case, the calculators of concrete predicates, D_R and D_R°, are reduced to

$$D_R(p) = ci \land p[a := f(c, v)]$$
$$D_R^\circ(p) = ci \Rightarrow p[a := f(c, v)]$$

This simplifies calculations of the assertion and assumption statements. For the nondeterministic assignment, the calculator $\mathcal{D}_R$ becomes the following:

$$\mathcal{D}_R(a, v := a', v' \bullet post) =$$
$$\{ci\};\ c, v := c', v' \bullet post[a, a' := f(c, v), f(c', v')] \land ci[c, v := c', v']$$

In particular, the data refinement of a deterministic assignment is again a deterministic assignment:

$$\mathcal{D}_R(a, v := e_1, e_2) =$$
$$\{ci\};\ c, v := e_1[a := f(c, v)], e_2[a := f(c, v)];\ [ci]$$

The guard statement at the end encodes the requirement that the assignment must preserve the concrete invariant.

Since $D_R(p) \Rightarrow D_R^{\circ}(p)$ is trivially true in the case of a functional relation R, no assumptions are needed in the alternation and loop statements. The calculational rule for the abstract action $g \to S$ becomes even simpler:

$$\mathcal{D}_R(g \to S) = D_{abs}(g) \to \mathcal{D}_R(S)$$

where $D_{abs}(g)$ is just $g[a := f(c, v)]$.

Adding Local Variables. A transformation that adds new local variables without removing old ones is a special case of data refinement. Since no variables are removed, the abstraction relation R is just a (concrete) invariant, ci, over the old and new program variables. The calculator $\mathcal{D}_R$ is then simplified for the nondeterministic assignment as follows:

$$\mathcal{D}_R(v := v' \bullet post) = \{ci\};\ c, v := c', v' \bullet post \ \wedge \ ci[c, v := c', v']$$

Moreover, predicate calculators D_R and D_R° become as below:

$$D_R(p) \ = \ ci \ \wedge \ p$$
$$D_R^{\circ}(p) \ = \ ci \ \Rightarrow \ p$$

The guards of alternations and loops remain unchanged.

As a result, the whole transformation introduces a block:

$$S \sqsubseteq \|[\ \mathbf{var}\ c \mid ci \cdot \mathcal{D}_R(S) \ ]\|$$

In combination with a rule for elimination of local variables, adding local variables can also be used as part of a two-step method for data refinement [17] with *auxiliary* (ghost) variables [16].

5 Implementation in HOL

Let the predicate r:'a#'c#'s→bool be the representation in the HOL logic of an abstraction relation R. We then define corresponding abstraction and representation predicate transformers:

$$\vdash \text{abst r q} \ \overset{\text{def}}{=} \ (\lambda v.\ \exists a.\ r(a, \text{FST } v, \text{SND } v) \wedge q(a, \text{SND } v))$$
$$\vdash \text{repr r q} \ \overset{\text{def}}{=} \ (\lambda w.\ \forall k.\ r(\text{FST } w, k, \text{SND } w) \Rightarrow q(k, \text{SND } w))$$

Intuitively, repr r operates as an inverse of abst r and replaces the abstract component of a program state by the concrete component according to the relation r.

Calculation of Data Refinement. For a monotonic predicate transformer c, the following theorem corresponds to the principle of data refinement given in Sect. 2:

    block p c ⊑ block (abst r p) (abst r ; c ; repr r)

For readability, we use the symbol ⊑ for the refinement relation ref and semicolon for the operator seq.

We have written a HOL conversion (i.e., a program in the metalanguage ML that generates a theorem from the input arguments) called DR_CALC that represents the data refinement calculator for statements. As indicated in the Fig. 2, where *wp* gives to a statement its (weakest precondition) meaning in HOL, this conversion calculates a new predicate transformer c' from (abst r ; c ; repr r) and proves the refinement theorem

    ⊢ abst r ; c ; repr r ⊑ c'

The predicate transformer abst r corresponds now to the predicate calculator D_R. Rewriting abst r p gives us a new initialization p' of the block. Since the block construct is monotonic in its body argument, the predicate transformer (abst r) ; c ; (repr r) can be replaced by its refinement c'. As a result, the whole block refinement is proved:

    ⊢ block p c ⊑ block p' c'

The conversion DR_CALC recursively pushes the pair abst r and repr r through the structure of the term c. The effect is that the resulting predicate transformer is a refinement of the original one. For each program statement, a theorem corresponding to the definition of the calculator D_R is used to distribute data refinement as, for example, in the case of sequential composition:

    ⊢ monotonic c1   ⇒   (abst r) ; (c1 ; c2) ; (repr r)
                        ⊑ ((abst r) ; c1 ; (repr r)) ; ((abst r) ; c2 ; (repr r))

Here, the side condition states that the refinement is valid only when the left argument of sequential composition is a monotonic predicate transformer. Monotonicity conditions also arise in the data refinement of loops. They are automatically discharged in the Refinement Calculator.

Inner Blocks. The state space of a program is extended within the block body. Thus, if an inner block, block p c, operates on the program state (a,v), then the predicate transformer c operates on the program state (b,a,v), where b is the local variable(s) of the block. Since the data refinement transformation replaces the first component of the program state, c has to be 'adapted' so that it operates on the state (a,b,v). The adaptation operator is defined as follows:

    ⊢ adapt f g c $\stackrel{\text{def}}{=}$ (assign f) ; c ; (assign g)

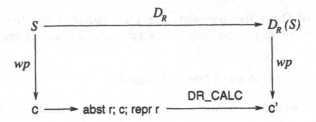

Fig. 2. Calculation of data refinement

where f and g are state functions of the types state1→state2 and state2→state1, respectively. The assignment assign f (assign g) stands for a transformation of the program state specified by the function f (g). The abstraction relation r is to be adapted as well:

$$\bar{r}(a,c,b,v) = r(a,c,v)$$

As adaptation functions, we choose a function f1 that moves the abstract component of the program state one position to the left and a function g1 that moves it back (i.e. $g1 = f1^{-1}$). Before data refinement, an adapted predicate transformer is automatically calculated from adapt f1 g1 c. After the transformation, a concrete predicate transformer must be 're-adapted' so that b is again the first component in the program state. To achieve this we define new adaptation functions, f2 and g2. The function f2 moves the concrete component one position to the right, whereas g2 moves it one position to the left. The refinement theorem for the the block construct is as follows:

⊢ (abst r); (block p c); (repr r)
  ⊑ block (dual(abst r̄) p) (adapt f2 g2 ((abst r̄); (adapt f1 g1 c); (repr r̄)))

Here dual(abst r̄) corresponds to the dual predicate calculator D_R°. The resulting predicate transformer is simplified so that there is no occurrence of adapt in it.

Recursive Construct. The recursive construct as a predicate transformer is represented by the least fixed point mu f. We then have the following refinement theorem for recursion:

⊢ regular f ⇒ (abst r); (mu f); (repr r)
            ⊑ mu (λy. (abst r); f((repr r); y; (abst r)); (repr r))

The side condition regular f which essentially requires that f is monotonic and maps monotonic predicate transformers to monotonic predicate transformers is proved automatically.

A concrete function is constructed from the abstract one by distributing data refinement over its structure. Therefore the concrete parameter y must be abstracted before the distribution as follows: (repr r); y; (abst r). This 'wrapping' is removed using the theorem

$$\vdash \text{monotonic } c \; \Rightarrow \; (\text{abst } r) ; ((\text{repr } r) ; c ; (\text{abst } r)) ; (\text{repr } r) \sqsubseteq c$$

whenever the distribution of the abstraction pair reaches a wrapped parameter (this agrees with the fact that the data refinement calculator maps a statement variable X to X itself).

Data Refinement Transformations in the Refinement Calculator. For the *Data Refine* transformation, the user has to supply three arguments: a list of variables to be replaced a, a list of new variables c, and an abstraction relation r. The arguments are translated into corresponding HOL terms, and the data refinement conversion is invoked. The focus must be a block for the transformation to be valid. The calculated predicate transformer is pretty-printed in our programming notation. Similarly, the rule *Add Block Inv* must be supplied with new variables c, and a concrete invariant ci. It can be applied to any focus and introduces a block with the local variables c under the invariant ci.

6   An Example of Data Refinement

As an example, we consider a program that finds the smallest natural number not occurring in a given array. We assume that the array $b : (num)array$ of natural numbers is given, whereas our goal is to find the smallest number not occurring in b. The specification is then

> **program** *find* **var** $x : num \cdot$
> $x := x' \bullet \neg(\text{elem } x' \; b) \; \wedge \; (\forall y \cdot \neg(\text{elem } y \; b) \; \Rightarrow \; x' \leq y)$

The function **elem** tests for occurrence of a value in an array; the definition is

$$\text{elem } z \; a \stackrel{\text{def}}{=} (\exists i \cdot i < |a| \; \wedge \; z = a[i])$$

Furthermore, we assume that all elements in the array b are within the range $0..M - 1$:

$$(\forall i \cdot i < |b| \; \Rightarrow \; b[i] < M)$$

Block Introduction. Consider the situation where $|b|$ is large while M is small. In this case, it is reasonable to collect information about numbers occurring in the array first, and then find the smallest number that is not among those. Using the *Block Introduction* rule we add a local variable $a : (num)set$ where the information is stored. Furthermore, the initialization of a is added as a nondeterministic assignment as well:

> $|[$ **var** $a : (num)set \; | \; T \cdot$
> $\quad a := a' \bullet (\forall y \cdot \text{elem } y \; b = y \in a');$
> $\quad x := x' \bullet \neg(\text{elem } x' \; b) \; \wedge \; (\forall y \cdot \neg(\text{elem } y \; b) \; \Rightarrow \; x' \leq y)$
> $]|$

The refinement is proved automatically (although it is intuitively obvious, it involves quite a number of proof steps since it relates two statements that work on different state spaces).

Using context handling rules the predicate in the second assignment is then rewritten to express the fact that x gets the smallest value not in the set a:

$$x := x' \bullet \neg(x' \in a) \ \wedge \ (\forall y \cdot \neg(y \in a) \ \Rightarrow \ x' \leq y)$$

Data Refinement. In the data refinement step, the set-valued variable a is replaced with a more concrete data structure – an array $c : (bool)array$ such that $c[x]$ is true if and only if x is an element of a. Thus, the abstraction relation is

$$a = \{y \mid y < M \ \wedge \ c[y]\}$$

Applying the *Data Refine* transformation with this relation produces the following program:

$$
\begin{aligned}
&|[\ \mathbf{var} \ c : (bool)array \mid T \cdot \\
&\quad c := c' \bullet (\forall y \cdot \mathbf{elem} \ y \ b = y < M \wedge c'[y]) \\
&\quad x := x' \bullet \neg(x' < M \wedge c[x']) \ \wedge \ (\forall y \cdot \neg(y < M \wedge c[y]) \ \Rightarrow \ x' \leq y) \\
&]|
\end{aligned}
$$

Note that basic rewrites of the set theory (the theorem $y \in \{x|b\} = b[y/x]$ in this case) were automatically applied in both assignments resulting in three subterms of the form $y < M \wedge c[y]$. The second assignment is actually a result of one additional refinement step which guarantees that the array c remains unchanged. More general refinement according to the rule for nondeterministic assignment from Sect. 3 would allow to change the value of the array c to any permutation of the initial array. Refinements similar to this rely on the Leibniz's rule ($u = u' \Rightarrow t[u] = t[u']$ for any term t). They are performed automatically whenever the corresponding option is selected in a transformation rule.

The form of the abstraction relation supplied to the *Data Refine* rule is very important. For example, the above abstraction relation is equivalent to

$$(\forall y \cdot y \in a = y < M \wedge c[y])$$

which is perhaps more intuitive, but written in nonfunctional form. The result of data refinement with such a relation would be a more complicated program. To derive the above program from it would require considerable user interaction.

As final steps we implement the two assignments as suitable loops using the *Loop Introduction* rule. The resulting program is:

$$
\begin{aligned}
&\mathbf{program} \ find \ \mathbf{var} \ x : num \cdot \\
&\quad |[\ \mathbf{var} \ c : (bool)array \mid T \cdot \\
&\qquad x := 0; \ \mathbf{do} \ x < M \rightarrow c[x], x := F, x + 1 \ \mathbf{od}; \\
&\qquad x := 0; \ \mathbf{do} \ x < |b| \rightarrow c[b[x]], x := T, x + 1 \ \mathbf{od}; \\
&\qquad x := 0; \ \mathbf{do} \ x < M \ \wedge \ c[x] \rightarrow x := x + 1 \ \mathbf{od}; \\
&\quad]|
\end{aligned}
$$

where the first loop has been introduced to initialize the array c. For details on how loop introductions such as these are carried out, we refer to [5].

7   Superposition Refinement

A *superposition* refinement step adds new state components and also adds computations over these new components. Superposition can be used to add detail to a program, for example in order to increase parallelism or implementability. In this section we describe how superposition refinement is implemented in our tool, and how it is used.

7.1   Data Refinement with Stuttering

The basis for superposition is the following rule for calculation of *data refinement with stuttering*:

$$\mathcal{D}_R(\text{do } A_1\#\ldots\#A_n \text{ od}) =$$
$$\text{do } \mathcal{D}_R(A_1)\#\ldots\#\mathcal{D}_R(A_n)\#$$
$$h \to c := c' \bullet t[c := c'] < t \ \wedge \ (\forall a \cdot R \Rightarrow R[c := c'])$$
$$\text{od}$$

where c is the concrete local variable and R is the abstraction relation. The second action in the refining statement is called a *stuttering action*, since it refines a skip step on the abstract level. In the rule, t is an expression ranging over the natural numbers (or some other well-founded set); it guarantees that the stuttering action cannot be repeated infinitely.

To our knowledge this is the first purely calculational formulation of superposition. We have proved the rule as a theorem in HOL. Although the rule is intuitively easy to justify, the formal proof is long and complicated. It follows the ideas of the proof of a similar rule given in [4], making use of a separate theory of iteration operators which is beyond the scope of this paper.

7.2   The Superposition Rule

Superposition is not a single rule, but a program development method. In its most basic form (which we use here), it involves replacing a program containing a loop with a block with local variables, such that the refined loop has an added stuttering action. A simple superposition refinement has the following form:

$$\text{do } A \text{ od} \sqsubseteq \ |[\ \text{var } c : T \ | \ ci \cdot \{ci\};$$
$$\text{do } \mathcal{D}_{ci}(A); \{ci\}$$
$$\# \ \ h \to c := c' \bullet t[c := c'] < t \ \wedge \ ci[c := c']; \{ci\}$$
$$\text{od }]|$$

Note that the concrete invariant in this case can be written as a loop invariant and be used as context information in subsequent transformations. The result is a more detailed and fine-grained program, since execution of the original action

A correspond to execution of $\mathcal{D}_{ci}(A)$ together with a finite number of executions of the stuttering action. The example below illustrates this.

We have implemented superposition as a transformation in the Refinement Calculator. The user provides four arguments:

1. a list of variables,
2. a concrete invariant,
3. a guard for the stuttering action, and
4. a termination function (variant) for the stuttering action.

The tool checks that the transformation can be applied, computes the new version of the program, proves that the refinement is correct, and updates the interface accordingly. The user can then move on to the next phase of the refinement (which typically means simplifying expressions in the resulting program).

7.3   Example: Subarray Search

As an example, we consider the problem of finding a certain subarray in a given array. To be able to handle subarrays, we define a constant sub in higher order logic, as follows:

$$\text{sub } x \ i \ k \ a \overset{\text{def}}{=} (\forall j \cdot j < k \;\Rightarrow\; a[i+j] = x[j] \;\wedge\; i+j < |a| \;\wedge\; j < |x|)$$

Thus, sub $x \ i \ k \ a$ holds when $x[0..k-1]$ is equal to $a[i..i+k-1]$ and no indices are out of range. The following recursive characterization, which is easily proved from the definition, turns out to be more useful in the refinement process:

$$\text{sub } x \ i \ 0 \ a \;\wedge$$
$$(\forall k \cdot \text{sub } x \ i \ k \ a \;\wedge\; a[i+k] = x[k] \;\wedge\; k < |x| \;\wedge\; i+k < |a|$$
$$\Rightarrow\; \text{sub } x \ i \ (k+1) \ a)$$

Our goal is to find an index i such that the array x occurs as a subarray in a starting at the position indexed by i. For simplicity, we assume (as a precondition) that such an index exists (which we name j). The specification is then

program *subarray* **var** $a, x : (num)array; i : num \cdot$
$\quad \{\text{sub } x \ j \ |x| \ a \;\wedge\; j + |x| \le |a|\};$
$\quad i := i' \bullet \text{sub } x \ i' \ |x| \ a$

Coarse-grained Implementation. Using the basic facilities of the Refinement Calculator (mainly a loop introduction), we refine the specification into the following implementation:

$\quad i := 0;$
$\quad \{\text{sub } x \ j \ |x| \ a \;\wedge\; j + |x| \le |a| \;\wedge\; i = 0\};$
$\quad \textbf{do } \neg\text{sub } x \ i \ |x| \ a \to i := i + 1 \ \textbf{od}$

The proof obligations that arise from this transformation are discharged by rewriting with standard theorems of arithmetic.

Superposition Step. What we have now is a coarse-grained program that compares subarrays directly. A superposition step can give us a more fine-grained program that uses only single-element comparisons. The idea is to introduce a new variable k and then incrementally compare the elements of x and $a[i..i+|x|]$. The inventive step (apart from coming up with this strategy) is to find a suitable invariant. We choose to use

$$Inv : \text{sub } x \ j \ |x| \ a \ \wedge \ j + |x| \leq |a| \ \wedge \ i \leq j \ \wedge$$
$$\text{sub } x \ i \ k \ a \ \wedge \ k \leq |x|$$

as our invariant. Since the idea is to increase k in the stuttering action, $|x| - k$ is a suitable termination function. The guard is

$$a[i + k] = x[k] \ \wedge \ k < |x|$$

The superposition transformation automatically calculates the following program and proves that it is a refinement of the above coarse-grain program:

$$
\begin{aligned}
&i := 0; \\
&\{\text{sub } x \ j \ |x| \ a \ \wedge \ j + |x| \leq |a| \ \wedge \ i = 0\}; \\
&\| [\ \mathbf{var} \ k : num \ | \ Inv \ \cdot \\
&\quad \{Inv\}; \\
&\quad \mathbf{do} \ \neg\text{sub } x \ i \ |x| \ a \rightarrow \\
&\qquad\qquad\qquad i, k := i', k' \ \bullet \ Inv'' \ \wedge \ i' = i + 1; \\
&\qquad\qquad \{Inv\} \\
&\quad \# \quad a[i + k] = x[k] \ \wedge \ k < |x| \rightarrow \\
&\qquad\qquad\qquad k := k' \ \bullet \ |x| - k' < |x| - k \ \wedge \ Inv'; \\
&\qquad\qquad \{Inv\} \\
&\quad \mathbf{od} \ \|]
\end{aligned}
$$

In the real program text the invariant Inv is expanded; here we abbreviate it to make the text easier to read. Note that Inv' stands for Inv with k' substituted for k. Furthermore Inv'' stands for Inv with i' and k' substituted for i and k, respectively.

Final Steps. At this point, we can start simplifying using context information. The initialization of the local variable k can be replaced by simply $k = 0$. In the Refinement Calculator, we focus on the initialization and offer $k = 0$ as a suitable replacement. The associated proof obligation

$$\text{sub } x \ j \ |x| \ a \ \wedge \ j + |x| \leq |a| \ \wedge \ i = 0 \ \wedge \ k = 0 \ \Rightarrow \ Inv$$

is trivial.

Both action bodies are also easily refined using basic features of the Refinement Calculator (they are replaced by the deterministic assignments $i, k := i + 1, 0$ and $k := k + 1$). The only more complex step is to strengthen the guard of the old (first) action to $a[i + k] \neq x[k]$. This requires the use of a general refinement rule that says we can strengthens a guard in a loop as long as we do not strengthen the disjunction of all the guards in the loop (in this reasoning the invariant *Inv* is used as context information). The remaining simplifications only make use of basic arithmetic together with the definition and the recursive characterization of sub.

The final result of all these steps is the following program for subarray search:

$i := 0;$
$|[\text{ var } k : num \mid k = 0 \cdot$
$\quad \text{do } a[i + k] \neq x[k] \rightarrow i, k := i + 1, 0$
$\quad \# \quad a[i + k] = x[k] \ \wedge \ k < |x| \rightarrow k := k + 1$
$\quad \text{od }]|$

where the assertions were removed using the general refinement rule $\{p\} \sqsubseteq \textbf{skip}$.

Note that this program is dependent on the assumption (precondition) that x does occur as a subarray in a. If the precondition is not satisfied, then the program loops. However, we can in a similar way use the Refinement Calculator to derive a program that terminates with $i = |a| - |x| + 1$ in the case when x does not occur as a subarray in a:

$i := 0;$
$|[\text{ var } k : num \mid k = 0 \cdot$
$\quad \text{do } a[i + k] \neq x[k] \ \wedge \ i + |x| \leq |a| \rightarrow i, k := i + 1, 0$
$\quad \# \quad a[i + k] = x[k] \ \wedge \ k < |x| \ \wedge \ i + k \leq |a| \rightarrow k := k + 1$
$\quad \text{od }]|$

8   Conclusions

We have described a tool for data refinement and superposition. It has been implemented as an extension to the Refinement Calculator, an existing tool for program refinement and general transformational reasoning. The tool supports a calculational style of data refinement: a concrete program is automatically constructed from an abstract one, using a user-provided abstraction relation. Furthermore, the tool proves the data refinement (superposition) as a HOL theorem which give us a high degree of confidence.

Data refinement proofs depend upon certain conditions (e.g., monotonicity and regularity) as described in Sect. 5. Since our tool is based on a shallow embedding of the refinement theory, these conditions are established (using the corresponding conversions) by induction on the structure of program statements. In a deep embedding, simple matching against a theorem would be sufficient in these cases. However, the shallow embedding strategy gives a number of advantages as well: (i) the programming notation is easily extendible with new constructs, (ii) we can reuse HOL types in programs. Besides, the current handling of program variables would not work (e.g., the definition of block) in a deep embedding.

A one-to-one correspondence between the structures of abstract and concrete programs is too restrictive in some cases. This is especially true for the loop statement where, for example, the introduction of new actions may be desirable. For this purpose, we have proved a refinement rule which introduces a stuttering action within the calculational style.

The complexity of the calculated program (predicates in the assignment, alternation and loop statements) depends essentially on the complexity of the abstraction relation used in the calculation. In the case of a functional relation, the calculated program usually does not require further simplifications. For more sophisticated abstraction relations, the concrete program needs subsequent transformations (refinements) as seen from the example in Sect. 7. A number of refinement rules depend on side conditions. Some of these are simple tautology checks. Otherwise, arising proof obligations require either reasoning about natural numbers (e.g., termination arguments for loops) or reasoning over the data types of the program variables. Basic rewrites related to the abstract and concrete data types can be easily incorporated into the tool. However, more advanced transformations cannot be easily automated, since the system allows us to declare program variables of any HOL type. Nevertheless, careful incorporation of simplifiers and decision procedures available in the latest HOL releases would certainly increase the level of automation.Therefore this must be considered for the tool to be applicable in practice.

A loop within a block can be thought of as an *action system* [2,3] which is a model for parallel and reactive programs. Since a refinement relation for such systems (trace refinement) is essentially reduced to data refinement and superposition, extensions to our tool that allow many-to-many mappings between abstract and concrete actions would make it possible to refine parallel and reactive programs as well. These extensions will be considered in the future.

The first tool which we are aware of that supported the calculational approach to data refinement is a tactic-driven refinement editor [9]. It is built upon Morgan's rules for data refinement [19]. However, this editor does not include formal proofs of transformations. Moreover, a concrete program is calculated in rather general form (without use of specialised techniques) and needs a number of subsequent refinements. The refinement tool PRT [6] is similar to the Refinement Calculator. It also includes a tool for data refinement [22] which is based on Morgan's rules. This tool does not support specialised techniques resulting in simpler programs and seems to be less automated compared to our system in general. Furthermore, to our knowledge its refinement rules remain unproven. In contrast to our tool, both above systems strictly preserve the structure of abstract programs and do not allow to introduce new computations as it is done in superposition refinement.

References

1. R. J. Back. *Correctness Preserving Program Refinements: Proof Theory and Applications*, volume 131 of *Mathematical Center Tracts*. Mathematical Centre, Amsterdam, 1980.

2. R. J. Back and R. Kurki-Suonio. Decentralisation of process nets with centralised control. In *2nd ACM SIGACT-SIGOPS Symp. on Principles of Distributed Computing*, pages 131–142, 1983.
3. R. J. Back and K. Sere. Stepwise refinement of action systems. *Structured Programming*, 12:17–30, Sept. 1991.
4. R. J. Back and J. von Wright. Reasoning algebraically about loops. Technical Report 144, Turku Centre for Computer Science, November 1997.
5. M. J. Butler, J. Grundy, T. Långbacka, R. Rukšėnas, and J. von Wright. The Refinement Calculator: Proof support for program refinement. In L. Groves and S. Reeves, editors, *Formal Methods Pacific'97, Discrete Mathematics and Theoretical Computer Science*, 1997. Springer-Verlag.
6. D. Carrington, I. Hayes, R. Nickson, G. Watson, and J. Welsh. A tool for developing correct programs by refinement. In H. Jifeng, editor, *BCS FACS 7th Refinement Workshop*. Springer-Verlag, July 1996.
7. E. W. Dijkstra. *A Discipline of Programming*. Prentice-Hall Series in Automatic Computation. Prentice Hall, 1976.
8. M. J. C. Gordon and T. F. Melham, editors. *Introduction to HOL: A theorem proving environment for higher order logic*. Cambridge University Press, 1993.
9. L. J. Groves, R. G. Nickson, and M. Utting. A tactic driven refinement tool. In C. B. Jones, B. T. Denvir, and R. C. F. Shaw, editors, *5th Refinement Workshop*, Workshops in Computing, pages 272–297, London, Jan. 1992. BCS-FACS, Springer-Verlag.
10. J. Grundy. The HOL window library. In *The HOL System*, volume Libraries. SRI International, Cambridge, England, 2.01 edition, July 1991.
11. C. A. R. Hoare. Proof of correctness of data representations. *Acta Informatica*, 1(4):271–281, 1972.
12. C. A. R. Hoare, He Jifeng, and A. Sampaio. Normal Form Approach to Compiler Design. *Acta Informatica*, 30(8):701–739, 1993.
13. H.-M. Järvinen and R. Kurki-Suonio. DisCo specification language: marriage of actions and objects. in *Proc. of 11th Int. Conf. on Distributed Computing Systems*, pages 142–151, IEEE Computer Society, 1991.
14. C. B. Jones. *Systematic Software Development using VDM*. Prentice-Hall, 1986.
15. L. Laibinis and J. von Wright. Context handling in the refinement calculus framework. Technical Report 118, Turku Centre for Computer Science, June 1997.
16. P. Lucas. Two constructive realizations of the block concept and their equivalence. Technical Report TR 25.085, IBM Laboratory Vienna, 1968.
17. C. C. Morgan. Auxiliary variables in data refinement. *Information Processing Letters*, 29:293–296, 1988.
18. C. C. Morgan. *Programming from Specifications*. Prentice Hall, 2nd edition, 1994.
19. C. C. Morgan and P. H. Gardiner. Data refinement by calculation. *Acta Informatica*, 27(6):481–503, 1990.
20. J. M. Morris. Laws of data refinement. *Acta Informatica*, 26(4):287–308, 1989.
21. J. K. Ousterhout. *Tcl and the Tk Toolkit*. Addison Wesley, 1994.
22. J. Shield, R. Nickson and D. Carrington. Supporting Data Refinement in a Program Refinement Tool. In L. Groves and S. Reeves, editors, *Formal Methods Pacific'97, Discrete Mathematics and Theoretical Computer Science*, 1997. Springer-Verlag.
23. J. von Wright. Program refinement by theorem prover. In D. Till and R.C.F. Shaw, editors, *6th Refinement Workshop*, Workshops in Computing, pages 121–150, London, Jan. 1994. BCS-FACS, Springer-Verlag.

Mechanizing Relevant Logics with HOL

Hajime Sawamura and Hajime Aramine

Dept. of Information Engineering and Graduate School of
Science and Engineering, Niigata University
8050, Nihono, Ikarashi, Niigata 950-2181, Japan
{sawamura,aramine}@cs.ie.niigata-u.ac.jp

Abstract. Relevant logics are logics a class of logics whose motivation is
to remove logical fallacies caused by the classical 'implication'. In this
paper, we propose a method to build an interactive theorem prover for
relevant logics. This is done first by translating the possible world semantics for relevant logics to the higher-order representation of HOL,
then make the HOL theory obtained by this translation. Relevant
formulas are shown to be valid using the powerful HOL proof capabilities
such as backward reasoning with tactics and tacticals. Relevant logics we
deal with here include a Routley and Meyer's R system (originally
with extra type axiomatization), and Read's R system (basically, Gentzen-
type axiomatization). Our success in formalizing relevant logics as
in HOL and their success yield a powerful proof heuristics for their
formalizations that allowed us to prove a formula which has been
known to be difficult for traditional theorem provers, and even relevant
logicians.

1 Introduction

Relevant logics [1, 3, 9] form a class of logics belonging to the so-called non-
classical logics, whose main concerns are to remove logical fallacies caused by
the classical 'implication'. Nowadays, they are also studied from the structural
viewpoint of logics, that is, a set of substructural logics. In any views, relevant
logics may be said to deal with the problem of implications such as what a logical
implication is and what a logical inference is.

As logic for computer science, relevant logics have been been potentially and
practically expected to provide useful concepts and models for various logical ideas
appearing in computer science as well. In this paper, we present a promising
method to build an interactive theorem prover for relevant logics, since the decidability results are lost, for systems of relevant logics, R and B [14].
This is done first by translating the possible world semantics for the R system
(Relevant logic) to the higher-order representation of HOL [6], and then makes
the HOL theory obtained by this translation. relevant formulas are shown to be
valid using the powerful HOL proof capabilities such as backward reasoning with
tactics and tacticals. In particular, we give a powerful and useful proof heuristics
for relevant logics, which was obtained through our various proof experiences in
relevant logics by HOL and their proof analyses.

Mechanizing Relevant Logics with HOL

Hajime Sawamura and Daisaku Asanuma

Dept. of Information Engineering and Graduate School of
Science and Engineering, Niigata University
8050, Ninocho, Ikarashi, Niigata, 950-0021, Japan
{sawamura,asanuma}@cs.info.eng.niigata-u.ac.jp

Abstract. Relevant logics are non-classical logics, whose motivation is to remove logical fallacies caused by the classical "implication". In this paper, we propose a method to build an interactive theorem prover for relevant logics. This is done first by translating the possible world semantics for relevant logics to the higher-order representation of HOL, and then under the HOL theory obtained by this translation, relevant formulas are shown to be valid using the powerful HOL proof capabilities such as backward reasoning with tactics and tacticals. Relevant logics we have dealt with so far includes Routley and Meyer's **R** system (originally Hilbert-type axiomatization) and Read's **R** system (basically Gentzen-type axiomatization). Our various proof experiences of relevant formulas by HOL and their analyses yielded a powerful proof heuristics for relevant logics. It actually allowed us to prove a formula which has been known to be difficult for traditional theorem provers and even relevant logicians.

1 Introduction

Relevant logics [1, 3, 9] form a class of logics belonging to the so-called non-classical logics, whose main concerns are to remove logical fallacies caused by the classical "implication". Nowadays, they are also studied from the structural viewpoint of logics, that is, as a part of substructural logics. In any views, relevant logics may be said to deal with the profoundest questions such as what a logical implication is and what a logical inference is.

As logics for computer science, relevant logics have been both potentially and practically expected to provide concepts and methods for various logical issues appearing in computer science as well. In this paper, we present a promising method to build an interactive theorem prover for relevant logics, since the decidability results are lost for typical systems of relevant logics, **E** and **R** [14]. This is done first by translating the possible world semantics for the R system of relevant logics to the higher-order representation of HOL [5], and then under the HOL theory obtained by this translation, relevant formulas are shown to be valid using the powerful HOL proof capabilities such as backward reasoning with tactics and tacticals. In particular, we give a powerful and useful proof heuristics for relevant logics, which was obtained through our various proof experiences in relevant logics by HOL and their proof analyses.

Two approaches have been attempted so far for mechanizing relevant logics. One is by implementing the proof theory of **LR** (a decidable fragment of the relevant logic **R**) [11]. Our approach, however, can deal with the full system **R** including **LR** and others, differently from [11]. The other is by utilizing a first order resolution theorem prover with a specially tailored proof search strategy for an efficient proof search [7]. In mechanizing relevant logics in an interactive manner, we instead provide a proof heuristics proper to relevant logics. The semantic encodings are essentially same in both [7] and our approach. In a word, the past two approaches aim at automatic provers for relevant logics, but our approach is interactive and it is natural or even indispensable for us to retain initiatives in proof search on our side, given the undecidability of relevant logics. Therefore we seek a better combination of machine-supported and human-guided proof search method for relevant logics.

The paper is organized as follows. In the next section, we discuss briefly the difficulties in mechanizing substructural logics such as linear logics and relevant logics. In Sects. 3 and 4, following closely Routley and Meyer's paper [10], we introduce the syntax and semantics of the relevant logic **R**. In Sect. 5, we describe how to embed the possible worlds semantics of **R** into the higher-order representation. In Sect. 6, we illustrate how proofs go under the HOL, employing the validity proof of the contraction axiom, where we suggest some of our proof heuristics for relevant logics. In Sect. 7, we give our proof heuristics in detail, which plays a central role in the proof construction of relevant logics. We also show an interactive proof of the converse of construction which is known to be difficult in the automated reasoning circle and even relevant logicians. The last section includes some concluding remarks.

Along the paper, we assume that readers are familiar with relevant logics. Some familiarity with HOL may also be helpful.

2   Difficulties in Mechanizing Relevant Logics

Groote [6] discusses the difficulties encountered when implementing linear logics in Isabelle [8], and explains why the sequent-calculus implementation is mandatory. The difficulties arise from the facts that Isabelle's meta-logic is a fragment of intuitionistic higher-order logic and Isabelle is natural deduction oriented. It, however, is not possible to give a natural deduction-oriented specification of linear implication in Isabelle, if we confine ourself to the pure form of natural deduction without introducing any other device for controlling inferences. This applies to relevant logics as well. For example, in the natural deduction-oriented formalization of relevant logics [3] we often encounter the following awkward inference schemata that are to guarantee relevant implication and relevant inference.

$$\frac{A^\alpha \quad B^\alpha}{A \,\&\, B^\alpha}$$

$$[A]^k$$
$$\vdots$$
$$\frac{B^s}{A \to B^t}$$

, where t = s-{k} and k ∈ s. It is worth noting that these inferences can be smoothly defined in a generic proof assistant system, EUODHILOS [13] since it provides a way to allow us to define various forms of the dependency of a conclusion on assumptions.

On the other hand, for relevant logics, it is not clear yet if its sequent-calculus formulation can be handled like for the sequent-calculus of linear logic within the framework of Isabelle. Basin, Matthews and Vigano recently studies how to reformulate relevant logics as labelled deductive systems [4] and how to implement them in Isabelle [2]. Their systems of relevant logics, then, may as well be said to be hybrid ones of proof theory and semantics. But for the moment, it is not clear how powerful they are in proving various relevant formulas and to what extent they have been successful. In this paper, apart from these we take such a purely semantic approach that the semantics of relevant logics is embedded into the higher-order representation provided by HOL [5] rather than the proof theory of relevant logics is.

3 Syntax and Proof Theory of Relevant Logic R

The language **L** of **R** is a triple $\langle S, O, F \rangle$, where S is a denumerably infinite set of propositional variables, O is a set of logical connectives: the relevant negation $\sim$, the truth-functional connectives & and $\lor$, and the relevant implication $\to$, and a set of formulas F is constructed as usual. We use 'p', 'q', 'r', etc., to refer to propositional variables of **R** and 'A', 'B', etc., to refer to arbitrary formulas of **R**.

The axiom schemata of **R** are:

A1. $A \to A$ (Self-implication),

A2. $A \to ((A \to B) \to B)$ (Assertion),

A3. $(A \to B) \to ((B \to C) \to (A \to C))$ (Suffixing),

A4. $(A \to (A \to B)) \to (A \to B)$ (Contraction),

A5. $A \& B \to A$ (Conjunction elimination),

A6. $A \& B \to B$ (Conjunction elimination),

A7. $(A \to B) \& (A \to C) \to (A \to B \& C)$ (Conjunction introduction),

A8. $A \to A \lor B$ (Disjunction introduction),

A9. $B \to A \lor B$ (Disjunction introduction),

A10. $(A \to C) \& (B \to C) \to (A \lor B \to C)$ (Disjunction elimination),

A11. $A \& (B \lor C) \to A \& B \lor A \& C$ (Distribution),

A12. $(A \to \sim B) \to (B \to \sim A)$ (Contraposition),

A13. $\sim\sim A \to A$ (Double negation).

The choice of the implicational axioms can be varied in a number of informative ways [3]. A2(Assertion), A3(Suffixing) and A4(Contraction) may be replaced by A2'(Permutation), A3'(Prefixing) and A4'(Self-distribution) respectively.

A2'. $(A \rightarrow (B \rightarrow C)) \rightarrow (B \rightarrow (A \rightarrow C))$ (Permutation),

A3'. $(A \rightarrow B) \rightarrow ((C \rightarrow A) \rightarrow (C \rightarrow B))$ (Prefixing),

A4'. $(A \rightarrow (B \rightarrow C)) \rightarrow ((A \rightarrow B) \rightarrow (A \rightarrow C))$ (Self-Distribution).

As for negation, the following formula called Reductio is often included into R, although it of course can be proved from other axioms above.

A14. $(A \rightarrow \sim A) \rightarrow \sim A$ (Reductio).

The inference rule schemata are:

R1. From $A \rightarrow B$ and A, infer B,

R2. From A and B, infer $A \& B$.

A proof is defined in the usual way.

4   Semantics of Relevant Logic R

Some semantic theories for relevant logics are known, such as algebraic semantics by de Morgan monoid, operational semantics by semi-lattice and relational semantics by possible worlds [3]. There is no big difference among these. This paper, therefore, deals with the third since it is somewhat easier to understand and implement analogously with the possible worlds semantics for modal logics.

The *relevant model structure* for $\mathbf{L}$ is a quadruple $\langle 0, W, R, * \rangle$, where W is a set of worlds (or set-ups), $0 \in W$ is called a real world, R is a ternary relation on W, $*$ is a unary operation on W, satisfying postulates p1–p6 below with definitions d1 and d2 [10]. For all $a, b, c, d \in W$:

d1. $a < b \overset{def}{=} R0ab$,

d2. $R^2abcd \overset{def}{=} \exists x (Rabx \& Rxcd \& x \in W)$,

p1. $R0aa$,

p2. $Raaa$,

p3. $R^2abcd \Rightarrow R^2acbd$,

p4. $R^2 0abc \Rightarrow Rabc$,

p5. $Rabc \Rightarrow Rac^*b^*$,

p6. $a^{**} = a$.

Let $\mathbf{L} = \langle S, O, F \rangle$ be a language defined in Sect. 3 and $\{T, F\}$ the set of classical truth-values. A *valuation* v of $\mathbf{L}$ in $\langle 0, W, R, * \rangle$ is a function from $S \times W$ to $\{T, F\}$ which satisfies the following heredity condition, for every propositional variable $p \in S$ and $a, b \in W$:

v1. $a < b$ and $v(p, a) = T \Rightarrow v(p, b) = T$.

The interpretation I associated with v is a function from $F \times W$ to $\{T, F\}$ which satisfies the following conditions, for all $p \in S$, $A, B \in F$ and $a \in W$:

i1. $I(p, a) = v(p, a)$,

i2. $I(A \& B, a) = T$ iff $I(A, a) = T$ and $I(B, a) = T$,

i3. $I(A \vee B, a) = T$ iff $I(A, a) = T$ or $I(B, a) = T$,

i4. $I(A \rightarrow B, a) = T$ iff $\forall b, c \in W$, $Rabc$ and $I(A, b) = T \Rightarrow I(B, c) = T$,

i5. $I(\sim A, a) = T$ iff $I(A, a^*) = F$.

A formula A is *true* on a valuation v or on the associated interpretation I at a set-up $a \in W$, if $I(A, a) = T$, otherwise A is *false* at a. A is *verified* on v or on the associated I if $I(A, 0) = T$, otherwise A is *falsified* on v. A is *valid* in a relevant model structure $\langle 0, W, R, * \rangle$ if A is verified on all valuations therein. Finally, A is **R**-*valid* if A is valid in all relevant model structures, otherwise A is **R**-*invalid*.

The following lemma, a generalization of the condition v1 above, is beneficial to the semantic embedding of the **R** semantics into the higher-order representation.

Lemma 1 (Routley and Meyer). [10] *For an arbitrary formula A and $a, b \in W$: $a < b$ and $v(A, a) = T \Rightarrow v(A, b) = T$.*

Theorem 1 (Routley and Meyer). [10] **R** *is sound and complete.*

5   Realizing Relevant Logic R with HOL

The possible worlds semantics of **R** above is translated into the HOL representation as follows, obtaining the HOL theory for **R**. Throughout the translation, we identify the semantic phrase $I(p, a) = T$ simply with pa, for example, in terms of a functional and applicative form. Here we construct a HOL theory for **R**, annotating each line of the HOL session.

Invoking HOL, we start creating a new theory called "R_system" with the command.

```
#new_theory 'R_system';;
() : void
```

We define a set of possible worlds or set-ups to be a 0-ary type operator named 'world'.

```
#new_type 0 'world';;
() : void
```

A ternary relation R on the world and a real world 0 are introduced as follows, where bool is a boolean type of the HOL logic.

```
#new_constant('R',":world#world#world -> bool");;
() : void
#new_constant('zero',":world");;
() : void
```

The unary operation * named "star" on W is defined as a new constant.

```
#new_constant('star',":world->world");;
() : void
```

The following is a direct translation of a quaternary relation R^2. We do not need a translation of d1 since we always use the R notation only.

```
#new_definition('R2','"R2(a,b,c,d)=?x.R(a,b,x)/\R(x,c,d)");;
|- !a b c d. R2(a,b,c,d) = (?x. R(a,b,x) /\ R(x,c,d))

#new_axiom('V1',"R(zero,a,b) /\p a ==> p b");;
|- !a b p. R(zero,a,b) /\ p a ==> p b
```

This is meant to be a translation of v1 expanded by any formulas, thanks to Lemma 1 described in the previous section. So from now on we will not have any concern about the phrase "for every propositional variable p" in the definition of the valuation function v1.

The remaining part of **R** is literally translated into the HOL representation as follows.

```
#new_infix_definition('IMP',"$-->p q =\x:world.!y:world.
               !z:world. R(x,y,z) ==>(p y==>q z)");;
|- !p q. p --> q = (\x. !y z. R(x,y,z) ==> p y ==> q z)
#new_infix_definition('AND',"$&p q =\x:world.p x /\ q x");;
|- !p q. p & q = (\x. p x /\ q x)
#new_infix_definition('OR',"$or p q =\x:world.p x \/ q x");;
|- !p q. p or q = (\x. p x \/ q x)
#new_definition('NOT',"not p = \w.~(p (star w))");;
|- !p. not p = (\w. ~p(star w))

#new_axiom('P1',"R(zero,a,a)");;
|- !a. R(zero,a,a)
#new_axiom('P2',"R(a,a,a)");;
|- !a. R(a,a,a)
#new_axiom('P3',"R2(a,b,c,d) ==>R2(a,c,b,d)");;
|- !a b c d. R2(a,b,c,d) ==> R2(a,c,b,d)
#new_axiom('P4',"R2(zero,a,b,c) ==> R(a,b,c)");;
|- !a b c. R2(zero,a,b,c) ==> R(a,b,c)
#new_axiom('P5',"R(a,b,c) ==> R(a,(star c),(star b))");;
|- !a b c. R(a,b,c) ==> R(a,star c,star b)
#new_axiom('P6',"star(star a)=a");;
|- !a. star(star a) = a
#close_theory();;
() : void
```

6   Proving Formulas under the HOL Theory for R – A Proof Example

The role of this section is twofold; (i) we simply illustrate how to use many definitions and axioms of the HOL theory for **R** described in the previous section, and (ii) we reveal some of the difficulties to be resolved in proving relevant formulas. These, therefore, serve as an introduction to understanding the next section. The method described here will be generalized to a useful proof heuristics for relevant formulas which we describe in the next section. Throughout the paper, we use not the usual mathematical notation but the standard notation of HOL since it can easily remind us of the original expressions.

A relevant formula we take up is A4 (Contraction) [10]:

$$|- \;\; (P \;\text{-->}\; (P \;\text{-->}\; Q)) \;\text{-->}\; (P \;\text{-->}\; Q)$$

1. Apply the routine tactics initially.

```
#set_goal("(P --> (P --> Q)) --> (P --> Q)zero");;
#e(REWRITE_TAC[IMP]);;
#e(BETA_TAC);;
#e(REPEAT STRIP_TAC);;
"Q z'"
4 ["R(zero,y,z)" ]
3 ["!y' z''.R(y,y',z'') ==>P y' ==>(!y'' z'. R(z'',y'',z') ==> P y'' ==>
 Q z')" ]
2 ["R(z,y',z')" ]
1 ["P y'" ]
```

From the forms of the assumptions and the conclusion, we can now see that we need to derive some more ternary relations in addition to the assumptions numbered 2 and 4 above to get to the conclusion. In the next section, we will elaborate on how the appropriate forms of those ternary relations should be determined. Here we just present the necessary steps.

2. Construct the specialized R2 relation 2 below from the assumptions 2 and 4 above, using the R2 definition, "R2(a,b,c,d)= ?x.R(a,b,x)/\R(x,c,d)". Hereafter, we will list only the assumptions to be paid attention. For the actual proofs, defining "Weakening rule" for the left of turnstile symbols would be helpful since it could prune lots of assumptions which obviously are not used in proofs and suppress a combinatorial explosion of formulas generated by tactics such as IMP_RES_TAC, RES_TAC, and so on.

```
#e(IMP_RES_TAC R2);;
"Q z'"
2 ["R2(zero,y,y',z')" ]
```

3. Derive the assumption 1 below from the assumption 2 above, using the definition P4, "R2(zero,a,b,c) ==> R(a,b,c)".

```
#e(IMP_RES_TAC P4);;
"Q z'"
1 ["R(y,y',z')" ]
```

4. Derive a property of the ternary relation R, "R(a,b,c) ==> R(b,a,c)" as a lemma named lemma3.

5. Derive the assumption 3 below from the assumption 1 in the step 3, using the lemma3.

```
#e(IMP_RES_TAC lemma3);;
"Q z'"
3 ["R(y',y,z')" ]
```

6. Add the assumption 1 below to the assumption list, using the definition of P2, "!a.R(a,a,a)". Here "y'" is substituted for "a" in P2. The reason for this ingenious step will be explained in detail in the next section.

```
#e(ASSUME_TAC (SPEC "y':world" P2));;
"Q z'"
4 ["R(y',y,z')" ]
1 ["R(y',y',y')" ]
```

7. Derive the assumption 7 below from the assumptions 1 and 4, using the definition R2.

```
#e(IMP_RES_TAC R2);;
"Q z'"
7 ["R2(y',y',y,z')" ]
```

8. Derive the assumption 3 below from the assumption 7 above, using the definition P3, "R2(a,b,c,d) ==> R2(a,c,b,d)".

```
#e(IMP_RES_TAC P3);;
"Q z'"
3 ["R2(y',y,y',z')" ]
```

9. Derive the assumptions 23 and 24 below from the assumption 3 above, using the definition R2. It is noted that the tactic IMP_RES_TAC promotes the elimination of existential quantifiers in the assumption part, introducing new variables. It is a new variable x''' in the assumptions 23 and 24 for this case.

```
#e(IMP_RES_TAC R2);;
 "Q z'"
24 ["R(y',y,x''')" ]
23 ["R(x''',y',z')" ]
```

10. Derive the assumption 7 below from the assumption 24 above, using the lemma3.

```
#e(IMP_RES_TAC lemma3);;
"Q z'"
71 ["!y' z''.R(y,y',z'') ==> P y' ==>(!y'' z'. R(z'',y'',z') ==> P y''
==> Q z')" ]
69 ["P y'" ]
40 ["R(x''',y',z')" ]
7 ["R(y,y',x''')" ]
```

11. Resolve the assumptions 7, 40, 69 and 71 and obtain the conclusion.

```
#e(RES_TAC);;
OK..
goal proved
```

7   A Useful Proof Heuristics for Relevant Logics

In this section, we present a useful proof heuristics for the relevant logic **R** which we have found by proving a number of relevant theorems with HOL. It enabled us to prove the converse of the contraction as well, which is known to be difficult for both traditional theorem provers and even relevant logicians [7]. First we deal with the case of formulas in which only the implication symbols appear, and then other cases in which conjunctions, disjunctions and negations appear in addition to the implication symbols. Finally we discuss another useful proof method, so called "proving by analogy". We will consider this from the standpoint of the proof method for relevant logics by tactics and tacticals.

7.1   How to Handle Implication

We will explain this by using proof examples, for the ease of description and understanding.

Step 1. Initial step

This is a step common to every formula to be proved. Hence, the following series of tactics is initially applied to it.

set_goal("(A)zero");;, letting A be a formula to be proved.

e(REWRITE_TAC[IMP]);;

e(BETA_TAC);;

e(REPEAT STRIP_TAC);;

Step 2. Eliminate the real world.

This step is divided into two substeps, Step 2.1 and Step 2.2. Step 2.1 deals with the case in which there exists one ternary relation in the assumption list and one formula related with that relation. Step 2.2 deals with the other cases. For example, the validity proof of the axiom A1(Self-implication) can be shown at Step 2.1 as follows. After Step 1, we have:

```
"P z"
2 ["R(zero,y,z)" ]
1 ["P y" ].
```

Hence, the next tactics enables us to prove it, using the definition of the heredity condition, V1.

e(IMP_RES_TAC V1);;

We illustrate Step 2.2, using the following result of the A4 (Contraction) proof obtained immediately after Step 1.

```
"Q z'"
4 ["R(zero,y,z)" ]
3 ["!y' z''.R(y,y',z'') ==>P y'==>(!y'' z'.R(z'',y'',z') ==>
  P y'' ==> Q z')" ]
2 ["R(z,y',z')" ]
1 ["P y'" ]
```

In the assumption list, there exist two ternary relations, 4 ["R(zero,y,z)"]
and 2 ["R(z,y',z')"], sharing the variable "z".

Then we can obtain a quaternary relation R2(zero,y,y',z') by the definition R2, and hence a new ternary relation R(y,y',z') by the definition P4. The
tactics of Step 2.2 is as follows.

e(IMP_RES_TAC R2);;
e(IMP_RES_TAC P4);;

Thus, we have, omitting unnecessary assumptions

```
"Q z'"
7 ["!y' z''.R(y,y',z'') ==>P y'==>(!y'' z'.R(z'',y'',z') ==>
  P y'' ==> Q z')" ]
5 ["P y'" ]
1 ["R(y,y',z')" ].
```

Here, it might be convenient to prepare a new ternary relation derived from this
R(y,y',z') by applying the lemma3 (|- R(a,b,c) ==> R(b,a,c)) after Step 2.2,
since it is often used as done in the previous section.

This step was used, for example, in the validity proofs of A2, A3, A4, A2',
A3', A4', the converse of the contraction, etc.

Step 3. Decide if we should derive new ternary relations.

As can be seen in the assumption list after Step 2.2, there exist one implicational formula, one atomic formula and some ternary relations. The implicational
formula numbered 7 above and the assumption numbered 5 above suggest us to
derive two new ternary relations of the form, R(y, y', u) and R(u, y', z'), where
the universally quantified variable "u" stands for a place temporarily left undetermined. Then we surely can get to the conclusion. We describe how to derive
these in Step 5 below. It might also be interesting to note that in our proof experience, we have observed that every atomic assumption in the assumption list
except ternary relations is necessarily used to derive a conclusion, and hence the
number of the atomic assumptions except ternary relations is less than that of
the atomic assumptions except ternary relations appearing in the implicational
formula. An exception is the proof of the converse of the contraction described
below that we came across so far. If the necessary ternary relation to be derived
is only one, we may go to Step 6, omitting Step 4 and 5 below. For example,
the A2 (Assertion) proof applies to this case.

Step 4. Decide if we should use the definition P2.

Here we decide if we should use the definition P2, |-!a.R(a,a,a) and if so we
determine a new variable to be substituted for the quantified variable 'a'. First
we compare the number of variables in the assumption list after Step 2.2 with
that of variables in the necessary ternary relations to be derived, whose forms
were made explicit in Step 3 above. For example, comparing R(y,y',z') in the
assumption list above with two desired relations, R(y, y', u) and R(u, y', z'), we
can know that one more variable "y'" would be needed to derive them, where the

new variable "u" is not taken into account. This increment can be attained by the following tactics, resulting a new assumption list with "R(y',y',y')" numbered 1 below.

```
e(ASSUME_TAC (SPEC "y':world" P2));;
"Q z'"
11 ["!y' z''.R(y,y',z'')) ==> P y' ==>(!y'' z'. R(z'',y'',z') ==>
        P y'' ==> Q z')" ]
9 ["P y'" ]
5 ["R(y,y',z')" ]
4 ["R(y',y,z')" ]
1 ["R(y',y',y')" ]
```

This step was used, for example, in the validity proofs of A4, A4', the converse of the contraction, etc.

Step 5. Derive new ternary relations.

This step will be repeated until necessary ternary relations are derived, if their number is more than two. We illustrate this step for our A4 example. By applying the following series of tactics, the above proof result produces a new assumption list with "R(y',y,x''')" and "R(x''',y',z')" numbered 24 and 23 respectively below.

```
e(IMP_RES_TAC R2);;
e(IMP_RES_TAC P3);;
e(IMP_RES_TAC R2);;
```

This is due to those inferences that the assumptions numbered 1 and 4 above yields the assumption 39 below by R2, then it yields the assumption 31 below by P3, and finally it yields the assumptions 23 of the form R(u, y', z') and 24 of the form R(y, y', u) below by R2, where the new variable "x'''" is generated to eliminate the existential quantifier and plays the role of the variable "u".

```
"Q z'"
54 ["!y' z''.R(y,y',z'')) ==> P y' ==>(!y'' z'. R(z'',y'',z') ==>
        P y'' ==> Q z')" ]
52 ["P y'" ]
48 ["R(y,y',z')" ]
47 ["R(y',y,z')" ]
44 ["R(y',y',y')" ]
39 ["R2(y',y',y,z')" ]
31 ["R2(y',y,y',z')" ]
24 ["R(y',y,x''')" ]
23 ["R(x''',y',z')" ]
```

Here again, it might be convenient to prepare new ternary relations derived from these ternary relations by applying the lemma3. This step was used, for example, in the validity proofs of A2', A3, A3', A4, A4', etc.

Step 6. Resolve among assumptions

The very powerful resolution-like tactics "RES_TAC", put it differently, a sort of an extended modus ponens, leads to the desired conclusion, as can be seen in the last step of the previous section.

```
e(RES_TAC);;
```

This step will be repeated in the necessary number of times. In fact, this tactics was used once, for example, in the validity proofs of A2, A2', A3', A4, and twice in the validity proofs of A3, A4' and the converse of the contraction.

Practically, prior to this step we had better apply the predefined WEAKEN-ING_TAC with ADD_ASSUM as a justification, in order to avoid unnecessary derivations caused by many assumptions.

Figure 1 depicts the overall flow structure of our proof heuristics for relevant logics in the case of implicational formulas. This heuristic proof procedure has not been implemented as a tactic yet since it still includes a process which has a difficulty of selecting appropriate worlds successfully leading to a proof.

7.2   Modification of Step 3 for More Complicated Formulas

At Step 3 above, we gave a guiding principle to derive necessary ternary relations from a given assumption list. For harder to prove formulas, we need to augment it. For the proof of the converse of the contraction,

$$(A->(B->B))->(A->(A->(B->B)))$$

we show how to do it.

After Step 2, we have, as the result of rewriting and simplifying the formula

```
"B z'"
13 ["!y' z''.R(y,y',z'') ==> A y' ==>(!y'' z'. R(z'',y'',z') ==>
    B y'' ==> B z')" ]
11 ["A y'''  " ]
10 ["R(z''',y'',z'')" ]
9  ["A y''  " ]
8  ["R(z'',y',z')" ]
7  ["B y'"]
1  ["R(y,y''',z''')" ].
```

In the assumption list, we have two atomic formulas, 9 ["A y''"] and 11 ["A y'''"]. However, there appears only one atomic formula "A y'" in the implicational formula of the assumption list. So, following our guiding principle stated in our original Step 3, we have two possibilities for this case: (i) From the assumptions numbered 7, 9 and 13, the new ternary relations to be derived are of the form R(y,y'',u) and R(u,y',z'), (ii) from the assumptions numbered 7, 11 and 13, the new ternary relations to be derived are of the form R(y,y''',u) and R(u,y',z'), where u is a new universally quantified variable. The previous method suggests that either (i) or (ii) could lead to a success, without considering both (i) and (ii). This, however, violates the fact that every initial atomic

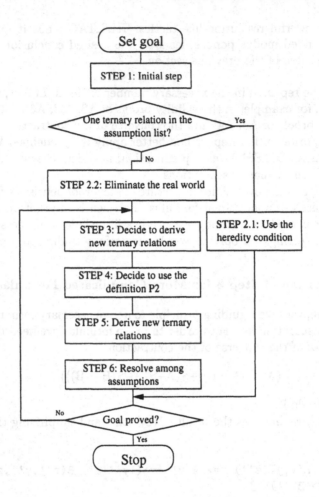

Fig. 1. Flow of a heuristic proof procedure for relevant logics – Case of implicational formulas

assumption except ternary relations has to be used according to our proof experiences on relevant logics proof done so far, as we mentioned earlier. As a matter of fact, it does not work for this formula. So we consider a way to use both assumptions 9 ["A y' ' "] and 11 ["A y' ' '"] as follows. First, from the assumptions numbered 7, 11 and 13, we can foresee that the new ternary relations to be derived are of the form R(y,y''',u) and R(u,y',v), where u and v are new universally quantified variables. Then from the following assumptions we can have an atomic formula "B v".

```
!y' z''.R(y,y',z'') ==> A y' ==> (!y'' z'. R(z'',y'',z') ==>
  B y'' ==> B z')
R(y,y''',u)
```

```
A y'''
R(u,y',v)
B y'
```

Next we can foresee that from the assumptions numbered 9, 13 and the obtained "B v", the new ternary relations to be derived are of the form R(y,y'',w) and R(w,v,z'), where v and w are new universally quantified variables. Then from the following assumptions we can have our desired atomic formula "B z'".

```
!y' z''.R(y,y',z'')) ==> A y' ==> (!y'' z'. R(z'',y'',z')
   ==> B y'' ==> B z')
R(y,y'',w)
A y''
R(w,v,z')
B v
```

Therefore, the necessary ternary relations to be derived are found to be R(y,y''',u), R(u,y',v), R(y,y'',w) and R(w,v,z').

The following output displays the proof state in which the four ternary relations to be derived and the atomic formula "B v" became present in the assumption list.

```
"B z' "
59 ["!y' z''. R(y,y',z'') ==> A y'==>(!y'' z'. R(z'',y'',z')
         ==> B y'' ==> B z')" ]
57 ["A y''' " ]
55 ["A y'' " ]
53 ["B y' " ]
44 ["R(y,y''',x')" ]      %R(y,y''',u) with u = x'
37 ["R(y,y'',x''')" ]     %R(y,y'',w) with w = x'''
23 ["R(x',y',x''''''')" ]    %R(u,y',v) with v = x'''''''
22 ["R(x''',x''''''',z')" ]  %R(w,v,z')
1  ["B x''''''' " ]       %Bv with v = x'''''''
```

Immediately after this step, the following tactics derives our conclusion.

```
#e(RES_TAC);;
goal proved
```

In summary, the overall proof script is as follows, together with some annotations on steps and derivatives.

```
#g("((A-->(B-->B))-->(A-->(A-->(B-->B))))zero");;
  %Step 1
#e(REWRITE_TAC[IMP;AND;OR;NOT]);;
#e(BETA_TAC);;
#e(REPEAT STRIP_TAC);;
  %Step 2.2
#e(IMP_RES_TAC R2);;
```

```
#e(IMP_RES_TAC P4);;
  %Step 4
#let th1 = SPEC "y:world" P2;;
#e(ASSUME_TAC th1);;
  %Step 5(modified)
  %Derivation of a new lemma from lemma 3.
#let lemma5 = TAC_PROOF
    (([],"R(x,y,z)/\R(z,a,b)==>?x'.R(x,a,x')/\R(y,x',b)"),
    (REPEAT STRIP_TAC) THEN IMP_RES_TAC R2 THEN IMP_RES_TAC P3
    THEN IMP_RES_TAC R2 THEN IMP_RES_TAC lemma3
    THEN EXISTS_TAC"x':world" THEN ASM_REWRITE_TAC []);;
%Derivation of one of the ternary relations of the form R(y,y''',w).
#let th2 = GENL ["x:world";"y:world";"z:world";"a:world";
 "b:world"] lemma5;;
#let th3 = SPECL ["y:world";"y:world";"y:world";"y''':world";
 "z''':world"] th2;;
#e(ASSUME_TAC th3);;
#e(RES_TAC);;
%Derivation of one of the ternary relations of the form R(y,y'',u).
#let th4 = SPECL ["y:world";"x'':world";"z''':world";
 "y'':world";"z'':world"] th2;;
#e(ASSUME_TAC th4);;
#e(RES_TAC);;
%Derivation of the remaining ternary relations of the forms R(u,y',v)
  and R(w,v,z').
#let th5 = SPECL ["x'':world";"x''':world";"z'':world";
 "y':world";"z':world"] th2;;
#e(ASSUME_TAC th5);;
%Derivation of the atomic formula of the form B(v).
#e(RES_TAC);;
  %Step 6
#e(RES_TAC);;
```

The readers may have noticed that the lemma5 is used many times in the core part of the proof, together with the appropriate substitutions. This is because the lemma5 permits the exchanges of variables among ternary relations. In every proof of A2', A3, A3', A4 and A4' which are basic axioms characterizing the implication, we actually have used the lemma5 at Step 5. In the proof of the converse of contraction, note that in the latter half of the proof script, Step 5 is mixed with Step 6 in order to reduce a combinatorial explosion of the results by RES_TAC.

7.3 How to Handle Conjunction and Disjunction

In the relevant logic **R**, the conjunction & and disjunction ∨ connectives, are truth-functional (classical). Therefore, it is not difficult to prove formulas including them. In fact, the validity proofs of A5, A6, A8 and A9, for example, were done by going through Step 1 and Step 2.1. A7, A10 and A11 can be proved by a simple case analysis after Step 1.

On the other hand, it should be noted that although conjunction and disjunction seem simple in semantic terms, systems added them are far from trivial as they become undecidable according to Urquhart's results about the decision problem for **R** and its neighbors [14].

7.4 How to Handle Negation

The relevant negation $\sim$ deserves a special treatment although its semantic definition is less difficult than the relevant implication. Naturally, the proper definitions for the relevant negation P5 and P6 are used very often. For example, the validity proofs of A12 and A13 go through Step 1, Step 2.1 together with P5, P6 and the usual HOL tactics. The validity proof of A14 is somewhat different from these. It goes through Step 1, Step 3, Step 4, Step 2.2, Step 5 and Step 6, where the definitions used are P2, P5 and P6 in order.

7.5 Proving by Analogy

In looking for a proof of a theorem, it is very helpful to find analogies with proofs of already proved theorems in order to guide the proofs of the new proof. In the HOL proof environment, however, there seems to be no work on how tactics and tacticals can deal with analogical reasoning. In analogical reasoning, the proof of one theorem is used to guide the proof of a similar theorem by suggesting analogous steps. When a step suggested by a guiding proof cannot be applied, we bring the proofs back into correspondence, often by adding intermediate steps. Here we just list some case studies in constructing proofs of relevant logics, showing potential usefulness of proving by analogy.

In Sect. 3, we have stated that A2 (Assertion), A3 (Suffixing) and A4 (Contraction) may be replaced by A2' (Permutation), A3' (Prefixing) and A4' (Self-distribution) respectively in the axiom system of the relevant logic **R**. So, we can expect that A2 and A2', A3 and A3', and A4 and A4' might have similar proof structures at the proof script level as well, respectively. In fact, we have observed that

• A2 (Assertion) and A2' (Permutation): A2 proof goes through Step 1, Step 2.2, use of the lemma 3 and Step 6. A2' proof goes through Step 1, Step 2.2, Step 5 and Step 6. The only difference is the third part of the proof steps, that is, use of the lemma 3 and Step 5.

• A3 (Suffixing) and A3' (Prefixing): A3 goes through Step 1, Step 2.2, Step 5 and Step 6. A2' goes through Step 1, Step 2.2, Step 5, use of the lemma 3 and Step 6.

• A4 (Contraction) and A4' (Self-Distribution): A4 goes through Step 1, Step 2.2, Step 5 and Step 6. A4' goes through Step 1, Step 2.2, three times of Step 5 and Step 6. For the cases like this, the tacticals REPEAT of HOL would become usable when yielding a generalization from some proof scripts

• A11 (Distribution) and a variant of it, A & (B ∨ C) → A & B ∨ A: these go through the same proof steps and tactics.

Therefore those proof scripts as series of tactics or tacticals could be effectively used for structure-similar formulas to be proved and performance-similar formulas if we save them for later use. For the moment, it is up to us to determine when and how they should be applied, closely looking at similarities.

8   Concluding Remarks

We have shown a new and promising direction to a theorem prover for relevant logics which are in general undecidable. Our mechanization method for relevant logics could be used for a wide range of relevant logics as well by changing the semantic postulates in obvious ways. Such generality might be of effective use as a proof tool of logicians and computer scientists.

In particular, through various proof experiences, we have found a useful proof heuristics with which many relevant formulas could be proved along the following outline:

Stage 1. Split a formula into assumptions and a conclusion.
Stage 2. Derive relevant properties of R.
Stage 3. Do derivations among assumptions with R properties added.
Stage 4. Go to Step 2 if we still do not get to a conclusion.

The most crucial step in the heuristics lies in Stage 2 which is concerned with when new worlds should be introduced and what they should be. We gave a specialized but promisingly powerful method to these questions. However, it is still not clear to what extent the heuristics would be successful for more long and difficult formulas we have not dealt with. This is left to us as a future work.

In addition to Routley and Meyer's **R** system, we attempted to formalize Read's axiom system for relevant logics in terms of HOL. It is formulated syntactically by employing Gentzen-like system and bunches of formulas [9]. Semantically, however, this is essentially the same as Routley and Meyer's semantics. The only differences are: (i) He uses two sorts of world relations: a binary relation and a ternary relation, (ii) he uses bunches of formulas where sequences of formulas (sequents in Gentzen system) are to be delimited by two kinds of commas. The semantic encoding of Read's system into the higher-order representation brings about some minor differences only in Step 2 of our proof heuristics. For example, in the step 2.1 which eliminates the real world, we need to apply the following series of tactics in Read's system:

```
e(IMP_RES_TAC d1);;
e(IMP_RES_TAC d3);;
e(IMP_RES_TAC V1);;
```

where d1 is "$DR(a,b,c) = ?x.D(a,x) \land R(x,b,c)$" and d3 is "$a \leq b = DR(zero,a,b)$" in place of "e(IMP_RES_TAC V1);;" in Routley and Meyer's system. To other proof steps, the same tactics can be applied as in the case of Routley and Meyer.

Acknowledgements

We would like to express our gratitude to Prof. R. M. Meyer, ANU, for suggesting us the converse of the contraction as a challenging problem of interactive theorem provers, as well as fruitful discussions on the theory and implementation of relevant logics. We also thank the anonymous referees for their constructive comments.

References

[1]   A. R. Anderson and N. D. Belnap, Jr. *Entailment: The Logic of Relevance and Necessity, Vol. 1*, Princeton Univ. Press, 1975.

[2]   D. Basin, S. Matthews, and L. Vigano. *Natural Deduction for Non-Classical Logics*, to appear in Studia Logica, 1998.

[3]   J. M. Dunn. *Relevance Logic and Entailment*. In D. Gabbay and F. Guenthner (eds.), Handbook of Philosophical Logic, Vol. III, D. Reidel Publishing Company, pages 117–224, 1986.

[4]   D. M. Gabbay. *LDS – Labelled Deductive Systems (Volume 1 – Foundations)*, Clarendon Press, 1996.

[5]   M. J. C. Gordon. and T. F. Melham. *Introduction to HOL*, Cambridge University Press, 1993.

[6]   P. de Groote. *Linear Logic with Isabelle: Pruning the Proof Search Tree*, LNAI 918, Springer, pages 263–277, 1995.

[7]   H. J. Ohlbach and G. Wrightson. *Solving a Problem in Relevance Logic with an Automated Theorem Prover*, LNCS 170, Springer, pages 496–508, 1984.

[8]   L. Paulson. *Isabelle, a Generic Theorem Prover*, LNCS 828, Springer, 1994.

[9]   S. Read. *Relevant Logic*, Basil Blackwell, 1988.

[10] R. Routley and R. Meyer. *The Semantics of Entailment*, In Leblanc (ed.), Truth, Syntax and Modality, North-Holland, pages 199–243, 1972.

[11] P. B. Thistlewaite, M. A. McRobbie, and R. K. Meyer. *Automated Theorem-Proving in Non-Classical Logics*, Pitman Publishing, 1988.

[12] H. Sawamura, T. Minami, K. Yokota, and K. Ohashi. *A logic programming approach to specifying logics and constructing proofs*, Proc. of the Seventh International Conference on Logic Programming, The MIT Press, pages 405–424, 1990.

[13] H. Sawamura, T. Minami, and T. Ohtani. *EUODHILOS: A general reasoning system for a variety of logics*, LNAI 624, Springer, pages 501–503, 1992.

[14] A. Urquhart. *The undecidability of entailment and relevant implication*, JSL, 49:1059–1073, 1984.

Case Studies in Meta-Level Theorem Proving*

Friedrich W. von Henke, Stephan Pfab, Holger Pfeifer, and Harald Rueß**

Universität Ulm, Fakultät für Informatik
D-89069 Ulm/Donau, Germany
{vhenke,pfab,pfeifer}@informatik.uni-ulm.de
ruess@csl.sri.com

Abstract. We describe an extension of the PVS system that provides a reasonably efficient and practical notion of reflection and thus allows for soundly adding formalized and verified new proof procedures. These proof procedures work on representations of a part of the underlying logic and their correctness is expressed at the object level using a computational reflection function. The implementation of the PVS system has been extended with an efficient evaluation mechanism, since the practicality of the approach heavily depends on careful engineering of the core system, including efficient normalization of functional expressions. We exemplify the process of applying meta-level proof procedures with a detailed description of the encoding of cancellation in commutative monoids and of the kernel of a BDD package.

1 Introduction

Many of the proof techniques we discover in the process of proving theorems with mechanized support are potentially useful for improving the overall performance of the underlying proving system. Thus a mechanism that allows users of such a system to incorporate specialized or even new automated proof techniques into the system would be helpful. It is crucial, however, that system modifications do not alter soundness of the system at hand, since uncontrolled insertion of unverified new proof procedures can be entirely fatal to the usefulness of such a system. A mechanized theorem prover is said to be *soundly extensible* if a meta language can be employed to extend reasoning capabilities and if these extensions can be shown to be correct with respect to some correctness criterion. There are basically two different mechanisms for soundly extending theorem provers, namely tactics and reflective systems.

Tactics have first been introduced in EDINBURGH LCF [13], and since then successfully applied to extend mechanical theorem provers in a sound way [10, 13, 12, 20, 21]. A *tactic* is a function written in a procedural meta-language (mostly some version of ML) that splits a goal into a set of subgoals, and provides a

---

* This work has been partially supported by the Deutsche Forschungsgemeinschaft (DFG) project *Verifix* and by the Deutscher Akademischer Austauschdienst (DAAD).
** Current affiliation: SRI International

justification to ensure soundness of each tactic invocation. This reduction step corresponds to backwards application of rules in the sense that the given goal may be inferred by basic rules from the subgoals. Tactics and strategies built from them do not have to be proved correct since a *safety kernel* of the basic tactic mechanism assures that these proof search procedures may fail but will never produce incorrect proofs. In effect, each successful tactic invocation is expanded into a proof of the original goal from the proofs of all computed subgoals, using the primitive inference rules of the underlying logic.

It has been observed in the past, however, that tactics may not be the most appropriate technique for constructing proofs of many facts that are expressible as meta-level statements [1, 3, 4, 16]. An example may help to illustrate this. Consider proving the equality of two terms that contain some associative commutative operator. A tactic that solves such a task must chain together appropriate instances of lemmas and rules. Using the analogy of tactic invocation with application of a meta-lemma, a tactic re-computes a proof object in terms of primitive rules for every instance of this *meta-lemma*, instead of taking the natural approach of simply instantiating its proof. This results in sometimes rather messy construction of tactics and obliges the tactic writer always to concern himself with generating proofs in terms of basic inference rules; this can increase the intellectual effort involved in constructing theorem-proving procedures. Moreover, all programming knowledge is implicitly contained in the tactic code. This complicates maintenance and modification of deductive systems based on the tactics approach; furthermore, even though the user of a tactic may know, or be able to verify, that a given tactic will construct a correct proof of a given goal, the implementation must still execute the tactic and verify the result. Finally, it may be hard to achieve the *efficiency* required to complete large verifications at reasonable cost using the LCF approach [6].

An alternative to purely procedural tactics is to encode theorem-proving methods as verifiable meta-functions in a *self-referential* system. Such a system is able to refer to (parts of) itself; it consists of a base system, the so-called *object level*, an internal representation of (parts of) itself, the *meta level*, and a *reflection* mechanism that expresses the relationship between the object level and its corresponding meta-level encoding. In such a framework it is possible to make formal statements about the behavior of meta-functions and verify their correctness. The main advantage of this approach lies in the fact that meta-theoretic results, once proven, can be used without further justification. Consider again the associative-commutative example mentioned above. A natural approach is to view the left-hand and right-hand sides of an equation as trees and to check whether their fringes are permutations of each other.

There are basically two different paradigms of encoding theorem-proving capabilities as verifiable meta-functions. *Computational reflection* uses an interpreter to associate meta-level representations with the values they denote [8, 15, 23]. In this approach meta-level representations are used to make the syntactic structures of object-level entities amenable to inspection and manipulation. Consequently, computational reflection frameworks do not permit statements about provability and the existence of proofs. The other approach can be termed *deductive reflection*. The idea here is to encode a meta-level *provability predicate*, say *Pr*, for a certain subset of the object-level theory. This predicate *Pr* is used to reduce the provability of a goal ϕ to the provability of $Pr('\phi')$; here, $'\phi'$ is the meta-level representation of the object-level entity ϕ. In a *deductive reflection* system the transitions between the meta-level and the object level are established by *deductive reflection rules*. These rules can usually be shown to be admissible in the object-level calculus by proving the *correctness* and *completeness* of the meta-level encoding, and, consequently, the extended reflective system is a *conservative extension* of the base-level system. While such a conservative approach can not give a *reflection principle* in the logicians' sense,[1] it allows a single system to simulate a large amount of meta-reasoning and gives the assurance that the resulting system remains consistent.

Sound extension by means of a self-referential system has several pragmatic advantages over tactics. First, theorem-proving procedures are ordinary programs of the object language that examine and manipulate representations of object-language expressions. Second, verified meta-programs do not have to deal explicitly with justifications. Instead, the procedures are justified by separate correctness arguments. Correctness is established *once and for all* and its proof "reused" every time the procedure is called. In contrast to LCF tactics, proofs are not re-computed but merely instantiated. This is especially important, since formal proofs of interesting developments in both mathematics and computer science tend to be rather large objects. Last but not least, for the very same reasons as for any other piece of software, formalized proof procedures permit building up and modifying libraries in a controlled and mathematical way, and formalized and (mechanically) proved properties of the procedures help in understanding their effects.

Despite these apparent advantages of verified meta-programs over tactics, reflective systems have had almost no impact on the design of theorem proving systems and sound extension by means of reflection is not yet ready to push back the boundaries of what is feasible in mechanized theorem proving [14]. There are two main reasons for this failure. First, although the underlying techniques of reflection needed to guarantee sound extension are well understood it is a towering (and rather thankless) task to build a reflective system: starting from a small kernel system enriched with some notion of reflection, a plethora of verified proof procedures must be added in the bootstrapping process in order to provide a useful initial system. Second, the practicality of reflective systems relies heavily on a notion of fast execution of the encoded proof procedures, since the basic idea of reflection is to replace deduction at the object level by meta-level computation. Unfortunately, many existing theorem proving systems – like HOL, COQ, LEGO, PVS, all of which are based on some sort of type theory – do not support efficient evaluation, although their underlying calculi clearly include

---

[1] The logicians' use of *reflection* is a way of extending theories by adding axioms and rules which are not derivable in a conservative extension of the system under consideration [17, 25].

the notions of evaluation and normalization. Consequently, a successful reflective system can be built only by taking the "programming" part of theorem proving systems serious and treating it as full-fledged programming language.

The purpose of this paper is to demonstrate by examples that existing theorem provers can be extended to provide a useful and practical notion of reflection in order to soundly extend theorem proving capabilities. Our starting point is the PVS system. We first extend the implementation of this system by an efficient evaluation mechanism to get *Lisp*-like speed of function evaluation. This extended system forms a suitable basis for verifying formalized proof procedures and applying them in the proof process. Proof procedures work on representations of a – rather small – part of the underlying logic and correctness thereof is expressed at the object level using a computational reflection function. Typically, showing correctness of such a meta function involves showing that the function is equality-preserving or that the target expression is a refinement of the source expression. We distinguish three phases of applying formalized proof functions. In the *reification* phase, PVS strategies are used to compute representations of some parts of the current proof goal; the subsequent *normalization* and *reflection* phases rely exclusively on evaluation. We exemplify this process with a detailed description of the encoding of cancellation in commutative monoids and applications of the resulting proof procedure. In a similar manner, the kernel of a BDD package has been encoded as a meta function that can be used as a decision procedure for propositional logic.

The remainder of the paper is structured as follows. Section 2 provides an informal introduction to the PVS system. The implementation of an evaluation mechanism for functional expressions of PVS is described in Sect. 3. Section 4 discusses in detail the encoding, verification, and application of a proof procedure for cancelling in Abelian groups, while Sect. 5 gives a tour through our encodings of a BDD package. Section 6 closes with a comparison to related work and final remarks.

2   Formal Background

The PVS system combines an expressive specification language with an interactive proof checker; see [19] for an overview. This section provides a brief description of the PVS language and prover, and introduces some of the concepts needed in this paper. More details can be found in [11].

The PVS specification language builds on classical typed higher-order logic with the usual base types, bool, nat, int, among others, the function type constructor [D → R], and the product type constructor [A,B]. The type system of PVS is augmented with *dependent types* and *abstract data types*. In PVS, predicates over some type A are, as usual, boolean-valued functions on A, and pred[A] is an abbreviation for the function type [A → bool]. A distinctive feature of the PVS specification language are *predicate subtypes*: the subtype {x:D | P(x)} consists of exactly those elements of type D satisfying predicate P. The expression (P) is an abbreviation for the predicate subtype {x:D | P(x)}. Predicate subtypes are used for explicitly constraining domains and ranges of operations in a specification and for defining partial functions. In general, type-checking with predicate subtypes is undecidable; the type-checker generates proof obligations, so-called *type correctness conditions* (TCCs), if satisfaction of the restricting predicate cannot immediately be derived. A large number of TCCs are discharged by specialized proof strategies; a PVS expression is not considered to be fully type-checked until all generated TCCs have been proved. PVS specifications are packaged as *theories* that can be parametric in types and constants.

Consider, for example, the theory `alist` in ⌐1⌐ for implementing association lists.[2] This theory is parameterized with respect to two nonempty types D and R and defines an abstract datatype `maybe` with two constructors `yes` and `no`.

```
alist [D,R : TYPE+] : THEORY                                            1
BEGIN
  maybe : DATATYPE
  BEGIN
    yes(arg:R) : yes?
    no         : no?
  END maybe

  alist : TYPE = [D → maybe]

  v : VAR D;  c : VAR R;  a : VAR alist

  empty          : alist = λv: no
  update(a,v,c)  : alist = a WITH [v := yes(c)]
  insert(a,v,c)  : alist =
    CASES a(v) OF
      yes(y) : a,
      no     : update(a,v,c)
    ENDCASES
END alist
```

Furthermore, `alist` is defined to be the type of functions with domain D and codomain `maybe`, the clause `v : VAR D` declares the type of variable `v` to be D, the expression `a WITH [v := yes(c)]` denotes the update of function `a` at position `v` with value `yes(c)`, and the insert operation is defined through a simple case split such that an alist is updated at position `v` unless a binding for `v` already exists.

A theory can use the definitions and theorems of another theory by *importing* it. Parameterized theories can be imported in either of two ways: as an instance of the theory by providing actual values for the formal parameters, or uninstantiated. In the latter case, all possible instantiations of the imported theory may be used, and ambiguities can be resolved by qualification. A built-in *prelude* and loadable *libraries* provide standard specifications and proved facts for a large number of theories.

---

[2] To increase the readability of PVS specifications the syntax has liberally been modified by replacing some ASCII codings with a more familiar mathematical notation.

Proofs in PVS are presented in a sequent-calculus style. The atomic commands of the PVS prover include induction, quantifier instantiation, conditional rewriting, simplification using arithmetic and equality decision procedures and type information, and propositional simplification. PVS has an LCF-like strategy language for combining inference steps into more powerful proof strategies. The strategy combinator (then <strat-list>), for example, successively applies a list of strategies, while (spread <strat> <strat-list>) applies the strategy <strat> to the current goal and then pairs the strategies in <strat-list> with the subgoals. Furthermore, the strategy language includes the constructs if for branching and let for binding variables in the body of a strategy to the results of Lisp computations. The most comprehensive strategies manage to generate many proofs fully automatically.

3   Efficient Evaluation

A subset of the PVS specification language can be considered as an executable, functional programming language; it includes all kinds of operations on expressions of basic types, several forms of conditionals (IF, CASES, COND, TABLE), total recursive functions (by means of measure recursion), and homomorphic functionals [27] on abstract datatypes. Although the PVS prover provides basic strategies like beta – which is based on an (inefficient) implementation of a substitution calculus – for executing these functional programs, it has been observed many times that efficient evaluation has the potential of speeding up and automating many proofs, e.g. simulation proofs. For this reason we have extended PVS to considerably improve on the speed of computing normal forms. Hereby, we use the idea of *inverse evaluation* by Berger and Schwichtenberg [5] and compute a normal form for a PVS expression in three successive steps: first, an expression is translated into the corresponding Lisp program, second, the Lisp program is executed using Lisp's evaluation function *eval*, and, finally, the result of Lisp evaluation is translated back to a corresponding PVS expression. In this way, we obtain Lisp-like execution speed for normalizing PVS expressions, and we may readily use Lisp compilers to produce efficient machine code for PVS functions. In addition to normal programming languages constructs, the evaluator also handles uninterpreted constant and function symbols; conditions involving uninterpreted symbols may be decided by calling the PVS prover; these features, however, are not used in the sequel. For the purpose of this paper it suffices to presuppose an efficient symbolic evaluator for normalizing PVS expression that faithfully implements the reduction relation of the underlying PVS logic (including abstract datatypes); technical details can be found in [22].

As interface to the efficient evaluator described above, we have extended the PVS prover with a new basic strategy (NORM). This strategy takes as argument a PVS expression e and replaces it with its corresponding normalized expression.

4 Cancellation in Commutative Monoids

Cancellation in the particular structure $(\mathbb{Z}, +, 0)$ has already been considered in the context of COMPUTATIONAL LOGIC [7] by Boyer and Moore [8]. They develop a meta function *cancel* that reduces, for example, the equation

$$(a + i) + (b + k) = j + (k + (i + x))$$

to

$$a + b = j + x$$

The main step in the *cancel* algorithm is to compute the fringes of both sides of the source equation, to delete all common terms, and to compute the simplified target equation by means of a meaning function that associates syntactic representations of equations with an equation. Boyer and Moore's *cancel* function is restricted to the particular structure $(\mathbb{Z}, +, 0)$, but the abstraction mechanisms of PVS permit generalizing their development to arbitrary commutative monoids satisfying the left cancellation property.

The development of the cancel function is carried out in a generic theory cancel (see 2) that takes the components of a commutative monoid (A, •, e) as arguments. Here, • is a binary operator on A and e is the identity; the semantic constraints on the theory parameters are stated in the assumption part of the theory.

```
cancel [A:TYPE, •:[A,A → A], e:A] : THEORY              2
BEGIN
  ASSUMING
    A: ASSUMPTION associative?(•)
    C: ASSUMPTION commutative?(•)
    I: ASSUMPTION left_identity?(•)(e)
    L: ASSUMPTION ∀(x,y,z:A): x•y = x•z ⇒ y = z
  ENDASSUMING
```

The first step is to define types trm and equality (see 3) for representing terms built up from the binary operator • and equations, respectively. These (meta-level) representations simply make the internal structure of equations on terms of type A explicit and permit inspecting and manipulating the structure of equalities on expressions of type A.

```
vars: TYPE = nat        % Infinite supply of meta variables      3

trm : DATATYPE
BEGIN
  mk_neutral                 : neutral?
  mk_var(name : vars)        : var?
  mk_app(left,right : trm)   : app?
END trm

equality : TYPE = [# lhs, rhs : trm #]
```

In the next step, we encode denotation functions for computing object-level terms from corresponding representations of types equality and trm. These functions require, besides a representation, a context that associates elements of type vars with terms of the object level. Here, a context c of a term t is represented as a function of type alist: TYPE = [vars → A], with the additional requirement that all variables occurring in t also occur in c.

```
x : VAR vars;   c  : VAR alist;      v : VAR A;                        4
t : VAR trm;    eq : VAR equality;

contains_all_vars?(t)(c) : bool =
  ∀x: occurs?(x,t) ⇒ ∃v: c(x) = yes(v)

TrmContext(t) : TYPE = (contains_all_vars?(t))

contains_all_vars?(eq)(c) : bool =   % Note the use of overloading here
  contains_all_vars?(lhs(eq))(c) ∧ contains_all_vars?(rhs(eq))(c)

EqContext(eq) : TYPE = (contains_all_vars?(eq))
```

Now it is a simple matter to define the (overloaded) functions $[\![\,t,c\,]\!]$ and $[\![\,eq,c\,]\!]$ to compute denotations of representations of terms and equations, respectively, with respect to a context c.

```
[ ](t:trm,c:TrmContext(t)) : RECURSIVE A =        % Reflection         5
  CASES t OF
    mk_neutral     : e,
    mk_var(x)      : arg(c(x)),
    mk_app(t₁,t₂)  : [ t₁,c ] • [ t₂,c ]
  ENDCASES MEASURE t BY ≪

[ ](eq:equality,c:EqContext(eq)) : bool =
  [ lhs(eq),c ] = [ rhs(eq),c ]
```

Recall that cancellation works by computing fringes from terms. These fringes can be represented conveniently by bags. We omit here the realization of bags in terms of lists. In the following, we use $b_1 \cup b_2$ to denote the union of two bags, $.\diagdown.$ for the difference and $.\cap.$ for the intersection of bags; the definitions of the functions are omitted. The functions fringe and tree in 6 are simple conversions between terms and bags.

```
IMPORTING bags[vars]                                                    6

fringe(t:trm) : RECURSIVE Bag =
  CASES t OF
    mk_neutral    : null,
    mk_var(x)     : cons(x,null),
    mk_app(t₁,t₂) : fringe(t₁)∪fringe(t₂)
  ENDCASES MEASURE t BY ≪

tree(b:Bag) : RECURSIVE trm =
  CASES b OF
    null      : mk_neutral,
    cons(x,l) : mk_app(mk_var(x),tree(l))
  ENDCASES MEASURE b BY ≪
```

Now we have collected all the ingredients to encode the `cancel` function in $\boxed{7}$. Cancellation works by computing two bags of argument terms of • from the left hand side and the right hand side of the equality under consideration. Now, common terms are cancelled in both bags, simplified terms are computed from these bags, and the target equality is formed from these simplified terms.

```
cancel(eq:equality) : equality =                                        7
    LET b₁       = fringe(lhs(eq)),
        b₂       = fringe(rhs(eq)),
        common   = b₁ ∩ b₂,
        new_lhs  = b₁ ∖ common,
        new_rhs  = b₂ ∖ common
    IN
        (# lhs := tree(new_lhs), rhs := tree(new_rhs) #)
```

Theorem `preserves_eq` in $\boxed{8}$ states that the function `cancel` preserves equality, i.e. the denotations of some source equality `eq` and the corresponding target equality `cancel(eq)` are equivalent.

```
preserves_eq: THEOREM                                                   8
    ∀(eq:equality,c:EqContext(eq)): ⟦eq,c⟧ = ⟦cancel(eq),c⟧

END cancel
```

The proof of the correctness theorem follows closely the one described by Boyer and Moore [8]. The main step is accomplished using lemma `meaning_difference` in $\boxed{9}$, which essentially states that splitting a term into two arbitrary parts preserves the denotation.

```
meaning_difference : LEMMA                                              9
    ∀(b₁,b₂:Bag, c:TrmContext(tree(b₂))):
        subbag?(b₁,b₂) ⇒ ⟦tree(b₂),c⟧ = ⟦tree(b₁),c⟧ • ⟦tree(b₂∖b₁),c⟧
```

Theorem `preserves_eq` is used to define the strategy `cancel` in Fig. 1. This strategy takes three strings `typ`, `op`, and `e`, selects the formula `fml` of the current proof sequent (line 3), and type checks the argument strings (lines 4 and

```
1: (defstep cancel (typ op e &optional (fnum 1))
2:    (let ((sforms (s-forms (current-goal *ps*)))
3:          (fml    (formula (car (select-seq sforms (list fnum)))))
4:          (op1    (typecheck (pc-parse op 'expr)))
5:          (e1     (typecheck (pc-parse e 'expr))))
6:      (if (not (equality? fml)) (skip)
7:         (let ((rep-alist  (quote-eqn fml op1 e1))
8:               (rep         (first rep-alist))
9:               (alist       (second rep-alist)))
10:        (spread (lemma "preserves_eq" :subst ("c" alist "eq" rep))
11:               ((then (NORM -1)
12:                      (replace -1)
13:                      (hide -1))
14:                (then (auto-rewrite "update" "insert" ...)
15:                      (reduce))))))))) ...)
```

Fig. 1. Defined strategy for cancellation.

5). If these operations are successful and fml is indeed an equality (line 6) then
the call to function quote-eqn (see Appendix A) yields a representation rep
for fml of type equality and an association list for all argument terms of the
operator op1 in fml (lines 7–9). This information is used to instantiate theorem preserves_eq (line 10), followed by a call to the normalization strategy
NORM (see Sect. 3) and term rewriting with this normalized equality. Finally,
the newly introduced equation is hidden from the current sequent (lines 11–13).
The PVS prover generates a type correctness condition for the instantiation of
preserves_eq, since the association list computed by quote-eqn must be a context for rep. This TCC, however, is easily proved by unfolding the definitions
involved (lines 14 and 15).

Consider, for example, simplification of the following proof goal, where f is some
uninterpreted function, by means of the cancellation strategy.

```
|-------
{1}    x + (f(y) + z) = (z + f(u)) + (z + f(y))
```

Applying the strategy (cancel "real" "+" "0") yields the simplified sequent

```
|-------
{1}    x = f(u) + z
```

together with four TCCs corresponding to the assumptions on the parameters
of theory cancel (see [2]) instantiated with the actual parameters real, +, and
0. One way to avoid repetitive generation of identical TCCs when applying the
cancel strategy is to import an instance of the cancel theory – e.g. IMPORTING
cancel[real, +, 0]. This causes the PVS type checker to suppress TCCs corresponding to theory instantiation, since it is able to detect that identical TCCs
have already been generated; in those cases, calls to the cancel strategy yield
exactly one subgoal, namely the simplified equation.

If the basic strategy NORM has been implemented correctly, the strategy cancel is "correct by construction" since it obeys the PVS prover interface; in particular, Lisp functions like quote-eqn can not alter soundness of the system as long as they do not update internal prover structures. The major difference between PVS strategies and LCF-like tactics is that in PVS there is no safety kernel to guarantee that some defined strategy conforms to the specified interface.[3]

5   Ordered Binary Decision Diagrams

Ordered Binary Decision Diagrams (OBDDs) represent Boolean functions in a form that is both canonical and compact for many practical cases. They have found widespread use in CAD applications such as formal verification, logic synthesis, and test generation, since OBDDs are manipulated by efficient graph algorithms. Here, we encode OBDDs together with a core library of verified OBDD manipulations in PVS and use these functions as a verified decision procedure for propositional logic. Our OBDD implementation follows the description in [2].

An OBDD is a rooted, directed acyclic graph with one or two terminal nodes labeled 0 and 1 of out-degree zero, a set of non-terminal nodes of out-degree two with one outgoing edge labeled *low* and the other *high*, a variable name attached to each non-terminal node such that on all paths from the root to the terminal nodes these variables respect a given linear order. Furthermore, no non-terminal node has identical 0 and 1-successor.

OBDDs may be represented by a function tab that maps node indices to nodes (see [10]) and satisfies the additional properties concerning variable ordering and reduction of common successors as mentioned above. The first two entries in the OBDD table are reserved for the terminal nodes 0 and 1, whereas the remaining indices point to non-terminal nodes. The latter are elements of type Node comprising triples of variable names (encoded as numbers with the ordering on natural numbers) and the two successor nodes. Technically, the function tab is defined as the inverse of a function lookup, which computes for every node a unique node index by a twofold application of Cantor's diagonalization technique. Since lookup is strictly monotonically increasing in all of its arguments the corresponding graph is assured to be acyclic.

---

[3] It is straightforward, however, to write such a checker.

```
bdd : THEORY                                                          10
BEGIN

  name       : TYPE = nat
  index      : TYPE = nat
  nodeindex  : TYPE = upfrom(2)
  Node       : TYPE = [# variable: name, low: index, high: index #]

  l,h,i : VAR index;  n : VAR nodeindex;  v : VAR name;

  pairing(l,h)  : index     = ((l+h)*(l+h+1))/2 + l
  lookup(v,l,h) : nodeindex = 2 + pairing(pairing(v,l),h)

  tab(n) : Node =
    LET T = inverse(lookup)(n) IN
      (# variable:=PROJ_1(T), low:=PROJ_2(T), high:= PROJ_3(T) #)

  leaf?(i) : bool = i < 2
  rank(i)  : nat = IF leaf?(i) THEN 0 ELSE 1+variable(tab(i)) ENDIF

  ordered?(i) : RECURSIVE bool =
    IF leaf?(i) THEN TRUE
      ELSE LET t = tab(i) IN
              (leaf?(low(t)) ∨ variable(t) > variable(tab(low(t))))
           ∧ (leaf?(high(t)) ∨ variable(t) > variable(tab(high(t))))
           ∧ ordered?(low(t)) ∧ ordered?(high(t))
    ENDIF MEASURE rank(i)

  reduced?(i:(ordered?)) : RECURSIVE bool =
    IF leaf?(i) THEN TRUE
      ELSE low(tab(i)) ≠ high(tab(i))
           ∧ reduced?(low(tab(i))) ∧ reduced?(high(tab(i)))
    ENDIF MEASURE rank(i)

  OBDD : TYPE = (reduced?)
```

Given an environment ρ of type [name → bool] for associating variable names
with some boolean expression, one can easily define the meaning $[\![b]\!](\rho)$ of an
OBDD b by recursively computing the corresponding *if-then-else* normal form.

```
[ ](b:OBDD)(ρ:[name → bool]): RECURSIVE bool =             11
  IF      b = 0 THEN FALSE
    ELSIF b = 1 THEN TRUE
    ELSIF ρ(variable(tab(b)))
         THEN [ high(tab(b)) ](ρ)
    ELSE     [ low(tab(b))  ](ρ)
  ENDIF MEASURE rank(b)
```

We have encoded in PVS a number of fundamental functions for building up
OBDDs. The apply function (see [9,2]), for example, combines two source

OBDDs into a target OBDD according to the binary Boolean operation •; this fact is expressed and formally verified in theorem apply_correct.

```
• : VAR [bool, bool -> bool];  b,l,h : VAR OBDD                    | 12 |

decr?(v)(b) : bool = leaf?(b) ∨ v > variable(tab(b))

makenode(v,(l,h:(decr?(v)))): {b | rank(l) ≤ rank(b) ∧ rank(h) ≤ rank(b)}
= IF l = h THEN l ELSE lookup(v,l,h) ENDIF

apply(•,l,h) : RECURSIVE {b | rank(b) ≤ rank(l) ∨ rank(b) ≤ rank(h)} =
  IF leaf?(l) ∧ leaf?(h) THEN
    bool2bit(bit2bool(l) • bit2bool(h))
  ELSIF leaf?(l) ∧ ¬leaf?(h) THEN
      makenode(variable(tab(h)),
                  apply(•,l,low(tab(h))), apply(•,l,high(tab(h))))
  ELSIF ¬leaf?(l) ∧ leaf?(h) THEN
      makenode(variable(tab(l)),
                  apply(•,low(tab(l)),h), apply(•,high(tab(l)),h))
  ELSIF variable(tab(l)) = variable(tab(h)) THEN
      makenode(variable(tab(l)),
                  apply(•,low(tab(l)),low(tab(h))),
                  apply(•,high(tab(l)),high(tab(h))))
  ELSIF variable(tab(l)) < variable(tab(h)) THEN
      makenode(variable(tab(h)),
                  apply(•,l,low(tab(h))), apply(•,l,high(tab(h))))
  ELSE makenode(variable(tab(l)),
                  apply(•,low(tab(l)),h), apply(•,high(tab(l)),h))
  ENDIF MEASURE rank(l) + rank(h)

apply_correct : THEOREM
  [[ apply(•,l,h) ]](ρ) = [[ l ]](ρ) • [[ h ]](ρ)
```

END bdd

The OBDD encodings can be used to construct a verified – and reasonably efficient – procedure for deciding validity (or unsatisfiability) of some propositional formula p by means of computational reflection. Since the overall structure is a straightforward variant of the application of cancellation in Sect. 4, we restrict ourselves to a rough outline of this procedure; details of the PVS definitions can be found in Appendix B.

First, a specialized tactic computes a syntactic representation rep of p together with an environment ρ for associating variable names with the arguments of the Boolean operators in p such that p = [[rep]](ρ). The meaning [[rep]](ρ) of representation rep (with respect to ρ) is computed by recursing on rep. Second, compute an OBDD build(rep) by recursively applying the OBDD constructor apply. Theorem apply_correct in | 12 | is used to prove the correctness of this procedure:

$$[\,\mathtt{rep}\,](\rho) = [\,\mathtt{build(rep)}\,](\rho)$$

Third, depending on whether the original formula p is valid or unsatisfiable, the evaluation of the right hand side of the equation above yields TRUE or FALSE, respectively. In all other cases one has the choice of replacing p with an equivalent *if-then-else* normal form or leaving p unchanged.

It is not hard to see how this procedure can be expressed – as a variant of the definition of the cancellation strategy in Sect. 4 – as a defined strategy bddprop. We have applied this strategy to numerous examples. Table 1, for example, states the run times[4] for deciding various pigeon hole formulas (with n holes and $n + 1$ pigeons). These numbers indicate that our verified decision procedure is efficient enough to be used for a number of problems that occur in practice.

Table 1. Deciding pigeon hole formulas

n	1	2	3	4	5	6	7	8	9	10	11	12
sec.	1.48	7.83	23.73	20.62	39.84	68.59	154.93	151.81	184.09	293.57	418.18	489.49

6 Conclusions

The main thesis of this paper is that current theorem provers like PVS can readily be extended to provide a reasonably efficient and practical notion of reflection in order to soundly extend theorem proving capabilities. To substantiate this claim, we have extended the PVS system by verified proof procedures – such as cancellation of equations and a decision procedure based on OBDDs – and demonstrated how to apply these procedures through (PVS) tactics and computational reflection. More precisely, the proof procedures are functions encoded in the underlying logic that work on representations of parts of this logic itself. Functional proof procedures are applied by sequencing a number of PVS strategies to compute a representation from the current proof goal, to compute the normal form of the proof procedure applied to this representation, and to compute a corresponding simplified term by means of computational reflection. The practicality of such an extension depends heavily on efficient normalization of functional expressions.

The overall architecture of computational reflection is essentially a re-casting of computational reflection as described in [8]. Our mechanism, however, is much more flexible – and therefore more widely applicable – in that we can abstract meta theorems with respect to classes of structures. Moreover, our approach allows for defining different representations, lifting of terms/formulas to these

---

[4] Run times on a Sparc Ultra-II as reported by PVS. Disturbances in the expected monotonicity are due to garbage collection.

representations, and suitable correctness criteria; there are examples for which equivalence reasoning is not appropriate and the result of the computational reflection process should rather be some "refinement" of the original formula.

The concept of reflection has been used in several proof systems and has been applied to various examples; see [14] for a good survey. In particular, the extraction mechanism of COQ has recently been used to translate proofs into executable CAML programs [6, 26].

Much work remains to be done. Specialized OBDD packages written in C are an order of magnitude faster and more effective than the encodings given in this paper. This is mainly due to aggressive use of tabulation techniques, specialized garbage collection algorithms, and variable reordering techniques. There is no conceptual reason, however, not to extend the verified OBDD package described above with more advanced features like efficient garbage collection. Another desirable goal would be to encode and verify complete OBDD packages and symbolic model-checkers inside PVS, thereby eliminating the error-prone task of connecting external (and unreliable) decision procedures. Similarly, it seems feasible to internalize and formally verify algorithms for combining decision procedures such as those described in [24, 18].

Acknowledgements

We would like to thank S. Owre from SRI International for invaluable help with implementing the symbolic evaluator and integrating it with PVS. We also thank the anonymous reviewers for their helpful comments.

References

1. S. F. Allen, R. L. Constable, D. J. Howe, and W. E. Aitken. The Semantics of Reflected Proof. In *Proc. 5th Annual IEEE Symposium on Logic in Computer Science*, pages 95–105. IEEE CS Press, 1990.

2. H. R. Anderson. An Introduction to Binary Decision Diagrams. Available at: ftp.id.dtu.dk/pub/hra, September 1994.

3. D. A. Basin. Beyond Tactic Based Theorem Proving. In J. Kunze and H. Stoyan, editors, *KI-94 Workshops: Extended Abstracts*. Gesellschaft für Informatik e.V, 1994. 18. Deutsche Jahrestagung für Künstliche Intelligenz, Saarbrücken.

4. D. A. Basin and R. L. Constable. Metalogical Frameworks. Technical Report TR 91-1235, Department of Computer Science, Cornell University, September 1991.

5. U. Berger and H. Schwichtenberg. An Inverse of the Evaluation Functional for Typed λ-calculus. In *Proceedings, Sixth Annual IEEE Symposium on Logic in Computer Science*, pages 203–211, Amsterdam, The Netherlands, 15–18 July 1991. IEEE Computer Society Press.

6. S. Boutin. Using Reflection to Build Efficient and Certified Decision Procedures. In M. Abadi and T. Ito, editors, *Theoretical Aspects of Computer Software*, volume 1281 of *Lecture Notes in Computer Science*. Springer-Verlag, 1997.

7. R. S. Boyer and J. S. Moore. *A Computational Logic*. Academic Press, New York, 1979.

8. R. S. Boyer and J. S. Moore. Metafunctions: Proving Them Correct and Using Them Efficiently as New Proof Procedures. In R. S. Boyer and J. S. Moore, editors, *The Correctness Problem in Computer Science*, chapter 3. Academic Press, 1981.
9. R. E. Bryant. Symbolic Boolean Manipulation with Ordered Binary Decision Diagrams. *ACM Computing Surveys*, 24(3):293–318, September 1992.
10. R. L. Constable, S. F. Allen, and H. M. Bromley et al. *Implementing Mathematics with the Nuprl Proof Development System*. Prentice–Hall, 1986.
11. J. Crow, S. Owre, J. Rushby, N. Shankar, and M. Srivas. A Tutorial Introduction to PVS. Presented at WIFT '95: Workshop on Industrial-Strength Formal Specification Techniques, Boca Raton, Florida, April 1995.
12. M. J. C. Gordon and T. F. Melham. *Introduction to HOL : A Theorem Proving Environment for Higher-Order Logic*. Cambridge University Press, 1993.
13. M. J. C. Gordon, A. J. R. Milner, and C. P. Wadsworth. *Edinburgh LCF: a Mechanized Logic of Computation*, volume 78 of *Lecture Notes in Computer Science*. Springer-Verlag, Berlin, 1979.
14. J. Harrison. Metatheory and Reflection in Theorem Proving: A Survey and Critique. Technical Report CRC-053, SRI Cambridge, Millers Yard, Cambridge, UK, 1995.
15. D. J. Howe. *Automating Reasoning in an Implementation of Constructive Type Theory*. PhD thesis, Cornell University, 1988. Available as technical report TR 88-925 from the Department of Computer Science, Cornell University.
16. T. B. Knoblock and R. L. Constable. Formalized Metareasoning in Type Theory. In *Proceedings of LICS*, pages 237–248. IEEE, 1986. Also available as technical report TR 86-742, Department of Computer Science, Cornell University.
17. G. Kreisel and A. Lévy. Reflection Principles and Their Use for Establishing the Complexity of Axiomatic Systems. *Zeitschrift für math. Logik und Grundlagen der Mathematik*, Bd. 14:97–142, 1968.
18. G. Nelson and D. C. Oppen. Simplification by Cooperating Decision Procedures. *ACM Transactions on Programming Languages and Systems*, 1(2):245–257, October 1979.
19. S. Owre, J. Rushby, N. Shankar, and F. von Henke. Formal Verification for Fault-Tolerant Architectures: Prolegomena to the Design of PVS. *IEEE Transactions on Software Engineering*, 21(2):107–125, February 1995.
20. L. C. Paulson. *Logic and Computation: Interactive Proof with Cambridge LCF*. Number 2 in Cambride Tracts in Theoretical Computer Science. Cambridge University Press, 1987.
21. L. C. Paulson. *Isabelle: A Generic Theorem Prover*, volume 828 of *Lecture Notes in Computer Science*. Springer-Verlag, 1994.
22. S. Pfab. Efficient Symbolic Evaluation of Formal Specifications and Its Interrelationship with Theorem Proving. Master's thesis, Universität Ulm, Fakultät für Mathematik, January 1998.
23. H. Rueß. Computational Reflection in the Calculus of Constructions and Its Application to Theorem Proving. In J. R. Hindley P. de Groote, editor, *Proceedings of Typed Lambda Calculus and Applications (TLCA'97)*, volume 1210 of *Lecture Notes in Computer Science*, pages 319–335. Springer-Verlag, April 1997.
24. R. E. Shostak. Deciding Combinations of Theories. *Journal of the ACM*, 31(1):1–12, 1984.
25. C. Smorynski. *Self-Reference and Modal Logic*. Springer-Verlag, 1985.
26. C. Sprenger. A Verified Model Checker for the Modal μ-Calculus in Coq. In B. Steffen, editor, *Tools and Algorithms for the Construction and Analysis of Systems*, volume 1384 of *Lecture Notes in Computer Science*. Springer-Verlag, 1998.

27. F. von Henke. An Algebraic Approach to Data Types, Program Verification, and Program Synthesis. In *Mathematical Foundations of Computer Science, Proceedings*, volume 45 of *Lecture Notes in Computer Science*. Springer-Verlag, 1976.

A   Auxiliary Functions for Cancel Strategy

```lisp
(defun argument1 (app) (first (exprs (argument app))))
(defun argument2 (app) (second (exprs (argument app))))

(defun quote-eqn (eqn op e &key (modinst ""))
  "Compute a representation together with an association list for a
  equality."
  (multiple-value-bind (rep1 trms1)
      (quote-trm (argument1 eqn) op e :modinst modinst)
    (multiple-value-bind (rep2 trms2)
        (quote-trm (argument2 eqn) op e :trms trms1 :modinst modinst)
      (let* ((rep
               (format nil "(# lhs := ~a, rhs := ~a #):~a.equality"
                   rep1 rep2 modinst))
             (trms   (union trms1 trms2 :test #'tc-eq))
             (alist (generate-alist (reverse trms) :modinst modinst)))
        (list rep alist)))))

(defun quote-trm (trm op e &key trms (modinst ""))
  "Compute a representation together with an association list for
  argument terms of an equation."
  (cond ((tc-eq trm e)
         (values (format nil "~a.mk_neutral" modinst) trms))
        ((and (application? trm) (tc-eq (operator trm) op))
         (let ((arg1 (argument1 trm))
               (arg2 (argument2 trm)))
           (multiple-value-bind (rep1 trms1)
               (quote-trm arg1 op e :trms trms :modinst modinst)
             (multiple-value-bind (rep2 trms2)
                 (quote-trm arg2 op e :trms trms1 :modinst modinst)
               (let ((rep (format nil "~a.mk_app(~a,~a)"
                               modinst rep1 rep2)))
                 (values rep trms2))))))
        (t (let* ((new-trms (adjoin trm trms :test #'tc-eq))
                  (pos (position trm (reverse new-trms) :test #'tc-eq))
                  (rep (format nil "~a.mk_var(~a)" modinst pos)))
             (values rep new-trms)))))

(defun generate-alist (l &key (acc "empty") (count 0) (modinst ""))
  "Compute an association list for the  list of terms t1,...,tn
  of the form (insert(...insert(insert(empty, t1, 0), t2, 1),...))."
  (if (null l) acc
    (let ((newacc (format nil "~a.insert(~a,~a,~a)"
```

```
                    modinst acc count (car l))))
    (generate-alist (cdr l) :acc newacc :count (1+ count)
                    :modinst modinst)))))
```

B   Auxiliary Definitions for BDD Package

Datatype for representing Boolean expressions:

```
                                                                    13
BExpr : DATATYPE
BEGIN
  mk_true                          : true?
  mk_false                         : false?
  mk_var(i : name)                 : variable?
  mk_not(arg : BExpr)              : negation?
  mk_and(left,right : BExpr)       : conjunction?
  mk_or(left,right : BExpr)        : disjunction?
  mk_implies(left,right : BExpr)   : implication?
END BExpr
```

The meaning of representation rep with respect to an environment ρ:

```
                                                                    14
[ ](rep:BExpr)(ρ:[name → bool]) : RECURSIVE bool =
  CASES rep OF
    mk_false         : FALSE,
    mk_true          : TRUE,
    mk_var(x)        : ρ(x),
    mk_not(v)        : ¬[v](ρ),
    mk_and(v,w)      : [v](ρ) ∧ [w](ρ),
    mk_or(v,w)       : [v](ρ) ∨ [w](ρ),
    mk_implies(v,w)  : [v](ρ) ⇒ [w](ρ)
  ENDCASES MEASURE rep BY ≪
```

Function build computes an OBDD for a representation rep by recursively applying the OBDD constructor apply.

```
                                                                    15
build(rep:BExpr): RECURSIVE OBDD =
  CASES rep OF
    mk_false         : 0,
    mk_true          : 1,
    mk_var(v)        : lookup(v,0,1),
    mk_not(v)        : apply(λx,y: ¬x, build(v), 0),
    mk_and(v,w)      : apply(∧, build(v), build(w)),
    mk_or(v,w)       : apply(∨, build(v), build(w)),
    mk_implies(v,w)  : apply(⇒, build(v), build(w)),
  ENDCASES MEASURE rep BY ≪
```

Formalization of Graph Search Algorithms and Its Applications

Mitsuharu Yamamoto[1], Koichi Takahashi[2], Masami Hagiya[3],
Shin-ya Nishizaki[4], and Tetsuo Tamai[5]

[1] Faculty of Science, Chiba University, Chiba 263-8522, Japan
[2] Electrotechnical Laboratory, Tsukuba, Ibaraki, 305-8568 Japan
[3] Graduate School of Science, The University of Tokyo, Tokyo 113-0033, Japan
[4] Graduate School of Information Science and Engineering
Tokyo Institute of Technology, Tokyo, Japan
[5] Graduate School of Arts and Sciences, The University of Tokyo, Tokyo, Japan

Abstract. This paper describes a formalization of a class of fixed-point problems on graphs and its applications. This class captures several well-known graph theoretical problems such as those of shortest path type and for data flow analysis. An abstract solution algorithm of the fixed-point problem is formalized and its correctness is proved using a theorem proving system. Moreover, the validity of the A* algorithm, considered as a specialized version of the abstract algorithm, is proved by extending the proof of the latter. The insights we obtained through these formalizations are described. We also discuss the extension of this approach to the verification of model checking algorithms.

1   Introduction

There are two approaches to the verification of computer systems. One is to verify the correctness of a system using an interactive proof checker such as HOL [8], NQTHM [2], or PVS [14] and so on. This approach is of wide use but has a high cost with respect to human efforts. The other is to ensure correctness by an exhaustive search of the state space with a model checker, without human interaction. This approach is restricted to the specific properties of computer systems, but is highly practicable for finite-state systems with a limited number of states.

The use of the former approach in software verification has shifted from the verification of concrete programs (codes) to that of designs and algorithms. One reason is that the verification of programs is of little importance when considering the reliability of an entire software system, while verification requires very precise inferences.

This study focuses on a graph search algorithm. Although search algorithms usually aim at finding solutions, they are sometimes used to ensure that "no solution exists under the given conditions". When the aim is to find solutions, one can confirm whether the computed solutions satisfy the given conditions, regardless of the correctness of the search algorithm. On the other hand, it is essential to state the correctness of the algorithm when one is trying to rigidly assert the absence of solutions.

Model checking is nothing but to show the absence of solutions (e.g., deadlock states) using some search algorithms. In general, the algorithms and software used for model checking are elaborately tuned, with many optimized strategies, in order to improve efficiency. Hence, it becomes non-trivial to ensure the correctness of such algorithms and softwares used in a real world.

In order to deal with several graph search algorithms uniformly, based on the work by Kildall [11], Tamai [15] formulated a class of graph search problems and then characterized two kinds of solutions: fixed-point solutions and a path solutions. This formulation captures several well-known problems of graph searches such as shortest path problems and data flow analyses. Tamai also characterized an abstract algorithm that computes a fixed-point solution, and informally showed its correctness.

In this study, we formalize Tamai's formulation with the HOL system. The two kinds of solutions and the abstract algorithm are formalized and the correctness of the algorithm is proved. Moreover, we obtain a formal proof of the A* algorithm, an optimized algorithm for solving a class of shortest path problems, by extending the proof of the abstract algorithm.

Since a formalization is usually hard work, we generally try to reduce the load by simplifying or making things more abstract. This sometimes leads to better abstraction or the more general settings of problems. For example, we managed to weaken the premises of the abstract algorithm, and thereby obtained insights on the correctness of the A* algorithm. This algorithm is characterized by the question of how to select a vertex from a pool of unprocessed vertices. However, through our formalization we found that this selection does not affect the correctness of the algorithm. This result can then be applied to the correctness of some variants of the A* algorithm, e.g., one that selects a vertex with certain heuristics in order to avoid falling into an infinite loop.

The usefulness of formalizations by proof checkers has been criticized mainly because of their high cost. However, if the verification of basic (abstract) algorithms can be used to derive the correctness of variants of the algorithm with relatively low cost, then we believe that the original verification is worth the costs of a great deal of human interaction.

This paper is organized as follows. Section 2 briefly reviews the formulation of problems on which our work based. This section also outlines the HOL system by which the formal proof is written. The actual formalization is described in Sect. 3 and Sect. 4, and is divided into the verification of the abstract algorithm and that of the A* algorithm. Section 5 reveals the insights that we obtained from this work. This paper ends with related work, concluding remarks and our probable future direction in Sect. 6 and Sect. 7.

2   Preliminary

2.1   Graph Algorithm

This section describes a brief overview of Tamai's paper [15], on which our formalization is based. Some parts of his formulation are omitted or changed from the original ones so as to make them more abstract or to facilitate the formalization. We will mention such changes in Sect. 5.1.

First we formulate the general setting of a search problem, consisting a (possibly cyclic) directed graph, a semi-lattice, and edge functions. Then we explain two kinds of solutions of a problem: fixed-point solutions and path solutions. After showing some examples of the problem, we explain an abstract algorithm which computes a fixed-point solution of the problem.

General Setting. Let $G = (V, E)$ be a directed graph; let V be a set of vertices and E a set of edges. The starting vertex and the ending vertex of an edge $e \in E$ is expressed as $h(e)$ and $t(e)$, respectively. A set of incoming edges $\text{in}(v)$ and outgoing edges $\text{out}(v)$ of a vertex $v \in V$ is defined ordinarily.

$$\text{in}(v) = \{e \in E \mid t(e) = v\}, \qquad \text{out}(v) = \{e \in E \mid h(e) = v\}.$$

We assume that there is a distinguished vertex $s \in V$ such that $\text{in}(s) = \emptyset$. Afterwards this vertex is treated as a starting point in a search problem.

A path $p = (v, [e_1, \ldots, e_n])$ $(n \geq 0)$ in the graph G is a (possibly empty) finite sequence of edges equipped with an entry vertex such that adjacent edges share the same end point, i.e. $v = h(e_1)$ and $t(e_i) = h(e_{i+1})$ for $i = 1, \ldots, n-1$. Note that a path $p = (v, [e_1, \ldots, e_n])$ starts from a vertex v and ends with a vertex w, where $w = t(e_n)$ when $n > 0$ and $w = v$ otherwise. A vertex w is said to be "reachable from v" when there is a path that starts from v and ends with w.

Let L be a semi-lattice, i.e., an underlying set L equipped with a meet operation $\wedge$ that satisfies the following conditions[1]:

1. $\forall x, y \in L.\, x \wedge y = y \wedge x$;
2. $\forall x, y, z \in L.\, x \wedge (y \wedge z) = (x \wedge y) \wedge z$;
3. $\forall x.\, x \wedge x = x$.

The partial order relation $\leq$ on L is defined as:

$$\forall x, y \in L.\, x \leq y \iff x \wedge y = x.$$

We further assume the existence of a top element $\top$ in L, i.e., $\forall x \in L.\, x \wedge \top = x$.

In a given problem, each edge $e \in E$ is associated with a monotonic function f_e from L to L, where $f_e(x) = \top$ only if $x = \top$. This function is naturally extended to a function f_p for a path p as $f_p = f_{e_n} \circ \cdots \circ f_{e_1}$ for $p = (v, [e_1, \ldots, e_n])$.

---

[1] In Tamai's paper [15], a (full) lattice is used instead of a semi-lattice. However we use only semi-lattices since the join operation $\vee$ is not used in this formalization.

The problem we are to formalize is formulated as follows. Given a graph $G = (V, E)$, a lattice L, a distinguished vertex $s \in V$ and an initial value $b_s \in L \setminus \{\top\}$ for the vertex s, and a function assignment for each edge $f_e \in L^L$ for $e \in E$, then compute an assignment of an element $x_v \in L$ for each vertex $v \in L$ that satisfies a certain condition. Such a condition determines a kind of solution of the problem, and two kinds of solutions are explained below.

Fixed-Point Solution. An assignment $x_v \in L$ (for $v \in V$) is a *fixed-point solution* if it satisfies the following equations.

$$\begin{cases} x_s = b_s \\ x_v = \bigwedge_{t(e)=v \text{ and } h(e) \text{ is reachable from } s} f_e(x_{h(e)}) \quad (v \neq s) \end{cases}$$

The second equation is slightly inaccurate and misleading. It should be read as "the right hand side exists and equals to x_v" here.

Path Solution. An assignment $x_v \in L$ (for $v \in V$) is a *path solution* if it satisfies:

$$x_v = \bigwedge_{p \in \text{path}(s, v)} f_p(b_s)$$

where $\text{path}(s, v)$ is a set of paths from vertex s to vertex v. Again, the above equation means "the right hand side exists and equals to x_v."

Problem Examples. Several concrete problems can be characterized as special cases of the general setting formulated above. We show some examples here.

1. **Reachability on graphs** Let L be a lattice $\{\bot, \top\}$ with $\bot \leq \top$, f_e be an identity function for all $e \in E$, and b_s be $\bot$. Then the solution x_v for $v \in V$ is $\bot$ if v is reachable from s. Moreover, $x_v = \top$ if we consider the path solution x_v and v is unreachable from s.
2. **Shortest path problem** Let L be a set of real numbers $\mathbb{R}$ with an additional top element, equipped with the total order on $\mathbb{R}$. When distance d_e is associated with each edge e, define $f_e = \lambda x. x + d_e$. If $b_s = 0$, the solution x_v coincides with the distance of the shortest path from s to v.
3. **Finite State Automaton** Consider a finite state automaton whose edge e is labeled by an element a_e of alphabet Σ. Let L be set of all the subsets of Σ^*, equipped with superset ordering "$\supseteq$", and b_s be a singleton set consisting of an empty string ϵ, where s is the initial state, and define $f_e = \lambda x. \{wa_e \mid w \in x\}$. Then the path solution x_v corresponds to a set of strings accepted at a final state v.
4. **Dataflow analysis** Let us explain by taking the reachable definition problem as an example. Let L be a set of all the subsets of value definitions in a program, equipped with the subset ordering "$\subseteq$". The execution flows of the

For each $v \in V$, $x_v \leftarrow \top$
$x_s \leftarrow b_s$
$S \leftarrow \{s\}$
While $S \neq \emptyset$ do
      Take and remove an arbitrary vertex v from S.
      For each $e \in \mathrm{out}(v)$ do
          If $x_{t(e)} \not\leq f_e(x_v)$ then
             $x_{t(e)} \leftarrow x_{t(e)} \wedge f_e(x_v)$
             Add $t(e)$ to S.

Fig. 1. Algorithm P

program form a directed graph as usual. A function assigned to each edge e is

$$f_e(x) = (x \cap K_e^c) \cup G_e$$

where K_e^c is a complement of a set of killed definitions and G_e is a set of generated definitions by a program fragment corresponding to the edge e. Then the path solution gives a vertex a set of definitions that is reachable at the execution point corresponding to the vertex. More examples can be found in [11].

Iterative Solution Algorithm. An abstract algorithm (Algorithm P) that computes fixed-point solution is given in Fig. 1

The correctness of the algorithm is shown in [15].

2.2 A* Algorithm

As we mentioned, a class of graph problems in Sect. 2.1 subsumes shortest path problems. Here we explain the A* algorithm [13], one of the algorithms for solving shortest path problems using heuristic information to reduce search space, as an extension of the iterative solution algorithm (Fig. 1).

In the A* algorithm, heuristic information is given as estimation of distance $\mathrm{h}(v)$ from each vertex v to the fixed goal vertex. The algorithm can be formulated by replacing the following line in Fig. 1

      Take and remove an arbitrary vertex v from S.

with

      Take and remove a vertex v from S such that
          $x_v + \mathrm{h}(v) \leq x_{v'} + \mathrm{h}(v')$ for $v' \in S$.
      If v is the goal vertex, the algorithm stops.

(Recall that $x_v \in L = \mathbb{R} \cup \{\top\}$.)

If this estimation $\mathrm{h}(v)$ gives a lower bound of distance from v to the goal, the above algorithm computes one of the shortest paths if the algorithm terminates and such a path exists.

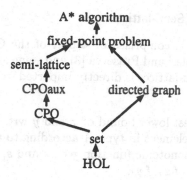

Fig. 2. Overall structure of our formalization

2.3 HOL

Our formalization is done by the HOL system, a tactical theorem prover based on Church's simple theory of types [6].

Some algebraic structures are used in the formalization: directed graphs and semi-lattices. We used the abstract theory library [16] that is bundled with the standard HOL90 distribution. With this library, one can make a predicate characterizing an algebraic structure more or less implicit, and obtain facilities of instantiating the abstract structure to a concrete one. Although instantiation of theorems is not used in this formalization, it will be useful when we try to apply this formalization to concrete problems.

We here introduce notations used in the later sections. By attaching the turnstile mark ⊢, we will specify that its following sentence is a theorem. The mark ⊢$_{def}$ is used for definitions and constant specifications similarly. We use Greek letters, $\alpha, \beta, \gamma, \ldots$, as type variables, **bold** font letters for type constants and sans serif font letters for term constants. Inside a definition or a constant specification, the defined term constant is written by an underlined symbol. Conditional expressions are denoted as "if A then B else C" where B and C must be of the same type, and A must be a boolean, whereas such expressions are written as "$A \Rightarrow B \mid C$" in the HOL system. Sometimes we put comments "*(** here is comments **)*" between term expressions for readability.

3 Formalization of the Abstract Algorithm

3.1 Overall Structure

Our formalization is comprised of five parts: partial order, semi-lattice, directed graph, fixed-point problem, and A* algorithm. Each of which corresponds to a theory, and as a whole they construct a hierarchical structure illustrated in Fig. 2.

The rest of this section describes the actual formalization for each part.

3.2   Partial Order and Semi-lattice

Theory of partial order is comprised of a part of the CPO (Complete Partial Orders) theory by Camilleri and Prasetya [3] and some auxiliary theorems. Most of the operations on semi-lattices is directly imported from those of CPOs in the library.

- Cap $r\,x\,y$: the greatest lower bound of x and y wrt. r;
- Top r : the greatest element in type A according to a relation r on A;
- Mono $r\,s\,f$: f is a monotonic function wrt. r and s,
  i.e., $\forall x\,y.\,r\,x\,y \Longrightarrow s\,(f\,x)(f\,y)$;
- Distrib $r\,s\,f$: f is a distributive function wrt. r and s,
  i.e., $\forall x\,y.\,f\,((\mathsf{Cap}\,r)\,x\,y) = (\mathsf{Cap}\,s)\,(f\,x)\,(f\,y)$.

where r and s are partial order relations. All of these but the last one are from the CPO library. Since a partial order relation is the only algebraic structure in CPO, almost all operations on CPO take partial order relations as arguments.

Using the abstract theory library, a semi-lattice is defined as an abstract entity with the following theory obligation (i.e., predicate specifying the conditions the abstract operations should satisfy).

$$\vdash_{def} \forall(l : \alpha\,\text{semilattice}).\ \underline{\text{semilattice\_oblig}\,l} \Longleftrightarrow$$
$$(\forall x\,y.\ \text{meet}\,l\,x\,y = \text{meet}\,l\,y\,x)\ \wedge$$
$$(\forall x\,y\,z.\ \text{meet}\,l\,x\,(\text{meet}\,l\,y\,z) = \text{meet}\,l\,(\text{meet}\,l\,x\,y)\,z)\ \wedge$$
$$(\forall x.\ \text{meet}\,l\,x\,x = x)$$

An element l of the type $\alpha\,\text{semilattice}$, which is automatically defined by the abstract theory library, represents a semi-lattice whose underlying set is α. The meet operation "$\wedge$" of a semi-lattice l is denoted by meet l, which is the only abstract operation of a semi-lattice. Note that the type of elements x, y, z of a lattice $l : \alpha\,\text{semilattice}$ is α.

With the help of the library, we can make theory obligation predicates implicit. As a result, the statement

$$\forall(l : \alpha\,\text{semilattice}).\ P\,l$$

actually means

$$\forall(l : \alpha\,\text{semilattice}).\ \text{semilattice\_oblig}\,l \Longrightarrow P\,l.$$

In the rest of this paper, we omit theory obligation predicates for brevity.

Although meet corresponds to the "$\wedge$" operation and it determines a semi-lattice, this operation is not so frequently used. Instead the partial order relation LEQ, derived from "$\wedge$" as follows, is used throughout the formalization, since almost all operations in CPO library takes partial orders as arguments as we mentioned above, and we extensively use the CPO library.

$$\vdash_{def} \text{LEQ}\,l\,x\,y \Longleftrightarrow (\text{meet}\,l\,x\,y = x)$$

As a result, operations on a semi-lattice are denoted less compactly as "Top(LEQ l)" and "Cap(LEQ l) $x\,y$".

On the other hand, the assumption on the existence of the top element in a lattice l is denoted as "HAS_Top l".

3.3   Directed Graph

Our basic definition of directed graphs follows Wong's work [17]. The most significant difference is that a directed graph is defined as an abstract entity as in the case of semi-lattices.

$$\vdash_{def} \forall g.\ \underline{\text{graph\_oblig}}\, g \iff (\forall e.\ e \in \text{ES}\, g \implies \text{es}\, e \in \text{VS}\, g \wedge \text{ed}\, e \in \text{VS}\, g)$$

Here is a summary of important operations on directed graphs.

- VS g : set of vertices of a graph g;
- ES g : set of edges of a graph g;
- es e : starting vertex of an edge e (formerly denoted as $h(e)$);
- ed e : ending vertex of an edge e (formerly denoted as $t(e)$);
- INCIDENT_FROM $g\,v$: set of outgoing edges from a vertex v in a graph g (formerly denoted as $out(v)$);
- EMPTY_PATH v : constructs an empty path $(v, [\,])$;
- PATH_SNOC $p\,e$: constructs a path $(v, [e_1, \ldots, e_n, e])$ by adding an edge e at the end of a path $p = (v, [e_1, \ldots, e_n])$.

3.4   Fixed-Point Problem

The abstract algorithm is formalized as a predicate that has the following form:

$$\text{POTENTIAL}\, n\ g\ l\ s\ bs\ fe\ open\ closed\ outv\ xv.$$

Arguments of the predicate can be classified into the following three categories.

The first one is the execution counter. The argument n belongs to this category. This records number of steps in the execution. This also makes it possible to define the predicate by a recursive definition on natural numbers.

The second is that of parameters given as parts of specification of the problem. These values do not change during the execution. Arguments g, l, bs, and fe belong to this category, and the meaning of each argument is as follows:

- g : directed graph;
- l : semi-lattice;
- s : start point of search;
- bs : initial value at s;
- fe : assignment of a function to each edge ("$fe\,e\,x$" corresponds to $f_e(x)$).

The last category means internal states of the execution. These values are updated at each step of the execution. Arguments $open$, $closed$, $outv$, and xv belong to this category, and the meaning of each is as follows:

$\vdash_{def}$ $(\forall g\ l\ s\ bs\ fe\ open\ closed\ outv\ xv.$
    <u>POTENTIAL</u> $0\ g\ l\ s\ bs\ fe\ open\ closed\ outv\ xv \Longleftrightarrow$
    $(open = \{s\}) \wedge (closed = \{\}) \wedge (outv = \{\}) \wedge$
    $(xv = (\lambda v.\ \text{if}\ (v = s)\ \text{then}\ bs\ \text{else}\ (Top(LEQ\,l))))) \wedge$
$(\forall n\ g\ l\ s\ bs\ fe\ open\ closed\ outv\ xv.$
    <u>POTENTIAL</u>$(SUC\ n)\ g\ l\ s\ bs\ fe\ open\ closed\ outv\ xv \Longleftrightarrow$
    $(\exists open'\ closed'\ outv'\ xv'.$
    POTENTIAL $n\ g\ l\ s\ bs\ fe\ open'\ closed'\ outv'\ xv' \wedge$
    $(\text{if}\ (outv' = \{\})$
      then
      $(\text{if}\ (open' = \{\})$
        $\text{then}\ ((open = open') \wedge (closed = closed') \wedge (outv = outv') \wedge (xv = xv'))$
        $\text{else}\ (\exists v.v \in open' \wedge (closed = \{v\} \cup closed') \wedge$
            $(open = open' \setminus \{v\}) \wedge (outv = INCIDENT\_FROM\ g\ v) \wedge (xv = xv')))$
      $\text{else}\ (^{**}\ (outv' \neq \{\})\ ^{**})$
      $(\exists e.\ e \in outv' \wedge (outv = outv' \setminus \{e\}) \wedge$
        $(\text{if}\ (LEQ\,l\ (xv'\ (ed\,e))\ (fe\ e\ (xv'\ (es\,e))))$
          $\text{then}\ ((open = open') \wedge (closed = closed') \wedge (xv = xv'))$
          $\text{else}\ ((open = \{ed\,e\} \cup open') \wedge (closed = closed' \setminus \{ed\,e\}) \wedge$
            $(xv = (\lambda v.\ \text{if}\ (v = ed\,e)$
                $\text{then}\ (Cap(LEQ\,l)\ (xv'(ed\,e))\ (fe\ e\ (xv'\ (es\,e))))$
                $\text{else}\ (xv'\ v)))))))))$

Fig. 3. Definition of abstract algorithm

- *open* : not-processed vertices (corresponds to S in Fig. 1);
- *closed* : vertices processed at least once, but not in *open*;
- *outv* : edges incident from the expanded vertex and not processed yet;
- *xv* : assignment of an element of l to each vertex ("*xv v*" corresponds to x_v).

This predicate is defined by a recursive definition on natural numbers as in Fig. 3. This algorithm is considered to be terminated when both *open* and *outv* become empty sets. In this case, all of the internal states remain the same values as the previous states.

Note that the original algorithm introduced in the previous section forms a doubly-nested loop, while the predicate is defined by a single loop. The inner loop of the original one is assimilated to the outer one, and an internal state *outv'* of the previous step determines which loop we are executing; we are in the outer loop if and only if *outv'* = {}.

With this definition, we proved the following theorem that ensures the correctness of solutions.

1. Algorithm POTENTIAL gives a fixed-point solution when it terminates.

   $\vdash \forall g\ l\ s\ bs\ fe.\ s \in \mathsf{VS}\ g \land (\forall e.\ \mathrm{ed}\ e \neq s) \land \mathsf{HAS\_Top}\ l \land (bs \neq \mathsf{Top}(\mathsf{LEQ}\ l)) \land$
   $(\forall x\ e.\ e \in \mathsf{ES}\ g \land (fe\ e\ x = \mathsf{Top}(\mathsf{LEQ}\ l)) \implies (x = \mathsf{Top}(\mathsf{LEQ}\ l))) \land$
   $(\forall e.\ e \in \mathsf{ES}\ g \implies \mathsf{Mono}(\mathsf{LEQ}\ l)\ (\mathsf{LEQ}\ l)\ (fe\ e)) \implies$
   $\quad (\forall n\ closed\ xv.\ \mathsf{POTENTIAL}\ n\ g\ l\ s\ bs\ fe\ \{\}\ closed\ \{\}\ xv \implies$
   $\quad \mathsf{IS\_FPSOLN}\ l\ g\ fe\ bs\ s\ xv)$

2. Algorithm POTENTIAL gives the path solution when it terminates.

   $\vdash \forall g\ l\ s\ bs\ fe.\ s \in \mathsf{VS}\ g \land (\forall e.\ \mathrm{ed}\ e \neq s) \land \mathsf{HAS\_Top}\ l \land (bs \neq \mathsf{Top}(\mathsf{LEQ}\ l)) \land$
   $(\forall x\ e.\ e \in \mathsf{ES}\ g \land (fe\ e\ x = \mathsf{Top}(\mathsf{LEQ}\ l)) \implies (x = \mathsf{Top}(\mathsf{LEQ}\ l))) \land$
   $(\forall e.\ e \in \mathsf{ES}\ g \implies \mathsf{Distrib}(\mathsf{LEQ}\ l)\ (\mathsf{LEQ}\ l)\ (fe\ e)) \implies$
   $\quad (\forall n\ closed\ xv.\ \mathsf{POTENTIAL}\ n\ g\ l\ s\ bs\ fe\ \{\}\ closed\ \{\}\ xv \implies$
   $\quad \forall v.\ v \in \mathsf{VS}\ g \implies \mathsf{IS\_PATHSOLN}\ l\ g\ fe\ bs\ s\ v\ (xv\ v)))$

Predicates IS_FPSOLN and IS_PATHSOLN mean the last argument is a fixed-point solution and a path solution respectively. Note that distributivity is required in the case of path solution.

The first theorem required 13 intermediate lemmas (two of them are mentioned in Sect. 4). The second required additional 1 definition and 8 lemmas. Most of these lemmas are proved by induction over the number n of steps. As a whole, proofs of these theorems are accomplished by a HOL script approximately 1300 lines long.

4   Verification of A* Algorithm

In this section, we define the A* algorithm and show theorems we proved about that. Although the algorithm is defined on $\mathbb{R} \cup \{\top\}$ in general, we here formalize it on a general semi-lattice.

Since the A* algorithm can be expressed as an extension of the abstract algorithm as we mentioned in Sect. 2.2, its formalization becomes similar one to that of the abstract algorithm (Fig. 4). In the definition, IS_MINIMAL $r\ X\ x$ means $x \in X$ is a minimal element in a set X wrt. an order relation r.

Compared with the predicate POTENTIAL in the previous section, ASTAR has 4 additional arguments: $goal$ and hv as parts of specification, $stat$ and po as internal states. The meaning of each argument is as follows:

- $goal$: the goal vertex
- hv : assignment of an estimation function to each vertex
- $stat$: status of the execution
- po : assignment of an optimal path from s to each vertex

Arguments hv and $stat$ should be explained in further detail. In Sect. 2.2, estimation $\mathrm{h}(v)$ for a vertex v was a real number, and $x_v + \mathrm{h}(v)$ was used as a measure when selecting a vertex from S. In the formalization, however, we do not restrict the lattice L to $\mathbb{R} \cup \{\top\}$, but make $hv\ v$ a function from l to l and

$\vdash_{def}$ ($\forall g\, l\, s\, bs\, fe\, goal\, hv\, open\, closed\, outv\, xv\, stat\, po.$
   $\underline{\text{ASTAR}}\, 0\, g\, l\, s\, bs\, fe\, goal\, hv\, open\, closed\, outv\, xv\, stat\, po \Longleftrightarrow$
   $(open = \{s\}) \wedge (closed = \{\}) \wedge (outv = \{\}) \wedge$
   $(xv = (\lambda v.\ \text{if } (v = s) \text{ then } bs \text{ else } (\text{Top}(\text{LEQ}\, l))))) \wedge (stat = 0) \wedge$
   $(po = \lambda v.\ \text{EMPTY\_PATH}\, s)) \wedge$
($\forall n\, g\, l\, s\, bs\, fe\, goal\, hv\, open\, closed\, outv\, xv\, stat\, po.$
   $\underline{\text{ASTAR}}(\text{SUC}\, n)\, g\, l\, s\, bs\, fe\, goal\, hv\, open\, closed\, outv\, xv\, stat\, po \Longleftrightarrow$
   $\exists open'\, closed'\, xv'\, outv'\, stat'\, po'.$
   $\text{ASTAR}\, n\, g\, l\, s\, bs\, fe\, goal\, hv\, open'\, closed'\, outv'\, xv'\, stat'\, po' \wedge$
   $(\text{if } (stat' = 0)$
     then
    $(\text{if } (outv' = \{\})$
      then
     $(\text{if } (open' = \{\})$
       then $((open = open') \wedge (closed = closed') \wedge (outv = outv') \wedge$
          $(xv = xv')) \wedge (stat = 2) \wedge (po = po'))$
       else $(\exists v.\, v \in open' \wedge$
         $(\text{IS\_MINIMAL}(\text{LEQ}\, l)\, \{hv\, v_1\, (xv'\, v_1) \mid v_1 \in open'\}(hv\, v\, (xv'\, v))) \wedge$
         $(\text{if } (v = goal)$
          then $((stat = 1) \wedge (open = open') \wedge (closed = closed') \wedge$
            $(outv = outv') \wedge (xv = xv') \wedge (po = po'))$
          else $((stat = stat') \wedge (closed = \{v\} \cup closed') \wedge$
            $(open = open' \setminus \{v\}) \wedge (outv = \text{INCIDENT\_FROM}\, g\, v) \wedge$
            $(xv = xv') \wedge (po = po')))$
     else (** $(outv' \neq \{\})$ **)
    $(\exists e.\, e \in outv' \wedge (outv = outv' \setminus \{e\}) \wedge (stat = stat') \wedge$
    $(\text{if } (\text{LEQ}\, l\, (xv'\, (ed\, e))\, (fe\, e\, (xv'\, (es\, e))))$
      then $((open = open') \wedge (closed = closed') \wedge (xv = xv') \wedge (po = po')$
      else $((open = \{ed\, e\} \cup open') \wedge (closed = closed' \setminus \{ed\, e\}) \wedge$
         $(xv = (\lambda v.\ \text{if } (v = ed\, e)$
             then $(\text{Cap}(\text{LEQ}\, l)\, (xv'(ed\, e))\, (fe\, e\, (xv'\, (es\, e))))$
             else $(xv'\, v)) \wedge$
         $(po = (\lambda v.\ \text{if } (v = ed\, e)$
             then $\text{PATH\_SNOC}(po'\, (es\, e))\, e$
             else $po'\, v)))))) \wedge$
  else (** $(stat \neq 0)$ **)
  $((open = open') \wedge (closed = closed') \wedge (outv = outv') \wedge$
  $(xv = xv') \wedge (stat = stat') \wedge (po = po'))))$

Fig. 4. Definition of A* algorithm

$hv\,v\,(xv\,v)$ is used as a measure for the selection. Obviously this formalization generalizes the usual formulation; set $hv\,v = \lambda x.\,x + \mathrm{h}(v)$. Execution status *stat* has one of 0, 1 or 2 as its value. Value 0 means the execution is now proceeding, 1 means that we have already reached the goal vertex and the execution has been finished, and 2 means we could not reach the goal vertex (i.e., *goal* is not reachable from s in the given problem.), and the execution has been finished.

Internal values are updated as in POTENTIAL's case while *stat* = 0, and these values stop changing when *stat* becomes 1 or 2. The most significant difference between ASTAR and POTENTIAL is how to select vertex from *open* as we mentioned in Sect. 2.2. Here we select a vertex $v(\in open)$ such that $hv\,v\,(xv\,v)$ is *minimal* in the sense of the order "LEQ l" in the semi-lattice l, since there may be no *minimum* value(here we do not restrict "LEQ l" to a total order). We later discuss this decision in Sect. 5.2.

Most of the properties of POTENTIAL can be imported to that of ASTAR, using the following theorem:

$\vdash \forall g\,l\,n\,s\,bs\,fe\,goal\,hv\,open\,closed\,outv\,xv\,stat\,po.$
(ASTAR $n\,g\,l\,s\,bs\,fe\,goal\,hv\,open\,closed\,outv\,xv\,stat\,po \implies$
($\exists m.$ (POTENTIAL $m\,g\,l\,s\,bs\,fe\,open\,closed\,outv\,xv$)))

The above theorem itself can be proved by expanding ASTAR and POTENTIAL with their definitions, and by induction over n. With the above theorem, a theorem whose form is "$\forall g\,l\,\ldots\ldots$ ASTAR $\ldots \implies P$" can be derived from a theorem "$\forall g\,l\,\ldots\ldots$ POTENTIAL $\ldots \implies P$".

The following two theorems, which are used in the proof of the correctness of POTENTIAL, also play important roles in the correctness of ASTAR. They correspond to Assertions 1 and 3 in [15].

- For each edge $e = (v, w)$, $x_w \le f_e(x_v)$, if e have already been processed.

$\vdash \forall g\,l\,n\,s\,bs\,fe\,open\,closed\,outv\,xv.$
POTENTIAL $n\,g\,l\,s\,bs\,fe\,open\,closed\,outv\,xv$
$\implies \forall e.\,e \in ES\,g \wedge es\,e \in closed \wedge e \notin outv$
$\implies (\text{LEQ}\,l)\,(xv\,(ed\,e))\,(fe\,e\,(xv\,(es\,e)))$

- For each edge $e = (v, w)$ such that $v \in closed$, either $w \in open \cup closed$, or e is being processed.

$\vdash \forall g\,l\,s\,bs\,fe.\ \text{HAS\_Top}\,l \wedge (bs \ne \text{Top}(\text{LEQ}\,l)) \wedge$
$(\forall x\,e.\,e \in ES\,g \wedge (fe\,e\,x = \text{Top}(\text{LEQ}\,l)) \implies (x = \text{Top}(\text{LEQ}\,l))) \implies$
$\forall n\,open\,closed\,outv\,xv.$
POTENTIAL $n\,g\,l\,s\,bs\,fe\,open\,closed\,outv\,xv$
$\implies \forall e.\,e \in ES\,g \wedge es\,e \in closed$
$\implies ed\,e \in open \vee ed\,e \in closed \vee e \in outv$

With importing the above theorems from POTENTIAL, we proved the following lemma.

$\vdash \forall g\, l\, n\, s\, bs\, fe\, goal\, hv\, open\, closed\, outv\, xv\, po.$
  $\mathsf{ASTAR}\, n\, g\, l\, s\, bs\, fe\, goal\, hv\, open\, closed\, outv\, xv\, 1\, po \wedge$
  $\mathsf{HAS\_Top}\, l \wedge (bs \neq \mathsf{Top}(\mathsf{LEQ}\, l)) \wedge$
  $(\forall x\, e.\, e \in \mathsf{ES}\, g \wedge (fe\, e\, x = \mathsf{Top}(\mathsf{LEQ}\, l)) \Longrightarrow (x = \mathsf{Top}(\mathsf{LEQ}\, l))) \wedge$
  $(\forall e.\, e \in \mathsf{ES}\, g \Longrightarrow \mathsf{Mono}(\mathsf{LEQ}\, l)\, (\mathsf{LEQ}\, l)\, (fe\, e)) \wedge$
  $(\forall bv\, v.\, \mathsf{IS\_LEQ\_PATHSOLN}\, l\, g\, fe\, (hv\, v\, bv)\, bv\, v\, goal) \wedge$
  $(\forall v.\, (v \in open) \Longrightarrow (\mathsf{LEQ}\, l)\, (xv\, goal)\, (hv\, v\, (xv\, v)))$
  $\Longrightarrow \mathsf{IS\_LEQ\_PATHSOLN}.l\, g\, fe\, (xv\, goal)\, bs\, s\, goal$

where $\mathsf{IS\_LEQ\_PATHSOLN}\, l\, g\, fe\, x\, b\, v\, w$ means x is a lower bound of

$$\{((fe\, e_n) \circ \cdots \circ (fe\, e_1))(b) \mid (v, [e_1, \ldots, e_n]) \text{ is a path from } v \text{ to } w\}.$$

A condition that uses this predicate in the above lemma corresponds to the condition that "h(v) gives a lower bound of distance from v to the goal."

The main theorem on the A* algorithm is that it gives a path solution when it normally terminates (i.e., when $stat = 1$). Since a path solution is expressed as the greatest lower bound of a certain set, we have to assert 1) the solution is a lower bound of the set, and 2) it is the greatest one among any lower bound of the set. The former condition is achieved by the above lemma. Then the latter one is asserted by adding an extra condition that "LEQ l" is total, which enables us to prove that "*po goal*" actually records a path from s to *goal* and its distance coincide with "*xv goal*". As a result, we obtain the following theorem:

$\vdash \forall g\, l\, n\, s\, bs\, fe\, goal\, hv\, open\, closed\, outv\, xv\, po.$
  $\mathsf{ASTAR}\, n\, g\, l\, s\, bs\, fe\, goal\, hv\, open\, closed\, outv\, xv\, 1\, po \wedge$
  $\mathsf{HAS\_Top}\, l \wedge (bs \neq \mathsf{Top}(\mathsf{LEQ}\, l)) \wedge$
  $(\forall x\, e.\, e \in \mathsf{ES}\, g \wedge (fe\, e\, x = \mathsf{Top}(\mathsf{LEQ}\, l)) \Longrightarrow (x = \mathsf{Top}(\mathsf{LEQ}\, l))) \wedge$
  $(\forall e.\, e \in \mathsf{ES}\, g \Longrightarrow \mathsf{Mono}(\mathsf{LEQ}\, l)\, (\mathsf{LEQ}\, l)\, (fe\, e)) \wedge$
  $(\forall bv\, v.\, \mathsf{IS\_LEQ\_PATHSOLN}\, l\, g\, fe\, (hv\, v\, bv)\, bv\, v\, goal) \wedge$
  $(\forall b.\, hv\, goal\, b = b) \wedge (\mathsf{IS\_TOTAL}\, l)$
  $\Longrightarrow \mathsf{IS\_PATHSOLN}\, l\, g\, fe\, bs\, s\, goal\, (xv\, goal)$

5   Insights from Our Formalization

This section describes some insights resulting from our formalization. We mention two topics: Modification of the original proof and an observation on the formalization of the A* algorithm.

5.1   Modifications to the Original Proof

As mentioned before, we made several modifications to [15]. This section describes these modifications in detail.

First, we modified the definition of fixed-point solutions in Sect. 2.1, so that reachability from s is taken into account. The original definition of a fixed-point solution is characterized by the following equation [15]:

$$\begin{cases} x_s = b_s \\ x_v = \bigwedge_{t(e)=v} f_e(x_{h(e)}) \quad (v \neq s) \end{cases}$$

However, the algorithm P (Fig.1) may not compute a fixed-point solution, if there is no restriction on reachability, since an isolated vertex can have non-⊤ value of L.

In the original work, directed graphs were restricted to be finite. This was because the existence of the GLB (Greatest Lower Bound) of an arbitrary subset of L was used when proving propositions having the following form:

For each step n, if a is the GLB of a set $X(n)(\subseteq L)$ then $P(a)$

If we try to prove the above proposition by induction over n, we should prove "$P(a)$ holds" from the following assumptions:

- (Assumption1) For each step n, if a' is the GLB of a set $X(n)$ then $P(a')$
- (Assumption2) a is the GLB of a set $X(n+1)$.

Then nothing can be derived from Assumption1, since we cannot assert the existence of the GLB of $X(n)$ without using some kinds of completeness on L or finiteness of a directed graph.

Therefore, we replace the above proposition with a more general one:

For each step n, if a is a LB (lower bound) of a set $X(n)(\subseteq L)$ then $P(a)$

Note that the new version results in no loss of generality whenever the GLB of $X(n)$ exists. Then all we have to do is to prove "$P(a)$ holds" from the following assumptions:

- (Assumption1') For each step n, if a' is a LB of a set $X(n)$ then $P(a')$
- (Assumption2') a is a LB of a set $X(n+1)$.

Since it is easy to prove that "each LB of $X(n+1)$ is also a LB of $X(n)$" in our case, one can use Assumption1' and prove the new version without assuming finiteness of a directed graph.

5.2   A* Algorithm

In Sect. 4, we gave a lemma on the A* algorithm with respect to the predicate ASTAR. However, if we examine its proof carefully, we notice that properties of ASTAR are not used in the proof. In fact, we can prove this as a property of

POTENTIAL:

$\vdash \forall g\, l\, n\, s\, bs\, fe\, goal\, hv\, open\, closed\, outv\, xv.$
    POTENTIAL $n\, g\, l\, s\, bs\, fe\, open\, closed\, outv\, xv\ \wedge$
    HAS_Top $l \wedge (bs \ne \text{Top}(\text{LEQ}\, l)) \wedge$
    $(\forall x\, e.\, e \in \text{ES}\, g \wedge (fe\, e\, x = \text{Top}(\text{LEQ}\, l)) \implies (x = \text{Top}(\text{LEQ}\, l))) \wedge$
    $(\forall e.\, e \in \text{ES}\, g \implies \text{Mono}(\text{LEQ}\, l)\, (\text{LEQ}\, l)\, (fe\, e)) \wedge$
    $(\forall bv\, v.\, \text{IS\_LEQ\_PATHSOLN}\, l\, g\, fe\, (hv\, v\, bv)\, bv\, v\, goal) \wedge$
    $(outv = \{\}) \wedge (goal \notin closed) \wedge$
    $(\forall v.\, (v \in open) \implies (\text{LEQ}\, l)\, (xv\, goal)\, (hv\, v\, (xv\, v)))$
    $\implies \text{IS\_LEQ\_PATHSOLN}\, l\, g\, fe\, (xv\, goal)\, bs\, s\, goal$

In the definition of the A* algorithm (Fig. 4), a vertex that is minimal in some sense is selected from a set *open*. However, the above theorem means that vertex selection is not essential to the *correctness* of the A* algorithm (it only affects its efficiency, i.e., the size of the search space), while a condition

$$\forall v.\, (v \in open) \implies (\text{LEQ}\, l)\, (xv\, goal)\, (hv\, v\, (xv\, v))$$

at the final stage (i.e., when the goal vertex is selected) is. The above condition means the value assigned to the goal vertex is less than or equal to $hv\, v\, (xv\, v)$ for all $v \in open$. Note that this condition is satisfied at the final stage in the usual A* algorithm with an assumption that LEQ l is a total order.

This fact implies the possibility of variants of the A* algorithm that may not select a vertex v such that $x_v + h(v)$ attains the minimum value in *open*. For example, one can consider an algorithm that selects a vertex from *open* so that the search may not fall into an infinite loop, even for a problem when the usual A* algorithm fails to terminate. All we should state is that the above condition is satisfied at the final stage, i.e., selection criteria at the middle of execution have nothing to do with the correctness of the solution.

In Sect. 4, we added an assumption that "LEQ l" is a total order to assert the computed solution is the greatest one among any lower bound of a certain set. However it can be achieved without a total order condition, but with a distributivity on "LEQ l". The theorem about this fact is also expressed as an property of POTENTIAL, and can be used both in POTENTIAL's case and in ASTAR's case:

$\vdash \forall g\, l\, s\, bs\, fe.\, s \in \text{VS}\, g \wedge \text{HAS\_Top}\, l \wedge$
    $(\forall e.\, e \in \text{ES}\, g \implies \text{Distrib}(\text{LEQ}\, l)\, (\text{LEQ}\, l)\, (fe\, e))$
    $\implies \forall n\, open\, closed\, outv\, xv.$
    POTENTIAL $n\, g\, l\, s\, bs\, fe\, open\, closed\, outv\, xv$
    $\implies \forall v\, a.\, \text{IS\_LEQ\_PATHSOLN}\, l\, g\, fe\, a\, bs\, s\, v$
    $\implies (\text{LEQ}\, l)\, a\, (xv\, v)$

This observation was made by Bruno Martin [12]. We are now planning to rewrite the proof of the correctness of the A* algorithm according to this observation.

6   Related Work

Formalizations on graphs and graph algorithms have been achieved for several theorem proving systems as an end in themselves or as a basis for other work. Formalizations of several kinds of graphs (directed [17], undirected [4], and planar [18]) can be seen even in a single system. Hesselink [10] constructed a mechanical proof of a distributed algorithm for minimum-weight spanning trees in NQTHM. Basin and Kaufmann [1] compared two systems, NQTHM and Nuprl, using Ramsey's theorem on graphs as an example. Graph algorithms can also be used as a target of program verification. An algorithm that tests the acyclicity of a graph with an efficient depth first search algorithm is verified by the KIV system [9] and an executable program is then extracted. Chou and Peled [5] verified the partial order reduction algorithm as an example of model-checking algorithms in HOL. As in our work, they also verified a meta-theory (abstract level of the algorithm) that led to a deeper understanding of the algorithm.

7   Concluding Remarks

We have succeeded in formally verifying the correctness of the A* algorithm. The verification of A* is based on that of the abstract algorithm, POTENTIAL. In particular, most properties needed for the correctness of A* could be verified as properties of POTENTIAL. This process led us to realize that some assumptions on the A* algorithm were redundant for its correctness, because the related properties of POTENTIAL could be demonstrated without them.

The definition of A* was written by hand, and the basic relation between A* and POTENTIAL, i.e., the fact that any property that holds for POTENTIAL also holds for A* was also proved, though not automatically. However, the definition of A* was derived from that of POTENTIAL by the addition of some parameters and conditions. If we could define A* by specifying only such differences, it would be possible to derive automatically the relation between the two as a theorem. Since the definitions are inductive, we need a mechanism to give a new inductive definition from an existing inductive definition by stating such differences. In other words, "inheritance" of inductive definitions should be supported.

We have not proved the termination of the A* algorithm. In order to demonstrate this, we need another formulation of A* that contains additional internal states such as a trace of the execution. Such a formulation should also be derived from the original definition of A*.

The efficiency of A* has also not been formalized. We showed that some assumptions on A* were not necessary for its correctness, but they are required for the arguments on its efficiency. Formalizing efficiency arguments in general will be our future work. For the efficiency arguments on A*, we will need yet another formulation of A*.

This work is also motivated by the goal of verifying the correctness of the verifiers such as model checkers based on computation tree logic. We plan to formalize the semantics of computation tree logic [7], and verify the correctness of the algorithm for model checking as a concrete example of the abstract algorithm in our framework.

Assume that a state transition graph is given. Generate a new graph by reversing the direction of each edge, and adding a new vertex s and edges from s to the original vertices. The added edge from s to v is denoted by e_v. Let P be a predicate on a state, i.e., a function from each state to a truth value. We use the boolean lattice $\{\top, \bot\}$ as the lattice for assigning values to vertices. If a transition from a vertex v to a vertex v' exists in the original graph, the generated graph has an edge e from v' to v. For such an edge, define $f_e(x) = \mathsf{P}(v) \wedge x$. As for a newly added edge e_v from s, define $f_{e_v}(x) = \top$. We show that the formula $\mathsf{A}\square\,\mathsf{p}$ (p always holds on any infinite path) corresponds to the path solution under this setting. Let x_v be the path solution of the above problem. Then

$$x_v = \bigwedge_{p' \in \mathrm{path}(s,v)} f_{p'}(b_s) \leq f_p(b_s) = \mathsf{P}(v_1) \wedge \ldots \wedge \mathsf{P}(v_n)$$

holds for any path $p = v_0, v_1, \ldots, v_n$ from $s(= v_0)$ to $v(= v_n)$. Hence if $x_v = \top$,

$$\mathsf{P}(v_1) = \ldots = \mathsf{P}(v_n) = \top$$

holds. This means that p holds at vertices $v_n(= v), \ldots, v_1$.

Conversely, if p holds at all the vertices on a path from v to v' for any v' in the original state transition graph, then

$$f_p(b_s) = \mathsf{P}(v_1) \wedge \ldots \wedge \mathsf{P}(v_n) = \top$$

holds in the generated graph. Therefore, $x_v = \bigwedge f_p(b_s) = \top$ holds for the path solution x_v. As a result, $x_v = \top$ if and only if the formula $\mathsf{A}\square\,\mathsf{p}$ holds at the state v.

The formula $\mathsf{E}\square\,\mathsf{p}$ (p always holds on a certain infinite path), however, corresponds to a solution of the following equation.

$$x_v = \bigvee_{t(e)=v} f_e(x_{h(e)})$$

The correspondence between the formula and a fixed-point solution also exists in this case. If x_v is the maximal solution of the above equation (maximal fixed-point), then $x_v = \top$ holds if and only if there exists an infinite path on which p always holds. Defining an algorithm that computes the maximal solution will also be our future work.

Acknowledgements

We thank Bruno Martin from ENS Lyon, who was visiting the University of Tokyo. The first formal verification of the A* algorithm is done by him using another strategy. We also thank anonymous referees for constructive comments.

References

1. David Basin and Matt Kaufmann. The Boyer-Moore prover and Nuprl: An experimental comparison. In Gérard Huet and Gordon Plotkin, editors, *Logical Frameworks*, pages 89–119. Cambridge University Press, 1991.
2. Robert S. Boyer and J Strother Moore. *A Computational Logic.* Academic Press, New York, 1979.
3. Albert J. Camilleri and Wishnu Prasetya. Cpo theory, 1994. Available from http://www.cl.cam.ac.uk/ftp/hvg/hol88/contrib/cpo/.
4. C.-T. Chou. A formal theory of undirected graphs in higher-order logic. In *Proceedings of the 7th International Workshop on Higher Order Logic Theorem Proving and Its Applications*, volume 859 of *LNCS*, pages 144–157, Valletta, Malta, September 1994. Springer-Verlag.
5. Ching-Tsun Chou and Doron Peled. Verifying a model-checking algorithm. In *Tools and Algorithms for the Construction and Analysis of Systems*, number 1055 in LNCS, pages 241–257, Passau, Germany, 1996. Springer-Verlag.
6. A. Church. A formulation of the simple theory of types. *Journal of Symbolic Logic*, 5:56–68, 1940.
7. E. Allen Emerson. *Handbook of Theoretical Computer Science*, chapter 16. Elsevier Science Publishers B.V., 1990.
8. M. J. C. Gordon and T. F. Melham, editors. *Introduction to HOL: A theorem proving environment for higher order logic.* Cambridge University Press, 1993.
9. R. Hähnle, M. Heisel, W. Reif, and W. Stephan. An interactive verification system based on dynamic logic. In J. Seikmann, editor, *8th International Conference on Automated Deduction*, number 230 in LNCS, pages 306–315, Oxford, 1986. Springer-Verlag. Also note http://www.informatik.uni-ulm.de/pm/kiv/kiv.html.
10. Wim H. Hesselink. The verified incremental design of a distributed spanning tree algorithm — extended abstract. Computing Science Reports Groningen CS-R9602, November 1997. Available from http://www.cs.rug.nl/~wim/ghs/whh168.ps.
11. G. Kildall. A unified approach to global program optimization. In *POPL*, pages 194–206, 1973.
12. Bruno Martin, July 1997. Private Communication.
13. Nils J. Nilsson. *Principles of Artificial Intelligence.* Tioga Publishing, 1980.
14. N. Shankar, S. Owre, and J. Rushby. The PVS proof checker: A reference manual. Technical report, Computer Science Lab, SRI Intl., 1993.
15. Tetsuo Tamai. A class of fixed-point problems on graphs and iterative solution algorithms. In *Logic and Software Engineering*, pages 102–121. World Scientific, 1996.
16. P. Windley. Abstract theories in HOL. In *Higher Order Logic Theorem Proving and its Applications: Proceedings of the IFIP TC10/WG10.2 Workshop*, volume A-20 of *IFIP Transactions*, pages 197–210, Leuven, Belgium, September 1992. North-Holland/Elsevier.
17. W. Wong. A simple graph theory and its application in railway signalling. In *Proceedings of the 1991 International Workshop on the HOL Theorem Proving System and its Applications*, pages 395–409, Davis, California, USA, August 1991. IEEE Computer Society Press, 1992.
18. Mitsuharu Yamamoto, Shin-ya Nishizaki, Masami Hagiya, and Yozo Toda. Formalization of planar graphs. In *8th International Workshop on Higher-Order Logic Theorem Proving and Its Applications*, volume 971 of *LNCS*, pages 369–384. Springer-Verlag, 1995.

Author Index

Asanuma, Daisaku 443

Bachmair, Leo 277

Beauvais, Jean-René 387

Benini, Marco 33

Bhargavan, Karthikeyan 49

Boulton, Richard J. 67, 87

Bundy, Alan 87

Caldwell, James L. 105

Dufourd, Jean-François 401

Gordon, Mike 87

Griffioen, David 123

Gunter, Carl A. 49

Gunter, Elsa L. 49, 143

Hagiya, Masami 479

Harrison, John 153, 171

von Henke, Friedrich W. 461

Homeier, Peter V. 189

Howe, Douglas J. 207

Huisman, Marieke 123

Jackson, Michael 49

Jackson, Paul B. 225

Kalvala, Sara 33

Konrad, Karsten 245

Liang, Chuck 263

Lifantsev, Maxim 277

Martin, David F. 189

Mikhajlova, Anna 295

Moten, Roderick 315

Müller, Olaf 331

Naraschewski, Wolfgang 349

Narasimhan, Naren 367

Nipkow, Tobias 1

Nishizaki, Shin-ya 479

Nowak, David 387

Nowotka, Dirk 33

Obradovic, Davor 49

Pfab, Stephan 461

Pfeifer, Holger 461

Puitg, François 401

Rueß, Harald 461

Rukšėnas, Rimvydas 423

Sawamura, Hajime 443

Slind, Konrad 87

Takahashi, Koichi 479

Talpin, Jean-Pierre 387

Tamai, Tetsuo 479

Vemuri, Ranga 367

Wenzel, Markus 349

von Wright, Joakim 17, 295, 423

Yamamoto, Mitsuharu 479

Zave, Pamela 49

Springer
and the
environment

At Springer we firmly believe that an
international science publisher has a
special obligation to the environment,
and our corporate policies consistently
reflect this conviction.
We also expect our business partners –
paper mills, printers, packaging
manufacturers, etc. – to commit
themselves to using materials and
production processes that do not harm
the environment. The paper in this
book is made from low- or no-chlorine
pulp and is acid free, in conformance
with international standards for paper
permanency.

Lecture Notes in Computer Science

For information about Vols. 1–1397

please contact your bookseller or Springer-Verlag

Vol. 1398: C. Nédellec, C. Rouveirol (Eds.), Machine Learning: ECML-98. Proceedings, 1998. XII, 420 pages. 1998. (Subseries LNAI).

Vol. 1399: O. Etzion, S. Jajodia, S. Sripada (Eds.), Temporal Databases: Research and Practice. X, 429 pages. 1998.

Vol. 1400: M. Lenz, B. Bartsch-Spörl, H.-D. Burkhard, S. Wess (Eds.), Case-Based Reasoning Technology. XVIII, 405 pages. 1998. (Subseries LNAI).

Vol. 1401: P. Sloot, M. Bubak, B. Hertzberger (Eds.), High-Performance Computing and Networking. Proceedings, 1998. XX, 1309 pages. 1998.

Vol. 1402: W. Lamersdorf, M. Merz (Eds.), Trends in Distributed Systems for Electronic Commerce. Proceedings, 1998. XII, 255 pages. 1998.

Vol. 1403: K. Nyberg (Ed.), Advances in Cryptology – EUROCRYPT '98. Proceedings, 1998. X, 607 pages. 1998.

Vol. 1404: C. Freksa, C. Habel. K.F. Wender (Eds.), Spatial Cognition. VIII, 491 pages. 1998. (Subseries LNAI).

Vol. 1405: S.M. Embury, N.J. Fiddian, W.A. Gray, A.C. Jones (Eds.), Advances in Databases. Proceedings, 1998. XII, 183 pages. 1998.

Vol. 1406: H. Burkhardt, B. Neumann (Eds.), Computer Vision – ECCV'98. Vol. I. Proceedings, 1998. XVI, 927 pages. 1998.

Vol. 1408: E. Burke, M. Carter (Eds.), Practice and Theory of Automated Timetabling II. Proceedings, 1997. XII, 273 pages. 1998.

Vol. 1407: H. Burkhardt, B. Neumann (Eds.), Computer Vision – ECCV'98. Vol. II. Proceedings, 1998. XVI, 881 pages. 1998.

Vol. 1409: T. Schaub, The Automation of Reasoning with Incomplete Information. XI, 159 pages. 1998. (Subseries LNAI).

Vol. 1411: L. Asplund (Ed.), Reliable Software Technologies – Ada-Europe. Proceedings, 1998. XI, 297 pages. 1998.

Vol. 1412: R.E. Bixby, E.A. Boyd, R.Z. Ríos-Mercado (Eds.), Integer Programming and Combinatorial Optimization. Proceedings, 1998. IX, 437 pages. 1998.

Vol. 1413: B. Pernici, C. Thanos (Eds.), Advanced Information Systems Engineering. Proceedings, 1998. X, 423 pages. 1998.

Vol. 1414: M. Nielsen, W. Thomas (Eds.), Computer Science Logic. Selected Papers, 1997. VIII, 511 pages. 1998.

Vol. 1415: J. Mira, A.P. del Pobil, M.Ali (Eds.), Methodology and Tools in Knowledge-Based Systems. Vol. I. Proceedings, 1998. XXIV, 887 pages. 1998. (Subseries LNAI).

Vol. 1416: A.P. del Pobil, J. Mira, M.Ali (Eds.), Tasks and Methods in Applied Artificial Intelligence. Vol.II. Proceedings, 1998. XXIII, 943 pages. 1998. (Subseries LNAI).

Vol. 1417: S. Yalamanchili, J. Duato (Eds.), Parallel Computer Routing and Communication. Proceedings, 1997. XII, 309 pages. 1998.

Vol. 1418: R. Mercer, E. Neufeld (Eds.), Advances in Artificial Intelligence. Proceedings, 1998. XII, 467 pages. 1998. (Subseries LNAI).

Vol. 1419: G. Vigna (Ed.), Mobile Agents and Security. XII, 257 pages. 1998.

Vol. 1420: J. Desel, M. Silva (Eds.), Application and Theory of Petri Nets 1998. Proceedings, 1998. VIII, 385 pages. 1998.

Vol. 1421: C. Kirchner, H. Kirchner (Eds.), Automated Deduction – CADE-15. Proceedings, 1998. XIV, 443 pages. 1998. (Subseries LNAI).

Vol. 1422: J. Jeuring (Ed.), Mathematics of Program Construction. Proceedings, 1998. X, 383 pages. 1998.

Vol. 1423: J.P. Buhler (Ed.), Algorithmic Number Theory. Proceedings, 1998. X, 640 pages. 1998.

Vol. 1424: L. Polkowski, A. Skowron (Eds.), Rough Sets and Current Trends in Computing. Proceedings, 1998. XIII, 626 pages. 1998. (Subseries LNAI).

Vol. 1425: D. Hutchison, R. Schäfer (Eds.), Multimedia Applications, Services and Techniques – ECMAST'98. Proceedings, 1998. XVI, 532 pages. 1998.

Vol. 1427: A.J. Hu, M.Y. Vardi (Eds.), Computer Aided Verification. Proceedings, 1998. IX, 552 pages. 1998.

Vol. 1429: F. van der Linden (Ed.), Development and Evolution of Software Architectures for Product Families. Proceedings, 1998. IX, 258 pages. 1998.

Vol. 1430: S. Trigila, A. Mullery, M. Campolargo, H. Vanderstraeten, M. Mampaey (Eds.), Intelligence in Services and Networks: Technology for Ubiquitous Telecom Services. Proceedings, 1998. XII, 550 pages. 1998.

Vol. 1431: H. Imai, Y. Zheng (Eds.), Public Key Cryptography. Proceedings, 1998. XI, 263 pages. 1998.

Vol. 1432: S. Arnborg, L. Ivansson (Eds.), Algorithm Theory – SWAT '98. Proceedings, 1998. IX, 347 pages. 1998.

Vol. 1433: V. Honavar, G. Slutzki (Eds.), Grammatical Inference. Proceedings, 1998. X, 271 pages. 1998. (Subseries LNAI).

Vol. 1434: J.-C. Heudin (Ed.), Virtual Worlds. Proceedings, 1998. XII, 412 pages. 1998. (Subseries LNAI).

Vol. 1435: M. Klusch, G. Weiß (Eds.), Cooperative Information Agents II. Proceedings, 1998. IX, 307 pages. 1998. (Subseries LNAI).

Vol. 1436: D. Wood, S. Yu (Eds.), Automata Implementation. Proceedings, 1997. VIII, 253 pages. 1998.

Vol. 1437: S. Albayrak, F.J. Garijo (Eds.), Intelligent Agents for Telecommunication Applications. Proceedings, 1998. XII, 251 pages. 1998. (Subseries LNAI).

Vol. 1438: C. Boyd, E. Dawson (Eds.), Information Security and Privacy. Proceedings, 1998. XI, 423 pages. 1998.

Vol. 1439: B. Magnusson (Ed.), System Configuration Management. Proceedings, 1998. X, 207 pages. 1998.

Vol. 1441: W. Wobcke, M. Pagnucco, C. Zhang (Eds.), Agents and Multi-Agent Systems. Proceedings, 1997. XII, 241 pages. 1998. (Subseries LNAI).

Vol. 1442: A. Fiat. G.J. Woeginger (Eds.), Online Algorithms. XVIII, 436 pages. 1998.

Vol. 1443: K.G. Larsen, S. Skyum, G. Winskel (Eds.), Automata, Languages and Programming. Proceedings, 1998. XVI, 932 pages. 1998.

Vol. 1444: K. Jansen, J. Rolim (Eds.), Approximation Algorithms for Combinatorial Optimization. Proceedings, 1998. VIII, 201 pages. 1998.

Vol. 1445: E. Jul (Ed.), ECOOP'98 – Object-Oriented Programming. Proceedings, 1998. XII, 635 pages. 1998.

Vol. 1446: D. Page (Ed.), Inductive Logic Programming. Proceedings, 1998. VIII, 301 pages. 1998. (Subseries LNAI).

Vol. 1447: V.W. Porto, N. Saravanan, D. Waagen, A.E. Eiben (Eds.), Evolutionary Programming VII. Proceedings, 1998. XVI, 840 pages. 1998.

Vol. 1448: M. Farach-Colton (Ed.), Combinatorial Pattern Matching. Proceedings, 1998. VIII, 251 pages. 1998.

Vol. 1449: W.-L. Hsu, M.-Y. Kao (Eds.), Computing and Combinatorics. Proceedings, 1998. XII, 372 pages. 1998.

Vol. 1450: L. Brim, F. Gruska, J. Zlatuška (Eds.), Mathematical Foundations of Computer Science 1998. Proceedings, 1998. XVII, 846 pages. 1998.

Vol. 1451: A. Amin, D. Dori, P. Pudil, H. Freeman (Eds.), Advances in Pattern Recognition. Proceedings, 1998. XXI, 1048 pages. 1998.

Vol. 1452: B.P. Goettl, H.M. Halff, C.L. Redfield, V.J. Shute (Eds.), Intelligent Tutoring Systems. Proceedings, 1998. XIX, 629 pages. 1998.

Vol. 1453: M.-L. Mugnier, M. Chein (Eds.), Conceptual Structures: Theory, Tools and Applications. Proceedings, 1998. XIII, 439 pages. (Subseries LNAI).

Vol. 1454: I. Smith (Ed.), Artificial Intelligence in Structural Engineering. XI, 497 pages. 1998. (Subseries LNAI).

Vol. 1456: A. Drogoul, M. Tambe, T. Fukuda (Eds.), Collective Robotics. Proceedings, 1998. VII, 161 pages. 1998. (Subseries LNAI).

Vol. 1457: A. Ferreira, J. Rolim, H. Simon, S.-H. Teng (Eds.), Solving Irregularly Structured Problems in Prallel. Proceedings, 1998. X, 408 pages. 1998.

Vol. 1458: V.O. Mittal, H.A. Yanco, J. Aronis, R-. Simpson (Eds.), Assistive Technology in Artificial Intelligence. X, 273 pages. 1998. (Subseries LNAI).

Vol. 1459: D.G. Feitelson, L. Rudolph (Eds.), Job Scheduling Strategies for Parallel Processing. Proceedings, 1998. VII, 257 pages. 1998.

Vol. 1460: G. Quirchmayr, E. Schweighofer, T.J.M. Bench-Capon (Eds.), Database and Expert Systems Applications. Proceedings, 1998. XVI, 905 pages. 1998.

Vol. 1461: G. Bilardi, G.F. Italiano, A. Pietracaprina, G. Pucci (Eds.), Algorithms – ESA'98. Proceedings, 1998. XII, 516 pages. 1998.

Vol. 1462: H. Krawczyk (Ed.), Advances in Cryptology - CRYPTO '98. Proceedings, 1998. XII, 519 pages. 1998.

Vol. 1464: H.H.S. Ip, A.W.M. Smeulders (Eds.), Multimedia Information Analysis and Retrieval. Proceedings, 1998. VIII, 264 pages. 1998.

Vol. 1465: R. Hirschfeld (Ed.), Financial Cryptography. Proceedings, 1998. VIII, 311 pages. 1998.

Vol. 1466: D. Sangiorgi, R. de Simone (Eds.), CONCUR'98: Concurrency Theory. Proceedings, 1998. XI, 657 pages. 1998.

Vol. 1467: C. Clack, K. Hammond, T. Davie (Eds.), Implementation of Functional Languages. Proceedings, 1997. X, 375 pages. 1998.

Vol. 1468: P. Husbands, J.-A. Meyer (Eds.), Evolutionary Robotics. Proceedings, 1998. VIII, 247 pages. 1998.

Vol. 1469: R. Puigjaner, N.N. Savino, B. Serra (Eds.), Computer Performance Evaluation. Proceedings, 1998. XIII, 376 pages. 1998.

Vol. 1470: D. Pritchard, J. Reeve (Eds.), Euro-Par'98: Parallel Processing. Proceedings, 1998. XXII, 1157 pages. 1998.

Vol. 1471: J. Dix, L. Moniz Pereira, T.C. Przymusinski (Eds.), Logic Programming and Knowledge Representation. Proceedings, 1997. IX, 246 pages. 1998. (Subseries LNAI).

Vol. 1473: X. Leroy, A. Ohori (Eds.), Types in Compilation. Proceedings, 1998. VIII, 299 pages. 1998.

Vol. 1475: W. Litwin, T. Morzy, G. Vossen (Eds.), Advances in Databases and Information Systems. Proceedings, 1998. XIV, 369 pages. 1998.

Vol. 1477: K. Rothermel, F. Hohl (Eds.), Mobile Agents. Proceedings, 1998. VIII, 285 pages. 1998.

Vol. 1478: M. Sipper, D. Mange, A. Pérez-Uribe (Eds.), Evolvable Systems: From Biology to Hardware. Proceedings, 1998. IX, 382 pages. 1998.

Vol. 1479: J. Grundy, M. Newey (Eds.), Theorem Proving in Higher Order Logics. Proceedings, 1998. VIII, 497 pages. 1998.

Vol. 1480: F. Giunchiglia (Ed.), Artificial Intelligence: Methodology, Systems, and Applications. Proceedings, 1998. IX, 502 pages. 1998. (Subseries LNAI).

Vol. 1482: R.W. Hartenstein, A. Keevallik (Eds.), Field-Programmable Logic and Applications. Proceedings, 1998. XI, 533 pages. 1998.

Vol. 1483: T. Plagemann, V. Goebel (Eds.), Interactive Distributed Multimedia Systems and Telecommunication Services. Proceedings, 1998. XV, 326 pages. 1998.

Vol. 1487: V. Gruhn (Ed.), Software Process Technology. Proceedings, 1998. VIII, 157 pages. 1998.

Vol. 1488: B. Smyth, P. Cunningham (Eds.), Advances in Case-Based Reasoning. Proceedings, 1998. XI, 482 pages. 1998. (Subseries LNAI).